Human Relations Today

Concepts and Skills

Human Relations Today

Concepts and Skills

Samuel C. Certo
Crummer Graduate School of Business at Rollins College

IRWIN
Chicago • Bogotá • Boston • Buenos Aires • Caracas
London • Madrid • Mexico City • Sydney • Toronto

Publisher: William Schoof
Acquisitions Editor: Mary Fischer
Production Manager: Bob Lange
Marketing Manager: Kurt Messersmith

Development, design, and project management provided by Elm Street Publishing Services, Inc.

Compositor: Elm Street Publishing Services, Inc.
Typeface: Stempel Garamond
Printer: Von Hoffmann Press, Inc.

Library of Congress Cataloging-in-Publication Data
Certo, Samuel C.
Human relations today: concepts and skills/Samuel C. Certo.
p. cm.
Includes bibliographical references and index.
ISBN 0-256-14588-1
1. Psychology, Industrial. 2. Personnel management.
3. Interpersonal relations. 4. Organizational behavior. I. Title
HF5548.8.C336 1995
158.7—dc20 94-31961

Printed in the United States of America
1 2 3 4 5 6 7 8 9 0 VH 9 8 7 6 5 4

Address editorial correspondence:
Austen Press
18141 Dixie Highway
Suite 105
Homewood, IL 60430

Address orders:
Richard D. Irwin, Inc.
1333 Burr Ridge Parkway
Burr Ridge, IL 60521

Austen Press
Richard D. Irwin, Inc.

Table of Contents Photos: Part 1, © Jonathan Pite / Gamma Liaison; Part 2, Courtesy of Ebony Glass & Mirror, Inc.; Part 3, Courtesy of McDonald's Corporation; Part 4, John Moss / Tony Stone Images; Part 5, Terry Vine / Tony Stone Images; Part 6, Photo by John Dickerson.

Cover source: "Color Weave" background image taken from Photoshop Filter Finesse (CD-ROM) by Bill Niffenegger, New York: Random House Electronic Publishing, 1994.

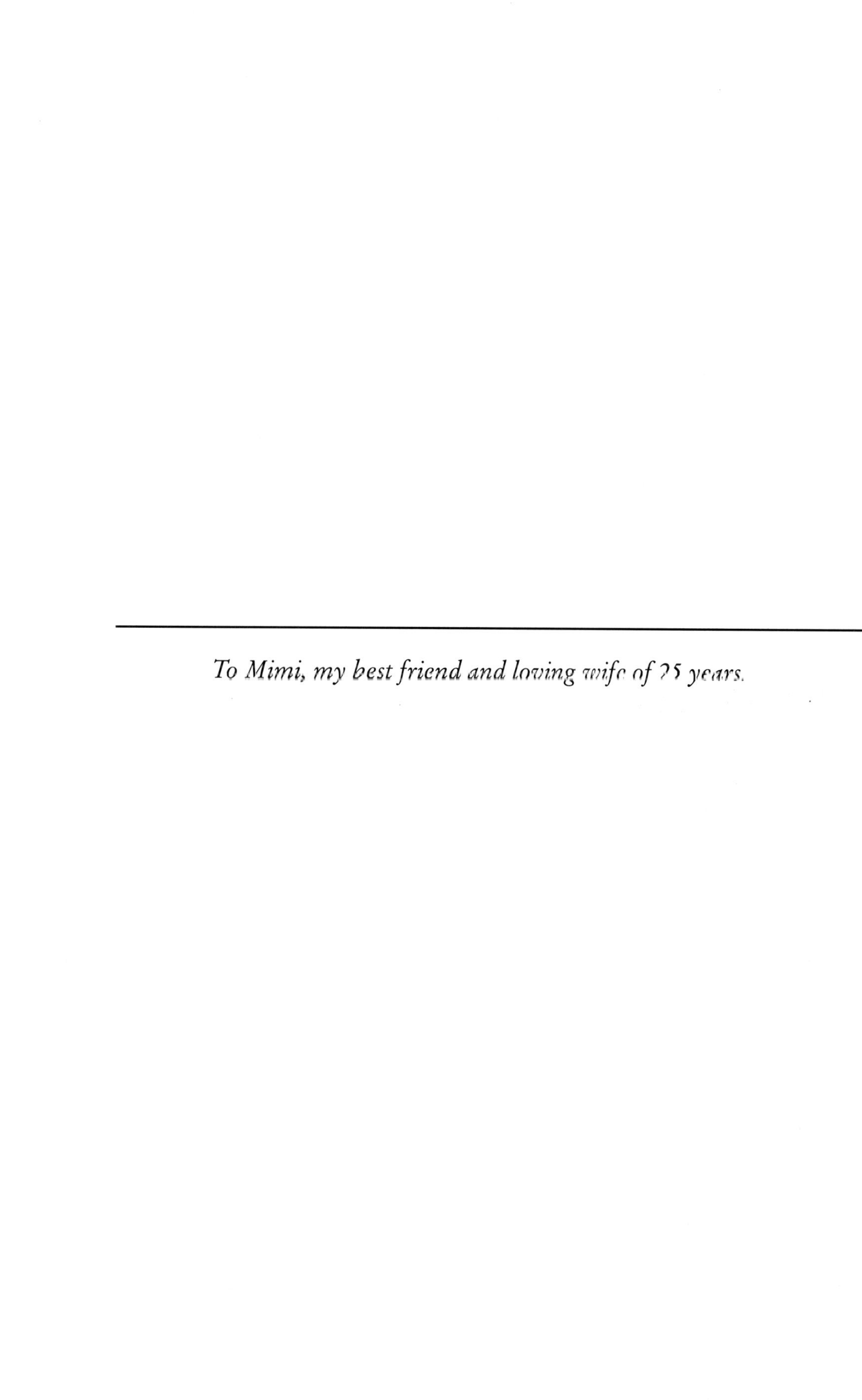

To Mimi, my best friend and loving wife of 25 years.

Preface

The purpose of *Human Relations Today: Concepts and Skills* is to prepare students to work with people. This book contains a wealth of practical suggestions about working with people that are based not only on scholarly research but on experiences of real individuals working in many different sizes and types of organizations. Emphasis throughout this book is on acquiring comprehensive and useful knowledge of how to work with people, along with developing the skill to apply the knowledge.

I am very proud to be publishing the *Human Relations Today* Learning Package—this book and its related ancillaries. Beyond any doubt, these learning materials meet the high standards that I have been using to develop business-related textbook materials for colleges and universities for almost twenty years. Within this learning package, important human relations concepts are presented clearly and concisely, learning materials reflect an empathy for and enhancement of the student learning process, and instructional support materials facilitate the design and conduct of only the best possible human relations courses.

The process followed to publish the *Human Relations Today* Learning Package is noteworthy. First, to accomplish my mission of providing human relations students with the most comprehensive and timely learning materials possible, I designed and implemented a detailed but preliminary project plan in cooperation with Austen Press. Input for this plan came from human relations instructors via mail surveys, telephone surveys, and focus groups. Second, this preliminary project plan was reviewed extensively by human relations professionals, refined based on comments from the reviewers, and then finalized. Next, a team of professionals was formed to make sure that the final publication plan was implemented efficiently and effectively. Figure A highlights the members of this team of professionals and generally illustrates how team members interacted. Video experts, supplements coordinators, market researchers, academic reviewers, and professional writers all worked with me to ensure that *Human Relations Today* and its ancillaries were the best in the marketplace.

Figure A The *Human Relations Today* Learning Package: A Professional Team

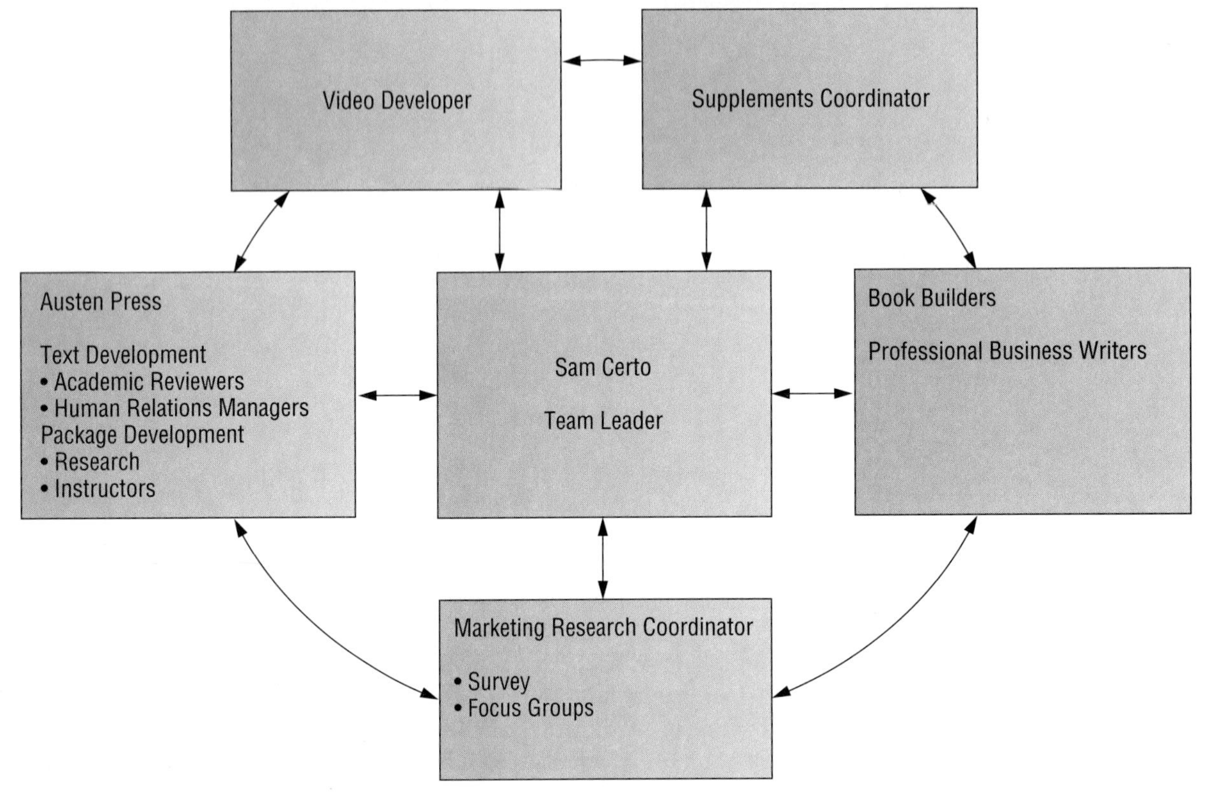

The following sections discuss, in detail, the major components of the *Human Relations Today* Learning Package, beginning with the text.

The Text

This book was designed and developed along two important dimensions—text content and text learning aids. A discussion of each of these dimensions follows.

Text Content

Deciding on which human relations concepts to include in this text was very difficult. Insights about what concepts to include came from reports and opinions of professional agencies such as the American Assembly of Collegiate Schools of Business (AACSB), trends in human relations research as reported by human relations scholars, accounts by human relations practitioners regarding the challenges they face in working with people and the ways they meet those challenges, and advice from colleagues through both formal channels such as text reviewing and informal channels as basic as conversations with successful managers.

Human Relations Today: Concepts and Skills is divided into six parts: "Defining Human Relations," "Modern Human Relations Challenges," "Foundations of Human

Relations Processes," "The Organizational Social System," "People Working Together," and "Special Topics." The following paragraphs highlight each part.

Reviewer Highlight: Roberta Kuhlman of Chafey College likes the division of the material within each part into small bits of information and says there are very few textbooks in human relations that do this.

Part 1, "Defining Human Relations," tells students what is meant by the term *human relations.* In Chapter 1, "Human Relations: Your Key to Success in Organizations," *human relations* is defined as interaction with people in much the same way that customer relations can be defined as interaction with customers or international relations can be defined as interaction with other countries. *Human relations skill* is defined as the ability to work effectively with people.

Reviewer Highlight: Jacqueline Stutzman of South Texas Community College feels that a strength of this chapter is the inclusion of contemporary developments in the field of human relations, especially the transitions made in the workplace environments in the last 30 years and the coverage of the quality approach.

Part 2, "Modern Human Relations Challenges," focuses on major human interaction issues that are typical of today's work environment. For example, Chapter 2, "Maintaining Quality and Productivity: Emphasizing TQM," discusses the recent and growing emphasis on quality within modern organizations; the relationships among productivity, motivation, and quality; and challenges in quality improvement.

Reviewer Highlight: Martin Greenan of Martin University says, "The discussion of giving employees 'ownership' of quality is significant."

Chapter 3, "Integrating People and Technology," outlines the effects of technological advancement on organizations and the information age. The chapter concludes by addressing what lies ahead for people and technology.

Reviewer Highlight: "I like the discussion of technostress and cyberphobia and the way in which these phenomena affect certain individuals," says Jacqueline Stutzman of South Texas Community College.

Chapter 4, "Managing Diversity," describes the transformation of the American work force, with special focus on women, racial and ethnic minorities, older workers, and physically challenged workers.

Reviewer Highlight: John Miller of Edison Community College says that this chapter "deals more effectively with the development of the cultural issue by looking at it from the broader perspective of the moral responsibility to be oriented to the need of diversity in the workplace rather than just the legal responsibility."

Part 3, "Foundations of Human Relations Processes," describes several basic processes involved in building effective working relationships with people. The first two chapters in this part focus on communication, the most fundamental means that people use to interact. Chapter 5, "Interpersonal Communication," explains fundamentals of the communication process.

Reviewer Highlight: "The cultural orientation of non-verbal communication is extremely strong. The section devoted to interpersonal communication reinforces the whole non-verbal concept and gives interpersonal communication skills a more practical focus," writes John Miller of Edison Community College.

Chapter 6, "Organizational Communication," discusses interpersonal communication that takes place in organizations.

Reviewer Highlight: "The content and organization is done very well; the topic coverage is excellent," says Ross Higa of Leeward Community College.

Chapter 7, "Processes and Tools of Motivation," includes the ideas of theorists such as Maslow, McClelland, Herzberg, Vroom, Adams, and Skinner in explaining how people are motivated in organizations.

Reviewer Highlight: "Coverage of empowerment is unsurpassed," says Ross Higa of Leeward Community College.

Chapter 8, "Principles and Styles of Leading," discusses various ways that individuals can lead in organizations.

Reviewer Highlight: Writes Jacqueline Stutzman of South Texas Community College, "The organization of this chapter is logical in its flow from the more general [leadership traits and styles] to the more specific [theories and characteristics involving leaders, employees, situations] to the final solution of becoming a leader."

The last chapter in this section, "Stress Management," explains what stress is and outlines how it should be handled.

Reviewer Highlight: Ruth Dixon, Diablo Valley Community College, says that "the coverage of the organizational role of stress is excellent."

Part 4 is "The Organizational Social System." This part emphasizes both individuals and groups as the primary units that make up any organization. Understanding the characteristics of both individuals and groups provides insights about how to further build effective working relationships in organizations. Discussion of individuals (Chapter 10) emphasizes personality, values, intelligence, learning, and perception.

Reviewer Highlight: "Excellent. I'm glad to find a text which dedicates a chapter to such an important topic," writes Ross Higa of Leeward Community College.

Discussion of groups (Chapter 11) focuses on the nature of groups, dynamics of groups, informal groups, and organizational behavior and culture.

Reviewer Highlight: "Including a section on 'norms' is GREAT! So many of the current texts do not," says Don Kelly of North Hennepin Community College.

Part 5, "People Working Together," emphasizes building a work environment in which people can be productive. Chapter 12, "Team Building," outlines concepts useful in turning groups into work teams.

Reviewer Highlight: "The information on teams in trouble is excellent!" says Mary Tranquillo at Commonwealth College.

Chapter 13, "Conflict and Change," discusses the character of conflict, managing conflict, the inevitability of change, downsizing, relocation, and overcoming resistance to change.

Reviewer Highlight: Martin Greenan thinks that the discussion of change is an important addition and that the section on "Traits That Help You Change" is excellent.

The last chapter in this part, "Job Design and Enrichment," discusses guidelines concerning how jobs can be structured to enhance the commitment and productivity of workers performing those jobs.

Reviewer Highlight: "This chapter is excellent because it provides a wonderful example of what job enrichment is about," writes Jacqueline Stutzman of South Texas Community College.

Part 6, "Special Topics," contains Chapter 15, "International Opportunities," and Chapter 16, "Ethics and Social Responsibility." Chapter 15 discusses the world of globalism, going global, cultural awareness, and the international work force.

Reviewer Highlight: All reviewers applauded the inclusion of this chapter.

Chapter 16 emphasizes "doing the right thing" when dealing with people.

Reviewer Highlight: The relationship of ethics and social responsibility is a plus for both Martin Greenan and Jacqueline Stutzman.

Text Learning Aids

The features of this text have been designed to make the study of human relations effective, efficient, interesting, and enjoyable. In no particular order, these features are listed and explained here.

Chapter Outlines. The beginning pages of each chapter contain a chapter outline. The outline is intended as a tool that students can use to preview textual materials and to keep material in perspective while it is being read.

Learning Objectives. At the beginning of each chapter is a set of learning objectives. These objectives are intended as guidelines to help students develop a method for studying each chapter.

Opening Vignettes. The opening pages of each chapter contain a short situation drawn from the work world that introduces the reader to human relations issues related to chapter content. The vignettes are referred to in the chapters to help students see how human relations concepts might relate to human relations challenges. Also, a photo accompanies each vignette.

A Second Look. To enhance the quality of learning for each chapter, a feature called "A Second Look" was designed to help students reflect on the opening vignette. "A Second Look" is a question or questions at the end of a chapter that help students apply chapter content to the opening vignette. "A Second Look" can be used independently by students to enhance learning or by instructors to enrich classroom discussion.

Photo Exercises. Photo exercises are a NEW pedagogic feature to human relations texts. There are approximately two Photo Exercises per chapter. A Photo Exercise is an engaging photograph used to provide visual support for student learning (see page 58 for an example). Accompanying each Photo Exercise photograph is a caption that helps students to relate the picture to chapter content, plus a thought-provoking question. These questions can be used by students to apply their learning of chapter material as well as by instructors to enliven classroom discussion.

Highlights. Each chapter features a rich mix of highlights, or real-life examples, of human relations situations. Highlights are integrated throughout the text, usually three per chapter.

Diversity Highlights. These examples illustrate human relations issues related to diversity. As an example, on page 166 the leadership chapter contains the "Diversity Highlights" boxed feature describing how the owner of Ruppert Landscaping helped recognize the Hispanics in his work force by donating his work team and materials to rehab a community soccer field.

Quality Highlights. These examples illustrate human relations issues related to quality programs in organizations. As an example, on page 266 the "Quality Highlights" in the chapter on groups discusses how Maurice Dake, a General Electric plant manager, believes that allowing groups to be a real force in an organization is a key to building a successful quality program.

International Highlights. International issues affect the functioning of virtually all modern organizations. These highlights illustrate human relations issues related to international factors. To illustrate, the "International Highlights" in Chapter 10, "Individual Behavior," (page 234) discusses how individual differences of people in Latin America, Asia, Europe, and the Middle East influence how people should do business in those countries.

Teamwork Highlights. In attempting to maintain competitiveness with organizations throughout the world, many organizations are attempting to turn their work forces into work teams. These highlights illustrate human relations issues surrounding work teams. An example is the "Teamwork Highlights" that appears on page 14. This highlight emphasizes how work teams are built at Chrysler.

Quick Quiz. "Quick Quizzes" appear periodically within each chapter. A Quick Quiz is a brief self-test of three or four short-answer questions. The questions cover each main section of a chapter and appear after the student has just finished reading the section. Answers to Quick Quiz questions appear at the end of the chapter. For an example of a Quick Quiz, see page 5, along with related answers appearing on page 22.

Self-Portrait. In order for students to reach the objective of developing human relations skills, they must have feedback about themselves as human relations practitioners. "Self-Portraits" are self-test questionnaires, one per chapter, that students can use to assess themselves along various human relations dimensions. For example, the "Self-Portrait" on page 309 lets students explore how they handle conflict.

Key Terms. At the end of each chapter is a list of key terms. This list can help students preview terms they will encounter or review them after the chapter has been read. Page numbers on which the term is defined are included in the list. For an example, see page 18.

Margin Glossary. Key terms are presented in the margin along with their definitions. Students can use this text feature as a way of testing their understanding of key terms and as a method of quickly finding where terms are discussed. See the definition of human relations in the margin on page 4 to see an example of a margin glossary term.

Figures and Tables. Line drawings and tables are used extensively to thoroughly explain and clarify human relations concepts.

Chapter Summary by Learning Objectives. Learning objectives are recapped at the end of the chapter in the Summary. By reviewing each objective and its summary, students can determine whether they have reached chapter learning objectives.

Review and Discussion Questions. At the end of each chapter is a set of review and discussion questions that tests understanding of chapter concepts and asks students to apply the principles learned. These questions can be used independently by students or by instructors as a method of reviewing chapter content.

Chapter-Ending Learning Exercises. To help students develop an understanding of human relations and related skills, three types of learning exercises are included at the end of each chapter: Independent Activities, Skill Builders, and Group Activities.

Independent Activities. Independent Activities are a variety of assignments or exercises that students can perform individually to further develop their understanding of and to become aware of human relations. Types of activities range from crossword puzzles to observation exercises and applications.

Skill Builder. Following the Independent Activities is also an experiential exercise called "Skill Builder" that can be used to help students develop their human relations skills. For example, the Skill Builder in Chapter 5 on page 116 asks students to observe and analyze the interpersonal communications in their classroom.

Group Activities. Instructors can use the Group Activities appearing as in-class assignments for groups of students. Activities encompass role-playing and teamwork exercises as well as class discussions. Examples of the types of group activities appear on page 90.

Concluding Cases. The concluding pages of each chapter contain two cases that further illustrate how chapter concepts can apply to real-life human relations situations. All cases are undisguised situations in real organizations. This feature can also be used independently by students or by instructors for course assignments or classroom discussion.

Photographs. Photographs are used to depict various human relations situations throughout the text and to help bridge the gap between theory and practice.

Color. A quick inspection of this text reveals that it is in full color. Color has been used not simply for the sake of color but to help students learn more through an engaging presentation of human relations concepts.

Glossary. Major human relations terms and their definitions are presented at the end of the text.

The *Human Relations Today* Video Series

To better engage students in the learning process, a series of specially designed videos has been developed to help students see how human relations is practiced in actual companies. These tapes have been carefully scripted to illustrate major sections of the text and to arouse student interest in human relations concepts. Each school using *Human Relations Today* receives a FREE copy of the videos. Titles and corresponding summaries for each tape follow:

Video 1: Introduction to Human Relations

Students are introduced to human relations by viewing what it is like to work with people at Specialized Bicycle Components, an international bicycle company in Morgan Hill, California.

Video 2: Quality

Not only is Aleta Holub in charge of quality at the First National Bank of Chicago, she is one of the nine members of the Malcolm Baldrige Award Committee. Quality at First Chicago starts with the chairman and is the primary responsibility of every employee at the bank. The video demonstrates how the department supervisors implement, maintain, and control quality.

Video 3: Motivation

Motivation is the key to being competitive in the new global marketplace. In this program, J.C. Penney demonstrates how it uses nonfinancial incentives to motivate its retail sales associates, and Nucor Steel, the nation's fastest-growing and most profitable steel company, explains how its unique financial incentive system has motivated its employees to be the most productive in the world.

Video 4: Groups and Teamwork

Southwest Airlines is the only company ever to win the coveted Triple Crown from the Department of Transportation: for best on-time performance, best baggage handling record, and fewest customer complaints. Southwest demonstrates how their use of teamwork has won them the distinction of being one of the ten best companies to work for in America.

Video 5: Job Design

This video demonstrates how increased teamwork and job redesign helped Detroit Diesel transform its production process and increase its market share.

Video Instructor's Manual

A *Video Instructor's Manual* accompanies the video series. Each segment includes a synopsis of the video, teaching notes on how to integrate the video with the chapters and other package components, a list of the chapter concepts covered in the video, and in-class exercises to use with each video, with accompanying handouts.

Other Learning Package Ingredients

Instructor's Manual and Transparency Masters

The *Instructor's Manual* includes an overview of how to use the manual. Each chapter contains the following:

- Chapter Outline
- Learning Objectives from the text
- Opening Vignette synopsis
- Chapter Overview, which summarizes the chapter
- Key Terms list with text page numbers
- Lecture Outline keyed to the transparencies and videos
- Notes on the "Highlights" boxed material
- Answers to the Review and Discussion Questions and "A Second Look"
- Synopsis of Independent Activities, Skill Builders, and Group Activities and suggested solutions
- Synopsis of the Cases and suggested solutions and answers
- Teaching notes to the Transparency Masters

Transparency masters of key exhibits from the text and teaching notes for each exhibit that describe the exhibit and draw out key points are also included. In addition, five to seven NEW transparency masters are included for each chapter with teaching notes. Natalie Hunter of Portland State University is the author of the *Instructor's Manual and Transparency Masters.*

Test Bank

The *Test Bank* contains over 1,200 questions. Each chapter contains true/false, multiple choice, fill-in-the-blank, and short essay questions. In addition, a short quiz is included for each chapter; quiz questions are pulled from the chapter questions.

Included for each question are answers with text page references, rationale for the answer, level of difficulty (easy, medium, hard), the learning objective to which the question pertains, and the type of question (recall, comprehension, calculation, or application). Natalie Hunter of Portland State University is the author of the *Test Bank.*

Acknowledgments

A project of this scope could not have been undertaken without the support of a great team. First, I'd like to thank the Austen Press staff, in particular, Bill Schoof for his belief in the project and ongoing encouragement. Bill's experience and knowledge set the tone for the team. Next, a special thanks to Mary Fischer and John Weimeister for their guidance and insight throughout the project. Their day-to-day work helped direct the team and keep the project on track. Thank you also to Natalie Hunter, Portland State University, for preparing the *Instructor's Manual, Transparency Masters,* and *Test Bank* which accompany this text.

Thanks to Elm Street Publishing Services for their dedication and skills: Linda Buchanan Allen, Jan Sellers Ashton, Maxine Barber, Karen Hill, Jan Huskisson, Maggie Jarpey, JoAnn Learman, Kathy Mitchell, Ted Murach, Jerry O'Mara, Stephanie Riley, Rebecca Smith, and Julie Webber.

Finally, I'd like to thank the reviewers and survey respondents, whose valuable insights have helped guide the team and shape the project. I appreciate their comments and suggestions.

First Draft Reviewers

Suzanne Bradford
Angelina College

Steve Branz
Triton College

Betty Dierstein
Commonwealth College

Ruth Dixon
Diablo Valley College

Sunnie Drake
McHenry County College

Don Kelly
North Hennepin Community College

Edward LeMay
Massasoit Community College

Beverly Nelson
University of New Orleans

Sheila Powell
Commonwealth College

Connie Sitterly
Texas Woman's University

Mary Tranquillo
St. Petersburg Junior College

Leslie Werner
Commonwealth College

Don Witkowski
Cape Cod Community College

Second Draft Reviewers

Bonnie Chavez
Santa Barbara City College

Martin Greenan
Martin University

Ross Higa
Leeward Community College

Roberta Kuhlman
Chafey College

John Miller
Edison Community College

Jacqueline Stutzman
South Texas Community College

Survey Respondents

Leonard Ackerman
Clarion University of Pennsylvania

Agnes Albany
Hartford Graduate Center

Lyle Alberts
University of Northern Iowa

Phyllis C. Alderdice
Jefferson Community College

Horace Alexander
City College of San Francisco

William Almarez
Southwestern College

William Anderson
Langston University

Verl Anderson
Eastern Oregon State College

Patty Anderson
Valdosta State College

Bob Ash
Rancho Santiago College

William Bachman
Adrian College

R. J. Bartusch
Pierce College

Joseph E. Benson
New Mexico State University

Bill Bergman
Pine Technical Institute

Arthur Berman
Chemeketa Community College

Mark Bershadsky
Portland Community College

Joseph Billingiere
Oxnard College

R. Blue
Lehigh County Community College

Albert A. Blum
New Mexico State University

Lana Boardman
Davis Junior College

Pamela A. Braden
Parkersburg Community College

Suzanne Bradford
Angelina College

Richard T. Braley
Eastern Oklahoma State College

William Breitling
Keuka College

Dennis C. Bromley
Central Wyoming College

Cindy Brown
South Plains College

Russell Bruce
Triton College

Elmer Burack
University of Illinois at Chicago

Randy Busch
Lee College

Stephen C. Bushardt
University of Southern Mississippi

Brad Campbell
Career Training Institute, Orlando

Ann Canty
University of Mississippi

Donald Caruth
East Texas State University

Bonnie Chavez
Santa Barbara City College

Robert A. Cisek
Mercyhurst College

Coleen Coorough
Lewis-Clark State College

Valinda Copeland
Colorado Mountain College, Breckenridge

Pam Crawford
Montana State University

Gary Cutler
Dyersburg State Community College

Christy De Vader
Loyola College

Robert Dean
Illinois Central College

Betty Dierstein
Commonwealth College, Virginia Beach

Glenna Dod
Wesleyan College

Dorothy Dodds
Dakota County Technology College

H. Leroy Drew
Central Maine Technical College

Leo Dumdum
Norfolk State University

Dee Dunn
Commonwealth College, Norfolk

Jean Egan
Asnuntuck Community College

Max Elden
University of Houston

Patrick G. Ellsberg
Lower Columbia College

Donna Everett
Texas Tech University

Mike Farley
Del Mar College East

Dave Fewins
Neosho County Community College

Robert L. Finkelmeier
Regis College

Joseph Flack
Washtenaw Community College

J. Flowers
Richland College

Dana Fogg
University of Tampa

Carson Gancer
Kalamazoo Valley Community College

Carol Garner
Orange Coast College

Donna Giertz
Parkland College

Ernst Gottmann
Texas State College

Dent Green
Charles S. Mott Community College

Martin Greenan
Martin University

Calvin Hall
Langston University

E. C. Hamm
Tidewater Community College

Donna Harr
McCook Community College

John Harrington
New Hampshire College

Carol Harvey
Assumption College

James A. Healey
Chabot College

Ronald Herrick
Mesa Community College

Ross Higa
University of Hawaii, Leeward Community College

Dan Hochstetter
Mima Management Assoc.

Gene Holand
Columbia Basin College

Russ Holloman
Augusta College

James Hostetter
Illinois Valley Community College

George Huxel
Midway College

Barry Jones
Florida National College, Hialeah

Lloyd Kalugin
Middlesex County College

Bernard G. Keller, Jr.
Southwestern Oklahoma State University

George Kelley
Erie Community College City Campus

Don Kelly
North Hennepin Community College

Corliss Keown
Morgan Community College

Bobbie Kuhlman
Chaffey College

Rosalie Lapone
Pima Medical Institute

Grant L. Learned
Defiance College

Edward J. LeMay
Massasoit Community College

Rick Lester
University of North Alabama

Mark Lipton
New School for Social Research

Terry Lowe
Lincoln College

Gloria J. Lynch
Mount Aloysius Junior College

Rex R. Mahlman
Northwestern Oklahoma State University

Marvin Mai
Empire College

Kathy Malenky
Cape Cod Community College

Dan Marrone
State University of New York at Farmingdale

Kristi Maruska
Mankato Tech College

Robert Mathis
University of Nebraska at Omaha

Nicholas Mathys
De Paul University

Eugene C. McCann
Louisiana State University and A&M College

James K. McCollum
University of Alabama in Huntsville

Mike McCuddy
Valparaiso University

Melvin McKnight
Northern Arizona University

Professor Milanowski
Detroit College of Business, Dearborn

John A. Miller
Edison State Community College

Michael J. Miller
Indiana University—Purdue University at Fort Wayne

Richard V. Miller
Harford Community College

Allan Milsop
Greater Hartford Community College

Kathleen Montgomery
University of California, Riverside

Susan Morse
University of Hartford

James Motroni
Golden Gate University

Abbas Nadim
University of New Haven

Hershel Nelson
Polk Community College

Robert Nixon
Prairie State College

Dwight Norris
Auburn University

C. O'Kelly
Providence College

Brian O'Neil
Clarkson University

Gerald E. Parker
St. Louis University

Dianna Parker
Branell College Tampa

Vera Pearson
Labette Community College

Newman S. Peery, Jr.
University of the Pacific

Yolanda Penley
Chandler Gilbert Community College

Marilyn Price
Kirkwood Community College

Ross Prizzia
University of Hawaii, West Oahu College

Sandy Reyna
McLennan Community College

Sharon Reynolds
Minot State College

Pat Rittenbach
Blue Mountain Community College

Anthony Rizzi
Central Missouri State University

Elizabeth A. Robinson
West Liberty State College

Richard Roder
Kalamazoo Valley Community College

Donald P. Rogers
Rollins College

Al Rosenbloom
Lewis University

James L. Ross
University of North Carolina at Charlotte

Wendell Roye
Franklin Pierce College

Charles Ryan
Anoka Ramsey Community College

William J. Scheela
Bemidji State University

Shirley Schooley
Samford University

John Scruggs
Pierce College

William Searle
Asnuntuck Community College

Jane Senger
Northwest Technical College Bemidji

Mary Shannon
Wenatchee Valley College

Pradip Shukla
Chapman University

Connie Sitterly
Texas Woman's University

Leanne Skinner
Columbus Area Vocational Technical School

J. North Smith
George Corley Wallace State Community College at Selma

Leon L. Smith
University of North Alabama

Paul Smith
Park College

Taggart Smith
Purdue University

Susan Somers
Quincy College

Daniel Spicer
University of Central Florida

Deborah St. John
Pierce College at Fort Lewis

H. T. Stanton, Jr.
Barton College

David Starr
Shoreline Community College

Alfred F. Steirt
Lamar University

Anita Sterchi
Albuquerque Technical-Vocational Institute

S. Stover
Cleary College

Bill Stull
Midway College

Jacqueline Stutzman
South Texas Community College

David Surges
Truckee Meadows Community College

Chen Teck Tan
Cumberland College

Parsram Thakur
Community College of Rhode Island

Jerry Thomas
Arapahoe Community College

B. Terry Thornton
Darton College

James Thornton
Champlain College

Patricia Trachy
Pensacola Junior College

Mary Tranquillo
St. Petersburg Junior College

Joseph G. Trebes
Catonsville Community College

Ray F. Tyler
Pennsylvania College of Technology

Maurice F. Villere
University of New Orleans

Francis Von Moll
Tidewater Community College

Richard Voth
Pacific Union College

Cindy Waesner
Ursuline College

Marie Wagner
Allan Hancock College

Lee Ward
Columbia Junior College of Business

Elzberry Waters
Marymount University

Bill Weisgerber
Saddleback College

Alan Winter
Connecticut College

Mary Jane Witter
College of Health Sciences

David Wright
West Liberty State College

Cheryl Wyrick
California State Polytechnic University, Pomona

Experience indicates that the highest quality human relations courses expose students to appropriate human relations concepts, give students an opportunity to apply such concepts to solve human relations problems, and provide an opportunity for students to learn from their application attempts. I have designed the *Human Relations Today* Learning Package, this book and its ancillaries, to allow individuals the flexibility to emphasize any or all of these components within a human relations course to the extent deemed appropriate. I sincerely wish you well in building your course around *Human Relations Today: Concepts and Skills.* Have a great class! Please let me know how I can make this book better in the next edition.

Samuel C. Certo
Professor of Management
Crummer Graduate School of Business
Rollins College
Winter Park, Florida
December 1994

About the Author

Dr. Samuel Certo is a Professor of Management and former Dean at the Roy E. Crummer Graduate School of Business at Rollins College. He has been a professor of management for more than fifteen years and has received prestigious awards, including the Award for Innovative Teaching from the Southern Business Association, the Instructional Innovation Award granted by the Decision Sciences Institute, and the Charles A. Welsh Memorial Award for outstanding teaching at the Crummer School. Dr. Certo's numerous publications include articles in such journals as *Academy of Management Review, The Journal of Experiential Learning and Simulation*, and *Training*. He has also written several successful textbooks, including *Modern Management: Quality, Ethics, and the Global Environment, Strategic Management: Concepts and Applications*, and *Supervision: Quality and Diversity through Leadership*. A past chairman of the Management Education and Development Division of the Academy of Management, he has been honored by that group's Excellence of Leadership Award. Dr. Certo has also served as president of the Association for Business Simulation and Experiential Learning, as associate editor for *Simulation & Games*, and as a review board member of the *Academy of Management Review*. His consulting experience has been extensive, with notable experience on boards of directors.

BRIEF CONTENTS

CONTENTS

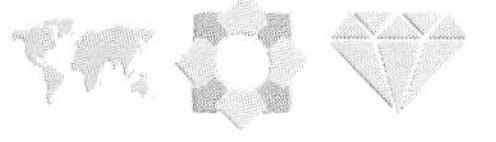

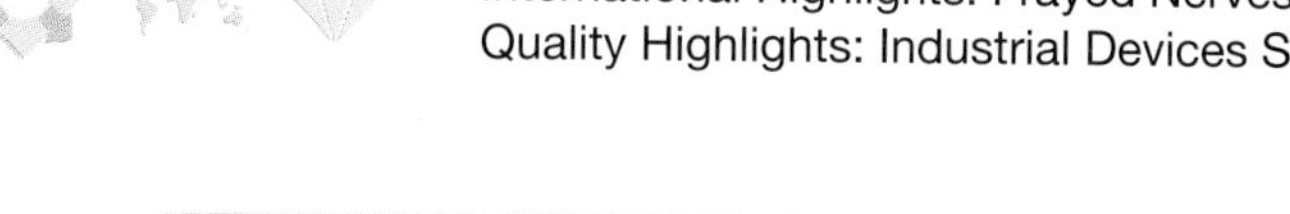

CITIZEN

Note to the Instructor

Austen Press texts are marketed and distributed by Richard D. Irwin, Inc. For assistance in obtaining supplementary material for this and other Austen Press titles, please contact your Irwin sales representative or the customer service division of Richard D. Irwin at (800) 323–4560.

PART OUTLINE

1

Defining Human Relations

CHAPTER

1

Human Relations: Your Key to Success in Organizations

CHAPTER OUTLINE

Introduction: The Importance of Human Relations Skills

History of the Human Relations Function

Scientific Management

Hawthorne Studies: A Turning Point in Human Relations

The 1960s to 1980s: Changes in Work Force, Technology, and Competition

Current Trends in Human Relations

The Quality Emphasis

Teamwork

Diversity in the Workplace

The Globalization of Business

A Book about You

Summary

Self-Portrait: Your Starting Point

International Highlights: Hitachi's Company Family

Teamwork Highlights: Work Teams Make Chrysler Hot

Diversity Highlights: La Romagnola's Melting Pot

Learning Objectives

- Define *human relations skills* and explain why they are important to your success in an organization.
- Define *scientific management* and explain how it differs from today's methods of dealing with human relations.
- Explain why the Hawthorne studies were a turning point in human relations.
- Explain how changes in work-force composition, advances in technology, and increased competition changed the nature of human relations during the period from the 1960s to the 1980s.
- Explain the importance of the quality emphasis, teamwork, diversity in the work force, and the globalization of business to human relations today.

MSJ Cooks Up a Happy Crew

Michael Natale, an apprentice chef at the Waldorf Astoria in New York, was used to arriving at work and finding the air conditioner had been on all night; he knew that the last person to leave had been so overworked he'd forgotten to turn it off. Natale was frustrated by the waste of people, time, and money. But as a lower-level employee, his comments about the restaurant industry's poor understanding of "people issues" went unheard.

Today, Natale may be the only CEO in America who talks to dishwashers. Now chief executive of MSJ Organization, which operates a chain of restaurants in South Carolina, Natale views his employees as the source for ideas that make his business work better. There may be six layers of organizational structure at MSJ, but Natale firmly believes that the employees closest to the customer are a company's most important asset. "There's wasted dollars lying around everywhere—from the front door to the garbage can—but you're not going to find them unless you get the people involved," he says.

Profits are slim in the restaurant business, but MSJ's restaurants are making money by saving money. Focusing on employee relationships and behavior as much as on menu and value helps keep down expenses. MSJ emphasizes open lines of communication, constant and consistent training, and competitive salaries and incentives.

Advances in technology are not feared. "The best technology is expensive. But once you set it up, the work gets done faster and with less labor," says Natale. In addition, MSJ employs a consulting group that runs on-site behavior evaluations and shows managers how to nurture the psychological needs of the staff. The result? Productivity has soared while labor has remained at 10 percent of sales.

Source: Jack Hayes, "California Dreaming Links Employees with Success," *Nation's Restaurant News,* July 26, 1993, pp. 7, 53. Photo source: © Jonathan Pite/Gamma Liaison.

Introduction: The Importance of Human Relations Skills

human relations
Interactions with other people.

human relations skills
The ability to work effectively with other people.

You get together with friends and confide or argue, eat dinner, or study. You sign up for the intramural softball league and help decide who should play which position on your team. You join a theater group and learn how important the stage crew, lighting designer, costume designer, and understudies—as well as the lead actors—are to the success of the whole production. You participate in class discussion of a controversial topic, taking the lone stance on one side of an issue. You walk through the doors of a company on your first day at a new job and meet your supervisor and colleagues. Without being aware of it, you are experiencing **human relations**—interactions with other people. Like everyone else, you've undoubtedly had both successes and failures in your working relationships with other people. Like Michael Natale in the opening vignette, you've probably encountered "people issues" that need to be addressed. This book will show you the importance of consciously developing your **human relations skills**—the ability to work effectively with other people. It will turn your experience into expertise.

Regardless of what field you enter when you graduate from college, you need to know how to work effectively with other people. You may discover that you enjoy dealing with human relations issues so much that you decide on a career in that field, or you may simply use your human relations skills to build a career in another area. In either case, the personal growth you gain through a well-developed ability to relate to coworkers, supervisors, and members of work teams as well as people from diverse cultural, geographic, and economic backgrounds will go a long way toward ensuring a successful career. In addition, your human relations skills will contribute to the overall success of the organization for which you work. Take some time now to assess your starting point in human relations by taking the short quiz in the "Self-Portrait" box.

organization
A group of individuals brought together for a common purpose and structured in a way that should best serve that purpose.

An **organization** is a group of individuals brought together for a common purpose and is structured in a way that should best serve that purpose. Thus, an organization is a living creature: its structure is its skeleton, its people are its flesh and blood. In order for the organization to reach its greatest potential, the people must work together efficiently and effectively. This may seem obvious, but many aspects of human relations were historically ignored or handled as afterthoughts by company managers. For example, in years past, an employee with a drug-abuse problem might simply have been dismissed by an employer; now, the employer might very well provide on-site treatment for the problem. Moreover, companies are increasingly providing managers with the training to recognize signs of substance abuse in a poorly performing employee so as to correct the problem sooner rather than later. Thus, the human relations approach values the employee as an important resource rather than viewing him or her as a disposable piece of company machinery.

Many companies now encourage employee involvement in decision making, support the use of teams to detect and solve problems, and teach employees to respect and value cultural diversity. As more and more firms cross international boundaries, employees who are able to understand and get along with other people are viewed as crucial to success. Table 1.1 lists work skills and characteristics most valued by employers. Note how many of these have to do with human relations!

Self-Portrait

Your Starting Point

Rate your human relations knowledge and skills on a scale of 1 to 5, with 5 the highest score. Half the questions provide an overview of the material to be covered in this course; the remainder concern your personal skills.

_____ I deal with everyone in an honest, ethical manner.

_____ I understand how to communicate effectively.

_____ I can build a productive, no-conflict relationship with people who have a different set of personal values.

_____ I understand the various types of groups, and the roles they play in organizations.

_____ I can identify the stages of group development.

_____ I do not take human relations mistakes personally.

_____ I understand how to use motivational techniques.

_____ I repair an injured relationship as soon as possible.

_____ I can describe a time-management system.

_____ I can describe several ways to handle stress.

_____ I can release my frustrations without hurting others.

_____ I can manage my career successfully.

_____ I avoid ethnic or sexual remarks that could be misinterpreted.

_____ I understand how to create better human relations.

_____ I can develop productive relationships with workers who are older or younger than I am.

_____ I can explain the relationship and differences between sexism and sexual harassment.

_____ I know how to gain power in an organization.

_____ I understand how attitudes and personal behavior affect human relations and organizational performance.

_____ I can list several ways to overcome resistance to change.

Top score is 95, but you are not expected to be an expert and will probably score much lower. You will take a similar test at the end of this course to compare your skills now and then.

Quick Quiz 1.1

1. What are the two main components of an organization?
2. In Table 1.1, all of the following desirable characteristics involve human relations skills except:
   a. influential personality
   b. time management
   c. group effectiveness
   d. communication skill

History of the Human Relations Function

People have been working together since the beginning of civilization. At first they cooperated as hunters and gatherers, then as subsistence farmers, to secure food, shel-

Table 1.1 Work Skills/Characteristics Most Valued by Employers

Skill/Characteristic	Application
Influential personality	Leadership
Group effectiveness	Negotiation
Time management	Goal setting
Adaptability	Problem solving
Communication skill	Writing, leadership
Learning ability	Job competence

Source: Adapted from A. P. Carnevale, L. J. Garner, and A. S. Meltzer, *Workplace Basics: The Essential Skills Employers Want* (San Francisco: Jossey-Bass, 1990).

ter, and clothing. In these early economic systems, people worked together in small groups with other family or tribe members to produce what they needed for survival. If they were lucky enough to produce more than they needed, they might trade with neighbors who had a surplus of something else. For instance, they might trade surplus eggs with a neighbor in return for surplus butter. Work relationships were very simple and direct; most people dealt on a daily basis with family members or others they knew well.

As trade developed, craftworker and merchant classes developed. Someone would set up a small workshop to produce, say, metal implements or perhaps a small store to sell imported cloth. Even these enterprises tended to be a family affair. However, some outsiders did come to work for these small businesses, usually as apprentices. A young worker attached himself or herself to the older, more experienced worker in order to learn the trade. Again, however, the work force for these small businesses tended to be small and close knit, and working relationships remained rather simple.

It wasn't until industrialism emerged in England during the 1800s that a different economic system began changing people's work lives. The new industrial manufacturers needed people to run the machines in their factories. People moved from the countryside to the cities to work in these factories. Jobs became more specialized: one person might work all day unloading raw materials into a hopper and another might remove partially finished products from one machine and place them in another. These workers didn't get a chance to see the whole production process from beginning to end. Instead, supervisors and managers were given the specialized job of making sure the workers under them did all the small tasks required to complete the larger process.

This was a very efficient process for producing large quantities of standardized products, but it introduced some new circumstances for the people working in the factories. Moving into large urban areas, people often felt uprooted at first. Eventually, instead of relying on family and neighbors for social support, they came to rely on coworkers who might have quite different backgrounds from their own. Instead of talking directly to the family patriarch or the master craftsman when a work-related problem arose, people had to talk to a boss who knew little or nothing about them as individuals. In addition, people who performed only narrow pieces of the production process often became alienated from the end results. It was harder to take pride in producing hundreds of bolts of fabric when one had merely watched over the whirring and clacking machines than it was to take pride in the single length of cloth one had produced by harvesting the cotton, cleaning it, spinning it, and weaving it on a loom in homey surroundings. For these reasons, workers in the new industrial workplace often felt stresses that had not affected workers in earlier economic systems.

Early in the Industrial Revolution, human relations skills were not considered important, and working conditions were hard. These girls in a southern cotton mill often worked up to 13-hour days.

Scientific Management

scientific management The merging of people and the work environment to produce optimum results.

At first, the owners and managers of factories had little understanding of these stresses and their effect on both people and production. Supervisory responsibilities were mainly geared toward achieving the greatest manufacturing output possible. The well-being of workers was secondary to the efficiency of the plant. Thus, if rest periods increased productivity, workers were allowed rest periods. If plant layout could be redesigned to eliminate wasted motions, then machinery and people would be moved around accordingly. This practice was called **scientific management**, the merging of people and the work environment to produce optimum results.

Frederick W. Taylor, often called the "father of scientific management," could also be called the first efficiency expert.[1] His approach was to break down jobs into simple, specialized steps, and then match these smaller jobs with appropriately skilled people. This way, a worker with the skill for one step in the production process did not need any other skills. Management considered employees' motivation to be based solely on pay incentives tied to units produced. So jobs were kept simple, and workers were expected to perform them as quickly as possible in order to earn as much money as possible. It seemed like such a logical plan! But workers were exploited, generally considered to be no more important than the machines themselves. Long hours, dangerous working conditions, and low pay were commonplace. Factory workers certainly did not participate in decision making or problem solving. Human relations skills were not only not a priority, they weren't even an issue.

People are not machines. Most enjoy variety, challenge, and the satisfaction of feeling responsible for a job well done. Workers interact with each other in a way that affects their job performance. During the days of scientific management, many workers did not respond to pay incentives to increase production because they were afraid that management would raise production standards. Newcomers were quickly advised, "Don't ruin it for all of us." Thus, scientific management created a vicious circle in the workplace.

But some of the principles of scientific management were indeed valid, even if they were practiced poorly. Frank B. and Lillian M. Gilbreth's "one best way"[2] was based on sound principles of efficiency that they tested on their own 12 children (recounted in the family's book, *Cheaper by the Dozen*).[3] Their idea was to avoid unnecessary motions in accomplishing a task; they recommended this approach for everything from childrearing to surgery to golf.[4] And certainly, Taylor's practice of matching job requirements to employee skills in order to meet precise standards was valuable as well. His time studies provided insights that led to necessary specialization in many jobs (though, taken too far, this specialization eventually led to the numbing boredom of the assembly line). Taylor, like the Gilbreths, also applied his efficiency ideas to golf: he designed his own clubs to reflect economy of movement. Further, his development of a "more efficient" overhand pitch in baseball changed the game forever.[5]

So we can see that the tenets of scientific management had merit. But they were just too narrow to explain or predict the important aspects of human behavior. It took the Hawthorne studies to suggest some of those.

Hawthorne Studies: A Turning Point in Human Relations

Hawthorne effect
An improvement in job performance resulting from feelings of self-worth.

The **Hawthorne effect**—an improvement in job performance resulting from feelings of self-worth—was discovered by accident. In 1927, researchers (led by Elton Mayo of Harvard) isolated a group of workers at the Western Electric Company in Chicago from the rest of the company to test the effects of various changes in the work environment (such as light and heat) on their productivity.[6] The researchers were surprised to find that production kept increasing no matter how they changed the environment. They concluded that *simply paying special attention to these workers increased their motivation to produce.* Just being noticed made the workers want to do well. Their enhanced feelings of self-worth led to pride in their work that transcended changes in the physical surroundings.

This discovery was the birth of human relations as we know the field today. Elton Mayo became known as the "father of human relations." Because of Mayo's (and his colleague, Fritz J. Roethlisberger's) work, humans took center stage in management studies. From here on, the psychological and sociological aspects of management would figure prominently.

Keep in mind that the business community was still unaware of social issues that would later have a profound effect on management practices as they relate to human relations. Most manufacturers and business owners felt no obligation to make employment a satisfying experience for workers, nor did they yet connect job satisfaction with performance. But gradually, from the 1930s to the 1970s, companies began to recognize this link. The human relations function in business, at first confined to a "personnel" employee or department, steadily gained recognition as an important part of an organization's operation. Later, the term *human resources* entered the general business vocabulary, signifying a deepened respect for the worker. He or she was to be regarded as a precious resource, not an easily replaceable cog in the machinery of a company.

The 1960s to 1980s: Changes in Work Force, Technology, and Competition

The transition from the term *personnel* to *human resources* in many companies showed the increasing authority and importance human relations skills had assumed. In addition, social movements that produced changes in the work force, technology, and the competitive environment all influenced human relations in the workplace.

In the 1960s, the civil rights movement threw a spotlight on human relations at work. New laws prohibiting discrimination against minority workers in areas such as hiring and promotion held employers accountable for their actions. The women's movement, which gained tremendous momentum during the 1970s, lobbied for equal pay and opportunities for women in the workplace. Although the equal rights amendment to the Constitution (which would have made employment discrimination unconstitutional)

International competition is forcing changes in human relations. Korea, for example, is no longer able to compete in the world marketplace on the basis of workers' low wages, but must focus on such issues as quality and human resources. Samsung's Chairman Lee Kun Hee (on the video screen) is applying what he calls "shock therapy" by sending his managers to visit U.S. retailers to study product quality and by recruiting women managers.
Photo source: Ki Ho Park-Kistone.

was defeated twice, a number of discrimination suits filed by women against their employers were successful. The Americans with Disabilities Act (ADA), designed to provide more employment opportunities for disabled workers, further deepened the complexity of human relations issues at work. As more doors opened for more different types of people, human relations skills—among employees as well as between workers and management—grew increasingly important to the overall success of an organization.

The importance of human relations was often manifested by formal programs. Employee assistance programs (EAPs) as well as counseling and referral programs were initiated to help employees with particular problems such as substance abuse. Preventive health programs—to promote both physical and emotional health—were instituted to help keep satisfactory employees from developing problems. Efforts were made to reduce stress in the workplace.

During these years, the rapid advance of technology in many fields necessitated the retraining of employees. Technological advances in Japan and other countries led to organizational restructuring of American companies to cut costs and allow quicker responses to environmental changes and to a new emphasis on the value of creativity and technical skills among employees. Downsizing a company meant the loss of traditional job categories as well as the restructuring of work roles. Thus, business owners realized that they needed to upgrade employees' skills to fill the more technically demanding jobs being created. Human relations professionals were often called upon to organize educational or retraining programs. Chapter 3, "Integrating People and Technology," discusses this issue in greater detail.

As more and more companies entered the global marketplace, domestic and international competition also forced changes in human relations. As mentioned earlier, technological advances intensified competition and necessitated restructuring and retraining. Also, as American businesses came into contact with businesses and governments abroad, people of different nations began to interact on a regular basis, further changing the composition of the work force. Never before was there a greater need for understanding among people and for more sophisticated human relations skills.

Quick Quiz 1.2

1. Which of the following is an example of scientific management?
   a. Shorten lunchtime by 15 minutes to increase the number of units shipped each day.
   b. Lengthen lunchtime by 15 minutes to give workers time to do errands.

Figure 1.1 **Personal and Organizational Growth**

The personal growth of the employee can contribute to the growth of the organization.

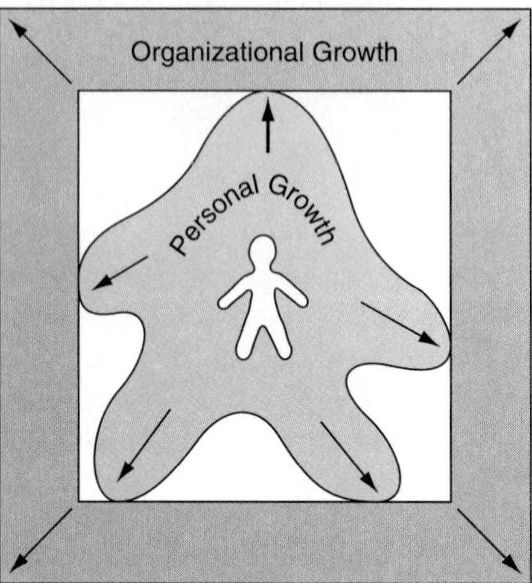

c. Redesign the plant layout so more workers are near windows and can benefit from natural light.

2. What major discovery did the Hawthorne studies make?
3. What three major social movements of the 1960s to 1980s changed the work force?

Current Trends in Human Relations

Current trends in human relations continue to reflect a rapidly changing world. Today, the concept of human relations embraces both the individual worker and the entire organization. Managers who adopt a human relations point of view try to nurture employees and motivate them to reach their full potential—not just to satisfy them in their current jobs, but to encourage them to set and reach higher goals. This benefits the organization because the result is more capable, motivated workers. The personal growth of the individual employee leads to a more profitable company (see Figure 1.1). As an employee develops all possible talents, he or she becomes more productive, more cost efficient, more creative. As personal growth leads to greater self-esteem, employees are also likely to be more productive. With each success, they work harder and better.

Projections for the year 2000 show that personal growth will indeed be a concern for more and more workers as a growing number of jobs require higher education and more sophisticated training. Table 1.2 shows that employment is expected to rise in occupations such as health care and computer services, while it will decline in manufacturing and retail jobs. Employees will have to develop their talents in order to fulfill the new, more demanding jobs.

This emphasis on personal growth in the workplace focuses attention on professionals in the human relations field. These specialists explore the various aspects of

Table 1.2

Employment Change in Selected Industries, 1988–2000

Industry[a]	1988 Level (Thousands)	Annual Rate of Change, 1988–2000
Fastest Growing		
Computer and data processing services	678	4.9
Outpatient facilities and health services, n.e.c.[b]	675	4.7
Personnel supply services	1,369	4.1
Water and sanitation including combined services	152	3.9
Residential care	391	3.8
Offices of health practitioners	1,850	3.5
Arrangement of passenger transportation	175	3.4
Research, management, and consulting services	811	3.2
Individual and miscellaneous social services	571	3.2
Personal services, n. e. c.	294	3.2
Nursing and personal care facilities	1,319	3.1
Credit reporting and business services, n.e.c.	776	3.1
Miscellaneous publishing	79	3.1
Security and commodity brokers and exchanges	449	3.0
Advertising	237	2.8
Legal services	852	2.8
Automotive rentals, without drivers	164	2.7
Accounting, auditing, and services, n.e.c.	530	2.7
Miscellaneous transportation services	141	2.7
Detective and protective services	464	2.6
Most Rapidly Declining		
Tobacco manufacture	56	–2.8
Telephone and telegraph apparatus	111	–2.3
Miscellaneous textile goods	56	–2.3
Alcoholic beverages	72	–2.2
Office and accounting machines	56	–2.2
Footwear, except rubber and plastic	90	–2.1
Railroad transportation	299	–2.1
Tires and inner tubes	84	–2.0
Photographic equipment and supplies	112	–1.8
Coal mining	151	–1.8
Luggage, handbags, and leather products, n.e.c.	54	–1.8
Miscellaneous transportation equipment	62	–1.7
Engines and turbines	94	–1.6
Electronic home entertainment equipment	85	–1.6
Sugar and confectionery products	98	–1.6
Apparel	893	–1.6
Knitting mills	211	–1.5
Sawmills and planing mills	206	–1.5
Automotive stampings	102	–1.5
Metal cans and shipping containers	53	–1.5

Source: Bureau of Labor Statistics, *Outlook 2000* (Washington D.C.: U.S. Government Printing Office, 1990), p. 30.

[a]Ranking is based on industries with employment levels of more than 50,000 in 1988.

[b]n.e.c. = not elsewhere classified

International Highlights

Hitachi's Company Family

However good your human relations skills are at home, applying those skills abroad can bring about culture shock. In the United States, the rights and responsibilities of the individual are prized; in other countries, the collective good is paramount.

A Canadian graduate student on an eight-month assignment in Japan with Hitachi Ltd. was taken aback by the influence of a country's culture on its human relations. Ming Ho was especially surprised by the extent to which the company involves itself in the lives of its workers. At Hitachi, employees between the ages of 20 and 33 are eligible to live in company-subsidized dormitories until they marry—at which point they are given a larger, subsidized apartment.

Since workers rarely socialize outside the office and almost all marry within it, Hitachi runs a tea-ceremony club as a way for male workers to meet their female counterparts. Japanese women are expected to quit work as soon as they become engaged, Ho says. At Hitachi, he remembers one female coworker with a master's degree in computer science who was gradually given less and less responsibility as she became older but did not marry.

In return for its generosity to workers, Hitachi expects total dedication. Ho says the workday typically runs 11 or 12 hours, and many people also work weekends.

In addition, employees must leave phone numbers where they can be reached at all hours, even when on vacation. "It doesn't matter what you're doing," Ho insists. "As a Japanese employee, the company has the ultimate right to interfere in your private life in order to fix a problem."

Hitachi's paternalistic role also requires employees to sweep their own offices and empty their own trash, which Ho says is aimed at instilling pride and a sense of ownership. That encouragement helps develop incredible loyalty. "What we have going for us [in the West] is a lot of creativity, but Japanese managers can keep their employees inside the company."

Source: Danielle Bochove, "Culture Shock Proves a Major Component of Work-Study Tour," *The Globe and Mail,* July 6, 1993, p. B16.

personal growth in order to help an organization achieve its goals. It's likely that, as companies demand more of their employees in the future, employees will continue to demand more of the companies for which they work. Perhaps these mutual demands will spark a new kind of loyalty between employer and employee, which all but disappeared during the downsizing and restructuring of the 1980s. The "International Highlights" box takes a look at how the relationship between employer and employee varies within different countries and cultures.

There are four important human relations areas in which to keep track of current trends: the quality emphasis, teams in the workplace, diversity in the workplace, and the globalization of business. You'll read discussion of these areas throughout this book; in addition, you'll encounter boxed highlights that feature them. All relate to personal growth and organizational growth through the interaction of people—in other words, human relations skills.

The Quality Emphasis

quality approach
A business orientation in which all members of the organization are involved in improving quality in order to satisfy customers.

empowerment
Giving employees the authority to make decisions that affect their jobs.

Quality as a formal approach to business practices emerged during the 1980s, gaining full steam toward the end of the decade and in the early 1990s. The **quality approach** is a business orientation in which all members of the organization are involved in improving quality in order to satisfy customers.[7] Although Chapter 2, "Maintaining Quality and Productivity: Emphasizing TQM," discusses in more detail the quality approach to managing people, for now keep in mind that part of the quality approach involves employee **empowerment**—giving employees the authority to make decisions that affect their jobs. This goes a step further than just trying to make employees happy. (In fact, some studies have shown that happiness itself doesn't make workers more productive.[8]) When workers have the power to make decisions, they also have the

Figure 1.2 **Reasons for Implementing Employee Participation**

*Responded 4 or 5 on a 5-point scale: 1 = little or no extent; 5 = very positive; "no basis to judge" also a possible response.

Source: Reprinted with permission from the September, 1992 issue of *Total Quality,* Lakewood Publications, 50 South Ninth St., Minneapolis, MN 55402. All rights reserved.

power to develop their talents and contribute more fully to the company as a whole. Managers who practice effective human relations skills allow their employees at least a certain degree of empowerment. Figure 1.2 shows reasons why companies decide to empower employees by encouraging them to participate more fully in all aspects of the business. Note how many reasons refer to human relations!

Teamwork

Building teams in the workplace is also part of the quality emphasis, and in many cases goes hand in hand with empowerment. There are as many different kinds of employee teams as there are organizations, but all are designed to accomplish the organization's short-term or long-term goals. A team may be cross-functional, made up of employees from different departments or areas of expertise. It may be permanent or temporary, formed to accomplish a particular task and then disbanded. The story of one cross-functional team, whose success in creating a product helped turn around the image and financial fortunes of a company, is recounted in the "Teamwork Highlights" box.

Being part of a team helps people develop their human relations skills, thus increasing their own effectiveness. Milacron Inc., a well-established manufacturer of factory machine tools, fell into decline during the 1980s. In staging its comeback, it embraced the idea of teamwork so seriously that it code-named its team-based efforts

Teamwork Highlights

Work Teams Make Chrysler Hot

When a hose can't be found, a team effort—the bucket brigade—is the most effective way to put out a fire. Likewise, a team effort is increasingly the way organizations are putting out fires and solving problems. Chrysler Corp. is among the companies discovering teams can *start* fires, as well.

Since the automaker changed to a work-team structure in 1989, it has significantly reduced its product-development cycle, increased its market share and profits, and won acclaim from car experts.

When Chrysler converted its work force into four horizontally structured, cross-functional teams, it also created a special projects group. "Team Viper" pulled together 80 volunteers from various departments to work quickly, strategically, and cost effectively. In a radical departure from the usual practices of the Big Three automakers, Team Viper put all the players—marketers, manufacturers, and engineers—in one room to tackle a project.

The team developed the Viper, from concept to showroom, in only three years, an unheard-of time frame for the industry. The project cost $50 million— a fifth of the cost of a conventional project—although only 2,000 cars are produced annually versus 200,000 by conventional car assembly. All 1993 models of the $50,000 car were sold before they were built. "It demonstrated that the team concept works," says Jean Pascal Mallebay-Vacqueur, who headed the team.

Team Viper's success has boosted Chrysler's bottom line, as well as its morale and confidence. Car buyers, critics, and industry experts "put us down four years ago, claiming we couldn't do anything right," says Mallebay-Vacqueur. "Because of the Viper project, we no longer accept mediocrity in ourselves or our products."

Source: Dawn M. Baskerville, "Why Business Loves Work Teams," *Quality Digest,* October 1993, pp. 41–43.

Operation Wolfpack. "It's not a joke to us," remarks CEO Daniel J. Meyer. "Wolves are survivors. They work in teams, and they go out to kill." Company management formed teams of workers—called focus factories—that were given the power to engineer, produce, and service a particular product line. Each focus factory made its own decisions about purchasing supplies, designing machines, and pricing its product. Team members were keenly aware that the survival of the organization depended on how effective they were, and indirectly, how well they worked together. Although it will take several years for the company to achieve a complete turnaround, by the early 1990s the wolfpack teams had helped Milacron cut production costs on many products by as much as 30 to 40 percent.[9]

Diversity in the Workplace

Human relations skills involve getting along with many different kinds of people. (Chapter 4, "Managing Diversity," discusses this topic in depth.) As more and more people enter the work force through opportunities created by legislation (such as the Americans with Disabilities Act), through opportunities created by special training or education, and through the globalization of business, organizations must constantly adjust to meet the human relations demands brought about by these changes. (Figure 1.3 depicts the increases in work-force diversity in American companies.)

For instance, Umanoff & Parsons, a small bakery and catering company in New York City, began hiring employees from diverse backgrounds in the early 1980s, when the company was just getting started. "Our original [full-time] staff was quite incredible," recalls Jane Umanoff, one of the owners, speaking of the Haitian workers they first hired. Now the company does $2 million in business each year and has 35 employees from Haiti, Trinidad, Jamaica, Grenada, the Dominican Republic, and Russia. Across the country, in San Diego, Debi Kelly, the human resources director for magazine publisher Trader Publications, explains that her firm has two major

Figure 1.3

Increases in Work-Force Diversity

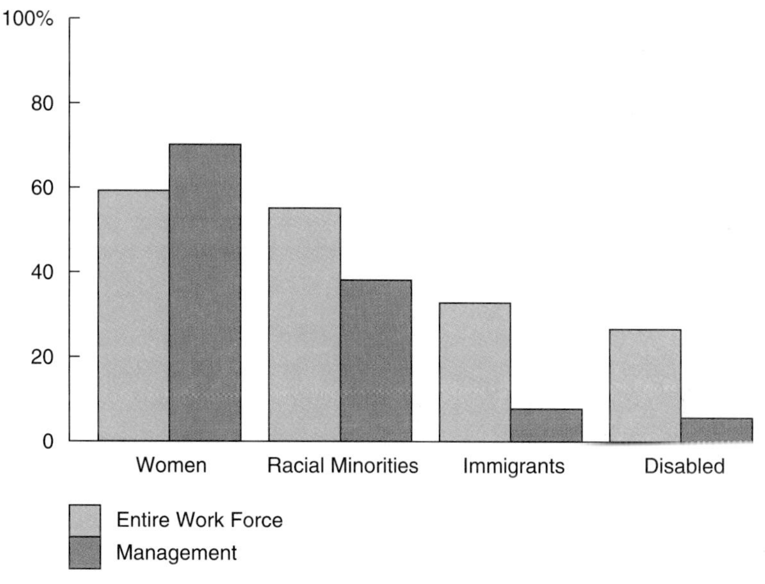

Source: Reprinted by permission, Nation's Business, September 1992. Copyright 1992, U.S. Chamber of Commerce.

objectives: to foster effective teamwork among its 200 employees, who are white, black, Hispanic, and Asian; and to manage human relations with customers, who now also come from more diverse backgrounds.[10] Clearly, as the work force becomes more complex, so do human relations issues. But a diverse work force enriches the organization, contributing to the personal and professional growth of employees, who learn from each other. The "Diversity Highlights" box profiles a company making a deliberate effort to diversify its work force.

The Globalization of Business

The business world seems to grow smaller and smaller every year as more countries open their doors to each other for trade. American firms that want to do business overseas must cope with a maze of regulations, economic and political differences, traditions, and languages in order to be successful. Overcoming all of these potential obstacles involves human relations skills.

When McDonald's (which has 13,000 restaurants worldwide) opened its first restaurant in Beijing, it was touted by communist newspapers as a model employer in a society that was struggling toward a form of capitalism. But suddenly, the *Beijing Youth News* published an exposé accusing McDonald's of low pay and poor working conditions. "Are we going to keep swallowing our complaints and listen to these cheats, or are we going to spit out the complaints in our hearts?" cried Dong Tao, 23, a McDonald's employee, in a related circular. The accusations were a human relations nightmare for McDonald's. Tim Lai, managing director of the Beijing restaurant,

Diversity Highlights

La Romagnola's Melting Pot

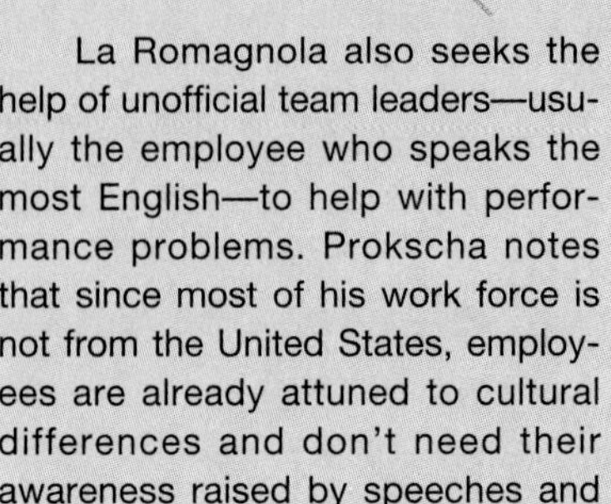

Changing demographics are forcing workers and their employers to get used to a work force that isn't white, male, and English speaking. Some companies, however, have embraced change by deliberately creating a diverse work force.

The employees at La Romagnola, a $5-million pasta maker based in Winter Park, Florida, include immigrants from Vietnam, Puerto Rico, Romania, and Bulgaria. Yet a common thread binds this group: these workers—who comprise two-thirds of the company's 30 production workers—are refugees, hired through the Catholic Refugee Service in Orlando.

Owner Herb Prokscha has combined his decision to diversify La Romagnola's work force with a realistic sense of diversity's difficulties. Language barriers are overcome with the help of translators; training is done by demonstration. As in many companies, new hires start in the least desirable jobs and move into other areas as their skills develop. Recognizing that immigrants who don't speak English well will gravitate toward others in their same ethnic group, the company has used those natural inclinations to encourage a strong sense of teamwork.

La Romagnola also seeks the help of unofficial team leaders—usually the employee who speaks the most English—to help with performance problems. Prokscha notes that since most of his work force is not from the United States, employees are already attuned to cultural differences and don't need their awareness raised by speeches and newsletters. Instead, the company focuses on the individual, such as by helping an employee schedule work hours around English classes.

Source: Ellyn E. Spragins, "Managing Diversity," *Inc.*, January 1993, p. 33.

countered that the Beijing employees are paid a higher rate than the average Beijing wage and even receive a housing allowance, as well as medical and education benefits.[11] It's easy to see how misunderstandings between workers and management of two very different cultures can arise. But most of these conflicts can be resolved through good human relations skills. As you read further in this book, you'll learn more about how people from all kinds of backgrounds—and in all kinds of situations—learn to work together effectively.

Quick Quiz 1.3

1. Which aspect of the quality approach gives employees the authority to make decisions that affect their jobs?
2. Being part of a team in the workplace is beneficial in all of the following ways except:
   a. It helps develop good human relations skills.
   b. It can help increase effectiveness.
   c. It guarantees career advancement.
3. In order to foster good human relations, an American company that wants to conduct business overseas should:
   a. hire managers who are native to the host country, if possible.
   b. require workers overseas to follow a rigid set of standards and practices that are customary in the United States.
   c. pay overseas workers more than company employees in the United States.

A Book about You

A book about human relations is a book about you. It is a book about the interactions you have with other people in any kind of organization: at work, in class, as a member

Matsushita, a Japanese electronics and appliance giant, has built more than 150 plants in 38 countries and has adapted to distant markets and diverse cultures. Listed first among Matsushita's six lessons for being global is, "Be a good corporate citizen in every country, respecting cultures, customs, and languages." Shown are Muslim workers at midday prayer in a Matsushita plant in Malaysia.

Photo source: © 1994 Alan Levenson.

Photo Exercise

Imagine that you are the manager of your company's new shoe manufacturing plant in Guadalajara, Mexico. What tactics would you initiate to "respect the culture, customs, and languages" of your Mexican employees?

of a club, as a player on a sports team. This book is designed to make you more aware of these interactions and improve your skills.

You've just completed Part 1, "Defining Human Relations," which introduces the different facets of human relations and how these skills are key to your success in an organization. Part 2, "Modern Human Relations Challenges," raises human relations issues of the contemporary business world: maintaining quality and productivity, integrating people and technology, and managing cultural diversity. Part 3, "Foundations of Human Relations Processes," walks you through the process of communicating with others and introduces you to the skills of motivating, leading, and managing stress at work. Part 4, "The Organizational Social System," explains how people behave in organizations. Part 5, "People Working Together," shows you how teamwork, conflict and change, and enriched jobs all contribute to a positive work experience—and success. Finally, Part 6, "Special Topics," focuses on international opportunities and the ethical and social responsibility aspects of the human relations function in organizations.

Look for yourself in these chapters. Take note of ways in which you might differ from others and ways in which you are similar. Use the knowledge you gain from this book to sharpen your people skills in every organization to which you belong. As you begin your professional career—in human relations or in any other field—remember that the way you relate to other people will be the key to your success.

Summary

- **Define *human relations skills* and explain why they are important to your success in an organization.** Human relations skills are the ability to work effectively with other people. The personal growth you gain through a well-developed ability to relate to coworkers, supervisors, members of work teams, and people from diverse cultural, geographic, and economic backgrounds helps you become a more effective employee.

- **Define *scientific management* and explain how it differs from today's methods of dealing with human relations.** Scientific management is the merging of people and the work environment to produce optimum results. Today's methods of dealing with human relations focus on personal growth of employees as a route to success for the employees and the organization as a whole.

- **Explain why the Hawthorne studies were a turning point in human relations.** The Hawthorne studies concluded that attention from management or others increased workers' motivation to produce. The enhanced feelings of self-worth led to pride in their work that transcended changes in the physical surroundings. This discovery shifted the focus from productivity to the worker.

- **Explain how changes in work-force composition, advances in technology, and increased competition changed the nature of human relations during the period from the 1960s to the 1980s.** Major social movements such as the civil rights and feminism movements and the Americans with Disabilities Act opened more doors to different types of workers. The rapid advance in technology necessitated the retraining of many employees. Intensified competition, especially as companies entered the global marketplace, required workers to be able to communicate with and understand more and more different types of people. All of these factors made human relations more complex but also more important to the success of organizations.

- **Explain the importance of the quality emphasis, teamwork, diversity in the work force, and the globalization of business to human relations today.** employees—giving them the authority to make decisions that affect their jobs. When workers have the power to make decisions, they also have the power to develop their talents and contribute more fully to the organization. Working in teams helps people develop their human relations skills, thus increasing their own effectiveness. Diversity in the workplace demands that people be able to communicate with and understand coworkers from different backgrounds. It also means that companies must try to meet the needs of a diverse work force in a way that contributes to the success of the organization. As more American firms seek to do business overseas, they must cope with a maze of regulations, economic and political differences, traditions, and languages. Expert human relations skills can go a long way toward contributing to the success of these ventures.

Key Terms

human relations (4)
human relations skills (4)
organization (4)
scientific management (7)
Hawthorne effect (8)
quality approach (12)
empowerment (12)

Review and Discussion Questions

1. Define *human relations.* Provide some examples you see in everyday life.
2. List four ways that developing human relations skills can help you in your future career.
3. How did industrialism change the workplace and working relationships?
4. What are the benefits of the scientific management movement to today's work force? What are its limitations?
5. Explain the source of the term *Hawthorne effect.* What is unusual about the findings of the Hawthorne studies?
6. How have social changes in the period from the 1960s to the 1980s affected human relations?
7. List four important trends in today's workplace. How can human relations skills help meet these challenges?

A SECOND LOOK

At MSJ Organization, front-line employees are considered an asset. How does CEO Michael Natale use them to improve his business? What other ideas for using this asset might Natale glean from current trends in human relations?

Independent Activity

Crossword Puzzle

To become familiar with the new terms you have learned in Chapter 1, complete the following crossword puzzle:

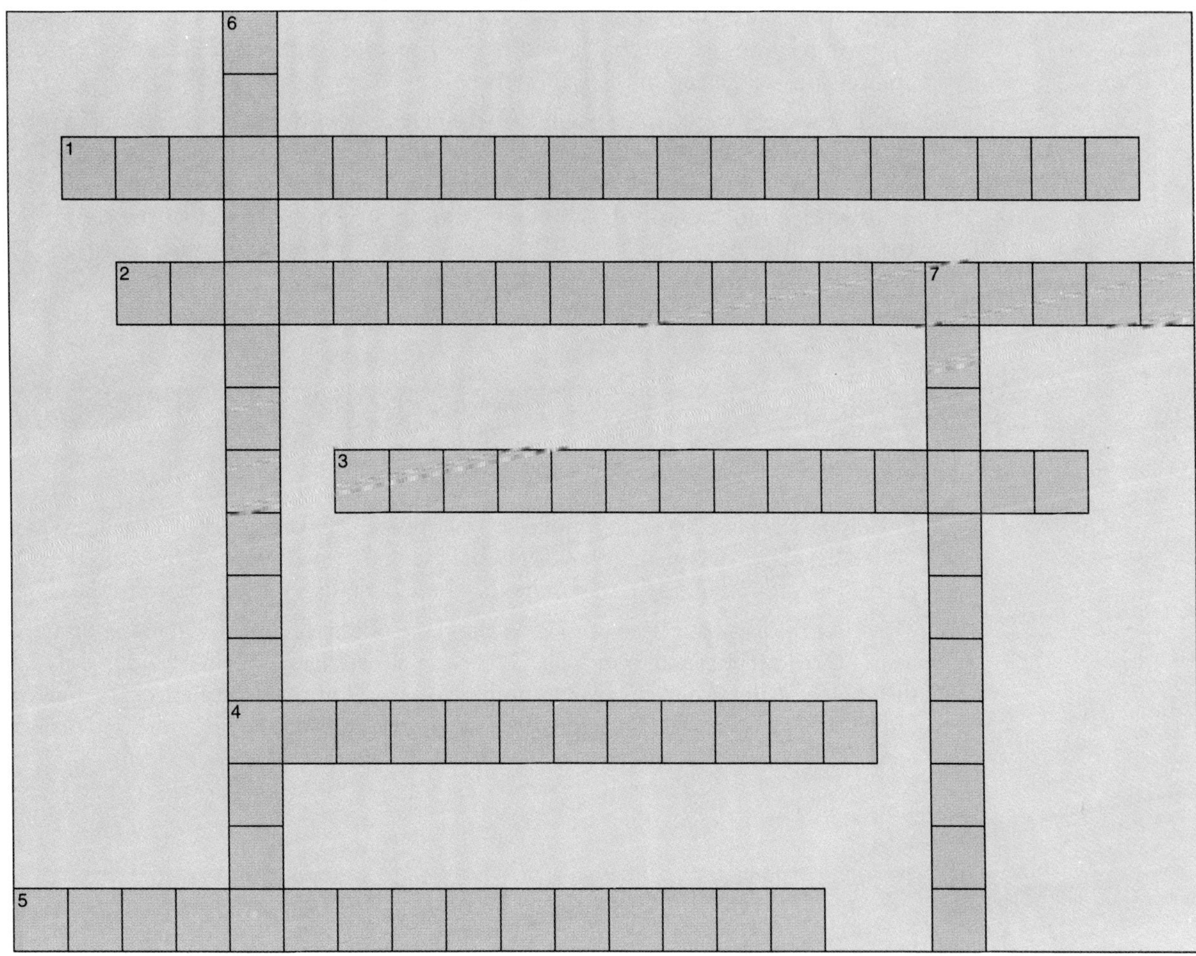

Across

1. The ability to work effectively with other people is _____ _____ _____ .
2. Frederick Taylor, the father of _____ _____, can be called the first efficiency expert.
3. Interactions with other people are called _____ _____.
4. A(n) _____ is a group of individuals brought together for a common purpose and structured in a way that should best serve the purpose.
5. Elton Mayo and his colleagues at the Western Electric Company in Chicago discovered that feelings of self-worth enhanced employee performance, a phenomenon called the _____ _____.

Down

6. A current business orientation in which all members of an organization are involved in improving quality to satisfy customers is _____ _____ .
7. _____ is the act of giving employees the authority to make decisions affecting their jobs.

Skill Builder

Your Human Relations Laboratory

Take some time in this, your first week of class, to look at the state of human relations in your classroom. In future chapters, you will be asked to make similar observations, using what you have learned, to evaluate how human relationships evolve in your "human relations laboratory." Keep all these memos on file. The class will compare its impressions at the end of the semester.

In this first week, write yourself a memo noting where you are sitting in relation to other students and the instructor. Take note of where others are sitting, and make observations on individual and group behavior. For example, are certain groups, such as athletes, minorities, or older students, sitting together? How does the room appear to you in this first week of class? What are your impressions of the classroom? How does the instructor address the students now?

Group Activity

Human Relations and Decision Making (30 minutes)

Divide the class into several groups of one, two, four, and eight people. Each group is to draft a list of possible benefits and drawbacks to employee empowerment in the workplace. The group will then present its top three benefits and drawbacks to the class.

After the lists have been presented, the class should discuss how each group selected its top three benefits and drawbacks. Did certain members' human relations skills affect the choice of the group? Did the number of people in the group affect the outcome? How? What has the class learned about human relations as a result of this activity?

Case Study

State Farm Insures Loyalty

You wouldn't normally think of an insurance company as "radical," but State Farm's focus on customer value as the center of its business strategy has been called just that. The numbers speak for themselves at the insurance company that insures more than 20 percent of the nation's households.

State Farm's success in building customer loyalty is not new. It was important when the company was founded more than 70 years ago, and it is still reflected in retention rates that exceed 90 percent—consistently the best of all the national insurers that sell through agents. State Farm agents make more money by operating in a system engineered for superior loyalty, making them more productive and earning them higher compensation while the company actually pays lower expenses. The result is a 10 percent cost advantage over competitors.

That system of loyalty extends to customers. Agents have the incentive to keep good customers, because commissions are structured to encourage long-term thinking. They receive the same compensation for new auto and fire policies as for renewals, a reward for serving existing customers, not just drawing in new business.

Retention rates are high for agents, too. State Farm agents are loyal, with an average 13 years of tenure, compared with 6 to 9 years for the industry. More than 80 percent of newly appointed agents remain through their fourth year, compared with 20 percent to 40 percent for the rest of the industry. The agent's commitment to a long-term relationship with the company underscores State Farm's lasting relationship with its customer. Agents obviously like being part of a system that consistently delivers superior value to customers: their productivity is 50 percent above industry norms.

A final note: all this emphasis on loyalty and customer service has earned State Farm the largest capital base of any financial services company in North America.

Case Questions

1. What message is State Farm communicating to its agents, its new customers, and its existing customers?
2. State Farm's business philosophy was part of its founding 70 years ago. Can its competitors, or other businesses, create the same kind of loyalty-based system today?
3. Are there any disadvantages to this system?

Source: Frederick F. Reichheld, "Loyalty-Based Management," *Harvard Business Review*, March–April 1993, pp. 68–73.

Case Study

The Little Things Matter at Southwest

"Whenever I tell anyone about the lengths we go to, the first thing I hear is, 'How can a no-frills airline afford it?' My response is, 'How can we *not* afford it?'" says Colleen Barrett, executive vice-president for customers at Southwest Airlines. Barrett is adamant about preserving the service culture that has made the no-frills airline a success and landed it on the most recent list of America's most employee-driven companies.

A secretary in 1971 when the company took off, Barrett oversees all areas dealing with customers—not only the external ones known as passengers, but the internal ones known as employees. Among her innovations are "culture committees" composed of a wide range of employees who meet quarterly to develop ways to maintain Southwest's special spirit. That spirit includes a game book for employees to turn to when bad weather strikes and planes are grounded. Trivia contests and ugly drivers' license pictures aside, the company takes its responsibility to its customers seriously, aiming to get its planes out of the gate within 15 minutes of scheduled departure times, versus 45 minutes for competitors.

Southwest also takes care of its own, sending birthday cards to frequent fliers and employees, a small gesture that resonates. Says Barrett, "A pilot once told me that the card we sent was the only one he got."

Training employees to be a little zany, Southwest works hard at getting them to relate to the public they're serving. "We ask flight attendants, all of whom have to stay overnight at a hotel two or three times a week, what kind of service they get. And we say, 'Remember that customer who wanted that third cup of coffee? Did you serve it with the same smile that the desk clerk gave you when you checked in?' It sounds hokey, but it really helps people to see things from a fresh perspective."

Case Questions

1. How is Southwest achieving the goal of good human relations?
2. How does the social system at Southwest contribute to its success?

3. How effective is Southwest management in human relations?
4. Through its human relations management, what message is Southwest communicating to its internal and external customers?

Source: "Pampering Customers on a Budget," *Working Woman,* April 1993, pp. 19–22.

Quick Quiz Answers

Quick Quiz 1.1

1. people and structure
2. b

Quick Quiz 1.2

1. a
2. Paying special attention to workers increased their motivation to produce.
3. The civil rights movement, women's movement, and the ADA

Quick Quiz 1.3

1. empowerment
2. c
3. a

2

Modern Human Relations Challenges

PART OUTLINE

CHAPTER

2

Maintaining Quality and Productivity: Emphasizing TQM

CHAPTER OUTLINE

Learning Objectives

- Define *total quality management.*
- State how Deming, Juran, and Crosby each influenced the quality movement.
- Define *employee involvement teams* and describe the three main features of a successful team.
- Explain how productivity, motivation, and quality are related.
- Describe the major variations on quality control and improvement.
- Explain how benchmarking, ISO 9000, and the Malcolm Baldrige Award are used to evaluate total quality.

Coleman Produces at Light Speed

In the spring of 1992, Kathleen Stone was looking at the biggest production challenge she could remember. The materials manager at Coleman Co., the Wichita, Kansas, camping equipment maker, had just received a huge rush order for lanterns. A prolonged drought had sapped Colombia's hydroelectric power, and the South American country needed backup lighting.

But 100,000 lanterns, produced and delivered in six weeks? That would mean expanding Coleman's daily output by 30 percent at a time when most of its produced goods went to Wal-Mart stores nationwide.

Five years ago, says Stone, Coleman probably would not have been able to fulfill such a huge order "unless we already had the inventory sitting there." But because the company had spent the past few years learning and mastering new quality techniques, it could rise to the challenge. Adopting the Japanese practice of "just-in-time" manufacturing, Coleman had emptied its warehouses of excess inventory and finished products and overhauled its assembly lines to permit quick changes in production. Equal emphasis was placed on training workers and forging partnerships with suppliers and transportation companies that shared Coleman's quality goals.

As a result, when the Colombian order arrived, Coleman was able to tool up an extra production line and ask about a dozen suppliers to step up shipments of parts for the lamps. In June, Coleman dispatched the last of the orders. "I'm not saying it went off without a hitch, but we got the order and it went out on time," says Stone.

Source: Jon Jacobs, "Making It Just in Time," *Quality Digest,* March 1993, p. 35. Photo source: Courtesy of Coleman Company, Inc.

TQM: Quality and People

Chapter 1 introduced you to the quality approach in the business world: an orientation in which all members of an organization are involved in improving quality in order to satisfy customers.[1] The preceding story about Coleman illustrated how adopting new quality techniques and ideas can help an organization succeed. Table 2.1 defines the eight dimensions of quality that customers find important in a product or service: performance, features, reliability, durability, serviceability, conformance, aesthetics, and perceived quality. In this chapter, you'll learn more about quality as it relates to people—employees, managers, and customers—such as those in the story that opened this chapter.

total quality management (TQM) An organizationwide focus on continuously improving every business process involved in producing and delivering goods or services.

Total quality management (TQM) is about quality and people. TQM is an organizationwide focus on continuously improving every business process involved in producing and delivering goods or services. You might say that "TQM applies quality principles to everything a company does, even the way its departments work together on the inside ... a stem-to-stern approach."[2] In other words, it takes quality people to produce quality products and services.

The lifeblood of TQM is *feedback,* both objective and subjective. Some of the feedback is about the product or service itself; other feedback concerns the performance of employees. Subjective feedback comes from managers, coworkers, and customers themselves and often deals with cooperation, attitude, initiative, and communications skills. Objective feedback is provided by techniques such as:

- *process-flow analysis,* which identifies each decision and action necessary to complete a task and can reveal unnecessary steps in a process
- *cause-and-effect diagrams* that generate a list of all the possible causes of a problem, which can then be evaluated
- *Pareto charts,* which list possible causes of problems by the frequency of their occurrence
- *histograms,* which display distributions of large sets of data grouped in categories
- *scattergrams,* which show the relationship between two variables, events, or different pieces of data.

Many well-known companies use TQM to keep their organizations strong: Federal Express, Hewlett-Packard, Motorola, 3M, Westinghouse, and Xerox. During the Persian Gulf War, the U.S. Navy taught TQM to 1,200 of its leaders, including every admiral and general.[3] It is the "leading business philosophy of the 1990s," according to some experts.[4] And since TQM is a philosophy—not just a single skill—it must spread gradually throughout an organization: one Chicago company estimates that getting started with TQM takes five years, and establishing it firmly takes ten.[5] Finally, for the quality approach (and TQM) to be successful in a business, everyone must be working together toward the same goal. Richard C. Buetow, senior vice-president and director of quality at Motorola, says, "You have to internalize and institutionalize these concepts ... make them part of the corporate environment ... otherwise they are just meaningless formulas."[6] It takes people who believe in what they are doing to make the quality philosophy work.

Quick Quiz 2.1

1. An informal discussion between manager and employee about the thoroughness with which the employee completed a task would be an example of ____________ feedback.
2. A process-flow analysis used to streamline manufacturing steps is an example of ____________ feedback.

Table 2.1 **Dimensions of Quality**

Dimension	Explanation
Performance	The product's primary operating characteristic, such as an automobile's acceleration or the picture clarity of a television
Features	Supplements to the product's basic operating characteristics—for example, power windows on a car or the ceremony with which a bottle of wine is opened in a restaurant
Reliability	The probability that the product will function properly and not break down during a specified period—a manufacturer's warranty is often seen as an indicator of this
Durability	The length of the product's life—for example, whether a stereo lasts for 5 years or 25 years
Serviceability	The speed and ease of repairing the product—for example, whether a computer store will send out a repairperson, service the computer in the store, or provide no maintenance service at all
Conformance	The degree to which the product's design and operating characteristics meet established standards, such as safety standards for a crib
Aesthetics	The way a product looks, feels, tastes, and smells, such as the styling and smell of a new car
Perceived quality	The customer's impression of the product's quality, such as a buyer's belief that an Audi is a safe and reliable car

Source: Adapted from David A. Garvin, "Competing on the Eight Dimensions of Quality," *Harvard Business Review*, November–December 1987.

History of the Quality Challenge: At Home and Abroad

TQM didn't appear overnight; rather, it developed from the trials and errors of the original quality movement in business.

Deming, Juran, and Crosby

statistical quality control Looking for defects in parts of finished goods selected through sampling.

Shortly after World War II, the U.S. statistician W. Edwards Deming taught something called **statistical quality control**—looking for defects in parts of finished goods selected through sampling—to businesspeople in Japan. In doing so, he became an important contributor to the quality improvement efforts that were emerging there. (Table 2.2 shows Deming's 14 principles of quality management.) In fact, Deming so impressed the Japanese with his lectures on quality that they named a prize after him: the Deming Prize is Japan's prestigious international quality award.

But it wasn't until decades after Deming introduced his principles that they became widely discussed in the United States. In the meantime, Japan forged ahead, using the principles of Deming as well as those of Joseph M. Juran. Juran taught Japanese businesses how to improve quality and control the "mission" of each department in an organization. He emphasized studying symptoms of quality problems to identify underlying causes and formulate solutions. The difference between the way American and Japanese companies traditionally dealt with quality problems is illustrated by Zenith, an American television manufacturer. Zenith decided to manufacture TV sets that were easy to repair; the malfunctioning component could be slid out of the machine. But Japanese manufacturers chose to produce televisions that were unlikely to need repairs in the first place; consumers, of course, preferred this option.[7]

Table 2.2 **Deming's 14 Guiding Principles**

1. Create constancy of purpose toward improvement of product or service.
2. Adopt the philosophy embedded in these 14 points.
3. Cease dependence on mass inspection to achieve quality.
4. End the practice of awarding business on the basis of price tags alone.
5. Improve constantly and forever every process for planning, production, and service.
6. Institute training on the job.
7. Adopt and institute leadership.
8. Drive out fear, so that everyone may work effectively for the company.
9. Break down barriers between departments.
10. Eliminate slogans, exhortations, and targets for the work force.
11. Eliminate numerical quotas for the work force and numerical goals for management.
12. Remove barriers that rob people of pride of workmanship.
13. Institute a vigorous program of education and self-improvement.
14. Put everybody in the organization to work to accomplish the transformation.

Source: From DR. DEMING: The American Who Taught the Japanese About Quality by Rafael Aguayo. Copyright © 1990 by Rafael Aguayo. Published by arrangement with Carol Publishing Group.

Philip B. Crosby, who pioneered the quality movement in the United States, summed up the Japanese approach in his advice: "Do it right the first time."[8] He pointed out the costs saved by *prevention of errors* and saw the value of *statistical quality control.* He proposed that **zero defects**—a quality-control technique based on the view that all members of the organization should work toward creating products and services free of problems—was the only ultimate goal worth pursuing.

zero defects
A quality-control technique based on the view that all members of the organization should work toward creating products and services that are free of problems.

These three giants of the quality movement—Deming, Juran, and Crosby—agreed on many essentials. When we discuss the various techniques of quality improvement later in this chapter, we will see reflections of all three men's thinking. Deming's thesis was foundational—that an organization should continually improve its product's design as well as its process of production, and that to do this, top management had to be involved and employees had to be encouraged to act in a spirit of cooperation.[9] Although the term *human relations* was not yet popular, Deming was, to some extent, talking about exactly that. As recently as 1990 he reiterated the importance of management's recognizing individual "self-esteem, dignity, and an eagerness to learn" in employees as the path to improved quality.[10] The paramount importance of the individual in creating quality is illustrated in the "Quality Highlights" box.

Today's emphasis on building teams within the workplace comes to mind when we reflect on Deming's assessment of Japanese success as arising from "cooperation ... not the everybody-for-himself approach."[11] Team spirit flourishes in the Japanese culture, and it is being nurtured in American corporate cultures today—with a twist here and there to reflect traits of American society. And that brings us to the subject of Theory Z.

Ouchi and Theory Z

Theory Z
A method of management that emphasizes formal planning, employee participation, frequent cross-training, and a focus on long-term results.

William G. Ouchi proposed a compromise between the best features of typically Japanese and typically American styles of management—a compromise he called **Theory Z.** He melded together the American characteristics of formal planning and control mechanisms and technologically advanced information and accounting systems with the Japanese philosophy of ensuring long-term employment. Theory Z emphasizes employee participation in all aspects of decision making, along with fre-

Quality Highlights

Policing with a TSQ Attitude Adjustment

Quality is an all-encompassing challenge, usually thought of in terms of products and services. But at its core, achieving quality often means developing and improving human relations skills.

Take, for example, the problems of the police department in Brighton, Colorado. An agency directly responsive to and responsible for the safety of its citizens found itself lacking the respect and esteem of the community it served.

After Brighton's police chief was fired in 1985, the new chief, Robert Galloway, had to confront a lack of people skills among the department's 28 sworn and 10 nonsworn officers. His goal was to build those skills and change the department's focus from a policy of enforcement to a policy of service. Galloway introduced a total service quality (TSQ) program to develop his officers' interpersonal skills.

"When we started this in 1986, people didn't talk about total service quality or total quality management," Galloway reports. "But as we started to develop an approach to improve services, these programs influenced what we did."

Galloway disagrees with Deming's view that quality means fixing the process, not the people. "In government, we can't start with the assumption that people are OK; that isn't always the case. We have to concentrate on the people, not the process."

Yet even "fixing" people has its limits. Galloway says that recruits with strong interpersonal skills can be trained to be good police officers, but no matter how talented recruits may be at law enforcement, without interpersonal skills, no amount of training can help them deliver good service.

Source: "Total Service Policy Rejuvenates Police Department," *Quality Digest,* May 1993, p. 10.

quent cross-training and a focus on longer-term results. Theory Z organizations tend to adopt *job rotation* to provide job security: instead of firing an unsatisfactory worker, these companies retrain the employee and rotate him or her to another job where success is more likely.

Employee Involvement Teams

employee involvement teams Teams that plan ways to improve quality in their area of an organization.

Employee involvement teams are exactly what they sound like—teams of employees who plan ways to improve quality in their area of an organization. These teams, which originated in the United States during the 1920s, were based on the ideas of Walter Shewhart of Bell Laboratories (and later expanded upon by Deming).[12] Most employee involvement teams are composed of two to ten people and a manager who acts as team leader (schedules meetings, prepares agendas, encourages participation, and so forth).

The successful employee involvement team has several characteristics: (1) support from management (which provides rewards and takes action on the team's ideas); (2) employees who desire to participate; and (3) the skills necessary for effective participation.

The Quality Movement in Retrospect

Improving quality has become a crucial goal for all businesses, both in the United States and abroad. As competition becomes increasingly stiff worldwide, companies recognize that they must address quality issues in order to stay in the ring. A spokesman for Germany's Cologne Institute of the German Economy explains, "Before, we could always rely on our competitors' errors, but in the interim, these competitors have stopped making the mistakes."[13]

Whatever the distinctive characteristics of a country's society, all businesses are trying to coax a better performance out of their employees, for that is where the quality edge lies now that technological advances sweep the industrialized world so quickly. The quality push is likely to continue. Certainly, the customer—whether in Europe, Asia, or the United States—has benefited from the quality movement. Employees have

To improve the quality of its semiconductor chips, Hewlett-Packard initiated statistical process control (SPC) during manufacturing. In SPC, operators are trained to interpret data and have a plan of attack if problems occur. These three employees were among the first to graduate as SPC-trained operators for Hewlett-Packard.
Photo source: © 1993 Ron Schwager.

as well, since the quality movement encompasses human relations issues. As part of the quality movement, employers have improved working conditions and provided incentives for employees to work harder and better at satisfying customers.

Quick Quiz 2.2

1. Name the three pioneers of the quality movement.
2. What business philosophy represents a compromise between American and Japanese management styles?
3. What are the three characteristics of successful employee involvement teams?

Productivity, Motivation, and Quality

To survive, an organization has to be productive; it must not only meet its own standards for satisfactory productivity, it must also match or exceed the productivity of its competitors. The consumer, the employee, and the employer all reap the benefits of this need for productivity. Let us consider the consumer first. In a country where the productivity of organizations is improving, citizens can obtain goods and services at lower prices than before. They also have access to more and better goods and services. As for employees, they tend to receive higher wages and enjoy better working conditions when their organization is a productive one. Finally, increased productivity naturally means higher profits for the employer.

Stiff competition from abroad has forced American businesses to pay close attention to productivity. Although innovations in technology can help increase productivity, human beings have a far greater impact. Motivated employees are productive employees. Unmotivated ones are less productive, and sometimes even wasteful.

Recently, many organizations have taken an active approach to applying human relations to productivity. Instead of solving productivity problems by applying human relations solutions like Band-Aids, they rely on human relations professionals to help formulate companywide strategies for production goals. Increasingly, top managers and executives express an understanding of the role that human relations plays in giving their organization the competitive edge. Cultural diversity plays an important role in helping companies compete; see the "Diversity Highlights" box.

Diversity Highlights

Levi's Unbuttoned Mind-set

Getting a job at Levi Strauss & Co. was simple back in 1908. Its brochure made employment requirements quite clear: "None but white women and girls are employed."

Today, job ads for the San Francisco clothing manufacturer "strongly encourage" minorities to apply. Believing that companies that want to hire the best people must be open to an increasingly diverse work force, Levi's has become one of the most ethnically and culturally diverse companies in the world.

At the end of 1991, 56 percent of Levi's 23,000 U.S. employees belonged to minority groups. Top management was 14 percent nonwhite and 30 percent female; those percentages are climbing as CEO Robert B. Haas continues to eliminate the glass ceiling that he believes has prevented some qualified women and minorities from reaching the company's top ranks. But numbers don't tell the whole story: Levi's supports in-house networking groups of blacks, Hispanics, lesbians, and gay men and has created a Diversity Council, made up of two members of every group, that regularly meets with Levi's executives on raising awareness of diversity issues.

Promoting diversity makes good marketing sense, too, as the best way to learn about and understand different markets. It also invites new viewpoints and ideas. For example, Levi's credits an Argentine employee with thinking up its line of Dockers casual pants—now worth more than $1 billion a year.

Levi's commitment to diversity can get it into trouble with outsiders. The company's recent cutoff of funding for the Boy Scouts, prompted by the group's ban on homosexual troop leaders, has prompted threats of a boycott by Christian groups. But Levi's executives are standing firm to send an important message to their employees of all races and lifestyles.

Source: Alice Cuneo, "Diverse by Design," *Business Week/Reinventing America,* 1992.

The United States versus Other Countries

The United States is still the most productive nation in the world.[14] Figure 2.1 compares the *gross domestic product (GDP)* per person in nine different countries. Note that Japan's output is about 25 percent less than that of the United States. Germany's output is about 33 percent less than that of the United States. Germany, long considered a strong competitor in the marketplace, has in recent years suffered from declining output, falling investment, and rising unemployment.[15] Germany has the highest labor costs in the world—the shortest workweek, longest vacations, most holidays, earliest retirement age, and oldest students.[16] In addition, the costs of unifying East and West Germany are now being felt throughout the economy after an initial boom that lasted about two years.

Although the United States still leads the world in actual productivity, that doesn't mean businesses can afford to relax or rest on their laurels! They must count on motivated employees to continue producing at a high level; to do that, they must be masters at handling human relations issues. Take some time to test your own productivity by taking the "Self-Portrait" test.

Productivity and Change

When employees must learn new skills in order to enhance their productivity, good human relations policies can prevent problems during the transition period. When laws regulating a certain type of business change, good human relations policies can help compliance go smoothly. By nature, humans don't like change, but skilled management of human relations in a company can help people through the upheaval it creates.

Good management of human relations does more than fix problems or help employees simply accept changes that are thrust upon them. It can encourage employees to seek change—to look for opportunities for training and advancement, search for innovations that can help productivity, and seek solutions to problems. For a discussion of the effect of self-managed work teams on productivity, see the "Teamwork Highlights" box.

Figure 2.1 **Gross Domestic Product per Person for Selected Countries, 1990**

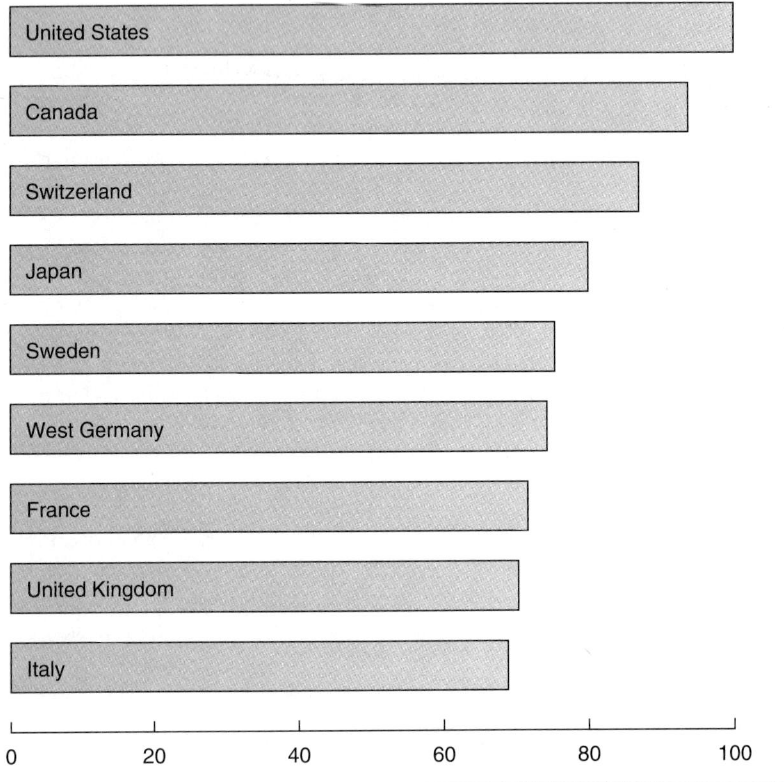

Source: Reprinted with the permission of The American Enterprise Institute for Public Policy Research, Washington, D.C.

Incentives and Disincentives for Productivity

Productivity lends itself to precise mathematical measurement (the equations in Figure 2.2 are two examples). But boosting productivity takes a lot more than crunching numbers; it takes motivation. After a certain amount of training or experience, all employees may be capable of equal productivity in many types of jobs. Incentives such as higher wages, bonuses, and promotions or privileges are then necessary to increase productivity. Human relations professionals understand the principles of motivation and are trained to identify what incentives work best in any given situation. Thus, human relations professionals can save a company from hit-and-miss trials that may cost a lot of time and money.

Disincentives are deterrents to productivity. Look at the cost of the employee productivity figures in the equation in Figure 2.2. A good company manager will avoid assigning the higher-priced employees to tasks that can be handled by lower-priced ones. In fact, a good manager resists taking on those tasks himself or herself and delegates them to more appropriate workers.

Knowledge of human relations helps all employers allocate human resources in a way that minimizes waste. Self-knowledge, a benefit reaped from the study of human relations, often helps in that regard.

Another drain on the productivity of an organization occurs when the productivity of a key employee is unnecessarily damaged. Laura Henderson, chief executive officer of a biomedical research and communications firm, observes that greater demands for productivity cause some workers to take on an unrealistic workload in

Self-Portrait

How Productive Are You?

Answer each question with a yes or no.

Y N 1. Does it often take you more than ten minutes to unearth a particular letter, bill, report, or other paper from your files (or from the pile of paper on your desk)?

Y N 2. Do things amass in corners of closets or on the floor because you cannot decide where to put them?

Y N 3. Are there papers on your desk, other than reference materials, that you have not looked at for a week or more?

Y N 4. Has your electricity or other utility ever been turned off because you forgot to pay the bill?

Y N 5. Within the last two months, have you forgotten any scheduled appointment, anniversary, or specific date you wanted to acknowledge?

Y N 6. Do your magazines and newspapers pile up unread?

Y N 7. Do you frequently procrastinate so long on a work or class assignment that it becomes an emergency or panic situation?

Y N 8. Has anything ever been misplaced in your home or office for longer than two months?

Y N 9. Do you often misplace keys, glasses, gloves, handbags, briefcases, or other items?

Y N 10. Does your definition of working in an organized space mean fitting as many objects as possible into a limited area?

Y N 11. Do you feel that your storage problems would be solved if you had more space?

Y N 12. Do you want to get organized but feel everything is in such a mess that you do not know where to start?

Y N 13. Do you regularly receive letters, comments, or calls that begin: "You haven't gotten back to me yet, so ..."?

Y N 14. Do frequent interruptions—phone calls or visitors—affect your ability to concentrate?

Y N 15. Are you so busy with details that you are ignoring opportunities for new school or work activities?

Y N 16. When you get up in the morning, do you know what your two or three primary tasks are?

Y N 17. By the end of the average day, have you accomplished at least the most important tasks you set for yourself?

For questions 1 to 15, give yourself one point for each Y you circled. For questions 16 and 17, give yourself one point for each N you circled. Here is how to interpret your total:

4 or less	Systems are under control!
5–8	Disorganization is troublesome.
9–11	Life must be very difficult.
12 or more	Your disorganization verges on chaos.

Source: Adapted from Stephanie Winston, *Getting Organized: The Easy Way to Put Your Life in Order* (New York: Warner Books, 1978) and *The Organized Executive: New Ways to Manage Time, Paper and People* (New York: W.W. Norton & Co., 1983).

order to gain a promotion. The result is an overworked employee with diminished decision-making ability. "People who have balance in their lives are more productive than those who spend every night and every weekend at the office," says Henderson.[17]

Teamwork Highlights

Redefining the Job at Johnson Wax

When he became head of human resources at S. C. Johnson Wax, the $3-billion-a-year maker of household products such as Raid and Pledge, Earl VanderWielen redefined the job of the human resources manager.

In a traditional system, a human resources manager is often divorced from day-to-day business, spending his or her time supervising companywide pay systems and making sure everyone adheres to government regulations. By contrast, VanderWielen knows the business inside and out—he spent ten years as a manufacturing manager—and gets deeply involved in operations.

When the company decided to move toward self-managed teams eight years ago, VanderWielen and his staff worked long hours in the factory, teaching line managers and workers about such management techniques as statistical analysis and pay-for-skills. In one instance, a team of workers figured out how to switch a line from liquid floor wax to a stain remover in 13 minutes instead of three days.

Overall results in those eight years have been startling. At its plant in Racine, Wisconsin, Johnson Wax has increased productivity 30 percent while reducing the number of middle managers from 140 to 37.

Source: ***Fortune***, February 22, 1993.

Carol Olmstead, an employment consultant, agrees. People who accept too much work "become resentful, [and their] productivity drops."[18] Deming's spirit of cooperation can come to the rescue here. "It is important for companies and employees to understand that there is a shared destiny between them," notes Henderson, who is also chairperson of the National Foundation for Women Business Owners. "We have to look for rational ways that we can work together, so employers and employees are successful."[19] It's clear that a major key to productivity is making sure that the best person is chosen for a job and that stress and workloads are kept at a manageable level.

Productivity and Quality

In advice to sales managers, one writer urges: "Instead of preaching quota, teach quality—and do it by example."[20] Quality and productivity are not only interdependent, they are inseparable. But note that this equation works both ways. Florida Power and Light, the only American company to win the Deming Prize, learned this the hard way. Nancy K. Austin, a management expert, tells the story: "Even some of the savviest firms have gone overboard in their single-minded pursuit of total quality. Probably the most infamous example is Florida Power and Light. … Reportedly, FPL threw nearly a million dollars into the effort but ended up with a massive quality bureaucracy [now dismantled], mutinous employees, and the dubious distinction of teaching the rest of us what not to do."[21] The Saturn Corporation is another example. Although the company is now doing relatively well, it has had to address problems of lower productivity and quality even after establishing extremely successful empowerment policies.[22]

controlling function Making sure that work goes according to plan.

performance standards Measures of what is expected in terms of quantity and quality.

The **controlling function**—making sure that work goes according to plan—brings productivity and quality together. First, a company must set **performance standards,** measures of what is expected in terms of quantity and quality. Then, actual performance is monitored and compared with those standards. If the standards have been met, the success is reinforced or rewarded; if they haven't, corrective action is taken.

To use a simple example, suppose Ron, a grocery store checker, is encouraged to meet quantity standards (to check a certain number of items per hour) and quality standards (to obtain a certain level of accuracy in items checked). His attitude toward customers might also be included in the quality standards. If Ron falls behind in either standard, his manager might talk with him about ways he could improve. If Ron does particularly well at his job, he might be named "Employee of the Month." As long as some response is made to Ron's performance, the controlling function is serving to boost both productivity and quality.

Figure 2.2 **Equations for Measuring Productivity**

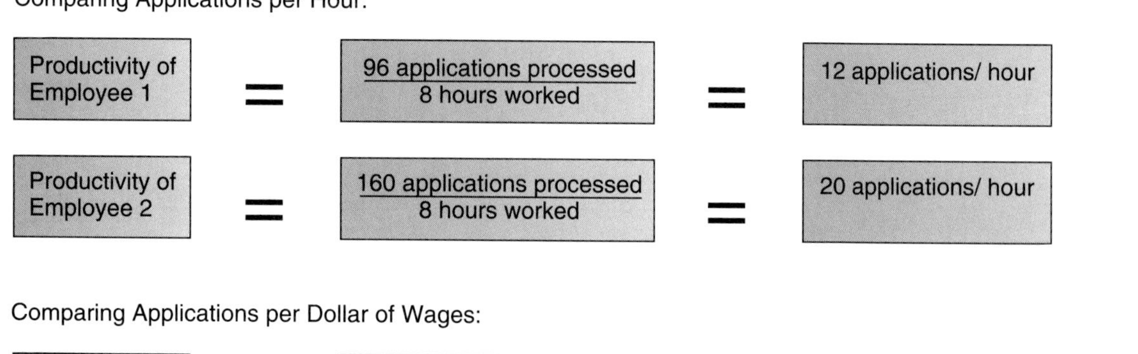

Comparing Applications per Dollar of Wages:

Productivity of Employee 1 = $\frac{\text{96 applications processed}}{\text{(\$6 / hour)(8 hours worked)}}$ = $\frac{96}{48}$ - 2.0

Productivity of Employee 2 = $\frac{\text{160 applications processed}}{\text{(\$8 / hour)(8 hours worked)}}$ = $\frac{160}{64}$ = 2.5

Quick Quiz 2.3

1. According to Figure 2.1, which country has the highest GDP? The lowest?
2. What function brings quality and productivity together?

Variations on Quality Control and Improvement

quality control
An organization's efforts to prevent or correct defects in its goods and services.

Quality control is an organization's efforts to prevent or correct defects in its goods and services, or to improve them. Decades of theorizing on the best way to do this have produced many techniques and programs, with just as many names. Organizations often have a manager devoted to supervising quality; larger companies may have an entire department devoted to monitoring quality. Regardless of corporate structure, all managers are pressed to take responsibility for quality control and improvement in their own area of operation. Expert David L. Goetsch makes some practical suggestions for managers:

- Emphasize quality to your employees. Make sure they know it is your top priority.
- Demonstrate a commitment to quality by using visual reminders such as posters. Before the posters get so familiar that employees stop noticing them, replace them with new ones.
- Make sure employees understand the quality standards that have been set. Encourage them to exceed the standards.
- Even if the organization has quality-control personnel to conduct inspections, periodically examine employees' work yourself.
- When you see something wrong, act on it immediately.
- If your employees' work involves producing a batch of parts or products, inspect the first item in the batch so that you can spot any problems before further work takes place.
- Make sure all your employees are aware of their role in improving quality. Work with them to develop their commitment to that role.[23]

Figure 2.3 **Quality Control—Product and Process**

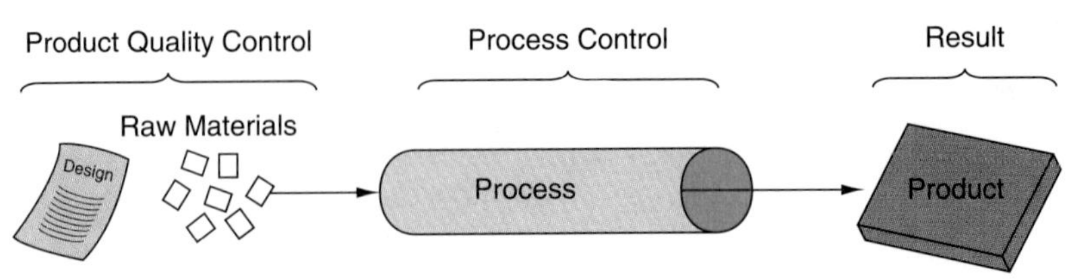

Notice how important good human relations skills are in carrying out most of the suggestions listed by Goetsch. Communicating to employees the priority of quality, making sure they understand quality standards, and helping them develop a commitment to their role in maintaining quality all require that managers work well with their employees—and vice versa.

Product and Process in Quality Control

product quality control Improving the product itself.

process control Improving the process of production.

Quality control can be considered from two main perspectives: the product and the process (see Figure 2.3). **Product quality control** focuses on ways in which the product itself can be improved. **Process control** focuses on ways in which the process of production can be improved. So you might use product quality control to manufacture a better lawnmower—one that cuts neatly in a wide radius. Then you might use process control to fit the parts together more quickly, so your costs are reduced and you can offer customers a better price.

Techniques of quality control and improvement include:

- total quality management (TQM), which embraces many or all of the other techniques
- statistical quality control—including statistical process control (SPC)
- the zero-defects approach
- employee involvement teams (or variations, such as empowerment and participative management)
- continuous quality improvement (CQI).

Total quality management was introduced and discussed in the first section of this chapter; statistical quality control, the zero-defects approach, and employee involvement teams were discussed briefly as part of the history of the quality movement.

Statistical Quality Control

statistical process control (SPC) Method in which operators use statistics to monitor quality on an ongoing basis during manufacturing.

It's impossible to check every single item that a company manufactures before it is shipped. So, organizations often use statistical quality control, a sampling method in which completed items are inspected at random. Some organizations take this a step further, using **statistical process control (SPC)**, in which operators use statistics to monitor quality on an ongoing basis during manufacturing. Using SPC empowers workers by giving them the responsibility for monitoring quality during production.

Zero-Defects Approach

"Zero defects should be the goal," said Philip Crosby, not "that's good enough."[24] The SPC technique just described aids the zero-defects approach, which views everyone in an organization as being responsible for delivering such high quality that no defects will occur. Thus, in a manufacturing organization using the zero-defects approach, the goods produced would be of excellent quality not only because workers and management are seeking ways to avoid defects but also because the purchasing department is ensuring a timely supply of well-crafted parts, the accounting department is seeing that bills get paid on time, the human resources department helps to find and train highly qualified personnel, and so on.

Employee Involvement Teams and Empowerment

As mentioned earlier in the chapter, employee involvement teams, which plan ways to improve quality in their own area of the organization, were the brainchild of Walter Shewhart of Bell Laboratories and were later expanded upon by Deming. Each team consists of a group of employees and a supervisor, who serves as team leader.

Employee involvement teams can take several forms. *Quality circles* focus on quality with a side benefit of improved productivity. Roles assumed by circle members are circle leader, circle facilitator, and steering committee members. The steering committee consists of managers and nonmanagers who select the facilitator. The facilitator should be experienced in principles of organizational development. The circle leader is usually, but not always, a supervisor.

In a quality circle, the opinions of all members receive equal hearing. All members are trained in group decision making and problem solving, and the leaders are given additional training. Each quality circle focuses on a particular area of production and meets regularly to deal with quality issues.

Other types of employee involvement teams include *process involvement teams* and *self-managed work groups.* These will be mentioned in other chapters because they are variations on the trend toward giving employees more autonomy in order to allow them to do their best work.

Saturn Corporation, despite its difficulties, is a good example of how this philosophy functions in a real company. Each work team is responsible for its own budget and hiring, representing a high degree of empowerment. The added responsibility appears to have had many good effects (in addition to improving product quality). Absenteeism has declined, and problems are fixed quickly. When a malfunction in the plant's powerhouse recently interrupted the flow of cooling water to the paint shop, a maintenance team worked 36 hours straight to fix the flaw as quickly as possible.[25]

Participative Management

participative management A management style that involves managers working with employees as a team in setting objectives and planning how to achieve them.

Participative management is a management style that involves managers working with employees as a team in setting objectives (including quality objectives) and planning how to achieve them. This is another way of giving employees more rein in decision making. Management consultant Peter Grazier suggests six steps for helping overcome managers' resistance to this style (shown in Table 2.3). Notice the wide range of Grazier's suggestions, from attacking problems (not people) to inviting guest speakers to talking openly about successes and failures. It's true that not every manager will have the skills to tackle all these recommendations, but Grazier's list presents some goals for managers to strive toward in improving human relations between themselves and their employees.

Continuous Quality Improvement (CQI)

continuous quality improvement (CQI) Closely allied with TQM, with emphasis on the notion that quality can—and should—always be improved.

The quest for zero defects and never-ending improvements is embodied in the idea of **continuous quality improvement (CQI).** CQI is closely allied with total quality management, with emphasis on the notion that quality can—and should—always be improved. The Japanese version is called *kaizen.*

Table 2.3 **Six Steps for Overcoming Managerial Resistance to Participative Management**

1. Establish a policy of attacking the problem, not the person.
2. Give managers experience in brainstorming.
3. Provide training in communication, interpersonal relations, personality types, personal values, and other human factors.
4. Bring in speakers from organizations that have successful participation programs, or send managers to visit those organizations.
5. Give managers and supervisors experience working on improvement teams.
6. Talk openly about successes and failures and what people should expect as they move further into worker participation concepts.

Source: Reprinted with permission from the April, 1993 issue of *Total Quality,* Lakewood Publications, 50 South Ninth St., Minneapolis, MN 55402.

Quick Quiz 2.4

1. A restaurant that switches suppliers in order to upgrade the quality of its beef is practicing
   a. process control
   b. product quality control
   c. the controlling function.
2. A manufacturing plant where machine operators use statistics to monitor quality on an ongoing basis is using
   a. a zero-defects approach
   b. statistical quality control
   c. statistical process control.
3. At a mountain bike manufacturer, a group of people who meet to discuss how to improve the bike's brakes is called
   a. an employee involvement team
   b. a participative management team
   c. a CQI team.

Evaluating Total Quality

Quality control techniques provide information about the rate of defects occurring, but how does an organization measure its success in a long-term process such as TQM or CQI? Three possible approaches are benchmarking, ISO 9000 standards, and the Malcolm Baldrige National Quality Award process.

Benchmarking

benchmarking
The practice of using examples of successful competitors to spur continuous improvement.

"Benchmarking," said one wit, "makes it kosher to steal a nifty idea from somebody else and do it even better. It's sometimes called market intelligence."[26] Actually, **benchmarking** is the practice of using examples of successful competitors to spur continuous improvement. It involves identifying, learning, and carrying out the practices of top performers. Xerox, for example, benchmarked the highly successful distribution system of L.L. Bean.[27]

Individual managers can benchmark in their careers, just as a company benchmarks as a whole. A good source of information on the procedure is the business-supported International Benchmarking Clearinghouse of the American Productivity and Quality Center, based in Houston, Texas.[28] The clearinghouse has developed a model

Xerox first began benchmarking when it discovered Japanese manufacturers able to sell midsize copiers in the United States for considerably less than Xerox's production cost. A team of line managers was sent to Japan to study Xerox's own joint venture, Fuji-Xerox. Facing facts marked the beginning of the Xerox recovery, and benchmarking has served the company as a key tool ever since.

Photo source: COURTESY, XEROX CORPORATION.

Photo Exercise

Since benchmarking can be used for an individual's career, think of one businessperson you would like to benchmark. What qualities make this person a good choice for benchmarking?

called Process Classification, designed to standardize the language that companies use to compare performance in 13 broad areas. The model outlines more than 100 activities and procedures categorized as operating or management and support processes.[29]

ISO 9000

ISO 9000
A series of criteria for quality systems.

The International Standards Organization (ISO) in Geneva, Switzerland, publishes **ISO 9000**, a series of criteria for quality systems.[30] Companies trading outside the United States need official ISO 9000 certification to have a chance at succeeding against competitors.[31] To be certified, an organization is visited by independent audit teams; if the auditors determine that the key elements of the standard are in place, they issue certification compliance. (Note that they are evaluating quality *processes,* not product quality.[32]) Ninety countries and more than 95 percent of the world's industrial population are members of the ISO.[33]

Malcolm Baldrige Award

Malcolm Baldrige National Quality Award
An annual award administered by the U.S. Department of Commerce.

An annual award administered by the U.S. Department of Commerce, the **Malcolm Baldrige National Quality Award** is given to companies that show the highest-quality performance in seven categories:

1. leadership
2. information and analysis
3. strategic quality planning
4. human resources development and management
5. management of process quality
6. quality and operational results
7. customer focus and satisfaction.

Established in 1987, the award recognizes companies in three categories: manufacturing, small business, and service. Besides the approximately 100 organizations that apply for the award each year, many others use the evaluation categories as a basis for assessing their own performance. In effect, organizations use the guidelines for the award as a kind of textbook for what needs to be done to improve quality. As one expert put it, the Baldrige award "provides companies with a comprehensive framework for assessing their progress toward the new paradigm of management."[34]

Guidelines for the Baldrige award are obtained from the National Institute of Standards and Technology. They are rigorous, serving as a good incentive for many companies. But several have pointed out some dangers in striving too single-mindedly for the award. First, the endeavor can be very costly.[35] Second, the goal of winning the award can sometimes compete with overall company goals. For example, David Williams of Cigna Corporation says, "The attention it takes to go for the award over and above the effort of creating a total quality–management process would take us off the track."[36] This is why some companies choose to use the Baldrige award as an inspiration, almost a benchmark, without actually contending for it.[37]

Quick Quiz 2.5

1. Name three ways of measuring an organization's success at total quality improvement.
2. An international set of quality standards is published by the ___________.
3. List the seven categories of the Baldrige award.

Challenges in Quality Improvement

How can a system that sounds so right go wrong? Organizations often stumble and fall in the race toward quality improvement. Four reasons have been identified:

1. Performance is usually measured in terms of quantity rather than quality.
2. Employees are held accountable for results that they do not completely control.
3. Rewards for employees' efforts are not financially commensurate with their contributions.
4. Rewards for employees' efforts are not directly connected to business results.[38]

In addition, researcher Leonard Berry identifies five reasons for failure in quality improvement:

1. incorrect prioritizing (and consequent incorrect allocation of resources)
2. failure to design high quality into a service system
3. choice of the quickest and easiest solution instead of searching for better, long-range solutions to quality problems
4. insufficient attention to customer and employee feedback
5. underinvestmen in leadership development.[39]

Berry blames the "tunnel vision" of managers for most failures, created by a false confidence in their own experience, which keeps them from listening and asking questions.[40] He explains that the dynamic nature of customers' expectations and perceptions necessitates continual monitoring. Not surprisingly, we have encountered a familiar face in our look at quality improvement—communication. The face of communication will become even more familiar as we explore other facets of human relations in this text.

Quick Quiz 2.6

1. What is a common temptation for organizations trying to solve quality problems?
2. Managerial failures in quality improvement usually stem from a lack of attention to ___________.

Pier 1 Imports focuses on exceeding customers' expectations in product selection, merchandise value, and customer service. The company continually uses customer focus groups, refund questionnaires, in-store "How are we doing?" brochures, customer letters, and telephone calls to Customer Service to monitor and fine-tune its approach to customer satisfaction.

Photo source: Photo courtesy of Pier 1 Imports.

Summary

- **Define *total quality management.*** Total quality management is an organizationwide focus on continuously improving every business process involved in producing and delivering goods and services.
- **State how Deming, Juran, and Crosby each influenced the quality movement.** Deming taught statistical quality control to businesspeople in Japan and became an important contributor to the quality improvement efforts that emerged there. Juran taught Japanese businesses how to improve quality and control the mission of each department in an organization. Crosby pioneered the quality movement in the United States.
- **Define *employee involvement teams* and describe the three main features of a successful team.** Employee involvement teams are teams of employees who plan ways to improve quality in their area of an organization. A successful team has three main characteristics: (1) support from management (which provides rewards and takes action on the team's ideas); (2) employees who desire to participate; and (3) the skills necessary for effective participation.
- **Explain how productivity, motivation, and quality are related.** To survive, an organization must be productive; motivated employees are productive employees. Good management of human relations motivates employees to improve quality and productivity. The controlling function helps bring productivity and quality together.
- **Describe the major variations on quality control and improvement.** Quality control is an organization's efforts to prevent or correct defects in its goods and services, or to improve them. Product quality control focuses on ways in which the product itself can be improved. Process control focuses on ways in which the process of production can be improved. Statistical process control allows workers to use statistics to monitor quality on an ongoing basis during manufacturing. The zero-defects approach views everyone in an organization as being responsible for delivering such high quality that no defects will occur. Participative management involves managers working with employees as a team in setting objectives and planning how to achieve them. Continuous quality improvement is closely allied with total quality management, with emphasis on the notion that quality can always be improved.
- **Explain how benchmarking, ISO 9000, and the Malcolm Baldrige Award are used to evaluate total quality.** Benchmarking is the practice of using examples of successful competitors to spur continuous improvement. ISO 9000 is a series of criteria for quality systems. Companies trading outside the United States need official ISO 9000 certification in order to remain competitive. The Malcolm Baldrige Award is an annual award administered by the U.S. Department of Commerce, given to companies that show the highest-quality performance in seven categories.

Key Terms

total quality management (TQM) (26)
statistical quality control (27)
zero defects (28)
Theory Z (28)
employee involvement teams (29)
controlling function (34)
performance standards (34)
quality control (35)
product quality control (36)
process control (36)
statistical process control (SPC) (36)
participative management (37)
continuous quality improvement (CQI) (37)
benchmarking (38)
ISO 9000 (39)
Malcolm Baldrige National Quality Award (39)

Review and Discussion Questions

1. Timberlake Knitwear is trying to boost production for the upcoming fall season while staying price-competitive. To keep costs down, the firm's president has told production to keep the assembly line moving; an inspector will be on hand to catch the mistakes later. What are the likely consequences for Timberlake as a result of this approach to manufacturing?

2. The manager of a supermarket wants to make sure his employees are delivering good service to customers, but he doesn't have the time to check up on the service given to every customer. Instead, every Tuesday and Thursday at 3 p.m., he helps bag groceries and asks those customers if they are satisfied with their service. Because he is talking to a sample of customers, this is a form of statistical quality control. How can the manager improve the accuracy of the information he gets from this quality-control technique?

3. What is the difference between product quality control and process control? Is balancing a checkbook a type of product quality control or process control? Why?

4. Jackie Martinez supervises a staff of eight claims processors at an insurance company. Jackie's boss has asked her to set up an employee involvement team with her staff members.
   a. What activities can Jackie expect that she and her employees will perform as members of the team?
   b. What kinds of training should Jackie consider for herself and her staff so the team can work effectively?

5. What is the zero-defects approach to quality control?

6. What is total quality management (TQM)?

7. One of the key values of TQM is a focus on meeting or exceeding customers' expectations. Who would be the customers served by each of the following employees or groups of employees?
   a. a hairdresser in a beauty salon
   b. a maintenance crew in a factory
   c. a telephone operator at city hall
   d. the human resources department of a nursing home

8. Describe how organizations can use the Malcolm Baldrige National Quality Award as a tool for measuring their success at continuous quality improvement.

9. David Ruff, the head pharmacist at the local drugstore, has received a number of complaints about mistakes in customers' prescriptions. To improve the quality of service, he can either do a better job of catching errors in the future or do a better job of avoiding those errors altogether. Which approach should he take? Why? To motivate his employees to improve the quality of their performance, what kinds of behavior and accomplishments should Ruff reward? Give some examples.

10. Explain how management can improve quality by the way it sets and enforces standards.

A SECOND LOOK

Thanks to its earlier adoption of quality techniques, Coleman Co. was able to meet the staggering production challenge of producing and delivering 100,000 lanterns to Colombia in just six weeks. What specific quality improvements enabled Coleman to succeed? What lessons did it learn from this episode?

Independent Activity

Ensuring Quality and Productivity through Training

Pick a company in your community. Imagine that you are an employee of that company and have just been asked to help train a new employee. The employee is a coworker of yours and will do the same job. What can you do to help the new employee learn the job and become acquainted with his or her coworkers? Provide a list of 20 things you can do to make sure quality and productivity are ensured.

Skill Builder

Enhancing Personal Productivity

Keep a log of your activities for two days. In the morning, write down a list of what you need to accomplish that day. At the end of each hour, write down what you did. At the end of the day, go through the list to see whether you actually completed the tasks you assigned yourself. Review your hourly log.

- If you did check off all of the tasks, ask yourself what helped you achieve your goals.
- If you did not accomplish everything you expected, see what hindered you.

Group Activities

Quality and Productivity Role Playing (30 minutes)

For this role-playing exercise, the class will divide into small groups of four to eight people. The groups are employee involvement teams that are to work on solving problems. One group member will play the role of team leader; the remaining members will be employees. Using strategies presented in the chapter, the employee involvement teams should work together to solve one of the following problems:

1. Xerocopy Repair Service has received repeated complaints from customers that its machines break down too frequently. Service calls have increased 50 percent in the past three months. Team members notice that repeat calls seem to be a particular problem. How can Xerocopy reduce repeat service calls?
2. Dazzle Shoelace Company has just introduced a new line of neon shoelaces. In the past month, the graveyard shift's productivity in making the laces has lagged behind the other shifts'. How can Dazzle improve productivity?
3. Jiffy Express Package Delivery has noticed an increase in complaints regarding lost and mangled packages. The electronic tracking system has been checked for defects and is fine. What can Jiffy do to fix the problem?
4. Vega Genesis Computer Games has noticed that its new video game, Destroyers of the Universe, has an unusually high defect rate. Programmers and manufacturing personnel are having trouble figuring out why the program crashes. What can Vega Genesis do to correct the problem?
5. Spreck's Nurseries has recently received complaints that its mail-order service has delivered the wrong bulbs. Customers say that the packages were labeled incorrectly. How can Spreck's fix the problem?

Classroom Teamwork Challenge—Airplane Project (20 minutes)

Divide the class into a production team, a management team, and groups of suppliers, buyers, and competitors. The project is to build paper airplanes. The production team must negotiate with management concerning materials, numbers to be completed, and time allotted. While production works, management should negotiate with suppliers and buyers and also watch the actions of competitors. At the end of production, the airplanes should be checked for quality. They are then bought, and profits or losses are shared. Watch for the tension that may result from any changes in production goals and problems in communication.

Case Study

Asking the Right Questions at R.R. Donnelley

An old-school manager often told people what to do, how to do it, and when. A new-style manager asks the questions that will get people to solve problems and make decisions on their own. Dee Zalneraitis, the information group manager at a Hudson, Massachusetts, division of R.R. Donnelley & Sons, America's largest printer, is a good example.

Her division began converting to self-managed teams last year. Zalneraitis's new role is to teach, train, cajole, and comfort her 40 people until they feel confident enough to do the things she now does—hiring, firing, scheduling vacations, and the like. Once Zalneraitis feels her people can handle the responsibility, she hopes to move on to another equally challenging post in the company. Says she: "I'd like to manage my way out of my current job in two years."

One of the hardest things about being this kind of manager, Zalneraitis has found, is letting people figure things out on their own when she knows the answer. But it's the only way people can really learn, she says. A worker once went on vacation without scheduling someone to cover for her. Although Zalneraitis saw the problem right away, she had to sit and listen to the phones ring until her people figured it out.

Another of her goals is to involve as many of her people as possible in decision making. This makes her work life harder. "You always have to ask yourself, 'Should I invite them to participate in the process?'" she says. Under the old system, Zalneraitis at budget time would spend a week and a half behind closed doors feeling harassed. Now she shows all her people the budget and asks them how they can save money. They respond: an employee helped her balance the budget by suggesting they do away with some scheduled trips to an unreasonably demanding customer.

If Zalneraitis does her job right, her hourly people will soon take over budgeting.

Case Questions

1. Are these self-managed teams an example of participative management, empowerment, or both? Why?
2. What is the motivation at this company for increasing productivity? What is the reward?
3. Can all of the activities Zalneraitis is passing on to her staff be described as steps toward quality improvement?
4. Why is it likely that Donnelley's adoption of self-managed teams will ensure its continued success as America's largest printer?

Source: *Fortune,* February 22, 1993.

Case Study

Motorola's Universal Language of Quality

There is little doubt about how successful Motorola Corp. has been at internalizing the ideas of quality gurus who preach the sermon of total quality management. Once a year, hundreds of engineers, accountants, factory workers, office clerks, and executives dress up in costumes ranging from hospital uniforms to Japanese headbands and happi coats for a kind of in-house quality Olympics that Motorola calls its "Total Customer Satisfaction Team Competition."

The purpose of the event is to ensure that the principles of total quality management that Motorola adopted in the 1980s continue through the 1990s and into the next century. Twenty-two finalist teams were pared down from more than 3,000 Motorola teams worldwide. Together, they represent the full range of Motorola's corporate structure: from the semiconductor sector to corporate finance, from sales and repair to distribution.

"There are no losers in this kind of competition," according to Gene Simpson, a member of Motorola's total customer satisfaction staff. Everybody wins when thousands of employees work together in teams to come up with new processes that enhance quality.

A corporate finance team created a new PC–based software package that reduced cycle time for financial reports 60 percent to 70 percent and cut the annual cost of the reports by $233,000. The team from Malaysia reduced defects in its operation by 62 percent, while a team from Northbrook, Illinois, reduced cycle time for filling orders by 65 percent.

To an outsider, it may all seem a bit obsessive, but the chairman of Motorola Japan says that this kind of corporatewide teamwork and enthusiasm regarding quality and excellence is the key to Motorola's success.

Case Questions

1. How has management institutionalized the concept of quality?
2. How well does Motorola meet the criteria for the Baldrige quality award?
3. What kind of challenges do you think Motorola faced in translating its message of TQM and teamwork to all its global divisions?

Source: *Chicago Tribune*, January 1, 1992.

Quick Quiz Answers

Quick Quiz 2.1

1. subjective
2. objective

Quick Quiz 2.2

1. Deming, Juran, and Crosby
2. Theory Z
3. support from management, desire to participate, skills needed to participate

Quick Quiz 2.3

1. United States; Italy
2. the controlling function

Quick Quiz 2.4

1. b
2. c
3. b

Quick Quiz 2.5

1. benchmarking, meeting ISO 9000 standards, and contending for the Malcolm Baldrige National Quality Award
2. International Standards Organization (ISO)
3. leadership, information and analysis, strategic quality planning, human resource development and management, management of process quality, quality and operational results, customer focus and satisfaction

Quick Quiz 2.6

1. to choose the quickest and easiest solution rather than searching for a better, long-term solution
2. customer and employee feedback

CHAPTER

3

Integrating People and Technology

CHAPTER OUTLINE

The Effects of Technological Advancement

Historical Trends in Technology

Modern Trends in Technology

Ergonomics and Technology

The Information Age

Preventing Errors in the Use of Information Systems

Reengineering

Emotional Reactions to Technology

Alienation

What's Ahead for People and Technology?

Summary

Teamwork Highlights: Making Leaders at Paslode

Quality Highlights: Mid-South Plunges into the Nineties

Self-Portrait: Your Technological Comfort Zone

International Highlights: California Sunshine Goes to Russia

Learning Objectives

- Explain how job specialization and standardization are related to the assembly line.
- Define mechanistic technology, automated technology, and cybernetic technology.
- Explain how computers made possible the phenomenon of telecommuting.
- Define ergonomics.
- Explain how to prevent errors in the use of information systems.
- Define business-process reengineering and explain why it is important to integrating people and technology.
- Explain why emotional reactions to technology are important.
- List the five major changes expected as a result of technological advances in the coming years.

Veterinary Centers Ring Up Business

For Bob Antin (pictured at left), investing in technology wasn't fun and games, nor was it a bid to keep his business growing. Technology was a way to counter new, unwanted competition.

Antin, chief executive of Veterinary Centers of America, a 20-unit chain of animal hospitals based in Santa Monica, California, was used to competing with other veterinary clinics for pet owners in need of medical services for their animals. Pet stores, breeders, and shelters were the sources for the animals that Veterinary Centers cared for. So the news that local pet stores were offering limited storefront veterinary services, including vaccinations, was alarming. At first, Antin thought the best way to fight back was by advertising the chain's services on television. But mass advertising, he reasoned, might work too well, and he couldn't afford the operators necessary to handle phone calls 24 hours a day.

Figuring his veterinary offices had the medical edge over pet stores, Antin determined that they should have the technological edge as well. He invested $100,000 in a state-of-the-art phone system that automatically routes calls to the nearest Veterinary Center location. Previously, each hospital had handled its own calls. Antin anticipates that the new phone system backing up his ads will help boost his million-dollar business by 45 percent.

Source: "The Big Squeeze on Small Business," *Business Week,* July 19, 1993, p. 67. Photo source: © Steve Goldstein.

The Effects of Technological Advancement

Technological advancement has affected every type and size of business, as it did in the case of Veterinary Centers of America. The days when people made their own products and created their own services seem light-years removed from today's technologically sophisticated lifestyle. People built everything they needed themselves, grew the food they ate, wove cloth and sewed their own clothes, even made their own soap from lye.

Technology has brought us a mixed bag of good and bad things. It has allowed more products to be developed and manufactured faster, thus giving consumers more choice. It has reduced the risk of injury at manufacturing plants and allowed workers to abandon assembly-line jobs to retrain for jobs requiring more skills. It has increased the capacity for communication worldwide. Technology has also cost people their jobs, in cases where they were phased out or could not be retrained. Increased communication also means increased competition and stress.

In the end, the individual can decide whether to make a friend or foe of technology. In the workplace, employers can help bring out the friendlier aspect of technology's face. Many are working hard to do just that. We will explore some of their attempts in this chapter.

Historical Trends in Technology

Adam Smith, author of the first book on modern economic theory, *The Wealth of Nations* (1776), drew attention to the benefits of *job specialization,* or *division of labor,* in his analysis of production in a pin factory.[1] He saw that whereas one worker could produce 20 complete pins a day, ten workers could produce 48,000 if the process was divided into several different operations and each worker concentrated on only one or a few of those operations. When inventions such as Eli Whitney's cotton gin (in 1793) allowed machine labor to replace human labor for certain processes, job specialization became even more practical. Jobs could be broken down into a small number of tasks that could be repeated by certain workers, then combined with a similarly limited number of tasks repeated by other workers, with the machine performing certain other tasks. The result was a much faster production process than if each worker had completed an entire product himself or herself.

Whitney also invented machinery to build interchangeable—that is, *standardized*—parts for muskets. Together with job specialization, this standardization made possible a forerunner of the assembly line in the factory that Whitney built under a government contract to manufacture firearms. Henry Ford used these ideas to develop the first true assembly line in producing his Model T automobile during the years from 1908 to 1927. Other industries successfully copied the assembly line, and productivity soared.

The result was a plethora of goods and services. As advances kept coming, the human role in production kept diminishing. The machine could do it better; the machine could do it faster. Assembly-line workers performed only the parts of the process that the machines couldn't. The machine gained prominence over the worker.

Modern Trends in Technology

Today's management styles, with their emphasis on employee empowerment and participation, attempt to meld technology with human potential. The idea is to work with the machines—keep all their advantages, such as standardization and specialization—but use human relations knowledge about job enrichment to keep workers motivated. This represents an attempt to combat the problem of *alienation,* discussed later in this chapter. In being responsible for an entire product, or at least an entire

Teamwork Highlights

Making Leaders at Paslode

When *Money* magazine named Illinois Tool Works of Chicago one of the country's most competitive companies, the magazine cited the company's research and development prowess. A closer look at one of the company's autonomous divisions, Paslode, would have revealed a far greater success—continued growth in an industry hit hard by the recent economic downturn: homebuilding.

Paslode's success was fueled by management's vision of developing leadership, building teamwork, and being the best at meeting customers' needs.

The high productivity and solid teamwork at Paslode's new manufacturing facility in Arkansas are a firm indication of the program's results. The plant's employees have gone beyond self-directed work teams by setting their own self-governing policies and work rules. For example, the plant's three shifts of workers together established their own absentee policy. In 1992, three years after the empowerment process began, the absentee rate at the plant was 0.0008 percent, compared to the national average of 1.8 percent.

Leadership training required the plant's staff—both management and labor—to become trainers. From controllers to shift supervisors, no one with any management responsibility or potential for it was overlooked. Being team-taught, the instructors learned from one another and involved the whole organization in the team-building process. "Our aim was to involve everyone at Paslode in our common goal of being the best at meeting customer needs," says Gean Stalcup, Paslode's operations manager.

Making the training a process, not an event, the program has been repeated, leaving its imprint on the organization. Today, Paslode has advanced beyond the system.

"We still use the leadership system as an agent of change with new people who come from other companies," explains Stalcup. "But for us as an organization, we've internalized the system and gone beyond it. It helped us make it obsolete. And that's good."

Source: James M. Cusimano, "Creating Leaders through Employee Empowerment," *Quality Digest*, March 1993, pp. 65–68.

aspect of a product, the workers gain more job satisfaction. At some companies, workers' names even go on the components they assemble.

Several companies in the apparel industry are trying the *whole-job concept* on for size. Recently, Levi Strauss, Russell, and Hanes have begun to use teams of 30 to 50 workers to make an entire garment, with operators deciding how to use the machinery themselves, moving among the machines as they see fit to eliminate bottlenecks.[2] Levi Strauss reports that its plants can now make a bundle of 30 jeans in seven hours from start to finish instead of the six days it often took because of bottlenecks.

Saab-Scania is another company notable for its employment of this whole-job concept. In the 1970s, selected assembly workers from Ford, General Motors, and Chrysler corporations in Detroit were sent to the Swedish plant to study its successful system in which each worker could elect to assemble a whole engine or one-third of an engine (few chose the latter).[3] To learn how one company used leadership training to boost its labor force to new heights via self-governing work teams, see the "Teamwork Highlights" box.

By keeping the labor-saving advantages of technology but redesigning jobs to supply variety and challenge, companies have the best of both worlds. The machines speed production, and wise job design keeps the workers motivated.

mechanistic technology Technology that allows some types of human labor to be performed by a machine, usually with human input.

automated technology Technology that allows some types of human labor to be performed mechanically or electronically, generally by a computer, with little or no human input.

cybernetic technology Technology that allows machines to be self-regulating; labor performed by a machine is controlled by another machine, further reducing human input.

The Second Industrial Revolution. **Mechanistic technology**, which allowed people to use machines to replace some types of human labor, ushered in the Industrial Revolution. Industry then progressed to **automated technology**, in which the computer replaced still more human labor, including certain computational tasks once thought to be beyond the range of a machine. Automated technology allows the human worker to be completely eliminated from many more steps of production. **Cybernetic technology**, in which machines control other machines, further reduces the human role (see Figure 3.1). Some experts say that automated technology has ush-

Figure 3.1 **Three Stages in Technological Advancement**

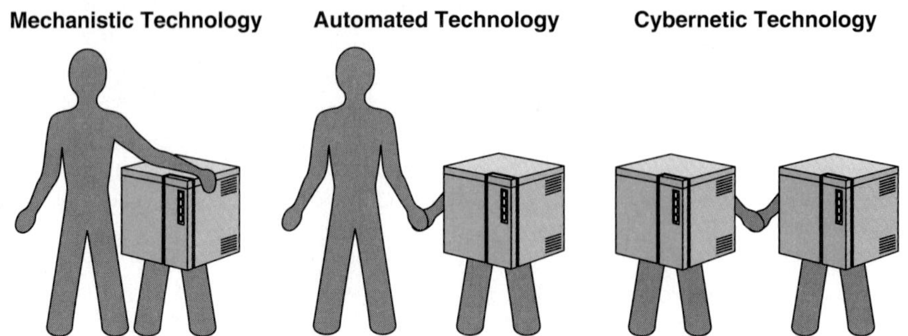

ered in the Second Industrial Revolution. Stephen R. Barley, a professor at Cornell's School of Industrial and Labor Relations, sums it up this way:

> [Until recently] the economies of the advanced industrial nations revolved around electrical power, the electric motor, the internal combustion engine, and the telephone .... [Now] our growing knowledge of how to convert electronic and mechanical impulses into digitally encoded information (and vice versa) and how to transmit such information across vast distances is gradually enabling industry to replace its electromechanical infrastructure with a computational infrastructure.[4]

robotics
The specific field of automated technology that utilizes robots: machines that duplicate, or better, human physical movements.

artificial intelligence
A computer's version of human reasoning and thinking.

The science of **robotics**, in which mechanical equipment (a *robot*) duplicates, or betters, human movements, has also become more sophisticated. Once confined to relatively simple spot-welding or spray-painting jobs, some robots can now handle sensitive work such as assembling electrical relays. Other robots are sent into hazardous environments such as volcanoes, oceans, and nuclear power plants to gather data in places where humans might be in danger or could not survive. A robot actually "discovered" the Titanic, and robots have "walked" on the moon.

Can machines "think" like humans? **Artificial intelligence**, in which a computer engages in its version of reasoning, is still totally dependent on the flexible reasoning of the human programmer. Once thought to be the wave of the future—in which "thinking" computers would replace people on the job—artificial intelligence was found to be lacking in many ways. Now, computer companies have focused on producing hardware and software that simplifies work for people but doesn't replace them. Researchers have turned their attention to other types of "intelligent" computers as well, such as chemical-based computers that use chemicals to store data much the same way DNA stores information about each human being.[5]

Although technology does eliminate some jobs, it opens up many new ones. AT&T has cut 21,000 low-skilled jobs since 1984 because of improved technology, but it has also expanded white-collar hires by 8,000.[6] When possible, most companies will provide training to employees phased out of lower-skilled jobs by technology to equip them for higher-skilled jobs. And then there is the home-based office, made possible by telecommunications.

telecommuting
Working at home by means of a computer and telephone linkup.

Telecommuting. With the advances made in personal computers and communications devices such as fax machines and modems, many people are now able to work at home. Some have their own businesses, but many are employed by companies that supply the home computer and telephone linkup for **telecommuting.** This is a great solution for people with children or invalids at home, those with physical limitations that make traveling to the office difficult, and those who simply enjoy working in their home environment. Music consultant Gaylon Horton quit his high-powered job and

Marion Merrell Dow, a Kansas City drug company, downsized for the first time in the spring of 1994, with as many as 1,300 employees leaving the company. Janet Mills, an executive administrative assistant still "gets the creeps" when she walks by empty cubicles, a common reaction of survivor's syndrome.
Photo source: © Max Aguilera-Hellweg.

set up his own home-based business after his three-year-old son called him at work to ask, "Dad, you wanna come over to my house this weekend?"[7]

Now that personal computers have become so much more affordable, people such as Horton have the option of home-based work. But you have to have the personality for it. Some people are relieved to exit the corporate environment. "Office politics and slow decision making drove me nuts," says Mary Logeland, who owns a wood-puzzle company with her husband, Doug. Says another home-worker, a CPA, "Meeting new people was hard work. I did not enjoy meetings—I was much better when I was analyzing something. Working at home is a lot easier for me."[8] Many miss the social aspects of the office, though. "The first two years on my own were especially hard. You miss your chums," says Rollene Saal, who left her job as editor in chief of Bantam Books to start her own literary agency from home.[9]

According to Link Resources Corporation, the number of full-time, home-based business owners was 12.1 million in 1992.[10] Counting part-time home-workers, the total for self-employed households was 23.8 million, an increase of 12 percent over 1991. It is predicted that 44 percent of all U.S. households will support some form of office activity by 1995. Employers generally report good results from telecommuting arrangements.

downsizing
Cutting the size of an organization by eliminating jobs in order to give it a flatter structure and make it more responsive to change.

Downsizing. Some home-based business owners are laid-off middle managers. **Downsizing,** the trend toward a "lean and mean" organizational structure (theorized to be more responsive to change) has cost the jobs of many such middle managers in their fifties—too young for retirement, too old to compete for new jobs. The threatening face of technology that cost them their jobs has turned benign for the many who have put technology to work in their own homes. In a recent survey, 20 percent of home-based business owners cited job loss as their major reason for beginning their home jobs.[11]

Projections call for downsizing to intensify.[12] Technology makes it possible and desirable in more and more areas. Thomas A. Malone of MIT's Sloan School suggests that the true value of computers is their capacity to take over "coordination activities" such as processing orders, keeping track of inventory, and posting accounts.[13] The result is a smaller company and a "flatter" organizational structure, that is, a less hierarchical one. James Brian Quinn, from Dartmouth's Tuck School of Business, predicts a "radically flat organization" for the future, a so-called *network organization* in which lots of separate sites transmit information to a single headquarters where decisions are made—a "spider's web" organization.[14]

One of the unfortunate results of downsizing is the *survivor's syndrome* that has been noted among those employees who do not lose their jobs. Rather than feeling relief, they tend to feel increased insecurity. Watching coworkers leave makes them feel uncertain about their own job security, even with corporate assurances that no more layoffs are planned. Once again, however, it should be noted that the unemployment threatened by downsizing trends is outweighed by the new jobs generated by technological advances.

Quick Quiz 3.1

1. Adam Smith and Eli Whitney both brought attention to the merits of ______________________.
2. Henry Ford instituted the first true ___________ in his factory for making Model T automobiles.
3. The original idea of using computers with artificial intelligence to replace humans on the job has now been modified to making computers that ______________________.
4. A parent who has small children at home might prefer ___________ to traveling to an office every day.

Ergonomics and Technology

hygiene factors
According to Herzberg's two-factor theory, aspects of employment that produce dissatisfaction by virtue of their absence.

ergonomics
The science of designing and arranging things used in the workplace so that they can be used most effectively and safely; also called *human engineering*.

In the 1950s, Frederick Herzberg's *two-factor theory* of motivation introduced the concept of **hygiene factors**, aspects of employment that produced dissatisfaction by virtue of their absence. One of these factors is particularly relevant to our discussion of technology—that of "satisfactory working conditions," as it applies to physical aspects of the workplace. Around this factor has grown up an entire science, **ergonomics** (also called *human engineering*), the designing and arranging of things used in the workplace so that they can be used most effectively and safely.

Some consulting firms specialize in office ergonomics. The computer figures largely in their consultations. For example, it has been shown that intensive work at a video display terminal (VDT) can lead to repetitive motion (or stress) injuries such as carpal tunnel syndrome, a painful disorder of the wrist and hand.[15] Once confined to such occupations as meat-packing and assembly-line jobs, this syndrome has spread to the modern office and now accounts for more than half of all occupational injuries recorded by the Department of Labor. (Figure 3.2 illustrates how this and other such disorders, like tendinitis, can develop.)

Technology caused these problems, so technology came to the rescue. Adjustable computer accessories and adjustable chairs and desks have been designed to prevent or minimize such occupational injuries. Special chairs with wrist supports are available (Figure 3.3), or wrist rests—thick rolls of foam—can be purchased to place along the edges of a worktable.[16] Special keyboards arranged to minimize strain on the forearms and wrists have been invented, too (Figure 3.3). Better yet, more than one keyless computer system is under development. Speech-controlled computers are in their infancy, but research on these continues at a rapid pace. One recent breakthrough is the ability to process continuous speech (words spoken at a normal speed); such a computer could take dictation. Other speech-controlled computers can translate languages on the spot, for instance, during phone calls between parties who speak different languages.[17]

Some of the problems created by working with computers are easily solved. Eye strain from prolonged work with a VDT can be reduced by glare-reducing screens or filters placed over the monitor.[18] A footrest can reduce the discomfort of sitting in one position for a long time. In addition, people who work at VDTs are advised to take fre-

Figure 3.2 **How Repetitive Stress Injuries Are Caused**

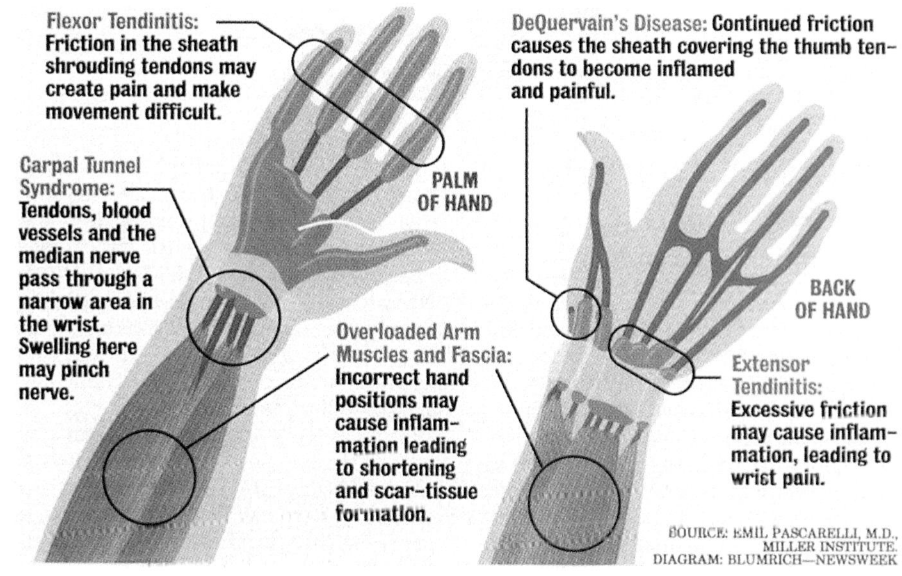

Source: NEWSWEEK, December 7, 1992, Artist: Blumrich.

quent breaks.[19] At the *Los Angeles Times* newsroom, terminals automatically remind staffers to take breaks, and a room with exercise equipment and ice packs is provided.[20]

Concern exists about the low-frequency radiation emitted from VDTs.[21] The National Institute for Occupational Safety and Health has found no proof of hazard, but neither has it been ruled out to the satisfaction of consumers. In response to that concern, "by the end of [1993], all terminals on the market will use low-emission tubes," says Louis Selsin, editor of *VDT News,* an industry newsletter.

Computers are not the only source of ergonomic problems. Since cubicles are replacing offices in so many companies, office designers are finding ways to improve cubicle space.[22] To make up for the loss of doors, Cubicle Cues— plastic signs saying "Open" or "Closed"—can be hung outside the entrance. Steelcase is designing cylindrical cubicles with sliding glass doors big enough for one person and a desk, with control panels to allow the temperature and even the stereo system to be adjusted to the individual's liking. Another design provides semicubicles that hold two or three employees each, situated so that they can easily consult with each other, catering to the current emphasis on teams.

Individual preferences guarantee that the science of ergonomics will never resolve all inadequacies in the hygiene factor of physical working conditions. But a company that does its best to solve the most glaring problems not only improves the health of individuals, it improves the health of the organization as a whole. An employee who isn't suffering from headaches or eye strain is much more likely to produce accurate work. As long as the human mind is housed in a physical body, ergonomics will be an important concern.

Quick Quiz 3.2

1. Which of Herzberg's hygiene factors does the science of ergonomics address?
2. Name some aids to relieve physical problems related to computer use.
3. How do some companies solve the problem of cubicles that lack doors?

Figure 3.3 **Aids to Prevent Repetitive Stress Injuries**

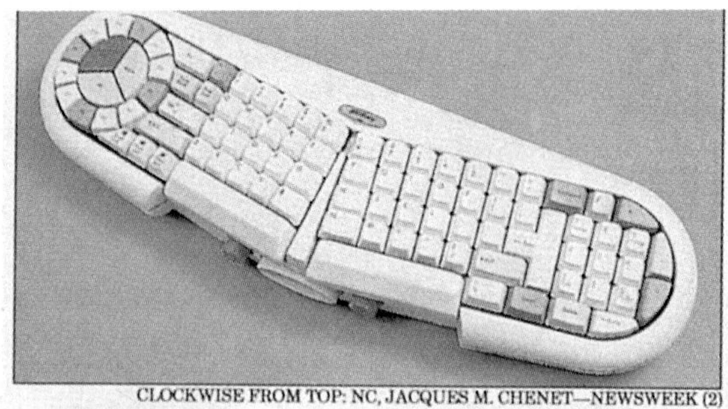

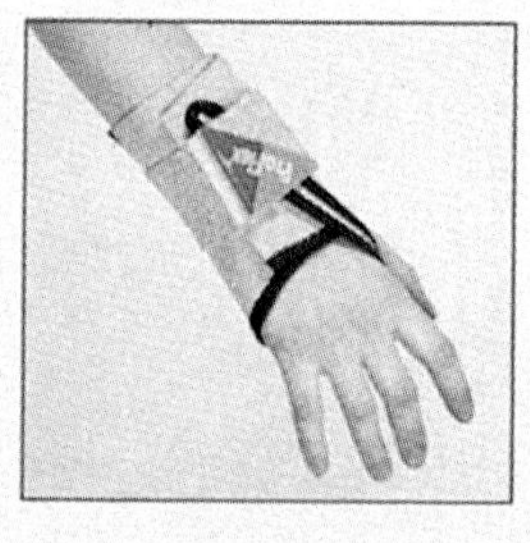

Source: NEWSWEEK, Photographer: Jacques M. Chenet.

The Information Age

The Computer Age is also the Information Age. The computer has given us access to more information than ever before, and businesses today need more information than ever before. A **management information system (MIS)** is a formal method of gathering, processing, and disseminating all the information an organization needs, both for its own use and to meet the needs of customers. The more timely that information is, the more valuable it is. The more precise it is, the more useful it is. The people operating the MIS will determine these issues of timeliness and precision. The decision makers who use the MIS will determine how valuable it is.

management information system (MIS)
A formal method of gathering, processing, and disseminating all the information an organization needs.

All the information in the world is not a substitute for good judgment! Edward C. Johnson III, chairman and CEO of Fidelity Investments and chairman of National Quality Month 1993, offers this insight:

> Technology's success depends on the hand that guides the tool. If you put a Stradivarius violin in the hands of the average six-year-old, you would not expect beautiful music. It's not much different with a technology tool. It may be able to do wonderful things. But in the hands of an unskilled user, it's worthless.[23]

Fernando Bartolome, professor of management at Bentley College in Waltham, Massachusetts, notes that "using information well is primarily a matter of not *misusing* it."[24] He further notes that "consuming, disseminating, and creating information" are all important to good managers and related to the issue of building trust between subordinates and their superiors.[25] To read about a company whose plunge into technology came only when its main customer demanded it, see the "Quality Highlights" box.

Quality Highlights

Mid-South Plunges into the Nineties

Jerry Weaver had a simple formula for success—sell a good product at a good price while staying chummy with the customer. His philosophy had helped him build Mid-South Industries, a contract manufacturer of everything from toaster ovens to plastic bottles, into a $110 million business in the 1980s.

But the business world had changed by the 1990s. In June, one of his biggest customers, Xerox Corp., sent a team of auditors into Mid-South's Gadsden, Alabama, plant. Its findings were sobering. Mid-South did not measure up to the new efficiency standards Xerox had set for its suppliers to help trim costs. "They took me behind the woodshed over quality problems and a high cost structure," admits Weaver.

Faced with losing Xerox's business, Weaver spent the next two years finding ways to cut costs and improve productivity. He upgraded his assembly line with robotics and other computer automation—a $400,000 investment. A further $1 million went toward efficiency training for his workers. Though he trimmed his annual operating costs by 5 percent while nearly eliminating product defects, the costs of training and new equipment had shrunk Mid-South's margins to only 2 percent, down from 6 percent in 1989. But Weaver says the squeeze is worth it. Sales are up 55 percent, to $170 million, at least partly due to an appreciative Xerox.

Thanks to his investment in training and adoption of new technologies, Weaver is optimistic about profit margins, too. "We've got systems in place that are going to keep getting us more and more efficient each year."

Source: "The Big Squeeze on Small Business," *Business Week*, July 19, 1993, p. 66.

Many companies are experimenting with *sales and marketing automation (SMA)* or, specifically, *sales force automation (SFA).* General success and high enthusiasm have been reported by most.[26] Table 3.1 gives some responses from a recent survey on SFA. Note that almost 90 percent of the respondents dismiss fears that computers could diminish original thinking. Some experts believe the computers actually enhance creative thinking:[27]

> Sales questions are generally not black-and-white issues. Therefore, one will always be able to exercise creativity and judgment. The creativity and original thinking come in asking the computer the right questions.
>
> —Joyce Nikola,
> marketing analyst for Wang Labs

> Accountants have used computerized applications for years, and no one accuses them of lacking original thinking. Providing data via laptops and simplifying communications with e-mail offers more time for the human aspects of thinking.
>
> —Frances Morgan,
> manager of information and communications
> systems for Coors Brewing

> Computers do the drudgery and give users the luxury of more time to think at a higher level.
>
> —Dave Prichard,
> section leader for sales systems
> at Hoechst Celanese

> Computerization will push users to think at higher levels. Without computers, users spend 90 percent of their time gathering information and only 10 percent analyzing.
>
> —David A. Lacey,
> manager of corporate sales
> technology for Clorox

Still, some cautions seem valid. Computers induce salespeople "to take the path of least resistance," says John Coulson, local sales manager at WXYV/WCAO Radio.[28] As always, the benefits or drawbacks of technology seem to depend on how an individual approaches the technology and how a company presents it to its workers. Certainly no one would dispute the overall value of computerized systems in general. Take the

Table 3.1 **Survey on Reactions to SFA**

1. Some experts feel salespeople will soon carry all they need in the field in their portable computers and will be less dependent upon branch offices as we now know them. This will enable companies to save millions of dollars by having fewer, smaller, or no branch offices. Do you agree or disagree with this statement?

Response	Total	Computer Users	Computer Nonusers
Agree	61.5%	68.5%	51.0%
Disagree	36.1	27.4	49.0
Undecided	2.5	4.1	0.0

2. Until now, computer applications have primarily been those that benefited the salesperson. However, some users feel the emphasis should shift to sales management, training, and other applications that help the sales department as a whole. Where do you think the emphasis should be placed?

Emphasis on ...	Total	Computer Users	Computer Nonusers
Individual salespeople	14.5%	18.7%	8.2%
Sales dept. as a whole	73.4	66.7	83.7
Both	10.5	13.3	6.1

3. As computers become more widely used in sales and marketing for problem solving and decision making, there's a danger users will become less likely to do their own original thinking. Do you think that threat is real or overstated?

Response	Total	Computer Users	Computer Nonusers
Real	11.2%	5.3%	20.4%
Overstated	88.8	94.7	79.6

4. It's almost an article of faith among computer vendors that "using computers in sales and marketing is essential because they give you a competitive edge." Do you agree or disagree with this statement?

Response	Total	Computer Users	Computer Nonusers
Agree	70.4%	74.3%	64.7%
Disagree	25.6	23.0	29.4
Undecided	4.0	2.7	5.9

Source: Reprinted with permission of Sales and Marketing Management, 355 Park Avenue South, NY, NY 10010–1789.

improvements they offer in customer service. Gene Schnabel, director of field information systems for Rosemount Inc., speaks for many when he says, "In order for any company to be competitive in customer service, it must improve its information systems."[29]

Preventing Errors in the Use of Information Systems

Efforts at computerization such as sales force automations (SFAs) can fail because of some very common errors that can be prevented. Stephen Gondert, an expert in sales and marketing automation, has identified ten such errors:[30]

1. *Giving one person responsibility for designing and implementing a program but not the real power and authority necessary to see the project through.* In other

Figure 3.4 **Example of a Flowchart for a Book Design**

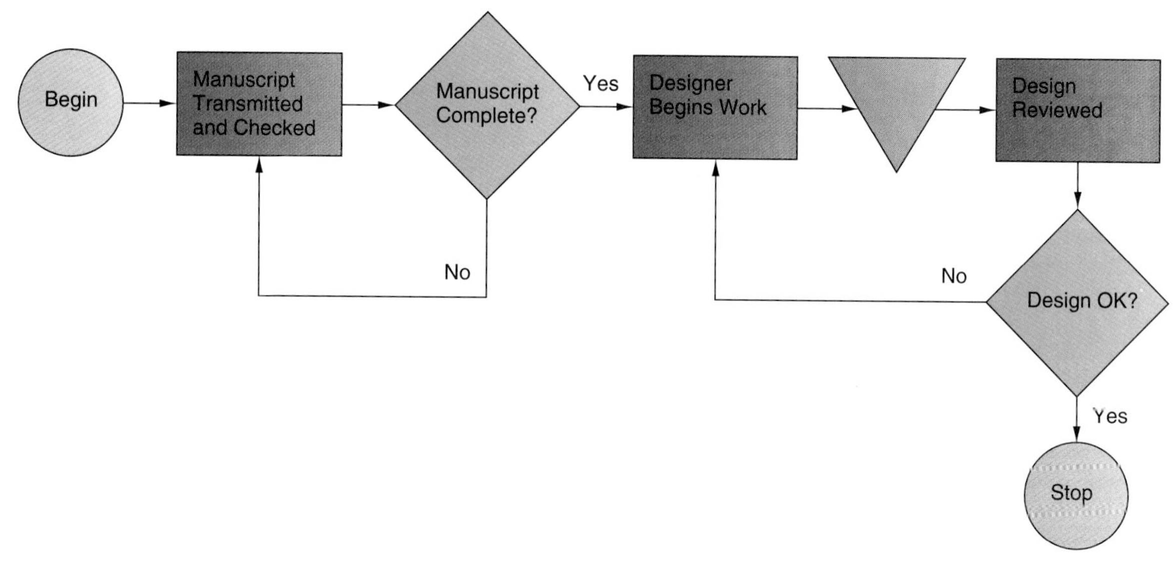

words, a person is asked to do a job without the proper tools. If a manager gives an employee an assignment, he or she should also give the employee enough authority to do the job.

2. *Failing to define information needs clearly enough.* People who are in charge of designing a program for gathering information should make sure they communicate with those who need the information. *Flowcharts* like the one in Figure 3.4 can help.
3. *Automating a flawed manual system instead of starting over.* If the manual system in place is inefficient, merely automating it is unlikely to make it efficient. It's often better to start anew, with a fresh approach.
4. *Failing to complete all steps of the planning process.* Every step of the planning process must be thoroughly carried out in order to head off as many problems as possible. Extra time spent in the planning stage will save time (and maybe money) later on.
5. *Failing to obtain strong top management support.* Since upper management usually approves funds for a program, this is a good time to gain its enthusiastic support.
6. *Focusing on technical problems to the exclusion of potential "people" problems.* Good employees ensure the smooth running of a system, so good human relations skills are vital to the project's success.
7. *Allowing fear of "Big Brother" to build.* If the new system is perceived as a watchdog, it may produce problems in motivation and job satisfaction that will outweigh its benefits. Allow workers to befriend the system, learning how it can help them perform their jobs more easily.
8. *Failing to control related departmental rivalries.* Create camaraderie rather than competition among departments, making sure that all users of the system have equal access to the information and equal opportunities to benefit from it.
9. *Bypassing the pilot test.* A pilot test is costly and time consuming, but it is essential to speedy and smooth implementation of the real thing. It is far more costly and time consuming to make corrections and to fine-tune the system after it is in place throughout the organization. Once people become accustomed to operating a certain way under the system, it is best to avoid major changes. For the pilot test, choose employees who are enthusiastic about the program and eager to try it.

Union Carbide has used reengineering to scrape $400 million out of fixed costs in three years. When these maintenance and operating workers at Carbide's Taft, Louisiana, plant tore up their old process map and redrew it, they found savings of more than $20 million.

Photo source: John Chiasson/ Gamma Liaison.

Photo Exercise

The text lists several companies that have used reengineering successfully. Think of a company where you've worked. How and where could reengineering be applied?

10. *Scrimping on training and support.* Make adjusting to the new system as easy for workers as possible. Provide tutorials, courses, access to hot lines, tips from experts on the best ways of operating, and anything else that can help.

Some changes will inevitably become necessary as organizational needs evolve, so a good support system is essential. Management should evaluate and act on suggestions from employees as they use the system and discover flaws or have ideas for improvements. Support personnel can also help keep enthusiasm for the program high.

Reengineering

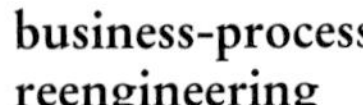

business-process reengineering
A complete redesigning of business processes rather than refinement or adjustment of existing processes. It focuses on the continuing nature of such processes rather than viewing them as many discrete tasks.

Michael Hammer is the management consultant who coined the term **business-process reengineering,** meaning a complete redesign of business processes rather than refinement or adjustment of existing processes. Such a redesign focuses on the continuing nature of business processes rather than breaking them into discrete tasks. He admits the concept is not new. "These ideas are obvious. No one disputes them. The trouble is, until recently no one followed them either."[31] The decade of the 1990s is seeing plenty of firms following them, though, including AT&T, Texas Instruments, Ford, Citicorp, Aetna Life, and IBM.[32]

Wal-Mart and Dell Computer are two prime examples of this approach. In both cases, managers decided how the computer could completely change their operations for the better, and it did. Sears certainly knows that it did for Wal-Mart, which lured so many Sears shoppers away with its greater variety of goods at lower cost.[33] Dell showed the other companies how it is done by evading the expensive dealer network or salespeople and selling directly to consumers.[34] And Levi Strauss pioneered the use of *electronic data interchange (EDI),* in which customers can tap into supplier computers to check inventories, order supplies, and generate invoices. A "director of quick response" was created to coordinate electronic links to suppliers and customers.[35]

Such reengineering is the answer to a major reason for failures in computerization, "automating a flawed manual system instead of starting anew," as described in the preceding section. Texas Instruments learned from an earlier mistake in this area, and enjoyed tremendous success after it "pretty well nuked the existing process."[36] With its leading-edge business software, Texas Instruments has likewise helped other companies to reengineer. For example, Xerox Corporation used TI's Information Engineering Facility (IEF) software, which comes with complete follow-up support, including training, to configure the company's wide range of products and options according to its multinational customer needs. This *decision support system* uses artificial intelligence to coordinate marketing, engineering, and distribution. Its integrated "toolsets" automate the entire development life cycle. The result is that customers are far better served with a flexible approach that allows applications to be easily modified to reflect changing business conditions.[37]

Ford is also happy with its decision to reengineer the procedure it used to pay its thousands of suppliers. From 500 people shuffling purchase orders and invoices among themselves, the company is down to 125 using a computer to do the same job faster.[38] Still another example of successful reengineering is Britain's Royal Mail: A "Customer First" quality program led to a complete reorganization in which 64 postal regions were replaced by 18 business units, each regarded as a profit center; headquarters staff was reduced from 2,500 to 160; and process-driven management replaced a functional approach—all supported by sophisticated information technology. Royal Mail's profits soared along with its customer satisfaction; independent surveys rate it Britain's top public service provider in terms of customer satisfaction.[39]

Emotional Reactions to Technology

Ned Ludd, they say, smashed the new machine that would have taken away his job. He may be a mythical character—no one knows for sure. At least 17 of the "Luddites" who destroyed new textile-industry machines in Great Britain during the early 1800s for the same reason were real enough to be hanged for the capital crime of destroying machinery. Today's Luddites usually behave themselves around the machines they fear or dislike, but emotional reactions can be manifested in other damaging ways: "this stupid machine" is blamed for errors. A resentful attitude blocks learning how to operate a computer program. A suspicious attitude further complicates the learning process. Test your own technological comfort zone by taking the accompanying "Self-Portrait" quiz.

Stress-reduction expert Craig Brod calls this phenomenon *technostress.*[40] *Cyberphobia* was the term used by H. L. Capron in reporting on a study that revealed actual physical symptoms of nausea, dizziness, cold sweat, and increased blood pressure occurring in people subject to this "disease."[41] Good human relations skills on the part of managers can help here. People need to be assured that they will not be left to sink or swim, that plenty of support will be available as they adjust to working with the computer. A company that invests in career development for its employees will probably have less trouble with cyberphobia related to fears of job loss.

Surveys show clerical workers are more subject to technostress and cyberphobia than professionals,[42] and this is a realistic fear, since it is their jobs that are most likely to be replaced by computer technology. Most technostressed workers are women, a logical outcome since most clerical workers are women. The phenomenon is twice as common among those over age 50 as among those under age 30, another logical outcome given the increased resistance to change that generally accompanies age.[43]

Fortunately, many companies are providing the kind of training that will equip such workers for better jobs, using the technology that took over their old jobs. Levi Strauss has created a "training for technology" curriculum to provide the needed skills for the 1,800 "knowledge workers" it expects to need in the future as a result of computer technology. This company and others actually use the technology of an information system as a tool for empowering their employees.[44]

Self-Portrait

Your Technological Comfort Zone

Our acceptance of workplace technology often depends on how old we are and how long ago we entered the work force. But other factors also come into play. Sometimes, the way we utilize our home technologies influences our acceptance of work technologies. Answer the first two questions with the appropriate number, and answer the remaining questions with a yes or no.

_____	1. How old are you?
_____	2. What year did you enter the work force?
Y N	3. If you have one, can you program your own VCR?
Y N	4. Do you use your microwave for cooking, not just defrosting and warming?
Y N	5. Have you read the manuals for your home electronics?
Y N	6. Do you take the time to learn how to use a new piece of office technology (fax machine, copier, computer) instead of "winging" it?
Y N	7. In your job, do you understand how to do just enough technologically to get by?
Y N	8. Do you think trying to better understand technology is hopeless?
Y N	9. When a deadline looms, are you overwhelmed by relying on technology to speed things along?
Y N	10. Do you often lose your work in the computer?
Y N	11. Does it seem as though the copier always has a paper jam when you are using it?
Y N	12. Do you feel that life and work would be easier without the bells and whistles of computers, fax machines, etc.?
Y N	13. Do you find voice mail impersonal and resent not talking to a live person?
Y N	14. Do computerized cash registers make you nervous about the nation's future math skills?
Y N	15. Are you sometimes afraid that technology will surpass your skills and put you out of a job?

Answering yes to questions 3 through 6 indicates an ease and familiarity with technology, at home and at work. Answering yes to a majority of questions 7 through 13 indicates uneasiness with technology. A yes to the two final questions illustrates fears common to many workers—even those comfortable with technology.

The days of computer fear may be just about gone. In one recent survey, 93 percent of respondents from all levels of business, clerical to management, reported no fear or reluctance to work with computers, although 14 percent said that such was not the case initially.[45] The only computer-related fear for today's younger generation, growing up with Nintendo, will probably be the fear of a computer breakdown. An older generation, far removed from the fast-paced technologies of Western countries, can make global business a more personal affair, as seen in the "International Highlights" box.

An interesting variation on cyberphobia is *cyberphrenia,* an addiction to computers rather than a fear of them, leading even to an identification with them.[46] Nicholas J. Curtis, vice-president of marketing at Lion Apparel, worries that sales reps sometimes find "quantification is easier to defend than creativity."[47] Craig Brod explains that people who become intensely interested in computers sometimes "begin to adopt a mind-set that mirrors the computer itself."[48] This overemphasis on computers reduces an employee's ability to relate successfully to coworkers and customers, so a manager may want to limit the employee's time with the computer and encourage him or her to redevelop creative thinking and good human relations skills.

International Highlights

California Sunshine Goes to Russia

Being serious about doing business in the newly emerging democracies of Eastern Europe means understanding that the technologies Americans use on a daily basis—telex, fax, even the telephone—are new, exotic, and often unavailable or unreliable in these countries. Sometimes using telecommunications even generates distrust. Doing business there means appearing personally.

Mats Engstrom, owner of California Sunshine, one of the world's largest private producers of caviar, knows that patience, caution, flexibility, and determination are the real key. Since he began doing business in Russia, he says he's learned that "the key to success is to stay as far away from Moscow as possible."

After eight years of fishing for sturgeon on the Chinese side of the Amur River, which separates Manchuria and Siberia, Engstrom decided he wanted to sample the Russian fish. He wrote to the Ministry of Fisheries in Moscow, suggesting a joint venture. Six months later, he received a letter from the ministry stating that because there were no fish in the Amur River, the ministry was not interested. After several attempts to plough through Moscow's bureaucracy, Engstrom finally traveled to Siberia with a trade mission and set up the joint venture with the help of local officials.

Engstrom's problems continued, however, when he discovered that the country's technological problems were not confined to telecommunications. Russian water-filtration devices, canning materials, and salt were not up to world standards. To ensure the consistency of his caviar, Engstrom now imports the materials.

Source: Armin A. Brott, "How to Avoid Bear Traps," *Nation's Business*, September 1993, pp. 49–50.

Alienation

alienation
Feelings of powerlessness and isolation and a view of one's work as meaningless and devoid of satisfaction.

In addition to the sometimes warranted fear of losing one's job, technology inspires a conglomeration of undesirable reactions that can be lumped together under the term **alienation**—feelings of powerlessness and isolation and a view of one's work as meaningless and devoid of satisfaction.[49] Attempts at empowerment can help employees feel more powerful and satisfied with their jobs (see Figure 3.5). Participative management can relieve feelings of isolation. Not surprisingly, workers in mass-production industries suffer the most alienation—automobile assembly-line workers being a prime example.[50] This is why participative management programs like those at Saturn are receiving so much attention.

Quick Quiz 3.3

Mark the following statements "true" or "false".

1. The beauty of today's management information systems is that they require very little human judgment to operate efficiently. ____________
2. If a clothing manufacturer's manual sales information system is flawed, it might be best to start with a fresh approach and design a new system for automation. ____________
3. People suffering from technostress or cyberphobia may actually exhibit physical symptoms such as dizziness and increased blood pressure. ____________
4. An employee who feels alienated in a job might be helped through attempts at empowerment by his or her manager. ____________

What's Ahead for People and Technology?

More than half of the people currently employed in the United States have seen their jobs change as a result of technology.[51] It has been estimated that technology will cause the loss of 30 percent of existing jobs.[52] New jobs will emerge, but projections indicate that they will be primarily in the service sector—the sector where growth has

Figure 3.5 **Empowerment's Effect on Job Satisfaction**

"They don't actually do anything. I just like the way they make me feel."

Source: David Brion.

slowed the most. Another matter of concern for the United States is the tendency of today's students to choose fields other than science, mathematics, and engineering. (According to the National Academy of Sciences, American students score poorly in these fields compared with students from other countries.[53]) Advanced computer skills don't make up for knowledge in these basic areas.

Future advances may hold the answers to some of our projected problems. Research and development (R&D) departments of organizations, where the technological innovations usually occur or are developed into practical applications, have assumed increasing importance and commanded correspondingly greater funding. Moreover, an increasing emphasis on social responsibility is prompting greater involvement from business in the education and training of future and present employees. A young employee of Rohn & Haas, for example, was helped to work his way up from a janitorial job to studying agricultural biology.[54]

computational infrastructure A computer-based system supporting the routine operations of a business.

We know that technology created a host of brand new jobs in the recent past, such as air traffic controller and nuclear technician. We also know that the **computational infrastructure** surrounding computers and supporting more and more of the routine operations of all types of businesses has likewise spawned many new jobs. What other new jobs might the future hold? One interesting prediction from Thomas W. Malone of MIT's Sloan School is that "the increasing use of information technology appears likely to increase the importance of market mechanisms as a way of coordinating economic activ-

Technology is an increasing part of the workplace. Hand-held devices such as the one this British Airways agent has will make flight reservations and check-in quicker. The networks use radio signals that travel between computer devices and receivers dotted around a service area.

Photo source: © John Abbott.

Photo Exercise

How have wireless data networks changed other people's jobs?

ity."[55] We can only speculate on how this might affect the welfare of our nation, and the world. It does suggest an unrelenting increase in the importance of technology, however.

Essentially, five major changes are expected as a result of technological advances in the coming years:

1. Jobs will require more skills and involve more responsibility.
2. The use of work teams will increase.
3. Managers will lean increasingly toward "coaching" and serving as resources.
4. The trend toward flatter corporate structures will continue.
5. Information systems will increase in importance and in scope of application.

Thus, technology and people will continue to be interrelated, because these changes can't take place without the help of human beings.

Quick Quiz 3.4

1. More than ______ of workers in the United States have seen their jobs change as a result of technology.
   a. 10 percent
   b. 50 percent
   c. 75 percent
2. Which of the following changes is most likely to take place in the workplace of the future?
   a. Work teams will be disbanded.
   b. Jobs will require fewer skills and less responsibility.
   c. Managers will be viewed as "coaches."

Summary

- **Explain how job specialization and standardization are related to the assembly line.** Job specialization, also called division of labor, breaks down whole jobs into a small number of tasks that can be repeated by certain workers, then combined with a similarly limited number of tasks repeated by other workers. Standardization refers to manufacturing parts that are interchangeable. On the assembly line, workers in specialized jobs perform part of a process using standardized parts.

- **Define mechanistic technology, automated technology, and cybernetic technology.** Mechanistic technology allows some types of human labor to be performed by machine, usually with human input. Automated technology allows some types of human labor to be performed mechanically or electronically, generally by a computer, with little or no human input. Cybernetic technology allows machines to be self-regulating; labor performed by a machine is controlled by another machine.

- **Explain how computers made possible the phenomenon of telecommuting.** Affordable personal computers, combined with a telephone linkup, made it possible for people with children at home, those with physical limitations, and those who simply enjoy the home environment to work at home.
- **Define ergonomics.** Ergonomics is the science of designing and arranging things used in the workplace so that they can be used more efficiently.
- **Explain how to prevent errors in the use of information systems.** A manager should delegate authority along with responsibility to the person designated to design and implement the program; people who are in charge of designing the program should make sure they communicate with those who need the information; if the manual system in place is inefficient, start over rather than just automating it; complete all steps of the planning process; obtain strong top management support; focus on human relations issues as well as technical problems; allow workers to befriend the system; create camaraderie rather than rivalry among departments using the system; use the pilot test; provide training and support for employees who use the system.
- **Define business-process reengineering and explain why it is important to integrating people and technology.** Business-process reengineering is a complete redesign of business processes rather than refinement or adjustment of existing processes. It focuses on their continuing nature rather than viewing them as many discrete tasks. Reengineering can make jobs easier, helping employees do their jobs better and faster.
- **Explain why emotional reactions to technology are important.** Emotional reactions affect how well the technology is used by employees, and ultimately how well they do their jobs. Technostress or cyberphobia can actually produce physical symptoms of distress, such as nausea and increased blood pressure. Cyberphrenia, in which people become addicted to computers, reduces creative thinking. Alienation—feelings of powerlessness and isolation and a view of one's work as meaningless and devoid of satisfaction—can also limit an employee's performance. Empowerment and participative management, along with other human relations skills, can help resolve these emotional problems.

Key Terms

mechanistic technology (49)
automated technology (49)
cybernetic technology (49)
robotics (50)
artificial intelligence (50)
telecommuting (50)
downsizing (51)
hygiene factors (52)
ergonomics (52)
management information system (MIS) (54)
business-process reengineering (58)
alienation (61)
computational infrastructure (62)

Review and Discussion Questions

1. What is the difference between whole-job and assembly-line concepts? Which uses a human relations approach?

2. Which of these people would fare best working at home? Why?
   a. a laser consultant with a national clientele
   b. a systems analyst who hates meetings
   c. a CPA with a heart condition
   d. a real-estate appraiser with two small children

3. What is downsizing? How is it related to technology?

4. In what ways has technology made the workplace more comfortable? Less comfortable?

5. What is an MIS?

6. When Gabe Hernandez calls up quarterly service reports on his computer, he sees that Georgette, his youngest clerk, has outproduced Jim, his oldest clerk, by nearly two to one. However, customer satisfaction questionnaires reveal that Jim's clients were happier with his level of service than Georgette's were with hers. How should Gabe use this information in his staff evaluations?

7. The new voice-mail system at Globbax Inc. was a hit with the employees, who were no longer tied to their desks during lunch to take incoming calls. One day, when the CEO called in from the road, he was bounced from mailbox to mailbox, unable to reach a single human voice. The next day, the system was yanked. Was the pullout a hasty decision, or was the system's implementation not well thought out? What errors did Globbax make?

8. What is business-process reengineering?

9. When Jean Allen's top salesperson is reluctant to modernize his methods through automation, the rest of the sales force follows suit. How can she persuade the sales force to overcome its reluctance?

10. What human relations challenges have been brought about by the rapid changes in workplace technology?

A SECOND LOOK

Bob Antin, chief executive of the Veterinary Centers of America chain, used technology to fight back when local pet stores began offering limited veterinary services. How did Antin turn technology to his advantage? How do you imagine the staff at the centers feel about this technological change? Why?

Independent Activity

Interviews

Interview a parent, grandparent, or other older person about the work they did. What types of tasks did workers do before machines and computers were available? How was the majority of their workday spent? After you have an idea of what a typical workday was like, observe today's workplace. What changes do you notice? How has technology changed the work people do? What additional changes are likely in the future?

Skill Builder

Expanding Your Technology Horizons

Odds are that you do not fully utilize all the bells and whistles on your own home technology. Take a half hour and sit down with the instruction manual that came with your tape player or CD player, VCR, personal computer, or microwave oven. Read a section of the manual describing an application you have not used or do not use often. After reading the section, put what you have read to work—dub a tape, program your VCR, move between file windows, or autocook a meal.

Group Activities

Technology Discussion (20 minutes)

The class should discuss ways technology has helped or hindered their daily lives. The instructor will compile a list of benefits and drawbacks of technology from students' stories. Afterwards, students should discuss ways in which the problems could be minimized.

Company Competition (30 minutes)

Divide the class into four or five "companies." Each company should brainstorm about a new high-tech product or service to improve people's lives. To help the companies get started, members should consider the following questions:

- What is something that people hate doing now that could benefit from machine or computer help?
- What can high-tech equipment do better than humans, freeing them to do the things they do best?
- Can a process or service be designed to give the company an advantage over its possible competitors?

Case Study

Breaking the Information Dam in Bow Valley

Battered by low prices for oil and gas, Bow Valley Industries, a Canadian energy company based in Calgary, decided two years ago to rethink the way it did business.

The company stripped out three layers of management and flattened the firm's corporate structure, just as business school gurus recommend. Previously organized along functional lines, Bow Valley restructured into separate business units, each an autonomous profit center.

The goal was a flatter, less hierarchical organization that would free up the flow of information that managers need to make decisions, helping the firm respond more quickly to the changes in the energy business. The reality? "We were drowning in data but starved of information," says Gary Moore, now Bow Valley's information systems manager.

A management team found that aging mainframe computers were preventing data from crossing functional and divisional boundaries. The company had become flatter, but its information systems remained stubbornly hierarchical.

To break down these "us-and-them" barriers, Bow Valley reengineered the way it processed and distributed information. At the heart of the strategy was replacing the company's mainframe computers with networks of high-powered desktop workstations. Rather than do this piecemeal over several years, Moore chose to complete the process in five months flat.

He counts many benefits of this swift "cutting and reseeding." By forcing employees to think in new ways and to cooperate with other business units, divisional barriers are being blurred and breached. New cross-divisional groups are forming to take advantage of the freshly freed-up data. The result? Information is being analyzed more efficiently, allowing decisions to be made more swiftly. And as a bonus, information technology costs have been cut by 40 percent.

Some snags remain. Some of the company's employees expect too much of the system and are disappointed when it fails to deliver miracles. And other employees—mostly those who feel threatened by the new processes—remained convinced that the rapidly installed new order will collapse into chaos. But Bow Valley management is certain that a gradual transition, rather than the wholesale reengineering for which it opted, would not have transformed the firm's information systems so effectively.

Case Questions

1. Did Bow Valley avoid any or all of the ten classic errors of computerization? How?
2. Could a slower transition to the new computer system have been as successful? Why? How would employee reaction have differed?
3. How can Bow Valley management reconcile the extremes of employee reactions to the new systems?

Source: *The Economist,* May 1, 1993, p. 68.

Case Study

Voicing Technology Concerns at Bell Labs

If Arno Penzias had arrived at AT&T Bell Laboratories in 1991 instead of 1961, he would never have won a Nobel Prize in physics. Today he is a top manager at Bell Labs with a substantial research budget, but he probably wouldn't fund the kind of heady astrophysics for which he got a Nobel in 1978.

The Bell Labs he first joined, and that many Americans cherished as a national treasure, is no more. Before the 1984 breakup of AT&T, it was supported by a hidden tax included in phone bills from America's monopoly telephone company. Bell Labs' innovations—the transistor, the laser, the solar cell, cellular radio, etc.—were meant to benefit the nation. Now the emphasis is on products and getting them to market first.

But the labs' competence in research is unimpaired. In 1989, Bell's inroads into computer recognition of human speech led to the invention of a technique known as word spotting. A phone caller might mumble, "I wanna maga collecall." The software can pick out the key word "collect" from a mass of unrelated sounds and ask the caller for further instructions, eliminating the need for an operator. Next year, word-spotting computers will handle over a billion calls nationwide, for both AT&T and such customers as New Jersey Bell.

Among those most affected by this new operatorless "operator-assisted" technology are AT&T's other employees. Maggie Wilson of Youngstown, Ohio, became a jobless telephone operator when AT&T began installing the word-spotting machinery that can understand words like "collect" as well as she can. Technologies such as this voice-recognition system were projected to eliminate 3,500 operator jobs by March 1994. Under AT&T's union contract, many of the operators were to be placed in other open positions; in Wilson's case, the company paid for retraining to help her find a new job.

Case Questions

1. Why does AT&T have a responsibility to those workers whose jobs have been eliminated by the company's own research efforts?
2. Is Maggie Wilson unemployed because the "friendly" face of technology has become "unfriendly"?
3. If technology can replace the human voice, do you think it can replace any worker?
4. What kinds of jobs are most threatened by technology?
5. What are the implications for future employment as technology keeps advancing?
6. What are the roles of human relations management here?

Source: *Fortune,* May 17, 1993, p. 63; *Chicago Tribune,* June 7, 1993, sec. 4, pp. 1–2.

Quick Quiz Answers

Quick Quiz 3.1

1. job specialization, or division of labor
2. assembly line
3. make work easier and faster for people to do
4. telecommuting

Quick Quiz 3.2

1. satisfactory working conditions
2. adjustable chairs with wrist supports, wrist rests, nonglare monitors, special keyboards that minimize forearm and wrist strain
3. by using plastic signs that say "Open" or "Closed"

Quick Quiz 3.3

1. false
2. true
3. true
4. true

Quick Quiz 3.4

1. b
2. c

CHAPTER

4

Managing Diversity

CHAPTER OUTLINE

Learning Objectives

- Identify four factors that are making the American work force more diverse than ever.
- Identify four benefits of workplace diversity.
- List three effects of discrimination on workplace minorities.
- Describe the three historical approaches to managing diversity.
- Describe three human relations challenges facing organizations attempting to institute diversity programs.
- List five techniques for promoting diversity.

Ebony Glass Breaks Through

Arthur Queen did all the right things in 1986 when he started Ebony Glass Corp. in Norcross, Georgia. (See photo at left.) But despite his impeccable reputation and the company's innovative commercial-glass services, Queen wasn't landing the contracts he needed to succeed. Believing the problem to be racial barriers, he soon discovered that less than one-third of 1 percent of the construction jobs in Georgia were granted to women and minorities.

Determined that his company would break through this barrier, Queen turned for help to minority programs such as the National Association of Minority Contractors, the Atlanta Business League, and the Georgia Minority Supply and Development Center.

Ebony Glass is a million-dollar success story today, boasting contracts with the Georgia Dome, the World Congress Center, Evander Holyfield's gymnasium, and the Atlanta Committee on the Olympic Games. That success, says Queen, is a direct result of the requirements that minority participation programs place on businesses. "Out of the twenty jobs contractors choose to bid on each month, only one or two will go to minorities, by requirement of minority participation programs," he says. "Take those requirements out, and the phone stops ringing."

Minority organizations that train, mentor, and fund programs, Queen says, are great stepping stones for entrepreneurs: "Their strength is in unity." Yet no matter how good the program, he points out, success comes down to the individual entrepreneur. "If you're fortunate enough to get a job, you have to do it well."

Source: "Glass Ceiling," *Entrepreneur,* March 1993, p. 77. Photo source: Courtesy of Ebony Glass & Mirror, Inc.

Instead of having a garden with just one type of flower, wouldn't you rather have a garden full of all *different* kinds of flowers—roses and daisies and petunias and marigolds, reds and blues and pinks and yellows? Variety is indeed appealing in the garden, but in the workplace, the "roses" have often preferred an office or shop full of other roses. "No daisies allowed here," they might have said, "and no roses that are not the exact same shade of red that we are." Many resent workplace **diversity**, the coexistence of many different types of people, because they feel more comfortable with others like themselves.

diversity
The coexistence of many types of people in a particular setting.

As any study of human nature and behavior will reveal, however, superficial similarities of appearance are less important in human bonding than the deeper ones of values, experiences, and interests. Yet, it takes time to get to know another person's values or interests, and people are often disinclined to take that time. **Stereotyping**, or making a judgment about an individual based on preconceived ideas about a group to which that individual belongs, is much easier. Unfortunately, stereotyping often leads to errors in judgment, and it frustrates the people who aren't being judged on their individual merits—as in the case of Arthur Queen of Ebony Glass Corp. One of today's biggest human relations challenges is learning how to overcome stereotypes and give all members of a diverse work force a chance to exercise their special skills.

stereotyping
Making a judgment about an individual based on preconceived ideas about a group to which that individual belongs.

Transformation of the American Work Force

The American work force has never been made up entirely of "red roses." Native Americans and European colonists on this continent were soon joined by African slaves. Then immigrants from Asia, the Pacific Islands, South America, the Middle East, and every other area of the world came to this country, attracted by its reputation as a "melting pot." But those of English and Northern European descent were for a long time a dominant majority in both the total population and the workplace, and every other group remained a minority in both numbers and influence. Their alien customs and values and languages were often barriers to success.

The situation is changing dramatically, however. In the past couple of decades, we have had a huge influx of immigrants, most of them non-European. And birth rates among the majority have been significantly lower than those of minority groups. Figure 4.1 shows the ethnic and racial makeup of today's U.S. population; it also shows that between 1980 and 1990, the minority population increased nearly four times as fast as the majority population.

Society and the workplace are likely to become even more racially and ethnically diverse in coming years. Today, only 76 percent of full-time workers in their early twenties are white, as opposed to 80 percent of workers of all ages.[1] By 2050, Hispanics are projected to account for one out of every six Americans, as opposed to one out of every twelve today.[2]

The makeup of the American work force has also become more diverse in other ways. For instance, the proportion of the work force that is young is declining as the numbers of new graduates drop relative to the numbers of middle-aged and older workers. People who are physically challenged or whose lifestyle differs from the majority's are also more visible in the work force than they once were. And women have also become more dominant. Although the work force has always included some women, their ranks began expanding dramatically in the 1970s. In the past couple of decades, women have taken a greater role in nearly all industries and occupations. Though a majority in the general population, women are still technically a minority in the workplace, as Figure 4.2 shows. Yet, like racial and ethnic minorities, they are catching up by joining the work force more than twice as fast as men are.

Figure 4.1 **Ethnic and Racial Minorities in the United States**

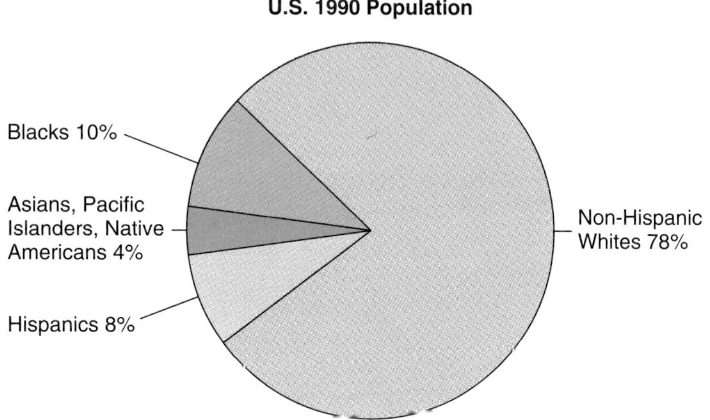

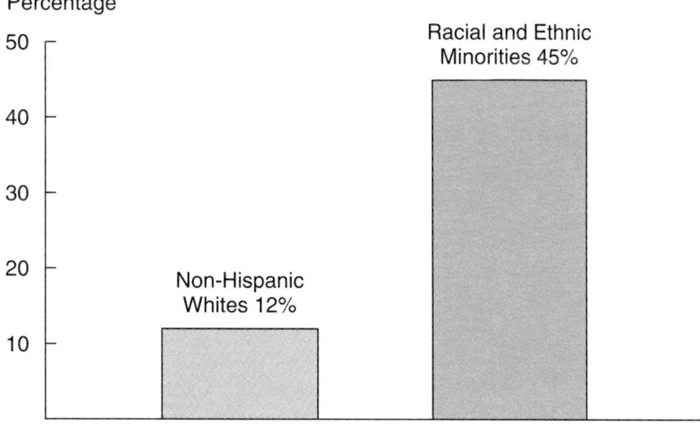

Source: Data from Warren A. Brown, "How to Write an Affirmative Action Plan," *American Demographics,* March 1993, p. 57.

Quick Quiz 4.1

1. What two factors account for the growing proportion of racial and ethnic minorities in the work force?
2. What ethnic minority is most likely to predominate in the twenty-first-century work force?
3. Women are a __________ in the general population and a __________ in the work force.

Benefits of Diversity

These trends in the general population are forcing businesses to accept diversity in the workplace. Some of them have been wise enough to learn how to value it as well. They

Figure 4.2 **Women in the U.S. Work Force**

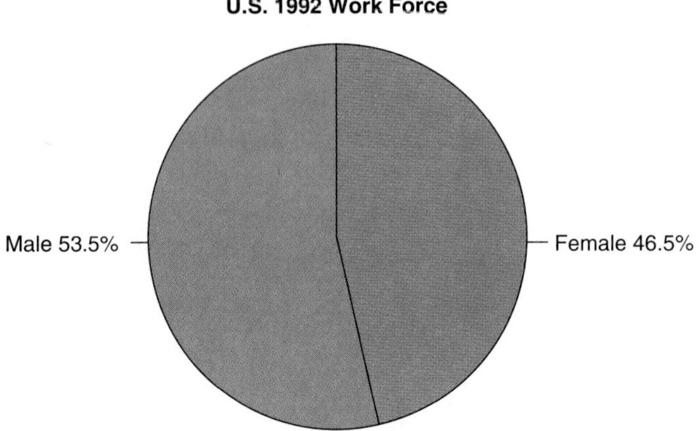

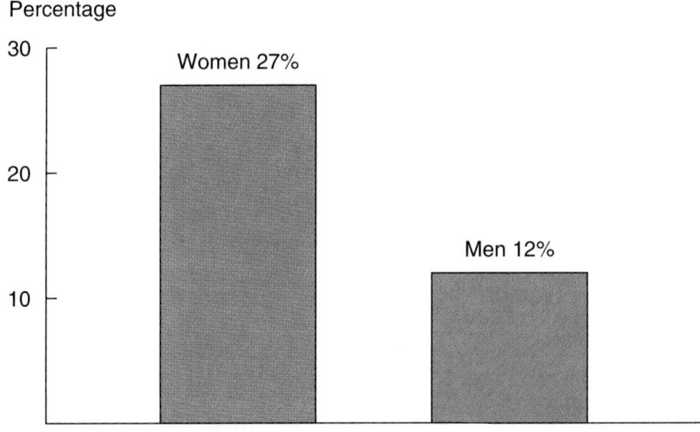

Source: Data from U.S. Bureau of Labor Statistics, *Work Experience of the Population in 1992* (Report no. USDL 93–444), Washington, D.C.: U.S. Department of Labor, 1993, table 1; Warren A. Brown, "How to Write an Affirmative Action Plan," *American Demographics,* March 1993, p. 57.

realize that, in a competitive world, what matters is an employee's skill, not superficialities. The bigger the pool from which they draw talent, the more likely they are to find the best workers. If they arbitrarily decide not to hire, say, people in wheelchairs, they might let a person ideally suited to their needs slip away.

A diverse team of workers also has some advantages when it comes to solving problems. Robert L. Lattimer, managing director of Towers Perrin, an international consulting firm, offers a thought-provoking reason:

> There is a growing sentiment that diverse employee teams tend to outperform homogeneous teams of any composition. Managers tell us that homogeneous groups may reach consensus more quickly, but often they are not as successful in generating new ideas or solving problems, because their collective perspective is narrower.[3]

In other words, a group of people with diverse viewpoints may be able to come up with more creative solutions than a group of people who have the same background and who see things the same way.

International Highlights

L'Oreal Recognizes the World's Diversity

Just as the world seems to be getting smaller and more homogenized—with everyone from Swedes to Brazilians to Malaysians drinking the same soft drinks and wearing the same athletic clothing—recognition is growing of the distinct differences between the world's peoples.

L'Oreal has found that marketing its cosmetics to Africa involves obstacles ranging from confusing distribution channels and inadequate infrastructure to the difficulty of translating name-brand marketing, aimed at ultrasophisticated buyers in high-tech societies, to Africa's more rural populace.

In Africa, local custom is vitally important in defining the marketing mix, according to L'Oreal's Valerie Banino. "When we launch a product, we have to factor in several parameters: the predominantly rural and community-based character of African societies, the African taste for close contacts, and a different way of thinking about time."

Sometimes only small changes are made when introducing products to Africa. L'Oreal's skin-care line Plenitude was brought into the Ivory Coast market just as it had appeared in France, with the same packaging and the same perfume. It was a success, but only because of L'Oreal's research. After local testing, a basic line was launched. More sophisticated products, already available in France, followed. Within the basic line, however, only products deemed likely to meet the expectations of African women were put on the market. "The Plenitude product line includes a non-greasy skin moisturizer that proved very successful because it is suited to African weather," says Banino.

L'Oreal also has launched a line of products specifically tailored to Africa. Based on the well-entrenched Mixa brand of shampoos, soaps, and shower gels, the company developed a line called Mixa-Paris. "All our efforts have focused on strengthening it—putting more emphasis on the idea of freshness, for example, by adding a lotion and a body cream, since African women are very sensitive to skin softness."

Source: Nathalie Boschat, "Catering to Africa's Customers," *World Press Review,* June 1993, p. 40.

Another reason to value diversity is the improved ability to reach customers. "If the work force is changing, the customer base is changing," says Ann M. Morrison, who directs research in leadership diversity.[4] A more culturally diverse group of employees attracts a broader segment of the buying public. A company with older workers on the payroll, for example, seems more welcoming to the older consumer. Older employees understand things about the older consumer that can be very helpful to the organization. Another example of how diversity helps win customers is the nation's largest pension fund, California Public Employees Retirement System. It turned over about 1 percent of its $57 billion in assets to ten new firms run by minorities or women. In their first six quarters, these firms achieved higher returns as a group than the fund's other domestic equity managers.[5] The new firms reached customers who were formerly untapped by the pension fund.

Finally, an expanded understanding of ethnically diverse customers also has benefits in the global marketplace. As one observer puts it, "Most employers are gradually facing the fact that the future of America in a global economy will rest with people who can understand cultural differences and can function across racial, ethnic, cultural, and linguistic lines."[6] In today's increasingly interdependent world, it behooves employers to remember that white people of European descent are not a majority in the world, but rather a minority. Multinational companies are finding that the usual way of doing business doesn't always work with a global customer base, as illustrated in the "International Highlights" box.

Quick Quiz 4.2

1. What are four benefits of hiring a diverse work force?
2. How does a diverse group of employees help a company market to a diverse American population?

3. How does a diverse group of employees help a company compete in the global marketplace?

Notable Groups in Today's Workplace

In times past, the typical worker was assumed to be an able-bodied, white family man of European descent. Indeed, most were. The problem was that employment policies and procedures were designed around this assumption, and people of a different gender, race, ethnic background or age group or with different physical abilities or lifestyles faced unfair **discrimination**. Minority group members were often limited to certain categories of jobs (usually the lowest paid and least desirable)—if they were hired at all—solely on the basis of stereotypes.

discrimination
The practice of limiting people to certain categories of jobs (usually the lowest paid and least desirable)—if they are hired at all—solely on the basis of stereotypes.

Today, workers are protected from employment discrimination by federal laws such as the Equal Pay Act of 1963 and the Civil Rights acts of 1964 and 1991, as well as by various directives of the executive branch and precedents set in court cases. Still, minority workers often are not fully accepted in the American workplace, which affects their ability to get good jobs and be promoted, their compensation, and their on-the-job relationships. If we are to reap the benefits of workplace diversity, we need to understand some of the special circumstances faced by minorities.

Women

Women undeniably have a large and growing presence in the American workplace. Gender discrimination in the workplace receives abundant attention, and women have more opportunities than ever. However, they still face a number of problems, including artificial limits on their career advancement and pay, conflicts between family life and work life, and sexual harassment.

The Glass Ceiling. No longer are women stuck at the very lowest rungs of career ladders. They are being promoted to supervisory and management positions, and they are joining the ranks of such professionals as doctors and lawyers. But they are not reaching the highest levels in numbers reflecting their presence in the work force. Although 43 percent of managers are now women, they account for only 3 percent of the nation's top corporate executives.[7] Even in fields dominated by women, such as nursing, the highest positions are usually filled by men.[8] This subtle form of discrimination is called the **glass ceiling**, an unspoken agreement among senior managers to prevent certain subgroups from rising to the upper ranks.

glass ceiling
An unspoken agreement among senior managers to prevent women or minorities from rising to their ranks.

Beliefs in stereotypes have built the glass ceiling. One such belief is that women are less likely than men to stay with a company because of their family concerns. But in the 1980s, 73 percent of women who left large companies did so to take a job promising career advancement, and only 7 percent quit in order to stay home.[9] Another stereotypical belief that has held women back is that they lack the aggressive characteristics that make a good manager. Although this is no longer a popular viewpoint (in fact, many now believe that nurturing qualities are essential for managers), the existence of the glass ceiling in so many organizations indicates that a residue of that belief may persist.

Some women break the glass ceiling or avoid it altogether by starting their own company. Heidi Neumann Hansen, who majored in human development at college, began a direct marketing firm called Letterworks International, based in Portland, Maine. Her business grew 20 to 30 percent annually during the 1980s and now reaps $1 million a year in sales.[10] Another female entrepreneur is profiled in the "Quality Highlights" box.

Quality Highlights

A Woman of Steel Guides Anko Metal Services

Anna Garcia finds nothing exotic about her role as founder, president, and majority owner of Anko Metal Services Inc. in Denver. For her, it was a natural step when, in 1981, after a career with three separate steel companies, she decided to hammer out her own fortunes. With her husband, she started Anko, a steel distribution company.

It was slow going the first seven years. Coupled with a deep recession in the Denver area, Garcia says, "a lot of fabricators didn't take us seriously."

Things have since turned around. During the past five years, Anko has grown 329 percent to annual sales of $2.8 million; Garcia predicts another 200 percent growth within the next five years. Part of her strategy is keeping overhead as lean as it was in the early days, keeping the office to a skeleton staff of only four employees, including herself.

Anko looks for niches in the marketplace and answers with quality service. "There is a place in the Denver market for people who will focus on customers' needs, whether it be one piece of iron or a truckload. We are willing to do the small jobs as well as the big."

Customers testify to Anko's personal service—Garcia has delivered metal from her car when competitors demanded that customers would have to pick it up. And flexibility. When commercial construction slowed, Anko shifted to marketing aluminum and alloys to the aerospace industry. When that market softened and public-sector construction boomed, Anko switched to commodity-grade metals.

"We are not that big that we carry millions of dollars worth of inventory, so we weren't stuck with high-specialty alloys earmarked for the space industry," Garcia says. Inventory, like Garcia and the company she built, is just "bread and butter ... nothing exotic."

Source: Steve Bergsman, "100 Fastest Growing Companies," *Hispanic Business*, August 1993, p. 48.

The Pay Gap. Women's salaries overall have persistently been lower than men's overall (see Figure 4.3), although the Equal Pay Act of 1963 and court decisions addressing pay discrimination did raise women's pay relative to men's. At present the figure is about 70 cents for every dollar a man makes. Being in a higher-paid field is no guarantee of equal pay, as Figure 4.3 also shows.

Why does this pay gap persist? At one time, women were assumed not to need the money to support a family, but the main reason these days is that women generally hold lower-paying jobs. Even within well-paid fields, women tend to have the jobs at the lower end of the pay scale. In fact, a recent study shows that the better-paying the field is, the greater the male-female salary gap. Nor is job title a guarantee of equal pay:[11]

- Female vice-presidents are usually in the lower-paying departments of an organization, such as corporate communications, rather than, say, corporate finance.
- Female physicians are more numerous in pediatrics than in surgery—and far less likely to be picked to run hospitals.
- Female attorneys are more likely to specialize in taxes or trusts and estates and far less likely to be groomed as star litigators.
- Female financial experts on Wall Street are usually analysts, "writing the reports that tell better-paid money managers how to invest."
- Female money managers generally work for wealthy individuals rather than banks, insurance companies, and mutual funds, where the money mounts into the billions.

The issue that must be considered in any discussion of this pay gap is women's occupational choices. For example, why do so many female doctors enter pediatrics, a lower-paying medical specialty than surgery? Probably because they enjoy it more, although to some extent, women may be subtly pressured to enter fields where their "nurturing instincts" (a stereotype) or other "female" characteristics are presumed to be useful.

Figure 4.3 **The Pay Gap between Women and Men**

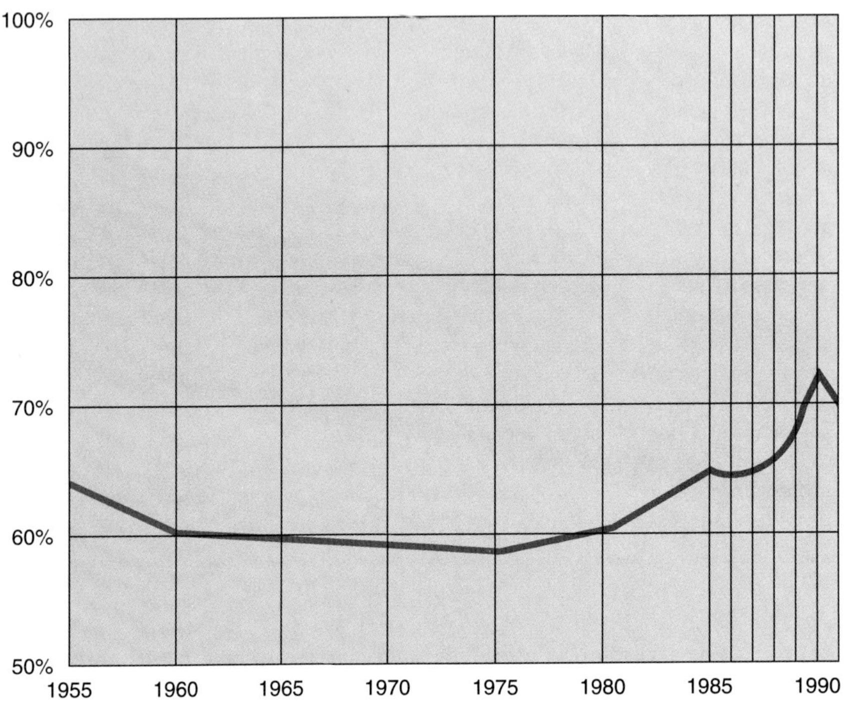

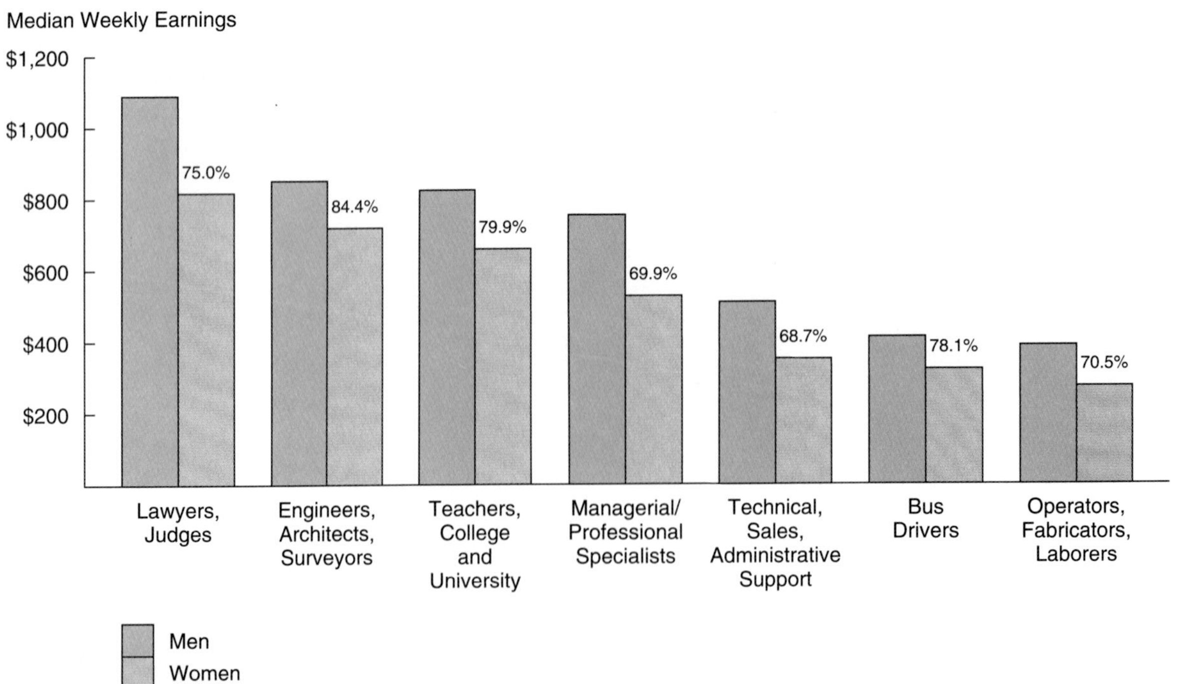

Source: Maggie Mahar, "The Truth about Women's Pay," *Working Woman,* April 1993, pp. 52–53.

Work-Family Conflict. Another issue that affects today's working women is the difficulty of balancing work and family life. Most women today work full time and then return home to face most of the housekeeping chores, for a conservatively estimated average of 65 hours in a week of "double days."[12] In addition, wives typically are still expected to subordinate their jobs to their husbands' when rescheduling or relocation is required.

The biggest problem for many working women is child care (although care of elderly parents is becoming an issue too). By law, women are guaranteed six weeks of unpaid maternity leave to bear a child and a comparable job when they return to work. However, they have no guarantee that they will be able to find an affordable, convenient, reliable caretaker for a child when they do return. Working mothers may therefore be absent from work more often than other workers or have more incentive to take extended breaks from their career.

sexual harassment Unwelcome sexual advances or physical or verbal conduct of a sexual nature that in any way influences a person's employment situation.

Sexual Harassment. Another problem that affects women workers is **sexual harassment**, or unwelcome sexual advances or physical or verbal conduct of a sexual nature that in any way influences a person's employment situation. In the worst cases, a person in a position of power (typically a man) uses that position to coerce sexual favors (typically from a woman). But sexual harassment also includes smaller acts that create an atmosphere constraining women from feeling like men's equals in the workplace. The number of sexual harassment lawsuits won suggests that these problems are widespread.

Sexual harassment is a hot topic for employers because it is still being defined. Does asking for a date more than twice constitute sexual harassment? Bettye Springer, a partner in a law firm that specializes in sexual harassment charges, notes that the influx of women into the workplace means that the workplace is often where people who begin dating first meet. The potential for harassment—and perceptions of harassment—under these circumstances is great. And exactly when are off-color jokes and sexual innuendo a problem? Some women participate to a degree but complain when the talk reaches a certain point, says Springer.[13] A sensitivity to people's feelings and old-fashioned courtesy—on the part of both men and women—should help reduce the problem. Table 4.1 presents some guidelines that employers can follow to prevent sexual harassment lawsuits and to deal with them if they come.

Racial and Ethnic Minorities

Some of the problems affecting women—namely, the glass ceiling and the pay gap—also affect racial and ethnic minorities; usually, their female members face a double-whammy. In addition, some racial and ethnic minorities, although not all, face significant disadvantages in even getting a job. Again, discrimination based on stereotypes keeps many able individuals from finding a job to which they would be well suited.

The four racial and ethnic minorities discussed here—blacks, Hispanics, Native Americans, and Asians—are the ones most often studied by social scientists and marketing researchers. Keep in mind, however, that people with other ethnic backgrounds—such as Middle Easterners and Eastern Europeans—may also face discrimination, especially if they are not well educated, do not speak English well, or have not adopted the customs of the American workplace.

Blacks. The unemployment rate for blacks, or African-Americans, is roughly double the rate for whites. It is especially high for young black men. Part of the problem is discrimination on the part of employers, but other factors are also involved. One is that jobs are generally scarce in the inner cities, where black populations are concen-

Table 4.1 **What Companies Can Do to Deal with Sexual Harassment**

To prevent a lawsuit:

- Develop and post a policy and establish procedures on sexual harassment and discrimination.
- Develop employee information/training on the subject, including supervisory training and/or employee meetings that encourage employees to speak out if they feel they've been sexually harassed or discriminated against.
- Respond swiftly and effectively to claims of sexual harassment.

If a lawsuit is filed:

- Take quick action. Court decisions usually require "prompt" remedial action. EEOC guidelines require "immediate" remedial action.
- Investigate the allegations. Employers who fail to investigate allegations of unwanted sexual attentions are often held by the court to have violated Title VII of the Equal Opportunity Act. Failure to investigate or act implies the employer approves of the illegal actions.
- If you investigate and find no need for disciplinary action, it may be appropriate to issue, revise, and/or reissue the company's policy on sexual harassment and discrimination. This reinforces to the court that there is an intention to provide a workplace free of discriminatory practices.

Source: Reprint Courtesy of the Fort Worth Star-Telegram.

trated. Another is a vicious circle linking education and socioeconomic status. In the past, most blacks were from lower-class or working-class families, which either did not value a higher education or could not afford to buy one for their children. Without an education, those children could not find high-paying jobs, and so they did not earn enough to send their children to college. Immigrants have often faced this same dilemma, but black families were at a particular disadvantage because of pervasive racial discrimination. Today, more and more blacks are breaking out of this circle and joining the middle and upper classes, but they leave behind many young people who still do not have access to good jobs.

Once hired, blacks confront such barriers as the glass ceiling, a pay gap, and stereotyping. Although a few prominent blacks have attained power and rank in the business world, most do not rise beyond middle management. Compared with college-educated white men, college-educated black men earn roughly three-quarters as much—sadly, even more of a gap than existed a decade ago.[14] Finally, coworkers often treat blacks differently from whites or even other minorities, which makes black workers feel self-conscious and contributes to job dissatisfaction.[15]

Hispanics. The fastest-growing ethnic minority in the country is the Hispanics. This large minority can itself be subdivided into a number of groups with different characteristics and concerns: recent immigrants versus people whose families have long lived in the United States; people of Mexican, Cuban, and Puerto Rican descent, among others; poorly educated people at the bottom of the socioeconomic ladder versus well-educated, well-paid people. Generally, however, Hispanic workers are not paid as well as majority workers and do not have the same opportunities for advancement.

Cultural and language differences between Hispanics and the majority are a distinct barrier. Some Hispanics, especially recent immigrants, speak English poorly. In addition, their culture traditionally places family and friendship ahead of work.[16] In the workplace, that tradition may be perceived as loyalty to other workers of their own ethnic group instead of to the company as a whole.

The Davis-Bacon Act requires union-scale wages on federally funded construction projects. Adopted in 1931, the act prevents unorganized construction workers from competing with the organized construction unions. Some believe that this creates labor union gains and great losses for the low-wage minorities. On many New York construction sites, the ongoing battle between these two groups has reached a state of near warfare.

Photo source: © Sygma, Les Stone.

Photo Exercise

What suggestions do you have for solving this low-wage minority versus higher-paid union member argument? How would a solution to this problem affect the unions: would it strengthen or weaken them?

Native Americans. The workplace problems faced by Native Americans are similar to those faced by blacks and Hispanics: a history of discrimination in hiring, the glass ceiling, a pay gap, and stereotyping by coworkers. And like Hispanics, some Native Americans have difficulty reconciling the values of their traditional culture with the values of the American workplace. What sets Native Americans apart from these other minorities is the current romanticization of their history. Books and movies about Navajos, Sioux, Apaches, the Mohawk, and many other tribes paint an image that is sometimes inaccurate and often has no bearing on the life of an individual Native American. It can be very difficult for a flesh-and-blood human being to live up to the mythology.

The Native Americans who continue to live on the large, isolated reservations may be the most unemployed ethnic minority in the country. Industry is scarce; the economy is dominated by government services, tourism, and arts and crafts. Educational opportunities are also often limited for reservation children, although a coalition of 27 Native American colleges is seeking to bring them affordable education that teaches the skills needed for success in the larger economy while preserving their culture and values.[17]

Asian-Americans. The problems of Asian-American workers are somewhat different from the problems of blacks, Hispanics, and Native Americans. Because Asian culture traditionally values education and work, they often have less trouble than other minorities in acquiring the skills they need to get well-paid, white-collar jobs as technical experts, managers, and professionals. But the glass ceiling keeps them, too, from the highest positions in the corporate world.

It is as difficult to generalize about Asian-Americans as it is to generalize about Hispanics. Some are recent immigrants who speak English poorly or not at all; some were born here and speak English like the natives they are. There are also significant differences in Asian languages and cultures—for example, the traditions of Japan, China, Vietnam, and the Philippines are all quite different. Understandably, individual Asian-Americans resent being stereotyped, just as individuals of other ethnic minorities do.

Older Workers

Although today's vigorous 40- and 50-somethings may resent being called "older," the fact remains that they are in a group that often suffers discrimination, especially in hiring. In the great wave of corporate downsizing of the 1990s, many of the laid-off workers were middle-aged middle managers. As they made the rounds looking for a new job, they often found that employers prefer younger workers with a more up-to-date education and lower salary expectations. Workers who are in their 60s and beyond face an even tougher time convincing recruiters that they have the energy and skill to handle a responsible job.

But employers had better find a place for older workers. For one thing, they are still capable of working. Says Joan Kelly of the American Association of Retired Persons (AARP):

> Age is a different thing than it used to be. The 50-year-old of today is like the 35-year-old of 20 years ago. People are living longer; therefore, they're going to be working longer.[18]

Second, by law employers can't discriminate against older workers. The Age Discrimination Act of 1967, with an amendment, protects employees of 40 to 70 years of age from discriminatory treatment and mandatory retirement. Third, they often have valuable qualities to offer employers, such as greater experience and stability than younger workers, better judgment, and a particularly strong work ethic. Finally, employers will find it increasingly difficult to hire people in their twenties and thirties, given the drop-off in birth rates following the "baby boom." In 1970, the median age of employees was 28; by the year 2000, it will be nearly 40.

The differences between 28-year-olds and 40-year-olds will necessitate some adjustments in all aspects of human resource management. For example, incentives may have to be modified; older workers may prefer time off over financial rewards. Supervisory style may have to become more participative to accommodate independent-minded older employees with many established ideas of their own. Energy levels of older employees may be lower, necessitating other changes. Some speculate that an older work force may be less adaptable or mobile. Problems could stem from management of older people by younger and from a decline in career opportunities at the top levels of companies. Another, quite costly disadvantage of an older work force may be its increased health-care needs.[19]

Still, "a company needs both older and younger workers," says Joan Kelly of AARP. "It's the mix that makes it work."[20] Older people have experience to offer; younger ones have an eagerness and facility for learning new things. It would seem that an organization could use both traits to advantage. Kelly points out that many organizations have regretted downsizing because they lost the "company memory" when older employees left.

Physically Challenged Workers

Employers seeking the best possible people to do the job cannot afford to overlook the physically challenged—people with hearing, speech, or vision difficulties and people in wheelchairs or with other limitations on mobility. In the past, employers have discriminated against the physically challenged because of misperceptions. For example, they have equated physical disabilities with mental disabilities; they have assumed the physically challenged would require sky-high premiums for company-provided health care; they have feared that customers and coworkers would react negatively to the presence of the physically challenged in the workplace. These sorts of beliefs are hard to change, but the "Diversity Highlights" box introduces one organization that is making the effort.

Employment discrimination against the physically challenged (as well as the mentally and emotionally challenged) became illegal in 1990 with passage of the Americans with Disabilities Act. A major provision is that employers make "reasonable accommodation" for physically challenged people who are qualified to do a job. For example,

Diversity Highlights

The NRH Helps Companies Adapt to the Disabled

It goes against the myths most people carry in their heads about people who are different. But the fact is that about 90 percent of corporate department heads and equal-employment officers rate handicapped workers as good or excellent workers.

Edward A. Eckenhoff, left a paraplegic by a 1963 car accident, is leading the battle against those myths. "People see a brace on my leg and think there's a brace on my brain," says the chief executive of the National Rehabilitation Hospital. Eckenhoff and the NRH are trying to show big companies how wrong that perception is. "It's easy to adapt with a disability," says Eckenhoff, who counts his only handicap as the one he battles on the golf course.

Under Eckenhoff's leadership, the NRH has become a specialist in showing large companies such as Gannett, AT&T, and Hewlett-Packard how simple it is to adapt to the needs of handicapped workers. The physical therapy and research facility in Washington, D.C., helps employers grapple with the 1990 Americans with Disabilities Act requiring companies to make the workplace accessible to physically challenged workers. Eckenhoff has steered the NRH toward finding low-tech ways for wary companies to comply with the law. Dispensing paper cups, for example, is cheaper than lowering water fountains.

Changing hardware is one thing. The biggest challenge for Eckenhoff and other disabled workers remains one of human relations—changing attitudes and perceptions.

Sources: *The Wall Street Journal,* May 19, 1987; Christine Del Valle, "Ed Eckenhoff: Champion for the Physically Disabled," *Business Week,* April 26, 1993, p. 99.

they might provide special computer software to help a visually impaired employee read documents.[21] What the law did not address is people's stereotyping of the physically challenged as mentally deficient, helpless, and depressing to have around. But perhaps, if more of the physically challenged are in the workplace, others will become accustomed to seeing them and learn for themselves how foolish the stereotypes are.

Quick Quiz 4.3

1. What are the four most notable minorities in today's workplace?
2. What is the glass ceiling?
3. Which four racial and ethnic minorities are of most concern to social scientists and marketing researchers?
4. Why is it imperative to deal with the issue of older workers?

Approaches to Managing Diversity

Given population trends and federal rules, nothing can prevent the workplace from becoming more diverse. The question of prime importance here is how to deal with that diversity. Historically, employers have used three methods: assimilation, affirmative action, and multiculturalism.[22] The underlying approach colors hundreds of other aspects of work life, including employment decisions and human relations.

Assimilation

assimilation
The belief that minorities should become as much like the majority as possible.

Instead of valuing diversity, organizations that adopt the **assimilation** approach believe that minorities should become as much like the majority as possible. These are the main assumptions:

- Diversity is an organizational weakness.
- Diversity is a threat to organizational effectiveness.

Until mayors and governors in over 20 cities and states enacted rules to spread business among firms owned by women and minorities, small minority-owned firms used to find it difficult to enter the muni-bond business, which generates fees exceeding $1 billion a year. For smaller firms, just getting started is "a matter of life and death," says Norma Yaeger, founder of Yaeger Capital Markets Inc. in Los Angeles.
Photo source: © Amy Etra.

- Members of minority groups want to and should be more like the majority.
- Minorities who are uncomfortable with the majority's values are overly sensitive.
- Equal treatment of employees means the same treatment for all.
- Managing diversity means changing the people rather than the organization.[23]

Minority workers in organizations that take this approach tend to be concentrated at the bottom of the hierarchy in low-paying positions without much power. Because the organization does not value diversity, individual workers do not value it either; as a result, each subgroup tends to stick together. Not surprisingly, the "out" groups don't feel much loyalty to the organization. The organization may operate smoothly when all the decisions are made by people with a similar perspective, but it also loses the creativity that comes when people of varied viewpoints are encouraged to participate in problem solving.

Affirmative Action

Assimilation has traditionally been the favored method of handling a diverse work force, but it was fairly obvious by the 1970s that it wasn't the best possible method. Thus **affirmative action** gained popularity. Affirmative action is a method of providing equal employment opportunities to certain groups of people hurt in the past by unfair, discriminatory employment practices. As one professor of human relations observed, "The notion of affirmative action arose historically because we realized that our country would never 'drift into' nondiscriminatory behaviors and practices."[24]

affirmative action
A method of providing equal employment opportunities to certain groups of people hurt in the past by unfair, discriminatory employment practices.

Executive orders and court decisions have since provided guidance on how an organization can implement affirmative action. Some organizations have been specifically singled out by the courts to implement affirmative action programs that ensure certain minorities, particularly women and blacks, are hired and promoted in numbers reflecting their presence in the population.

An affirmative action program is implemented by first evaluating the status of minorities in the organization and determining how many should be working for the organization at different levels, given their representation in the general population. The organization then makes a concerted effort to recruit, hire, and promote minorities from underrepresented groups. Sometimes, to give everyone a fair chance, jobs must be redesigned and people must be retrained.

The merits of affirmative action have been hotly debated. Some feel that it leads to *reverse discrimination,* which unfairly penalizes qualified white men who have had no individual responsibility for past discrimination. Furthermore, the results of affirmative action programs appear to be mixed. Employment gaps for racial and ethnic minorities and for women have narrowed, particularly among officials and managers.[25] However, minorities of all kinds are still underrepresented at the highest levels and overrepresented among laborers and service workers. And although women have increased their numbers in professional occupations, the percentage of racial and ethnic minorities in those jobs has not increased since the 1980s. Pay gaps also persist. Finally, affirmative action does nothing to help minorities feel like valued members of the organization; instead, they often feel like tokens who have been hired and promoted because they must be, not because they have valued skills and perspectives. Majority-group employees find it all too easy to resent a minority-group member who is in a position they would like to have, dismissing that person's merits and crediting success to race, ethnicity, or gender alone.

Multiculturalism

multiculturalism
The belief that the diversity of employees is an asset and policies promoting diversity and equality create a competitive advantage.

As organizations begin to see the shortcomings of affirmative action, that approach is gradually giving way to **multiculturalism**, which is the belief that the diversity of employees is an asset and policies promoting diversity and equality create a competitive advantage. Affirmative action is essentially a negative approach—a reaction to government and court mandates, a response to a problem, an attempt to inject minorities into a structure developed and dominated by the majority (in other words, to assimilate them). Multiculturalism, in contrast, is essentially positive—a voluntary effort to take advantage of our society's diverse population, a view that diversity is a strength and that minorities' perspectives are just as valid as the majority's.[26]

In the multicultural workplace, everyone is encouraged to contribute and to achieve. Employees are given the tools they need to do the job, are offered the training they need to succeed, and are hired, paid, and promoted without regard to stereotypes. Because diversity is valued, employees of all stripes relate more easily both formally and informally. Thus they learn to value alternative perspectives and lifestyles. Loyalty to the organization is quite high, because members of all groups have a stake in decision making and problem solving.

These are the assumptions of multicultural organizations:

- Work-force diversity helps in meeting the needs of a diverse customer base and in recruiting the best employees.
- The organization must adapt to the needs of its people rather than change the people.
- Deriving benefits from diversity is a long-term process, so the organization must be open to constant renewal.[27]

Multiculturalism is not necessarily the easiest approach to handling diversity, especially for organizations that have had an entirely different approach in the past. But multiculturalism does offer solid benefits.

Quick Quiz 4.4

1. What is wrong with assimilation as an approach to workplace diversity?
2. What are the three main drawbacks of the affirmative action approach?
3. What is the underlying belief of multiculturalism?

Human Relations Challenges

In the process of shifting from assimilation or affirmative action to multiculturalism, various challenges are likely to arise. Most relate to the human relations in an organization. Indeed, few tasks are more in need of human relations skills. Changing people's hearts and minds and the way they work together requires unity of purpose, flexibility, patience, and a true appreciation of people's differences.

Hiring and Promoting without Bias

It is one thing to know about antidiscrimination laws and to agree that some people are treated unfairly. It is quite another to overcome your own built-in biases. What we are talking about here is personally avoiding stereotypes when making employment decisions. For example, don't assume that an Asian-American applicant will be a hardworking, detail-oriented drone; she may be a brilliant and erratic visionary. Don't assume that a guy in his fifties can no longer do the job because he doesn't know anything about the latest technology; he may in fact have experience that gives him a deeper perspective on new developments than recent graduates would have. Don't assume that a visually impaired person will be unable to keep watch over other workers; she may be able to see well enough with technology that is now available, and she may have just the sort of "vision" needed to deal sensitively but firmly with other employees. Each person in an organization (and each job applicant) deserves to be considered on his or her own merits.

Remember, when you are the person with the power to hire, promote, and generally control others' work lives, your stereotypes and prejudices can do a lot of harm. Take a few minutes to explore your own feelings on stereotyping and workplace diversity by completing the accompanying "Self-Portrait" exercise.

Compensating Workers Fairly

Discrimination has produced a pay gap that won't go away, despite efforts to close it. In part, the pay gap persists because women, racial and ethnic minorities, and other disadvantaged groups tend to choose lower-paying jobs or to be shunted into them by a biased system. Even in the same jobs as similarly qualified white men, however, minorities often receive less pay. The discrepancy could relate to the fact that minority workers may be generally younger than white men holding the same jobs, because antidiscrimination efforts are relatively recent; these minority workers have therefore had less time to get pay raises. They may also lose ground during maternity leave or during economic downturns, when the last hired is often the first fired. In addition, some employers play hardball and withhold or limit raises from people who don't demand them. It is easy to imagine how a person lacking confidence because of workplace discrimination or desperately needing the job might just accept whatever pay is offered, even if it is less than other people in the same position earn.

comparable worth
The concept that equal pay should exist not just for the same jobs but for jobs of equal importance to society and demanding equal levels of knowledge and skill.

The fact that many minorities still tend to be channeled into the lower-paying occupations has given rise to the issue of **comparable worth**—equal pay not just for the same jobs but for jobs of equal importance to society and demanding equal levels of knowledge and skill. It is based on the idea of fairness: why should one job pay more than another if both require the same degree of intelligence and training and are equally important to the world? The problem is that the marketplace determines salaries to a great degree. The employer may value one job more highly than another or have more trouble finding people with certain skills and pay accordingly.

Self-Portrait

How Open-Minded Are You?

Answer the following questions on a scale of 1 to 5:

1—strongly disagree
2—disagree
3—neutral
4—agree
5—strongly agree

_____ I have an open mind and do not consider myself prejudiced.
_____ Qualifications and experience should be the only factors in determining whether someone gets a job.
_____ People often mistake friendly overtures for sexual harassment.
_____ I think people should be paid equal pay, regardless of their gender, race, or marital status.
_____ If a member of a minority group was promoted over me, I would assume his race played a role in it.
_____ Women are less committed to their work than men.
_____ Older workers cost more in benefits and take more sick leave.
_____ Asians are intellectual and poorly suited for blue-collar jobs.
_____ The increase in working women has caused rising unemployment among men.
_____ Affirmative action and quota systems are not necessary if you really want to get ahead in the business world.

Total your score. Any score over 30 indicates that while you are aware of the problems created by diversity in the workplace, you are less sensitive to the opportunities it presents. Any score between 20 and 30 indicates that you are thinking about the workplace from the point of view of others; keep trying. A score between 10 and 20 shows that you refuse to accept the so-called conventional thinking about diversity in the workplace and are not afraid of the changes and challenges that lie ahead. Congratulations.

Nevertheless, many enlightened organizations are working to establish pay equity for jobs requiring similar knowledge and skills.

Promoting Workplace Harmony

ethnocentrism
The belief that one's own culture is superior to all others.

Unfortunately, new diversity programs sometimes have a rocky start. Majority employees feel anxious and confused. For some, any change is threatening (see Chapter 13). If nothing else, a program that promises to open opportunities to minorities challenges the majority's assumptions about responsibilities, power, and promotion. These entirely human feelings may be supplemented by **ethnocentrism,** which is the belief that one's own culture is superior to all others. The majority employees may wonder why the "outsiders" can't just adapt to things as they have always been. At the extreme, a few majority employees may actively resist change.

In dealing with minorities, understand that a long string of disappointments may make them skeptical about any new program. They are likely to be especially wary of any program that does not seek their input about problems and solutions. Minorities might also be conditioned to misinterpret guidance ("You need to be more thorough in your reports") as bigoted criticism.

ServiceMaster recognizes and manages diversity and recently highlighted its commitment through an annual report entitled, "Unity in Diversity." When Maria Burany joined the company, she had limited formal education, no regular work history, and was unable to speak English. Today, she is an award-winning manager, is proficient in English, and has mastered college-level courses. Here, she discusses career development with service partner Allen McDonald.

Photo source: Courtesy of The ServiceMaster Company.

Negative reactions among both the majority and minorities may take many forms, including apathy or passive resistance, conflict between groups, subtle acts of discrimination against individuals of the "wrong" group, and blatant cruelty based on stereotypes. Over time, however, these stresses can be overcome with the judicious application of both sensitivity and firmness.

Quick Quiz 4.5

1. Whose stereotypes and biases can do a lot of harm?
2. What is an alternative to the unsuccessful effort to reduce the pay gap between minority workers and white men?
3. How do majority workers often feel when confronted with an increasingly diverse work force or with new employment policies that promote diversity?

Techniques for Promoting Diversity

Although workplace diversity presents a challenge for today's organizations, multiculturalism can be achieved. It doesn't happen by itself, however; the organization has to make an effort to include minorities. Examples abound:[28]

- Levi Strauss & Company has a "Valuing Diversity" educational program required for all employees, a "Diversity Council" of selected representative employees that meets regularly with Levi's executive committee, and an "Aspiration Statement" that sets appreciation of diversity as a goal and ties managerial bonuses to evidence of its achievement.
- Kraft General Foods has a program to encourage first-year Hispanic M.B.A. candidates to study marketing to boost its percentage of Hispanic hires among suitable graduates.
- Dun & Bradstreet has a summer internship program for minority M.B.A. students, and it is gathering data on how its methods of recruiting different groups have fared in order to see how to improve.
- Avon sends racially and ethnically diverse groups of 25 managers to regular sessions at the American Institute for Managing Diversity and has arranged for networks of black, Hispanic, and Asian employees from all 50 states to elect representatives to speak to top management on diversity issues. Capitalizing on

the diversity of its employees, Avon gave black and Hispanic managers increased authority over its unprofitable inner-city markets, which are now among Avon's strongest performers.

- Digital Equipment Corporation encourages celebrations of ethnic diversity by observing Hispanic Heritage Week and Black History Month. Voluntary groups work through their prejudices with company-trained facilitators in a program called "Valuing Differences."
- Xerox sets goals for the number of minorities (and women) in each division and at every level. In a particularly imaginative move, it identified the key lower-level positions that had been held by its successful managers and set goals for assigning minorities and women to those key jobs.
- Burger King has a board game, "The Diversity Game," to encourage an appreciation of diversity among its employees. More concrete proof of its commitment to diversity is its increase in business with minority-owned suppliers from $2 million in 1986 to $74 million.
- La Romagnola, a $5 million pasta maker based in Winter Park, Florida, hired two-thirds of its 30 production workers through the Catholic Refugee Service in Orlando: Vietnamese, Puerto Ricans, Romanians, and Bulgarians among them.[29] The company employs translators to help with language barriers and seeks opportunities to promote understanding of the different cultures among all employees.

See the case studies at the end of this chapter to learn more about how businesses successfully deal with a diverse work force.

Here are some suggestions for making a diversity program work (see also Chapter 16):

- *Take a long-term perspective.* As the saying goes, when you want to do it right, you can't do it overnight. Diversity programs take time to succeed. When Procter & Gamble launched its Corporate Diversity Strategy Task Force, it discovered that diversity at the company was more complex than expected and that managing diversity would entail a long-term process of organizational change. However, says John Smale, "If we can tap the total contribution that everybody in our company has to offer, we will be better and more competitive in everything we do."[30]
- *Involve all levels of the organization.* A few people operating apart from the rest of the organization cannot make a diversity program work any better than they could play a symphony or a football game operating on their own. There must be companywide commitment, at least of the formal and the informal leaders. Those personally unenthusiastic must be convinced to support the program for the sake of their own department's smooth functioning as well as the organization's overall welfare. A commitment from top managers is essential, because only they have the power to reward managers who help institute the program and to pressure those who don't. At the same time, input must also come from the bottom, because that's typically where the minorities are.
- *Educate and coach employees.* Employees frequently need guidance to adopt the new attitudes and new ways of behaving that are a part of diversity programs. According to various industry reports, about 40 percent of U.S. companies have some sort of diversity training. In addition, several colleges and universities now offer courses on the subject. But be careful about the message such training sends. Consultants Michael Mobley and Tamara Payne recommend that companies assign both white males and members of minority groups to conduct diversity training, so that "employees won't dismiss diversity as being only about women and minorities."[31]
- *Revise employment policies.* Past policies have not been good enough to smash the glass ceiling and to close the pay gap. To ensure equal opportunity for everyone,

Teamwork and communication among multicultural employees at Andersen Consulting are natural outgrowths of its multinational employment policies. This multinational class has completed Andersen's tough introductory training course.
Photo source: © John Abbott.

make sure they all know about job opportunities: Advertise job openings in minority publications, encourage employees (including minority employees) to tell people they know about openings, post notices of promotion opportunities in all departments. It may also be necessary to revise job descriptions so that outdated, irrelevant qualifications are deleted. Then take a look at compensation plans: are jobs requiring comparable skill levels paid similarly? Finally, undertake a program that identifies and nurtures promising employees—men and women of every race and ethnic background, old and young, physically challenged or not—and puts them on track for promotion.

- *Encourage teamwork and communication.* Give employees of different backgrounds opportunities to work together and socialize together. Help members of the majority understand the concerns and values of minority-group members, and help minorities understand the anxieties of the majority. Often, the organization has to mediate this effort at first. But by consistently demonstrating its commitment to all employees, it will eventually foster trust.

Workplace diversity is steadily increasing—that fact cannot be debated or controlled by any organization. What organizations can control is the way they respond. Those that come to value diversity and actively promote it will gain a competitive edge over those that do not.

Summary

- **Identify four factors that are making the American work force more diverse than ever.** The American work force is becoming more diverse because of immigration, higher birth rates among racial and ethnic minorities, a decreasing proportion of younger workers, and an influx of female workers.
- **Identify four benefits of workplace diversity.** Employers that embrace diversity have a larger pool of skilled workers to draw from, a broader range of perspectives to call on for solving problems, better rapport with a diverse customer base, and workers who are familiar with the languages and customs of other countries with which they may do business.
- **List three effects of discrimination on workplace minorities.** Women, racial and ethnic minorities, older workers, and physically challenged workers all face fewer employment opportunities, the glass ceiling (which confines them to the lower and middle levels of organizations), and the pay gap between minorities and white men.
- **Describe the three historical approaches to managing diversity.** Assimilation is the practice of forcing

minorities to adapt to and become like the majority. Affirmative action is the practice of hiring and promoting minorities to meet government mandates. Multiculturalism is the practice of restructuring employment policies so that the work force is as diverse as the population at large and so that all employees' perspectives are valued.

• **Describe three human relations challenges facing organizations attempting to institute diversity programs.** To hire and promote without bias, human relations professionals must examine their own stereotypes and prejudices. To compensate workers fairly, they must restructure pay systems so that jobs of comparable value to the company and requiring comparable skills receive equal pay. To promote workplace harmony, they must deal sensitively but firmly with anxiety, confusion, and conflict.

• **List five techniques for promoting diversity.** Take a long-term perspective. Involve all levels of the organization. Educate and coach workers. Revise employment policies. Encourage teamwork and communication.

Key Terms

diversity (70)
stereotyping (70)
discrimination (74)
glass ceiling (74)
sexual harassment (77)
assimilation (81)
affirmative action (82)
multiculturalism (83)
comparable worth (84)
ethnocentrism (85)

Review and Discussion Questions

1. Why is the diversity of the American work force projected to increase in coming years?
2. How might a homogeneous group perform differently than a heterogeneous group?
3. What prevents minorities from breaking through the glass ceiling and closing the pay gap?
4. Theresa Lopez aspires to run the credit department for the store where she works, but her boss jokes that she's too valuable dealing with customers to spend all her time behind a desk going over reports. What message is Theresa's boss sending her? Is she hitting the glass ceiling or encountering sexual harassment?
5. What is the vicious circle that keeps blacks and some other minorities from getting well-paid, white-collar jobs?
6. What diversity issues do Hispanics and Asian-Americans encounter in the workplace?
7. What changes in employment policies might be required as the work force ages?
8. What stereotypes do the physically challenged face?
9. How do affirmative action and multiculturalism differ?
10. What is the role of the human relations manager in making a diversity program successful?
11. What is the goal in making comparable worth the basis for setting pay, and why is it difficult to achieve?
12. Why is the change to multiculturalism so difficult for some organizations?

A SECOND LOOK

In what ways has Arthur Queen, owner of Ebony Glass Corp., fared better as an entrepreneur than he would have as an employee? How might the idea behind minority participation programs be applied by organizations seeking to promote multiculturalism and diversity among employees?

Independent Activity

Human Relations TV

The next time you sit down to watch TV, detach yourself from your usual viewing habits. Watch as a human relations manager and observe how diversity is portrayed on TV. How are women shown in commercials and TV shows—as housewives concerned only about clothing stains or as multifaceted working women, wives, and mothers? How about African-Americans? What, if any, percentage of commercials feature Hispanics or Asian-Americans? How are older people shown? How are the physically challenged shown? Does the world portrayed on television reflect the diversity you see every day at school or in the workplace? Why or why not? Would you prefer TV to be more racially diverse?

Skill Builder

Human Relations Lab

You are now nearly a quarter of the way through this text, and you have been sitting in this class with the same group for several weeks. It is time for your second memo in the human relations laboratory.

Take a few minutes to read your previous entry. Study the classroom as you write yourself a memo on how things have changed since Week 1. Specifically, are certain identifiable groups, such as minorities or older students, still sitting together? Have the small-group exercises in the three previous chapters affected relationships? Why or why not? Do you notice specific problems between certain groups? Do members of these groups interact or ignore one another? Where do you fit in? Are you still in the same seat, surrounded by the same people? How do you think this diverse classroom could be melded into a smooth-running organization?

Group Activities

Classroom Diversity Challenge (25 minutes)

Divide the class into three kinds of groups: groups in which everyone is the same sex, groups in which everyone is the same race, and mixed groups. Each group should come up with a way to use $500 to benefit everyone in the class. The class will then evaluate each group's idea and rate it on a scale of 1 to 10 (10 being the highest). Which group's idea was most creative? The class should discuss the reasons for this. A discussion of the value of diverse viewpoints within an organization should follow.

Stereotypes in Print (20 minutes)

Class members should collect several ads and cartoons from newspapers and magazines that portray stereotypes and bring them to class for discussion. How prevalent are stereotypes in the print media today? Are there any counteracting influences at work?

Gender and Managerial Ability (20 minutes)

The class should brainstorm a list of characteristics of an effective manager. The instructor should write down the characteristics so that the entire class can see them. The class should then picture first a woman who has these characteristics and then a man. Does the gender affect their perceptions of the manager? If so, how? A discussion of these issues should follow.

Case Study

When Leo Burnett Talks, Management Listens

The push for diversity gained force among American businesses in the 1990s, but Leo Burnett, founder and chairman of Leo Burnett Co., a Chicago-based advertising company, described it four decades ago when he talked about a workplace where everyone has a chance to succeed, regardless of race, gender, sexual orientation, or ethnic background.

"We recognize that everyone here is looking for human dignity, a feeling of belonging, an open-minded attitude, an atmosphere of human and friendly relationships, a sense of participating and a feeling of 'worthwhileness' about his or her efforts," he said in 1956.

So perhaps it's not surprising that Leo Burnett USA, a division of Leo Burnett Co., is on the cutting edge in dealing with diversity. It reaches out to a diverse employment pool by offering internships to women and minorities and recruiting them at colleges. The result: 18 percent of Burnett's 2,200 Chicago employees are minorities. Of its nonsupport staff professionals, 128 are women and minorities, who make up 12 percent of client service employees and 11 percent of media employees. Between June 1990 and February 1993, minority hiring was up by 3 percent in client services, 7 percent in media, 14 percent in creative services, and 5 percent in research. Female and minority suppliers won more than $5 million in contracts in 1991.

This year, the company instituted an eight-hour, one-day training session, held during work hours, to sensitize the professional staff to diversity issues. Other vital ingredients in the diversity mix—openness, mentoring programs, family-friendly policies, and interaction among all levels of employees—are part of the Burnett organization.

Don Richards, a senior vice-president and director of resource development, says that while some initially questioned the diversity programs, there was no real resistance. "Although we have a fairly diverse managerial corps, historically most of the managers have been white males, and many of those who will implement our diversity policies will be white males."

As an African-American who entered the professional world in 1960, Richards is encouraged by the changes he has seen during the past 30 years. "We have a long way to go, but my hope is that one day diversity will not be a special effort but the norm—just part of doing business."

Case Questions

1. How might an advertising agency such as Leo Burnett benefit creatively from diversity?
2. Through Burnett's policies, is it likely that in the future more top managerial spots will be staffed by women and minorities?
3. If all companies followed such activist diversity policies, would affirmative action be necessary?

Source: Carol Kleiman, "Burnett Takes Lead in Push for Diversity," *Chicago Tribune,* May 9, 1993, sec. 8, p. 1.

Case Study

New York Bakery Is a Melting Pot

Umanoff & Parsons, a New York City bakery and catering firm, doesn't ask its employees to conform to the organization; the company adjusts to fit its employees. "The culture of our company becomes who works for it; it's very, very employee oriented," says co-owner Bo Parsons.

When Parsons and Jane Umanoff founded the company 15 years ago, most of its employees were American-born whites who worked part time. Today, the company does $2 million worth of business a year and has 35 employees. About 90 percent of them were born in Haiti, Trinidad, Jamaica, Grenada, the Dominican Republic, and Russia. It's a percentage all the more remarkable because the partners listened to the hiring suggestions of their first full-time employee, a Haitian cleaning man.

As pleased as the partners are with the diversity, richness, and dedication of their work force, Umanoff and Parsons realized early on that they were being viewed by their Haitian workers as "the rich, white owners [who] didn't care about them." Overcoming that lack of trust meant changing their style of management and celebrating diversity. Naming blacks or Caribbeans as department managers wasn't enough because the new managers still felt they lacked authority. "What we had to do," says Umanoff, "was give people authority, responsibility, and accountability. It doesn't matter what race or color you are, that's what you need in order to do your job and feel good about it."

Umanoff & Parsons' senior management now includes four Caribbean immigrants, one of them a woman. Third in command to the owners is Jean-Baptiste Brouard, a civil engineer who fled Haiti in 1980 and worked his way up to operations manager after starting at the bottom, glazing baked goods.

There have been problems. Umanoff and Parsons assumed that because of the oppression they had suffered in their own country, the Haitians would naturally be more compassionate toward other workers, especially black employees. But when the Haitians became a majority, they began treating the Senegalese like slaves. The bakery's owners held employee meetings to emphasize the spirit of teamwork for all employees and refocused on increasing the company's diversity.

That emphasis continues. A recent ad for a bookkeeper brought in 80 resumés—half of them from Russians. Next, says Parsons, will be people from what was Yugoslavia. Umanoff & Parsons is ready for them.

Case Questions

1. Could the bakery be accused of bias against white males?
2. How has diversity benefited the bakery?
3. Is Umanoff & Parsons a special case, or can other companies follow its lead in deliberately looking beyond the traditional base of white male job candidates?
4. Are certain types of companies better suited to a diverse work force, or is it a matter of management and attitudes?

Source: Sharon Nelton, "Winning with Diversity," *Nation's Business,* September 1992, pp. 18–22.

Quick Quiz Answers

Quick Quiz 4.1

1. immigration and higher birth rates
2. Hispanics
3. majority; minority

Quick Quiz 4.2

1. a bigger pool of talent to draw on, a broader range of perspectives for decision making, the ability to attract a more diverse customer base, the ability to operate more effectively in the global marketplace
2. It makes the company appear more welcoming and helps it better understand its customers.
3. It provides some familiarity with other cultures and languages.

Quick Quiz 4.3

1. women, racial and ethnic minorities, older workers, physically challenged workers
2. an unspoken agreement among senior managers to prevent women and minorities from rising to senior rank
3. blacks, Hispanics, Native Americans, Asians
4. The population is aging, and soon the average worker will be nearly 40 years old.

Quick Quiz 4.4

1. Discrimination persists, and minority employees aren't allowed or motivated to contribute.
2. reverse discrimination, limited effectiveness in creating equal opportunity for minorities, and alienation and resentment among employees
3. Diversity is an asset.

Quick Quiz 4.5

1. those with the power to hire, promote, and influence life on the job
2. comparable worth
3. anxious and confused

PART OUTLINE

Chapter 5
Interpersonal Communication

Chapter 6
Organizational Communication

Chapter 7
Processes and Tools of Motivation

Chapter 8
Principles and Styles of Leading

Chapter 9
Stress Management

3

Foundations of Human Relations Processes

CHAPTER

5

Interpersonal Communication

CHAPTER OUTLINE

Learning Objectives

- Describe the process of communication.
- Define *feedback*.
- Define *nonverbal communication* and explain why it is important.
- Define *active listening*, and list seven ways of improving listening ability.
- Describe Azar's categories of communicator styles.
- Discuss ways to improve interpersonal communication.

Beyond Skin Deep at Mary Kay

Dennis Boykin's first two weeks on the production line at Mary Kay Cosmetics left him "flabbergasted." He received a free calculator (given to all plant employees for no lost-time accidents in the previous month), a birthday card (signed by Mary Kay herself), and a Thanksgiving turkey.

Boykin had joined a company that runs on a mixture of recognition and rewards. Mary Kay Ash, the company's founder, spends a lot of time making sure her 1,600 employees feel important. One night might find her signing 400 birthday cards, each offering a free lunch for two at the company restaurant or free movie tickets. Any number of occasions warrant gifts: for a new child, she sends a duck-shaped silver bank; newlyweds receive a silver bowl. Every employee receives a turkey on the Monday before Thanksgiving, because Mary Kay knows it takes a full three days for a turkey to thaw properly.

Employees also receive a $100 U.S. savings bond after every five years of service. Ten-year veterans of the Dallas company are profiled in *Heartline,* the company newsletter, and honored in a special ceremony in Ash's office. Fresh flowers and tablecloths are standard in the cafeteria, as are perfume and makeup in the rest rooms. "Appreciation," says Ash, "is the oil that makes things run."

Making sure that the company's sales consultants and in-house employees feel appreciated was sparked by the lack of recognition Ash felt during the 25 years she spent with other door-to-door sales companies. She believes praising people—not just for what they have done but for what they can do—will lead them on to greater accomplishments. Pictured at left are a group of enthusiastic Mary Kay sales directors.

Source: Robert Levering and Milton Moskowitz, *The 100 Best Companies To Work For in America* (New York: Doubleday, 1993), pp. 269–273. Photo source: Nina Berman/SIPA.

interpersonal communication The process by which persons send, receive, and interpret messages.

Mary Kay Ash knows the importance of communicating with her employees. She gives that communication a personal touch. **Interpersonal communication** is the process by which persons send, receive, and interpret messages. Thus communication, even within the confines of a strictly business setting, is always an intensely *human* affair. That is why a textbook on "human relations" must be a textbook about interpersonal communication.

The Communication Process

communication process The process in which a sender encodes a message and transmits it to a receiver, who decodes the message and responds with feedback.

The **communication process** is the sequence of events in which someone (a sender) encodes a message and transmits it to someone else (a receiver), who decodes the message and responds with feedback. Figure 5.1 is a model of this process. Note that the process is subject to communication barriers, which are physical or psychological interferences or distractions.

Simply talking or writing does not necessarily constitute communication. The receiver determines whether communication actually took place. The concept is similar to that of the Hebrew word for "teach," which in fact incorporates the meaning of "learned." Thus, if the student does not learn, the teacher did not teach. And if the receiver does not understand the message of the sender, there was no communication—or there was incomplete or erroneous communication.

Sender

encoding Translating the ideas behind a message into such symbols as words, pictures, gestures, or facial expressions.

An act of communication begins with the sender. Thus, to a great extent, the quality of communication depends on the sender's skill. First, the sender must decide on the contents of the message, bearing in mind what the receiver already knows or might assume. Then the sender begins **encoding** the message, or translating the ideas into such symbols as words, pictures, gestures, or facial expressions. The sender also chooses how and when to send the message. The sender's final responsibility is to seek feedback and evaluate it carefully to make sure that the message transmitted is the one that was received.

Wise choices made in the encoding stage can make the difference between effective communication and ineffective (even harmful) communication. A well-intended message could go awry, for instance, if the sender assumes a lack of knowledge and provides unneeded information. Suppose a new manager hired from outside a company gives instructions to an old-timer on procedures the company veteran has been performing successfully for 15 years. This kind of communication can be harmful to working relationships.

Such mistakes can easily be avoided by keeping the receiver's viewpoint in mind during encoding. People have different experiences, values, priorities, and interests—all of which must be respected if communication is to be effective. Here are some ways to communicate from the receiver's viewpoint:

- Ask yourself what the receiver already knows, what questions you might want answered if you were in the receiver's place, and how you might interpret the message if you were the receiver.
- Use vocabulary that the receiver will understand.
- Refer to experiences that you share with the receiver.
- Address the receiver's interests instead of your own.

For example, if you are sending a memo on new office arrangements, you might mention that you, like the receivers, will be happy to give up the old crowded office for a

Figure 5.1 **The Communication Process**

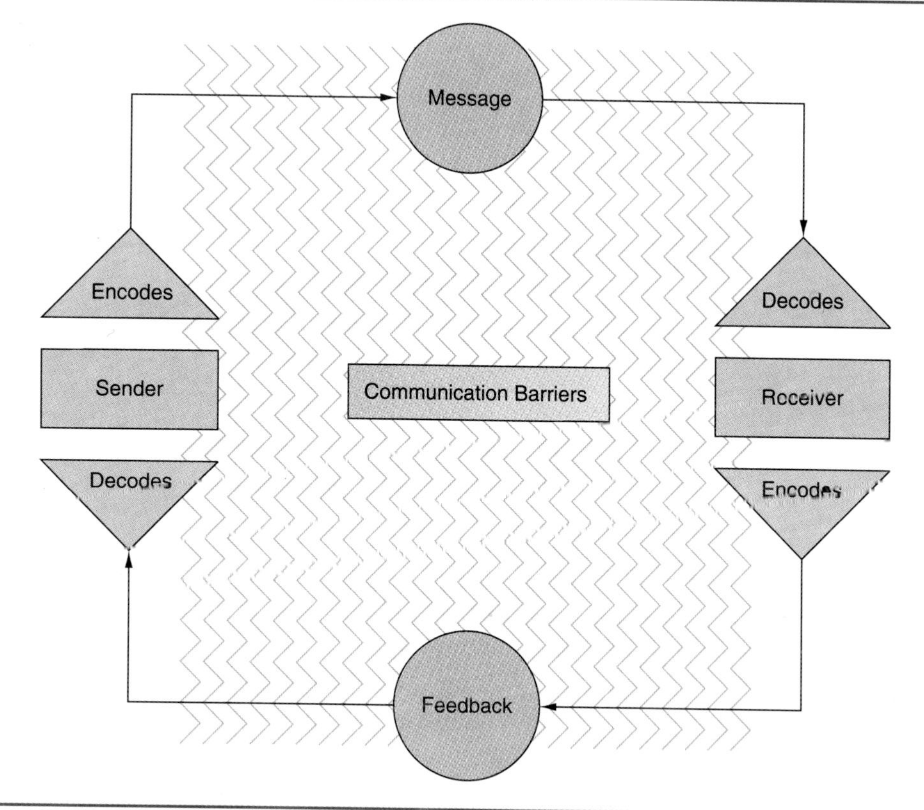

spacious new one. You could include a diagram showing exactly where everyone will be working to allay receivers' anxieties. And instead of dwelling on the difficulties you have had in coordinating the move, you could spell out all the steps you have taken to ensure that the receivers' things are moved safely and quickly, so they can become comfortable in the new space as soon as possible.

Receiver

decoding
Interpreting a message.

The communication process is not complete without the active involvement of the receiver, who takes responsibility for **decoding,** or interpreting, the message. The sender's choices determine to a great extent the receiver's success in decoding. If the receiver is lazy or hasty in the decoding attempt, however, even the clearest message may be misunderstood.

To ensure successful decoding, the receiver must truly listen to, not just hear, the message. Hearing is a physical process of taking in sounds, but listening is the mental process of paying attention to what is being said and trying to understand the full message. Here are some ways a receiver can aid the communication process:

- Make a commitment to listen carefully.
- Tune out distractions.

- Try to control emotions that may be stirred up by the sender's inept phrasing or lack of objectivity.
- Ask for more information if the message is unclear.

Additional information on the receiver's role appears later in this chapter, under the heading "Active Listening."

Message

The two main elements of the message are its content and the medium by which it is transmitted from sender to receiver. Both are determined in part by the *purpose* of the message. Three main categories of purpose can be identified:[1]

1. *To express an opinion or convey information that requires no response.* A financial report to stockholders is one example. A memo congratulating the department on a successful meeting or on exceeding a quota is another.
2. *To prompt action.* A verbal comment on the smallness of one's office to one's superior is intended to prompt action, not just convey information or express an opinion. Of course, the same comment to a coworker would represent only an emotional release.
3. *To support actions taken.* A video explaining how to use new equipment, a conversation about the reasons behind a new office policy, or a letter of resignation written after a heated conversation ending with, "I quit!," are all examples of this third category of purpose.

medium
The method chosen for transmitting a message.

Marshall McLuhan's famous pronouncement that "the **medium** is the message"[2] highlights the importance of the method chosen for transmitting a message. "It's not what you say, but how you say it" is a truism. The media used for business communication include written documents, presentations, meetings, telephone calls, and e-mail. Some messages are better conveyed in face-to-face oral communication than in a memo or report—because they are sensitive issues, because they require an immediate response, because the receiver's facial expressions will provide important feedback, because they are not important enough to warrant the time and effort involved in committing them to the printed page, because they are so urgent that the luxury of taking that time cannot be permitted. Other messages are better written down. If you need to document events or have any doubt that the message might be misinterpreted, lost, or forgotten, write it down. Messages that convey a great deal of information or complex information should also be written, and perhaps diagrammed or pictured as well. The number of receivers also affects the choice of medium. "Marsha, can we get together this afternoon?" is fine on the telephone for a meeting of two, but if the meeting requires nine people, a memo would be more efficient.

Still another choice in transmittal of a message is whether the receiver will be contacted directly or indirectly, through another person. Bypassing a supervisor to deliver a message directly to top management can create problems for all three parties. Many organizations have a chain of command dictating that messages must flow from one level to the next, so that they indirectly reach the person you really want to communicate with. In some organizations, people overcome the rigidities of this system by using the "grapevine" to transmit messages (see Chapter 11 for more on this subject). On the other hand, direct communication is usually more effective. If you wanted salespeople to know how to implement a new promotional program that you had just tested, you might get better results by meeting with them than by telling someone else what to tell the salespeople.

International Highlights

Giddings & Lewis Cases the Joint

Getting feedback is crucial to improving a presentation or a product. But sometimes, a history of indifference or a lack of listening skills can inhibit the process of give and take in communication.

Take, for example, Giddings & Lewis Measurement Systems Inc., a Dayton, Ohio, maker of precision measuring devices used in automobile production. In the mid-1980s, it achieved a technological breakthrough that enabled it to offer more accuracy at a lower price than could its competitors. But the premier automakers of Europe gave a collective yawn to the advanced product.

To find out why, John Bosch, vice-president and general manager of Giddings & Lewis, traveled to the Stuttgart Works of Daimler-Benz. It was quite a comeuppance. What he heard, he recalls, "would hurt your feelings if you didn't know they were trying to help."

Bosch was on the receiving end of a stern lecture about the decline of quality in American industry since the end of World War II and insensitivity to customer needs. By asking questions of his hosts, Bosch learned that it was not the technology of his company's device but the look of its casing that put off the design-conscious Germans.

Bosch was taken aback—after all, he was selling a precise instrument for use on a dirty shop floor, not a glamorous consumer product. Still, Giddings & Lewis hired a New York design firm and developed a new machine cover. The redesigned equipment now has $50 million in worldwide sales. "By getting everyone involved and breaking down barriers, the implementation easily fell into place," summarizes Bosch.

Source: Elizabeth Ehrlich, "The Quality Management Checkpoint," *International Business,* May 1993, p. 58.

Feedback

feedback
A message sent by the receiver in response to the sender's message.

Feedback is the message sent by the receiver in response to the sender's message. In effect, the receiver encodes a new message, which must be decoded by the person who sent the original message. Feedback is important because it helps ensure that messages are transmitted accurately. If the feedback seems inconsistent with the original message that was sent, the sender can once again encode the message.

Feedback can help prevent misunderstandings that might disrupt relationships within the organization or cost it money or time. Thus organizations are going to all kinds of lengths to gather feedback: employee surveys, supplier surveys, customer surveys, exit interviews with employees leaving the company, and performance appraisals, to name but a few. As a sender, you should always try to get feedback and evaluate its meaning carefully; as a receiver, you should try to accurately reflect your understanding of messages. One example of the importance of feedback to organizations is explored in the "International Highlights" box.

Feedback can be verbal or nonverbal. To get verbal feedback, a sender can listen carefully to what the receiver says or carefully read what the receiver writes. In the event that feedback is missing or unclear, the sender can ask the receiver a question or two or request a paraphrase. The responses would indicate whether the message was understood. To get nonverbal feedback, the sender can observe the receiver's behavior in response to the message. For example, a manager who has asked a worker to do a job in a different way can watch to see if the worker is indeed doing the job differently.

communication barriers
Things that disrupt the communication process—that create problems in encoding, transmitting, and decoding a message.

Communication Barriers

The things that disrupt the communication process—that create problems in encoding, transmitting, and decoding a message—are called **communication barriers**. One serious barrier is "noise," or physical disruption of the communication process. For instance, a bad telephone connection creates noise that complicates the job of decoding a message. Four other important communication barriers are information overload, misunderstandings, perceptions and prejudices, and denial.

Information Overload. These days, many more messages are competing for our attention than any one person can possibly handle. Every day, we are bombarded with news, entertainment, and ads on television and radio and in print; with signs on the road, in public places, and at work; with "junk mail" and telephone solicitations, as well as phone and mail messages we want to receive; and with letters, memos, reports, e-mail, phone calls, meetings, presentations, and many other types of messages at work. The result is **information overload**, an excess of information. The natural response is to tune out some of the messages.

information overload
An excess of information.

The best way to overcome this barrier is to be conservative in the amount of information you send out. Think carefully about what the other person needs to know and wants to know. You can also try to ensure that your messages are organized and presented in the most efficient way, so that the receiver can easily access the information they contain. When you suspect that the receiver is skeptical about your message or hostile toward it, you can also be sure that you clearly communicate the benefits or importance of your message.

As a receiver, you can also take steps to overcome information overload. Be aware of what information you need, and either seek it out or open yourself to it. Don't waste time trying to understand messages that aren't relevant to your needs. You can also make sure the feedback you provide is constructive; simply venting your emotions may not have any practical value.

Misunderstandings. Problems in decoding messages are often the result of misunderstandings. Misunderstandings have a number of possible causes:

- *Complexity of the message.* Some ideas are more complicated, and therefore harder to communicate, than others. For instance, a 15-step process for solving a technical problem has a lot more room for error than a single-step process.
- *Confused purpose.* If a sender doesn't really know what the goal of communicating is, the receiver may well get the wrong idea.
- *Deceptive purpose.* Some senders want the receiver to misunderstand and intentionally send a message that is vague or misleading. For example, an employee who is behind on a project might respond to a question about its progress by saying, "Everything's proceeding the way I thought it would"—neglecting to mention that he or she was originally skeptical about the schedule.
- *Poor word choice.* The words used to convey a message can also be vague or misleading. If someone asks, "Should I turn left?" and you say, "Right," what is the person to do? Words also have different meanings to different people. "A lot of money" could mean $20 or $200,000, depending on the context and the person's point of view. And words such as "loyalty" are also subject to interpretation.
- *Cultural differences.* A single message might mean different things to people of different cultures. For example, the Japanese value harmony and will say "yes" in a conversation as a polite way of signaling that they hear what the speaker is saying. But Americans interpret "yes" to mean agreement. Within American culture, there are subcultural differences as well. For instance, women frequently follow statements with such tag phrases as "Don't you think?" and "Isn't it?" Men may misunderstand the meaning of these phrases—which are requests for acknowledgment—and launch into full-blown opinions regarding the original statements.

- *Confusion between facts and inferences.* A fact is something that is objectively true; an inference is a subjective conclusion based on a fact. For example, the observation that quarterly sales figures for a business are lower than the previous quarter's would be a fact, but the statement "This company is going down the drain!" is an inference. Misunderstandings often arise when a sender or a receiver does not carefully distinguish between facts and inferences.

Both senders and receivers have a role to play in overcoming barriers based on misunderstandings. Senders must have a clear idea of the message they wish to transmit and construct it to suit their receivers' background and needs. For their part, receivers must pay careful attention to a message, try to understand both the words and the intent behind the words, and seek clarification with such phrases as "So you'd like me to ..." and "Are you saying that ...?"

perception
A way of seeing and interpreting reality; based on subjective factors, such as experiences and values.

Perceptions and Prejudices. A **perception** is a way of seeing and interpreting reality; it is based on subjective factors, such as experiences and values. A perception can be a communication barrier when it results in mistaken assumptions about the other person. For example, imagine that Janice, a supervisor, has decided to show more interest in her employees' day-to-day problems and successes. She stops by Mitchell's workstation and asks what he's doing. Mitchell's experience leads him to perceive Janice's question as the prelude to criticism of his performance, so he snaps, "My work, of course!" Janice, in turn, formulates a perception: that Mitchell has a hostile attitude.

prejudices
Negative perceptions based on stereotypes.

Negative perceptions based on stereotypes are called **prejudices**. For example, in our culture we often assume that men are more interested in career than in family. We might therefore interpret as sexism a man's complaint about allowing mothers time off to attend their children's school functions. In reality, the meaning of his message might be that he wants to be allowed to take such time off too.

To overcome barriers based on misperception and prejudice, communicators need to be aware of their assumptions. Are we framing a message for the particular receiver or for the group to which the receiver belongs? Are we responding to the words that were said or the words that we heard? Are we responding to the message or to the person sending it?

Denial. It's only human to ignore the things we don't want to hear. If a message contradicts our beliefs or destroys our hopes, we tend to shut it out. For example, if someone reports that a new motivational program isn't having the intended effect, we might proceed as if we had never even heard the message ("It's time to implement phase two") or discount it ("Elvin never did buy into the program") or interpret it in a way far different from the way it was intended ("The low turnout is actually a sign that employees have started taking their jobs seriously!").

To overcome denial, a sender should phrase messages carefully so they appeal to the receiver's self-interest and take biases into account. Elvin, for example, could begin his report on the failure of the new motivational program by pointing out the importance to the receiver of focusing on results rather than process; he could then point out the program's successful features and suggest "improvements." Receivers, on the other hand, should be aware of their own biases and try to remain open-minded. Free and open communication with others, after all, helps us expand our perspective and increase our understanding.

Quick Quiz 5.1

1. To encode a message, the sender does all of the following except ____________:
   a. selects message content
   b. selects the medium

Figure 5.2 **Relative Contributions of Several Factors to Total Impact of a Message**

When a message is both verbal and nonverbal, the nonverbal message may have more impact on the receiver than the words themselves. Psychologist Albert Mehrabian has found that the relative impact of words, vocal tones (tone of voice), and facial expressions is as shown in this pie chart.

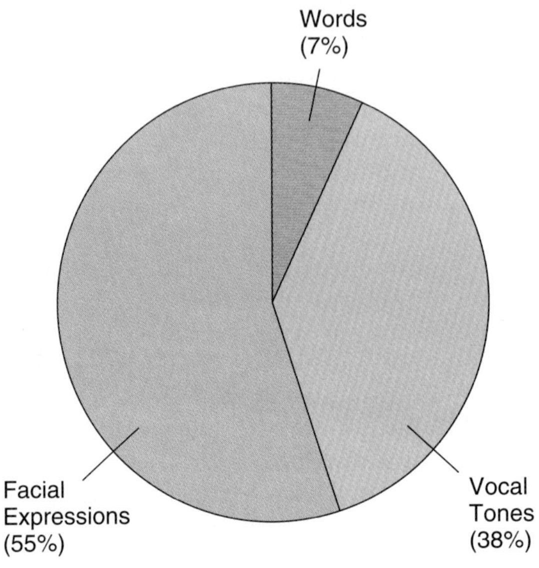

Source: Data from Albert Mehrabian, "Communication without Words," *Psychology Today,* September 1968, pp. 53–55.

c. translates the message into appropriate symbols
d. interprets the message

2. What is the name for the message sent by the receiver in response to the sender's message?
3. Communication ___________ disrupt the transmission of a message from sender to receiver.

Nonverbal Communication

nonverbal cues
Facial expressions, tone or pitch of voice, body positions, gestures, and degree of eye contact.

Nonverbal cues—facial expressions, tone or pitch of voice, body positions, gestures, and degree of eye contact—contribute significantly to communication. Sometimes a nonverbal message that accompanies a verbal one may even have more impact than the verbal one. A *Chicago Tribune* reporter found that it was common at city hall to send memos stating that needed repairs were emergencies, but the word "emergency" carried less weight than whether the memo was hand delivered or sent through the office mail system.[3] Figure 5.2 shows the weight that different components of a message may carry. If the relative importance of nonverbal communication seems surprising, imagine that someone is saying, "You're in trouble!" in an angry tone of voice. Now imagine the same person saying that while laughing.

Diversity Highlights

Communicating across Cultures

As the workplace grows more and more diverse, organizations must direct employees or serve customers who are from other cultures. In these situations, ignorance on both sides can muddy the message. The following suggestions can help you meet one of the newest challenges of human resources.

Stick to simple, basic words. Every culture has its own slang and idioms, such as "over the hill." These terms sound friendly to people who understand them, but people from other cultures usually don't know what they mean. Avoid using the jargon of your industry, whether it's diner shorthand or computer technospeak. Another mistake is using very formal language, such as "utilizing resources."

When speaking, make sure your listener understands. Talk slowly (not loudly), and pronounce words carefully. Seek feedback from your listener, but do not ask simply, "Do you understand?" Many people are too embarrassed to admit they don't understand. The following clues may indicate a lack of understanding:

- nodding and smiling in a way that isn't related to what you are saying
- a complete lack of interruptions or questions
- efforts to change the subject
- inappropriate laughter.

Give your listener plenty of time to come up with questions. If you have doubts that he or she has understood your instructions, check on the progress of his or her work in plenty of time to make any needed corrections or to clarify what you meant.

Make sure you understand what the other person is saying. Ask for clarification when you need it. Help the speaker to relax, and invite him or her to speak more slowly. If you are having trouble understanding a word pronounced by a nonnative speaker of English, try asking him or her to spell it. Most important, assume you can understand, and then *try.*

Learn about the communication style of different cultures, and try to match the different style of another person when appropriate. Don't make new English speakers do all the learning. Educate yourself, and avoid jumping to conclusions about an individual's character on the basis of cultural preferences.

Source: Rose Knotts and Sandra J. Hartman, "Communication Skills in Cross-Cultural Situations," *Supervisory Management,* March 1991, p. 12; and Sondra Thiederman, *Bridging Cultural Barriers for Corporate Success: How to Manage the Multicultural Work Force* (New York: Lexington Books, 1991).

An understanding of nonverbal communication is useful in many ways. Mike Woodruff, a management consultant, has half-humorously suggested that seating positions at a meeting allow some important types of nonverbal communication. The even-numbered seat farthest from the door is the one he picks as the leader spot, and if you want more influence in running the meeting but cannot take that spot, Woodruff advises sitting directly across from the person who does. "Just think about where Leland and Douglas sit during partners meetings on 'L.A. Law'." He further advises seating the person who rambles next to you, then staring at the side of his head when he talks too long. "He is guaranteed to turn and look at you, and when he does, don't blink. Works faster than a stun gun." On the other hand, someone you want to encourage to talk should be placed opposite you and made the object of frequent eye contact. Finally, if your boss's boss is sitting next to your boss, Woodruff cautions against taking the seat on the other side of your boss. Any questions directed to you by "the big cheese" are likely to be intercepted by your boss "due to table geography—and hierarchy."[4]

In a diverse workplace, it is very important to understand differences in nonverbal communication styles. For instance, African-Americans tend to look at the other person more while they are speaking than while they are listening; whites do the opposite. Under these circumstances, it would be dangerous to assume either that the person looking at you is hostile or that the person who is not looking at you lacks interest. Additional tips in communicating in today's diverse workplaces are in the "Diversity Highlights" box.

Downcast eyes in the United States is seen as submissive, even lacking in self-confidence. In Japan, downcast eyes are seen as a sign of attentiveness and agreement.

Photo source: Dan Bosler/ Tony Stone Images.

Photo Exercise

How do you interpret the nonverbal messages in this photo?

Nonverbal Communication with People from Other Countries

Cultural differences in nonverbal communication are extremely important to successful communication in all kinds of human relations situations. Here are some examples of differences:[5]

1. In *high-contact* cultures, as typified by Arabs, Latin Americans, and, in general, people from warmer climates (the Mediterranean, Eastern Europe, Indonesia), people tend to stand closer together and touch more. In *low-contact* cultures, such as North American and other cooler-climate cultures, such physical closeness might be upsetting. The distance maintained by the low-contact person might in turn be viewed with suspicion by a person from a high-contact culture.

   Generalizations about high- and low-contact countries cannot be made too broadly, since there are variations among subcultures. One study showed that Middle Eastern men typically stand only 18 inches or less apart when talking; Americans, 2 feet apart on average; and Asians and many people from African cultures, 3 feet or more apart.
2. The Taiwanese prefer side-by-side seating for two people of the same gender, while Americans prefer corner seating.
3. Smiling is more frequent in *individualistic* societies like the United States than in *collectivist* societies like China or Russia.
4. On the other hand, in countries with a more disparate distribution of wealth and power, subordinates tend to smile more at superiors, probably in an effort to appease them. Moreover, in one study, Japanese were found to mask negative emotions with smiles while Americans usually did not.
5. People from the countries with a more disparate distribution of wealth and power are more likely to find vocal loudness offensive than those from the opposite type of culture. Interestingly, Native Americans are more likely than other Americans to find vocal loudness offensive.
6. Downcast eyes in the United States are seen as submissive, even lacking in self-confidence. In Japan and Cambodia, downcast eyes are seen as a sign of attentiveness and agreement.

7. Asians often perceive Americans and Northern Europeans as being excessively talkative, while they, in turn, are perceived as secretive. In one study, more verbal people were rated as more attractive in the United States and less attractive in Korea. Asians tend to place more importance on nonverbal cues.

Gender Differences in Nonverbal Communication

Gender differences in nonverbal communication appear to depend partly on the culture. More "masculine" cultures (those that regard competition and assertiveness as more important than the "feminine" virtues of nurturance and compassion) encourage more gender differences.[6] Highly "masculine" countries are Japan, Australia, and Venezuela, to name a few; Sweden, Norway, and the Netherlands rank high in "feminine" values.[7] In general, whatever the culture, women seem to have the edge in noticing and interpreting nonverbal cues.

A disadvantage for women is the way their nonverbal communication may be interpreted differently. A woman's silence may be more likely to be interpreted as "yes" than would a man's. A tone of voice and other body language that would be interpreted as firmness in a man may be interpreted as inflexibility in a woman. A warmer, friendlier demeanor that would be interpreted as flexibility in a man might be interpreted as a lack of strength in a woman. An aggressive stance might be perceived as strength in a man, as autocratic in a woman. Bias needs no language to maintain its existence.

Quick Quiz 5.2

1. In responding to a mistake you made, if your supervisor clutched a pen tightly and frowned as she said, "It's not important," would you believe her words?
2 Would you be surprised if a Chinese customer laughed out loud at a silly joke you told?
3. Who usually has the edge in noticing and interpreting nonverbal cues—men or women?

Active Listening

active listening
Hearing what the speaker is saying, seeking to understand the facts and feelings the speaker is trying to convey, and stating what you understand that message to be.

We are capable of hearing more than 600 words a minute; we can speak only 125 words a minute. But effective listening doesn't come naturally. The problem is that most of us tend to think our own thoughts while waiting for the other speaker to stop. We begin formulating our response before we have really heard the speaker's complete message. Often we take our cue from the first sentence we hear and pay little heed to qualifying information that follows. **Active listening**, the term coined by psychologist Carl R. Rogers, involves hearing what the speaker is saying, seeking to understand the facts and feelings the speaker is trying to convey, and stating what you understand that message to be. Table 5.1 gives some of his examples. This kind of listening is work. If you are tired or uninterested, your listening will falter. If you can listen actively, you will reap incredible benefits. In our Information Age, the active listener has a fine competitive edge, a truly precious tool. Surely there can be no greater asset for human relations than the ability to really listen, for it not only mines the gold from the speaker's ore, but it also encourages the speaker to produce more "gold." The average listener decides what information is important to retain before hearing it all and that is often a mistake. Consider this example given by Diana Bonet, a listening consultant:

Table 5.1 Hearing versus Active Listening

Example 1: Hearing	**Word-Processing Operator**: Hey Wanda, is Finchburg kidding? He wants the whole report ready by the end of the day? That's impossible! **Supervisor**: But that's the job. You'll have to work as fast as you can. We're under terrific pressure this week. **Operator**: Doesn't he realize we're behind schedule already because of the quarterly reports? **Supervisor**: Look, Don, I don't decide what the managers want. I just have to see that the work gets done and that's what I'm trying to do. **Operator**: How can I tell my wife I'll be working late *again?* **Supervisor**: You'll have to handle that with her, not me.
Example 2: Active Listening	**Word-Processing Operator**: Hey Wanda, is Finchburg kidding? He wants the whole report ready by the end of the day? That's impossible! **Supervisor**: Sounds like you're pretty upset about it, Phyllis. **Operator**: I sure am. I was just about caught up after doing all these quarterly reports. And now this! **Supervisor**: As if you didn't have enough work to do, huh? **Operator**: Yeah. I don't know how I'm gonna meet this deadline. **Supervisor**: Hate to work late again, is that it? **Operator**: That's for sure. I made other plans two weeks ago. Seems like everything we do around here is a big rush. **Supervisor**: I guess you feel like your work cuts into your personal time. **Operator**: Well, yeah. I know Finchburg needs this report to land a big customer. I guess that means that this job really *is* important. Maybe if Joel will help me by doing the tables, I can get it out of here at a reasonable hour.

Source: Based on "Active Listening" by Carl R. Rogers and Richard E. Farson.

A $100,000 error was caused by a dispatcher who routed a fleet of drivers to deliver building materials to the wrong state. The dispatcher heard the city (Portland), but quit listening before he heard the state (Maine). The result was eight trucks 3,000 miles away in Portland, Oregon.[8]

"Millions of dollars are lost annually because people don't listen," says Letitia Baldrige, etiquette expert. Careless listening is not only rude, then, but costly.[9] So why is this deficiency so common? Probably because people just do not realize what they are losing by letting their attention wander when another is talking. Also, instead of waiting to respond, most of us respond too quickly.

US West Communications, a telecommunications company, reports that managers spend about 80 percent of each business day communicating; of that, 9 percent is spent writing, 16 percent reading, 30 percent speaking, and 45 percent listening.[10] A lot of time is spent listening, so when we don't do it well, a lot of time is wasted. The average recollection efficiency rate is only 25 percent. "Every day, orders are misinterpreted, relationships damaged, and meetings prolonged due to errors in listening," says Paul Friedman, a professor of communication studies. He puts the statistics into startling form: "If almost half our working time is spent listening, and a manager earns $50,000 a year, then more than $20,000 of that is listening pay."[11] Table 5.2 lists some common barriers to active listening.

Table 5.2 **Barriers to Active Listening**

1. *Our minds won't wait.* Our thoughts can race along from four to ten times faster than most people speak. So while we wait for the words to come, the mind tunes in and out. The result? Only a few words penetrate, and we miss the point.
2. *We think we already know.* We assume we know what a person will say, so we listen with only "half an ear." Yet, most of the time, our second guessing is wrong.
3. *We're looking, not listening.* How often in introductions has a name failed to register because your mind was occupied with its owner's appearance or mannerisms?
4. *We're busy listeners.* We try to listen while giving part of our attention to a report, book, or work project.
5. *We miss the big ideas.* We end up listening to words rather than ideas. Whether because we're impatient, distracted, apathetic, or upset, we catch a phrase here and there but miss the main point.
6. *Our emotions make us deaf.* When someone offers opposing ideas on a matter about which we feel strongly, we unconsciously feel it is risky to listen. We're busy planning our verbal counterattack and don't want to hear something that could make us question ourselves.

Source: Reprinted with permission from **Entrepreneur** Magazine, May 1992.

For a profile of how one company strives for quality by directly communicating with both its customers and its consumers, see the "Quality Highlights" box.

Listening Skills

To become skilled in human relations, you need to be an active listener. Some tips for improving listening ability follow:[12]

- Think like the speaker.
- Limit your own talking.
- Concentrate and focus.
- Respond while listening.
- Refrain from assumptions.
- Paraphrase what you have heard.
- Practice listening skills.

Think like the Speaker. You will retain what is said better if you keep the speaker's problems, needs, and viewpoints in mind while listening. This is particularly apt advice for salespersons listening to customers. Jodi Solomon, president of a lecture and performing arts agency, explains: "Projecting your own opinion onto customers and assuming you know what they want often prevents you from meeting their needs."[13] Another expert proposes some questions to ask yourself in order to think like the customer—or any other communicant:[14]

1. This is what the message means to me, but what does it mean to him (or her, or them)?
2. What would I mean if I said what he (or she) is saying?
3. Does my interpretation of his (or her) words coincide with what I understand to be his (or her) viewpoint?

Quality Highlights

Quality Is The Real Thing at Coca-Cola

Active listening and equally active responses have helped the Coca-Cola Company stay on top in the global soft-drink market. As Roberto C. Goizueta, chairman and CEO, says, "Satisfied customers and consumers are the lifeblood of our worldwide system."

Twenty miles from the company's Atlanta headquarters, 225 customer service representatives staff the Customer Communications Center, staying close to Coca-Cola's 350,000 U.S. fountain customers 24 hours a day, 364 days a year. No sales force could do what they do—handle more than three million customer calls a year on a special toll-free line, in minutes dispatching one of 1,100 agents across the nation to help the customer.

Coca-Cola was one of the first companies in the nation to set up a consumer hot line (1-800-GET-COKE, printed on all product packages). Less than 15 percent or nearly half a million consumer calls the center handles each year involve quality issues. Another hot line, created by Coca-Cola to enlist its U.S. employees and retirees in the quest for quality and customer service, may be responsible.

When an employee or retiree discovers a vending machine out of order or hears of a problem at a fountain outlet, he or she dials a special hot-line number called "Coca-Cola Cares." The special line provides a quick, efficient mechanism for that information to be directed for prompt handling. Since the program began in March 1992, more than 1,500 reports have come in from the "quality army" on everything from out-of-order equipment to out-of-stock products.

Coca-Cola's work force is proud of its quality efforts. USA division employees recently identified as a principal area of strength the company's commitment to a high standard of quality in customer service.

Source: "Keeping in Touch at Coca-Cola," *Fortune,* September 20, 1993, pp. 126–127.

Limit Your Own Talking. Since you cannot talk and listen at the same time, you'll know you are sacrificing the chance to gain information from the speaker if you hear the sound of your own voice too often and for too lengthy a time. "What gets you to the top is both what you say and what you don't say," says Debra Benton, founder of a management development company. She offers this gem of advice: "When someone stops talking, people think they have to fill in the quiet, but it takes more courage to remain silent. People resent being cut off. Most people are too polite to call you on it, but they will remember."[15] Benton further notes that when you talk less, what you do say is more effective.

Concentrate and Focus. It is tempting to work on other tasks while listening to someone (especially on the telephone), but being able to *do* several things at a time does not mean you can *concentrate* on all of them. We either give our speaker 100 percent of our attention or we give less than 100 percent as we apportion some other percentage to the competing task. Thinking like the speaker, the first item discussed in this section, can help with the goal of concentrating and focusing. "By engaging yourself in the topic and challenge at hand, by putting yourself in the client's position, you ensure that the big picture stays in focus," remarks Richard Kuhn, co-owner of a successful graphic design firm.[16]

Taking notes is helpful in concentrating and focusing. You must decide what you are hearing before you can write it down, so this forces you to concentrate.

Respond While Listening. Maintain frequent eye contact, respond with appropriate facial expressions, and use reflective responses like "I see" and "Uh-huh." In other words, give the speaker evidence that you are listening actively to what he or she is

To demonstrate active listening, maintain frequent eye contact, respond with appropriate facial expressions, and use reflective responses like "I see" and "Uh-huh."

Photo source: © 1992 Comstock, Inc.

saying and are thinking about it. Such responses encourage a person to continue talking. If, on the other hand, it is time to *discourage* someone from continuing, you might ask a pointed question that requires a summing-up statement, such as, "So the project should take exactly how long and cost how much?"

Refrain from Assumptions. Try to guard against bias and prejudice. Learn to recognize when someone is pushing your "buttons" so that you can control emotional reactions that might cloud your interpretation of a message. Remind yourself that it is easy to come to a mistaken conclusion if you fail to listen to the complete message.

Paraphrase What You Have Heard. "Verifying by restating the information or asking for clarification is safer in almost any transaction," advises Cheryl Chepeus of US West Communications.[17] This is the surest way to discover if you have misheard something. It allows the speaker to see immediately where a misinterpretation has occurred.

Practice Listening Skills. Get in the habit of active listening by consciously practicing it with everyone, not just those at work. It is a habit that will stand you in good stead in your personal life anyway. Moreover, since active listening does not come easily to most of us fairly self-centered individuals, it is something that we probably need to practice before we are going to be any good at it.

Test your own listening skills by taking the "Self-Portrait" exercise.

Telephone Techniques

Telephone conversations require total concentration on the speaker's words and tone of voice because you cannot see his or her body language. Pauses are worth noting as well. Sometimes there is much to learn from what a person *doesn't* say.

mirroring
A technique for creating rapport by feeding back the same kinds of phrases and style of talking, including the same speed and volume of speech, to the other speaker.

Mirroring has been suggested as a good telephone technique for listening and understanding, much like paraphrasing. In mirroring, the listener feeds back to the speaker the same kinds of phrases and style of talking, including a similar speed and volume of speech. A sales expert explains, "The reason mirroring works is that we like doing business with people we feel comfortable with, and usually these are people who we perceive to be like ourselves. No, it's not mimicking. Rather, it's a way of pacing

Self-Portrait

Are You an Effective Listener?

For each statement, circle Y for Yes if the statement is true about you or N for No if the statement does not describe you. Mark your answers as truthfully as you can in light of your behavior in the last few meetings or gatherings you have attended.

Y N 1. I frequently attempt to listen to several conversations at the same time.
Y N 2. I like people to give me only the facts and then let me make my own interpretations.
Y N 3. I sometimes pretend to pay attention to people.
Y N 4. I consider myself a good judge of nonverbal communication.
Y N 5. I usually know what another person is going to say before he or she says it.
Y N 6. I usually end conversations that do not interest me by diverting my attention from the speaker.
Y N 7. I frequently nod, frown, or whatever to let the speaker know how I feel about what he or she is saying.
Y N 8. I usually respond immediately when someone has finished talking.
Y N 9. I evaluate what is being said while it is being said.
Y N 10. I usually formulate a response while the other person is talking.
Y N 11. The speaker's delivery style frequently keeps me from listening to the content of what he or she is saying.
Y N 12. I usually ask people to clarify what they have said rather than guess at the meaning.
Y N 13. I make a concerted effort to understand other people's point of view.
Y N 14. I frequently hear what I expect to hear, rather than what is said.
Y N 15. Most people feel that I have understood their point of view when we disagree.

According to communication theory, you are a good listener if you answered No to questions 1, 2, 3, 5, 6, 7, 8, 9, 10, 11, and 14 and Yes to questions 4, 12, 13, and 15. If you missed only one or two questions, you strongly approve of your own listening habits, and you are on the right track to becoming an effective listener. If you missed three or four questions, you have uncovered some doubts about your listening effectiveness, and your knowledge of how to listen has some gaps. If you missed five or more questions, you are probably not satisfied with the way you listen, and your friends and coworkers may not feel you are a good listener either. Work on improving your listening skills.

Source: *Supervisory Management,* January 1989, pp. 12–15.

what the person is doing and saying in order to sound more alike and create that rapport."[18] Mirroring allows you to communicate in the style that the other person prefers.

Dennis Fox, another sales management expert, warns against talking too much: "Say as little as you can get away with. In the interest of business efficiency—both yours and [the other party's]—be brief and to the point."[19] On the phone, just as in person, it is wise to limit your own talking.

Quick Quiz 5.3

1. Define *active listening.*
2. List the seven techniques for active listening.
3. What is mirroring?

Communicator Styles

Brian Azar, president of a training and consulting firm that specializes in sales, has come up with a helpful way of categorizing visual, auditory, and kinesthetic communicators.[20]

1. *Visual* people tend to talk faster and may interrupt more. They ask questions. They tend to make decisions faster. Some 60 percent of Americans fall in this category.
2. *Auditory* people are natural "listeners" and thus talk a little more slowly and interrupt less frequently. They tend to wait until you finish a thought before asking a question, and then their questions tend to be more pointed and thoughtful. Only about 20 to 25 percent of Americans are judged to be auditory communicators.
3. *Kinesthetic* people depend more on their emotional feelings about what you are saying, talk the slowest of the three groups, and have the most difficulty in making decisions. They might have difficulty defining their questions also, opting instead for an objection like, "I can't really get a grasp on what you're saying."

David W. Johnson categorizes communicator styles according to dominance. *Low-dominance* communicators have the advantages of being cooperative and accommodating but the disadvantages of being shy, submissive, and easily controlled or influenced—even intimidated. *High-dominance* communicators have the advantages of being very free with advice and opinions—that is, expressive, assertive, decisive, and bold—but the disadvantages of being too hasty, demanding, and controlling.[21]

Still another description of communicator style is based on sociability. *High-sociability* people seek and value social relationships and tend to express themselves freely. *Low-sociability* people are more reserved and formal in their style of communicating. Gerald Manning and Barry Reece developed a sociability continuum and then put it together with a dominance continuum to identify the four styles of *emotive* (high dominance and high sociability), *director* (high dominance and low sociability), *reflective* (low dominance and low sociability), and *supportive* (low dominance and high sociability) communicators.[22]

No doubt other systems of classification for communicator styles will emerge regularly, since the infinite variety of human personality allows for many combinations of communicating among two or more unique human beings. All these views can expand our understanding of the dynamics of the communication process.

Quick Quiz 5.4

1. Who makes decisions more quickly, a visual type of person or a kinesthetic type?
2. A shy, easily influenced person can be described as a ____________ communicator.

Improving Interpersonal Communication

Management expert Fernando Bartolome says communication is "a matter of keeping subordinates informed, providing accurate feedback, explaining decisions and policies, being candid about one's own problems, and resisting the temptation to hoard information for use as a tool or a reward."[23] There appears to be a lot of room for improving our interpersonal communication skills. Though Bartolome speaks from the viewpoint of a supervisor, the principles of good communication are the same for everyone within an organization.

Olivet Jones, a management consultant, notes that people sometimes "collide" because they use different, and conflicting, communicator styles.[24] Being sensitized to

Loretta M. Flanagan is executive director of West Side Future, a community organization sponsored by the YMCA. Flanagan supervises 32 employees and must communicate with employees, clients, the community, the government, and key funding agencies. She considers clear, brief, written directions to employees key to providing the communications necessary to complete assigned tasks.

Photo source: © Ted Lacey.

Photo Exercise

What advantages do you see in written communication versus oral communication? What disadvantages might exist?

the fact that people, including yourself, have different styles of communicating, can help you to modify your style when you should. If you need to write a memo to a manager who prefers a more formal style, catering to that person's formal style will probably help get your message across more effectively.

Laura Pederson, author of a new career-development book, advises asking questions "strategically." She means you should "pick your moments and your people." Additionally, "think about your questions in advance, and never take more than ten minutes of someone's time."[25] Her recommendations require not only thinking ahead, but also extending the common courtesy of respecting other people's time.

Avoiding Misunderstandings

Certainly, the most direct way to improve our communication skills is to prevent misunderstandings. These occur during the decoding of a message by the receiver. Misunderstandings are practically invited by needlessly complicated messages such as:

> The deterioration of maintenance practices will inevitably lead to conditions that will be injurious to our heretofore admirable safety record.

Much better would be:

> Because the maintenance workers are no longer tuning up the machines each month, the machines will wear out and cause injuries.

The Power of Words. *Simplicity* and *precision* are the two watchwords for avoiding misunderstandings. Words are the tools for creating either simplicity or complexity, precision or confusion. They can change a situation, a feeling, a relationship. They can determine the success or failure of a project. They can resolve a dispute or start one. As one poet said,

> Visionary power
> Attends the motions of the viewless winds
> Embodied in the mystery of words.[26]

A mistake more common in written than in oral communication is to use a long word where a short one would suffice. Like Winnie-the-Pooh, many receivers might say, "Long words bother me." Choose shorter words over longer ones unless the longer ones are truly more precise. Simpler is better, as long as it means no sacrifice of precision.

Table 5.3 "You" versus "I" Statements

	"You" Statements	"I" Statements
Examples	"You're so irresponsible!"	"I'm upset that you've missed the deadline for the third time. When someone in the department misses a deadline, the whole department looks bad. What can we do?"
	"At the next department meeting, you'd better be prepared and be on time, or you're going to be sorry when we review your salary."	"I was not pleased that you were late to the meeting and unprepared. I expect a higher standard of performance."
	"You're bugging the women with those dirty jokes, so knock it off before we get in trouble."	"I have received complaints from two of the employees in the department that you are embarrassing them by telling dirty jokes. Our company policy and the law both forbid that type of behavior."
Likely Response	Defensiveness, ignoring speaker	Listening, collaborating on a solution

Lazy thinking often leads to the use of vague or ambiguous wording. Take the time to evaluate the accuracy and clarity of what you are going to say or write. Do your words lend themselves to misinterpretation? Do they leave too much to the guesswork of the receiver?

Don't use words or expressions that are insulting or offensive to others. New Orleans lawyer Harry McCall, Jr., learned the hard way about the importance of how people are addressed. While representing the state of Louisiana in a prison-rights case being tried before the U.S. Supreme Court, McCall said he "would like to remind you gentlemen" of a legal point. "Would you like to remind me, too?" asked Justice Sandra Day O'Connor.[27]

It is smart to avoid using words that attribute negative characteristics to another person ("you" statements), substituting words that describe your own situation ("I" statements). Table 5.3 gives some examples. The idea is to identify a problem without making an accusation. Accusations make people defensive instead of cooperative.

inferences Conclusions drawn from available evidence, instead of statements based solely on that evidence.

Don't use words that represent **inferences** (conclusions drawn from available evidence) rather than words based solely on the evidence. If the available evidence is not the complete evidence, your inference may be faulty. For instance, if a coworker seems to be uninformed about the details of a project being discussed in a meeting, don't mutter, "She's always unprepared." You probably don't know what circumstances led to her lack of information, and she is probably prepared on other occasions. This example makes the point that precision in words means careful thinking and truthful speaking—that is, fact-based statements, not inferences.

Cross-Cultural Differences. In addition to the nonverbal communication differences across cultural groups, there are some differences in the connotations of words. *Connotations* are associations conveyed by words. In addition, the *way* in which words are used differs among cultures. As mentioned earlier, Japanese people often say "yes" during a conversation to signal that they hear what the speaker is saying, not that they necessarily agree with what is being said. An American businessperson dealing with a Japanese customer would be wise to determine whether a "yes" means agreement or merely that the message was received.

Gender Differences. Since assertiveness is generally viewed as favorable in men but unfavorable in women, most women tend to use a less assertive communication style than men do. Studies show that in mixed groups, women tend to speak less and to make more use of phrases such as "Don't you think?" and "Isn't it?" At one academic conference, men took an average of 53 seconds to ask questions, whereas women took only 23 seconds. And although half the audience was female, only one-quarter of the questions came from women.[28]

Becoming a "Great Communicator"

Preventing misunderstandings is not the only task in becoming a better communicator. Human relations goals such as establishing trust, motivating others, helping others do their jobs, and eliciting their help in doing yours are involved in improving interpersonal communication. You want to do more than just avoid errors. You want your communications to be an asset—a way to improve situations (your own and others'), to advance your career, to profit the organization you work for, and even to be a source of enjoyment and fulfillment for yourself and those you communicate with. A sense of humor is always welcome. A sensitivity to the feelings of others is always appropriate.

We do not have the luxury that Humpty Dumpty did in Alice's Wonderland, to insist, "When *I* use a word, it means just what I choose it to mean—neither more nor less." We have to discover the words that our *audience* will interpret as meaning exactly what we chose them to mean, neither more nor less; and we need to decipher the intended meaning behind the words chosen by others. Then we need to use our words, *and* our nonverbal communications, to build up relationships, clarify information, and enrich the world around us wherever possible. That's the job of a "great communicator."

Quick Quiz 5.5

1. The two watchwords for avoiding misunderstandings are ____________ and ____________.
2. Change the following statement to an "I" statement: "The meeting was canceled because you were so absentminded that you forgot to attend."
3. At the end of a group sales presentation, who would be more likely to ask several questions—men or women?

Summary

- **Describe the process of communication.** Communication takes place when a sender successfully encodes a message and transmits it to a receiver. The receiver then decodes the message and encodes a new message, or feedback, in response. Communication barriers may disrupt encoding, transmitting, and decoding of the message.
- **Define *feedback*.** Feedback is the receiver's response to the sender's message.
- **Define *nonverbal communication* and explain why it is important.** Nonverbal communication includes body language: facial expressions, tone or pitch of voice, body positions, gestures, and degree of eye contact maintained. It is important because it supplements or modifies verbal communication. Sometimes the nonverbal message is more significant than the verbal message. There are cultural differences and some gender differences in nonverbal communication.

• **Define *active listening*, and list seven ways of improving listening ability.** Active listening is hearing what the speaker is saying, seeking to understand the facts and feelings the speaker is trying to convey, and stating what you understand that message to be. Seven ways to improve listening ability are (1) think like the speaker; (2) limit your own talking; (3) concentrate and focus; (4) respond while listening; (5) refrain from assumptions; (6) paraphrase what you have heard; and (7) practice listening skills.

• **Describe Azar's categories of communicator styles.** Azar's categories of communicator styles are (1) visual people, who tend to talk faster and interrupt more; (2) auditory people, who are natural listeners, talk slowly, and interrupt less frequently; and (3) kinesthetic people, who depend more on their emotions, talk the slowest, and have difficulty making decisions.

• **Discuss ways to improve interpersonal communication.** Ways to improve interpersonal communication include asking questions strategically, preventing misunderstandings, using simple and precise words, avoiding inferences, and being aware of cross-cultural and gender differences in communicating.

Key Terms

interpersonal communication (96)
communication process (96)
encoding (96)
decoding (97)
medium (98)
feedback (99)
communication barriers (99)
information overload (100)
perception (101)
prejudices (101)
nonverbal cues (102)
active listening (105)
mirroring (109)
inferences (113)

Review and Discussion Questions

1. Marlena Saldana wants to enroll in a continuing education course that she feels will increase her skills on the job and benefit her career. She would like her company to pay for the course as part of its policy to support employees who want to further their education. Should she approach her supervisor or someone in top management about this? Should she make the contact in person or by memo? How can she communicate her wishes effectively?

2. Why is feedback important in communication? How can the receiver make feedback more effective? What can the sender do to encourage feedback?

3. Indicate whether each of the following is a verbal or nonverbal message. For each verbal message, indicate whether it is oral or written.
    a. a long silence accompanied by an icy stare
    b. a letter delivered by fax machine
    c. voice mail
    d. laughter

4. Every Tuesday morning, Ted Tsoumas must attend a departmental meeting to discuss progress and make plans. Ted finds that most people at the meetings are long-winded and that the meetings are boring overall. However, he needs to know what is going on in the department. What are some ways Ted can listen effectively, even though he is bored?

5. Face-to-face communication conveys the most information, because the people communicating can learn from each other's body language and tone of voice, as well as from the words themselves. However, why shouldn't a supervisor always choose face-to-face communication over other ways to communicate?

6. As the supervisor of the mail room, you need to report to your boss that a sack of mail has been misplaced (you are not sure how it happened). Would you want to send this message through oral or written communication? Would you want to deliver it face to face? Describe the form of communication you would choose and why you would choose it.

7. What are some techniques that can help you become a better listener?

8. Identify whether the following people are more likely to be visual, auditory or kinesthetic communicators:
    a. a housepainter quick to suggest colors to a customer
    b. a clothing-store clerk unable to offer helpful suggestions about color or size
    c. an insurance agent listening to a customer's claim
    d. a deli counter manager handling seven customers

9. Adam Sam, a classified-ad salesman, has a list of 20 prospects to telephone this morning. The first call goes badly when his verbal style and presentation overwhelm the prospective client. What telephone communication guideline would help Sam in his calls? How does it work?

A SECOND LOOK

Describe the message being sent at Mary Kay Cosmetics through its gifts to employees and recognition programs. If the goal is to foster interpersonal communication in the workplace, what else could management do?

Independent Activity

All Ears (Really)

Being a good communicator means being a good observer as well as a good listener. For the first part of this exercise, go to the library, a restaurant, or some other location where you can observe people in conversation but not actually hear what they are saying. Watch the nonverbal communications going on during the conversation you cannot hear. Look for smiling or frowning, eye contact, and facial expressions. How do those involved in the conversation hold themselves? Is the speaker's hand chopping the air while speaking? Is the listener tapping a pencil as he or she listens? What do these gestures and other aspects of nonverbal communication mean?

Next, sit down with a friend or relative. Ask about his or her childhood or a significant event, such as his or her wedding or first job, that will allow you to listen; speak only to prompt more of the story. Concentrate on listening to the story and observing what forms of nonverbal communication he or she uses to tell it. Afterward, ask the speaker to evaluate your listening skills by asking you some pertinent questions about the story just told. Illustrate your listening skills with answers that also reveal how the speaker told the story (such as what nonverbal gestures he or she made).

Skill Builder

Learning to Listen Better in Class

You have just begun the third part of the text, learning the foundations of the human relations process. It's no accident that the first two chapters in this part focus on communication, which is the bedrock of good human relations skills.

For this skill builder, begin to observe deliberately and carefully the process of interpersonal communication as it occurs in your own classroom. During class discussion, how well do you and your classmates communicate? When classmates are speaking, what kind of a listener are you? Write down the seven ways to improve active listening, then note the areas in which you feel you need improvement and one or two specific steps you can take in each.

Group Activity

Trying Different Communicator Styles (25 minutes)

What kind of communicator style comes naturally to you?

- Are you a *visual* person, who talks fast and interrupts?
- Are you an *auditory* person, who talks slowly and interrupts less frequently?

- Are you a *kinesthetic* person, who depends on emotions, talks even more slowly, and has difficulty making decisions?

Divide the class into groups of six. Each student in the group should choose a communicator style that does *not* fit his or her natural style of communication. Be sure that all three styles are represented within the group.

Each group should conduct a brief "staff meeting" to discuss whether smoking should be banned in the office, with students role-playing their chosen communicator styles. If there is time, students may want to switch roles partway through the meeting. Afterward, discuss as a class how it felt to adopt different communicator styles, which styles seemed to dominate the discussion, and whether a consensus on banning smoking was reached during the meeting.

Case Study

NeXT Opens Its Books

At NeXT Computer, when employees feel underpaid and underappreciated or think that perhaps the boss is getting paid a little too much, there's no reason for them to stew. All they have to do is ask the company. They may be relieved, pleased, or angry, but they'll know where they stand, in the pay scale and in management's eyes.

At NeXT, it isn't enough that every employee is privy to the company's sales, profits, and strategic plans. Taking an open company policy to its furthest extreme, NeXT gives everyone access to everyone else's salary and stockholdings. Kevin Grundy, a director of manufacturing and engineering at NeXT, believes the open-pay system helps morale. "The availability of salaries ensures that most inequities in the system get resolved. You don't want a lot of secret deals going on and one guy making more than the guy sitting next to him because he's a good negotiator."

At Grundy's factory, he and the human resources department keep a list of everyone's salary. Any employee can come see the list at any time. Grundy used to post it but found that reactions varied, with some people stalking off angrily. Now, the point is to make sure that the person with the list—Grundy or the HR staffer—is trained to offer explanations about salary discrepancies.

Very few people ask to see the list, perhaps assuming that they can't do much about their pay anyway or fearing negative feedback. But there are exceptions, and each disgruntled employee meets face to face with Grundy; the outcome of each complaint depends on the merits of the employee's individual work record. But all get a fair hearing.

In one case, a very good engineer working long, hard hours on a project saw his compensation was lower than someone else's on the project team. Grundy admitted to the engineer that it wasn't fair, but maintained that he couldn't just change it. "Give me some time to get you where you need to be. You have to trust me." It worked. The engineer remained a productive team member, knowing that he'd eventually get his raise.

When another worker wanted to know why he wasn't being paid more, Grundy bluntly told him that he didn't think he deserved more. Negative feedback has its place, after all, says Grundy. "You have to sit down with someone like that and talk about where he needs improvement. If he's only working 8 hours a day, and everyone else is putting in 12, you have to highlight the difference."

Case Questions

1. What kind of message is encoded in NeXT Computer's open-pay approach? What is the purpose of the message?

2. How effective is NeXT's method of providing performance feedback? Does it show employees they are valued?
3. How important has the element of face-to-face communication been in NeXT's open-salary policy? Why?
4. Would you enjoy working under this system of shared information?

Source: Brian Dumar, "The New Non-Manager Managers," *Fortune,* February 22, 1993, p. 82.

Case Study

Toyota's Low-Tech Touch

In Japan, lifetime employment with one large corporation is still the rule rather than the exception. There are pros to this system: knowing you have a job day in, day out. And cons: Japan's hierarchical social system, which keeps workers in their place.

But if some bosses cannot hear, others are listening. And watching. The production-line workers at Toyota's factory in Motomachi, Japan, for example, can thank Mikio Kitano, the so-called "guru" of Toyota's production lines, for making their working days a little more pleasant.

While in Motomachi, during one of his frequent walkabouts in Toyota factories, Kitano had puzzled over the workers' pained expressions. Workers installing instrument panels across the aisle from the inspection site seemed to grimace at him each time he went by. He didn't take it personally. This was body language for a reason. Then he noticed the inspection lights shining right in the eyes of the workers. The solution was easy—a fence of mismatched metal built to shield the rest of the factory from the intense lights of the plant's final inspection sites.

It was, Kitano says, a low-tech solution, the best part being that it was simple and cheap. Not that he minds spending money on making workers' jobs easier: in the early 1980s, he was among the first to push for adopting automation to take over the tasks workers found most numbing, such as body welding.

Kitano, who spent three years in California at Toyota's joint venture with General Motors, brings a peculiarly American sense of informality to the office as well. He has little patience for the perquisites or ceremony that go with his status at Toyota. For example, few Japanese businessmen would acknowledge their secretary's presence when she brings in tea; Kitano not only thanks his, he even introduces her to guests by name.

Case Questions

1. What type of communicator is Kitano? High- or low-dominance?
2. Does his people-oriented approach to business indicate he is an active listener? Why or why not?
3. Do you think American bosses have the same sense of their employees' comfort as Kitano? Why or why not? Would most executives—of any culture—look for and interpret body language as Kitano did?

Source: "The Factory Guru Tinkering with Toyota," *Business Week,* May 17, 1993, pp. 95–97.

Quick Quiz Answers

Quick Quiz 5.1

1. d
2. feedback
3. barriers

Quick Quiz 5.2

1. no
2. yes
3. women

Quick Quiz 5.3

1. Active listening is hearing what the speaker is saying, seeking to understand the facts and feelings the speaker is trying to convey, and stating what you understand that message to be.
2. Think like the speaker; limit your own talking; concentrate and focus; respond while listening; refrain from assumptions; paraphrase what you have heard; practice listening skills.
3. In mirroring, the listener feeds back the content and style of the speaker's message.

Quick Quiz 5.4

1. visual
2. low-dominance

Quick Quiz 5.5

1. simplicity; precision
2. "I was upset that you didn't attend the meeting, which had to be canceled."
3. men

CHAPTER

6

Organizational Communication

CHAPTER OUTLINE

Learning Objectives

- Name and describe the three directions of communication in an organization.
- Contrast formal and informal communication.
- Define networks and climate.
- Explain how technology enhances organizational communication.
- Explain the problems generated by technology-assisted communication.
- Explain the role of the gatekeeper in organizational communication.
- Discuss how the choice of language can aid or hinder communication with customers.

McDonald's Real Chain of Command

By the early 1960s, fast food had asserted itself into the American landscape, offering hamburgers, fries, shakes, and soft drinks to teens, families, and workers. McDonald's Golden Arches were sprouting everywhere. But one franchisee saw a niche not being addressed by the growing chain. In his devoutly Catholic area, there was a need for a nonmeat menu item for Fridays. The franchisee's request to test his homemade fish sandwich was approved by McDonald's executives. As sales soared, McDonald's Corporation simplified the franchisee's complicated preparation process into a national product—the Filet-O-Fish sandwich.

In years to come, McDonald's menu innovations, such as the Big Mac, would continue to come from franchisees. In 1975, one franchisee, located near an Air Force base, even changed marketing history. He developed "drive-thru" service in response to a military regulation that prohibited airmen from leaving their cars unless they were in uniform. Sales at that McDonald's jumped 28 percent in the first year. Now, approximately 90 percent of McDonald's free-standing restaurants in the United States have drive-thru windows.

Today, McDonald's corporate office in Oak Brook, Illinois, continues to listen. Though all company personnel must adhere to the chain's *Operations & Training Manual* and clear product introductions with corporate personnel, McDonald's has decided that regional franchisees can best judge their area's taste preferences and personalities.

Sources: Jack Falvey, "Field Intelligence," *Sales & Marketing Management,* November 1992, p. 10.; John F. Love, *McDonald's—Behind the Arches,* New York: Bantam Press, 1987, pp. 228–231; 295–296; 393–394. Photo source: Courtesy of McDONALD'S CORPORATION.

Like a good marriage, a good friendship, or any project that requires more than one person, an organization needs good communication to function effectively. McDonald's Corporation discovered this and devised a way for regional franchisees to communicate their customers' desires and meet them. Your supervisor or coworkers need to communicate the information you need to do your job properly. They need to communicate it pleasantly, too, if optimal production is desired. If you are working in a team, all team members need to warn each other about problems and suggest solutions where they can. They also need to make each other aware of personal issues wherever the work will be affected by them. Thus, there are two aspects to the importance of organizational communication: (1) the work itself and (2) the feelings and thoughts of the people involved. Both deal with human relations skills. In the case of the work itself, good organizational communication will help people do their jobs more effectively. In the case of thoughts and feelings, communication will encourage people not only to continue good work but to improve on their performance and develop their potential. It can be said that good communication is the lifeblood of an organization.

Patterns of Communication in an Organization

Communication in the organization, like blood in the human circulatory system, tends to follow certain patterns. Understanding these patterns can help you develop the human relations skills to use organizational communication effectively.

Directions of Communication: Up, Down, and Across

In an organization, communication generally travels downward, upward, or laterally (across).

downward communication
When someone at a higher level in the organization sends a message to someone at a lower level.

Downward Communication. **Downward communication** occurs when someone at a higher level in the organization (say, a marketing manager) sends a message to someone at a lower level (an administrative assistant). The marketing manager may *receive* downward communication from someone positioned even higher, say, the chief financial officer. Downward communication is vital to the organization for two reasons: (1) since the company's goals are set at the highest managerial level, they must be communicated downward to all employees; (2) employees must receive enough downward information so that they can do their jobs effectively, thus meeting the goals of the company. (Studies have shown that employees suffer less stress when they are well informed.[1]) At AT&T, Dana Becker Dunn, vice-president of Call Servicing, notes, "We understand that the more knowledgeable our operators are about AT&T services, the more value they offer the customer."[2]

If top management decides to introduce a new program to improve quality, production, or service, employees must be well informed about their role in the program, through downward communication. For instance, when Xerox instituted its Customer Satisfaction Measurement System, the company also taught employees how to use the system to solve problems and improve their own work. "We provide lots of cross-training to empower employees to adjust bills, correct forms, or take other steps to solve problems single-handedly," explains Roger Humbert, manager of National Customer Care Operations.[3]

The "Diversity Highlights" box looks at how one company established communication programs to improve and celebrate its employees' cultural diversity.

Diversity Highlights

Digital Programs Itself for Diversity

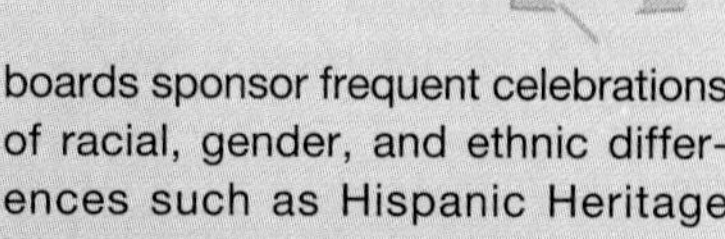

In the 1970s, Digital Equipment Corp. followed the government's directives of affirmative action and Equal Employment Opportunity (EEO) and began focusing on hiring more women and minorities. But by the next decade, managers at the Maynard, Massachusetts, computer company realized that recruitment was not the best—or only—way to make Digital the diverse workplace they wanted it to be.

Wishing to move beyond programs that seemed like "white males doing good deeds for minorities and women," the company decided it should not be an environment where individual differences were tolerated but, instead, one where they were valued, even celebrated.

The company's driving philosophy, Valuing Differences, has two components: Through voluntary Core Groups run by company-trained facilitators, Digital employees get in touch with the stereotypes and false assumptions they have of others. A second voluntary program, "Understanding the Dynamics of Diversity," has been taken by thousands of Digital employees. In addition, two new boards of directors have been created to celebrate cultural differences and promote openness. The boards sponsor frequent celebrations of racial, gender, and ethnic differences such as Hispanic Heritage Week and Black History Month.

Digital preserved its EEO and affirmative action programs. Valuing Differences focuses on personal and group development, EEO on legal issues, and affirmative action on systemic change. It is, the company believes, a winning combination, mixing corporate desire and legal need for diversity with the policies and procedures necessary to achieve it.

Source: R. Roosevelt Thomas, Jr., "From Affirmative Action to Affirming Diversity," *Harvard Business Review,* March/April 1990, p. 111.

upward communication Communication that flows from a lower level in the organization to a higher level.

Upward Communication. **Upward communication** takes place when someone at a lower level in an organization (say, a computer programmer) sends a message to someone who is higher up (a vice-president). Upward communication can take any number of forms, from the old-fashioned "suggestion box" to open meetings. As more and more companies emphasize team building and human relations, upward communication becomes more common and more important. Indeed, many companies are discovering that upward communication benefits the organization as a whole—after all, who knows more about how to improve production and service than the employees engaged in them? Consider the following examples:[4]

- Georgia Pacific Corporation shopworkers created a new source of revenue for their company by suggesting that sawdust from the lumber mills be sold to nurseries as mulch.
- At United Airlines, an employee team developed a plan for redesigning circuitry in galley elevators on the new 747s that reduced elevator malfunctions that had caused flight delays.
- A team of accounting employees at General Motors' Delco Remy Division came up with a way of identifying items that were exempt from sales taxes that saved the company $700,000 a year.

An innovative employee suggestion system developed by a St. Helena, California, consulting company is called Buck-A-Day, or BAD. It relies on friendly competition among employee teams to generate the most BAD ideas. Each employee receives a token prize for the first idea he or she submits, whether or not it is implemented—an "I had a BAD idea" coffee cup. After that, ideas are added to team totals. At the end of the month-long program, winning team members receive customized jackets.[5]

The BAD system has since been employed by Ohio-based Flexmag Industries Inc. as well, bringing in 254 cost-saving ideas from 80 employees. This successful system is based on the insight that many people are hesitant to make a suggestion because they are

Recently, four CEOs of major corporations, (second from left to right) Larry Bossidy of AlliedSignal, William Weiss of Ameritech, Jack Welch of GE, and Michael Walsh of Tenneco, met and discussed their management styles. Welch gave an example of upward and downward communication: "We give our people 360-degree evaluations, with input from superiors, peers, and subordinates. . . ."
Photo source: © John Abbott.

Photo Exercise

What are the advantages and disadvantages of such upward and downward communication?

unsure of its worth. "Most employees have good ideas," say Chris Tyler, division manager at Flexmag, "but normally only those who are outgoing will come forward. The others think, 'I won't mention my idea because it probably won't win.'"[6]

Boeing Commercial Airplanes has its supervisors act as "enablers" when employees make suggestions. For example, if a production worker has thought of a better way to produce a part, the employee tells his or her supervisor, who can invite someone from the engineering department to come to the shop floor and discuss the idea.[7]

The ultimate in suggestion-box ideas may be Reflexite Corporation's EARS (Employee-Assistance Request System), devised by manufacturing manager Matt Guyer and his associates after CEO Cecil Ursprung defined their task as follows: "Create a feedback loop where suggestions don't get lost, one that doesn't duplicate the existing structure for getting things done in the company." There is a form to fill out in the EARS system, but there is a lot more to the system than the form. The EARS system requires that all employees attend classes to learn the steps and skills necessary to solve a problem correctly. They learn how to document the problem, plot and graph its potential causes, and keep notebooks to track the amount of downtime it causes or how much scrap is wasted because of it. An "action leader" is assigned to help the person who has identified the problem conduct the studies and fill out the form. Teams of employees may be involved. Money is allocated to each EARS request, no questions asked. Progress in solving the problem is charted on bulletin boards and reviewed at weekly meetings.[8]

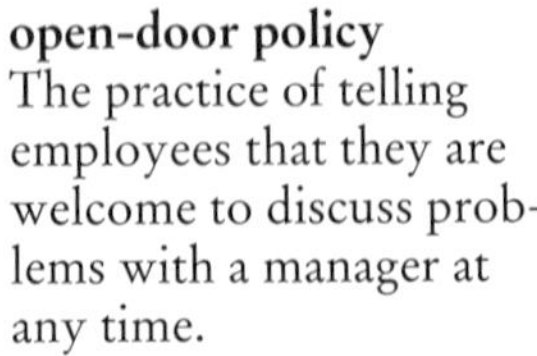

open-door policy
The practice of telling employees that they are welcome to discuss problems with a manager at any time.

As another way to encourage upward communication, a manager might establish an **open-door policy**, meaning that employees are welcome to discuss problems with the manager at any time. Obviously, someone who establishes this policy must be an active listener who is flexible enough to handle problems at any given moment.

Although the best methods may differ depending on the circumstances and the organization, it is always a good policy to encourage upward communication. Upward communication must be based on trust, which can be encouraged by providing plenty of downward communication. This is especially important when an employee needs to communicate bad news to a supervisor. How the supervisor responds to the negative message is crucial to keeping the lines of communication open and encouraging employees to come forward in the future. The exchange of information is so important that even bad news is better than no news at all, and receiving early news of a problem can result in its being solved before the problem mushrooms. Fernando Bartolome, professor of management at Bentley College, explains the importance of obtaining upward information this way:

> By far the simplest and most common way to find out about problems is to be told, usually by a subordinate .... Managers who can head off serious problems before they blow up in the company's face are two steps ahead of the game. Their employers avoid needless expense or outright disaster, and they themselves get the promotions they deserve for running their departments smoothly and nipping trouble neatly in the bud.[9]

The reward of the successful exchange of downward and upward communication, as Bartolome puts it, is that "information attracts information. Managers who are generous with what they know seem to get as much as they give .... The final positive outcome for information-rich individuals is that information flows to them as well as away from them."[10]

lateral communication Communication between two people at the same level in an organization.

Lateral Communication. In the case of **lateral communication**, one person sends a message to another person at the same organizational level. Often such communication takes place between departments or within teams. As with upward communication, lateral communication is playing a more vital role as companies emphasize human relations skills and team building. At CPC International, makers of Mazola corn oil, representatives from marketing, purchasing, packaging technology, engineering, manufacturing, and logistics management communicated their expertise to each other so successfully that they redesigned the Mazola bottle while reducing packaging by 32 percent, which not only implemented the company's commitment to environmental responsibility, but also saved money.[11] Of course, this lateral communication among team members also incorporated downward communication (the company's directive on environmental policies and cost control) as well as upward communication (management's acceptance of the team's ideas).

As a member of an organization, you will be affected by all three types of communication—downward, upward, and lateral. You'll also notice that in most companies, the three types of communication constantly overlap, often taking place at once. Throughout your career, you will learn to send and receive them all.

Test your ability to communicate by completing the "Self-Portrait" exercise now.

Formal versus Informal Communication

formal communication Communication specifically geared toward achieving the goals of the organization and that follows the lines of the organizational chart.

informal communication Communication directed toward meeting individuals' needs.

Formal communication is specifically geared toward achieving the goals of an organization and follows the lines of the organizational chart. For instance, a companywide memo, a written performance review, or a progress report delivered in a meeting are all formal communication. **Informal communication**, on the other hand, is directed toward meeting individuals' needs and does not necessarily follow the lines of the organization. A quick discussion among flight attendants about what time a flight is scheduled to depart or a conversation between accountants in the company cafeteria about long work hours before tax time are both examples of informal communication. (See Figure 6.1.) Informal communication can take several potentially sensitive forms: gossip, rumors, and the grapevine.

Gossip and Rumors. Gossip and rumors abound in the workplace. Allan J. Kimmel, a psychology professor at Fitchburg State College, defines *gossip* as "small talk about people."[12] People use gossip as a way to indicate what behavior is acceptable.[13] Thus, a conversation about two coworkers who are dating will reveal the general verdict on whether such intracompany dating is frowned upon or accepted. A conversation

Self-Portrait

How Well Do You Communicate?

In response to each item, write down always do (SA), often do (A), rarely do (D), or never do (SD). Your answer should reflect your own perceptions of the way you communicate. Be honest with yourself; you are the only one who will see the results.

SA A D SD

_____ 1. When people talk, I listen attentively; I do not think of other things or read or talk on the telephone.

_____ 2. I provide the information people need, even if someone else is its source.

_____ 3. I get impatient when people disagree with me.

_____ 4. I ask for and carefully consider advice from other people.

_____ 5. I cut off other people when they are talking.

_____ 6. I tell people what I want, speaking rapidly, in short, clipped sentences.

_____ 7. When people disagree with me, I listen to what they have to say and do not respond immediately.

_____ 8. I speak candidly and openly, identifying when I am expressing opinions and feelings rather than reporting facts.

_____ 9. I finish other people's sentences.

_____ 10. I find it difficult to express my feelings, except when stresses build up and I become angry.

_____ 11. I am conscious of how I express myself: facial expression, body language, tone of voice, gestures.

_____ 12. When people disagree with me, I avoid arguments by not responding.

_____ 13. During meetings, I prefer to listen rather than to talk.

_____ 14. When I talk, I am concise and to the point.

_____ 15. I prevent arguments during meetings.

Scoring: Agreeing (SA or A) with items 1, 4, 8, 11, and 14 and disagreeing (D or SD) with all the rest suggests you encourage openness. You communicate clearly and concisely.

Agreeing with items 2, 3, 5, 6, and 9 suggests you tend to be task oriented and dominating. You may be intolerant of disagreement and squelch involvement and discussion. Disagreeing with these items doesn't necessarily mean you encourage collaboration; you may block it by passive communication.

Agreeing with items 7, 10, 12, 13, and 15 suggests you squelch disagreement by avoiding it.

Source: *Supervisory Management,* May 1992. © 1992. American Management Association, New York.

about a coworker who wears hiking shorts and sneakers to the office reveals whether people admire the person's individuality or disapprove of such casual dress.

In contrast to gossip, *rumors,* says Kimmel, "are what people say among themselves to try to make sense out of what's going on around them."[14] For example, if a factory gets a visit from the company's president, employees may spread rumors that the factory is to be shut down or sold. When people are afraid, they spread rumors to soothe themselves by trying to explain the situation that is making them fearful. Thus rumors tend to circulate most during crises and conflicts. Unfortunately, this is when informal communication typically is at its least accurate.

Table 6.1 presents some guidelines for keeping rumors and gossip under control. In general, though, if a rumor or gossip situation could be harmful to anyone, try to

Figure 6.1 **Formal versus Informal Communication**

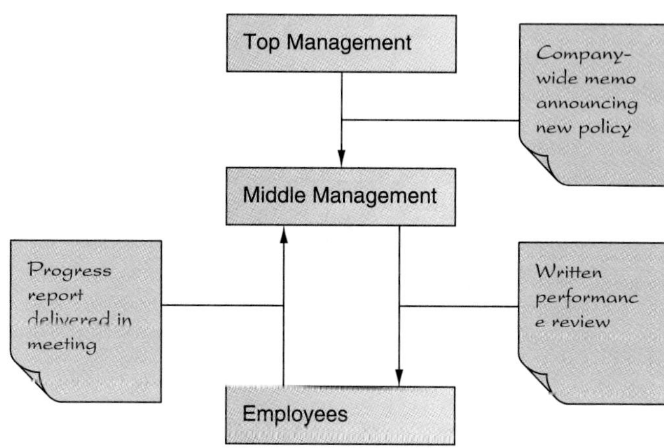

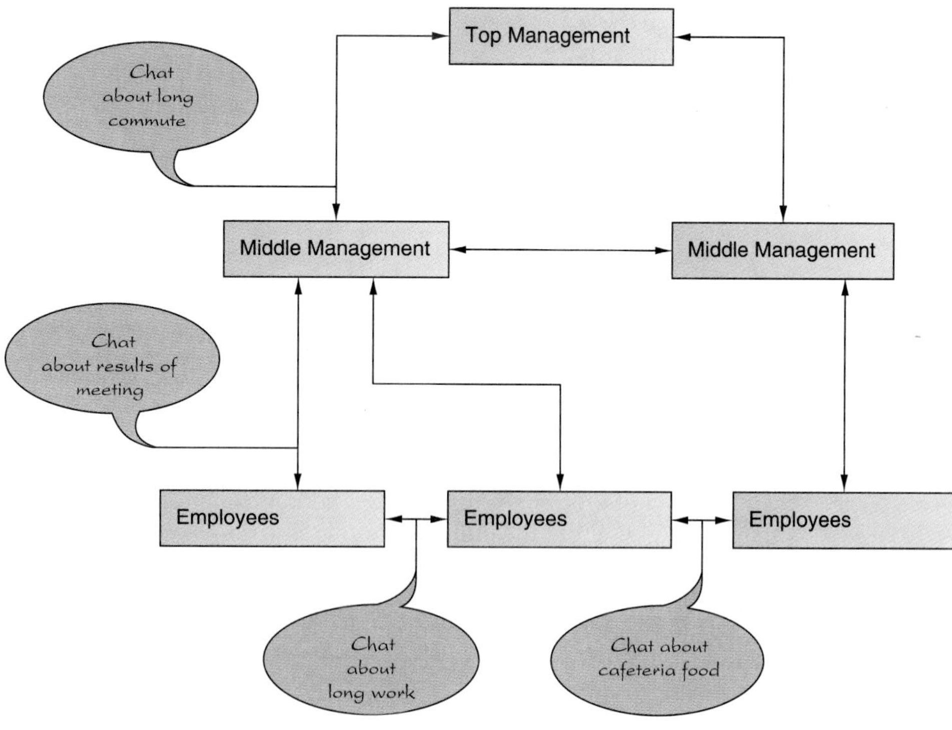

end the discussion or divert it to another topic. You may want to remind coworkers that there are usually two sides to a story or that they may not have all the information necessary to make a judgment. Don't spread rumors or gossip yourself.

Table 6.1 **Guidelines for Controlling Gossip and Rumors**

- Do not share any personal information about other employees, including your desire or intention to criticize or discipline an employee. Discuss the matters with others only when they truly need to know, as when you must discuss a personnel matter with your boss or someone in the human resources department.
- When you hear company information, such as plans for expansion or cutbacks, keep it to yourself until the organization makes an official announcement. Otherwise, if the information is inaccurate or the plans fall through, you could embarrass yourself and upset your boss or employees.
- If you hear a rumor, investigate it and find out the truth and the cause. The rumor may be a tip-off that employees are worried or angry about something, and it is the supervisor's job to address those concerns.

Source: Based on *The Front Line Supervisor's Standard Manual* (Waterford, Conn.: Bureau of Business Practice, 1989), pp. 42–43.

grapevine
The path along which informal communication travels in an organization.

The Grapevine. The path along which informal communication actually travels is called the **grapevine**. The term originated during the Civil War, when telegraph wires were strung between trees to resemble wild grapevines.[15] The mainstay of informal communication in any organization, the grapevine has been used and abused. More than a hundred years after the Civil War, the grapevine has snaked its way into electronic communication via the computer: e-mail now provides users with an infinite grapevine, filled with gossip, rumors, and all kinds of other informal communication.[16] A couple of decades ago, Keith Davis wrote a vivid description of the futility of trying to cut down the grapevine:

> [The grapevine] cannot be abolished, rubbed out, hidden under a basket, chopped down, tied up, or stopped. It is as hard to kill as the mythical glass snake that, when struck, broke into fragments that grew a new snake out of each piece.[17]

Why does the grapevine flourish so? Because it serves many purposes, binding people in an organization. It provides additional information not available through formal channels, and it delivers all of its information quickly. Long before the official memo reaches a department, its employees will know via the grapevine about the new policy or the new equipment ordered or the change in services being instituted.

Some people abuse the grapevine, enjoying the attention that some juicy bit of news brings them. But the grapevine can be used positively as well. Organizations can use the grapevine to gauge, and perhaps influence, employee reaction to new departmental rules by "leaking" proposed changes before finalizing or officially announcing them. Instead of ignoring it, managers who pay attention to the grapevine may gain valuable insights about the human relations situation in their organization. They may learn about a problem that, if brought to light, could be solved. They may discover the interests or ambitions of some employees, which have not been expressed openly but could be developed to the benefit of all. Here are some steps that supervisors can take to make the effects of the grapevine positive:[18]

1. Regularly use the tools of formal communication to inform employees of the organization's version of events.
2. Be open to discussion, becoming someone employees will turn to when they want a rumor confirmed or denied.
3. Use performance-appraisal interviews as a way to listen to employees as well as give them information.

Figure 6.2 **Basic Communication Network Patterns**

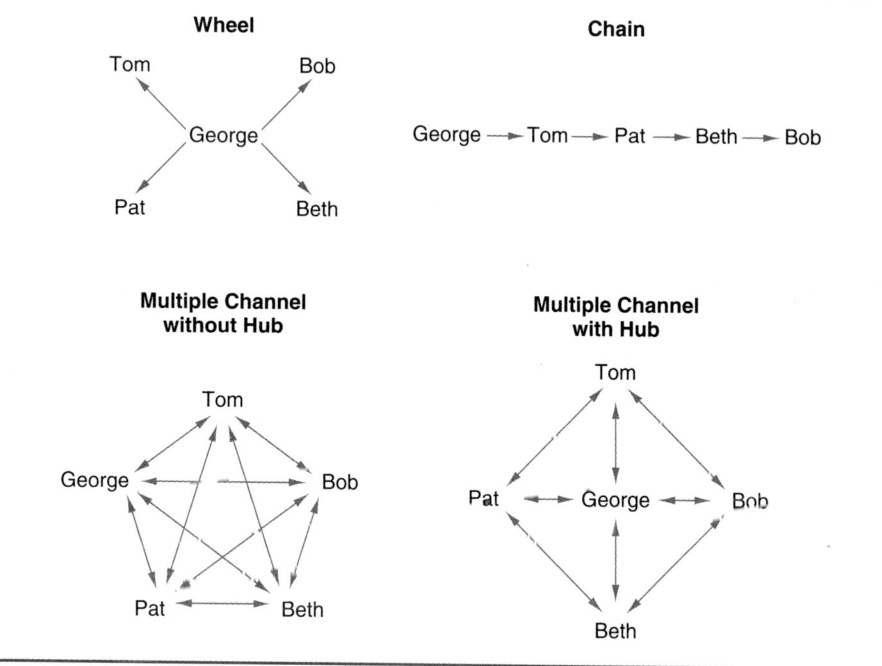

4. Have a trusted employee act as a source of information about the messages traveling the grapevine.
5. When necessary, issue a formal response to a rumor in order to clear the air.

Coworkers and team members can also use the grapevine in a positive manner, to communicate useful information along its lines. Although no one can cut down the grapevine, individuals with a strong sense of integrity can encourage its use for helpful information and discourage gossip or rumors.

liaisons
People who are the first to learn and pass on information in the informal communication system of an organization.

Liaisons. The people who are the first to learn and pass on information in the informal communication system of an organization are the **liaisons**. They exercise selectivity in deciding who will get the information and who will not. The bypassed people may be distrusted or disliked—or they may simply be those to whom the information is not likely to be relevant. For instance, the impending promotion of one person in a department is probably of interest to his or her immediate colleagues, but not to those in another department or division of the company. Whoever is acting as liaison for this information would bypass people outside the department.

networks
The channels used by people to send and receive messages.

climate
The emotional tone of the group where the communication occurs.

Networks and Climate

Two features of an organizational communication situation are its **networks**, or the channels used by people to send and receive messages, and its **climate**, or the emotional tone of the group where the communication occurs.

Networks. Figure 6.2 shows four basic networks. The first is a *hierarchical,* or *wheel,* pattern in which all communication seems to flow to and from one high-status person.

A nurturing climate is demonstrated by the formation of this JCPenney cross-functional team, which was created to enhance diversity and foster a multicultural environment. Such participative management encourages free expression of ideas and provides optimal communication.

Photo source: Courtesy of JCPenney.

Photo Exercise

If you were empowered by your manager to form such a cross-functional team, what criteria would you use for membership selection?

This network pattern doesn't allow for the most abundant flow of information. In a hierarchy, people with less power are naturally cautious about disclosing weaknesses or mistakes, so there won't be much opportunity for meaningful upward communication.

The *chain* pattern is likewise undesirable. It usually occurs in newly formed groups, where people feel comfortable communicating only with those nearest them. This inefficient pattern changes to one with more interaction as the newness of the group wears off. Lateral communication such as occurs here is of value only when it helps coordinate the work of the communicating employees.

The *multiple-channel* pattern is usually the best, providing upward, downward, and lateral communication, and involving all members of the group. It may or may not involve a "hub" person. If it does, that central person is sure to be a democratic type of leader.

networking
The process of developing a wide range of contacts inside and outside the organization.

Networking is the process of developing a wide range of contacts—or sources of information—both inside and outside an organization. Communication through networking can take place in any of the patterns just discussed, through formal and informal channels.

Climate. The climate, or emotional tone, of a communication situation can be described as either repressive or nurturing. A *repressive* climate inhibits those with less self-confidence or less status in the organization from speaking up. Suggestions for change are met with hostility. Questions are dealt with impatiently. The result is minimal, and even distorted, communication. Hierarchical communication patterns—and authoritative leaders—run the risk of creating this type of climate.

A *nurturing* climate encourages the free expression of ideas and is based on an egalitarian approach to all workers whatever their status in the organization. The *empowerment* and *participative-management* trends of today's business world require and inspire a nurturing climate for communication. It is the climate most conducive to the multiple-channel pattern described as being generally most effective.

One organization's belief in the team spirit has opened pathways of communication among its worldwide employees, boosting their ability to do their jobs effectively (see the "Teamwork Highlights" box).

Teamwork Highlights

The Whole Is Greater than the Sum at Andersen

Arthur Andersen Worldwide Organization considers itself one, big, established team, which takes great pride in the skills and abilities of its members. Teamwork is a feeling instilled from the day new hires join the Chicago-based company and begin intensive, three-week training at the Center for Professional Education in St. Charles, Illinois. There, standard methods and problem-solving approaches have been developed to allow Andersen personnel from any country to work together to develop unique, effective solutions designed to fit individual business challenges.

Herbert W. Desch, managing partner of the Professional Education Division (PED) and Andersen's chief training officer, says, "Individual brilliance is not as important as the ability to share different ideas and a variety of potential solutions through a worldwide team approach. As a global organization, we believe that clients ought to be able to get the same level of quality service from any of our offices."

That global approach is very much part of the Andersen training process. The cultural mix of trainees at the St. Charles facility leads to an international team spirit, says a British employee, "which is particularly of benefit as projects get larger and people from other offices are drafted to complete complex projects."

Part of the Andersen culture reinforced by training and work teams is the ability to pull from many resources to complete a job effectively. A junior staff member comments that "working with and as a team is extremely important here. If you challenge yourself as an individual and pull together as a team, you can get any job accomplished."

Teams are even used to develop training. To shorten the time between the recognition of new training needs and design and delivery of the actual training, PED has begun to use teams (called "group technology cells") composed of subject-matter experts, educational experts, and graphic artists to develop new training programs more quickly.

Sources: Patricia A. Galagan, "Training Keeps the Cutting Edge Sharp for the Andersen Companies," *Training and Development Journal* (January 1993): 30–35; Andersen Consulting, Your Career and Professional Development, Arthur Andersen & Co., S.C., 1991; "Training Counts," New Accountant, September 1991.

Quick Quiz 6.1

1. A worker at an auto assembly plant who approaches her supervisor with an idea on how to improve production is engaging in ___________ communication.
   a. downward
   b. upward
   c. lateral
2. A team made up of representatives from accounting, marketing, production, and customer service meets to discuss redesigning a product. They are engaging in ___________ communication.
   a. downward
   b. upward
   c. lateral
3. All of the following are examples of informal communication except:
   a. a heated discussion between supervisor and employee about overtime pay
   b. a rumor passed along the grapevine
   c. a written memo from the director of marketing outlining the promotion strategies for a new product
4. A discussion among coworkers about another employee who always arrives early and leaves late is an example of ___________.
   a. gossip
   b. rumor
   c. networking

Figure 6.3 **Technology and Communication**

Source: © 1994 by Sidney Harris.

Communication and Technology

impersonal communication Communication in which the recipients have no opportunity to respond with questions or express reactions.

Communications in an organization range from **impersonal communication**, in which the recipients have no opportunity to respond with questions or express reactions, to *interpersonal communication,* which takes place on an individual-to-individual basis. Technology makes possible a variety of impersonal communications, including electronic mail, bulletin boards, company newsletters, and so forth. These methods are good for transmitting large quantities of information quickly, but they can produce problems, too. If the recipient of a message misinterprets it, the misunderstanding might never be cleared up (unless there is immediate feedback). Technology can even slow down a process instead of speeding it up if it is not implemented properly, as we will discuss shortly in regard to *voice mail.* Figure 6.3 shows a twist on technology and communication.

Electronic mail, as mentioned earlier in this chapter, is an increasingly popular way for both organizations and individuals to communicate. It's fast, convenient, and inexpensive. But it has its downside. Many people use it for more than business communication, even on company time. One market research assistant started flirting through e-mail, until she got caught. "The messages weren't what you'd call torrid, but I got in a lot of trouble" with the employer, she says. She didn't lose her job, but now she uses e-mail only for business purposes.[19] The other side of this coin is the fact that someone other than the intended recipient of a message has access to that message. "I never, never put a personal thing on there," says Jim Moye, chief deputy comptroller for Orange County, Florida. "If you think nobody's reading it, you'd better wake up."[20] Researchers at 9 to 5, the National Association of Working Women based in Cleveland, have documented cases of employees who were reprimanded by supervisors, based on the content of the employees' e-mail. "Having your e-mail monitored is like having your supervisors look over your shoulder the entire day," notes Diana Roose, director of research for 9 to 5.[21]

Not all impersonal communication takes place electronically. An exploration manager for an oil company in Venezuela tells of the following use of the impersonal bulletin board to elicit some very personal and valuable input from employees: The building has two elevators in which every employee rides several times a day. The boss put a bulletin board in each one and posted frequent notices, including a weekly newsletter about office activities, personnel changes, and industry developments. He then let it be known informally that the bulletin boards were open to everyone—no approvals required—provided that all contributions were original (no newspaper or magazine clippings). Employees made good use of the bulletin boards, especially because they usually had a chance to ride an elevator alone from time to time. "The boss learned volumes about the problems and views of his staff and organization."[22]

Finally, while most communication via computer is impersonal, it is possible to conduct some interpersonal communications via computer as well. Video conference networks allow several different people to interact, while seeing and hearing each other. AT&T has developed a new telephone called the Picasso that is capable of sending a full-color, high-quality still image to another similar phone while simultaneously allowing a conversation. Users simply plug a video camera and a TV or other monitor into the phone. The obvious application will be within industries such as advertising, design, and photography, where photos and sketches are the subject of consultation. In addition, though, insurance-claims, medical, and educational applications are planned.[23]

Telephone Technology and Communication

One big problem with technology-assisted communication such as *voice mail,* in which the caller is asked to respond to a computer's questions by pushing certain buttons on the phone, is that people often become annoyed by it. Also, sometimes the voice-mail system is inefficient, leaving the caller in a maze of recorded voices that won't answer the actual question that needs an answer. This is even more of a problem for customers than among employees.

"Voice mail was originally designed to accommodate communication between individuals within the same company," says Tom Hunse, a Dallas-based telecommunications consultant. "Eventually, however, companies began using voice mail as a receptionist." Customers have been lost as a result. Hunse warns against the following mistakes, which apply to fellow employees as well as customers:[24]

- *Don't sentence your callers to voice-mail jail.* Offer the option of reaching a real, live operator at any time during the message.
- *Don't use voice mail as an excuse not to answer your phone or return calls.* Check for messages regularly—at least three times a day—and return all calls within 24 hours.
- *Don't leave the same tired greeting on your voice mail.* Change the message daily to reflect the specifics of your schedule: "Hello, it's Wednesday, March 10. I'll be out of the office until noon."
- *Don't prolong phone tag.* Ask callers to leave a detailed message; if you know what they need, you can have the information in front of you when you return the call.

Another expert, Karl Albrecht, comments, "When customers telephone your organization seeking help and receive instead one of those infernal push-button voice menus, they get the message, 'Our people are much too important to talk to you; we've turned you over to a machine.'" Obviously, voice mail has its place and can be quite valuable, but when it is misused, the results can be horrifying. Albrecht offers an example of a major health plan in California that asked the caller to choose from a lengthy listing

"For family practice appointments, push 1," etc.—that *ended* with, "If this is a life-threatening situation, push . . ." after a full minute of reciting other options.[25]

Quick Quiz 6.2

1. A company newsletter is an example of ___________ communication.
2. Giving callers the option to speak with a human operator is an example of something you can do to improve communication via ___________.

Gatekeepers and Organizational Language

Two factors that can either help or hinder organizational communication are gatekeepers and the choice of organizational language. The first factor primarily involves employees; the second primarily involves customers.

Gatekeepers

gatekeepers
Those who determine what information will be conveyed to the decision makers in the organization.

The **gatekeeper** of a department or an organization is the person who determines what information will be conveyed to the decision makers in the organization.[26] Often this is the secretary or administrative assistant, who occupies a far less imposing position on the organization chart than his or her power actually warrants. Placing the right person in this role can smooth the path for effective organizational communication.

The gatekeeper not only possesses information that people might need but also determines whether or not to pass on their information as requested. Information is the oil that lubricates the engine of a company, a department, and a specific job. The gatekeeper can help keep that oil flowing or create a dangerous blockage.

When it comes to sales, the gatekeeper is the person who can help a salesperson avoid "NARDs," that is, people "not able to render a decision," says Dennis Fox. He suggests a question such as, "So if I want to speak with the person responsible for buying copiers, who would that be?" rendered, of course, with the utmost respect and courtesy to the worthy gatekeeper.[27]

Organizational Language

Addressing the subject of quality improvement, Karl Albrecht notes a common stumbling block in communication with customers. "It's remarkable how many quality programs, even those purported to be customer-focused, overlook the simple yet profound importance of customer-friendly communication." He gives the following examples of "customer-hostile" messages:[28]

- "Children under three years old will not be accepted for babysitting." The message is, "We don't want your kid here if he or she is too much trouble."
- "This contract limits our liability—read it" (from a parking lot). "Gives you a real comfy feeling about the safety of your car, doesn't it?" comments Albrecht.
- "All accounts must be settled on the day services are rendered" (on a sign in the doctor's office). Albrecht suggests the message be phrased in cooperative rather than adversarial terms. His version: "We will appreciate payment of your charges on the day you receive treatment." (It wouldn't mean the office couldn't insist on payment; it's just a nicer way of saying it.)

Dennis Fox offers a related observation: "Client-centered phrases focus on the use of 'you' statements, followed by 'we' statements, followed at a distant third by 'I' statements." He further points out that words such as "learn about," "explore," and "consider" are less threatening to a customer than "tell you," "determine," or "decide," which may leave the customer feeling pressured and defensive. In other words, phrases such as "let me show you" and "I'd like to tell you how" should be replaced with "I'd like to hear what you have to say" and "I'd like to learn more about your business."[29]

Quick Quiz 6.3

1. Why is the gatekeeper so important to everyone?
2. Rewrite the following statement to change it from "customer hostile" to "customer friendly": "No blue jeans, tank tops, or sandals allowed in this restaurant."

Summary

- **Name and describe the three directions of communication in an organization.** Communication can be downward, upward, and lateral. Downward communication occurs when someone at a higher level in an organization sends a message to someone at a lower level. Employees depend on downward communication in order to receive enough information to do their jobs properly. Upward communication flows from a lower level to a higher level in an organization. Lateral communication, which occurs between people on the same organizational level, can help coordinate the work of different departments and speed up the exchange of information. Both upward and lateral communication have become more prevalent and important to organizations that focus on human relations issues.
- **Contrast formal and informal communication.** Formal communication tends to follow the organization chart. Through the grapevine, the informal system provides a lot of information not available from the formal system but also includes gossip and rumors that may be false. The informal system operates with much more speed than the formal system.
- **Define networks and climate.** Networks are the channels people use to send and receive messages. Climate is the emotional tone of the group where communication occurs. A repressive communication climate discourages the expression of ideas or questions, whereas a nurturing climate does the opposite and is based on an egalitarian approach to all employees regardless of status in the organization.
- **Explain how technology enhances organizational communication.** Technology makes possible a wide range of impersonal communications, including electronic mail and company newsletters. These communications can transmit a large amount of information to a lot of people quickly.
- **Explain the problems generated by technology-assisted communication.** Sometimes technologies such as voice mail can be inefficient by eliminating the human role too thoroughly and denying people the opportunity to clarify information. Another problem is that customers may feel slighted by the lack of human contact or may find the process of using the technology unwieldy. Many problems can be prevented by always providing the option of human contact, by responding promptly to messages left, and by giving and asking for complete information.
- **Explain the role of the gatekeeper in organizational communication.** Gatekeepers are people who decide what information will be conveyed to the decision makers in an organization. Gatekeepers are extremely important to the informal communication system, even though they may not occupy impressive positions on the organization chart.
- **Discuss how the choice of language can aid or hinder communication with customers.** Often organizational language is unintentionally "customer hostile" instead of "customer friendly." Choosing positive rather than negative phrasing and focusing on "you" sentences and nonthreatening terminology can help.

Key Terms

downward communication (122)
upward communication (123)
open-door policy (124)
lateral communication (125)
formal communication (125)
informal communication (125)
grapevine (128)
liaisons (129)
networks (129)
climate (129)
networking (130)
impersonal communication (132)
gatekeepers (134)

Review and Discussion Questions

1. Name the three directions that communication in an organization can take. Why are upward and lateral communication increasingly important in today's organizations?

2. Which of the following organizational communications are formal and which are informal?
   a. a memo providing information about the company picnic
   b. a meeting in which employees discuss the department's goals for the month
   c. a rumor about a new vacation policy
   d. a discussion between the headwaiter and a busboy about the World Series

3. What positive and negative roles does the grapevine play in an organization?

4. Why are informal channels of communication important?

5. Mallory Gray, a team leader, has heard a rumor through the company grapevine that the project her team is working on may be cancelled. What steps can Mallory take to confirm or deny it?

6. Name the three main types of network patterns. Which is considered the best? Why?

7. Why is a nurturing climate important in organizational communication?

8. Yesterday morning, when Donetta Simpson had to stay home and care for her sick child, she tried three times to call her manager so he could switch her schedule with another worker's. Each time, she was only able to reach his voice mail. She didn't get through to him personally until nearly noon; he was angry, and she was defensive. How could this situation have been averted?

9. Should a manager participate in informal communication? If so, when? If not, why not?

10. June Perez is representing a new line of heart medications. Trying to schedule an appointment with the city's leading heart specialist has been difficult; his secretary just says he's busy. Why is the secretary's role so important? What approach might June take to be more successful at obtaining an appointment with the specialist?

A SECOND LOOK

What innovations throughout McDonald's history can be traced to upward communication? How does a nuturing climate continue to generate innovations today?

Independent Activity

The Fast-Food Communication Flow

At the beginning of this chapter, you read about some McDonald's menu innovations which were suggested by franchise managers and then fine-tuned into national products by McDonald's top management. How do you think communication between managers and employees works in the restaurants themselves? Visit a fast-food restaurant; it can be part of a national chain or independently operated. Take a seat near the front, where you can observe the give-and-take among workers. Keep these questions in mind as you observe:

- What kind of interaction is there between fellow employees?
- How would you define the communications pattern here?
- Which appears to be stronger, the formal or informal communications network?

- Can you detect a grapevine? A gatekeeper or liaison?
- How would organizational communications here differ from that in a large office? A factory? Are there similarities? What factors account for those differences or similarities?

Skill Builder

Making Messages "Customer Friendly"

Organizational language can make or break a customer-oriented relationship; it can also affect communication between manager and employees and among team members. No one likes to be put off or threatened. Read the following "customer-hostile" statements, and rewrite them so that they are "customer friendly." Notice your own reaction to both.

1. "Rent our bicycles at your own risk."
2. "You break it, you buy it."
3. "Don't touch the merchandise."
4. "Not responsible for lost or stolen items."
5. "Children and pets not allowed."

Group Activity

Following the Grapevine (20 minutes)

Divide the class into teams of six or more. Make one person on each team the team leader. Designate another person to think of and start a rumor. The rumor starter may spread the rumor any way he or she chooses, using lateral communication, as long as the team leader is omitted. Then the team leader should try to learn what the rumor is, encouraging upward communication by trying to create a nurturing climate. Team members may choose to reveal bits and pieces of the rumor indirectly, tell the leader outright, or not tell the leader at all, creating a "chilly" climate. After about 15 minutes, the teams should examine their actions and reactions to the rumor grapevine. Was it a positive or negative experience? Did the team leader feel frustrated, left out of the grapevine? Did the grapevine function to spread the rumor among team members accurately or inaccurately?

Case Study

Coffee and Criticism for Eastern Realty

Its market was flat, its turnover high, and morale low. Pinpointing poor communication as the root of its troubles, Eastern Realty Investment Management Inc. began holding companywide breakfast meetings. "We had the best of intentions," says Ermena Walz, director of human resources for the Washington, D.C., company. "We reasoned that getting everyone together for an informal, relaxed meeting would help dissolve barriers between coworkers."

But Eastern quickly confronted an unexpected barrier. Although the mandatory meetings were held during work hours, turnout was low; many employees felt management was wasting their time. And the natural rift between the company's 40 white-collar workers and 20 blue-collar workers kept most of those 20 union laborers away.

CEO Christopher Whyman plugged away, opening the first meeting by asking employees to share their ideas and give feedback about the way the company operates. Breaking into smaller groups, the employees discussed customer expectations, as well as their own expectations of and experiences with Eastern—good and bad. Eastern's management, expecting helpful criticism and comments, was unprepared for the onslaught of counterproductive, sometimes angry comments, such as "Bulldoze the place and start over." Walz and a group of managers took notes and compiled a list of manageable issues, then distributed the copies to everyone as the agenda for discussion at the next meeting.

It was tough going, admits Walz, "but we knew we would strike the right button sooner or later, so we settled for every two inches of progress we could make." By the third meeting, attitudes were changing and attendance was growing. The turning point for union members was CEO Whyman's personal appeal for their participation in service training.

Since that time, the meetings have had the intended results—and then some. Morale has improved, turnover has declined, and several committees have been formed to deal with specific issues. Based on employees' requests, the company newsletter has been resurrected, corporate goals are openly discussed, and employee recognition efforts, such as a new employee-of-the-month program, have been stepped up.

Case Questions

1. How balanced are the amounts of downward and upward communication at Eastern? What kind of communication do the breakfast meetings provide? Do you think all employees' input is weighed equally?
2. Do Eastern's communication pattern and climate today differ from what it had before the meetings? How?
3. What effect will Eastern Realty's new communication efforts have on the company grapevine? Do you think communications inaccuracies and mistakes are more easily caught and corrected since these meetings began?
4. What other ways could Eastern have improved morale and reduced turnover?

Source: "Improved Communication Can Be Firm First Step Toward Quality," *Total Quality,* April 1993, p. 5.

Case Study

Ringing Phones Tumble Walls at Enrich

The phones never stop ringing at Enrich International, a products distributor based in Lindon, Utah. But until recently, the "territorial" walls erected between new-product development people and the order-taking team were causing repeated problems for the 80-person firm. Though the company took great pains to notify its distributors of new products, guaranteeing that its phones were flooded with orders the day the products were scheduled to be shipped, the order takers were often overlooked. As a result, those responsible for answering the ringing phones spent shipping days either frustrated by the jammed switchboard or, even worse, unfamiliar with what the callers were talking about.

Enrich tried to remedy the situation by putting together spec sheets on upcoming products and giving them to order takers, but that solution muddied the waters further because the shipping dates often changed. The company began to look for a long-term solution to its communications nightmare.

Building lines of communication through the barriers erected by the two departments meant breaking down those walls, brick by brick. Enrich put together a communications team that included managers from the customer service, order entry, and new-product development departments. Weekly meetings were set up to prepare a definite order rollout for the coming week.

Today, every employee in the telephone order-entry department is a step ahead instead of a step behind, according to Suzanne Dean, vice-president of field development and communications. Now that they are included in the order planning, she adds, "people are making wonderful suggestions about how they could promote and cross-sell over the telephone."

Case Questions

1. What type of communications system could have led to the problems suffered by Enrich? What type of communication was lacking within the company?
2. Why do you think walls were erected between the two departments? Was a gatekeeper, or the lack of one, at fault? Why or why not?
3. Does Enrich have a healthy communications climate today?

Source: Mark Henricks, "All Together Now," *Entrepreneur,* April 1993, p. 47.

Quick Quiz Answers

Quick Quiz 6.1

1. b
2. c
3. c
4. a

Quick Quiz 6.2

1. impersonal
2. voice mail

Quick Quiz 6.3

1. **The gatekeeper controls the flow of information to decision makers in the organization.**
2. **"Appropriate dress requested" or "Jacket and tie preferred."**

CHAPTER

7

Processes and Tools of Motivation

CHAPTER OUTLINE

Learning Objectives

- Explain the relationship between motivation and performance.
- Name and define the major motivation theories and categorize them as content or process theories. Describe the difference between content and process theories.
- Discuss the use of money to motivate employees.
- Name several types of financial incentives.
- List eight tools of motivation.

Commitment Motivates at Clorox

Cindy Ransom (pictured at left) is a middle manager "passionate" about her job at Clorox. She considers herself a coach or sponsor of people, rather than a manager. Three years ago, Ransom asked her workers at a 100-person plant in Fairfield, California, to redesign the plant's operations. Although she was available to answer the occasional question, Ransom stayed in the background, watching as a team of hourly workers took over her managerial work. They established training programs, set work rules for absenteeism, and reorganized the once-traditional factory into five customer-focused business units. Ransom used her growing amount of free time to take care of the needs of customers and suppliers.

Last year, Ransom's commitment to her job and her employees paid off: Clorox named the plant the most improved in its largest division, Household Products. Ransom's reward is not money or a job higher up in the Clorox hierarchy. Instead, she'll head overseas, to apply her skills at another Clorox plant. That's just fine with a manager who says her real motivation for the plant redesign was neither money nor personal glory, but the chance to see the people who work with her succeed.

"When I read about America losing its competitive edge, it really ticks me off," says Ransom. "It gets me motivated to make a difference in my little corner, to make my factory competitive enough so my people can be employed here until they retire."

Source: *Fortune,* February 22, 1993, p. 81. Photo source: © Brian Smith/Outline.

motivation
Giving people incentives to act in desired ways.

In a human relations context, **motivation** is giving people incentives that cause them to act in desired ways. Organizational goals of improving quality, enhancing productivity and innovation, and increasing efficiency all depend on motivated employees, as illustrated by Cindy Ransom's group at Clorox. Controlling them, monitoring them, instructing them, and evaluating them will never take the place of motivating them. The proverbial horse who is led to water will not drink unless he has the motive of thirst to do so.

The principle applies to you as well. You will always do a better job when you are motivated. So it is useful to understand the mechanics of motivation in order to arrange your own career to best advantage, as well as influence those around you.

When motivation is missing, an organization may never realize its employees' full potential. Work skills alone will take performance only so far. You can teach work skills and you can test them, and obviously a minimum level of such skills must be present to succeed in a given job. But motivation coupled with skills is what determines performance (see Figure 7.1).

We all know this because people are continually proving it. Consider the case of Pete Gray, a young boy with only one arm—and a love of baseball. Motivated nevertheless to "someday play in Yankee Stadium," he actually did, in 1945, with the St. Louis Browns. Consider Helen Keller. Blind and deaf from infancy, she learned to read and write and communicate to the extent that she one day graduated with honors from Radcliffe College, wrote several books, and helped countless others with similar disabilities overcome them the way she had.

In both of these dramatic cases, a *motivator* helped instill motivation in the hero of the story. Pete Gray had his older brother always working with him, reminding him, "A winner never quits." Helen Keller had Anne Sullivan, the teacher who broke into Helen's dark and silent world by tapping letters into her palm. In your own life, perhaps you have received or given motivation yourself. In your career, it is the factor that can lift you to success if you learn how to spark it in yourself and in others.

Now consider the case of Susan Khoo's dress shop. "I don't know what's wrong with these people," says Susan. I pay them good wages, but when we hit a busy season, nobody's willing to put forth the extra effort we need—giving up a break once in a while or even just moving a little faster."

Susan needs to determine what will motivate her employees to work harder. Perhaps the wages are not as satisfactory as she thinks. Perhaps her employees need some special incentive, whether money, praise, or recognition. Perhaps she needs to appeal to their team spirit. (In a recent survey, a lack of team spirit was blamed by a majority of respondents for their decreasing job satisfaction.[1])

Different types of motivation are effective with different groups of people and with different individual personalities, so Susan has to consider the unique characteristics of her employee group and workplace in determining appropriate motivators. As a framework for determining these specifics, though, she needs an understanding of basic motivational principles. Over the years many theories have been formulated and tested in the workplace in order to discover these principles.

Theories: What Motivates People and How?

Theories of motivation derive from studies of observed human behavior and are of necessity based on generalizations. Therefore, none of these theories is guaranteed to "work"—human beings are too complex for that. The challenge is to apply what is useful from them to a given situation, always bearing in mind the necessity of tailoring a general principle to the quirks and peculiarities, unique gifts, and potentials of the individual or group of individuals at hand.

content theories
Theories that focus on the incentives of motivation.

Many of the theories of motivation that have evolved can be divided into two categories: **content theories** focus on the incentives of motivation, or *what* motivates

Figure 7.1 **Relationship between Motivation and Performance**

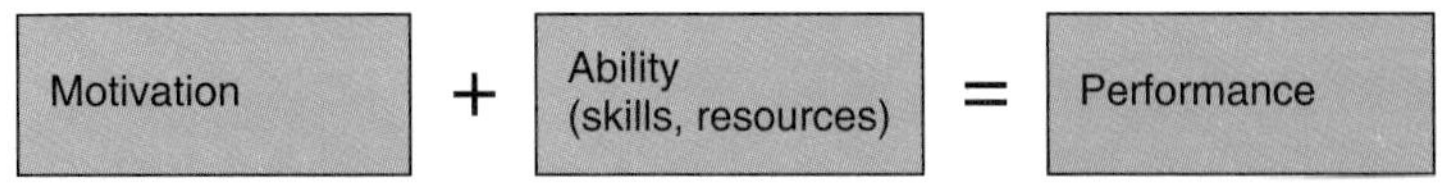

process theories
Theories that focus on the way motivation operates.

people, and **process theories** focus on the way motivation operates, or *how* people are motivated. The major theories are as follows:

1. *Content theories:* Maslow's hierarchy of needs, McClelland's achievement-power-affiliation theory, and Herzberg's two-factor theory.
2. *Process theories:* Vroom's expectancy-valence theory, Adams's equity theory, and Skinner's reinforcement theory.

Maslow's Hierarchy of Needs

Abraham Maslow based his pioneering content theory on the idea that what motivates people is unmet needs. Remember our proverbial horse? If he is thirsty, he will be motivated to drink. Human needs encompass those of animals but transcend them, too. Maslow categorized these needs in five basic ways:

1. *Physiological needs* refer to the things required for survival—food, water, sex, and shelter. Many physiological needs depend on having a job with a steady paycheck.
2. *Security needs* mean the need to keep oneself free from harm. In modern society, these needs might be met by insurance, a home in a safe neighborhood, and the steady paycheck mentioned earlier that pays for such things.
3. *Social needs* are the desire for love, friendship, and companionship. People seek to satisfy these needs through the time they spend with other people.
4. *Esteem needs* are the needs for self-esteem and the respect of others. Two ways these needs are met are through acceptance and praise.
5. *Self-actualization needs* describe the desire to live up to one's full potential.

hierarchy of needs theory
Theory that people first try to satisfy physiological needs, then security, social, esteem, and finally self-actualization needs.

Maslow believed these needs fall into a hierarchy of importance (Figure 7.2). The needs at the bottom of the hierarchy are the most basic needs, the ones people try to satisfy first. The needs at the top are the ones people try to satisfy only when most of their other needs have been met. Thus, the **hierarchy of needs theory** holds that people first try to satisfy their need for food and shelter, then their need for safety, and so on, until finally they seek to satisfy their need for self-actualization.

As many studies have since pointed out, though, people often seek to meet more than one category of needs at a time or a higher need before a lower one is thoroughly satisfied. You might forego the party or family gathering that would satisfy a social need and choose instead to fulfill an esteem need or self-actualization need by working overtime to complete a special project at the office.

People tend to rely on their job to meet a lot of the needs in Maslow's hierarchy. Their paycheck and benefits such as health insurance meet many physiological and security needs. Depending on the individual's life situation and personality, social needs may be met through relationships with coworkers. And, as just suggested, work may be a main avenue for meeting some esteem and self-actualization needs. The

Figure 7.2 **Maslow's Hierarchy of Needs**

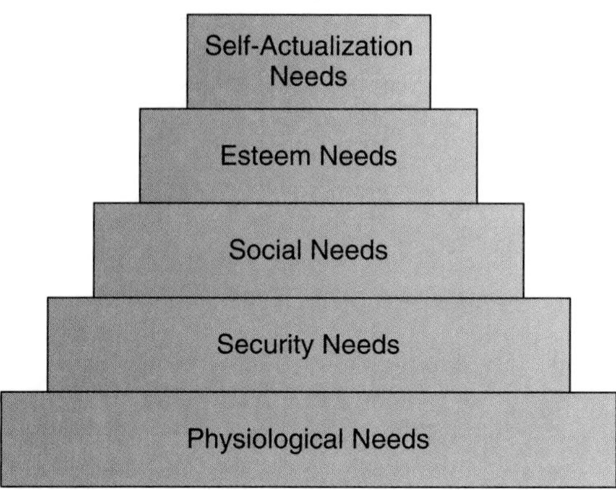

organization hopes it is; employees who meet those higher needs at work usually perform above average.

To discover your needs and prime motivators, complete the "Self-Portrait" exercise now.

Although Maslow's hierarchy provides some useful insights about motivation, Maslow himself cautioned against "swallowing whole" principles that he considered "tentative."[2] His research came from clinical studies of people suffering from neuroses, not the ordinary population. His basic principles nevertheless proved useful to other theorists who followed and still have much applicability.

For example, Maslow's theory explains why, during a serious recession, a factory supervisor may find that many employees are highly motivated just by their awareness of the tight job market. Factory workers facing a recession are motivated primarily by physiological and security needs. Employees who are less worried about keeping a job need other incentives, however. The Richard Michael Group, a Chicago placement firm, must meet higher needs in order to attract and retain its employees who are in demand in the job market, so it hosts spontaneous dinner parties to address esteem, and probably social, needs.[3] The firm credits its low turnover to these dinners. During a computer conversion period, the Berlin Packaging Company invited those who exceeded production goals to take three shots at a basketball hoop in the president's office and receive cash awards based on how many baskets they made. The money was secondary to the social and esteem needs that this contest satisfied.[4]

Many organizations today offer tuition reimbursement, which can help meet employees' self-actualization and self-esteem needs. In addition, tuition reimbursement may hold out the promise of meeting more basic security needs, since the schooling will better assure future employment. Some organizations have a "no-layoff" policy, directly addressing such physiological and security needs. Some boast a superior insurance and benefits package to the same end.

achievement-power-affiliation theory
A content theory based on the assumption that through their life experiences, people develop needs for achievement, power, and affiliation.

McClelland's Achievement-Power-Affiliation Theory

In the 1960s, David McClelland developed a content theory of motivation (called the **achievement-power-affiliation theory**) based on the assumption that through their life experiences, people develop the following three needs:

Self-Portrait

What Motivates *You?*

What makes a job appealing to you? Rank the following factors from 1 to 12, assigning 1 to the factor you consider most important and 12 to the one you consider least important.

_____ 1. Work that is interesting and meaningful
_____ 2. Good wages or salary
_____ 3. Authority to make important decisions
_____ 4. Comfortable work environment
_____ 5. Likable coworkers
_____ 6. Good relationship with supervisor
_____ 7. Clear understanding of company's goals
_____ 8. Appreciation and recognition for doing a good job
_____ 9. Opportunity to learn new skills
_____ 10. Prestigious title or occupation
_____ 11. Opportunity for advancement
_____ 12. Job security

---

1. *achievement:* the desire to do something better than it has been done before
2. *power:* the desire to control, influence, or be responsible for other people or results
3. *affiliation:* the desire to maintain close and friendly personal relationships.

According to McClelland, people have all of these needs to some extent. The intensity of the needs varies from one individual to the next, however, depending upon their early life experiences. And the relative strength of the three types of needs influences what will motivate a person.

Thus, people with a high need for achievement prefer to tackle difficult tasks. Many successful businesspeople exhibit this trait. If a job is too easy, these people tend to lose motivation. In this vein, Kenneth Blanchard, chairman of Blanchard Training and Development, Inc., believes that the ideal employee goals are those that have only a 70 percent chance of success and so require employees to "stretch."[5] Interestingly, McClelland found that training programs emphasizing the importance of achievement can strengthen this motivation in employees who initially seem to lack it.[6]

McClelland's Power Need Becomes Empowerment

The need for power, the second need in McClelland's theory, may mean the desire to control other people, but in a healthy personality this need is satisfied by assigning responsibility and providing a degree of control over circumstances. Some people crave more responsibility than others, but today's emphasis on *empowerment,* the responsibility for self-management, is based on the belief that most employees would welcome more responsibility than they currently have if it came with appropriate controls and support. Attempts at empowerment generally take the form of *work teams,* which, interestingly enough, often serve to satisfy McClelland's third need, for "affiliation," or close and friendly personal relationships. Moreover, some degree of empowerment is essential if one is to meet "achievement" needs. A company where employees feel empowered as a function of their pride in their product and their role as contributors to society is profiled in the "Teamwork Highlights" box.

Teamwork Highlights

Giro Employees Make a Contribution

Pride in an organization and passion for its products or services can do more than just enhance the workplace. It can motivate employees to go beyond the call of duty. Smart companies, such as Giro Sport Design, cultivate these emotions and help their employees feel good about what they do.

Many of the employees at the Soquel, California, bicycle-helmet manufacturer are hard-core cyclists. Tim Plaskett, the company's shipping supervisor, was among them; Monette Paparotti was not. Though she had little interest in cycling, Paparotti took the company up on its offer of a discounted helmet. By the end of her first year with Giro, after rubbing elbows with coworkers who were former world-class athletes and having designers seek her opinion on helmet colors, the customer-service representative was a convert. Now a mountain-bike racer, she finds herself waving down fellow cyclists wearing battered Giro helmets so she can tell them about the company's guarantee to replace damaged helmets for a nominal fee. "Here I am, out on the trails doing PR work for Giro!" she says.

Plaskett was already a Giro convert; he joined the company because he liked the product. But his appreciation and pride in it grew when he began dealing with helmets sent in under Giro's crash-replacement program. The damaged helmets are often accompanied by letters of thanks in which cyclists describe how the Giro helmets saved their lives. "This really makes you understand what you're doing," says Plaskett.

Giro posts and circulates the letters, building on Plaskett's constantly renewed sense of pride and encouraging all its employees to appreciate the importance of the product they make.

Source: Alessandra Bianchi, "True Believers," *Inc.*, July 1993, pp. 72–73.

Key to effective empowerment is the clear communication of valid performance standards. One expert suggests that customer feedback is the best basis for setting performance standards in some industries.[7] Certainly all agree that the goals must be specific and clearly communicated. "All too often, when you ask managers what they expect from their employees, and then you ask their employees what their managers expect of them, you get completely different answers," observes training expert Blanchard.[8]

Once the goals have been set and communicated, a system for monitoring progress must be established. Blanchard calls this the "recording" phase. "Almost any type of performance can be measured," he asserts. "And if you can't measure it, you can't manage it." Successful empowerment of employees means that they will do the recording themselves, evaluate their own and each other's progress, and adjust performance as necessary to reach the goals. One management expert adds another requirement for successful empowerment: encouraging and supporting demands for information and authority.[9]

Donnelly Corporation, an auto parts manufacturer, is enjoying great success with its empowerment emphasis. Workers set their own production goals, and they are accountable to coworkers, not bosses, for the quality of their work and for absences or tardiness. There are no time clocks to punch. Supervisors are available to advise, not to check up on, workers. "Equity committees," in which all votes are equal and the membership exactly reflects the ratio of white- and blue-collar workers, make final policy decisions and recommend wages, benefits, and bonuses (which are posted). The result of Donnelly's empowerment philosophy has been a healthy increase in sales despite the overall decline for the auto industry.[10]

Remmele Engineering Inc., is another example of effective empowerment. The company sponsors courses in basic math, statistical process control, computer programming, and blueprint reading that are taught on site, mostly during work hours, by

Today many Taco Bell outlets operate with no manager on site. Self-directed teams, known as "crews," manage inventory, schedule work, order supplies, and train new employees. Taco Bell's team-managed restaurants have lower employee turnover and higher customer satisfaction scores than conventionally run outlets. Shown is the Taco Bell kiosk on UCLA's campus.

Photo source: © Fritz Hoffmann/ JB Pictures.

Photo Exercise

Why would an employee-empowered, team-run outlet achieve higher employee and customer satisfaction ratings?

instructors from local community colleges. The aim is to make employees capable of self-directed work. The result for the employee can be a doubling of earnings. "Remmele has made training a part of being competitive," says Jerome M. Rosow, president of the Work in America Institute.[11]

Lev N. Landa, a former Russian educator who emigrated to the United States in 1976, is showing some other companies how to make empowerment a part of their training programs. In essence, he advises that every employee be turned into an expert—and he's proving that it can be done. At Allstate Insurance Co., his system has produced a corps of skilled workers who caused a 75 percent increase in productivity and a 90 percent increase in quality of work for a projected savings of $35 million a year.

Landa's empowerment tool is a "logic flowchart" of the decision-making process in a job. Landa says that workers soon "internalize" the principles of the chart and are then able to apply them in different situations. The secret lies in the thoroughness of the charts. In traditional training, experts unintentionally fail to inform workers of some very important steps. Landa discovered this phenomenon while analyzing the way people think. His method reverse-engineers the decision-making process to find the gaps in logic that cause problems for the trainee. By studying the expert, he is able to reconstruct the expert's thinking and incorporate it into the chart. His flowcharts gained wide acceptance in Russian academic circles and now are proving themselves in U.S. industry. Allstate is even considering a venture with Landa to market "Landamatics" to schools.[12]

Other empowerment success stories include the following:[13]

- Gaines Dog Food plant in Topeka, Kansas, which is built around self-managed work teams and has been 20 percent more productive as a result.
- AT&T's American Transtech subsidiary, which was able to cut its prices by 50 percent because of self-managed teams.
- Litel Communications (now LCI), which used such teams to cut processing time from two weeks to one day.

It is important for empowerment programs to be established for the right reasons. Unfortunately, sometimes empowerment programs are established for the wrong reasons—to eliminate jobs, for example. When this happens, the remaining workers' trust is shattered, and without employee trust, such programs will not succeed.

Sometimes the programs are incompletely, halfheartedly implemented. Many feel that U.S. companies in general give only lip service to the idea of increasing production workers' autonomy. If employees' decisions are not honored by top management, then they will lack motivation for effective self-management.

Glenn R. Englund, a senior engineering manager, pinpoints "honor" as the essential ingredient in a successful empowerment program. If team members expect the decisions they make to be honored, he observes, they will also honor the decisions made by others. Since they know their decisions will be carried out, they make them more carefully, seeking consultation where needed. "The effect that honor has on decision making, and thus on action, is powerful," Englund concludes.[14]

Historically, two-thirds of the nation's training goes for white-collar workers and managers. The ratio should be reversed, according to many experts.[15] If the United States does not train more blue-collar workers to learn greater autonomy, wages will continue to fall and social tensions increase, predicts the Commission on the Skills of the American Workforce.[16] "If our workers don't know more and can't do more than those in Indonesia, then there is no reason for international companies to pay them any more," says Marc Tucker, president of the National Center on Education and the Economy.

At present, only about 1 percent of payroll expenses of U.S. companies overall goes for training, and only one-half of 1 percent of the nation's 3.8 million companies carry out some form of training, according to the American Society for Training & Development. Furthermore, most of the $30 billion a year corporate America spends on training is accounted for by less than 10 percent of all companies. Again, it is noteworthy that a disproportionate share of that goes to professionals, not blue-collar workers.[17]

The United States has no comprehensive program to compare with, for example, Germany's apprenticeship system, which gives 1.8 million noncollege youths sophisticated training on the job, equipping them for high-level employment.[18] The typical German factory worker can do everything from programming computerized machinery to repairing the machines.[19] "These people think for themselves, adapt to changing markets, and take responsibility for expensive machinery," observes Anton Kathrein, owner and CEO of Kathrein Werke, a German antenna maker. In chilling contrast, consider the practice of U.S. machine-tool manufacturers who have handed over the computer programming for the latest equipment to technicians, not machinists, betraying their desire to keep management in control.[20]

The American Society for Training & Development recommends that at least $30 billion more should be spent on training by U.S. industry to bring some 50 million, mostly nonprofessional, workers up to the desired level of skill. This would require that most large and midsize companies allocate 1.5 percent of their payrolls to the effort. The percentage for Japanese and German companies is 3 to 4 percent. Remmele Engineering, discussed earlier, spends 2 to 3 percent, but most firms of its size do no training at all. "We have an undereducated, undertrained work force at the point of production and sales, which is where the competition is in the new world economy," says Anthony Carnevale, chief economist with the society.[21]

The Southport Institute for Policy Analysis found that for some companies a reluctance to spend money on training was not the problem; rather, the companies did not know how to establish an effective program. The Labor Department has already begun several programs to meet this need, and further joint efforts with several industries are under way. Some companies and workers have already benefited from the National Governors' Association's program called "Excellence at Work," which helps states integrate their various job-training services.[22] The National Safety Council, in an effort to prevent on-the-job accidents, is offering to help companies create and direct

Table 7.1 **Guidelines for Empowerment**

- Adapt any empowerment program to the individual department or organization.
- Ensure that goals are appropriate, specific, and clearly communicated.
- Reward team success rather than individual success.
- Anticipate and resolve conflict between self-managed teams and the existing organizational culture.
- Supply additional information and authority as requested where feasible.

Sources: Adapted from Clay Carr, "Planning Priorities for Empowered Teams," *Journal of Business Strategy* (September–October 1992): p. 43; and James A. Belasco, "How Do I Empower People?" *Supervisory Management,* January 1992, p. 12.

cross-departmental work teams to select personnel, identify issues, conduct and analyze research, and set and attain goals.[23] Apparently, the main problem with government programs is not a lack of quantity but a lack of coordination.[24]

Suggested guidelines for empowerment are presented in Table 7.1. Areas of industry that are particularly subject to change require more varied training and constant upgrading of employee skills to keep pace with market changes. Aetna Life & Casualty Co., for example, recently trained many of its workers in business writing techniques. "New systems like managed care require our claims processors to deal directly with doctors and hospitals," explained Willima McKendree, vice-president of Aetna Education. "Because the conditions of the jobs have changed, employees need better skills."[25]

Herzberg's Two-Factor Theory

job satisfaction
A favorable emotion toward work.

two-factor theory
Theory that dissatisfaction results from the absence of hygiene factors and satisfaction results from the presence of motivating factors.

motivating factors
Job characteristics that create job satisfaction.

Frederick Herzberg's research led him to conclude that employees' **job satisfaction**, a favorable emotion toward work, stems from different sources than their dissatisfaction. According to his **two-factor theory**, dissatisfaction results from the absence of hygiene factors, such as adequate or agreeable

- company policy and administration
- supervision
- relationship with supervisor
- relationship with peers
- working conditions
- salary and benefits
- relationship with subordinates.

In contrast, satisfaction results from the presence of **motivating factors**, such as

- opportunity for achievement
- opportunity for recognition
- work that is satisfying in itself
- responsibility
- opportunity for advancement
- opportunity for personal growth.

Herzberg found that employees are most productive when the organization provides a combination of desirable hygiene factors and motivating factors. With these factors

Table 7.2 **Job Characteristics Rated Most Important**

Characteristic	Percent
Good insurance and other benefits	81%
Interesting work	78
Job security	78
Opportunity to learn new skills	68
Annual vacations	66
Being able to work independently	64
Recognition from coworkers	62
Work that helps others	58
Regular hours and no nights or weekends	58
High income	56
Working close to home	55
Work that is important to society	53
Opportunity for promotion	53
Contact with a lot of people	52

Source: Adapted from Patricia Braus, "What Workers Want," *American Demographics,* August 1992, pp. 30–31.

in mind, take a look at Table 7.2, which presents the job characteristics rated important by U.S. workers in a recent survey. Note the mix of hygiene and motivating factors.

Herzberg's theory has come in for its share of criticism—namely that a motivating factor for one person could be a hygiene factor for another. It has been shown that hygiene factors themselves do not motivate people; they simply prevent a decline in performance. But many people are, indeed, motivated by money (one of the hygiene factors), and others actually report that a chance for advancement (one of the motivators) leads to their dissatisfaction. (Perhaps these workers do not want the added responsibility of a promotion.) Further, some managers may apply the theory rigidly, not allowing for differences in individual needs. But the theory has been influential, particularly in bringing to light the importance of helping employees fulfill more than just basic needs at work.

valence
The value a person places on the outcome of a particular behavior.

expectancy
The perceived probability that a certain behavior will lead to a certain outcome.

expectancy-valence theory
Theory that the strength of motivation equals the perceived value of the outcome times the perceived probability of the behavior resulting in the outcome.

Vroom's Expectancy-Valence Theory

Victor Vroom, another content theorist, believed that people are most motivated to seek results they not only value highly but also think they can achieve. Vroom called these two aspects of motivation valence and expectancy:

1. **Valence** is the value a person places on the outcome of a particular behavior. For example, a person may highly value the prestige of submitting a winning suggestion in a contest for improving quality. Another may more highly value the award money that goes to the winner. Both people will be motivated to enter the contest.
2. **Expectancy** is the perceived probability that a certain behavior will lead to a certain outcome. Both employees in our earlier example would have to believe that their idea had at least a 50-50 chance of winning. Without this expectancy, the valence of the prestige or money, or even both, would probably be insufficient motivation to enter the contest.

As shown in Figure 7.3, Vroom's **expectancy-valence theory** allows a human relations expert to roughly calculate the strength of a person's motivation to do some-

Figure 7.3 **Vroom's Expectancy–Valence Theory**

Strength of Motivation	=	Perceived Value of Outcome (Valence)	×	Perceived Probability of Outcome Resulting (Expectancy)

thing to achieve a goal. Imagine that a fast-food restaurant wants counter workers to sell more add-ons like side dishes and desserts. It institutes a contest that awards two tickets to a rock concert to the person who sells the most add-ons in a week. Dave wants very much to go to the concert, and so for him the reward has a valence of +1 (the highest possible valence). For Beatrice, who only likes classical music, the rock concert is of no personal interest; still, she thinks, she could give the tickets to her sister, and so for her the reward has a valence of +.6. The reward has a valence of –1 (the lowest possible valence) for Thomas, who believes that all rock musicians are decadent and should be banned from entertaining. It appears that Dave is most likely to be motivated to sell add-ons.

However, expectancy is a factor, too. Let's say that Dave has been working for the restaurant long enough to realize that sometimes the manager just forgets to add up the results at the end of the week. He thinks the contest winner has a 50–50 chance of actually getting the concert tickets (.50 expectancy). Beatrice and Thomas are both new employees, however, and they have every expectation (1.0 expectancy) that the manager will end the contest with an award of concert tickets. Here's how the strength of the motivation would be calculated for the three employees:

Dave: *Strength of motivation = 1.0 valence × .5 expectancy = .50*

Beatrice: *Strength of motivation = .6 valence × 1.0 expectancy = .60*

Thomas: *Strength of motivation = –1.0 valence × 1.0 expectancy = –1.0*

As you can see, Beatrice is the worker most likely to be motivated by this program, even though she values the reward somewhat less than Dave does.

Another element of expectancy-valence theory that is often overlooked is that employees must believe they can do what is required in order to achieve the rewards. Workers must believe that

Effort → Performance → Outcome

For example, if Beatrice believes that she doesn't have the kind of personality needed to succeed at selling add-ons, the strength of her motivation will suffer. She might be more inclined to compete in a contest rewarding the person with the lowest amount of cash shortages during a week.

Notice that this theory is based on employees' *perceptions* of the value and achievability of rewards. Thus, those who determine what the rewards will be must know how their employees are likely to perceive them. Here again, individual characteristics will determine the success of the motivational techniques, since perceptions will vary from one person to another. Expectancy theory allows for individual differences to a greater degree than most other theories. Indeed, its application demands an awareness on the part of the supervisor of the individual characteristics of a given group of employees.

Adams's Equity Theory

equity theory
Theory that people tend to compare the ratio of their rewards to their work effort against what they perceive to be the ratio for others.

Related to the idea of *perceptions* in Vroom's valence-expectancy theory is the basic premise of the **equity theory** proposed by J. Stacy Adams. He defined *equity* as a person's perception of the fairness of an employment situation. People tend to compare the ratio of their rewards (salary, prestige) to their work effort against what they perceive to be the ratio for others. Their motivation, or lack of motivation, is linked to this perception.

Perceptions of inequity most frequently center on money but can involve such things as promotions or work assignments, too. Therefore, anything that is used as a motivator could conceivably be made ineffective by a perception of inequity. The best way to prevent such perceptions is open, clear lines of communication.

Skinner's Reinforcement Theory

reinforcement theory
Theory that people behave as they do because of the consequences they experience as a result of their behavior.

From the field of psychology comes **reinforcement theory**, pioneered by B. F. Skinner, which says that people behave as they do because of the consequences they experience as a result of their behavior. Thus, they keep doing things that lead to consequences they like and avoid doing things that have undesirable consequences. Since praise is a desirable consequence, people tend to do things that will cause others to praise them. Since disapproval is undesirable, they tend to avoid doing things that produce that result.

Reinforcement involves either (1) giving a desired consequence in order to encourage the continuation of a desired behavior, or (2) ending a negative consequence in response to a desired change in behavior. *Punishment* involves giving an undesirable consequence in order to discourage the continuation of undesired behavior.

behavior modification
The use of reinforcement and punishment to motivate people to act in desired ways.

The use of reinforcement and punishment to motivate people is known as **behavior modification**, also referred to as "using the carrot and the stick." For long-term results, the "carrot" (reinforcement) appears more effective than the "stick" (punishment). In fact, psychologists have found that repeated punishment can lead to an unhappy consequence called "learned helplessness,"[26] in which the punished person comes to believe that he or she simply is unable to succeed at the job and therefore stops trying. Another unwanted consequence of punishment may be increased turnover and absenteeism rates.

Skinner's theory has been criticized for being too rigid, ignoring the differences in individual personalities and needs. It also has been assailed on ethical grounds for "manipulating" people and on practical grounds for not considering the ability of people to learn to manipulate the system in return. However, it undeniably offers some valuable insights into motivation.

Quick Quiz 7.1

1. What are the five needs in Maslow's hierarchy?
2. What are the three needs identified by McClelland, and which one is involved in today's emphasis on empowerment?
3. According to Herzberg's two-factor theory, job satisfaction is caused by the presence of ____________ factors and dissatisfaction by the absence of ____________ factors.
4. According to expectancy theory, the strength of motivation equals the perceived ____________ of the outcome times the perceived ____________ of the behavior resulting in the outcome.

At Marshall Industries, an electronics distributor in El Monte, California, commissions and every other incentive (cars, bicycles, VCRs, or trips to Hawaii) have been discontinued. Instead, their 600 salespeople earn salaries. Denise Stoll, one of Marshall's star salespeople, says she prefers the predictability of a salary.
Photo source: © Philip Saltonstall.

Photo Exercise

Under the commission system, Denise Stoll's salary last year would have been roughly $400,000, which is over twice her current salary. Would you be more motivated by predictability or by possible higher earnings of a commission system?

5. In what theory do people compare their work situation with that of others?
6. In the "carrot and the stick" metaphor, the carrot represents ____________ and the stick represents ____________.

Motivating through Money

The various theories of motivation have led to the use of many different motivation tools, some monetary and some not. Even nonmonetary motivators, however, often work better when a monetary aspect is present. For example, people who would choose shorter hours or more appealing work over a bigger paycheck will still usually require a certain minimum amount of money as a motivator.

financial incentives Payments for meeting or exceeding objectives.

Financial incentives, payments for meeting or exceeding objectives, are effective motivators only if employees believe they are capable of obtaining them. Thus, if a theater company offers its staff a bonus for selling a given number of season-ticket subscriptions over the telephone, the bonus will motivate the employees only if they believe they can sell that many tickets. This brings to mind the expectancy factor in Vroom's expectancy-valence theory.

Often financial incentives are tied to the pay plan in one of the following ways:

1. *Piecework system.* Employees are paid according to how much they produce, that is, exactly according to the units of production.
2. *Production bonus system.* In addition to a base salary, employees receive a bonus for each unit of work produced.
3. *Commissions.* Payments are linked to the amount sold by a salesperson (or the amount billed for a job in some other professions). In other words, the employee receives a percentage of the total sale, sometimes in addition to a base salary. Many companies welcome help in deciding on the best type of commission plan, and books on the subject are available. See James F. Carey's *Complete Guide to Sales Force Compensation* (Homewood, Ill.: Business One Irwin, 1992) and Robert J. Calvin's *Managing Sales for Business Growth* (New York: AMACOM, 1991).
4. *Payments for suggestions.* Employees receive payment for any suggestions that are implemented by the company.

Diversity Highlights

Colgate-Palmolive's Pay-as-You-Grow Plan

Linking pay to diversity performance is just one small part of an overall effort to show that Colgate-Palmolive values diversity. The New York consumer products company makes the link between pay and diversity through its Executive Incentive Compensation Plan. About 900 of Colgate's 30,000 employees in 80 operating units worldwide are in the plan, including about 550 managers in the United States.

For managers in the operating units, two-thirds of their annual award is based on financial results. The remaining third is based on four to six individual objectives related to key, year-long projects. Because staff managers' jobs are more project oriented, there is a 50-50 split between financial and individual project results.

Colgate began its incentive program in 1985. Robert Burg, vice-president of global compensation, says that as the eighties ended, "we mandated that one of the individual objectives for managers in the United States who had significant people responsibility be cultural diversity."

Diversity efforts focus primarily on women, African-Americans, and Hispanics. While Burg feels significant progress has been made in attracting more women at all levels, he admits that progress for minorities "has not been as good as we would like. It's a constant struggle; we're renewing our effort."

Colgate's push for diversity is fueled by its chairman, Reuben Mark, who believes that things that are measured get accomplished. Thus the goal setting and results tracking that reward cultural diversity.

The reactions of managers have been somewhat mixed. While many say linking pay to diversity efforts is the right thing to do, Burg admits that some "think it's crass to include social goals in incentive plans.... Others have the attitude that the bottom line is what's important and let's not deflect from that."

Linking pay to diversity performance is not the right approach for every company, he adds. But at Colgate, "it's an important communications tool. It tells what our goals are. Putting it in our incentive plan—in our culture—reinforces our serious intent."

Source: Stephanie Overman, "A Measure of Success," *HR Magazine,* December 1992, p. 39.

5. *Money awards for contests.* Payment is made to the winner of a contest (for most sales, most new customers, fewest defects in quality, etc.).
6. *Group incentive plans.* Employees receive a bonus if their work group exceeds its objectives. Profit sharing and gain sharing are examples of group incentive plans. The pay-consulting firm of Schuster-Zingheim and Associates, Inc., advises more emphasis on this approach. Its managers point out that incentives for individual compensation sometimes pits one employee against another, whereas incentives for successful teamwork and collaboration are more beneficial to a company. They recommend tying everyone's pay more directly to company performance. In a program of *group variable pay* installed on Schuster-Zingheim's advice by a health-care organization, for example, managers were rewarded only if the entire organization succeeded in cutting costs and improving productivity and customer satisfaction.[27]
7. *Cafeteria plans.* Employees are allowed to choose between taking all of their compensation as salary or selecting among a menu of benefits (medical and/or dental insurance, dependent care, and other benefits). These salary reductions to buy benefits are free of federal and state income tax and social security tax.

Linking managers' pay to their success at increasing cultural diversity among their employees is one way to underline the importance of such efforts and quantify progress. For an example, see the "Diversity Highlights" box.

A growing number of organizations tie raises and bonuses to success in retaining existing customers and meeting established quality goals.[28] Many, such as Quaker Oats' pet food plant in Topeka, Kansas, pay employees a higher rate for learning additional skills, including how to operate forklift trucks and computer-controlled machinery.[29]

Exabyte Corporation gives stock options to every new employee, the corporate philosophy being that when a personal investment is on the line, employees are likely to work harder. Says human relations manager Richard Shinton, "It makes a powerful statement to the people we're recruiting that we want them to be owners." In addition, the company gives annual profit-sharing bonuses based on its success that year, matching 401(k) contributions, partial tuition reimbursement, and insured benefits.[30]

The possibilities for financially based motivators are probably endless, and they are usually successful unless they are perceived as being inequitable. Here is where the equity theory discussed earlier comes in. It is noteworthy, for example, that in certain studies of companies where wages were kept secret, employees usually overestimated what coworkers earned.[31] The result was a perception of inequity, with disastrous consequences for motivation.

The *pay-for-performance* concept that is receiving favor lately for lower-level and middle-level employees rarely exists among the upper echelon. However, it may be gaining popularity. Nearly half of the executives from companies reporting losses or declines in profits in Sibson & Co.'s survey received a decline in their compensation as well. CEO Robert A. Bardagy of Comdisco suffered a 27 percent cut that matched his company's 27 percent decline in profits. Robert W. Burdick of Yellow Freight System of Delaware suffered a 32 percent cut that reflected his company's significant decline in profits. Many opposite examples exist, though, such as Wilton L. Parr of Piedmont Natural Gas Co., who received an 80 percent increase in pay despite a 19 percent decline in the company profits.[32] A survey by *Sales & Marketing Management* found that 1992 pay increases at smaller companies were greater than those reported for the large companies in the Sibson survey. Of course, pay levels are lower in the smaller companies (averaging about $75,000). Since well over half reported basing bonuses at least partially on profit performance—and some on customer satisfaction or market share—the pay-for-performance concept is apparently stronger among these smaller companies.[33]

Some large companies are extending the pay-for-performance idea to their board of directors. At American Express, a director forfeits 25 percent of his or her $48,000 annual retainer by missing more than 25 percent of board and committee meetings. Other companies, such as Whirlpool, link stock or stock-option grants for directors to improved financial performance of the company.[34]

Quick Quiz 7.2

1. What factor in Vroom's expectancy-valence theory needs to be considered in planning monetary incentives?
2. How does Adam's equity theory tie in with monetary incentives?
3. Is the pay-for-performance concept currently more popular for lower- or higher-echelon employees?

The Motivational Toolbox

By itself, of course, money may not be a sufficient motivator for some employees. Many people need the kind of rewards that are involved in meeting Maslow's self-actualization needs. Others value their leisure time more highly than added money. They may, for example, have an absorbing interest outside work that makes them prefer a less demanding job. Consequently, there is more to motivating people than just providing financial incentives, and some motivational techniques work better with certain individuals than others. Some tools of motivation are the following:

- job redesign
- customer contact
- high expectations
- valued rewards
- performance-linked rewards
- individualistic treatment
- participative decision making
- feedback system.

Job redesign, customer contact, participative decision making, and feedback systems are covered in detail in other chapters.

High Expectations

Pygmalion effect The direct relationship between expectations and performance.

A fact of human nature is that we perform better when more is expected of us than when less is expected. The direct relationship between expectations and performance is known as the **Pygmalion effect**. It refers to the motivational effect of having high expectations of employees. The name comes from the Greek myth of Pygmalion, a king of Cyprus who carved a statue of a beautiful maiden and then wished so fervently for her to be real that she became real. Thus, you might say Pygmalion created his own "dream girl." The musical *My Fair Lady* adapted from George Bernard Shaw's play *Pygmalion,* borrowed the idea. Professor Higgins' expectations of Eliza Doolittle turned the raw material of the bedraggled flower girl into his image of a "fair lady" of the highest station.

General H. Norman Schwarzkopf, who came to prominence during the Persian Gulf War, has described how he put the Pygmalion effect to work earlier in his career when he was in charge of helicopter maintenance. He asked how much of the helicopter fleet could fly on any given day, and the answer was 75 percent. Recalled Schwarzkopf, "People didn't come in at 74 or 76, but always at 75, because that was the standard that had been set for them. I said, 'I don't know anything about helicopter maintenance, but I'm establishing a new standard: 85 percent.'" Before long, 85 percent of the fleet could fly each day.[35]

Valued Rewards

Several of the theories of motivation suggest that not all employees will value the same rewards at the same time. Employees who have a high need for achievement (McClelland's theory) or are trying to meet esteem or self-actualization needs (Maslow's theory) may appreciate opportunities for additional training. Employees who have a high need for affiliation or who are seeking to meet social needs may appreciate being assigned to jobs that involve working with other people. Sometimes the opportunity for more flexible working hours or time off is prized. Monetary rewards, of course, are universally valued, and so is praise.

Performance-related Awards

Whatever rewards the supervisor uses, they should be linked to employees' performance. Unfortunately, according to a recent survey of about 5,000 employees, less than half saw a clear link between good job performance and higher pay.[36] As indicated in the "Motivating through Money" section, however, the pay-for-performance concept is receiving increasing attention.

International Highlights

Budget's Fair Compensation Dilemma

Implementing a new incentive plan for employees of international organizations brings cultural differences to the forefront. While an organization needs a global vision so it can create a business strategy that crosses national borders, it also must understand the impact of local cultural conditions. For example, Budget Rent-A-Car utilizes a philosophy of "think globally, act locally." It has been particularly useful while trying to develop a new plan for its French employees.

Budget's incentive plan was designed to reward salaried employees for achieving corporate goals. Its intent was to align its pay practices with business strategy and compensate its international employees in a fair, comparable manner. But France's state-mandated, compulsory profit sharing complicated Budget's plans to create a motivating environment with its incentive plan.

Budget worried about how profit sharing would affect motivation. Factoring in required compensation before incentives were determined would mean a double bonus for managers.

Jack McEnery, corporate vice-president of training and compensation at Budget's Lisle, Illinois, headquarters, saw a twofold problem. "I think it's important that we avoid underpayment since that will be frustrating and may be perceived as unfair by employees. On the other hand, overpayment is both inappropriate for Budget and possibly demotivating. Why, after all, if you already get a high reward for moderate effort make an extraordinary effort?"

His counterpart, Sylvia McGeachie, vice-president of human resources for Europe, the Middle East, and Africa, agreed. "We must try to ensure in France that approximately the same level of pay related to profit is at risk as in other countries." Although she cautioned that France's high income-tax rate also would have an effect on pay, McGeachie's global experience led her to conclude that French managers would react similarly to incentives as did other Europeans.

Sources: "The Quality Imperative—What It Takes to Win in the Global Economy," *Business Week*, October 25, 1991; D. J. Carey and P.D. Howes, "Developing a Global Pay Program," *Journal of International Compensation and Benefits* 1, no. 1 (1992): pp. 30–34; F. K. Hahn, "Shaping Compensation Packages in Global Companies," *Journal of Compensation and Benefits* (November/December 1991): pp. 11–16; J. S. Hyman and R. G. Kantor, "The Globalization of Compensation," *Journal of International Compensation and Benefits* 1, no. 1 (1992): pp. 25–29; M. J. Marquardt and D. W. Engel, *Global Human Resource Development* (Englewood Cliffs, N. J.: Prentice-Hall, 1993).

The intricacies of motivating employees through financial compensation are a challenge for globally operating companies. See the "International Highlights" box for an example.

management by objectives (MBO)
A system that provides rewards when employees meet or exceed the objectives they have helped set.

Rewards must be linked to realistic objectives. As Vroom's expectancy-valence theory described, motivation depends on a reasonable expectancy of achievement. The **management by objectives (MBO)** system operates on the theory that employees are more likely to meet objectives they have helped set for themselves. Thus, *participative decision making*, another motivational tool in our list, is involved in MBO. Actually, all motivational plans emphasize the importance of objectives. Consultant and trainer Will Kaydos writes, "You only have to imagine a basketball court without baskets to realize that motivating someone without clear goals and measures is practically impossible."[37]

Individualistic Treatment

Everyone appreciates being treated as an individual rather than a nameless cog in the corporate machine. Simply knowing they are seen as individuals often serves to motivate people. For example, a more experienced employee may be asked for suggestions or delegated extra responsibilities. A lateral transfer may be offered an employee with skills in more than one area, benefiting the organization and enriching the job for the employee.

The idea of individualistic treatment ties in with our earlier discussion of valued rewards—certain rewards are valued more highly by some people than by others. Everyone in a department may not be equally excited about cross-training or overtime

Although Chevron has reduced its work force by nearly half since 1984, CEO Kenneth Derr and others in top management hold periodic meetings with employees to explain how business is changing and how this affects career advancement and security. This individualistic treatment has promoted employee commitment at Chevron, even when news is bad. Pictured at right is Derr speaking with an employee in New Orleans.
Photo source: © 1994 Philip Gould.

pay. Some employees might prefer shorter hours or days off. Wherever rewards can be tailored to suit individual employees, their motivational value should increase.

Although we are calling individualistic treatment a "tool" of motivation, it is a principle that underlies all human relations interaction. Faithfully adhered to, it would eliminate cultural bias and would ameliorate a number of other "people" problems in organizations. Moreover, where a motivational theory or program breaks down, individualistic treatment can often come to its aid. With a little adjustment here and there to accommodate individual differences, the problematic program may be made effective after all.

Quick Quiz 7.3

1. A team leader who sets high goals for team members new to the job is basing motivation on the ___________.
2. To be effective, rewards must be linked to realistic ___________.
3. What motivational tool is a principle of human relations interactions?

Summary

- **Explain the relationship between motivation and performance.** Although ability (work skills) is essential to performance, the best performance possible cannot be achieved on the basis of ability alone; a person must be motivated to achieve his or her best.
- **Name and define the major motivation theories and categorize them as content or process theories. Describe the difference between content and process theories.** Content theories include Maslow's hierarchy of needs (in which people satisfy physiological needs before security, social, esteem, and self-actualization needs); McClelland's achievement-power-affiliation theory (which assumes that through their life experiences, people develop needs for achievement, power, and affiliation); and Herzberg's two-factor theory (which holds that dissatisfaction results from the absence of hygiene factors and satisfaction results from the presence of motivating factors. Process theories include Vroom's expectancy-valence theory (which says that the strength of motivation equals the perceived value of the outcome times the perceived probability of the behavior resulting in the outcome); Adams's equity theory (which states that people tend to compare the ratio of their rewards to their work effort against what they perceive to be the ratio for others); and Skinner's reinforcement theory (which holds that people behave as they do because of

the consequences they experience as a result of their behavior). Content theories focus on *what* motivates people, whereas process theories focus on *how* people are motivated, or the way motivation operates.

• **Discuss the use of money to motivate employees.** Money is the primary motivator for most people; however, financial incentives are effective only if people believe they are achievable. Also, despite its importance, money is often not a sufficient motivator in and of itself; many people require rewards that satisfy self-actualization needs, or McClelland's achievement, power, and affiliation needs.

• **Name several types of financial incentives.** The piecework system, production bonus system, commissions, payments for suggestions, money awards for contest winners, group incentive plans, and cafeteria incentive plans are some types of financial incentives.

• **List eight tools of motivation.** Job redesign, customer contact, high expectations, valued rewards (which may include money), performance-linked rewards (which may again include money), individualistic treatment, participative decision making, and feedback systems are eight tools of motivation.

Key Terms

motivation (141)
content theories (142)
process theories (143)
hierarchy of needs theory (143)
achievement-power-affiliation theory (144)
job satisfaction (149)
two-factor theory (149)
motivating factors (149)
valence (150)
expectancy (150)
expectancy-valence theory (150)
equity theory (152)
reinforcement theory (152)
behavior modification (152)
financial incentives (153)
Pygmalion effect (156)
management by objectives (MBO) (157)

Review and Discussion Questions

1. Describe the categories of needs that Maslow identified in his hierarchy. Does this hierarchy seem complete to you, or can you think of any other categories of needs that people try to meet?

2. What are the three categories of needs that McClelland identified in his theory? Which category is strongest for you?

3. What are the hygiene factors and motivating factors described by Herzberg? Consider your current job or the one you held most recently. Which of these factors are (were) present at that job? How would you say they affect(ed) your level of job satisfaction? Your level of motivation?

4. John Lightfoot believes he has a 75 percent chance of earning a bonus of $100. Young Yu believes she has a 75 percent chance of qualifying for a raise of $1,000 a year. According to Vroom's expectancy-valence theory, would it be correct to conclude that Young will be more intensely motivated by her potential reward than John by his? Explain.

5. How can the content theories of motivation guide managers and team leaders in motivating employees?

6. Duane Pickering, who supervises computer programmers, expects each programmer to turn in a progress report by quitting time each Friday.
   a. Name at least one way Duane can use reinforcement to motivate employees to turn in their reports on time.
   b. Name at least one way Duane can use punishment to motivate employees to turn in their reports on time.
   c. Which of these approaches do you think would be most successful? Why?

7. In which of the following situations do you think money would be an effective motivator? Why?
   a. A men's clothing store announces that the top sales performer in the month-long fall sale will have the best shot at a management job in the new store it is opening.
   b. An obstetrics nurse with three teenage children can earn an extra $500 this month by accepting a schedule that involves working weekends.
   c. With sales down and a recession looming, M&G Laminating tells its salespeople to cut any deal they can to make a sale; anyone who can get his or her sales up by 10 percent by the end of the week wins a $5,000 bonus.

8. Describe the following pay plans:
   a. production bonus system
   b. commissions
   c. group incentive plans

9. What is wrong with each of the following attempts at motivation?
   a. A sales supervisor believes that employees appreciate an opportunity to broaden their experience, so she rewards the top performer each year with an all-expenses-paid leadership seminar. The seminar lasts a week and is conducted at a hotel in a city 200 miles away.
   b. The manager of a hospital cafeteria awards one employee a $50 bonus each month. To give everyone an equal chance at receiving the bonus, she draws from a jar names written on slips of paper.
   c. A maintenance supervisor in a brewery believes that if employees are qualified, they should be able to tell whether they are doing a good job. Therefore, the supervisor focuses his motivation efforts on thinking up clever rewards to give out each year to the best performers.

10. What is the Pygmalion effect? How can a manager or team leader use it to motivate employees?

A SECOND LOOK

Now that you have read about the various theories of motivation, what would you say is the reason that Cindy Ransom's management techniques at Clorox have been so successful? What motivational tools does she appear to use?

Independent Activity

(L)earning Praise

Think about a work situation in which you did a good job—whether it was raking leaves, writing a report, or selling shoes. Perhaps you went above the call of duty, working a double shift or saving the company money. Did you receive the praise and recognition you deserved? Why or why not? Write a few paragraphs describing what happened, and conclude with praise you would give an employee for doing what you did.

Skill Builder

Achievement-Power-Affiliation

According to David McClelland, through our life experiences, we all develop the need for achievement, power, and affiliation. You can further understand what motivates you if you are aware of the influence of these three needs in your life.

In your notebook, jot down the three needs in order of importance to *you.* Then write specific examples of the ways in which those needs manifest themselves in your life and how you go about meeting them. For instance, what specific thing do you want to do better than ever before? What have you done to accomplish your goal? Do you have a strong desire to maintain close friendships? How do you go about this (for instance, do you try to please people by doing them favors)?

Finally, think about how these needs would (or do) affect your performance in the workplace. What areas are strengths? What areas are weaknesses?

Group Activity

Motivating Coworkers (30 minutes)

Divide the class into several teams of at least four employees. The teams are workers in either a product or service company. Each team should have members play the following roles:

- a team leader who organizes and records activities and strategies
- a "problem" employee who needs to be motivated
- a coworker who performs above expected levels
- a coworker whose work is satisfactory, although not exceptional.

Using concepts presented in the chapter, the teams should devise strategies to motivate all team members to perform acceptably. Teams should use their creativity in making up the problems and solutions. After 20 minutes, the class should reconvene to discuss the problems and strategies for motivation.

Case Study

Wal-Mart's Wealth of Associates

In 1990, Wal-Mart passed both Sears and K mart to become the world's largest retailer. It did this by relying on a very simple formula: provide low-cost items with superior service. The company's late founder, Sam Walton, called highly motivated employees the key to his business strategy.

In his autobiography, *Sam Walton: Made in America,* he said: "I think our story proves there's absolutely no limit to what plain, ordinary working people can accomplish, if they're given the opportunity and the encouragement to do their best."

Giving that encouragement has taken many forms. For example, Sam Walton's frequent store visits included employee meetings that invariably turned into pep rallies as he led them in a cheer: "Give me a W...!"

In addition, the Bentonville, Arkansas, company's employee handbook is a primer on how to make employees feel important. Called the *Associates Handbook,* each page has the same header, "We're glad you're here," and footer, "Our PEOPLE make the difference." Homilies reminding employees to smile and be happy are posted around every store.

Success can be fatiguing: store managers earn $100,000 a year but work 60-hour weeks, including time on the night shift. For many of Wal-Mart's lower-level employees, earning low to average wages, happiness takes on a monetary flavor. Sam Walton may have been the wealthiest man in America, but thousands of his "associates" have also gotten rich through Wal-Mart's profit-sharing and stock-ownership plans. Every year, Wal-Mart contributes an average of 6 to 8 percent of an employee's income to his or her profit-sharing accounts, investing about 80 percent in Wal-Mart stock.

It has proved to be one of the best investments around: between 1982 and 1992, the value of Wal-Mart stock multiplied 45 times. As a result, hourly associates with more than 10 years at the company have profit-sharing accounts worth more than $100,000. Sticking with your job at Wal-Mart means a comfortable retirement fund. When Shirley Cox retired in 1989 after 24 years at the register, she was earning $7.10 an hour. She received $262,000 in retirement benefits.

Case Questions

1. What type of financial incentive does Wal-Mart offer? Why is this type of incentive recommended? How responsible has it been for Wal-Mart's success?
2. Are Wal-Mart employees motivated to work by love of the company or love of money? Why?
3. Is Wal-Mart satisfying both parts of Herzberg's two-factor theory? Explain.
4. Is a six-figure salary and the likelihood of a large retirement fund enough incentive for you to work a 60-hour week?

Source: Robert Levering and Milton Moskowitz, *The 100 Best Companies To Work For in America,* (New York: Doubleday, 1993), pp. 475–480.

Case Study

Saturn Employees Take Charge

Empowering its employees to make decisions was a big step, but Saturn Corp. got more than it bargained for when production-line employee Annette Ellerby admitted her work load was too light. It's almost unheard of for workers to admit they're underworked, but Saturn's approach to employee empowerment allows for and encourages radical statements and innovative ideas. The General Motors subsidiary is organized as a collection of small, self-directed work teams that manage everything from their own budget and inventory control to hiring, without direct oversight from top management.

The added responsibility appears to have made workers more accountable. Absenteeism averages just 2.5 percent, versus 10 to 14 percent at other GM plants. Peer pressure helps: team members must take up the slack when coworkers don't show up.

Saturn workers are also motivated to show a remarkable commitment to the company. When a malfunction in the plant's powerhouse interrupted the flow of crucial cooling water to the paint shop, a maintenance team worked 36 hours straight to make repairs. According to the president of Saturn's United Auto Workers local, "You couldn't get people to do that in GM."

A comprehensive training program has provided workers with up to 700 hours of schooling in basic skills, such as problem solving. Saturn hopes to have workers spend at least 5 percent of their work time, or 92 hours a year, in further training.

Empowerment does run up against some workers and managers who find it impossible to make the switch from the traditional hierarchical approach to a team-oriented one. Some have left; others struggle on. The pay gap between union workers and vice-presidents who share some responsibilities causes friction, too.

Still, Saturn's push to empower its employees seems to be paying off. Saturns have sold so well dealers can't keep them in stock. In February 1993, sales were ahead of those for the Honda Accord. Saturn did experience a setback in August 1993, with a recall of vehicles to fix a wiring problem. However, Saturn's teams are attempting to locate and fix the problems. The company is optimistic its efforts will pay off.

Case Questions

1. Which of the major motivation theories is Saturn's empowerment strategy based on? Does Saturn fulfill all the needs of the theory?
2. Do you think Saturn's empowerment experiment is successful, or does it still need to prove itself over time? Why?
3. Is the pay gap between union and management workers a problem that will grow as the former become more empowered? Why? Should Saturn offer financial incentives to further motivate its production-line work force?

Sources: *Business Week/Reinventing America,* 1992, p. 66; O. Suris, "Recall by Saturn Could Tarnish Its Reputation," *The Wall Street Journal,* August 11, 1993, A3, A7.

Quick Quiz Answers

Quick Quiz 7.1

1. physiological, security, social, esteem, and self-actualization needs
2. achievement, power, affiliation; power
3. motivating; hygiene
4. value; probability
5. equity theory
6. reinforcement; punishment

Quick Quiz 7.2

1. expectancy
2. Employees may perceive inequity in each other's salaries, which can reduce motivation.
3. lower

Quick Quiz 7.3

1. Pygmalion effect
2. objectives
3. individualistic treatment

CHAPTER 8

Principles and Styles of Leading

CHAPTER OUTLINE

Learning Objectives

- Describe the three styles of leadership based on the degree of authority retained.
- Explain McGregor's Theory X and Theory Y assumptions.
- Describe the basic concept of the Managerial Grid.
- Define situational leadership, and compare Fiedler's contingency theory with Hersey-Blanchard's.
- Identify the three characteristics that should be considered in choosing a leadership style, and give examples of each.

Ryka's President Lets Others Fill Her Shoes

Sheri Poe (pictured at left) admits she used to overmanage. The founder of Ryka Inc., a Weymouth, Massachusetts, athletic footwear company, today runs her company like a good captain, with a highly skilled, handpicked crew. But her leadership philosophy wasn't always so laissez-faire: she used to have a hand in everything; however, Ryka's rapid growth—sales climbed from zero to $16 million in less than two years—forced her to start delegating.

The turning point came in 1988 at Ryka's second Sporting Goods Manufacturing Association trade show. Poe was juggling responsibilities, handling the myriad details of the show and trying to set up and conduct interviews with retailers. "I just couldn't do everything myself. I knew that if I didn't delegate, some area in my company would suffer."

With some reluctance and not a few worries, Poe handed over show planning to public relations manager Laurie Ruddy. Poe's decision to delegate some of her duties was reinforced when show orders exceeded her expectations.

Today, Poe lets staffers manage their posts as they see fit and keeps tabs on operations through weekly checkup meetings with the head of each department. "Good employees just need guidance and freedom to do their jobs right," she says.

Source: *Working Woman,* March 1990, p. 77. Photo source: Courtesy of Rykä Inc. 1994.

Are you a born leader? Even if you're not, you can probably become a good leader by learning the principles behind good leadership and identifying the styles that fit you and your situation best. The idea that people are born with or without leadership ability, much as we are born with or without musical or artistic ability, has been largely discredited. At one time, the *great man theory of leadership* was popularly held—that leaders such as Alexander the Great and Napoleon inherited their ability, and that

Diversity Highlights

Ruppert Landscaping Plants Goodwill

A leader is one who can influence the behavior of others in desired directions, but sometimes, a leader is also the catalyst to allow others to accomplish what they want to accomplish. As landscape company president Craig Ruppert discovered, sometimes leadership is best attained by giving back to your workers—with their help.

Ruppert Landscaping Inc. in Ashton, Maryland, traditionally hosts a "field day" for its employees, combining motivational games and training contests in a day of fun, but serious, play. This year, the company paid tribute to its Hispanic employees by helping them give a gift to their families and their community.

"Our work force has changed dramatically over the past three years," says Ruppert, who oversees a landscaping crew that is 60 percent Hispanic. "It is essential that we communicate our gratitude to that portion of our work force."

Fifty-three of Ruppert's 60 Hispanic employees live in central Washington, D.C., less than a mile from the Lincoln Multicultural Soccer Field. Employees' children play there so often and so vigorously that they have worn out the grass, spurring local fans to dub it *La Polvosa,* or "the Dust Bowl."

On this year's employee field day, Craig Ruppert saluted his diversified staff by giving a $35,000 facelift to the field. He volunteered his firm's entire staff of 300 and donated 6,100 square yards of sod, seven shade trees, and 143 new hedges. Two other landscaping companies also contributed foliage.

Ruppert employee Marco Garcia, who lives a block from the field, summed up the pride—in self and in company—felt by many volunteers. The gift, he said, "is something no one else can do for the community."

Source: "A Company's Gift to Its Diverse Work Force," *Nation's Business,* November 1992, p. 12.

others must inherit theirs, too. Behavioral psychology proved otherwise. People can learn leadership skills just as they can learn many other human relations skills. As Sheri Poe of Ryka learned, sometimes being a good leader means knowing when to back off.

What Makes a Good Leader?

leaders
Those who can influence the behavior of others in desired directions.

A **leader** is one who can influence the behavior of others in desired directions. According to business professor Paul B. Malone III, an important distinction between managers and leaders is that a manager focuses on just getting a task done, but a leader focuses on getting it done in a way that gives employees a feeling of accomplishment and willingness to follow the leader again.[1] In other words, a leader sees beyond the immediate job at hand. The followers' feelings about that job need to be considered. Obviously, the best managers will be skilled in leadership.

Some employers have found that leadership is best attained by appreciating their employees' work and providing them personal opportunities. One such organization is profiled in the "Diversity Highlights" box.

Figure 8.1 shows the results of a survey that asked over 5,200 top-level managers to identify the traits they most admire and look for in a leader. The trait deemed most important was honesty. Note that effective communication is necessary to convey honesty. Sometimes a charge of dishonesty is simply the result of a lack of communication. "You said—" "But I thought—" "You *told* me—" are the sounds of the kind of miscommunication that can lead to such a charge. Trust is essential in good working relationships, and honesty is the basis of trust.

Honesty *is* the best policy, especially in leadership. Hughes Aircraft Company's new CEO, C. Michael Armstrong, proves the adage. A 31-year IBM executive, he knew little about missiles, aircraft, or defense contracts. He was hired from outside the com-

Figure 8.1 **What Managers Admire and Look for in a Leader**

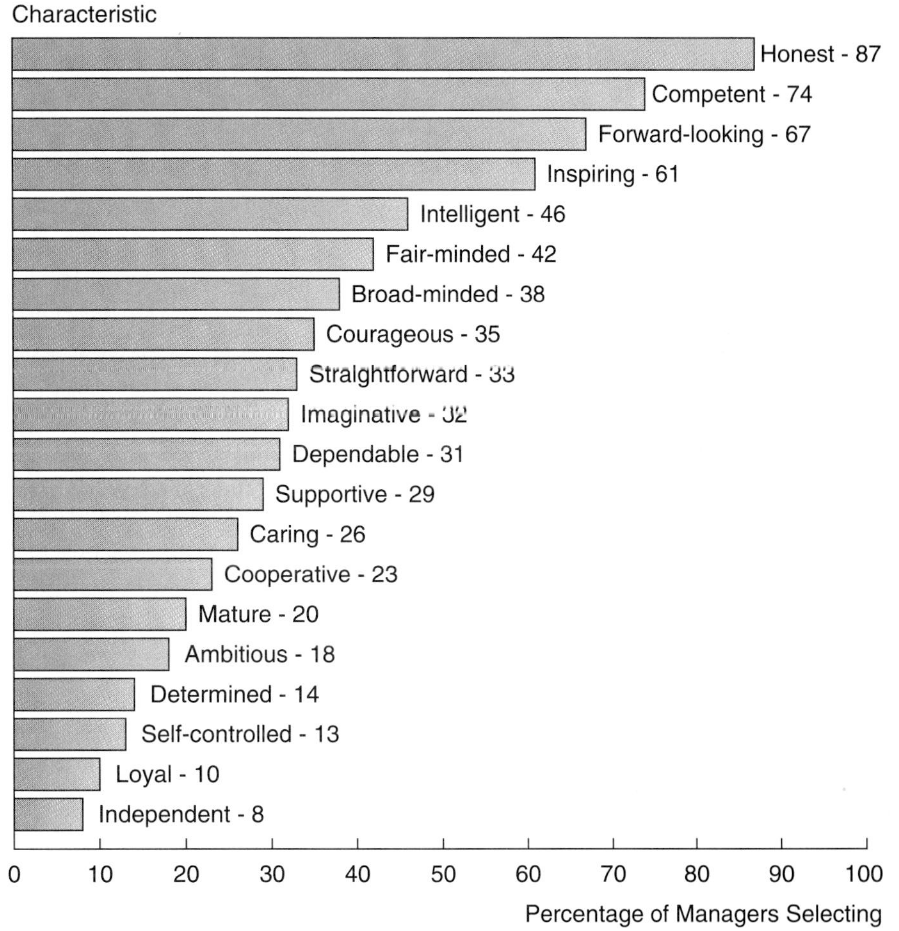

Source: Data from James M. Kouzes and Barry Z. Posner. "The Credibility Factor: What Followers Expect from Their Leaders," *Management Review,* January 1990, p. 33.

pany and was received coolly by his colleagues and employees. But Armstrong is an honest leader. The wariness at Hughes changed to enthusiastic acceptance. Jeffrey Heilprin, a manager director at Delta Consulting Group, which counsels companies with new leaders, offers an explanation based on his observation: "As much as charm, I'd say it's truth in the person" that helps win over subordinates. Confirms Anthony Iorillo, senior vice-president at Hughes, "He's straight up. He tells you what he thinks."[2]

The second most important trait in the survey shown in Figure 8.1 was competence. A leader must be worthy to lead. If you have been given leadership responsibility in an area where you feel unqualified, you are headed for trouble. Honesty is your ally here. Confess your lack of competence where appropriate and seek the counsel you need. Hughes Aircraft provides another example for us. Vice-chairman Michael T. Smith recalls that Hughes once hired a manager for its laboratories whose perceived lack of competence failed to engender the respect of researchers. The outcome was "organ rejection."[3]

Next in importance in the survey was the quality of being "forward-looking." Close behind was "inspiring." These terms bring to mind the observation of Paul

An entire group can be energized by an enthusiastic, confident leader. Herbert D. Kelleher (pictured in foreground at right), chairman of Southwest Airlines, has enthusiastically led his employees—the airline has won the Triple Crown: number one in on-time performance, number one in baggage handling, and number one in customer satisfaction.

Photo source: Courtesy of Southwest Airlines 1992 Annual Report.

Photo Exercise

What do you think makes an effective leader?

Malone, that good leaders focus on more than just getting a job done. A good leader checks the horizon as well as the next few steps and notices the well-being of his or her companions as they advance toward the goal. You will recall that Malone put it this way: "[a good] leader focuses on getting [the job] done in a way that gives employees a feeling of accomplishment and willingness to follow the leader again."

Social scientists who have studied the personalities of effective leaders have identified the following traits that seem common to most:

- *Sense of responsibility*—a willingness to be responsible for the work of others as well as one's own individual work. A good leader takes the blame for mistakes even when he or she did not commit them. If you have that attitude, you will try harder to prevent mistakes.
- *Self-confidence*—a belief in one's own ability, and in the ability of others, to get the job done. Such self-confidence should be justified by the "competence" just discussed. When self-confidence is well-founded, it is catching. An entire work group can be energized by an enthusiastic, confident leader who has faith in the ability of the group and himself or herself.
- *High energy level*—the physical and emotional toughness necessary to see a job through, even if it means longer than usual hours. The leader must attend to each of the workers he or she is leading as well as oversee completion of the project. A lot of energy is required.
- *Empathy*—an ability to understand the feelings and needs of coworkers and subordinates and thereby avoid making unrealistic demands or unwittingly creating resentment. Empathy can prevent a false charge of "dishonesty" by keeping communication lines open.
- *Internal locus of control*—the belief that you are in charge of whatever happens to you. This attitude is the opposite of an *external locus of control,* or the tendency to blame others or circumstances for any problems. It is an attitude that encourages a greater effort to take charge of events and prevent or fix problems.
- *Sense of humor*—an ability to laugh at oneself or the situation instead of losing one's temper when problems arise. Roger Ailes reports that among people who lose their jobs, the most common cause is personality conflicts, and the most common reason for disliking someone is that the person takes himself or herself too seriously. Observes Ailes, "It's important to take your *job* seriously. But people who take *themselves* too seriously tend to believe that their title or their intelligence makes them more important than others."[4]

Quick Quiz 8.1

1. How does leadership differ from simple management?
2. List the four most important traits common to most good leaders.
3. Self-confidence should be based on ___________.

Leadership Styles

Depending on our personality and our experience, most of us have already developed a certain leadership style—an approach that we automatically assume when charged with the responsibility for leadership. It may have been formed when we were entrusted with the care of a younger sibling, and it may consist of little more than a tendency either to "sweet-talk" or threaten someone into the desired behavior. Our inclination may even be to bypass the task of leadership and try to do all the work ourselves. Although people rarely fit into the neat categories devised by social scientists, it can be helpful to recognize yourself as leaning toward one primary style or another and then make adjustments as appropriate.

Authority—How Much Is Enough?

One way to describe leadership styles is in terms of how much authority the leader retains. Do employees get to make choices and control their own work? Or does the supervisor make all the decisions? To describe the possibilities, management theorists refer to autocratic (or authoritarian), democratic, and laissez-faire leadership.

autocratic leaders Leaders who depend primarily on their formal authority to lead others and tend to subscribe to Theory X assumptions.

Theory X assumptions Belief that people tend to dislike work and thus avoid it when possible, making tight control by a leader necessary.

Theory Y assumptions Belief that people tend to want meaningful work and can therefore be encouraged to use self-direction and self-control in accomplishing employment objectives.

democratic leaders Leaders who invite participation in planning from subordinates, delegate responsibility, and allow employees flexibility in carrying out their duties. They tend to subscribe to Theory Y assumptions.

Autocratic or Authoritarian Leadership. An **autocratic leader** depends primarily on his or her formal authority to lead others, issuing orders and instructions without much delegation of responsibility, and overseeing the efforts of others without displaying much trust in their ability or integrity.

Autocratic leaders operate on the **Theory X assumptions** that people tend to dislike work and thus avoid it when possible, making tight control by a leader necessary. The creator of the concept of Theory X, Douglas McGregor, believed it to characterize poor leadership. In contrast, **Theory Y assumptions** state that people tend to want meaningful work and can therefore be encouraged to use self-direction and self-control in accomplishing employment objectives. (Table 8.1 contrasts the two sets of attitudes.) It has been pointed out by others, though, that certain employment situations benefit from a Theory X style, at least temporarily.

Democratic Leadership. Democratic leaders invite more participation in planning from subordinates, delegate more responsibility, and allow employees more flexibility in carrying out their duties. They accept more of McGregor's Theory Y assumptions. More experienced or more highly skilled employees will respond far better to a democratic leader than an autocratic one. But, again, certain situations might not allow for the give-and-take of a democratic relationship.

Democratic leadership is inherent in the idea of empowerment. "Increasingly, involving employees in decisions that affect them is a requirement, not a luxury, for managers today—-the expectations on the part of today's employees are too great to do otherwise," comments Kenneth Blanchard, a management authority.[5] Autocratic leaders who cannot abide such *participatory management* may find themselves with fewer employment opportunities if this trend strengthens.

Recent studies have revealed a difference between the sexes when it comes to leadership. The "feminine way of leadership" is examined in the "Quality Highlights" box.

Table 8.1 **McGregor's Theory X and Theory Y Assumptions**

Theory X	Theory Y
People dislike work and try to avoid it.	Working is as natural an activity as resting or playing.
People must be coerced to perform.	People will work hard to achieve objectives they are committed to.
People wish to avoid responsibility and prefer to be directed.	People can learn to seek responsibility.
People's primary need is for security.	Many people are able to be creative in solving organizational problems.

laissez-faire leaders Leaders who expect employees to discharge their duties without prompting, to ask for guidance when they need it, and to perform well for the sake of their own self-esteem.

Laissez-Faire Leadership. The most freedom for employees is provided by a **laissez-faire leader,** one who expects workers to discharge their duties without prompting, to ask for guidance when they need it, and to perform well for the sake of their own self-esteem. Such leaders have complete trust in their followers' ability and integrity. Obviously, this degree of trust would be appropriate in some situations but not in others. An employee might be trustworthy but not capable of making the kinds of decisions a laissez-faire style requires. Or, under some circumstances, such a style might unfairly saddle the employee with more responsibility than his or her position warrants. On the other hand, certain highly qualified workers will bloom in a laissez-faire atmosphere, reaching their full creative potential and thus greatly benefiting the organization as well as themselves. Obviously, laissez-faire leaders thoroughly accept Theory Y assumptions.

coaching A leadership style that involves encouraging employees with lots of feedback and guidance.

The danger in laissez-faire leadership lies in the fact that most people need some encouragement—**coaching**—to fulfill their working potential. Even if an employee is performing adequately, he or she may need feedback or guidance in order to improve. The worker who is adequate under a laissez-faire leader might have been superior under a more involved leader.

Overview of the Role of Authority in Leadership. Years ago, Robert Tannenbaum and Warren H. Schmidt drew a graph showing the continuum, or range of possibilities, for the degree of authority a manager can retain. This continuum, shown in Figure 8.2, is still popular today as a way to picture the possibilities. Few leaders adhere to a strictly autocratic, democratic, or laissez-faire style at all times, and most jump around the continuum shown in the figure depending on the situation at hand. The *contingency theories of leadership,* discussed later in this section, are based on the premise that this is exactly what a good leader should do.

Theory Z

In the last decade, management experts have extended their view of leadership to include *Theory Z* as well as McGregor's theories X and Y. Inspired by the success of Japanese management, Theory Z has been proposed as a way of melding together the best of the Japanese and American approaches. It proposes to involve employees even more deeply and extensively in making decisions and give them much freedom in carrying out their duties. It emphasizes long-term goals, both for the organization and the employee.

Although Theory Z originally capitalized on the differences between Japanese and American approaches, the line between those two has in recent years become more blurred. For instance, the loyal Japanese company man who once toiled tirelessly in

Quality Highlights

Women in Charge

In the United States, the model for effective leadership has long been based on experiences in sports and the military. Such a model focuses on competition and winning at all costs. It assumes that you must be on top or be a loser—kill or be killed.

In a culturally diverse workplace, it isn't realistic to assume that the people in leadership roles can draw on these common experiences. Particularly noteworthy is the different set of values and experiences that most women bring to the workplace. A study of well-known women leaders, conducted by UCLA professor Helen Astin, found what she calls "a feminine way of leadership." Astin claims that women tend to focus on interpersonal issues and that this focus is precisely what leaders will need in the workplace of the future.

The most significant characteristic of "feminine" leadership that Astin identified was an emphasis on collective leadership, on empowering one's followers. The women leaders she studied tended to emphasize accomplishments as being those of the whole group, not just of the leader. Similar results came from a study at Purdue University, which found that the only significant difference in male-female leadership was that women tend to be more democratic.

In many cases, this leadership style is supported by a view that the people in an organization are interdependent, not independent of one another. A leader who believes in interdependence is more likely to respond to a problem by saying to employees, "Let's work out a solution."

While women have been rewarded by society for valuing humanistic qualities and emphasizing the individual, not just the goal, society hasn't encouraged men to manage in this way. Today's current emphasis on working in teams is helping more men adopt aspects of the leadership style that now characterizes women.

Source: Charlotte Taylor, "Taking the Lead," *Entrepreneurial Woman*, April 1992, pp. 42–47.

return for the guarantee of a lifetime job is now at risk of losing that job in the midst of Japan's economic slump. Conversely, if American business creates new opportunities for displaced workers, it could end up with an adaptable, flexible work force that is very competitive.[6]

Task versus People Orientation: An Organization Needs Both

Another way to look at differences in leadership styles is to consider what leaders focus on in making decisions and evaluating accomplishments. In general terms, leaders may be *task oriented,* focusing on the jobs to be done, or *people oriented,* focusing on the well-being of the people involved.

Of course, the organization expects that its leaders will care about meeting organizational objectives; however, it seems reasonable to assume that satisfied, motivated, cooperative workers will perform the best over the long run. In that regard, consultant Peter L. Thigpen has concluded that one source of the high level of commitment in the Marine Corps lies in the unwritten rules of behavior for the officers:[7]

- Never eat before your troops eat.
- Never bed down until your guards are posted and your troops are bedded down.
- Your job, up to and including the commandant of the Marine Corps, is to support the private rifleman on the front line.
- Never ask your troops to do something you wouldn't do.

The rules detected by Thigpen for leadership in the Marine Corps incorporate a people-oriented view together with a commitment to getting the job done. Every organization can benefit from such an attitude. Based on the premise that leaders should be strong in both people and task orientations, Robert R. Blake and Jane S. Mouton developed the **Managerial Grid** (shown in Figure 8.3). Along one axis is the leader's concern for people, and along the other is his or her concern for production. Five leadership possibilities are identified on this grid:

Managerial Grid
A device that identifies five types of leadership according to the degree of concern for people and for production.

Figure 8.2 **Possibilities for Retaining Authority**

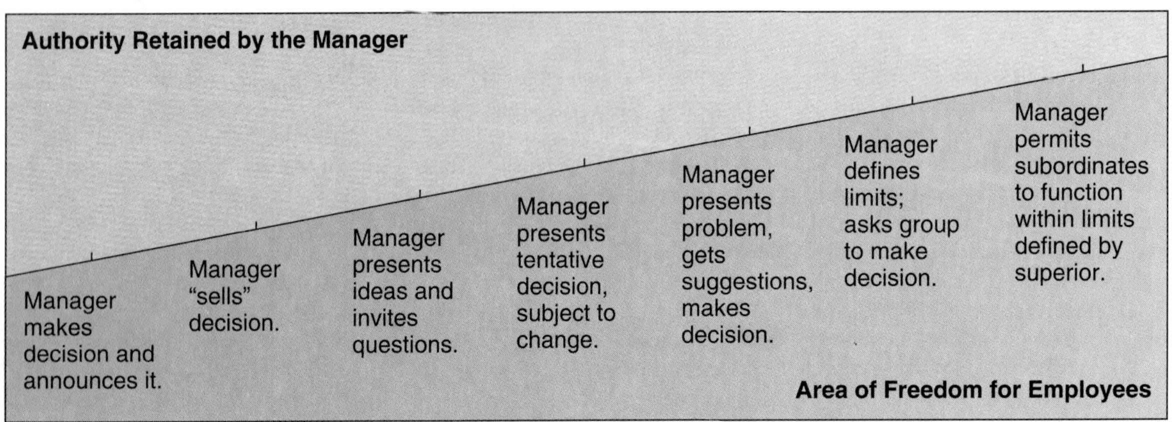

Source: Adapted from Robert Tannenbaum and Warren H. Schmidt, "How to Choose a Leadership Pattern," *Harvard Business Review,* May–June 1973.

- *Country Club Management*—low on production orientation and high on people orientation
- *Authority-Compliance*—high on production orientation and low on people orientation
- *Impoverished Management*—low on both orientations
- *Middle of the Road Management*—moderate on both orientations
- *Team Management*—high on both orientations

An autocratic leader primarily concerned with production would come under the "Authority-Compliance" heading. A democratic leader would have a people orientation as well, but not, it is hoped, at the expense of production. The grid concept is that both concerns are equally important. Blake and Mouton's research led them to conclude that productivity, job satisfaction, and creativity are highest with a "9,9" score on the grid, identified as a "Team Management" style.

Turn to the "Self-Portrait" exercise to discover your tendencies in leadership, and whether you are a task-oriented or people-oriented leader.

Contingency Leadership

situational leadership An approach in which the particular leader, followers, and situation determine the leadership style chosen. The term refers to *contingency theories of leadership.*

Just as some motivating factors are more effective with certain employees than with others, so are some leadership styles. Moreover, some styles are better suited to certain employment *situations* than others. When the situation changes, the leadership style should probably change as well. **Situational leadership**—in which the particular leader, followers, and situation determine the leadership style chosen—is generally accepted as the best approach. The term refers to *contingency theories of leadership,* stemming from Fred Fiedler's contingency model, shown in Figure 8.4.

Fiedler held that whether relationship-oriented (people-oriented) or task-oriented leaders perform better depends on leader-member relations, task structure, and the position power of the leader. *Leader-member* relations refer to the extent to which the leader has group members' support and loyalty. *Task structure* refers to whether there is a specified procedure to follow in carrying out the task. *Leader position power* refers to the leader's formal authority granted by the organization.

Figure 8.3 **The Managerial Grid**

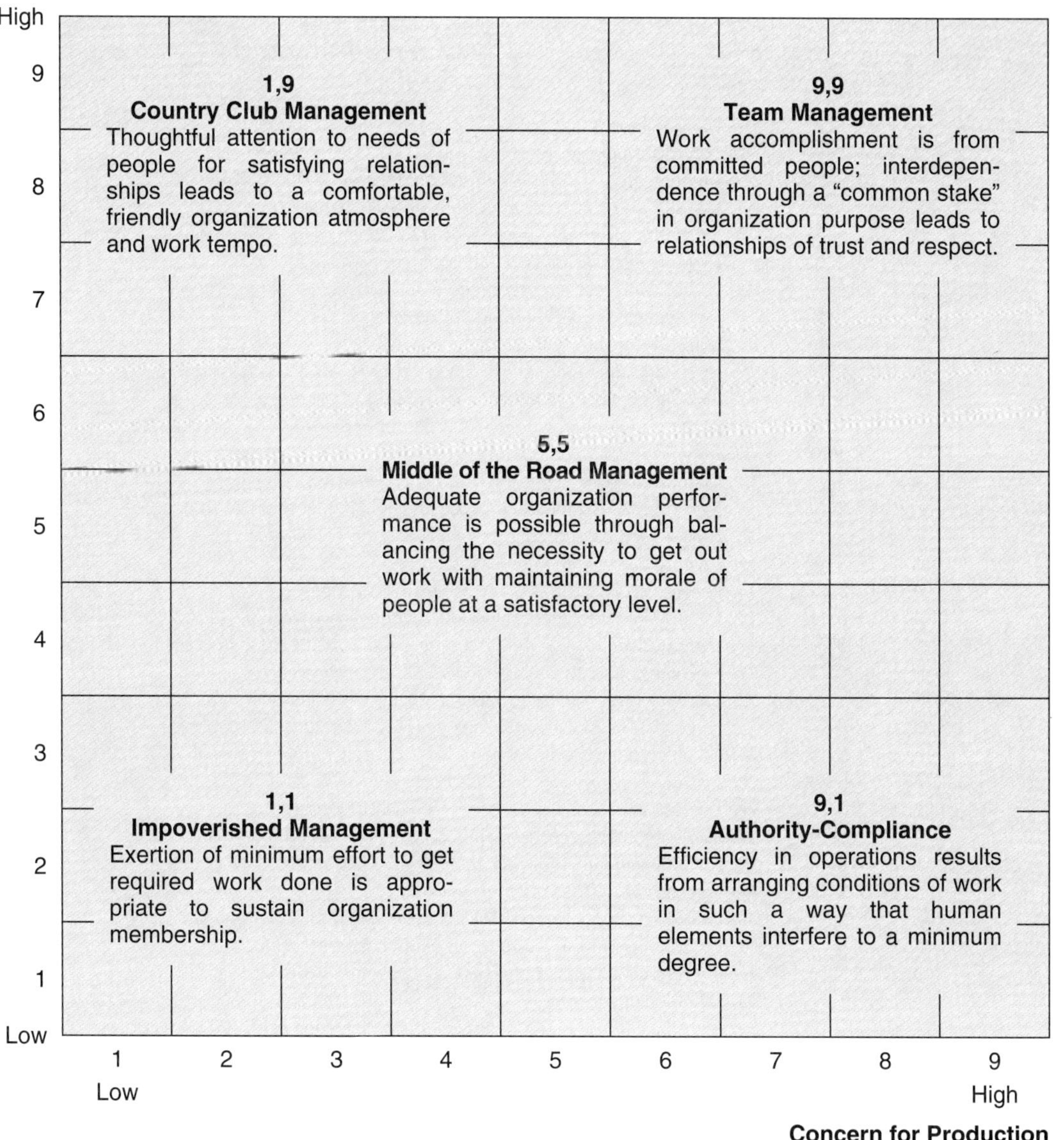

Source: The Leadership Grid® Figure for *Leadership Dilemmas—Grid Solutions,* by Robert R. Blake and Anne Adams McCanse. (Formerly the Managerial Grid figure by Robert R. Blake and Jane S. Mouton.) Houston: Gulf Publishing Company, Page 29. Copyright 1991 by Scientific Methods, Inc. Reproduced by permission of the owners.

Fiedler recommends that a leader determine whether his or her preferred leadership style fits the situation; if not, the leader should try to change the characteristics of the situation.

Another contingency theory, the *Hersey-Blanchard theory* of Paul Hersey and Kenneth Blanchard, takes the opposite position, contending that leaders should adapt their style to the situation rather than trying to change the situation. More specifically, this theory says that the leadership style should reflect the maturity of the follow-

Self-Portrait

What Is Your Leadership Style?

This is the T/P (task-oriented/people-oriented) Leadership Questionnaire. The following statements describe aspects of leadership behavior. Respond to each item according to the way you would most likely act if you were the leader of a work group. Circle whether you would most likely behave in the described way always (A), frequently (F), occasionally (O), seldom (S), or never (N).

A F O S N 1. I would most likely act as the spokesperson of the group.
A F O S N 2. I would encourage overtime work.
A F O S N 3. I would allow employees complete freedom in their work.
A F O S N 4. I would encourage the use of uniform procedures.
A F O S N 5. I would permit employees to use their own judgment in solving problems.
A F O S N 6. I would stress being ahead of competing groups.
A F O S N 7. I would speak as a representative of the group.
A F O S N 8. I would encourage members for a greater effort.
A F O S N 9. I would try out my ideas in the group.
A F O S N 10. I would let members do their work the way they think best.
A F O S N 11. I would be working hard for a promotion.
A F O S N 12. I would tolerate postponement and uncertainty.
A F O S N 13. I would speak for the group if there were visitors present.
A F O S N 14. I would keep the work moving at a rapid pace.
A F O S N 15. I would turn the members loose on a job and let them go to it.
A F O S N 16. I would settle conflicts when they occur in the group.
A F O S N 17. I would get swamped by details.
A F O S N 18. I would represent the group at outside meetings.
A F O S N 19. I would be reluctant to allow the members any freedom of action.
A F O S N 20. I would decide what should be done and how it should be done.
A F O S N 21. I would give some members some of my authority.
A F O S N 22. Things would usually turn out as I had predicted.
A F O S N 23. I would allow the group a high degree of initiative.
A F O S N 24. I would assign group members to particular tasks.
A F O S N 25. I would be willing to make changes.
A F O S N 26. I would ask the members to work harder.
A F O S N 27. I would trust the group members to exercise good judgment.
A F O S N 28. I would schedule the work to be done.
A F O S N 29. I would refuse to explain my actions.
A F O S N 30. I would persuade others that my ideas are to their advantage.
A F O S N 31. I would permit the group to set its own pace.
A F O S N 32. I would urge the group to beat its previous record.
A F O S N 33. I would act without consulting the group.
A F O S N 34. I would ask that group members follow standard rules and regulations.

T _____ P _____

The T/P Leadership Questionnaire is scored as follows:

a. Circle the item number for statements 8, 12, 17, 18, 19, 29, 33, and 34.
b. Write the number 1 in front of a *circled item number* if you responded S (seldom) or N (never) to that statement.
c. Also write a number 1 in front of *item numbers not circled* if you responded A (always) or F (frequently).
d. Circle the number that you have written in front of the following statements: 3, 5, 8, 10, 15, 18, 19, 21, 23, 25, 27, 29, 31, 33, and 34.
e. Count the *circled number 1s.* This is your score for concern for people. Record the score in the blank following the letter P.
f. Count the *uncircled number 1s.* This is your score for concern for task. Record this number in the blank following the letter T.

Source: The T/P Leadership Questionnaire was adapted by J. B. Ritchie and P. Thompson in *Organization and People* (New York: West, 1984).

Figure 8.4 **Fiedler's Contingency Model of Leadership**

Leader-Member Relations	Good	Good	Good	Good	Poor	Poor	Poor	Poor
Task Structure	Structured	Structured	Unstructured	Unstructured	Structured	Structured	Unstructured	Unstructured
Leader Position Power	Strong	Weak	Strong	Weak	Strong	Weak	Strong	Weak
Which Leader Performs Better?	Task-Oriented Leader	Task-Oriented Leader	Task-Oriented Leader	Relationship-Oriented Leader	Relationship-Oriented Leader	Relationship-Oriented Leader	Task- or Relationship-Oriented Leader	Task-Oriented Leader

Source: Adapted from Fred E. Fiedler, "Engineer the Job to Fit the Manager," *Harvard Business Review*, September–October 1965.

ers as measured by such traits as ability to work independently. It is called a *life-cycle theory* because it proposes that leaders adjust the degree of task-versus-people orientation in response to the growing maturity of employees as the project itself matures. That is, as workers gain experience and skill, the leader can decrease task orientation and increase people orientation.

Pitfalls in Leadership

One could argue that contingency leadership is only common sense, and perhaps good leaders have always employed it, whether or not they had a name for it. Sometimes, though, people are not aware of the way their natural style of leadership might be causing problems in a situation not suited for it. The theories serve to bring attention to the ways that a given style should be adjusted or situation adjusted to suit the leader's style.

If Daniel's caring, friendly style is being taken advantage of by people who could and should work harder, he might need the prompting that a knowledge of contingency leadership theory could supply. Suppose those under his authority have semi-skilled jobs that require little creativity. Perhaps a lot of freedom in carrying out their duties is not a good idea—at least not until the quota set for his department has been reached. Perhaps financial incentives might be employed along with a more authoritarian, task-oriented approach.

On the other hand, consider an office full of advertising copywriters and an authoritarian boss: "The rules are, no talking. If you people don't stop this chitchatting, we'll have to put partitions up around your desks!" A creative bunch, advertising copywriters can probably be led in better ways than that. Simply announcing a deadline for the copy due would probably do the trick. The "chitchatting" might well be inspiring some good advertising ideas. The authoritarian style simply is not appropriate in this situation. And the situation cannot really be changed to accommodate such a style.

The various leadership styles are prone to different pitfalls. For example, an autocratic leader is not likely to make the mistake that one college administrator with a different leadership personality did: In the spirit of democracy, he volunteered to be the

Teamwork Highlights

Estee Lauder's Sweet Smell of Success

Not every newly named CEO would put herself in a position to be kidnapped, bound and gagged, and delivered aboard a clanging fire truck into the hands of the opposition. It might not be a proper way to inspire authority and respect.

But Robin Burns is no ordinary CEO. In addition to holding the title of president at the Estee Lauder USA cosmetics company, she maintains an open mind and explosive energy—all at the service of her company, its products, and its employees. So like the rest of the Estee Lauder employees spending a week at the Vassar College campus, immersed in exercise, self-improvement, and corporate goals, Burns went through the whole drill, including predawn hikes.

Her vibrant personality and strong character are important in an industry of individual entrepreneurs such as cosmetic pioneers Elizabeth Arden, Helena Rubenstein, and Charles Revson. "When they passed on, so did their businesses. Others couldn't carry on in the same style," acknowledges Leonard Lauder, son of the octogenarian company founder, Estee. Lauder is determined to carry on and alter the company's staid, middle-aged image.

Burns is anything but staid. She is open and direct, believing that business life is simple and doesn't require plots or paranoia. Instead, Burns passes on a sense of wonder to almost everyone she works with, a feeling that anything is possible—at least for her team.

Burns promotes a team mentality despite describing herself as having "a very, very hands-on approach." She says launching Obsession when she headed the Calvin Klein fragrance line was the high point of her professional life, but it is also a testament to how she leads. Burns had put together a highly energized, fanatically devoted team. Kim Delsin, her successor as Calvin Klein president, says, "It was like the kids running the zoo. Robin had the ability to let her mind go—'What if we did this? What if? What if?'"

Burns herself is proud of the emotional bonding she felt at Lauder's Vassar seminar. "You know why? What we all wore there was sweats and T-shirts. Everyone. I loved that equality. It's what makes work fun."

Source: Martha Duffy, "Take This Job and Love It," *Time,* August 6, 1990, pp. 70–72.

target for a student pie-throwing contest. Since he no longer met the president's requirement for a "professional image," he was demoted to a counselor's job.[8]

The new CEO of an international organization went even further, allowing herself to be bound and gagged during a corporate team-building seminar. See the "Teamwork Highlights" box to find out why her behavior enhanced her leadership skills.

Another pitfall for the people-oriented leader is the temptation to become embroiled in controversial social or political discussions or to share confidences with employees that would have been better left unshared.[9] The excessively production-oriented leader, on the other hand, can miss important information by being distant from the people working for him or her. A good antidote is **management by walking around,** a style of management that involves just what it says—walking around the employment area and thereby making oneself accessible to employee questions and observations. The late Sam Walton, founder of Wal-Mart, made management by walking around his philosophy.

management by walking around
A style of management that involves walking around the employment area and thereby making oneself accessible to employees' questions and observations.

Quick Quiz 8.2

1. Would autocratic leaders subscribe more to Theory X or Theory Y beliefs?
2. What is the best way to describe Theory Z?
3. What is situational leadership?

Consider the Characteristics

In choosing a leadership style for a given situation, you need to consider the characteristics of (1) yourself as a leader, (2) the subordinates you intend to lead, and (3) the situation.

Characteristics of Leader

You can adjust your style, but only to the extent allowed by your personality. So it is helpful to know yourself well enough to, as Fiedler suggests, change the situation where you can to better accommodate your natural style and, as Hersey and Blanchard suggest, change your style as much as possible when necessary.

Darlene feels uncomfortable without clear rules, regulations, and schedules. June hates them. She would like to be free to come up with decisions on her own as needed, involving her subordinates as much as possible. "Just tell me what you want done and when you want it done, and then let me and my people do it!" is her attitude. Both women are good leaders—for certain situations. Darlene is great at getting her group of workers to meet short-term deadlines. They know just what is expected of them, and they deliver. June is wonderful at leading brainstorming sessions for long-term plans at her company.

Some of the characteristics distinguishing one leader from another follow:

- *Values.* What is most important to the leader? Is it the organization's goals? Being liked by subordinates? Feeling important? Doing a good job and helping others to do a good job? This subject is explored in depth in Chapter 10, on individual behavior.
- *Confidence in subordinates.* What is the leader's opinion of his or her subordinates? Does the leader subscribe more to Theory X or Theory Y beliefs? Does he or she respect subordinates' abilities and opinions? The answer will determine the degree to which the leader involves subordinates in decision making and planning.
- *Human relations skills.* How skilled is the leader at interpersonal relationships? Is he or she good at conducting a discussion group? At motivating subordinates? At explaining goals and procedures? We cannot escape the importance once again of communication skills.
- *Risk averseness.* How tolerant of uncertainty is the leader? How willing to take some risk? Delegating work and involving subordinates in decision making always involves some degree of risk. Some leaders are more comfortable with this aspect of leadership than others.

Characteristics of Employees

Dave coordinates the work of a dozen engineers. Dominique manages a secretarial pool of a hundred typists. Their approaches to leadership are bound to be different because their employees are so different. Moreover, within a given occupation, individual personalities may mean very different approaches to work, making different leadership styles appropriate.

In general, though, Dave's engineers are not likely to need prodding to do independent work. The very nature of their work is independent. Dominique's typists may need some encouragement to check the logic of any dictated passages rather than just blindly type them. Then again, some of those typists might automatically take as much initiative as allowed. A leader would be wise to modify his or her style accordingly in dealing with such subordinates. An overly autocratic style could crush their initiative and enthusiasm.

Keep in mind, too, that your expectations of employees could have a lot to do with their performance. If you believe an employee needs firm supervision, that person could begin behaving even less independently in response. If, on the other hand, you expect workers to be independent, you will probably communicate that expectation in many subtle ways and thereby encourage independence. The notion of a "self-fulfilling prophecy" (discussed further in Chapter 10) says that a person will tend to live up—or down—to the labels attached by others.

Occupation makes a difference in how a leader deals with employees or team members at work. Doug Morris, chairman of Time Warner Inc.'s Atlantic Music Group, leads a team that manages musical artists such as Pete Townshend, Stevie Nicks, En Vogue, Stone Temple Pilots, and All-4-One (in the photo). The music field requires employees to be more independent, but Morris still speaks of "empowerment" and "decentralization" to describe his role as leader.

Photo source: © 1994 Alan Levenson.

Photo Exercise

What special leadership challenges would you foresee in your chosen career?

Characteristics to consider in employees are as follows:

- *Need for independence.* People who want a lot of direction will appreciate autocratic leadership. Others most definitely will not. Some will find an autocratic style insulting and discouraging.
- *Need for responsibility.* People who are eager to assume responsibility will appreciate a democratic or laissez-faire style of leadership. For some highly creative jobs and for some highly motivated employees, the laissez-faire style will work well, but, as mentioned earlier, most people need some "coaching." People who eschew responsibility will be miserable under a democratic or laissez-faire style and will much prefer an autocratic style.
- *Understanding of and identification with goals.* People who understand and identify with organizational goals require less supervision than those who are concerned only with their own goals—unless, of course, their own goals happen to coincide exactly with the organization's.
- *Knowledge and experience.* The more knowledgeable and experienced employees usually fare better under a democratic style of leadership, and their input can be very valuable. New employees, however, are likely to need more autocratic leadership than others, although personality plays a part here, too.
- *Expectations.* Some employees expect to participate in making decisions and solving problems. Others think that a boss who does not tell them what to do is not a good boss. Cultural standards can also influence employees' expectations. For example, Arthur Edwards supervises Vietnamese immigrants at a computer company in California's Silicon Valley. To build more friendly relations with his employees, he took such actions as working alongside them and joining them for lunch in the employees' cafeteria. However, the Vietnamese culture expects managers to be more formal, and the employees distanced themselves from Edwards.[10]

Characteristics of Situation

There are so many possible characteristics of a situation that they could never all be listed. However, some major considerations are as follows:

- *Type of organization.* Organizations often lend themselves to one leadership style or another. If the organization expects supervisors to manage large numbers of employees, a democratic leadership style may be time consuming and unwieldy. If higher-level managers clearly value one style of leadership, the leader may find it difficult to use a different style and still be considered effective.

- *Effectiveness of group.* Regardless of the characteristics of individual employees, some groups are more successful in handling decisions than others. If a department or work group has little experience in making its own decisions, the leader may find that an authoritarian approach is easier to use. A democratic approach is best for groups that prove they can handle more responsibility.
- *Nature of problem or task.* Some problems are easily solved by the work group or individual employees without much guidance. Other problems or tasks might require that the leader retain more control. Consultant Hap Klopp cites the example of a Himalayan mountain-climbing expedition that fell apart because the leader asked the group to choose a route to the top and group members could not agree.[11] Unstructured tasks, such as generating ideas to improve customer service, benefit from the employee involvement sought by a democratic, people-oriented leader.
- *Time available.* An autocratic leader is in a position to make decisions quickly. Group decision making requires more time for discussion and the sharing of ideas. Thus, the leader should use a more democratic style only when time allows for it.

Quick Quiz 8.3

1. Name some characteristics of employees that should be considered in determining which leadership style to use.
2. Name some situational characteristics that determine leadership style.

Becoming a Better Leader

Companies like Monsanto are encouraging feedback between managers and their subordinates in an effort to prevent the kind of scenario that follows:

Anne Markle tried to be friendly with her subordinates, accessible, considerate. So she was shocked by the exit interview with Miriam Stoner, who had obviously dismissed her friendly gestures as an irrelevant phoniness.

"Your instructions are impossible to figure out," said Miriam, zeroing in on what she found most important, "and it's no use asking you to explain. Either you'll 'get back to me' and you never do, or you just say the same thing over again."

"I didn't realize—"

"And then you're never satisfied, no matter what I do. There's always something wrong with my work. I never hear about anything that I did right."

"Well, of course, you did a great many things right. Overall, I was very pleased with your work."

"You sure never showed it."

Anne reflected that she probably hadn't bothered to mention the things that were right. She had pointed out areas that needed improving, assuming that silence on other areas indicated approval.

"And some of these crazy changes that you wanted ..." Miriam gave an example of a change that from her point of view was senseless. Too late, Anne realized she could have explained the reason for the change quite easily—and thus changed Miriam's attitude toward making it. "Seems like you just wanted to make additional work for me sometimes."[12]

Anne Markle is a fictional character created by Adele Scheele, management consultant and career strategist, based on several real-life managers. She suggests the following questions for a management-assessment questionnaire designed to prevent this kind of situation:

1. Are my directions usually clear, or do you depend on your coworkers to help you figure out what your tasks are?
2. Do I often change my mind and alter your assignments after you've already begun them?
3. Do I usually edit your work without improving it?

Private discussions with employees can provide the feedback necessary to improve leadership ability.
Photo source: © Superstock.

4. Am I usually open to new ideas and innovative plans?
5. Do you think that I am disappointed in your work?
6. Do I provide constructive criticism?
7. Do you trust me?
8. Do I help develop your skills and promote you?
9. Am I available to you when you need additional assistance?
10. Do I create or operate in a crisis mode too often?

Employee advocacy manager Jennifer Luner has initiated a program wherein employees anonymously rate their bosses on a questionnaire, which is then shown to the managers for their perusal.

Even in companies without formal management-appraisement programs, it is possible to hold private interviews with each employee to seek the necessary feedback. Scheele recommends asking such questions as, "How can I help you perform your job better?" rather than, "What do you think of me?" She stresses the need to be an active listener, to note nonverbal cues, and to paraphrase what has been said in order to make sure you have understood the employee. In regard to the fictional Anne Markle, Scheele says, "Before Markle can figure out whether or not she is a bad boss, she needs to understand what a good one is. Recognizing that her greatest asset is a hardworking, enthusiastic staff, a good boss encourages, develops, and promotes her employees." Moreover, a good boss will regard employees' complaints as seriously as superiors'—and learn from them.

Although feedback from employees may be useful in improving one's leadership ability, a self-assessment can help, too. The insights to be gained from a study of personality and behavior cannot fail to translate into more effective leadership. Moreover, management literature abounds with information on all aspects of leadership. Many other chapters in this text tie in with the subject of what makes a good leader. Some final tips on becoming a better leader, used by ITW Paslode to build leadership throughout its work force, are presented in Table 8.2.

Quick Quiz 8.4

1. ___________ from employees and ___________ can be very useful in improving one's leadership ability.
2. According to Table 8.2, a leader should acknowledge the contributions of ___________ to a project.

Table 8.2 **Tips for Becoming a Better Leader**

- Recognize that you must confront incompetent employees, but do it in a way that builds their esteem. Don't seek to punish. Instead, redirect people to the desired behaviors by getting their opinion, agreeing on what should be done, observing the action, and positively reinforcing desired action.
- Acknowledge the contributions of everyone, not only the top performers.
- Recognize that all new employees are incompetent. They have to understand the job to perform it successfully. It's your responsibility to help them understand the job.
- Break job assignments into bite-sized pieces. In most organizations this means monthly interim goals that add up to the year's total.

Source: Reprinted with permission from *Quality Digest*. Based on A Foundation for Leadership, which ITW Paslode used to build leadership throughout its work force.

Summary

- **Describe the three styles of leadership based on the degree of authority retained.** Autocratic or authoritarian leadership retains the highest degree of authority. Such leaders issue orders and instructions without much delegation of responsibilities and oversee the efforts of others without displaying much trust in their ability or integrity. Democratic leadership invites more participation from subordinates, delegates more responsibility, and allows employees more flexibility in carrying out their duties. Laissez-faire leadership retains the least authority, allowing subordinates almost complete freedom in carrying out their duties, trusting them to ask for guidance when they need it and to do a good job without prompting or encouragement.
- **Explain McGregor's Theory X and Theory Y assumptions.** Theory X assumptions are that people dislike work and thus avoid it when possible, making tight control by a leader necessary. Theory Y assumptions are that people tend to want meaningful work and can therefore be encouraged to use self-direction and self-control in accomplishing employment objectives.
- **Describe the basic concept of the Managerial Grid.** The basic concept of the Managerial Grid is that the best leaders are equally strong in task or production orientation (focusing on the job to be done) and people or relationship orientation (focusing on the well being of the workers involved).
- **Define situational leadership, and compare Fiedler's contingency theory with Hersey-Blanchard's.** In situational leadership, the particular leader, followers, and situation determine the style of leadership chosen. Fiedler's contingency theory recommends that the situation be changed to accommodate a leader's natural style. Hersey-Blanchard's contingency theory recommends that the leader adapt his or her style to the situation and to the life cycle of the project and employees as they gain maturity.
- **Identify the three characteristics that should be considered in choosing a leadership style, and give examples of each group.** The characteristics of the leader, the subordinates, and the situation should be considered in choosing a leadership style. The leader's values, confidence in subordinates, human relations skills, and risk averseness should be considered. The subordinates' need for independence, need for responsibility, understanding of and identification with goals, knowledge and experience, and expectations should be considered. For the situation, the type of organization, effectiveness of the work group, and nature of the problem or task should be considered.

Key Terms

leaders (166)
autocratic leaders (169)
Theory X assumptions (169)
Theory Y assumptions (169)
democratic leaders (169)
laissez-faire leaders (170)
coaching (170)
Managerial Grid (171)
situational leadership (172)
management by walking around (176)

Review and Discussion Questions

1. What traits might be associated with successful leadership? Are there other traits you've encountered in your working experience that are not covered in the chapter?

2. The manager of an appliance store wants his staff to emphasize sales of a particular brand of dishwashers. How can he do this, using each of the following leadership styles?
   a. authoritarian leadership
   b. democratic leadership
   c. laissez-faire leadership

3. What are the beliefs associated with Theory X leadership? What beliefs are associated with Theory Y? What set of beliefs do you think is more correct?

4. Tamara Elstein heads the promotions department at a graphics company. During lean times, when layoffs are occurring, she decides to adopt a leadership style that is more people oriented than the style she normally uses. What does this change mean?

5. Is it more realistic to expect leaders to adjust the situation to meet their preferred leadership style, as suggested by Fiedler's contingency model of leadership, or to adjust their leadership style to fit the situation, as suggested by Hersey and Blanchard? Why?

6. In which of the following situations would you recommend using an authoritarian style of leadership? In which situation would you recommend a democratic style? Why?
   a. The supervisor's boss tells her that top management wants supervisors to ask the employees to suggest ways to improve quality in all areas of operations. Each department has wide latitude in how to do this.
   b. A supervisor is uncomfortable in meetings and likes to be left alone to figure out solutions to problems. His employees believe that a good supervisor is able to tell them exactly what to do.
   c. A shipment of hazardous waste is on its way to a warehouse. The supervisor is responsible for instructing employees in how to handle the materials when they arrive later that day.

7. Sam Bandur is uncomfortable when he has to tell someone what to do; he prefers a very democratic style of leadership. His solution as the owner of a small grocery store is to make his instructions as general as possible so that his employees will feel they have more control. At such times, he also tends to apologize for being authoritarian. Do you think this method of giving directions will be effective? Why or why not?

8. Why would "management by walking around" benefit a task-oriented leader and her employees? Which of the following situations would most benefit from this style of management?
   a. a fast-food eatery
   b. a commercial-loan office in a large bank
   c. a construction site
   d. the menswear department in a large clothier

9. You believe your boss is unfair and arbitrary in her treatment of you. How can you handle this problem?

10. Identify the human relations errors in each of the following situations. Suggest a better way to handle each.
   a. Joe Orlando's boss compliments him on the report he submitted yesterday. Orlando says, "Oh, it was no big deal."
   b. When Larry Jackson was promoted to supervisor, he told the other employees, "Remember, I was one of the gang before this promotion, and I'll still be one of the gang."
   c. The second-shift supervisor observes that the first-shift employees have not left their work areas clean for the last three days. She complains to her boss about the lax supervision on first shift.

A SECOND LOOK

How would you characterize the leadership style of Sheri Poe of Ryka Inc., using the various concepts introduced in this chapter?

Independent Activity

Being Boss

Assuming the mantle of leadership means trade-offs, giving up some of the basic rights of being an employee and taking on the responsibilities of leading employees. Think about previous jobs or organizations where you held a position of leadership. How did things change when you became a leader? What rights (such as the right to think of yourself first) did you give up to be a boss? What rights did you gain? If you have no experience in a leadership role, interview someone who does, and ask him or her to compare the pros and cons of the roles of supervisor and employee. What type of leadership style did he or she follow? Do you think it was appropriate for the situation?

Skill Builder

Ready, Set, Boss?

The "Self-Portrait" exercise assessed your leadership style. A more fundamental question, which should be answered first, is whether you are ready for leadership. Answer each of the following questions Yes or No.

1. Do you consider yourself a highly ambitious person?
2. Do you sincerely like and have patience with other people?
3. Could you assume the responsibility of decision making?
4. Is making more money very important to you?
5. Would recognition from others be more important to you than taking pride in doing a detailed job well?
6. Would you enjoy learning about psychology and human behavior?
7. Would you be happier with more responsibility?
8. Would you rather work with problems involving human relationships than with mechanical, computational, creative, clerical, or similar problems?
9. Do you desire an opportunity to demonstrate your leadership ability?
10. Do you desire the freedom to do your own planning rather than being told what to do?

Give yourself 1 point for each Yes answer. If your score is 6 or more, you might be happy in a leadership, or supervisory, role. If your score is 5 or less, you should think hard about your preferences and strengths before jumping into a supervisory job.

Source: Reprinted with the permission of Simon & Schuster from the Macmillan college text THE SUPERVISOR'S SURVIVAL KIT by Elwood N. Chapman. Copyright © 1993 by Macmillan Publishing Company, Inc.

Group Activity

Considering the Characteristics (20 minutes)

The "Self-Portrait" exercise and "Independent Activity" focus on your traits as a leader. But what about the characteristics of those you lead? Divide into groups of five or more. Imagine that each group faces the challenge of selecting and inviting the keynote speaker for college graduation. Designate a group leader, who should consider his or her own distinguishing characteristics: values, confidence in group members, human relations skills, and risk averseness. Each group member should assess his or her own characteristics as well: need for responsibility, understanding of and identification with goals, knowledge and experience, expectations. Based on these assessments, the group leader can assign group members various tasks related to obtaining a speaker. The group should discuss the outcome: Are members satisfied with their roles in the group? Did the leader delegate the most appropriate jobs to the most appropriate group members? Do group members feel that they would follow this leader again?

Case Study

"Renaissance Manager" Wins Respect at RCA

Thirty years ago, the title "general manager" meant what it said—the ability to manage anything. It was believed that an insurance executive could shape up a machine-tool company in no time. Today's leaders possess not quite so broad a palette of skills, sticking to their industry or core technology, such as pharmaceuticals or financial services.

Louis Lenzi is one of these so-called "renaissance managers." Based in Indianapolis at the U.S. headquarters of France's Thomson Consumer Electronics, he heads industrial design at the company's RCA television division. Lenzi's broad background of experience, including assignments in marketing, manufacturing, and engineering, brought him to the post, but he hasn't forgotten how to lead. When asked how he motivates people, Lenzi points to a life-size poster in his office of the Punisher, a horrific Marvel comic character, and starts spraying the room with a toy machine gun.

Levity aside, Lenzi says the key to working with people to get things done is to win their respect—especially if you have no direct authority over them. Lenzi accomplishes this by showing them how thoroughly he understands their jobs, skills, and needs.

For the past couple of years, Lenzi served on a cross-functional team of RCA managers to develop ProScan, a high-end line of TVs. Because each manager took turns being team leader, no one was really the boss. Lenzi had to win his teammates' respect not by wielding authority but by demonstrating a broad knowledge of the business.

The way he worked on the ProScan team contrasts with the way Lenzi was simultaneously handling his day-to-day job supervising 37 people designing other RCA products. "I had to build trust and confidence. Part of the trick is showing up only when crucially needed. If my people had an issue with the factory on, say, whether to paint the back of a TV—which the designers thought was a great idea and the manufacturers thought insane—I'd go to a meeting and raise hell where I had to raise hell and cajole where I had to cajole."

Difficult as it was working two jobs at once, Lenzi says the ProScan experience was valuable management experience. The line is a success, the team members have moved on to bigger and better things, but most importantly, he adds, "It made us all better generalists."

Case Questions

1. What style(s) of leadership does Lenzi use in his job? How did his approach on the ProScan team differ from that in his regular job?
2. Did Lenzi change his style or his situation when working the two jobs? Why did he make that choice?
3. Do you consider Lenzi a good leader? Explain.

Source: Brian Duma, "The New Non-Manager Managers," *Fortune,* February 22, 1993, p. 83.

Case Study

The Axeman Cometh to IBM

Lou Gerstner was only halfway through with what he once boasted was "the hardest job in America"—reshaping the bloated and heavily indebted RJR Nabisco—when he took on what some describe as the hardest job in the world: turning around IBM.

Gerstner's job was even more daunting than the financial reports revealed: Long the world's biggest business success, "Big Blue" had become its biggest disaster, losing $5 billion and half its stock-market value in 1992 alone. With the resignation of chief executive John

Akers, the world's biggest high-tech company turned to the first outsider in its 79-year history. IBM, which had always promoted company insiders to the top job, turned to Gerstner, who boasted not an iota of computer industry experience.

Although IBM isn't saying publicly why it went for outside leadership, Gerstner is using his appointment as a mandate for change within the company. He has turned to a diverse group of outsiders experienced in the automobile and banking industries, as well as politics, to help him manage the turnaround.

It won't be easy, but Gerstner is known as a task-oriented agent of change. He revived American Express's flagging credit-card operation in the 1980s before taking over RJR Nabisco in 1989 after its purchase from shareholders in the biggest leveraged buyout in history. He succeeded there in cutting costs and reducing debt but failed to produce much growth.

The job at IBM is similar. Analysts say that 100,000 more jobs will have to be chopped, on top of the 100,000 cut since 1987 when the firm employed 400,000 workers. But, as at RJR Nabisco, layoffs will not be enough. IBM has thousands of products but no discernible strategy to survive the quickening pace of technological change and competition engulfing the computer industry. Without a background in computers, Gerstner may not have the knowledge and skills necessary to develop a strategy. But he may be just the man to chop and trim a sprawling but unfocused company into separate, focused businesses.

Case Questions

1. What kind of leadership style will best serve Gerstner at IBM?
2. Which of the characteristics listed in Figure 8.1 will best serve Gerstner in his job?
3. How will the size of IBM affect Gerstner's management style? Could IBM benefit from a Theory X style of management, or would democratic leadership, in the form of empowerment, have a more positive effect? Explain.
4. According to Fiedler's contingency theory (see Figure 8.4), what situation best describes the one Gerstner inherits at IBM? Should Gerstner continue to be a task-oriented leader? Why?

Sources: *Time,* May 17, 1993, p. 21; *The Economist,* April 3, 1993, p. 64.

Quick Quiz Answers

Quick Quiz 8.1

1. **Leadership sees beyond the job at hand, but gets the job done in a way that makes people want to follow the leader again.**
2. **honesty, competence, being forward-looking, being inspirational**
3. **a belief in one's own ability**

Quick Quiz 8.2

1. **Theory X**
2. **a melding of Japanese and American leadership styles**
3. **Situational leadership occurs when the combination of leader, followers, and situation determine the best leadership approach .**

Quick Quiz 8.3

1. **need for independence, need for responsibility, understanding of goals, knowledge and experience, expectations**
2. **type of organization, effectiveness of group, nature of problem or task, time constraints**

Quick Quiz 8.4

1. **Feedback; self-assessment**
2. **everyone, not just the top performers**

CHAPTER

9

Stress Management

CHAPTER OUTLINE

Learning Objectives

- Describe the stress response.
- Contrast healthy stress and unhealthy stress.
- List some personal and some organizational stressors.
- Explain how personality type influences stress.
- Discuss the role of interpersonal relationships as stressors.
- Name some ways that organizations can reduce stress or help employees manage it.
- Name some ways that the individual can take responsibility for managing stress.

Pepsi Chief Puts the Lid on Tampering Scare

In mid June 1993, reports began emerging that syringes had been found in Diet-Pepsi cans. Within a week, more than 50 people would emerge with similar stories. Though the stories would later all prove fraudulent, they were starting to spread panic.

Craig Weatherup, president and chief executive officer of Pepsi-Cola North America, had already begun to sweat, but was reassured by a phone call from the commissioner of the Food & Drug Administration. "I'd never met David Kessler or talked to him," says Weatherup, "but it was clear we both knew the same thing: that for this to be happening defied logic."

They agreed that a product recall would not solve the problem. A recall would be a huge undertaking—and, says Weatherup, "dishonest," since the problem did not appear to be manufacturing-related.

When the TV networks called for Pepsi's statement the next day, Weatherup (pictured in foreground at left) was in control. He had his staff prepare video footage demonstrating the company's canning process. His own video appearances on the networks' morning and evening news shows displayed an earnest, straightforward manner that played well to the public. He also made a joint appearance on "Nightline" with Kessler, showing consumers that the company accused of wrongdoing and the government agency policing its actions were presenting a united front.

But the handwringing—and Weatherup's 20-hour-plus workdays—continued. He spoke with his boss, PepsiCo chairman D. Wayne Calloway, several times a day, and called him at home every night. Pepsi employees faxed updates to anxious bottlers twice a day. Some of those bottlers even opened their doors to show off their quality control to local consumers. And two dozen Pepsi employees worked the phones, taking calls from worried consumers, as well as various celebrity endorsers and supermarket chain CEOs calling to offer support.

By June 17, the FDA announced that there was no evidence of nationwide tampering. As the FBI began making a score of arrests for consumer fraud and tampering, Pepsi and its bottlers began running ads reassuring the public about the soft drink. By mid-July, Weatherup could even begin planning for a day off.

Source: Elizabeth Lesly and Laura Zinn, "The Right Moves, Baby," ***Business Week,*** **July 5, 1993, pp. 30–31.**
Photo source: Courtesy of Pepsi-Cola Company.

"Stress has become one of the most serious health issues of the twentieth century," proclaims the annual *World Labour Report* of the United Nations' International Labour Office.[1] It is a worldwide problem (see Figure 9.1), a big factor in absenteeism, turnover, accidents, illnesses, errors, burnout, and grievances among unionized workers. Certainly problems issuing from stress have always existed in the workplace as in the rest of life, but perhaps certain conditions of modern employment are exacerbating them. For example, California worker's compensation mental stress claims rose from 1,178 in 1979 to an estimated 35,000 in 1990.[2] Causes, in order of frequency, were as follows:

1. job pressures (69 percent)
2. harassment (35 percent)
3. being fired (15 percent)
4. discrimination (7 percent).

Without doubt, more attention is being trained on stress today as a human relations issue in the workplace. The ability of Pepsi executives to handle stress and work as a team was key to overcoming the tampering-fraud crisis. Stress management is a significant part of the health promotion programs that so many organizations have instituted. Human relations managers are expected to be experts on the subject. Organizations are asking them, "How can we reduce stress, and how can we teach our employees to better cope with it?"

What Is Stress?

stress
The body's response to environmental demands.

Stress is the body's response to environmental demands. Typically, a person under stress experiences a quicker heartbeat, increased blood pressure, and tense muscles. Although our response to stress may be physical, the stimuli causing stress may very likely be psychological, such as pressure to meet deadlines or fear of job loss. If we feel that there is nothing we can do to relieve the stress, we may get sick or discouraged, or may even turn to substance abuse to relieve our **distress**, the scientific term for excessive or undesirable stress.

distress
The scientific term for excessive or undesirable (unhealthy) stress.

eustress
The challenge that motivates us to reach for a goal.

There is actually a positive stress called **eustress**, which is the challenge that motivates us to reach a goal and adds excitement to our lives. All of life's major events are marked by either eustress or distress, or perhaps a combination of the two: first day of school, wedding day, giving birth. Numerous less major events are, too: learning to ride a bicycle produces fear and then, eventually, euphoria; being selected as team leader might quicken your heartbeat for a few seconds, especially if you have never served in that capacity before. So stress can be good or bad, healthy or unhealthy, pleasant or unpleasant.

Figure 9.1 **The Worldwide Problem of Stress**

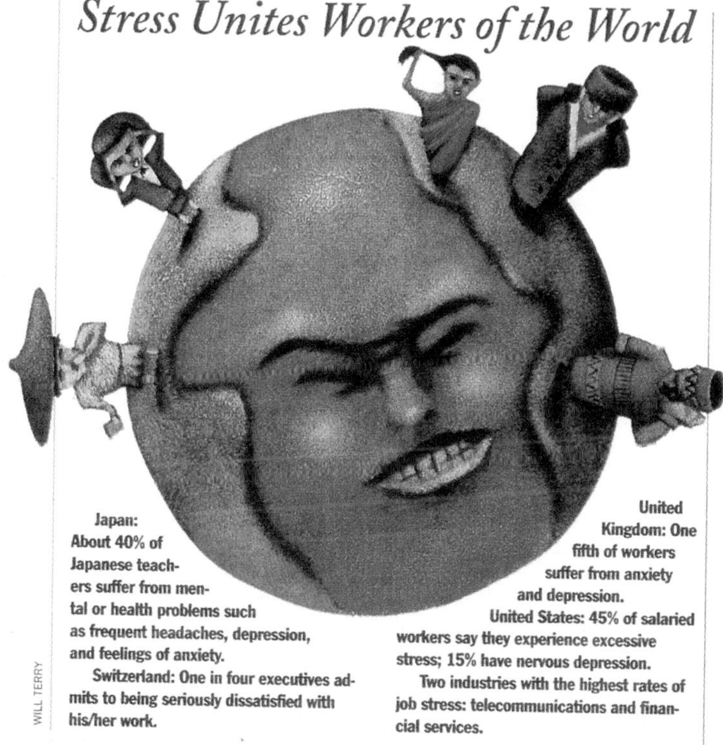

Source: REPRINTED WITH PERMISSION FROM PSYCHOLOGY TODAY MAGAZINE, May–June 1993, p. 15, Copyright © 1993 (Sussex Publishers, Inc.).

The Inevitability of Stress

Since stress is a response to environmental factors, its complete absence would leave us without a way to respond to the things that happen to us. Obviously, then, the healthy person must experience some amount of stress. No organization could design a job to eliminate all stress any more than you could arrange your personal life that way. Stress often translates into motivation. An employee encouraged to try for a promotion is placed under stress. If he or she succeeds in capturing the higher position, the first days on the new job will doubtless be stressful, too. Moreover, any challenge to step up production, reduce errors, or learn to use a new type of equipment is stressful to employees. There is simply no way to avoid stress at the workplace.

Finally, change produces both good and bad stress. Since change occurs often in today's workplace, through technological advances, mergers and buyouts, downsizing, and so forth, stress is bound to occur as well.

Physical and Psychological Aspects of Stress

Unhealthy stress can issue from either physical or psychological sources. In the workplace, for example, the physical sources of stress might include working in an uncomfortable office with too little light or too much noise, spending too many hours without a break at the computer, or performing a repetitive task that puts unusual

Figure 9.2 **Stages in the General Adaptation Syndrome (Stress Response)**

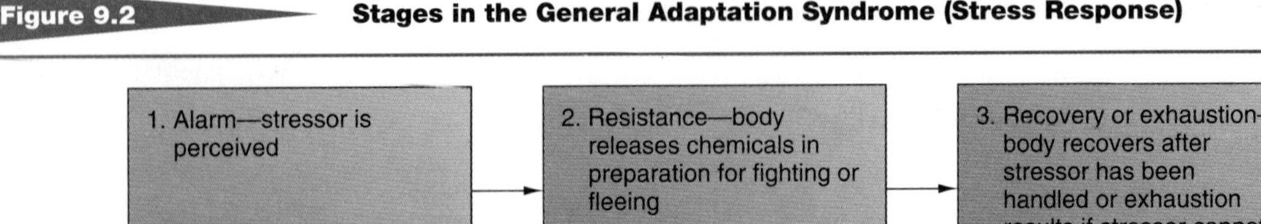

strain on some part of the body. Among the psychological sources are interpersonal conflict, time and budget pressures, and uncertainty about one's employment future.

Healthy stress—the type that motivates people and keeps them interested in life—can also turn destructive if it becomes too intense or too enduring. If an employee is pursuing an unrealistic goal, his or her physical and mental health may suffer. If a workload is consistently heavy and demanding, stress may heighten to the point of no return, in the sense that the employee can never relieve it. Consider an account representative who is galvanized into the stressed state by his boss's accusation, "How could you possibly lose the Clemson account?" He cannot *do* anything physically to relieve his stress. Even if he has a good answer to the accusation, his body is likely to suffer the stress reaction from being put on the defensive.

When a stressor is interpreted by the higher brain—the part involved in thinking, learning, emotions, and self-consciousness—as being threatening in some way, it signals the lower brain, which controls basic bodily functions. Therefore, the lower brain prepares the body for self-preservation. It sends forth a stress hormone that signals the adrenal glands to release adrenaline, causing muscles to tense, heart to pound, and so forth. A rapid heartbeat increases circulation, rapid breathing increases the rate of oxygen movement into the body, and an elevated level of blood glucose increases the energy available to active cells. Thus, the body is ready for strenuous physical activity.

general adaptation syndrome
Generalized reactions to any stressor; also known as the *stress response.*

This is the first stage of the **general adaptation syndrome**, or *stress response,* of all animals, which consists of generalized reactions to any stressor (see Figure 9.2). Unfortunately, human beings react in this physical way to purely psychological stressors; our lower brain does not distinguish between the two types of threat.

The *alarm* stage of the general adaptation syndrome is followed by the *resistance* stage, wherein the body tries to restore itself to its normal state by fighting or escaping the danger. Hormones are released during this stage to help the body cope. Keep in mind that these hormones can start flowing at the sound of a boss's angry voice or the approach of a deadline.

Finally comes the third stage of the syndrome, *recovery* or *exhaustion,* since the body cannot escape or fight the stressor forever. If the stressor cannot be eliminated or evaded, the body eventually reaches a state of exhaustion in which it is susceptible to various physical and psychological problems.

Unhealthy stress is often associated with such physical symptoms as headaches, high blood pressure, asthma, cardiovascular problems, and even a weakened immune system.[3] High blood pressure (hypertension) alone is estimated to account for a $20 billion loss in wages and productivity per year.[4] By the same token, many of the suggested ways of managing stress (detailed later in this chapter) employ the principle of doing something physical—such as taking a brisk walk at lunch—to help dissipate the chemicals that are physiologically responsible for stress.

frustration
An unsettled, dissatisfied feeling that produces a number of negative reactions.

Among the psychological responses to unhealthy stress are severe psychological problems and substance abuse. Another is **frustration**, an unsettled, dissatisfied feeling that produces a number of negative responses:[5]

- *Rationalization:* "Everybody else uses the phone for personal long-distance calls, so why shouldn't I?"
- *Compensation:* "I'll work twice as hard as those people with college degrees!"
- *Negativism:* "Sure, his report covers all the necessary topics and was submitted on time, but I found 17 typographical errors."
- *Resignation:* "Nobody pays any attention to my suggestions, so I'm just going to stop trying to solve the problems in our department."
- *Flight:* "I've been passed over for promotion twice now; I'm going to look for another job."
- *Repression:* "Oh dear. I forgot to tell my boss that those parts we need tomorrow haven't arrived yet."
- *Pseudostupidity:* "I'll just tell them that I forgot to call Elaine Briden, and then maybe they'll get somebody else to do their dirty work."
- *Obsessive thinking:* "Why didn't Steve say hello in the lobby this morning? I wonder if he's mad at me for contradicting him yesterday. Maybe he decided to give that project to somebody else. Or maybe he's going to ask that I be transferred to another department. I wonder if I should go ask him. Or maybe I should just go directly to Ms. Katz and tell her that Steve has been treating me unfairly lately. Or maybe ..."
- *Displacement:* "I'm sick and tired of being blamed for all the mistakes around here.... What are those nincompoops on my staff doing now?"
- *Conversion:* "I know I have to fire Walter, but I have a splitting headache. I guess I'll have to fire him tomorrow."

burnout
A state of emotional exhaustion in which motivation is lost and continued high performance is rendered impossible; it results from ongoing, excessive stress.

Unhealthy stress can also drive a good employee into that state of emotional exhaustion known as **burnout**, where motivation is lost and continued high performance is rendered impossible. A recent survey reported three out of four American workers as being "stressed out..., many to the point of burnout."[6] Typically, burnout occurs in three stages:

1. The employee feels emotionally exhausted.
2. The employee's perceptions of others become calloused.
3. The employee views his or her effectiveness negatively.

Being burned out is worse than just needing a vacation. Therefore, it is important to cope with stress before it leads to burnout. Those in the helping professions, such as health care and teaching, are especially vulnerable, since burnout is most likely to occur when people feel that they are giving of themselves all the time, with little or no returns.

Some of the workplace results of unhealthy stress are as follows:

- decline in work performance
- increase in sick days
- increase in errors and accidents
- moodiness and irritability
- fatigue
- loss of enthusiasm
- overly aggressive behavior
- difficulty making decisions
- family problems
- apparent loss of concern for others' feelings
- feeling of inadequacy to help others or oneself
- despair over the perceived impossibility of getting the work done in time.

Physical reactions to stress vary much less from one individual to another than the psychological reactions that lead to the physical ones. How we interpret various stressors is key. A new job assignment produces pleasant exhilaration (eustress) in one person, fear and anxiety (distress) in another. The way an organization presents the assignment may also make the difference in the kind of stress it produces. For example, if plenty of support is made available—if information sources are identified and advice offered—the employee can enjoy the challenge with a tingle of anticipation rather than dread of failure.

Quick Quiz 9.1

1. What are the scientific terms for healthy stress and unhealthy stress?
2. Name the three parts of the general adaptation syndrome, or stress response.

What Causes Stress?

The causes of stress can be categorized as personal or organizational. In other words, they can arise from an employee's personal life, or even personality type, or they can arise from his or her employment situation. The organization can do much to relieve both kinds of stress.

Personal Stressors

Stressors that arise from events in one's personal life include such things as work/family pressures resulting from societal changes and from individual life changes, physical or mental illness, and personal choices regarding career development and personal growth. In addition to that, personality type can be a cause of stress in the sense that some events act as stressors for some people but as motivators for others.

locus of control
Extent to which people feel in control of circumstances. Those with an external locus of control believe they are largely controlled by external forces; those with an internal locus of control believe they have much control over their circumstances.

Locus of Control. The **locus of control** is internal in people who believe they have much control over their circumstances and external in those who believe they are largely controlled by external forces. Generally, the latter type is more prone to stress, although it has been noted that "some people can find strength through strong spiritual or religious beliefs. In this case, they believe that the control starts from outside them, but they still benefit because they believe ... there *is* some control somewhere on their behalf over what is happening."[7]

The feeling that things are out of control causes a person to perceive challenges as threats. Thus, a reward system that elicits high performance from employees with an internal locus of control may place those with an external locus under almost unbearable stress—they want the rewards but they do not believe it is within their control to obtain them; thus, they tend not to strive for the rewards and then feel like failures for not obtaining them. People with an internal locus tend to thrive under an appropriate degree of stress, actually finding it stimulating, since they believe they have the capability within themselves of meeting it. Of course, the actual characteristics of a job come into play here. Sometimes too much of the job truly is out of the employee's control. In this case, excessive, harmful stress is unavoidable.

A heart attack is sometimes the ultimate expression of stress, and studies have found that people are more likely to have heart attacks if they hold high-demand, low-control jobs.[8] In other words, these people work under demanding conditions, but they have relatively little control over those conditions. Table 9.1 shows some of the most and least stressful jobs. Note that the nature of the least stressful jobs obviously offers more control over the work.

Type A
Classification describing people who are aggressive, competitive, and hard driving.

Personality Types A and B. One well-known way of classifying personalities is according to **Type A**, representing aggressive, competitive, hard-driving people, and

Table 9.1 **Most and Least Stressful Jobs***

Most Stressful	Least Stressful
Inner-city schoolteacher	Forest ranger
Security trader	Craftsperson
Air-traffic controller	Natural scientist
Medical intern	Architect
Newspaper editor	Actuary
Assembly-line worker	Librarian
Firefighter	Barber
Police officer	
Bus driver	

Source: Adapted from "In Search of Workplace Serenity," *Denver Post,* July 22, 1991, p. 8B; Steve Johnson, "You Think You've Got Stress—Join the Club," *Chicago Tribune,* March 25, 1993, p. 1.

*Note: No rank order is implied.

Type B
Classification describing people who are more easygoing and relaxed than Type A people, enjoy more non-work-related activities, and are more flexible in their attitude toward work.

Type B, representing more easygoing, relaxed people, who enjoy more non-work-related activities and are more flexible in their attitude toward work (see Table 9.2). Type A personalities are more prone to stress than Type B. Both types have their advantages and disadvantages in the workplace. Type A people might work longer hours and push harder to meet a deadline, but Type B people might have a better effect on coworkers or might make decisions with a cooler head.

One study of Type A employees found that they tend to achieve high job performance and satisfaction provided they perceive themselves as having adequate control over their job circumstances.[9] Their health reports were poorer than those for Type B,[10] however, indicating they indeed, as theorized, do suffer more from stress. Moreover, their characteristic impatience tends to create stress in their coworkers! For this reason, Type A employees are usually not the best choice for high-level positions. Certainly, Type B is better suited to be a human relations manager.

Although this theory has been disputed by some experts, and we can probably all think of some people who seem to combine Type A and Type B characteristics depending on the circumstances, it can be useful as a starting point to evaluate different approaches to work. Clearly, some Type A attitudes have value: when there is an emergency, Type A Kelly can be counted on to rev up her work group and get the job done, no matter what, whereas Type B Meghan might be sidetracked by a personal consideration or convey a less-than-emergency feeling to those in her work group. Then again, Type A attitudes if carried to the extreme can actually make a person prone to hostility. It is reported that Michael Milkin drove many of his coworkers into a severe state of stress through his hard-driving, critical attitude; people attempting to leave after "only" 12 hours of work, or, worse yet, requesting sick leave, were the targets of Milkin's hostility.[11] If one of Kelly's work group seems to be holding up the schedule, she might feel personal anger toward that person and show it by lashing out with sarcasm or perhaps taking a kind of revenge via an unfair job assignment in the future. And if she perceives herself as holding up the schedule, that hostility may be turned inward.

Self-Esteem. People with high self-esteem seem to handle stress better than those lacking it, often perceiving a stressful situation as a challenge and thus enjoying it rather than suffering from it.[12] A 10-year study of Illinois Bell executives found that those who adapted best to stress had "different worldviews than others, tending to be

Table 9.2 Behavior Patterns Associated with Type A and Type B Personalities

Type A	Type B
Moving, walking, eating rapidly	Having varied interests
Feeling impatient with people who move slower than you	Taking a relaxed but active approach to life.
Feeling impatient when others talk about something that is not of interest to you	
Doing two or three things at the same time	
Feeling unable to relax or to stop working	
Trying to get more and more done in less and less time	

Source: Adapted from Meyer Friedman and Ray H. Rosenman, *Type A Behavior and Your Heart* (New York: Fawcett Crest, 1974), pp. 100–101, summarized in Jane Whitney Gibson, *The Supervisory Challenge: Principles and Practices* (Columbus, Ohio: Merrill Publishing, 1990), p. 309.

committed to the world and their place in it—an attitude requiring self-esteem—rather than alienated from it, and to *see changes in life as challenges to be risen to, rather than threats* [emphasis added]."[13]

Even if the stress is too inappropriate to be viewed in a positive light, people with self-esteem are likely to weather it better, since they are less likely to worry over their performance. Thus, Carlos may shrug and think, "Oh, well, I did the best I could today," and go off to enjoy his daily racketball game without giving the job too much thought until the next morning, whereas Vernon might spend all evening with his family thinking of nothing but the job—"What will they think of me if I don't get it done on time?" After spending a restless night fretting over it, he returns to work the next day haggard and weary—stressed. Carlos's self-esteem is not dependent on any single event, such as meeting the deadline. Vernon's is shaky enough that any single event can topple it.

Vernon's performance may suffer as a result, but even if it doesn't—even if Vernon turns in a superior performance, actually completing the project within the unreasonable deadline—his body and mind will be ravaged by the stress of worry. No one is immune to worrying; in some strange way, we feel we are helping a project along by worrying about it. But people with high self-esteem do less worrying and endure less stress.

Societal Changes. Work/family balancing is a major stressor resulting from societal changes. It is the norm today for women to work outside the home while still taking care of the home, and this mean lots of stress for working women, particularly working mothers. Men are expected to take more responsibility for child care today, and that means more stress for men in an unaccustomed area. At one time the typical American father could concentrate on his job without concerns about his children's after-school activities or doctor appointments. Mom was taking care of all that. Those families are now in the minority.

Usually women bear the greater stress load in regard to work/family balancing. For one thing, many of them are single parents. For another, those who are married are still expected to take the most responsibility at home, yet employers hold them to the same standards as male employees at work. Something's got to give—and often it is the female worker's health. A survey of 311 female nurses aged 50 to 70 found that women who feel tension between demands from work and demands from home are at higher

Diversity Highlights

Pennzoil, Aetna Confront Sexual Harassment

The costs of sexual harassment go beyond anything that can be measured on a profit-and-loss statement. Women feel threatened by subtle—and not so subtle—sexual power trips men use to keep them in their place. But the majority of men would never dream of harassing anyone, most certainly not intentionally. It is a fine line, with both sides often confused and tense about whether it was crossed.

Many men are terrified of being falsely accused—with some reason. Companies sometimes overreact, and the ultimate punishment—termination—is often the first step.

From 1977 to 1984, Louis Kestenbaum was vice-president in charge of guest operations at a secluded ranch and spa operated by Pennzoil in northern New Mexico. In January 1984, an anonymous letter sent to the company's top management accused Kestenbaum of sexual harassment and other misdeeds. Kestenbaum denied the allegations but was fired anyway. He sued Pennzoil and won $500,000 in damages for wrongful discharge. In court, Pennzoil's in-house investigator admitted that she had relied on rumor and innuendo in putting together the report that got Kestenbaum fired. Wrote the judge, "No attempt was made to evaluate the credibility of the persons interviewed."

Of course, not all men are falsely accused of sexual harassment. An obvious instance of sexual harassment at an Aetna Life & Casualty golfing party shows the other side of the story. When four male managers vented their resentment at the presence of female managers at what had traditionally been an all-male event, Aetna responded by demoting two of the men, asking the other two to resign, and stepping up its sexual-harassment training course. According to one male trainee, "The guys in the class were absolutely not resistant to it, not at all. In fact, it's a relief to have someone spell out exactly what sexual harassment is. The men in my session were all saying, 'It's about time.'"

Source: Anne B. Fisher, "Sexual Harassment—What to Do," *Fortune,* August 23, 1993, pp. 84–88.

risk than other women of having serious heart disease. The risk was not associated with what the women achieved or how hard they worked, but with the degree to which they felt a conflict between career and family. At greatest risk were the women who believed that having a family interfered with advancement in their career.[14]

The growing role of women in the workplace has taken the natural stresses and tensions between the sexes to new heights. With confusion and misinterpreted intentions abounding, many employers are educating their employees to better understand what constitutes sexual harassment. See the "Diversity Highlights" box for more details.

The lack of job security characterizing this age is another stressor, especially for those with many financial responsibilities and dependent family members and those in endangered jobs or industries. Layoffs resulting from downsizing, acquisitions, and mergers have been a direct contributor to many employees' stress, including that of many managers and professionals.[15] Still another societal change contributing to stress is linked to technological advancements; the lack of the "human touch" in personal business affairs is stressful to many, as is the presence of machines at work that demand retraining or additional training. Technology always means change—and change always means stress.

Life Changes. As noted before, stress accompanies both favorable and unfavorable change. Researchers Thomas H. Holmes and Richard H. Rahe estimated the degree of change in certain major life events, as shown in Table 9.3. Obviously, some of these changes would produce mostly eustress and others mostly distress, but in every case, stress would definitely be present and would probably affect work. Human relations managers sometimes recommend policies that accommodate the stress of employees undergoing the death or sickness of a close family member, a divorce, or the birth or adoption of a child.

Table 9.3 **Social Readjustment Rating Scale**

Rank	Life Event	Mean Value	Rank	Life Event	Mean Value
1	Death of spouse	100	22	Son or daughter leaving home	29
2	Divorce	73	23	Trouble with in-laws	29
3	Marital separation	65	24	Outstanding personal achievement	28
4	Jail term	63	25	Spouse beginning or stopping work	26
5	Death of close family member	63	26	Begin or end school	26
6	Personal injury or illness	53	27	Change in living conditions	25
7	Marriage	50	28	Revision of personal habits	24
8	Fired at work	47	29	Trouble with boss	23
9	Marital reconciliation	45	30	Change in work hours or conditions	20
10	Retirement	45	31	Change in residence	20
11	Change in health of family member	44	32	Change in schools	20
12	Pregnancy	40	33	Change in recreation	19
13	Sex difficulties	39	34	Change in church activities	19
14	Gain of new family member	39	35	Change in social activities	18
15	Business readjustment	39	36	Change in sleeping habits	16
16	Change in financial state	38	37	Change in number of family get-togethers	15
17	Death of close friend	37	38	Change in eating habits	15
18	Change to a different line of work	36	39	Vacation	13
19	Change in number of arguments with spouse	35	40	Christmas	12
20	Foreclosure of mortgage or loan	30	41	Minor violations of the law	11
21	Change in responsibilities at work	29			

Source: Adapted and reprinted with permission from JOURNAL OF PSYCHOSOMATIC RESEARCH, Vol. 11, Thomas H. Holmes and Richard H. Rahe, "The Social Readjustment Rating Scale," (1967): Table 3, p. 216. © 1967, Elsevier Science Ltd., Pergamon Imprint, Oxford, England.

Career Development. Opportunities for stress buildup are more likely for the kind of employee who is seeking career development than for one who is satisfied with where he or she is. The relationship between stress and *career plateaus*—those points at which a person's career seems to have stalled—has been noted by several researchers.[16] Also, not knowing whether advancement is possible or in what direction realistic chances for advancement lie can generate stress.

The desire for career advancement is not universal, and some employees enjoy a period of less stress when they reach a plateau—a period where they feel confident about their ability to perform their duties and face no threatening new challenges.[17] Those who desire advancement, however, can become so frustrated at a plateau that their performance drops because of the stress their frustration produces. Human relations help in career planning can help employee and organization alike avoid this unhappy circumstance.

Another finding about the relationship between stress and career plateaus is that such plateaus are often caused by the kind of stress that produces burnout.[18] Human relations managers should watch for the signs of approaching burnout, as detailed later in this chapter, to head off this consequence.

Depression, rather than burnout, is a consequence of job loss, which for many is a more serious source of stress than a career plateau. Regardless of whether the organization, the individual, or outside factors are responsible for the job loss, an individual's sense of self-worth and ability to provide for his or her family are at stake. The "International Highlights" box illustrates one family's story.

International Highlights

Frayed Nerves at Electro-Wire

When Penny Reha took a job making wiring harnesses for trucks at Electro-Wire Products Inc. in 1986, she knew she wouldn't get rich quick. But the mother of three recognized how helpful her $6.35-an-hour wages could be when her construction-worker husband was between jobs. The job was secure as well: the year before, Electro-Wire had built a new $3 million plant in her hometown of Owosso, Michigan—triple the size of its old factory.

Quality ratings were high, but production slowed down as the firm steadily added plants in and moved production to Mexico. It was the company's success that by April 1990 led to the Owosso plant's closure and layoffs. Marketing director Richard J. Wheeler says Electro-Wire had to look at the big picture in deciding how to manage its 26 facilities and 4,000 employees scattered across North America. He argues that free trade will ultimately result in more U.S. jobs. "We try to be a good corporate citizen."

But more than 250 of Electro-Wire's former employees don't agree and are suing the company for allegedly failing to give them adequate notice of their layoffs. If they win, 60 days' pay will be only a temporary help; for Reha and others, unemployment benefits ran out long ago. Now, she and her unemployed husband scan the want ads daily. "You ain't got nothing if you ain't got hope," she says. "But I wonder what my kids are gonna do."

Source: Greg Bowens, "How Do You Compete with $1-an-Hour Wages?" *Business Week*, March 16, 1992, p. 103.

Organizational Stressors

Figure 9.3 divides various organizational stressors into four main categories: policies, structures, physical conditions, and processes. Human relations managers need to be involved in all of these areas. Just a few of the job factors linked to stress are unfair policies, ambiguous procedures, lack of opportunities for advancement, poor communication, and physically uncomfortable working conditions. Table 9.4 compares stressors across countries. As observed earlier, stress is a worldwide problem.

Note that some organizational stressors (all of those listed in Figure 9.3) can be eliminated or ameliorated, but others (many of those listed in Table 9.4) are an integral part of the job. In the latter event, responsibility to modify or cope with the stress of the job rests primarily with the employee. Many organizations are helping employees learn to do this. Refer again to Table 9.1 for a sample of some low-stress versus high-stress occupations. Personality type might point a person toward or away from many of these occupations.

Job Role. When a person's personality and skills match the requirements of a job, unhealthy stress is minimal, even if the job is high stress, such as air traffic controller. So that's the first human relations task: effective recruitment, selection, and job assignment.

Next is the kind of job design that keeps a person busy but not too busy, challenged but not intimidated. **Role overload** occurs when the requirements of a job are greater than the ability of the worker, whether that means too much work or too difficult work. Managers report that role overload, usually in the form of unreasonable deadlines, is the main stressor in their jobs.[19] Note that Table 9.4 also named "time pressures and deadlines" as the number one stressor across countries.

role overload
When the requirements of a job are greater than the ability of the worker.

Some people feel that too little work is as unpleasant—and stressful—as too much. **Role underutilization** occurs when the requirements of a job fail to fill the worker's time or utilize the worker's ability. Stress symptoms include weariness, depression, and even proneness to injury in some types of jobs. When a continual possibility of emergency demanding an alert response coincides with hours of uneventfulness and boredom, as in the case of operating a nuclear power plant, stress really escalates.

role underutilization
When the requirements of a job fail to fill the worker's time or utilize the worker's ability.

Figure 9.3 **Job Factors Linked to Stress**

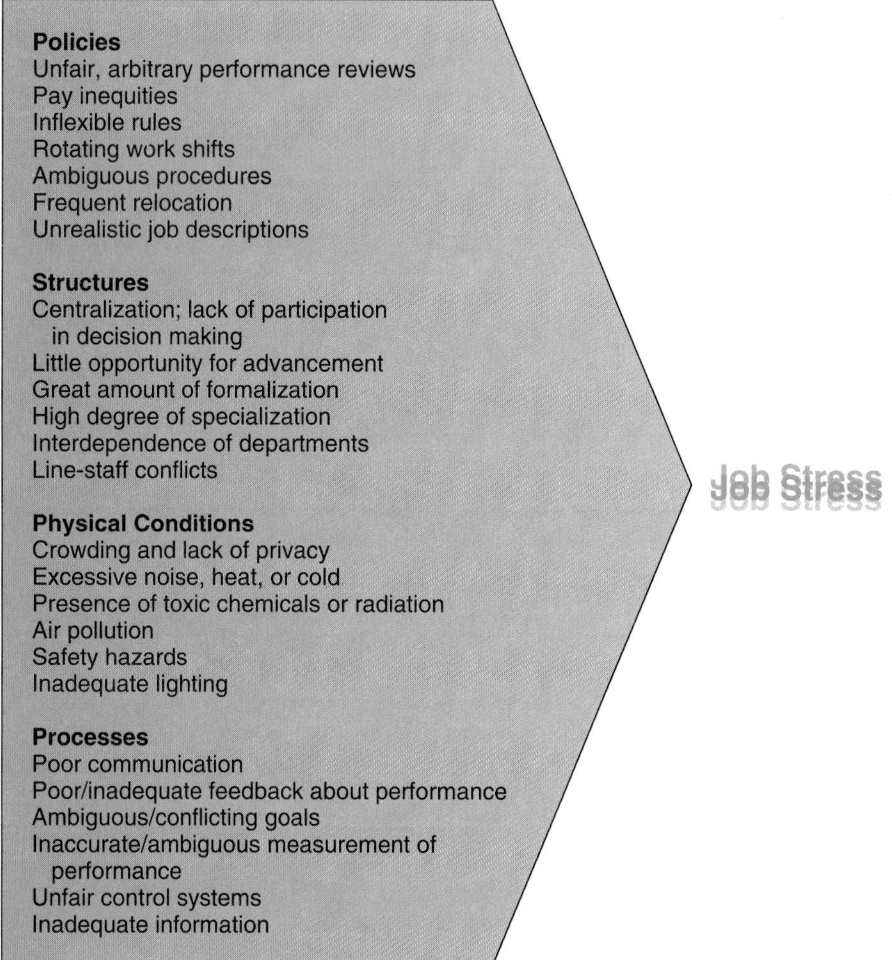

Source: Samuel C. Certo, MODERN MANAGEMENT: Diversity, Quality, Ethics, and the Global Environment, 6e. © 1994, p. 309. Reprinted by permission of Prentice Hall, Englewood Cliffs, New Jersey.

role ambiguity
When the job requirements are unclear to the worker.

Role ambiguity occurs when the job requirements are unclear to the worker. Some amount of role ambiguity is inevitable in high-level managerial or professional jobs that allow a great deal of freedom and flexibility in performance of duties. Exactly what constitutes satisfactory performance may not always be definable in concrete terms. Moreover, the consequences of undesirable performance may be unknown. Sometimes the worker has to set goals for herself or himself in order to combat role ambiguity.

It is possible for role ambiguity or a bad job match to produce role underutilization. In such a case, the employee fails to fulfill the needs of the job because he or she does not understand them or lacks ability and thus faces a lot of slack time at work. If the employee has high achievement needs, the result can be extremely stressful. Consider the following true story of a subtle mismatch and unrecognized role ambiguity:

Sarah was hired as assistant advertising manager for a greeting card manufacturer on the basis of her advertising copywriting experience, in which she had had many dealings with suppliers. Unfortunately, the job was a bad match, because Sarah's strength and interest lay in writing,

Table 9.4 Global Comparisons of Work Stressors

Source of Stress	Percentage of Respondents Mentioning Source	Most Often Mentioned by Managers in	Least Often Mentioned by Managers in
1. Time pressures and deadlines	55.3%	Germany (65.4%)	Japan (41.8%)
2. Work overload	51.6	Egypt (76.7%)	Brazil (38.1%)
3. Inadequately trained subordinates	36.4	Egypt (65.0%)	Britain (13.1%)
4. Long working hours	29.0	Nigeria (40.5%)	Brazil (19.6%)
5. Attending meetings	23.6	South Africa (28.5%)	United States (16.3%)
6. Demands of work on my private and social life	22.1	Sweden (31.7%)	Singapore (12.9%)
7. Demands of work on my relationship with my family	21.4	Nigeria (29.7%)	Brazil (8.2%)
8. Keeping up with new technology	21.4	Japan (32.8%)	Egypt (10.0%)
9. My beliefs conflicting with those of the organization	20.6	United States (30.2%)	Egypt (13.3%)
10. Taking my work home	19.7	Egypt (30.0%)	Japan (13.4%)
11. Lack of power and influence	19.5	United States (46.5%)	Sweden (11.0%)
12. Interpersonal relations	19.4	Japan (29.8%)	Singapore (12.9%)
13. The amount of travel required by my work	18.4	Nigeria (29.7%)	Brazil (9.3%)
14. Doing a job below the level of my competence	17.7	Brazil (23.7%)	Sweden (10.3%)
15. Incompetent boss	15.6	United States (30.2%)	Britain (9.1%)

Source: Reprinted with permission.

whereas the new job called primarily for managerial skills—coordinating the functions of the company to produce various products of advertising. Translated into specifics, this meant, for example, stopping by one department to prod certain people into producing something by Friday, then calling the out-of-state main office to check on something else due by Friday, then explaining what was wrong with something else produced by still another department and arranging to have it redone properly by Friday so that the whole package could go out Monday. Writing was only a part of the job, and not the main part.

Sarah was not good at prodding. She was not skilled on the telephone. Her conversations with the suppliers in her previous job had been totally focused on obtaining information. Now she was expected to motivate people. But that had not been spelled out to her, because her supervisors thought that the requirements of the job were obvious: you checked on the progress of various functions, gave a nudge here or there, and made sure everything came out on time. Sarah told everybody that the work was needed by Friday, then forgot about it while she devoted herself to the writing portion of her job—writing the copy to sell wedding cards and presents, a sideline of the company. It was pleasant work, but hardly enough to fill the hours. So she expanded the company newsletter—another small part of her job—into a full-time occupation, producing ever more lavish interviews with various employees, laboring over feature articles. The newspaper work was unnecessary but it saved her from the stress of underutilization. Meanwhile, no one was "watching the store," so to speak; no one was doing the assistant advertising manager's job!

If an employee is misdirecting his or her energies the way Sarah was, an effort at clearing up role ambiguity must be made, and if it fails, the only recourse is job reassignment. In Sarah's case, a conversation with the supervisor revealed to Sarah that the job required abilities she did not have, or at least did not wish to develop. She submitted her resignation and accepted a writing job somewhere else.

role conflict
When a worker has conflicting job requirements.

More difficult to resolve is the stress issuing from **role conflict**, which occurs when a worker has conflicting job requirements. For example, Zoe is told to see to it that quality is increased, which will require some expenditures on materials. But she is also told to keep costs down. Typically, role conflict occurs for middle managers in reconciling the demands of top management with the needs of lower-level managers.[20] It may also involve a conflict in ethics. The stress generated can wreck the interpersonal relationships necessary for good performance for the organization as a whole. Mutual trust and respect among coworkers can be shattered by role conflict.

Interpersonal Relationships and Organizational Politics. Highlighting the importance of human relations is the fact that any disruption in them— any problem with interpersonal relationships in the workplace— can create more stress than two or more other stressors combined. In numerous studies, at least 60 percent of workers of all types, in all industries, report this as their worst workplace stressor.[21] And, truly, an argument with a coworker, or resentment against one, can upset the most job-satisfied person. No matter how well matched your abilities and interests are with your job requirements, anger or disapproval, rudeness or mockery are sure to create some degree of stress. This is why discriminatory behavior from coworkers is so destructive even when it does not actually impede advancement on a job or affect a paycheck. And this is why sexual harassment has finally been recognized as intolerable. A good job, one well suited to a person, with good pay, good benefits, and comfortable working conditions, is immediately rendered undesirable by the stress of poor interpersonal relationships. And no one would want to sacrifice that good job because of that poor relationship if such a sacrifice could be avoided. One reason for human relations managers' presence in an organization is to prevent such sacrifices, especially in today's world of increasing cultural diversity.

Organizational politics, too, are part of many interpersonal relationships at work. Politics are usually inescapable, but good management can keep them strictly work related and therefore benign. When they get out of hand and power struggles rage, stress becomes a real threat to the organization's health as well as the individual employees'.

For a quick checkup on your own stress levels, turn to the "Self-Portrait" exercise.

Productivity and Stress. As Figure 9.4 shows, people tend to perform their best when they are experiencing a moderate degree of stress. Extremely high and extreme-

Figure 9.4 **Stress Levels and Performance**

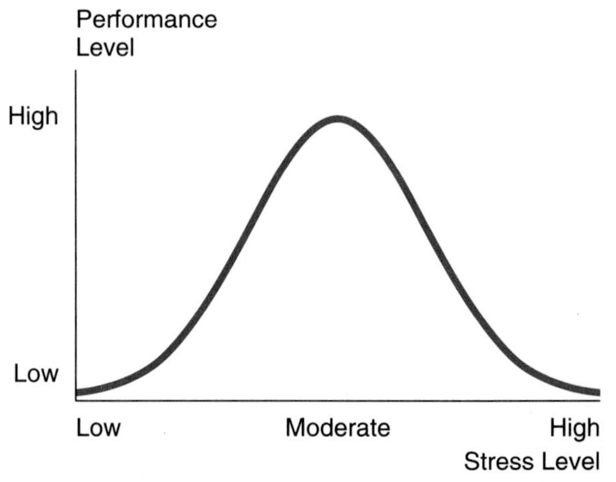

Self-Portrait

How Much Stress Are You Under?

No matter what your personality, everyone has some stress. Circle the answer that best applies to you.

How Often Do You Suffer From:	Never	Hardly Ever	Sometimes	Often
Aches in back, neck, or head	0	1	2	3
Stomachaches or indigestion	0	1	2	3
Thinking of too many things at once	0	1	2	3
Feeling tired	0	1	2	3
Chest pains	0	1	2	3
Less interest in physical intimacy	0	1	2	3
An urge to drink a lot of alcohol	0	1	2	3
Feeling anxious and uptight	0	1	2	3
Difficulty sleeping	0	1	2	3
Feeling depressed	0	1	2	3
Feeling overwhelmed	0	1	2	3
An inability to think clearly	0	1	2	3

Score: _____

A score of 12 or less indicates a low degree of personal stress reactions; between 13 and 24 reflects a moderate degree; higher than 24 indicates that you're experiencing a high degree of stress.

While your score may not altogether surprise you, it would be wise to consult your physician to determine whether you have a health problem that requires medical attention, one that may be contributing to both your stress level and your ability to withstand it.

Source: Sandra Lotz Fisher, "Vital Signs," *Sales & Marketing Management,* November 1992, p. 43.

ly low levels of stress tend to have negative effects on production. The benefits of some stress are varied. First, it provides motivation. It also provides interest. It contributes to job satisfaction and often brings out the best in people. For example, group leaders and members become more receptive to problem-solving information provided by others outside the group when they are subjected to some stress.[22]

So some stress is good, but how much is too much? That depends on the job and on the person. Human relations professionals should be equipped to advise an organization on how to ensure adequate eustress for job satisfaction and motivation while preventing excess, harmful stress.

Too much stress brings lower performance, along with increased absenteeism and all the potential health problems of stress, including the tendency of some stressed people to seek emotional relief in substance abuse. The organization's productivity is hurt by all of this. Indeed, the cost of stress-related problems has been estimated at $150 billion per year.[23] Sometimes continuing stress even leads to sabotage![24] Apparently, the stressed employee blames the organization for his or her symptoms and takes revenge. In one case that came before the Michigan Supreme Court, assembly-line workers purposely installed automobile parts labeled defective by a "compulsive perfectionist" boss in order to get even with him for his constant correction of their work.[25] We will discuss perfectionism in greater detail later in this chapter.

Quick Quiz 9.2

1. Which personality type is more prone to stress, Type A or Type B?
2. A person with ___________ of control is likely to manage stress well.
3. Role ___________ produces a particularly destructive type of stress, as it also erodes mutual trust and respect among workers.

How to Manage Stress: Organizational Role

At one time managing stress was considered to be wholly the employee's responsibility; indeed, for managers, being able to manage stress was an indication of fitness for the job. In recent years organizations have discovered their role in managing stress as a matter of financial necessity.[26] The cost of *not* helping is simply too great.

As touched on earlier, the organizational role in stress management has two main aspects: (1) eliminating unnecessary stress from the job and (2) helping employees cope with the unavoidable stress that remains. Ways in which stress can be eliminated or reduced are

- job matching
- job training
- job design
- organizational policies
- management style
- communication
- ergonomics.

Where stress cannot be eliminated or reduced, the employee can be helped to cope with it by means of

- career development plans
- employee assistance programs (EAPs)
- health promotion programs
- stress management programs.

Job Matching

Wisdom in hiring and selection is the first step in preventing undue stress from developing later. Not only skills and abilities, but also personality type, should be considered in job placement. Of course, the employee has an equal responsibility here. If Elena knows that she is going to want something more challenging after mastering the requirements of a certain entry-level job, she must take it upon herself to make sure there is a possibility of advancement.

Job Training

Lack of proper training guarantees unwanted stress on a job. Training can increase self-esteem and prevent the problems of role ambiguity and role conflict. It should be based on accurate job analysis and harmonize with a good job design. During training, potential problems that could create unhealthy stress on the job will likely emerge and can be dealt with. Many managerial and professional jobs cannot be specifically "trained" for, but courses and seminars on various pertinent subjects can help. *Mentoring* is often a good substitute for training in these kinds of jobs.

Napoleon Barragan (center), founder of Dial-A-Mattress, a company that sells mattresses by phone, likes to say "there are no secrets" at his company. He believes that the most successful company is the one that shares ideas and information. "In almost every instance, the cause of a problem is a lack of communication." Such open communication helps to keep stress levels down.

Photo source: Courtesy of Dial-A-Mattress.

Photo Exercise

Think of a time in your life when communication relieved stress. What especially helped?

Job Design

Careful job design also will prevent role ambiguity and role conflict, as well as job overload and underutilization. It should provide enough eustress to keep employees motivated and enough control over work scheduling and methods to prevent distress.[27] Participative management is helpful here.

Organizational Policies

Policies regarding sick leave, promotion, and so forth must be perceived as fair, or they may produce quite a lot of stress, even making employees hostile toward the organization. Sometimes people come to regard their employer as the enemy. Unsure of doing better elsewhere in the job market, they stay in their job, but their goal is to take advantage of the company rather than to help it—to obtain as many benefits, such as paid days off, as possible in return for as little work as possible. Since they feel the organization is prepared to take advantage of them, they return the favor. This is a horrible situation for everyone concerned, including coworkers, who may in fact become infected with the same attitude.

Management Style

For most employees, stress is bound to be lower in a participative-management atmosphere than in a traditional, hierarchical one. There are exceptions: some people find the added responsibility of participative management stressful. Most, however, interpret that responsibility as eustress rather than distress. Participative management gives employees more control over their jobs, plus opportunities to vent their feelings about such things as unfair organizational policies or the need for job redesign.

Communication

The feeling that the employer is withholding information about something vital to the employee, such as impending layoffs, certainly encourages a suspicious, hostile attitude and creates tremendous stress. Uncertainty is uncomfortable. Moreover, the imagination can paint a worse picture than would the facts. An atmosphere of open communication keeps stress levels down. Participative management is a great help in establishing this kind of atmosphere and in keeping communication channels open. The opportunity to express complaints to higher-ups is also an effective stress reliever.

Ergonomics

Safe, comfortable working conditions are a legal mandate as well as a wise business practice for reducing unhealthy stress in employees. Ergonomics is the science concerned with the human characteristics that must be considered in designing tasks and equipment so that people will work safely and effectively. Whatever the cost of establishing good ergonomics, the cost of not doing so is greater. Even if employees don't complain, file formal grievances, or sue—even if employees are not consciously aware of their uncomfortable working conditions, their performance will probably decline.

Career Development Plans

Some organizations offer assistance to employees wishing to advance in their career. Vocational tests may be offered, along with personalized guidance, including recommendations as to which training or higher education to pursue and tuition-reimbursement programs. Organizations offering this type of assistance may benefit themselves greatly. The awareness of being valued—and a career-development plan sends that unmistakable message—inspires a person to do his or her best. In addition, the motivation provided by a career plan may lead to the development of talents that the organization urgently needs. Finally, a good career-development program can head off stress-related burnout and stress issuing from career plateaus, as discussed earlier. Some such programs incorporate mentoring, in which an employee receives individual attention from a senior employee; mentoring has been found very effective in relieving stress.[28] Certainly, it helps prevent career plateaus.

Employee Assistance Programs (EAPs)

employee assistance programs (EAPs) Employer-provided programs that offer counseling for stress-producing problems.

Counseling for emotional and mental problems, for substance abuse problems, and for various non-work-related problems such as those involving work/family balancing is provided by some organizations through **employee assistance programs (EAPs)** as a way of preventing dangerous stress levels in employees. Counseling may be either in-house or by referral. Such programs may cover work-related issues as well, such as career or retirement planning. These programs do require someone with expert knowledge and human relations skills to administer them.[29]

Health Promotion Programs

health promotion programs Programs that encourage employees to practice healthy living habits; also called "wellness" programs.

Also called "wellness" programs, **health promotion programs** encourage employees to practice the kind of healthy living habits that can help them handle stress better. A well-nourished, rested, physically fit person can cope with emotional as well as physical stress far better than a physically vulnerable, run-down person. These kinds of programs stress exercise, nutrition, and the elimination of unhealthy habits such as smoking. Often screening programs are offered to detect high blood pressure, obesity, pulmonary malfunction, high cholesterol levels, and so forth. Even advice on back care, cancer detection, breast self-examinations, and moderate alcohol use may be included. Some companies install gyms with exercise equipment or even swimming pools for employees to use on lunch breaks and after work. Some even hire aerobics instructors and diet counselors for employees.

Stress Management Programs

stress management programs Programs that educate employees about stress and/or train them in stress management techniques.

Though their scope varies greatly from one organization to another, most **stress management programs** (or "interventions") tend to focus on either (1) educating employ-

Figure 9.5 **A Model of Stress Management Intervention**

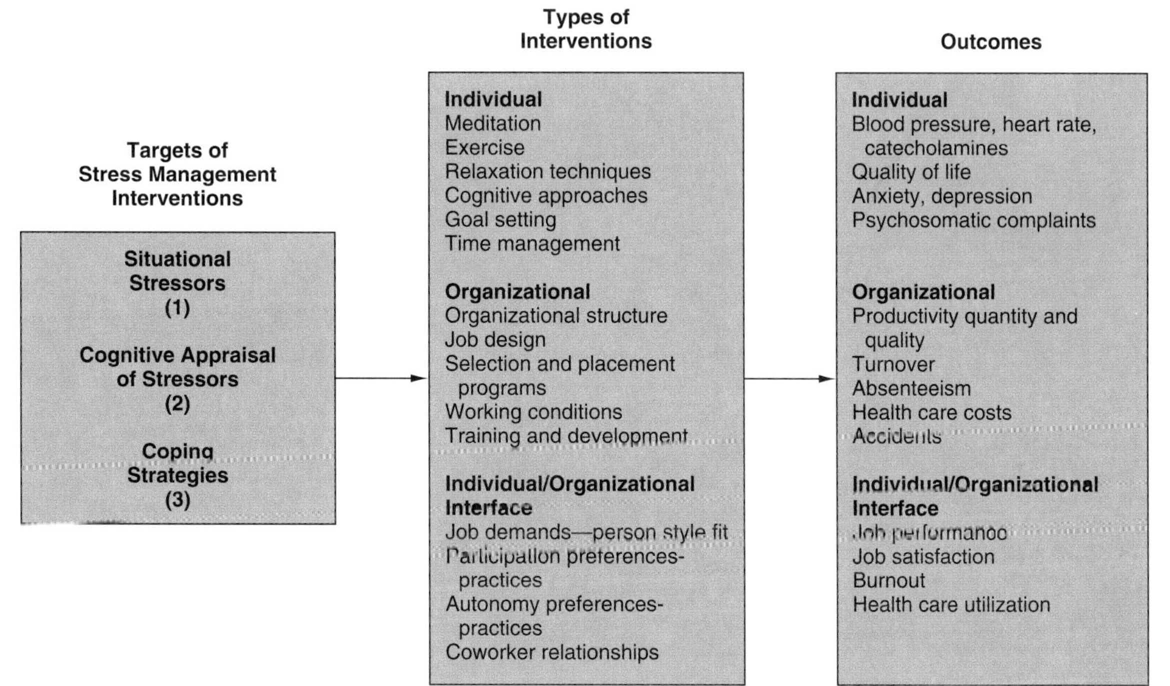

Source: From "Worksite Stress Management Interventions" by John M. Ivancevich, Michael T. Matteson, Sara M. Freedman, and James S. Phillips, *American Psychologist* 45, p. 254. Copyright 1990 by the American Psychological Association. Reprinted by permission.

ees about stress or (2) training them in stress management techniques, such as time management.[30] A psychological model has been proposed, categorizing such programs as focusing on the individual, the organization, or the "individual-organization interface"[31] (see Figure 9.5). The current recommendation of most experts is to focus on the organization—in other words, for the organization to take more responsibility in preventing and reducing stress.[32]

Techniques used in stress management programs include the following:

- meditation
- biofeedback
- relaxation techniques
- time management
- assertiveness training
- participative management.

meditation
A relaxation technique in which you focus your thoughts on something—a phrase, a word, a symbol, or even just the act of breathing—other than day-to-day concerns.

Meditation. An increasingly popular technique is **meditation**, in which employees are taught to focus their thoughts on something—a phrase, a word, a symbol, or even just the act of breathing—other than day-to-day concerns. At the consulting firm of Symmetrix in Massachusetts, executives daily close their office doors and spend 20 minutes in meditation. Symmetrix's CEO signed up his company for a $3,000 program from Harvard's Mind/Body Medical Institute to learn relaxation and meditation techniques when employees began complaining of stress. Marriott, Polaroid, and The Boston Company have all offered such training. Adolph Coors Company's extensive "wellness" program combines meditation, nutrition, and exercise to help treat stress-related problems.[33] Table 9.5 lists some of the principles for using meditation.

Table 9.5 **Meditation Techniques to Relieve Job Stress**

Job Stress? Shut the Door and ...

- Pick a calming focus word, phrase, image, or prayer (example: ocean).
- Sit quietly in a comfortable position, such as up straight with your hands in your lap.
- Close your eyes or focus on a single object.
- Relax your muscles.
- Breathe slowly and naturally, repeating your focus word.
- Assume a passive attitude. Do not worry about how well you are doing. When other thoughts come to mind, simply say to yourself, "Oh, well," and gently return to the repetition.
- Continue the meditation session for 10 to 20 minutes.
- Practice the technique once or twice daily.

Source: *The Wellness Book,* by Dr. Herbert Benson.

biofeedback
A technique of developing an awareness of such automatically controlled bodily functions as pulse rate, blood pressure, body temperature, and muscle tension and thus being able to control them to some extent.

Biofeedback. In **biofeedback**, employees are taught to develop an awareness of such automatically controlled bodily functions as pulse rate, blood pressure, body temperature, and muscle tension and thus be able to control them to some extent. In essence, conscious mental control of the body produces a relaxed state and dissipates stress.

Relaxation Techniques. In addition to meditation and biofeedback, other relaxation techniques exist as well, some mental, some physical, some a combination. Mental imagery, used by many athletes to perfect their skill, can be adapted to relaxation at work. Certain physical exercises relax the body and, it is theorized, relieve mental anxiety and stress as a consequence. Yoga combines mental with physical relaxation.

assertiveness training
Training that teaches how to say no to the demands of others when saying no is appropriate.

Assertiveness Training. **Assertiveness training** may be needed to equip a person to act on the necessity of saying no at appropriate times. Some people are too dependent on the opinions of others to risk their displeasure by saying no. As a result, they find themselves with an unreasonable workload. Obviously, low self-esteem is the problem here. Although the causes of low self-esteem are too complex to be dealt with by a simple organizational program, assertiveness training can help employees help themselves combat the problem. By explaining the validity of saying no at appropriate times and teaching nonconfrontational ways to do so, assertiveness training can give employees the tools they need to eliminate this source of stress.

Unusual Programs and Procedures. Some unusual tactics to relieve or prevent employee stress have been taken by organizations:[34]

- Instead of trying to prevent the barrage of telephone calls that working parents tend to make or receive around 3:00 p.m. as children return home from school, John Hancock Financial Services encourages employees to check on their children at that time.
- Chase Manhattan and Citicorp established lunchtime support groups for employees undergoing stressful situations, providing professional therapists in the company lunchroom.
- Circle Consulting Group believes in matinee outings on Broadway and brownie-tasting bake-offs to relieve stress and tension.

At the Symmetrix consulting firm in Lexington, Massachusetts, Alice Domar, a staff psychologist from a Boston hospital, teaches stress-reduction techniques to employees.
Photo source: © 1994 Bob Sacha.

Photo Exercise

What do you think is the future need for stress reduction in business? Why?

Quick Quiz 9.3

1. The organization's roles in stress management are __________ and __________.
2. What type of program might prevent the kind of stress that leads to substance abuse?
3. At one small company, employees routinely shut their office doors and focus their thoughts on a word or symbol for 20 minutes in order to relax; they are practicing __________.
4. __________ helps people learn how to say "no" at appropriate times.

How to Manage Stress: Your Personal Role

You have at your disposal both physical and psychological strategies for managing stress, whether or not your organization provides assistance in either area.

Nutrition, Rest, and Exercise

If no one else tells you that a sugary donut and coffee are insufficient to carry you through the morning, the TV commercials will! Good nutrition is popular today, at least in theory. So everyone knows that breakfast is good for you, but it is a difficult habit for some to acquire. Settling for a nutritious lunch (rather than potato chips and a soft drink, for instance) is better than nothing. Younger people can get away with abusing their bodies nutritionally for quite a while before it catches up with them, but eventually they either change their dietary ways or regret it.

Health promotion programs try to increase employees' awareness of the importance of what they eat. Your personal responsibility is to pay attention and use some discipline in acting on what you learn. (Have a chicken sandwich and a salad with those potato chips! Try a glass of water instead of the soft drink!)

Animals do not have to be admonished to rest when they are tired, but people may push themselves to keep going, for reasons of duty or pleasure, when their whole body is silently screaming at them to stop. It helps to realize that rest is a preventive measure: it recharges us mentally and physically so that we are less vulnerable to the destructive forces of stress. A task that is difficult when you are tired may be easy

Table 9.6 Possible Signs of Excess Stress

Decline in work performance
Increase in use of sick days
Increase in number of errors and accidents
Moodiness and irritability
Fatigue
Loss of enthusiasm
Aggressive behavior
Difficulty making decisions
Family problems
Apparent loss of concern for others and their feelings*
Feeling that it's impossible to help other people*
Feeling of inability to get your job done fully or well*

*Possible signs of burnout

when you are not. You will make errors when tired that you would never make when refreshed and well rested. You will catch errors when rested that you would never notice when you are weary. By law, organizations must provide rest breaks and set reasonable working hours. If we ignore them on a regular basis—not just when work emergencies occur—we will pay the price. And so will the organization, as our productivity and accuracy diminish.

Exercise is such a well-established virtue in today's society that no one would challenge its importance. But sometimes we all need encouragement to do it. Organizations that provide gyms for their employees doubtless reap the benefits of better work, since exercise undeniably improves physical health and appears to improve mental and emotional health as well.

Stress buildup results from a lack of physical movement. It is logical, then, that exercise would help in stress management. You cannot punch the boss who criticizes you, or run away from the clients who complain, but you may well find it helpful to take a walk or ride a bike before or after work, or during lunch. A sports activity or active recreation such as dancing during your off-hours may make you better able to handle stress during work, not only because such activities "let off steam," but also because they strengthen the organs so that they can better withstand stress.

Well-Rounded Life Activities

For someone who gets all of his or her satisfaction and rewards from working, job-related stress is more likely to be overwhelming. No job is going to be rewarding all the time, so it helps to have other areas in life that bring rewards. For example, if your boss is impatient and fails to praise you for completing an important project, it helps to enjoy the love of friends and family members or to hear the cheers of your softball teammates when you make a good play.

People who lead a well-rounded life are more likely to experience satisfaction in some area of life at any given time. This satisfaction can make stress a lot easier to cope with. Leading a well-rounded life means not only advancing your career but also devoting time to social, family, intellectual, spiritual, and physical pursuits. For example, one person might choose to read biographies, join a volleyball team, and volunteer in a soup

Table 9.7 **Risk Factors for Job Burnout**

Factor	Who Burns Out More
Sex	Females more than males
Age	Younger more than older (especially beyond age 50)
Pay	Lower paid more than higher paid
Position	Lower status more than higher status
Ethnicity	Hispanics more than any other race
Customer contact	Those with direct customer contact more than those with no customer contact
Seniority	Longer-term employees more than those with less than 10 years of service
Job preference	Those in a nonpreferred job more than those in a preferred job
Marital status	Singles more than marrieds
Potential	Those with low promotion potential more than those with high potential

Source: R. T. Golembiewski and R. F. Munzenrider, *Phases of Burnout: Developments in Concepts and Applications* (New York: Praeger, 1988), pp. 102–108. Reprinted with permission of Greenwood Publishing Group, Inc., Westport, CT. Copyright © 1988.

kitchen. Another person might take bicycle trips with the kids on weekends and be active at her temple and in a professional organization. These varied pursuits not only help people manage stress, they also make life more interesting and enjoyable.

Avoiding Burnout

Self-knowledge and *self-awareness* are powerful allies in personal stress management. In addition to what you already know about yourself, take a look at Table 9.6 to see some common signs of approaching job burnout. Now see Table 9.7, which presents some risk factors for burnout. You can use this knowledge not only in personal stress management but in noticing danger signs in coworkers. Human relations professionals are charged with the responsibility of noticing such signs.

perceptual adaptation Learning to condition your mind to handle stressors you cannot control.

Skill at **perceptual adaptation**, in which you learn to condition your mind to handle stressors you cannot control, is worth developing. Essentially, this consists of analyzing whatever is causing you stress in terms of its total life importance. The "thousand years test," for example, asks, "A thousand years from now, will this really matter?"[35] Or you might ask yourself, "What is the worst that can happen if I don't succeed here?" Usually, the stress-producing event—perhaps meeting a deadline for a certain project—is not capable of producing dire consequences. Rarely is a job, let alone a life, or one's happiness, in danger. Often, too, a solution to any bad consequence is available.

time management Controlling the use of time.

One way to help avoid burnout is to learn time management skills. **Time management**—controlling the use of one's time—can be as simple as putting things away as soon as you are done with them, using an appointment calendar to keep track of your schedule, and getting all the information you need before you start on a project.[36] Even if you really do not have enough time to accomplish all that you are supposed to, having a *plan*—a schedule, a "to do" list, an appointment calendar—keeps panic at bay. If necessary, something will simply have to be scratched off the list or schedule or postponed to another day, but at least you will feel you have approached the problem in a concrete way. In other words, you maintain a *sense of control* over your job if you have a means of controlling your time. And, recall, a sense of control is most important in combating stress. Several experts recommend focusing on retaining, or regaining, a sense of control to avoid job burnout.[37] Here are some specific suggestions:

1. Make a list of what is and is not within your control, then focus on what you can control—exactly the opposite of what most people do. Usually their thoughts compulsively return again and again to what they cannot control. A lot of emotional energy is expended this way, all to no avail.[38]
2. If others at work are creating a conflict that is the source of your stress, have a talk with them. Sometimes communication can work wonders. Beware of antagonizing them, though, by implying that everything is their fault. Simply lay out the problem and together look for solutions.[39]
3. Take a break. A slow walk, not for exercise but to unwind, or simply a few minutes of clearing the mind and thinking of something restful can make you more productive and better able either to resolve the conflict or to wait it out.[40]
4. Do something physical. A brisk walk or run or workout on an exercise machine at lunch can do wonders for your mental attitude. Even a few stretches behind the office door can be helpful. Remember all those hormones we talked about earlier that need something to do.
5. Because laughter is relaxing—genuinely, physically relaxing to the muscles of your body—it can help ward off stress's assault. Interviews with former hostages, war veterans, airplane crash survivors, and cancer patients have revealed a common coping mechanism of humor.[41] If you can think of something humorous to make yourself laugh, do it. If not, seek out the company of a friend who is able to do that for you.

procrastination
Putting off what needs to be done.

Time management also helps combat the tendency toward procrastination and perfectionism, two potential sources of unhealthy stress leading straight to eventual burnout. **Procrastination**, putting off what needs to be done, can be addressed by listing every task on a schedule. When the day and hour arrive for that task to be done, it must be done. No more procrastination!

The devastations of procrastination are many: High-priority jobs are neglected in favor of lower priority ones or a chat on the phone about personal matters. Small problems grow worse as time proceeds and they are neglected. Self-esteem is lowered, according to some experts: "It's not easy to summon positive thoughts about yourself when there's always something to be done that's making you feel inadequate," says one.[42] Certainly, by procrastinating, you lose control.

Understanding your own abilities and limits is key to controlling stress. An employer trying to compete while keeping up with and implementing new quality methods and techniques must also recognize what works best for that company and its employees. A small-business owner who does just that is profiled in the "Quality Highlights" box.

perfectionism
The attempt to do things perfectly.

Perfectionism, the attempt to do things perfectly, sounds noble, but since human beings are imperfect, the attempt to be perfect dooms a person to failure. Slaves to perfectionism cannot escape stress—that is, distress. They may also be prone to procrastination, putting off the project that they fear they will not be able to complete to perfection. Time management means starting the project at a specific point, whether or not it is the "perfect" time to begin, and ending it by a specific time, whether or not it is flawless. A deadline is a perfectionist's best friend. Some perfectionists would labor over one job for a lifetime if allowed to do so.

Quality Highlights

Industrial Devices Steers an Independent Road

Many small-business owners are so busy just getting through an eight-hour day that they have no time to study, let alone implement, quality techniques that might cut their costs and improve their productivity.

To stay current without being overwhelmed, they improvise. Rather than relying on labels and strict adherence to textbook models, they choose a handful of ideas that they think will work best for them.

Bernie Schnoll, president of Hackensack, New Jersey–based Industrial Devices, tries to keep up with all the latest trends. But he steers clear of tying his 375-employee company, a maker of indicator lights for dashboards and other uses, to any one theory.

Because it was required to adopt quality-control techniques eight years ago by one of its major customers—Ford Motor Co.—Schnoll says his company "is probably doing total quality management [now], but we don't use that term here."

Schnoll can cite the ideas of various management gurus. He gleans their theories from the three to four weeks he spends each year attending seminars and the required reading he assigns himself: at least one business book a month. But, he says, "I don't like to feel pressured with these things.... I try to pick among the ideas, while never losing sight of what I'm trying to do."

At Industrial Devices, as at many small businesses, the need for and application of quality techniques goes beyond the current management fads. Right now, Schnoll is studying ways to speed up design and production. "My customers need it," he says, "and if I can't, then I'm dead."

Source: Gilbert Fuchsberg, "Small Firms Struggle with Latest Management Trends," *The Wall Street Journal*, August 26, 1993, section B, p. 2.

Time management includes delegating work to others, but delegation is sometimes resisted by perfectionists, who often believe that they and they alone can do a given task perfectly (even though they constantly disappoint themselves). Of course, we can all use a touch of perfectionism; without it, there is not much chance of improving.

Making Stress Work for You

Although our bodies may respond to stressors without our permission, releasing hormones and getting ready for the fight or the flight that cannot take place, we can outwit our bodies by understanding stress and using the techniques of stress management. In addition, we should try to understand ourselves. If we are aware of our vulnerability to certain stressors, we can avoid them or prepare for them. Conversely, we can look for or elicit the kind of eustress that we know we need for motivation. As with all self-knowledge, learning how to manage our individual reactions to stress translates into a better understanding of how others react and how they can be helped. The human relations manager must beware of projecting his or her own feelings onto others; meditation might suit you well but seem like torture to someone of a more "Type A" nature. Bearing these individual differences in mind, human relations managers can use knowledge of the universal reactions to stress to advise organizations on ways of making stress productive where possible, eliminating it where not, and helping employees to manage it.

Quick Quiz 9.4

1. Three physical basics of personal stress management are nutrition, ____________, and ____________.
2. Are men or women at greater risk for burnout?
3. Procrastination and perfectionism can be helped by learning techniques of ________.

Participating in an exercise such as running before or after work, as this woman is doing, can be helpful to managing stress.
Photo source: © 1992 Mike Malyszko, FPG International Corp.

Summary

• **Describe the stress response.** Stress is a physiological reaction to environmental demands in which the heartbeat quickens, the blood pressure rises, and the muscles tense, preparing the body for physical action. Psychological stressors produce the same response in human beings as actual physical danger would, creating a stress buildup that often cannot be relieved and thus leads to various physical ills.

• **Contrast healthy stress and unhealthy stress.** Healthy stress, eustress, adds excitement and interest to life and serves to motivate employees. Unhealthy stress, distress, leads to a host of emotional and physical problems, including frustration, job burnout, and substance abuse. Studies have shown that a moderate degree of stress boosts productivity at work, whereas either too little or too much diminishes it. Some degree of stress is inevitable in life, and some degree appears to be desirable as well.

• **List some personal and some organizational stressors.** Personal stressors include reactions to societal change, including technological advancements and decreased job security; individual life changes and events; physical or mental illness; and concerns about career development and personal growth. Family/work balancing is a major source of stress for many employees, especially women with children. Organizational stressors arise from on-the-job role conflicts, role ambiguity, role overload, or role underutilization; unfair organizational policies; problems with interpersonal relationships at work and organizational politics; and dangerous or uncomfortable physical working conditions.

• **Explain how personality type influences stress.** Personality type can determine whether an event acts as a stressor or a motivator and influences how well a person is able to manage stress. More prone to stress are (1) hard-driving Type A personalities rather than more relaxed Type B personalities, (2) people with an external locus of control rather than those with an internal locus, and (3) people with low self-esteem rather than those with high self-esteem.

• **Discuss the role of interpersonal relationships as stressors.** The most frequently cited cause of stress is an interpersonal relationship at work, a fact that highlights the importance of human relations. Discriminatory behavior and sexual harassment can therefore produce severe stress despite other aspects of a job being favorable. Organizational politics, which involve interpersonal relationships, can also serve as a source of unhealthy stress.

• **Name some ways that organizations can reduce stress or help employees manage it.** Organizations can eliminate or reduce stress by wise job matching, proper job training, good job design, fair organizational policies, participative management, open communication, and good ergonomics. They can help employees manage unavoidable stress by means of career development plans, employee assistance programs (EAPs), health promotion programs, and stress management programs. Stress management programs may employ meditation, biofeedback, relaxation techniques, and assertiveness training.

• **Name some ways that the individual can take responsibility for managing stress.** The individual employee can better manage stress if he or she maintains good health by means of adequate nutrition, rest, and exercise; engages in non-work-related activities that provide satisfaction and pleasure; employs perceptual adaptation, in which the mind is conditioned to handle stress that cannot be eliminated; learns the techniques of time management so as to combat tendencies toward procrastination and perfectionism; and gains enough self-knowledge and self-awareness to recognize the onset of unhealthy stress and know how to cope with it.

Key Terms

stress (188)
distress (188)
eustress (188)
general adaptation syndrome (190)
frustration (190)
burnout (191)
locus of control (192)
Type A (192)
Type B (193)
role overload (197)
role underutilization (197)
role ambiguity (198)
role conflict (199)
employee assistance programs (EAPs) (204)
health promotion programs (204)
stress management programs (204)
meditation (205)
biofeedback (206)
assertiveness training (206)
perceptual adaptation (209)
time management (209)
procrastination (210)
perfectionism (210)

Review and Discussion Questions

1. Name five job factors that have been linked to stress. Which do you think an organization could have some control over?

2. Which of the following is a source of stress? Explain.
   a. having a boss who gives vague and confusing instructions and then criticizes your results
   b. buying a house
   c. working at a boring job
   d. getting a promotion to a managerial position you have been wanting for a year

3. What is ergonomics? Do you think it is an important factor in reducing stress? Why or why not?

4. Flight attendant Jesse Scott does not understand all the fuss about stress. He feels stimulated by a job that is exciting and contains many challenges. Does his attitude show that stress is not harmful? Explain.

5. Which job factors linked to stress might the following people encounter, and over which do they have control? Explain.
   a. Albert Menendez, principal of an inner-city high school
   b. Leslie Tanaka, head of a bank's loan department
   c. Tawana Williams, makeup artist at the city opera
   d. Mike O'Reilly, a hospital orderly

6. List at least five possible signs of excess stress. Are some more serious than others? List some ways to alleviate these stresses.

7. What are some jobs that would be unsuitable for Type A personalities? Explain.

8. What are some ways an organization can alleviate stress in its employees?

9. How can the following responses help you cope with stress?
   a. exercising
   b. biofeedback
   c. meditating
   d. participating in a wellness program

10. What is general adaptive syndrome? How can it help you deal with stress?

A SECOND LOOK

What were the causes of stress for Craig Weatherup during the Pepsi tampering scare? What measures helped him deal with the stress?

Independent Activity

Going, Going, Gone

One of the most stressful changes in a person's life is losing a job. Imagine that you have been laid off from a job that you really need—to pay college tuition, save for a wedding, support a child, or help care for your parents. Using the self-knowledge you have gained from the exercises and "Self-Portraits" throughout this text, evaluate your strengths and weaknesses and come up with a transition plan to deal with these aspects of the change:

- Dealing with anger and accepting your situation
- Telling your family and helping them cope
- Reassessing your job opportunities (or career path)
- Coping financially
- Finding a new job
- Relieving stress
- Staying motivated and optimistic.

Skill Builder

Stress Self-Management

Refer to your score on the "Self-Portrait" exercise. Did you score high or low? To what do you attribute your score and personality type?

Think objectively, as a psychologist or human relations counselor would, about your family background and work and living environments. What stress factors are present in your life? Have you learned to cope with them? How? If you have not learned to cope with stress, refer to pages 207–211 on managing stress, and map out a strategy for yourself.

Group Activity

Watching for Signs of Burnout (25 minutes)

Form groups of three or more. Instead of assessing yourselves for stress leading to burnout, assess each other. First, list out loud the stress factors in your own life and any signs that you may not be coping with them well (use Table 9.6). Discuss these with group members to determine each other's potential for burnout. Then, using some of the strategies discussed in the chapter, discuss ways of relieving any excess stress and avoiding burnout.

Case Study

John Deere Breaks the Pattern with Ergonomics Committee

On the face of it, the work force at John Deere & Co. is no different from anyone else's. The Moline, Illinois, company's 20,300 U.S. workers include service workers and factory employees. But unlike five million other working Americans, the work force at the farm-implement manufacturer is no longer suffering from injuries caused by repetitive motion.

John Deere began efforts ten years ago to reduce assembly-line injuries from repetitive motion. "We noticed in the early 1980s that we were making significant progress in reducing injuries such as cuts, lacerations, punctures, and fractures—but our workers' compensation costs were continuing to go up," says Ted Wire, Deere's manager of product and occupational safety. "We formed a team to analyze the problem and found the injuries were from repetitive motion, affecting soft tissue."

In 1984, the company formed a corporate ergonomics committee that included coordinators in the manufacturing units and awareness training programs for engineers, managers, supervisors, and the employees who do the actual labor. Using its own skilled tradespeople to pinpoint the work tasks that create discomfort was the fastest way to correct problems, says Wire.

Ergonomics has played a big role in reducing cumulative trauma at Deere. The company now uses tilt devices so employees don't have to reach overhead, bend over, or crawl under machinery to work. Parts and storage bins have been repositioned to minimize the number of times employees have to reach into them.

As things improved on the factory floor, Deere initiated training programs for workers using personal computers and word processors—a group that commonly suffers from neck, shoulder, and back pain, as well as the wrist and hand disorder known as carpal-tunnel syndrome. In 1992, Deere expanded its efforts to its warehouse workers and the more than 15,000 employees in its overseas operations.

Wire says the benefits of Deere's ergonomics and training programs have been substantial. While repetitive stress is responsible for nearly two-thirds of job injuries in American industry, Deere reports a 90 percent reduction in time lost from back problems and an 86 percent decrease in time lost from carpal-tunnel injuries. In addition, productivity has increased because workers are not overly tired. Several units have reduced cumulative trauma disorders 100 percent since the program began.

"These health problems can be prevented," Wire states. "All you have to do is identify the stressors and then minimize or eliminate them." It's not as simple as it sounds, he cautions, because it takes companywide awareness and teamwork to achieve results. But it's exciting, he admits, "because you can do so much for employees at a very minimal cost."

Case Questions

1. Would Deere's approach work in other organizations? Why or why not?
2. Do you think repetitive injuries on the factory floor are more important to solve than those in the office? Why?
3. Is ergonomics a human relations problem? Why or why not?
4. What do you think were the stressors identified by Deere's work force? Do you think they were similar to those at other companies?
5. How important is training in reducing repetitive stress injuries?

Source: Carol Kleiman, "John Deere Gets a Grip on Repetitive Stress Injuries," *Chicago Tribune,* June 6, 1993, sec. 8, p 1.

Case Study

Avoiding Stress from Day One at Nucor

When Nucor Corporation prepared to open the employment office for its new Crawfordsville, Indiana, steel mill in 1988, it faced some unusual concerns. Tracy Shellabarger, comptroller of the rural plant, says there were human resource implications for the start-up operation, including worries that the mill's working environment would strain the nerves of new workers.

Although its high wages guaranteed a large number of applicants, Shellabarger says Nucor was concerned "that potential employees would not be familiar with what it's like to work in a steel mill. Mills are very hot and loud. With sparks flying and the floor rumbling, there are people who will decide they don't care about the pay. They conclude that it's frightening, and they're out of there."

Early on, Nucor's management decided that new hires would be sent to visit other mills so they could see what the work would really be like. The visiting employees would spend two to three weeks observing, and after some training, actually performing some of the jobs.

To get that far, however, job hopefuls had their applications prescreened by teams of managers, who then conducted joint interviews. In addition, a meeting with a psychologist determined whether the applicant was interested in and capable of participating on a work team.

Ensuring psychological readiness for the culture of teams was important because, once hired, employees enter what Nucor's chairman and CEO, Ken Iverson, calls an "egalitarian" culture. Everyone gets the same vacations, holidays and health care programs. Nucor has no job descriptions, because Iverson thinks they limit people, telling them what they cannot do.

Work groups are responsible for decisions about work, because Iverson claims managers can make bad decisions, and workers should tell them if that is the case. Responsibility is pushed down to the lowest level, as communication travels up and down the hierarchy. There have been no layoffs in 20 years at Nucor. If business is slow, plants may work only a few days a week and workers' pay drops. But a program called "Share the Pain" ensures that during slow periods, *all* employees are affected: a foreman's pay can drop up to 25 percent, department heads' salaries drop 35 to 40 percent, and officers' pay dips 65 to 70 percent.

Although, at the time, managers and department heads found the hiring process time consuming, they recognized that the time invested was worth it for the future. Vincent Schiavoni, hot mill manager, says he knew that the success of the plant was as dependent on the attitudes and abilities of the people as it was on new technology. "People warned us that there would be high turnover the first year, but we had virtually none."

And, he adds, "the little turnover we've experienced is related to personal, not job-related, problems of employees and low performance."

Case Questions

1. What job factors at Nucor could be linked to stress? How well has Nucor controlled them?
2. What effect does the "egalitarian" culture have on reducing stress at Nucor? What effect does the "Share the Pain" program have?
3. Nucor couldn't change its physical plant, so it concentrated on its psychological environment. Did it go far enough? Explain.
4. How important has training and open communication been in reducing turnover at Nucor?

Sources: F. C. Barnes, in J. M. Higgins and J. W. Vincze, *Strategic Management: Text and Cases* (Fort Worth, Tex.: Dryden Press, 1993); "Empowering Employees," *Chief Executive,* March/April 1989, pp. 44–49; "Hot Steel and Good Common Sense," *Management Review,* August 1992, pp. 25–27; T. P. Pare, "Big Threat to Big Steel's Future," *Fortune,* July 15, 1991, pp. 106–108; T. M. Rohan, *Industry Week,* January 21, 1991, pp. 26–28; R. Wrubel, "Ghost of Andy Carnegie?" *Financial World,* September 29, 1992, pp. 50–52.

Quick Quiz Answers

Quick Quiz 9.1

1. **eustress, distress**
2. **alarm, resistance, recovery**

Quick Quiz 9.2

1. **Type A**
2. **internal locus**
3. **conflict**

Quick Quiz 9.3

1. **eliminating unnecessary stress from the job, helping employees cope with the unavoidable stress that remains**
2. **health promotion program**
3. **meditation**
4. **Assertiveness training**

Quick Quiz 9.4

1. **rest, exercise**
2. **women**
3. **time management**

PART OUTLINE

4

The Organizational Social System

CHAPTER

10

Individual Behavior

CHAPTER OUTLINE

Learning Objectives

- Name and define the factors that influence individual behavior.
- Contrast various personality types.
- List Spraunger's six categories of values.
- Name the areas of intelligence that aptitude tests measure.
- Explain biased, selective, and subjective perception.
- Describe the role of attribution in the process of perception.
- Explain the importance of self-concept to work attitude.
- Discuss transactional analysis and assertiveness training as they apply to interpersonal behavior in the workplace.

Keeping Business and Personality Separate at Minyard Foods

Better than most corporate executives, Liz Minyard knows what it's like to rush into the supermarket after a full day of work and try to figure out what to make for dinner. She knows what working women are up against. After all, Minyard and her sister are the co-chairs of Minyard Food Stores, a 78-store grocery chain in Dallas. But even Minyard can't always find what she wants in her own stores. It's a frustration that gives her insight into her customers, who—like most supermarket shoppers—are two-thirds female, and mostly work outside the home.

"Sometimes I don't think we are looking at what the shoppers, especially working women, need," she says. "I can relate to people who like one-stop shopping. I am the same way.... You leave work, you're tired, and you've put in a full day. You want to go home. You don't want to make four or five stops on the way."

But a change for the better may be coming, says Minyard, one of only a handful of women executives in the supermarket business who have moved beyond traditional female roles, such as consumer affairs directors. She points to the changing attitude of many in the industry toward bringing their daughters into the business. Minyard knows she would never have ascended to the top level at age 39 had she not had the dual advantage of being born into the Minyard family and not having any brothers.

Yet while she wants to be a symbol of encouragement to others that women can do the job, Minyard insists her role as symbol ends there. She draws a line between her professional behavior and her individual personality and lifestyle, making it plain that what she likes and dislikes should have no effect on decision making at her company or for any supplier.

Minyard also maintains that she does not speak for all women in the industry or for all women shoppers. She refrains from speaking out on certain issues because she doesn't consider herself a typical shopper: not only is she wealthier than most of her customers, but Minyard eats out most nights with her husband.

Source: Michael Sansolo, "In One Woman's Opinion," ***Progressive Grocer,*** **July 1993, pp. 44–48. Photo source: © Les Wollam/Gamma Liaison.**

As human beings, in one sense we are all alike—and in another, we are all different. Your fingerprints and DNA will never be duplicated in another human being. But the chemicals that make up your body are the same as in all human beings. We all experience birth and growth, disappointment and sadness. But at the same time, our life experiences are unique—a combination of what happens to us and how we interpret those events, which shapes our unique personalities. As you saw in this chapter's opening vignette, Liz Minyard understands and sympathizes with what her customers need, even though she has a lifestyle vastly different from most of them.

Of course, if certain patterns of behavior were not common to all human beings, there could be no study of human relations. Yet, since all human beings differ in their specific behaviors, the study of human relations involves both generalizing about people and taking into account individual differences. It sounds like a contradictory task. The challenge is to adjust the appropriate broad principle to the specific application. Therefore, an understanding of basic human nature must be blended with a reasonable knowledge of the individual employees.

The factors that influence individual behavior can be broken down as follows:

- personality
- values
- intelligence
- perceptions
- attitudes.

These influences overlap, of course. Values and intelligence, for example, help make up personality. Personality helps determine attitudes, and so forth. But some distinctions can be made among the various elements.

You've Got Personality!

personality
The behavioral and emotional characteristics that distinguish an individual.

The behavioral and emotional characteristics that distinguish an individual are his or her **personality**. Genetic and environmental factors are involved. To what extent each overshadows the other is a subject of continuing debate. Nevertheless, whatever the early role of environment, it is less influential after a person reaches adulthood. Therefore, in an employment setting, personality must be accommodated rather than changed; it appears remarkably resistant to change except in small degrees.

Table 10.1 lists some basic personality traits. Any one of these traits might be significant in a given employment situation. For example, an informal idea-gathering session might be squashed by a team leader with a very formal personality. A sympathetic person might suffer undue stress from the responsibility of announcing layoffs. A creative person will be stifled by a routine job, and a conforming one will panic if given too much autonomy.

Of course, each person is a unique mix of the traits common to all. Thus, again we return to the idea that generalizations about human behavior are useful only when an awareness of individual differences is maintained.

Table 10.1 **Ranges of Selected Personality Traits**

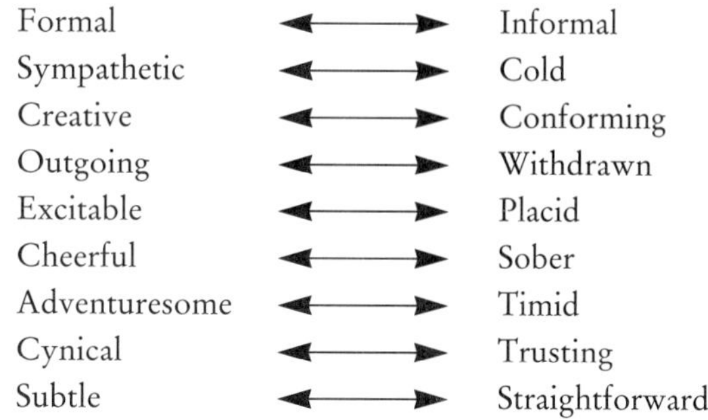

Formal	↔	Informal
Sympathetic	↔	Cold
Creative	↔	Conforming
Outgoing	↔	Withdrawn
Excitable	↔	Placid
Cheerful	↔	Sober
Adventuresome	↔	Timid
Cynical	↔	Trusting
Subtle	↔	Straightforward

Personality Types

One well-known way of classifying personalities is as *Type A,* representing aggressive, competitive, hard-driving people, or *Type B,* representing more easygoing, relaxed people. As discussed in Chapter 9, Type A personalities are more prone to stress than Type B. Both types have their advantages and disadvantages in the workplace. Type A people might work longer hours and push harder to meet a deadline, but Type B people might have a better relationship with coworkers or might make decisions with a cooler head. Then again, the individuals' intelligence, values, and so forth will determine how their Type A or B personalities are manifested.

internalizing Description of people who believe they have much control over their own circumstances; they have an internal *locus of control.*

externalizing Description of people who believe external forces largely control them; they have an external *locus of control.*

Personality types may also be described as emotional versus logical, passive versus active, introverted versus extroverted, and **internalizing** (people who believe they have much control over their own circumstances) versus **externalizing** (those who believe external forces largely control them). Internalizing and externalizing are also referred to as internal and external *locus of control* (see Figure 10.1). From this perspective, you would not assign a job that requires creativity and initiative to a passive, externalizing person. This type of personality is better suited to a job that comes with complete instructions. Nor would you waste a "self-starter" (internalizing type) on a routine job that requires no initiative.

Another way of describing personality types is according to their degree of *authoritarianism*—essentially, a respect for authority that transcends other feelings and values, leading to unquestioning obedience and an expectation of such obedience from others. The concept was linked by its creators to an intolerance for individual differences, specifically anti-Semitism, and to political conservatism. *Dogmatism* is a less politicized version of authoritarianism; it describes an inflexible, confident personality who is quick to make decisions where someone less dogmatic would seek further information—and perhaps others' opinions—first. Authoritarian or dogmatic employees tend to work better under supervisors of the same personality bent.

Some organizations actually hire psychological management consulting firms to help them select the right personality type for an important position. For example, a different type of person is needed to cut down the size of an organization than to recruit new employees or initiate a sensitivity training program.

Otto Kroeger Associates is one such consulting firm. Its Typewatching process is designed to "help individuals and companies understand and use personality differences constructively and creatively." Based on the *Myers-Briggs Type Indicator,* which identifies 16 psychological types according to Jungian theory, the Typewatching system "pigeonholes" people as

Figure 10.1 **Externalizing versus Internalizing Personality**

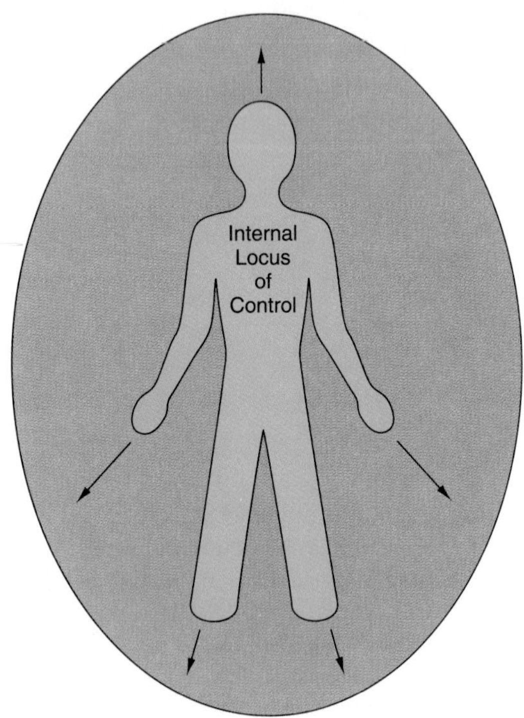

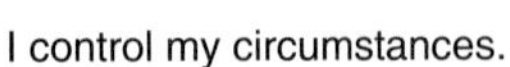

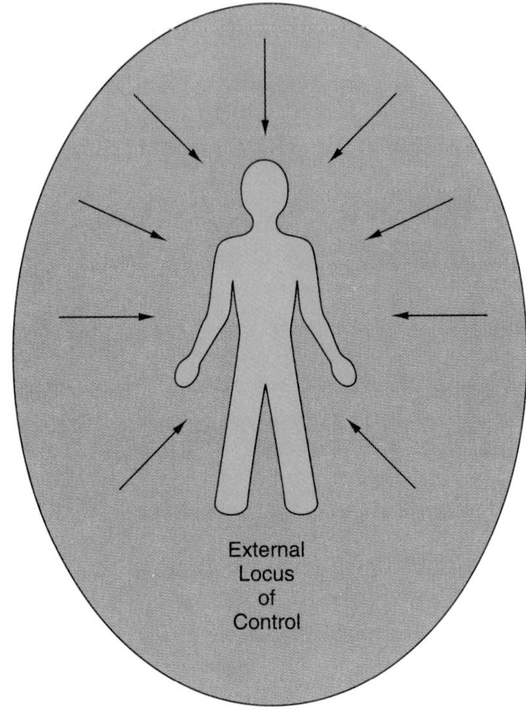

- *Extrovert type*—outgoing, verbal, and energized by other people or actions
- *Introvert type*—private, inward-looking, and energized by thoughts and ideas
- *Intuitive type*—visionary, figurative, and preferring possibilities and meanings
- *Thinker type*—logical, analytical, and driven by objective values
- *Feeler type*—subjective, interpersonally oriented, and driven by the impact of decisions on people
- *Judger type*—structured, scheduled, ordered, planned, and controlled
- *Perceiver type*—flexible, spontaneous, adaptive, and responsive.

It's important to keep in mind that one person might fit several categories, such as extrovert, intuitive, feeler, and perceiver. Also, a person with a combination of traits can use those traits to behave in the best way in a given situation. Or a person can choose to develop a trait that seems desirable or important in a work situation.

Pigeonholing people is something we do naturally anyway, according to Otto Kroeger, so "as long as we're going to label one another, we might as well do it as skillfully, objectively, and constructively as possible." Kroeger presents the example of Art, a typical Judger, whose rigid, controlling behavior was causing problems for coworkers and portending a possible stress-related problem for himself. The Typewatching system was used to help Art recognize and modify his extreme behaviors. He scheduled some relaxation time into his routine, and reminded himself to be on guard against excessive inflexibility or compulsive action. "We helped him take advantage of his personality strengths to tackle his weakness."[1] The idea of such personality evaluation, then, is that knowledge is power—power to use one's personality to best advantage and minimize bad results from any weaknesses.

Personality Tests

Personality tests are available, although their value is disputed. *Personality ratings* are scales on which an observer evaluates the degree to which a certain trait is present in the observed person. For example, Julie might be rated as extremely sensitive to the feelings of others, George as moderately sensitive, and Pete as insensitive. Obviously, the accuracy of the rating depends entirely on the perception of the rater, who may be biased in any number of ways.

Situational or *behavioral tests* also depend on the skills of an observer but offer more objectivity; behavior is directly observed in a setting designed to reveal personality traits. Usually the person being evaluated is not aware of being observed. These tests provide some valid information, but they are expensive to conduct and limited in what traits they can reveal.

Personality inventories depend on the perception (and honesty) of the person being evaluated. Respondents are asked if certain statements are true for them, such as, "Do you find it easy to make friends?" Checks against false answers are included but, of course, are not infallible.

Projective tests such as the Rorschach (inkblot) test, the story-telling thematic apperception test (TAT), and sentence completions probe more deeply into personality. The rationale behind these tests is that people will see in the inkblot, or reveal in the story or sentence, what is in their psyche. In other words, they project their feelings onto the device presented, much as a person who is feeling anger might perceive it in another's blank expression.

Effect of Personality on Performance

Surprisingly, research indicates that personality has only a moderate effect on performance. Possibly the personality tests fail to measure the traits that affect performance the most, or perhaps the test results do not correlate well with the performance tests. That is, the traits most important to performance may not be measurable on available tests, or the aspect of performance most affected may not be measurable. Another consideration is that many facets of personality, though they may dictate choice of occupation and other actions, are not relevant to actual performance.

The trait most directly linked with performance appears to be the aforementioned *locus of control*: internalizing people tend to perform better in most areas, although they may be more demanding of their environment. For example, they may resist management by an autocratic leader who allows them no participation in decision making. Efforts at correlating personality traits with job requirements have centered on *mechanistic* versus *impressionistic* approaches. Mechanistic approaches use mathematics to determine correlations; impressionistic approaches use intuition based on various data to make correlations. The former appear to have better results.[2]

Personality judgments and test results are not safe predictors of job performance. Other, more objective characteristics—namely, experience and education, or results of a work skills test—should be the primary guide for hiring or job-assignment decisions, with personality a significant, but secondary, consideration.

Effect of Stress on Personality

Although some degree of stress can be beneficial, serving to motivate an employee, too much stress can cause detrimental changes in personality that cripple job performance.

Self-Portrait

How Does Time Pressure Affect You?

To assess the degree to which time pressure influences your life, answer all the questions by circling the number of the best alternative, even if no single answer seems exactly right.

1. In a typical week, how often do you wear a watch?
   (1) regularly (2) part of the time (3) occasionally (4) almost never
2. How many hours do you sleep on an average weeknight?
   (1) 5 or less (2) 6 (3) 7 (4) 8 or more
3. When driving, how often do you speed?
   (1) regularly (2) often (3) seldom (4) almost never
4. While driving, as you approach a green traffic signal that is turning to yellow, you are most likely to:
   (1) speed up to get through before it turns red
   (4) slow down and wait for it to turn green
5. (1) When I have a train or plane to catch, I like to arrive as close as possible to the departure time so I won't have to waste time sitting around.
   (4) I always try to leave extra time to get to an airport or train station so I won't have to worry about missing a flight or train.
6. (1) At a restaurant, I like my food served as soon as possible after I've ordered.
   (4) I don't mind waiting a few minutes for the food I've ordered.
7. (1) I like microwave ovens because they cut down on meal preparation time.
   (4) I'd rather spend extra time preparing meals than use a microwave oven.
8. (1) I often use a remote-control device to scan a lot of television channels to see what's on.
   (4) To me, a remote control is a convenient tool for turning the TV on or off from a distance, adjusting the volume, or occasionally changing channels.
9. (1) With so many other demands on my time, I find it hard to keep up friendships.
   (4) I try to make time to see my friends regularly.
10. Compared with your life ten years ago, would you say you have more or less leisure time?
    (1) less (2) about the same (3) a bit more (4) a lot more
11. How would you compare the amount of time you spend running errands today with the amount you spent ten years ago?
    (1) more (2) about the same (3) somewhat less (4) a lot less
12. During the past year, how many books have you read for pleasure from beginning to end?
    (1) 0 to 2 (2) 3 to 5 (3) 6 to 10 (4) 11 or more
13. How good are you at glancing at your watch or a clock without anyone noticing?
    (1) very good (2) good (3) fair (4) not good at all
14. How would you rate your ability to conduct a conversation and appear to be paying attention while thinking about something else at the same time?
    (1) excellent (2) good (3) fair (4) poor

The result may be burnout, a state of emotional exhaustion that produces a complete loss of motivation. As discussed in Chapter 9, a recent survey reported three out of four American workers as being "stressed out..., many to the point of burnout."[3] Again, Type A personalities are more prone to stress than Type B. Take the "Self-Portrait" exercise above to see how the stress of time pressures affects you.

15. How often do you find yourself interrupting the person with whom you're talking?
    (1) regularly (2) often (3) occasionally (4) rarely
16. When talking on the telephone, do you:
    (1) do paperwork, wash dishes, or tackle some other chore?
    (2) straighten up the surrounding area?
    (3) do small personal tasks?
    (4) do nothing else?
17. In an average week, how many evening or weekend hours do you spend working overtime or on work you've brought home?
    (1) 16 or more (2) 11 to 15 (3) 6 to 10 (4) 0 to 5
18. On a typical weekend, do you primarily engage in:
    (1) work for income
    (2) errands, household chores, and child care?
    (3) leisure activities?
    (4) catching up on sleep and relaxation?
19. In a typical year, how many weeks of paid vacation do you take?
    (1) 1 or less (2) 2 (3) 3 (4) 4 or more
20. On the whole, how do you find vacations?
    (1) frustrating
    (2) tedious
    (3) relaxing
    (4) rejuvenating
21. How often do you find yourself wishing you had more time to spend with family and friends?
    (1) constantly (2) often (3) occasionally (4) almost never
22. During a typical day, how often do you feel rushed?
    (1) constantly (2) often (3) occasionally (4) almost never
23. Which statement best describes your usual daily schedule?
    (1) There aren't enough hours in the day to do everything I have to do.
    (2) On the whole, I have enough time to do what I have to do.
    (3) I can usually do the things I have to do with time left over.
    (4) The day seems to have more hours than I'm able to fill.
24. During the past year, how would you say your life has grown?
    (1) busier (2) about the same (3) somewhat less busy (4) a lot less busy

Scoring: Add the total of all the numbers circled. A score of 25 to 40 indicates you are *time-locked;* 41 to 55, *pressed for time;* 56 to 71, *in balance*; 72 to 86, *time on hands.*

The ravages of excessive stress include poor decisions, interpersonal conflict, and low morale. Furthermore, stressed people are often physically unhealthy people. Ulcers, headaches, and even a weakened immune system and cardiovascular problems can result from stress or be aggravated by it, along with a host of other disorders. Stress can even precipitate violence. According to the Society of Human Resource Management, between 1988 and 1993, physical violence (everything from sexual assault to murder) occurred in one-third of the workplaces surveyed.[4] This survey also noted that the violent incidents primarily stemmed from personality conflicts.

Levi Strauss & Co. tries to manage by values. Today in Bangladesh, 11- to 13-year-old girls are in classrooms. Not long ago, they were working full time sewing Dockers pants. In 1992, Levi Strauss extended its ethical code to its international businesses and disallowed employing children under 14 years. Realizing this meant the loss of the only income for some families, the company sent the girls to school and arranged with its contractors to pay their wages and hire them back at 14.

Photo source: Pablo Bartholomew/Gamma Liaison.

Photo Exercise

Do you think a U.S. company should apply its ethical standards to its international operations? Why or why not?

Companies now try harder to reduce stress in the workplace by providing such services as employee assistance programs, training, and counseling. But an organization can go only so far in reducing stress for its people. As we learned in Chapter 9, each of us must take responsibility for controlling stress in our life and on the job by making sure we get adequate rest, nutrition, and exercise. An optimistic attitude and a willingness to avail ourselves of the emotional support of friends and family help, too.

Quick Quiz 10.1

1. Is the Type A or Type B personality most prone to stress?
2. Name three types of projective personality tests.
3. ___________ is the personality trait most directly linked with job performance.

A Variety of Values

values
A person's beliefs about what is morally right and wrong or what has worth and what does not.

Values are a person's beliefs about what is morally right and wrong or what has worth and what does not. Notice that our definition covers two different ways of looking at values. There is (1) a moral aspect and (2) a practical aspect that may have nothing to do with morality. In the moral realm, a person may or may not value honesty, for example. Consider the following three scenarios:

1. Sandra's values would never permit her to steal from an individual. As a grocery checker, she called back the customer who was about to walk off without his change, even though she could have easily pocketed it. However, she has no scruples about pocketing a package of cookies from the store when she has the opportunity. And she accepted a paycheck error in her favor with delight.
2. Given the same opportunity as Sandra, Jeremiah would have kept the customer's change. But his values would not permit this action if the customer were a friend of his. Jeremiah regards stealing from an organization (in this case, the grocery store) the same way Sandra does—his values permit it. Unlike Sandra, he also gives himself license to steal from an individual, provided the individual is a stranger.
3. Delilah's values prohibit all stealing. Though she may be tempted by an opportunity to steal (as in the case of the paycheck error), she will probably resist the temptation in order to avoid an uneasy conscience.

Moral values are a legitimate area of concern to an employer, but they are hard to assess. Some employers administer a preemployment "honesty test," which is a form of personality test of debatable accuracy. Usually, though, values concerning the second part of our definition—that is, what has worth and what has not—are much easier to assess. An employee might value a prestigious title more than a high paycheck, extra money more than time off, an opportunity for advancement more than extra money—or vice versa. Recall the expectancy-valence theory of motivation. The *valence* of a motivating factor is the degree to which an employee *values* it.

Edward Spraunger identified six categories of values that often appear to dictate a person's choice of occupation:

1. *Theoretical values* emphasize the discovery of truth. Scientists probably have strong theoretical values.
2. *Economic values* emphasize the accumulation of wealth and/or the production of useful goods and services. Successful businesspeople probably have strong economic values.
3. *Aesthetic values* emphasize that which is beautiful, whether in art or literature or music or any other area. Creative, artistic people necessarily have strong aesthetic values.
4. *Social values* emphasize the welfare of humanity. People with strong social values are characterized by love and compassion for other people. These values may well be linked to religious values.
5. *Political values* emphasize power and need not involve government politics, although people with strong political values often do become politicians. However, anyone interested in positions that offer power over situations or other people has strong political values, according to this definition.
6. *Religious values* emphasize the beliefs of one religion or another. Obviously, clergy would have strong religious values, but people in almost any occupation might be found in this category.

Our values—moral and otherwise—are formed by our family and other social influences, our exposure to ideas in books and movies, our religious beliefs or lack thereof, plus that indefinable something that makes each of us uniquely ourselves. They may change with time and experience. We have all heard of cases in which a notorious lawbreaker reforms, or we may even find ourselves valuing something more than we used to—such as family time together or job security.

When it comes to moral values, those of top management in an organization can have far-reaching, even astounding implications involving many people and—in the case of pollution—the environment as well.

Values Related to Work Ethic

work ethic
An attitude of valuing work for its own sake and seeing virtue and dignity in any type of hard work.

The **work ethic** values work for its own sake, seeing virtue and dignity in any type of hard work. An interesting finding in regard to the work ethic was that negative feedback ("You're not performing up to expectations") produced an effort to improve in people who had expressed a belief in the work ethic, compared to a reduced performance in those who rejected such a belief.[5] Acceptance of the work ethic has diminished, especially among younger workers. On surveys asking whether people would continue working if they had no financial needs, few respond affirmatively, and more are choosing early retirement than in the past.[6]

"Entitled employees" is what management consultant Judith Bardwick calls those lacking the work ethic. These are "workers who feel their pay is something they are owed, not something they earn." She warns that although they are more prevalent in

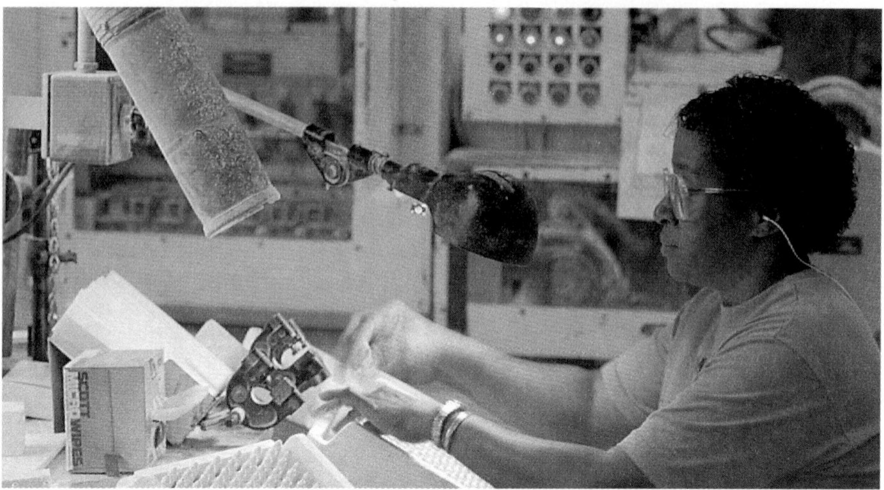

Rewarding performance provides motivation. At the Allied-Signal spark-plug plant in Fostoria, Ohio, the company cut the traditional 3 percent annual raise to 2 percent. However, the employees can boost their salaries as much as 6 percent a year if they meet productivity improvement goals.
Photo source: © 1994 Ted Rice.

Photo Exercise

Would you find it more motivating to receive a guaranteed raise or be paid for your increased productivity?

government and big business, they pop up even in the smallest shops today. Human resources consultant Dianne La Mountain agrees. "In many companies, we no longer see the old-fashioned notion of giving a fair day's work for a fair day's pay.... Yesteryear's work ethic no longer prevails."[7]

Bardwick offers these principles for combating the "entitlement" attitude:[8]

- *Increase employee accountability through regular performance evaluations.* The first step is to let employees know in detail what is expected of them and then hold them accountable for it. Frequent informal evaluations can also serve as a "crucial teaching tool."
- *Reward differentially.* A problem in most companies is that the performance differential between the highest and lowest performers is not reflected in their paychecks. Rewarding performance—perhaps by bonuses—provides motivation.
- *Visibly fire for nonperformance.* First, employees should be explicitly informed as to what kind of performance it takes to earn job security. Then, frequent evaluations should let them know how they are doing. Bardwick warns against the "sort of gloomy secrecy that usually accompanies terminations.... If George is let go because of chronic absenteeism, call a staff meeting ... and tell your people how often he was absent. Give them hard numbers. Workers fear irrational firings."
- *Create competition.* Most people perform best when competing, even if only against their own past levels of performance. Set "stretch" goals. "Competition can be used to jar people out of entitlement," says Bardwick, "especially when it's tied to differential rewards."

The entitlement issue may be related to workers' sense that they have no job security, and thus no longer possess the value of company loyalty. Downsizing certainly has contributed to this. For instance, IBM cut 25,000 jobs in 1993 and announced that another 47,000 workers would be offered "voluntary early retirement."[9] According to one national survey, 63 percent of middle managers feel less loyalty toward their companies than they did several years ago. In addition, 57 percent of American corporations feel less loyalty toward their employees.[10] This points to the importance of human relations in shifting employees' attitudes from entitlement to a more positive outlook.

Values Related to Moral Development

Lawrence Kohlberg's model for moral development proposes that people's values reflect their stage of "moral maturity." At the lowest stage, people adhere to ethical behavior in order to avoid punishment or receive rewards, whereas at the highest level they are motivated by a love of justice and universal principles of morality.[11] In between are stages where ethical behavior is chosen for various reasons of personal benefit or benefit to society at large.

Tests have been devised for measuring the stage of moral development. The obvious application to the workplace is that people in the lower stages may break company rules, steal or lie, and so forth, when they feel safe from detection. Thus, according to this model, Delilah in our previous example would be considered at a higher stage than Jeremiah, because her moral development prohibits her from all stealing. The more responsibility given a worker, the higher his or her stage of moral development should be. Although it is not always true, we expect the president of the United States to have achieved a high stage of moral development in order to carry out the job effectively. We don't want the president to declare war on another nation because of a personal vendetta, thus jeopardizing the lives of many people. And we expect the president to set a good example for other citizens by paying personal income taxes promptly.

Quick Quiz 10.2

1. Which of Spraunger's six categories of values might be predominant in a person who chooses a career as a social worker? An art director? A business executive?
2. An employee who feels that his or her paycheck is something that is owed, not earned, is referred to as an ____________.
3. A person who adheres to ethical behavior only to avoid punishment or receive rewards is in a lower stage of ____________ according to Kohlberg's model.

Intelligence and Learning

intelligence
A person's ability to learn and reason.

A person's ability to learn and reason is his or her **intelligence**. Unlike personality or values, this influence on behavior can be objectively measured as an *IQ score* (intelligence quotient) and matched with some accuracy to the demands of a given job. Personality can influence intelligence, though: a person with a hard-driving, ambitious personality might accomplish more than one with equal intelligence but less drive. Also, *attitude*, discussed later in this chapter, may determine how effectively a person's intelligence is used.

aptitude tests
Preemployment intelligence tests that aim to predict performance by measuring cognitive ability in verbal, numerical, perceptual, spatial, or reasoning areas.

Nevertheless, a certain minimum of intellectual ability required by a certain job can and should be ascertained. It would be unfair to the job candidate as well as to the organization to hire someone whose cognitive ability is inadequate for the job. Preemployment intelligence tests, called **aptitude tests**, measure cognitive ability in verbal, numerical, perceptual, spatial, or reasoning areas with a fair degree of accuracy. (They must be directly related to the tasks of the position to be legal.)

For some jobs, knowledge possessed is of prime importance; for others, capacity to learn is just as important or more important. But even for jobs that emphasize experience, some degree of on-the-job training, or capacity to learn, is involved. A new employee always faces learning tasks associated with the particular company or department, even when the substance of the job is the same as that of a previous job.

Different areas of intelligence are significant for different jobs. A mechanical engineer needs more spatial ability than an accountant, for example. However, communi-

Table 10.2 **Learning Styles and Occupations**

Characteristics	Sensing/Thinking (ST)	Intuiting/Thinking (NT)	Sensing/Feeling (SF)	Intuiting/Feeling (NF)
Is interested in:	Facts	Possibilities	Facts	Possibilities
Tendency to be:	Pragmatic, down to earth	Logical, but ingenious	Sympathetic, sociable	Energetic, insightful
Strengths:	Technical skills involving facts	Theoretical problem solving	Providing help and services to others	Understanding and communicating with others
Typical occupations:	Physician, accountant, computer programmer	Scientist, corporate planner, mathematician	Salesperson, social worker, psychologist	Artist, writer, entertainer

Source: Table from ORGANIZATIONAL BEHAVIOR, Second Edition by Robert P. Vecchio, copyright © 1991 by The Dryden Press, reproduced by permission of the publisher.

cations skills are important in almost every type of job. In fields that heavily involve human relations, they are a vital prerequisite.

Learning Styles

Learning styles are based on personality type. Carl Jung described the different learning styles as (1) sensing/thinking, (2) intuiting/thinking, (3) sensing/feeling, and (4) intuiting/feeling. *Sensing* refers to a preference for dealing with facts; *intuiting,* to a preference for dealing with possibilities. *Thinking* refers to a logical, analytical style; *feeling,* to a people-oriented style. Jung's theory was that everyone has a dominant style combined with a secondary, backup one. Table 10.2 shows some occupations typically chosen by people with the various styles.

Recall the Myers-Briggs Type Indicator, based on Jung's categories, which is used by consulting firms specializing in defining personality types. *Sensors* tend to be more practical types than *intuitives.* They prefer specific answers to specific questions and concentrate on short-term or immediate results and on tangible results, rather than getting excited about the future or the "big picture." Intuitives deal better with abstract concepts; they tend to be "visionary," and work better with ideas than facts (just the opposite of the sensor). *Thinkers* tend to be more objective, impersonal in their decision making; *feelers* are more subjective. Thinkers are less prone to panic and are more logical, but feelers are more likely to be considerate of other people. "Neither [sensor versus intuitive, or thinker versus feeler] is right or wrong," explains Otto Kroeger. "They're just different ways of dealing with the situation."[12]

An awareness of employees' learning styles is useful, since tasks can be assigned in a way that takes advantage of a particular style. Moreover, people with similar learning styles tend to work together better than those with dissimilar styles, so a joint project may proceed more smoothly if people with the same styles are assigned to it. Of course, the most effective learners are those who can change their learning style to fit the situation at hand and the people he or she will be working with.

The way different learning styles affect your skills and ability to work at home is described in the "Diversity Highlights" box.

Recall Brian Azar's categories of communication styles from Chapter 5; people are visual, auditory, or kinesthetic communicators.[13] These categories can be applied to

Diversity Highlights

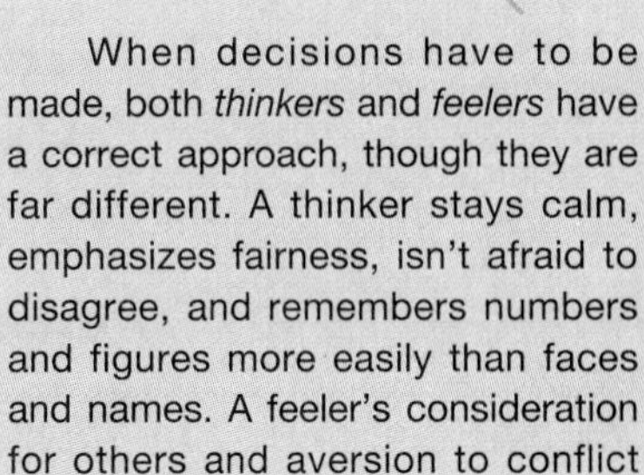

Homing In

Does having a personality well suited to working at home mean a person is antisocial, boring, unambitious? Or is the home-based worker an entrepreneur—focused, thrifty, a self-starter? It all depends on—what else? Personality.

For example, Arthur Perrone didn't last long as a home-based financial consultant. "I went from the whole 'power-tie' attitude to sitting on the floor in my spare bedroom," he says. "It drove me crazy to be on the phone talking to someone in Europe while the dog was barking and the kids were running around. I felt terribly unproductive."

Mary Logeland and her husband, Doug, had the opposite reaction, preferring the solitude and warmth of their home to the cold corporate world. She says, "Office politics and slow decision making drove me nuts."

Obviously, working at home has more pluses for some, more minuses for others. Though no one personality type is ideally suited to working at home and none totally prohibitive, some are more inclined than others.

Introverts, as a group, are better suited to working from home, says Otto Kroeger, a psychological and management consultant. Kroeger's Typewatching system reveals that introverts do best if their business relies heavily on the phone and demands self-motivation. *Extroverts* are better suited to home-based businesses that have heavy competition and require aggressive advertising and networking.

Sensors like the hands-on experience of working at home and bring to it practicality and the ability to distinguish the doable from the impossible. However, sensors can become overwhelmed by dealing with work and family in the same environment. *Intuitives* have the opposite problem. Lacking the discipline of an office setting, their excitement about the creative aspects of working can lead them to lose their grounding and become all hype.

When decisions have to be made, both *thinkers* and *feelers* have a correct approach, though they are far different. A thinker stays calm, emphasizes fairness, isn't afraid to disagree, and remembers numbers and figures more easily than faces and names. A feeler's consideration for others and aversion to conflict provides a sound counterbalance to the thinker's approach; partnering these two personality types covers the bases.

Judgers are more likely than others to become completely immersed in their work, perhaps never really leaving the "office." Their need for structure compels them to work until they finish. With their spontaneous nature, *perceivers* sometimes have problems prioritizing and are easily distracted, trying to make work as much fun as play.

Source: Janean Huber, "Homing Instinct," *Entrepreneur,* March 1993, pp. 83–87.

learning styles as well. A visual person learns well from charts and graphs. An auditory person learns from a lecture or tape. A kinesthetic person learns through emotion and intuition.

Learning Environment

Kenneth Blanchard identifies the following factors as contributing to an effective learning environment in an organization:[14]

- *Openness.* Organizations need an atmosphere of inviting questions and concerns. There must be no fear of retribution, no hidden agendas. Employees should feel free to question even the "pet projects" of top managers.
- *Recall.* Continuous learning is enhanced when there is good retention of what has already been learned. Blanchard notes that this "memory" is harder to achieve in an organization than in an individual. He recommends documentation of such past learning and wide communication of it in written form. A company newsletter can help.
- *Objectivity.* On emotional issues, Blanchard recommends systematically asking a set series of questions, such as, "What are we excited/nervous about?" "What is likely to go wrong?" "How could we make it work?"

Quick Quiz 10.3

1 A job applicant is asked to take an aptitude test in areas that are directly related to the job. Is this legal?
2. According to Jung's theory of learning styles, an entertainer such as Billy Crystal or Whoopi Goldberg would fit into which category?
3. What are three factors that contribute to an effective learning environment?

Perceptions: Do You See What I See?

Perceptions are people's interpretations of reality, or what they think about what they observe. Both the *equity theory* and *expectancy-valence theory* of motivation relate to people's perceptions of their work. Equity theory concerns the perceived fairness of an employment situation, and expectancy-valence theory the perceived value of rewards that are meant to motivate. Perceptions affect job performance in other ways, too. Problems arising in this area involve

biased perception Seeing only a stereotype and basing conclusions on that.

selective perception Seeing only what you want or expect to see.

subjective perception Seeing everything from your own point of view and discounting others' perceptions.

1. **biased perception**—seeing only a stereotype and basing conclusions on that
2. **selective perception**—seeing only what you want or expect to see
3. **subjective perception**—seeing everything from your own point of view and discounting others' perceptions.

Biased Perception

Biased perception involves the unwise practice of *stereotyping*, or judging an individual according to generalizations about the particular group to which he or she belongs. Even when valid, a generalization about a group can never be safely applied to an individual. You might read somewhere that most Scandinavians love to eat fish, but this valid generalization does not guarantee that your Scandinavian guest will want fish for dinner. Unfortunately, most stereotyping is more harmful than this example. In a survey of 11 major U.S. companies, including Aetna Life and Casualty, AT&T, Gannett, Kodak, and Mobil, every one cited bias based on stereotyping as a primary obstacle to upward mobility.[15]

Biased perception not only prompts invalid conclusions based on unfounded beliefs, it can also block out important information. Consequently, it is often the cause of *selective* perception, discussed next.

Selective Perception

One type of selective perception involves the tendency to see what you expect to see. Another harmful form of selective perception is seeing what you want to see. Although prejudices—the result of a belief in stereotypes—obviously can play a role in both kinds of selective perception, many other factors can be involved as well. Suppose Francesca unsuccessfully opposed Randall's new program and now has to report on its results. She wants to see any bad results—she's looking for them—but subtle benefits of the program may well escape her attention despite her determination to be fair and write a complete report. Suppose instead that she has seen Randall's program operate successfully in the past and expects it to do the same here. She expects to see benefits. If they do not at first appear, she will look harder for them. She may not have any personal feelings about whether or not she *wants* Randall's program to succeed; past experience simply leads her to *expect* its success.

Subjective Perception

In subjective perception, a person considers only his or her own point of view. Since one person's point of view might be based on only partial information, while another's conflicting point of view is based on equally important additional information, the disadvantage of subjective perception is clear. Even when subjective people are right in their conclusions, the inability to consider other points of view hampers them in persuading others and thus enlisting cooperation. It can also cause misinterpretation of a message. If I don't understand your point of view, I might think your words mean something you did not intend.

Subjective perception means you can't "put yourself in the other person's shoes." It is a severe handicap to communication, yet its cure lies in communication, too. The more information you can assimilate about the other person's point of view, the better you should be able to understand it. Sometimes enough information will even bring you around to that opposing point of view. Or it may give you the ammunition you need to convince the other person to come over to your side.

Perceptual Congruence

perceptual congruence The extent to which people share the same perceptions.

The problems presented by subjective perception can be avoided if coworkers enjoy a high degree of **perceptual congruence**, or a sharing of perceptions. Agreement on goals and on the best methods of reaching those goals is easier in the presence of perceptual congruence. Communication is better also, since there is less chance of misinterpreting messages. The issue of *sexual harassment* underscores how a lack of perceptual congruence can create problems. Studies have shown dramatic differences in male and female perceptions of what constitutes sexual harassment.[16]

Unfortunately, perceptual congruence has a negative aspect—if the perceptions are wrong, their flaws are less likely to be detected. Furthermore, perceptual congruence can lead to *groupthink*, where everyone is thinking so much along the same lines that an effort at brainstorming or some other technique for idea generation is stymied.

Cultural Differences in Perception

Sometimes perceptions are a direct result of an individual's culture, as people involved in international businesses quickly learn. Certain behaviors viewed favorably by one society might be disapproved by another. Although the emotions experienced may be the same, the way people express those emotions may differ greatly. For example, Americans manifest significantly more verbal and nonverbal reactions to various emotions than do Japanese people.[17] Many differences between Japanese and American culture have come to light in recent years as business dealings between the two nations have increased.

On a smaller scale, amid the cultural diversity of the American workplace some differences in perception have arisen, too. Being able to distinguish a difference in perception from some other difficulty makes all the difference in successful human relations interactions. For example, in one instance a specialist in managing cultural diversity was able to inform a company that its Asian employee's reluctance to give an oral presentation was motivated by cultural differences, not a professional inadequacy. The specialist suggested that the Asian be teamed with a colleague to give the presentation. The result was an "eloquent" performance by the Asian.[18]

One large American company learned the importance of cultural sensitivity when one of its television commercials—shown only in the United States—insulted the European town where it was filmed. Learn why background cultural research is needed even before market research can begin by reading the "International Highlights" box.

International Highlights

A Visa to Cultural Sensitivity

Citizens and merchants in the Italian town of Todi were angered by the way their young people were represented in a recent Visa credit-card commercial. American tourists might be silly enough to hand a camera to two "peasant" boys so they could be photographed with a donkey, but making it appear that the boys "took off" with the camera, as the announcer says, was insulting to the village. Protests—and a threatened boycott of Visa cards—led Visa to smooth over this incident of cultural insensitivity, but the spot continues to run.

However standards and values vary, respect for and understanding of another country and its culture is vital in human relations and the world of business. Market research studies and focus groups, the first steps in doing business internationally, are greatly affected by cultural differences. For example, doing business in Latin America requires a one-on-one effort, because Latins are more forthcoming in person than over the phone or by mail. At the same time, however, their face-to-face effusiveness often leads to overstatement and hyperbole.

When asked pointed questions, Asians prefer to be noncommittal. They are more inclined to tell the interviewer what they think he or she wants to hear instead of what they really think. Mixed age, mixed gender, or manager-subordinate focus groups do not work because one group will defer to the other.

Americans' and Europeans' shared history and heritage allows for a more familiar approach to the European market, though not as familiar and casual as Visa's. Small cultural differences distinguish each country; the Germans and the English tend to understate their emotions, while subjects from Italy and Spain tend to be overly complimentary. In addition, Europeans prefer a broad perspective in focus groups and use more than one moderator.

In Saudi Arabia, going door to door to sell a product or ask questions is illegal. Contact must be made with business executives at their offices; if you are interested in gathering information about consumers, you must ask these executives for an introduction to their wives and friends.

Sources: Nancy Millman, "Oops! Spots Can Trip Over Inadvertent Insults," *Chicago Tribune*, April 19, 1994, section 5, p. 2; Aimee Stern, "Do You Know What They Want?" *International Business*, March 1993, p. 103.

Relationship between Values and Perceptions

Values are closely related to perceptions. For example, if Howard values accuracy over speed, and Helen values speed over accuracy, the two will perform a job very differently according to their perceptions of what has priority. They will perceive another person's performance very differently, too. Helen will attach more importance to a team member's missed deadline than Howard, and he will be less inclined to forgive minor errors.

As another example, suppose Sharon greatly values social relationships at work and therefore admires socially adept people who supervise with charm and grace. How will she perceive a blunt-spoken supervisor who issues orders with no friendly warmup of "Hello, how are you today?"? Suppose she is entrusted with this supervisor's performance review. Even if his department runs smoothly and his employees have made no complaints about his brusque manner, Sharon may well deduct points for his lack of gracious manners. If Manuel, on the other hand, who values intelligence above all, reviews the same supervisor and is impressed with that supervisor's intelligence, he may totally discount the man's lack of social graces.

Ask yourself how values are related to different perceptions in the following scenario:

> "If your previous employers had to describe you with one word, what would they say?" asked the interviewer for a high-level management job in an advertising company.
>
> "She's hard working!" answered the candidate.
>
> It was not the answer the interviewer was looking for. "*My* previous employers," he commented, "would have said, 'He's creative!'"

The job candidate in this scenario might well be as creative as the interviewer, but she values hard work above creativity. The interviewer might be as hard working as the candidate, but he values creativity more. They therefore had different perceptions about the top requirements for the job.

Process of Perception

The process of perception begins with *sensory inputs,* that is, what your senses (vision, hearing, and so forth) tell your brain. Usually, so many sensory inputs bombard us that we must select those we will pay attention to, and this is called the *attention* phase of the perception process. The problem known as *information overload* occurs when too many sensory inputs worthy of our attention occur at one time.

The next phase in the process of perception is *construction,* in which information is organized and edited so as to make the final phase of *interpretation* possible. Necessary to construction is **perceptual grouping**, or organizing data received into familiar patterns. This is a way of reducing the data to manageable proportions.

perceptual grouping
Organizing data received into familiar patterns in order to facilitate interpretation.

Perceptual set, the expectations of the perceiver (discussed as "selective perception" earlier), influences construction. Biased perception and subjective perception may occur here. Other influences on construction include the following:

perceptual set
The expectations of the perceiver.

1. **Contrast effects**, in which contrast to a reference point makes something seem smaller or greater than it really is. For example, if Leroy received a 10 percent raise last year, a 3 percent raise this year will be perceived as less satisfactory than if last year's had been 1.5 percent.
2. **Anchoring-and-adjustment effects**, in which the perception represents an adjustment from an "anchoring" reference point. If Mary Lou hears that Leroy got a 10 percent raise and she knows her performance has exceeded his, she will adjust up from that 10 percent in her request for a raise, probably asking for at least 12 percent. If she hears instead that Leroy received only 1.5 percent, she probably will ask for far less than 12 percent—even if 12 percent would be a reasonable request in relation to her job performance.
3. **Halo effects**, a form of anchoring and adjustment, in which a perception in one area influences perceptions in other, unrelated areas. Physical attractiveness is the best example—it creates a "halo" around the person, causing more favorable perceptions of his or her character, competence, and so on, than would otherwise occur. The power of a positive first impression is connected to the halo effect in a sense. "Dressing for success" is a solid concept; the proper appearance gives a person an edge, and a proper first appearance gives a greater edge.

contrast effect
When contrast to a reference point makes something seem smaller or greater than it really is.

anchoring-and-adjustment effect
When the perception represents an adjustment from an "anchoring" reference point.

halo effect
A form of anchoring and adjustment in which a perception in one area influences perceptions in other, unrelated areas.

In *interpreting,* the last phase of the perception process, we give meaning to the construction. This entails assigning causes to outcomes, a process called **attribution**. If your supervisor is frowning when you enter her office, you might attribute the frown to disapproval of your latest piece of work, disapproval of you—or, if you happen to know she has an ulcer—stomach pain. Suppose you did perform poorly on your last piece of work. Your supervisor might attribute the poor performance to a lack of effort, a lack of ability, or—if she happens to know you are worried about a sick relative—an excusable lack of concentration.

attribution
Assigning causes to outcomes in the process of interpretation.

Our interpretations may be skewed by **self-serving attribution**, in which we assign causes in a way that reflects favorably on ourselves. If Jenny fails to meet her deadline, she attributes the failure to other people's slowness, conflicts at home, unclear instructions for the job, or simply an unreasonable deadline. Her self-serving bias demands that she interpret the failure in a way that will avoid casting blame on herself. The antidote is called **objective self-awareness**, meaning an awareness of one's own role in causing outcomes. A good feedback system can help employees develop their objective self-awareness.

self-serving attribution
Assigning causes in a way that reflects favorably on ourselves.

objective self-awareness
An awareness of one's own role in causing outcomes.

The power of image projection can be found in an employee's personal dress code and also in the appearance of the business premises. In the photo, Kevin Grace, president of Spring Engineers, Inc. a Dallas, Texas, spring manufacturer, dresses with a successful image in mind. He is also concerned with his office: "It's very important that we make an impression that although we're a small business, we're a substantial one."

Photo source: T. Michael Keza/ Nation's Business.

The externalizing personality type described earlier in this chapter tends to use self-serving attribution. Since the locus of control is believed to be external, this type of person perceives circumstances, or other people's actions, as the cause of distressing events in his or her life. Objective self-awareness leads a person to see himself or herself as in charge of life events (to have an internal locus of control).

A cultural study of Japanese versus American tendencies in this area showed that Japanese people tend to be more internalizing in attributing responsibility for failure, though not for success.[19] That is, they took the blame themselves, while Americans in the study blamed circumstances or others. However, a larger percentage of Japanese than Americans declined to make any attribution at all.

social comparisons
Influences on our perception by other people's expressed perceptions.

Other people often alter our interpretations. A coworker's suggestion, a friend's comment, a relative's opinion may subtly influence our thinking. Such influences on our perception by other people's expressed perceptions are called **social comparisons**. The previously described anchoring-and-adjustment effect is related to this idea of social comparisons. Someone's suggestion, however illogical, may serve as an anchoring reference point from which we make an adjustment, arriving at a conclusion far different than we might have without the suggestion—or with a different suggestion. For example, if Jim suggests a task force of eight people, Bill, who has the responsibility for the final decision, might adjust downward from that number to five, whereas he might otherwise have appointed only three. If he speaks to Dora instead of Jim, and she suggests fifteen, he might say, "That's ridiculous. We don't need that many." But he might end up appointing eight instead of five or three.

subliminal influences
Influences on our perception that we are not consciously aware of.

Finally, **subliminal influences** on our perception exist, influences we are not aware of. Sensory inputs may suggest to our subconscious a familiar pattern that is hidden from our conscious awareness. Usually, however, such influences appear overridden by those that occur to our conscious mind.

Image Projection and Perceptions

image
The way others perceive us.

If we want to take advantage of the *halo effect* described earlier and the power of first impressions, we will devote some care to our own **image**, or the way others perceive us. The two aspects of our image are appearance and behavior. Appearance largely involves clothing and grooming. Even beautiful people make a poor first impression when dressed inappropriately or exhibiting inadequate grooming.

Behavior, the second aspect of image, involves verbal and nonverbal communication. Your handshake, for example, contributes greatly to that all-important first impression. Gilda Carle, communications specialist, goes so far as to say, "Your handshake represents who you are ... and how much power you have."[20] But she warns that since your handshake projects your image—your personality—so strongly, you should be careful about projecting the wrong image. Though the dreaded "limp fish" handshake is always to be avoided, it is possible to be too firm as well. You can actually inflict pain on a person with arthritis, or someone wearing several rings. The two-handed shake, in which you take the other person's hand in both of yours, may be perceived by some as patronizing. Being sensitive to the individual and to the situation is all that is necessary to avoid handshake mistakes that might dim your "halo."

The more we understand about perception, the better we can prevent misperceptions and the projection of an undesirable image. A false image is not the goal, but rather the best possible representation of what we really are. Interestingly, behaving a certain way can change what we really are to an extent. If you tend to be thoughtless and inconsiderate but make an effort to project the opposite image, in the very action of thoughtfulness and consideration you have indeed become your image.

Quick Quiz 10.4

1. Racial and gender-based discrimination are based on what type of flawed perception?
2. What are the four stages of the process of perception?
3. Too many sensory inputs can lead to information ___________.
4. Projecting false perceptions about yourself creates a false ___________.

Attitude Affects It All

attitude
A specific emotion toward a person, object, or situation.

An **attitude** is a specific emotion toward a person, object, or situation. Possibly no behavioral influence, other than intelligence, is more pertinent to job performance. Indeed, the appropriate attitude can sometimes make up for deficiencies in other areas. Conversely, a destructive attitude can negate a person's strengths. Attitudes are inevitably influenced by perceptions, values, personality, and intelligence, and these qualities are in turn influenced by attitudes.

Self-Concept: Your Attitude toward Yourself

self-concept
The opinion you have of yourself and the way you picture yourself.

Your **self-concept**, which is the opinion you have of yourself and the way you picture yourself, reveals your attitude toward yourself. It is formed by *perceptions* gained from life experiences, especially family influences. Thus, the way you have been treated, especially in childhood, largely determines your self-concept. Nevertheless, experiences in adulthood can modify it. Recall the *Pygmalion effect* discussed in Chapter 7, in which expectations tend to determine results. The expectations of coworkers and supervisors can influence your self-concept and thus your work performance to some degree.

A positive self-concept, or *self-esteem,* is basic to motivation, which causes desired behavior. The attitude of someone with a poor self-concept is usually, "What's the use of trying? I'm sure to fail." People with low self-esteem generally have difficulty working with others. They may be suspicious of others' motives. For example, if Joel has a poor self-concept, he might think Maria and Kurt are laughing at him when they share a joke near his office. That belief will hamper his working relationship with

Teamwork Highlights

Kaytee's Growing Flock

Some people have a hard time taking credit for their achievements, believing that their individual talents have less to do with their accomplishments than do teamwork and the contributions of their coworkers and employees. It is an attitude that usually results in personal and professional success.

Despite a White House ceremony honoring him and his achievements as the country's Small Business Person of the Year, Bill Engler Jr.'s first thoughts when he returned home to Chilton, Wisconsin, were of his employees and customers.

The employees at the family-owned firm, Kaytee Products Inc., maker of foods and nutritional products for birds and small animals, were thinking of him. They organized a welcome-home parade, complete with fire trucks and the high-school band.

Engler had been honored by the Small Business Administration for his leadership; when he assumed the company's reins in 1984, Kaytee had 60 employees and $10.6 million in annual sales. Today it has more than 350 employees and sales for the fiscal year are up 30 percent over 1992's $70 million. In addition to growing the company, Engler has opened a state-of-the-art avian research center in Wisconsin, devoted to preserving exotic species and encouraging domestic breeding. Most of the center's 1,500 inhabitants are on the list of threatened or endangered species.

Yet Engler, who gave up a successful law practice to head Kaytee, says he's just carrying on his father's vision. He has difficulty describing his own contributions to Kaytee. "When you ask me a question like that, you're asking me to talk about myself, and that's always difficult," he says. "We try to think in terms of 'we' rather than 'me.'"

Engler reluctantly allows that his function at Kaytee is to create a vision and to establish and reinforce the company's culture. "We try to be sensitive to individuals for what they are and treat them in a respectful way."

Source: Sharon Nelton, "Flying High on Bird Food," *Nation's Business*, September 1993, pp. 16–17.

them. Paradoxically, Joel may act egotistically in an effort to counteract his lack of self-esteem. He may seek relief from the unpleasant feeling of doubting his own worth by downgrading Maria and Kurt—especially if they are his subordinates. Or he may boast about himself in an effort to convince himself, and others, that he is not the failure he fears he might be.

Positive self-esteem, and the security it gives an individual to share the credit and shoulder the blame, can bring success to individuals and organizations. One such company is profiled in the "Teamwork Highlights" box.

The Pygmalion effect turned upon oneself has the effect of a *self-fulfilling prophecy,* in which one's own expectations determine one's own failure or success. Jorie predicts, "I'll be terrible at this job; I just know it." She's more likely to fail and fulfill her own prophecy with that attitude than if she approached the job with an optimistic, "can do" attitude. The world is full of stories of people who achieved amazing goals simply because they believed they could.

Consultant Hanoch McCarty, a former psychology professor, claims, "Sustained productivity is a by-product of self-esteem. When employees have high self-esteem, they're much more productive." Gail Dusa, another consultant, agrees: "High self-esteem is the greatest single indicator of excellence in any activity, job performance included."[21]

A positive self-concept does not mean an unrealistically favorable one. Suppose Clarissa has taken an entry-level job that is appropriate for her level of experience, but she feels it is beneath her talents and resents its low prestige compared with that of other jobs requiring more experience. Clarissa believes she could handle those higher-status jobs without the prerequisite experience, but she is wrong. She has an unrealistic self-concept.

Consider the case of the buyer for a medium-sized clothing store whose self-concept allows no admission of inadequacy in any area. He is partially color blind, but rather than seek the advice of the store manager, he chooses the colors for the new spring line of clothes. His store suffers the results of his poor choice in lower sales than otherwise would have resulted.

Certainly, a realistic view of oneself is worth pursuing. A clear view of strengths and weaknesses allows a person to use his or her strengths to advantage while improving areas of weakness.

Components of Attitude

The components of attitude are cognitive, affective, and behavioral. The *cognitive* component is the belief that forms the basis of the attitude (Samantha believes her teammates are lazy and that they will try to avoid work whenever possible). The *affective* component is the emotion that accompanies that belief (Samantha distrusts her teammates). The *behavioral* component is the behavior that results from the emotion felt (Samantha constantly checks up on her teammates and speaks to them in condescending ways).

Self-concept is often (though not always) involved in the cognitive component and gives rise to the affective component of an attitude. If Samantha has a healthy self-concept, she is more likely to believe the best of her teammates unless given reason to withdraw her trust. The behavioral component of her attitude toward them may in turn influence the cognitive and affective components—and thus ultimately the behavioral component—of their attitudes toward their work.

Measuring Attitudes

graphic scale
An attempt to measure attitudes by offering the respondent a choice of positions ranging from strong agreement with a statement to strong disagreement; also called the *Likert Scale.*

semantic differential scale
An attempt to measure attitudes that offers a choice of positions ranging from one adjective (such as "good") to the opposite adjective (such as "bad").

The **graphic scale** (also called the *Likert scale* after its creator, Rensis Likert) attempts to measure attitudes by offering the respondent a choice of positions ranging from strong agreement with a statement to strong disagreement. The **semantic differential scale** offers a choice of positions ranging from one adjective (such as "good") to the opposite adjective (such as "bad"). Such tests seem to give fairly accurate results, especially when combined with follow-up interviews.

Changing Attitudes

Attitudes are more amenable to change than are personality or values. As with perceptions, communication—that is, more information—is key to changing an attitude. The factors that can effect a change are as follows:

1. *Source.* People are more influenced by information from certain sources than from others. The more credible the source, the more attention a person will pay to the information.
2. *Message.* The content of the information will either be persuasive or not.
3. *Medium.* Some methods of conveying information (written, face-to-face, or telephoned communication) are more effective than others.
4. *Audience.* Characteristics (age, sex, values, etc.) of the person or people whose attitudes are targeted for change will determine the effectiveness of the attempt.

Just between You and Me: Interpersonal Behavior

transactional analysis
The theory that there are three *ego states* in social transactions: the child, parent, and adult.

Individual behavior cannot be studied in isolation from the dynamics of human interaction, which includes our attitudes toward ourselves and others. A popular approach to the subject is **transactional analysis**, which presents three *ego states* in social transac-

Table 10.3 **Principles of Business Etiquette**

1. *Telephone etiquette.* Return all phone calls, or at least have someone else return them for you, even if just to say you received the call and need more time to respond. If your telephone conversation is likely to disturb neighboring coworkers, close your door.
2. *Voice-mail etiquette.* Leave concise, specific messages on other people's voice mail, and if you need to speak in person, suggest a specific time period for the person to return your call so that he or she will not be confronted with your own voice mail.
3. *Meetings etiquette.* Be on time. If you cannot be on time, call ahead (where appropriate) and ask if a delay is preferable to resetting the meeting. Arrange for someone to take phone calls for you during a meeting. And, remember, answering a phone while someone is in your office indicates that whoever is calling is more important than the person in your office.
4. *Handling interruptions.* Business etiquette does not require that you allow all work interruptions, but it does require that you acknowledge the interrupting person's presence and suggest another time for him or her to approach you, or say you will "get back to" that person at the specified time.
5. *Handling "hoverers."* If someone is hovering around you or your office while you are on the phone or in a meeting with someone else, do not ignore the "hoverer." Excuse yourself from the other party and ask the person waiting if you can "get back to" him or her at a specified time.

Source: Based on information in Kenneth Blanchard, "Remembering Business Etiquette," *Quality Digest,* November 1992, pp. 13–14.

tions: the child, parent, and adult. An awareness of which ego state is operating in a given transaction is helpful in understanding one's own behavior and the behavior of others.

The theory is that all of us are capable of behaving like the child we once were, like the parents (or parental figures) we have, or once had, and like the adult we now are. The most beneficial interactions occur between appropriate ego states. For example, an adult question from an employee should not be met with a parental reply, but with a similarly adult reply. A childish question, however, might indeed warrant a parental reply. Adult-adult transactions are the ideal on the job. It is helpful to recognize the child or parent in ourselves or others when it emerges so that we can deal with it appropriately—and encourage the adult ego state to take its place.

Assertiveness training, discussed in Chapter 9, is promoted as a way of improving interpersonal relations. It teaches people to determine what they are feeling, then act in appropriate ways to achieve legitimate goals. Assertive behavior differs from aggressive behavior, which can verge on rudeness or hostility. It corresponds with the adult ego state of transactional analysis.

Assertiveness is most effective when accompanied by courteousness, which is as important in the business world as in purely social relationships—maybe more so, since close friends are quicker to forgive an occasional lapse in manners. Table 10.3 lists some principles of business etiquette set forth by Blanchard Training and Development Inc. As the author of those principles notes, "In most instances, being polite only takes a minute, and you should never be too busy for that."[22]

Quick Quiz 10.5

1. Your ____________ reflects your attitude toward yourself.
2. Name the three components of attitude.
3. Name two scales used to measure attitudes.

4. Name the four factors involved in changing an attitude.
5. ___________ is a theory of interpersonal behavior that presents three ego states: child, parent, and adult.

Summary

• **Name and define the factors that influence individual behavior.** Personality, values, intelligence, perceptions, and attitudes influence individual behavior. Personality is the mix of behavioral and emotional characteristics that distinguishes an individual. Values are the deeply held beliefs of a person as to what is morally right and wrong or what has worth and what does not. Intelligence is the ability to learn and reason. Perceptions are people's interpretations of reality, or what they think about what they observe. Attitude is a specific emotion toward a person, object, or situation. These factors overlap in various ways.

• **Contrast various personality types.** Type A personalities are aggressive, competitive, hard-driving people who are particularly prone to stress. Type B personalities are more easygoing and relaxed. Other contrasting types of personalities are emotional versus logical, passive versus active, and introverted versus extroverted personalities. In addition, personalities can be characterized according to their degree of authoritarianism or dogmatism. The Myers-Briggs Type Indicator further classifies personalities according to a system based on Jungian theory.

• **List Spraunger's six categories of values.** Edward Spraunger identified theoretical, economic, aesthetic, social, political, and religious values, which often influence occupation choice.

• **Name the areas of intelligence that aptitude tests measure.** Aptitude tests measure verbal, numerical, perceptual, spatial, and reasoning ability. Verbal ability, which enhances communication, is important for almost every type of job.

• **Explain biased, selective, and subjective perception.** Biased perception involves stereotyping, or judging an individual according to generalizations about the particular group to which he or she belongs. Selective perception involves seeing only what you expect or want to see; thus, you may block out important information. Subjective perception involves seeing everything from your own point of view and discounting the validity of another's perceptions, which greatly impedes communication.

• **Describe the role of attribution in the process of perception.** Attribution entails assigning causes to outcomes and is a part of interpretation, the last phase of the perception process. In self-serving attribution, we assign causes in a way that reflects favorably on ourselves. Objective self-awareness, which can be facilitated by a feedback system, is the antidote to self-serving attribution.

• **Explain the importance of self-concept to work attitude.** A negative self-concept can create the attitude of "Why try?" as a result of a lack of self-confidence. A healthy self-concept allows for maintenance of self-esteem despite an awareness of one's faults or limitations (objective self-awareness). A lack of self-esteem causes problems in working with other people since it creates suspicion of their motives.

• **Discuss transactional analysis and assertiveness training as they apply to interpersonal behavior in the workplace.** Transactional analysis presents three ego states in social transactions: the child, parent, and adult. Working relationships should encourage adult-adult transactions, but it is helpful to recognize behavior issuing from the other two ego states so as to deal with it. Assertiveness training teaches employees how to obtain legitimate goals in working situations by operating in the adult ego state.

Key Terms

personality (220)
internalizing (221)
externalizing (221)
values (226)
work ethic (227)
intelligence (229)
aptitude tests (229)
biased perception (232)
selective perception (232)
subjective perception (232)
perceptual congruence (233)
perceptual grouping (235)
perceptual set (235)
contrast effect (235)
anchoring-and-adjustment effect (235)
halo effect (235)
attribution (235)
self-serving attribution (235)

objective self-awareness (235)
social comparisons (236)
subliminal influences (236)
image (236)
attitude (237)
self-concept (237)
graphic scale (239)
semantic differential scale (239)
transactional analysis (239)

Review and Discussion Questions

1. What are some job positions or work assignments that would be suitable or unsuitable for the following personalities:
    a. a Type B personality
    b. an externalizing personality
    c. a dogmatic personality
    d. an intuitive-type personality

2. What are the four types of personality tests? What are the benefits and drawbacks of each?

3. John Gamboa is eager to win his company's Salesperson of the Year award. Achievement at work is something he highly values; moreover, his family is in desperate need of the monetary award that goes with the recognition. John has the opportunity to increase his sales substantially by taking advantage of a customer's ignorance. Which of Spraunger's values might be in conflict here?

4. Abby Towers is an accountant and scores very high on numerical ability in intelligence tests. Her verbal ability tests low, however. How could this lack of verbal ability affect her work performance?

5. How do mechanistic approaches to matching personality traits with job requirements differ from impressionistic approaches? In which would you have more faith and why?

6. After seven years as vice-president of loans at a local bank, Carlton Franks has to relocate to a new city where the only banking job he can find is as assistant bank manager. What are his chances for success if he is a Type A personality? Type B? What personality traits might benefit him in this new role? What traits would be detrimental?

7. Although Devlin Wood Products pays well and provides excellent benefits for its employees, every day at lunchtime, one group of workers can be found complaining in the cafeteria. Today's complaint: "The least this company could do is provide decent silverware." What kind of employees are these? Why? How can the company deal with these attitudes?

8. How could a person register high job satisfaction despite delivering a substandard performance? What element is needed to prod this satisfied employee into improved performance?

9. After reluctantly assuming some promotional duties outside her area of expertise, Lourdes Pinella was upset to see her coworkers laughing as they read her brochures. After asking her boss not to give her future projects, Lourdes stopped talking to her coworkers; they, in turn, assumed she was too busy with her new duties to bother with them. How has Lourdes's poor self-concept disrupted the firm's productivity? Why? What would be the result if Lourdes had a positive self-concept?

10. Which of Jung's learning styles are the following people likely to have?
    a. Tom, a midshipman at the Naval Academy
    b. Teresa, a concierge at a large hotel
    c. Leslie, owner of a small art gallery
    d. you

A SECOND LOOK

Why does Liz Minyard of Minyard Food Stores resist being stereotyped as a typical female shopper? How could biased perception, selective perception, and subjective perception cause male owners to make errors in deciding what to stock in their grocery stores?

Independent Activity

The Concept of Self

As discussed in this chapter, your opinion of yourself is formed by the perceptions you gain from your life experiences, especially family influences. Learning about your self-concept can help you improve your attitude toward yourself or achieve a more realistic view of yourself. In the space provided, or on a separate sheet of paper, answer the following questions:

1. What do I like about myself? What are my strengths? What skills can I offer to others?
2. What are my goals? (Try to visualize them positively, as already accomplished.)
3. How can I achieve each of these goals?
4. What strengths and skills will help me achieve them? What behaviors must I change?

Skill Builder

Life's Ins and Outs

Indicate how strongly you agree with each of the following statements. Score 1 point each if you disagree, 3 points if you are neutral, and 5 points if you agree. There are no rights or wrongs; this exercise is just a simple exploration of your personal beliefs in internal and external forces.

1. Hard work, not luck, is the key to getting ahead in life.
2. I am in charge of what happens in my life, and I don't let other people and situations determine it.
3. Who you know won't get you a raise or a promotion; you earn it through your own hard work.
4. I decide what I say or do and don't allow other people or situations to affect my behavior.
5. Students earn their grades; teachers don't determine them.
6. How I live my life is up to me; my success or failure at whatever I do is my responsibility.

Your score should add up to between 6 and 30. The lower your score, the more strongly you believe you are controlled by external sources, such as fate, chance, or other people. The higher the score, the more strongly you believe you have complete control over your life. Do you agree with your score? Why or why not?

Group Activity

Classroom Perception Challenge (20 minutes)

The instructor should bring in three or four large photographs or images from magazines and mount them on the wall in front of the class. Each photograph should be evocative and feature people prominently; for example, fans at a sporting event, mother and child, a well-known celebrity. Each student should jot down any thoughts about each photo, focusing on how he or she perceives the person's personality, values, intelligence, and attitudes. A discussion of these perceptions should follow and should address whether or not these perceptions were biased or selective, and how the students arrived at their conclusions.

Case Study

AmEx Veteran Thumbs Ride to Fingerhut

The fast track seemed like the place to be for an Ivy League graduate. Within three years at American Express Co., Princeton alum Leo Toralballa was in charge of the company's lucrative corporate-card program for small companies. His marketing skills and success won him high marks from his supervisors, and colleagues believed him destined for bigger assignments and richer rewards at the New York-based company.

But after five years with the credit-card giant, Toralballa and his family packed their things and moved to Minneapolis, where he now heads marketing at Fingerhut Companies, one of the nation's largest catalog-sales organizations. Though some would question leaving a corporate giant like AmEx to sell merchandise to middle-and lower-income families, the native New Yorker's only regrets are leaving behind the Metropolitan Opera, the Sunday edition of *The New York Times,* and his home in Greenwich, Connecticut.

Personal finances and professional challenges were both factors in Toralballa's decision. "My wife and I talked about where we wanted to be financially in five to ten years," he says. "The new job had a high probability of giving us a fairly special position." Indeed, in his first six months at Fingerhut, company stock has earned Toralballa a tidy paper profit on his stock options.

The uncertainty and corporate upheaval at AmEx was making Toralballa's life difficult as well. Morale was slipping; an onslaught of new, competing bank cards caused the company's performance to slump—profits tumbled 42 percent in 1992. And questions and confusion over the successor to CEO James D. Robinson III were distracting. Toralballa believes AmEx will emerge from its current woes, but the process will be painful. "It's sort of like entering World War II. There will probably be significant gains for those who survive, but a great many will wither in the process." Toralballa, for one, decided not to stick around to find out which category he would fall into.

Case Questions

1. What type of personality is Toralballa? How would you "pigeonhole" him psychologically?
2. Which of Spraunger's values most likely dictated or influenced Toralballa's decision? Why?
3. What is your opinion of Toralballa's work ethic? His values?
4. Would you have made the decision Toralballa did? Why or why not?
5. Is Toralballa more influenced by internal or external forces? Explain.

Source: Leah Nathans Spiro, "For This AmEx Escapee, There's No Place Like Minneapolis," *Business Week,* February 22, 1993, p. 79.

Case Study

Lower Pay, Higher Horizons at LSII

Most people wouldn't take a new job that meant a pay cut, particularly if it meant undergoing 16 hours of testing just to get hired. Especially if the new company expected its workers to do every job in the factory, even jobs they didn't like and didn't care to learn.

But taking a pay cut was just what Dana Leavitt, Mary Croft, and Bryan Oiler did. They went to work at a plant where they designed their own jobs, their own pay systems, and their own schedules. And they earned less while they worked harder.

At the LSII electro-galvanizing steel plant in Columbus, Ohio, there is only one job classification among the work force: technician. Each of these technicians must train and ultimately qualify for every job in the plant. One day Croft might be doing maintenance, the next shipping huge rolls of steel. She and the others receive base pay plus incentive pay based on how many different jobs they have qualified for among LSII's six job areas, such as inspection or shipping and packaging, which must be mastered through detailed training programs. In sum, skill determines the level of pay.

Over the next several years, all the workers in the plant are expected to be able to do every job. This is not as easy as it sounds. "I don't think everybody *can* do everything," says Croft, who previously worked in a DuPont plant. Leavitt, for example, is strong at maintenance, but he finds electrical work difficult. If someone is deficient in an area, he says, "the aim is to bring that person up to your level. You have to have patience."

The idea behind LSII—ending the narrow, sometimes mind-numbing, assembly-line jobs that led to rigid work systems, high costs, and poor productivity and hobbled U.S. industry in the past two decades—was born of a joint venture between LTV Steel Co. and Sumitomo of Japan. Its first company, LSE Co., opened in Cleveland in 1986. LSII opened four years later.

Oiler came to LSII from a nonunion plant and found the new freedom astonishing. Some people took advantage of the system, he says, leading at times to absenteeism. It's true that the plant isn't perfect, agrees David Murdock, LSII's director of human resources. But, he says, workers "are getting to a level of competency now where their input will really begin to pay significant returns. For us, training isn't really a cost; it's an investment."

Case Questions

1. Which of Spraunger's values most likely dictated or influenced these workers' decision to go to LSII? Why? What do you think of their values? Why?
2. How does the work ethic shown by these LSII "technicians" contrast to that of other companies' workers?
3. Would you have made the decision these workers did? Explain.
4. What kind of learning style might be best suited for the varying and multifaceted job demands at LSII?
5. How will workers' different values and perceptions affect the way a specific job is done from day to day? Why?

Source: William Neikirk, "Workers Take Chance on Shaping the Future," *Chicago Tribune,* July 26, 1993, section 1.

Quick Quiz Answers

Quick Quiz 10.1

1. **Type A**
2. **Rorschach, TAT, sentence completion**
3. **Internalized locus of control**

Quick Quiz 10.2

1. **social values; aesthetic values; economic values**
2. **entitled employee**
3. **moral development**

Quick Quiz 10.3

1. **yes**
2. **intuiting/feeling**
3. **openness, recall, objectivity**

Quick Quiz 10.4

1. **biased perception, or stereotyping**
2. **sensory inputs, attention, construction, interpretation**
3. **overload**
4. **image**

Quick Quiz 10.5

1. **self-concept**
2. **cognitive, affective, behavioral**
3. **graphic scale, semantic differential scale**
4. **source, message, medium, audience**
5. **Transactional analysis**

CHAPTER

11

Groups and Organizational Structure

CHAPTER OUTLINE

Learning Objectives

- Describe the two main types of formal groups in an organization.
- List the five stages of a group's life cycle and the four features of a mature, effective group.
- Name six characteristics of a group, and explain the significance of each.
- Discuss the advantages and disadvantages of group decision making.
- Explain how informal groups differ from formal groups.
- List some ways that informal groups can benefit an organization.
- List some ways that informal groups can hinder the operation of an organization.
- Compare various types of organizational cultures.
- Compare various types of organizational structures.

Abacus Director Counts Success a Lonely Job

Despite graduating cum laude from Harvard and earning an M.B.A. in finance at the University of Chicago, after 11 years as a vice-president at a prominent Wall Street investment firm, Adela Cepeda found herself alone. Unlike her white, male bosses and coworkers, she had no network of support, no informal group of peers. Cepeda was in a group of one. Cepeda says her experience was typical of Hispanic women. "You usually are the only one at your level, and you have no peer groups or role models."

Finally exhausted from banging her head against a doubly thick glass ceiling, Cepeda left Wall Street in 1991. Today she is managing director of Abacus Financial Group Inc., an asset-management firm founded that same year. She had had enough of breaking barriers and was tired of always being "on trial."

Cepeda asserts that Hispanic women are set up for failure. "You're already viewed as different and even disadvantaged. In a corporate setting you're expected to fit in."

But Cepeda found that fitting in to the corporate structure, or even the informal give-and-take of the coffee room, was a career in itself. Her actions, work habits, and opinions were seen as representative of Hispanic women. Whenever she spoke, Cepeda says, she was viewed as "sounding like a woman *and* like a Hispanic. To communicate excellence every time becomes tiresome. When you're the only one in the group, you define the stereotype, and that's paralyzing."

Source: Carol Kleiman, "Hispanic Women Face Brick Wall," *Chicago Tribune,* June 17, 1993, sec. 3, p. 3. Photo source: John Moss/Tony Stone Images.

Figure 11.1 **Example of a Functional Group**

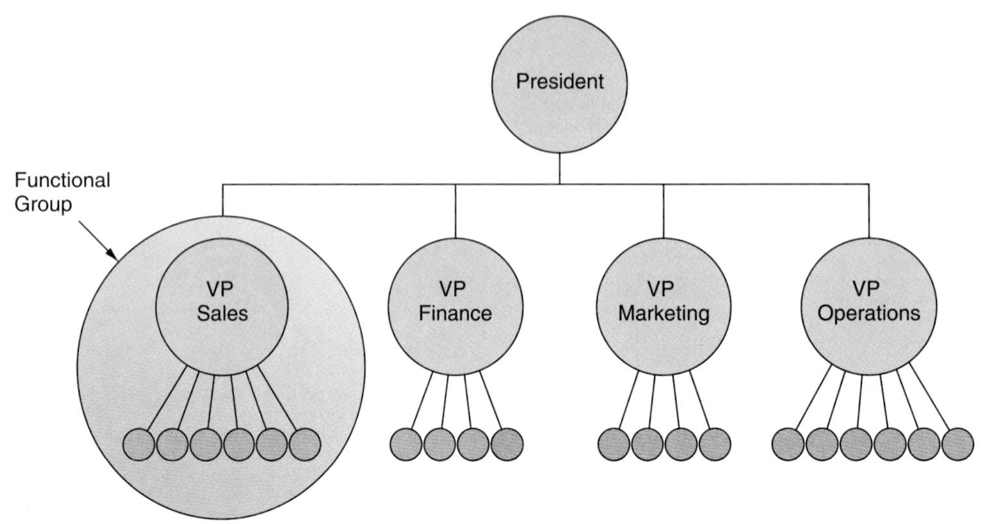

groups
Two or more people who in some way interact with one another and think of themselves as being a group.

formal groups
Groups set up by management in order to meet organizational objectives.

informal groups
Groups that result when individuals in the organization develop relationships to meet personal needs.

functional groups
Groups that fulfill the ongoing needs in an organization by carrying out a particular function.

task groups
Groups set up to carry out a specific activity and disbanded when the activity is completed; also called *project groups*.

Human beings operate in groups of many different types, often simultaneously. The group influences our behavior, and our behavior helps determine the group's actions. Sometimes good or bad actions are taken by a group that no single individual within the group would have performed. Consider a riot. Or consider a charitable organization. Sometimes a group can reach heights of inefficiency and snarled communications that no single person, however inept, could have duplicated. But the marvels of history—from the pyramids of Egypt to contemporary space travel—are the products of groups. They could never have been produced by one individual, however gifted.

Note that the study of human relations employs a plural noun, "relations." Thus, it entails the study of people in plural—in groups. A **group** consists of two or more people who in some way interact with one another and think of themselves as being a group. In this chapter, you'll see how important both formal and informal groups are in the workplace, as did Adela Cepeda in the opening vignette.

The Nature of Groups

Within an organization are both formal and informal groups. They share certain characteristics: all have group norms, for example, which we will discuss later in detail. **Formal groups** are set up by management in order to meet organizational objectives. **Informal groups** result when individuals in the organization develop relationships to meet personal needs.

Formal groups may be functional or task groups. **Functional groups** fulfill the ongoing needs in an organization by carrying out a particular function, such as producing goods, selling products, or investing funds. In most cases a functional group is one that appears on a company's organization chart (see Figure 11.1). The formal communication discussed in Chapter 6 involves these groups.

Task groups (also called *project groups*) are set up to carry out a specific activity and are disbanded when the activity is completed. For example, at Master Industries

Figure 11.2 **Profile of Organizations Using Task Groups**

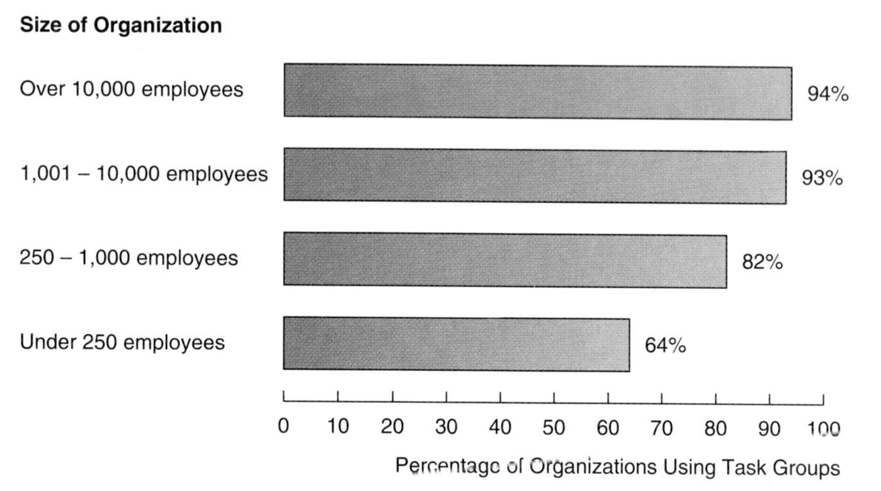

Inc. of Ansonia, Ohio, a task group was responsible for buying the company's brooms and dustpans and for finding places to hang them.[1] Presumably, such a task could be completed in a matter of weeks. Another task group might be formed to identify ways to promote safety in the workplace. This kind of task group could go on for years with no definite ending date, because it is unlikely the job of promoting safety would ever be finished. Figure 11.2 shows the percentage of organizations of various sizes that use task groups.

The Growing of a Group

In a sense, groups are living organisms with life stages. They grow, are subjected to stresses, and either mature or die as a result of the stresses. As illustrated in Figure 11.3, one view of group development is that groups may pass through the following five stages:[2]

1. *Orientation.* When a group first forms, its members tend to be highly committed to the group but do not yet have the experience to work together efficiently. Group members tend to be concerned about what the group is supposed to do and how they will fit in. Objectives need to be clarified and direction provided.
2. *Dissatisfaction.* At this stage, while group members are more competent at working together, their initial enthusiasm has given way to disappointment with the day-to-day reality of being part of the group. Encouragement and motivation are necessary.
3. *Resolution.* If group members are able to reconcile the differences between their initial expectations and the new realities they experience, the group moves to this stage of resolution. During this time, group members continue to be more productive, and their morale also improves. Conflicts need to be resolved, and group members should participate in planning and decision making.
4. *Production.* If group members continue to resolve conflicts and develop a workable structure for the group, their output and morale will continue to increase. The group at this point is effectively working as a team. When group structure must change or other issues arise, the group resolves them quickly.

Figure 11.3 Stages of Group Development

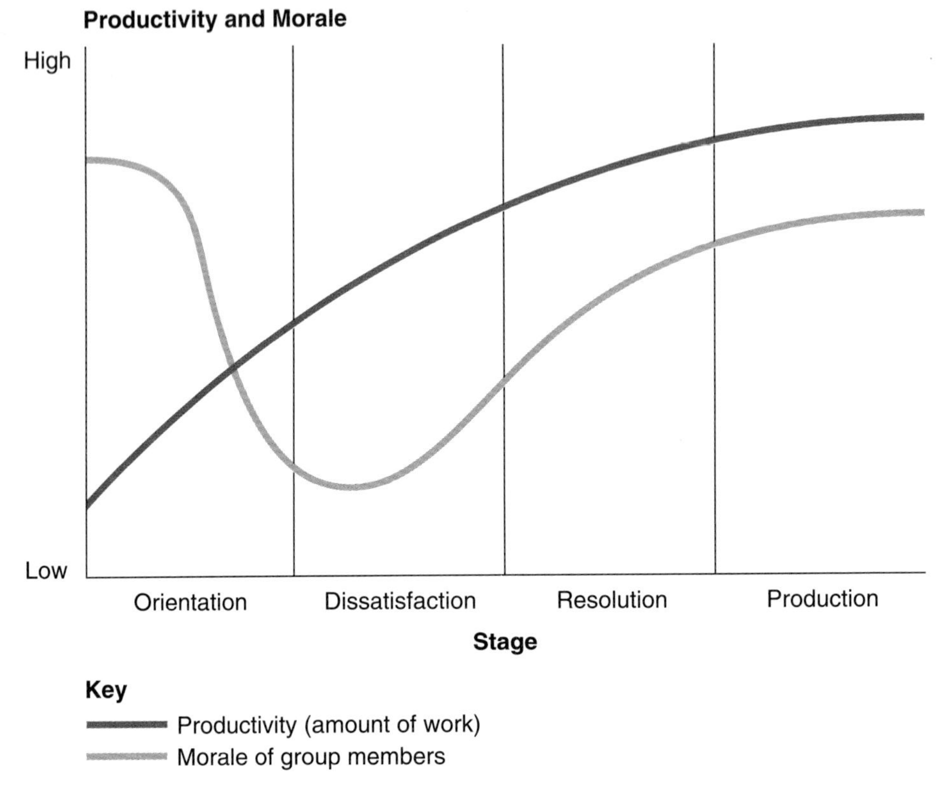

5. *Termination.* At some point, many groups must come to an end. If the group has reached the production stage before termination, group members will be sad. If the group ends before that stage, members are more likely to be relieved.

Six Main Group Characteristics

Figure 11.4 shows a six-pointed star indicating the main characteristics of a group: its members' roles, norms, status, cohesiveness, size, and homogeneity.

group roles
Patterns of behavior related to the member's position in the group.

Group Roles. Much as the characters in a play assume various roles, so do the members of a group. **Group roles** are patterns of behavior related to the member's position in the group. Some common group roles you may have encountered—or even held—include those of the (formal or informal) leader, the scapegoat, the class clown, and the shoulder people cry on. In terms of a formal organizational group, roles are commonly categorized as follows:

- *leader*—the one who influences the thinking of others
- *gatekeeper*—the one who oversees group communication, determining who receives what information
- *liaison*—the one who is the contact person, or link, to other groups
- *follower*—the one who is easily influenced to agree with others in the group
- *outsider*—the one who is generally ignored by others in the group.

Figure 11.4 **Six Characteristics of a Group**

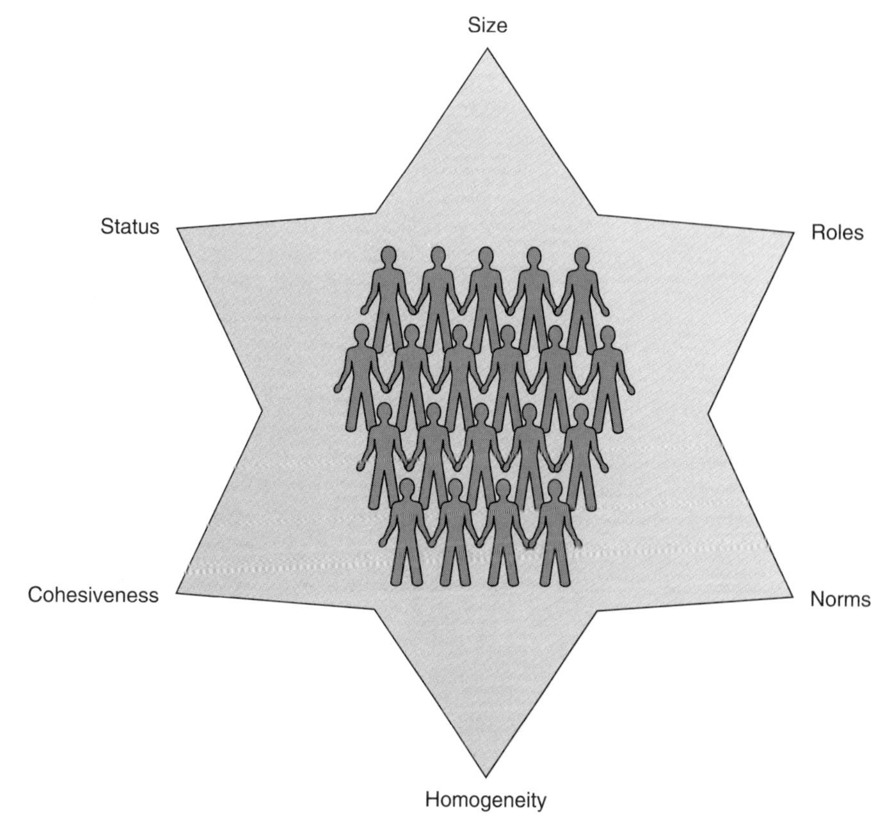

Sometimes a person's formal position in the organization dictates a certain role. For example, the member with the highest ranking position in the organization may be expected to take the role of leader. Sometimes personality dictates the role. A lower-ranking person with an aggressive personality might assume the leadership role.

There are many other group roles: planner, organizer, peacemaker, blocker, controller, encourager, compromiser—the list goes on and on. Depending on its function, a group might need people to fulfill certain roles. For example, a group entrusted with making a difficult, controversial decision might desperately need a compromiser or a peacemaker. One charged with creating a schedule will need a good planner. One engaged in brainstorming had better not be made up entirely of followers.

Role conflict occurs when a person has two different roles that call for conflicting types of behavior. Suppose that several employees have been members of a volleyball team for years. At work, one of them is promoted to be supervisor of the others. The supervisor's role as volleyball teammate may conflict with her role as a supervisor.

group norms
Standards for appropriate or acceptable behavior.

Group Norms. Groups typically have standards for appropriate or acceptable behavior, called **group norms**. These can be related directly to work performance, as in the acceptable quota of production. (Higher production on the part of one individual will mean a more intense effort on the part of others to keep up.) Norms can also apply to non-work-related issues such as whether members dress formally or informally.

International Highlights

At Semco, Autonomy Ties Workers to the Group

Group norms and beliefs can create peer pressures, which can keep group values in check and help ensure that freedoms granted are not freedoms abused.

At Semco, a Brazilian manufacturer of pumps, mixers, valves, and other industrial equipment, employees are more than simply empowered: they are in charge. Workers decide their own salaries and set their own working hours; groups of employees set their own productivity and sales targets. Workers even choose their own boss and then publicly evaluate his or her performance. All employees have unlimited access to the company's books and are trained to read balance sheets. Everyone knows what everyone else earns—and some workers earn more than their boss. Big corporate decisions, such as acquisitions and diversifications, are made by all employees.

It sounds radical and chaotic—especially in Brazil, where authoritarian management has never gone out of style. But Semco has thrived amid the turmoil of Brazil's hyperinflationary economy, which has destroyed thousands of other small companies. Owner Ricardo Semler would not call his company a great entrepreneurial success story, yet in 1993, it earned about $3 million on sales of $30 million.

Semler's experiment in employee involvement works because he combines it with old-fashioned hardheadedness. He demands healthy dividends—and because a large proportion of employee earnings is tied to the company's profits, there is enormous peer pressure on employees not to abuse their freedoms.

"It's really very simple," asserts Semler. "All we're doing is treating people like adults."

Source: "Treating People Like Adults Isn't Just Fantasy," *Toronto Globe and Mail,* July 6, 1993, p. BBB.

When a member of the group violates a norm, the group responds by pressuring the violator to conform. For a work-related issue, there may be an organizational policy in place to bring the rebel into line. Thus, one who is habitually tardy may be docked for the time he or she misses in the morning. Or if there is a dress code, the fellow who saunters in among the suits and power ties in his cut-offs and sandals can be officially reprimanded and warned to change his casual dress. If there is no official policy, the issue may become the focus of a test of wills. A group member who lunches at a steak house while the rest eat salads may feel subtle pressure to change his or her lunch habits. A company that has empowered its employees with all decision-making authority and uses peer pressure to keep work standards high is profiled in the "International Highlights" box.

Norms can be trivial or significant, positive or negative. Consider the case of a negative norm that could be cured only with a new organizational policy: The clerical employees in the catalog department of an office supplies company were supposed to take an hour lunch break but had drifted into the habit of taking far longer when they went out together to a favorite restaurant. At first, these events occurred only to celebrate someone's birthday, but soon the five or six workers in question were taking regular lunches of one-and-a-half to two hours every day. When reprimanded, their attitude was one of resentment—and defiance. They had become so accustomed to this practice that they had come to think of their long lunches as a right. A new secretary was quickly indoctrinated into the routine and automatically assumed the same attitude toward it. Further reprimands were simply ignored. Ultimately, the company had to install a time clock and punchcards for these hourly workers in order to break the long-lunch habit.

As this illustration shows, *attitudes* are frequently vulnerable to peer influence. A group of employees sometimes acquires a certain attitude—toward the company, a company policy, or a particular supervisor—that is infectious. For good or for ill, that attitude may become a group norm.

status
A person's rank, or importance, in the group.

Status. A person's rank, or importance, in the group is his or her **status**. Status is determined by a variety of factors, which may include the person's role in the group, position in the organization, reputation for job competence, education level, age, race, gender, and even physical appearance. In one group the person with the highest status might be a good-looking man with a summer home. The others are impressed by his physical presence and hope for an invitation to the summer home, so his status is great. In another group, a woman with an unprepossessing appearance may have the highest status as a result of her intelligence and connections with powerful business and political people.

Status is important in a group because those with the highest status have the most effect on the development of group norms. It is important in a larger sense, too, in the business world and in the organization. The editor in chief of *Industry Week* points out that the low status of industry jobs compared with service jobs is destructive to society. Industry is the primary source of a nation's wealth and the chief influence on standard of living. One job created in the manufacturing sector creates ten more jobs in the service sector and pays 44 percent more than the average service job. So it is obviously in a nation's best interest to encourage the development of manufacturing jobs. Yet the low status of such jobs does just the opposite.

"Status influences the skills we polish and praise, and those that we disdain, ridicule, and neglect. It influences the manner in which we teach those skills, and the quantity and quality of those we attract to teach them," says *Industry Week*'s editor.[3] And industry's "tattered status" is keeping talented people out. A Wharton professor says, "I've seen people who saw the only way to the top through marketing or financing even if they loved technology and manufacturing. Now it is significant that companies like Digital Equipment and Hewlett-Packard have replaced their CEOs with people who are manufacturers."[4]

cohesiveness
The degree of closeness among group members.

Cohesiveness. The degree to which people in the group stick together is the group's **cohesiveness**. This is the quality that makes members stay with the goals of the group and support one another even during stresses. Cohesiveness causes members to abide by group norms even when under pressure to follow other norms. Cohesive groups work harder and are more likely to accomplish their objectives. This desirable quality can be fostered in several ways:

- by emphasizing to group members their common characteristics and goals.
- by emphasizing areas in which the group has succeeded in achieving its goals. A history of success tends to improve cohesiveness.
- by keeping the group small enough so that everyone feels comfortable participating.
- by encouraging competition with other groups. Cohesiveness diminishes when group members are competing with one another; external, not internal, competition is the key.
- by encouraging less active members to participate in group activities. Groups tend to be most cohesive when everyone participates to about the same extent.

Size. Groups don't get smaller than two people, but they can grow to any size. Of course, not every size is effective for accomplishing a given objective. It is generally agreed that in a group of 15 or so, group members may have problems communicating with one another. In groups of beyond 10 or 12 members, there is a tendency for informal subgroups to form. This may be good or bad, depending on the purpose of the larger group. Small groups usually reach decisions faster and rely less on formal rules and procedures than large ones. Also, quiet group members are more likely to partici-

Figure 11.5 **Effects of Group Size**

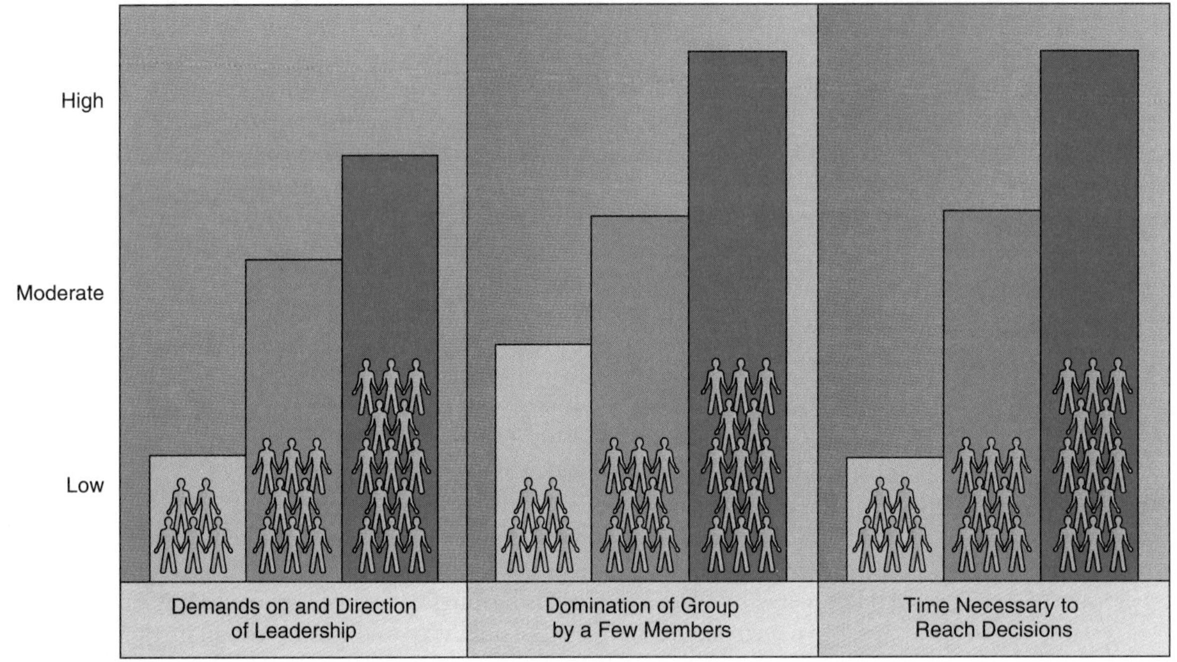

Key

Groups of 2 – 7 members

Groups of 8 – 12 members

Groups of 13 – 16 members

pate in a small group. On the other hand, a bigger group makes sense when a lot of work needs to be done and the individual group members can work independently most of the time. Figure 11.5 shows some differences in the way groups of different sizes operate.

homogeneous groups Those in which members have a lot in common.

groupthink A phenomenon in which the people in a group all think so much alike that new ideas are unlikely.

heterogeneous groups Groups made up of people of different ages, education levels, races, personalities, work experiences, and so forth.

Homogeneity. The more alike we are, the better we tend to get along in a group. Thus a **homogeneous group**, in which members have a lot in common, tends to operate more harmoniously and reach decisions more quickly. Unfortunately, too much alikeness can lead to the Orwellian-sounding phenomenon of **groupthink**, in which new ideas are stifled because everyone in the group finds it so comfortable to think alike. A more **heterogeneous group**, made up of people of different ages, education levels, races, personalities, work experiences, and so forth, may well be more creative—though it may also breed more conflict. Furthermore, a heterogeneous group can probably handle complex projects more effectively since it brings to bear on a problem a greater variety of skills, experience, and knowledge.

Making a group heterogeneous can be especially difficult, however, for the group members who differ in gender, race, ethnic background, age, or sexual orientation. To read about such culture shock, see the "Diversity Highlights" box.

Diversity Highlights

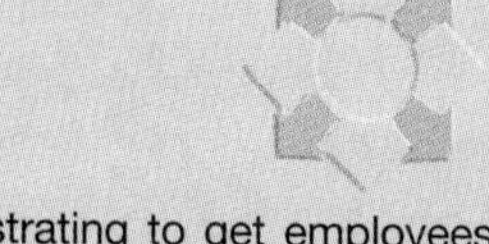

In with the In Crowd

Culture shock. Not a term you would normally associate with the workplace, but the multicultural and multigenerational diversity of the twenty-first-century workplace makes it an important human relations concern.

According to Sondra Thiederman, president of San Diego–based Cross-Cultural Communications, culture shock is "a state of mind that occurs when people find themselves immersed in a strange culture." Behavioral expectations differ: not only do others not respond to their behavior in the accustomed way, people in a strange culture no longer know how *they* are supposed to behave. Responses can range from depression and loneliness to aggression and frustration.

But culture shock doesn't apply only to immigrant employees. Others also have a hard time acclimating themselves to the organizational culture and the groups that function within it.

Employees from other than the dominant culture—blacks in a predominantly white workplace, women in a primarily male workplace, or older workers returning to the work force only to be supervised by people young enough to be their grandchildren—may also experience culture shock. Likewise, managers trained to manage according to the rules and norms that apply to white, mainstream U.S. workers may find themselves supervising workers from a broad spectrum of backgrounds. For example, it may be frustrating to get employees to participate in group decision making if they have a background that expects leaders to be authoritarian.

Healing culture shock requires exposure to a variety of groups and education about them. It is also helpful to be open and honest about the problem. Discussing feelings helps to defuse them and leads people to a better understanding of one another.

Source: Adapted from Sondra Thiederman, *Bridging Cultural Barriers for Corporate Success: How to Manage the Multicultural Work Force* (New York: Lexington Books, 1991), pp. 5–10.

Quick Quiz 11.1

1. Role ___________ may occur when a group member has more than one group role.
2. A person who arrives at work every day at 10:00 a.m. rather than 9:00 a.m., when everyone else arrives, is violating group ___________.
3. Groups that are too homogeneous are prone to the disadvantageous phenomenon of ___________.

Dynamics of Groups

What makes a group greater than the sum of its parts? Four features of a good, productive, mature group, one that becomes even more effective with time, are as follows:

1. *Acceptance.* Initial distrust is common for members of a new group. When that emotion has been transformed into mutual trust and general acceptance of one another, the group is off to a good start and can become productive. Of course, heterogeneous groups may take longer to reach this acceptance phase than homogeneous ones.
2. *Good communication.* Group decision making (which will be discussed shortly) cannot take place without good communication. Members must feel free to communicate frankly with one another, which means that there must be a basis of trust and acceptance established.
3. *Group solidarity.* Solidarity occurs naturally when acceptance prevails and communication is good. Satisfaction with membership in the group leads to a commitment to enhancing the group's success. Cooperation rather than competition

When using problem census to improve group effectiveness at meetings, it is helpful to list topics so they can be easily seen by all, and then prioritize the topics.
Photo source: Joseph Pobereskin/ Tony Stone Images.

prevails within the group. Competition with other groups, however, will enhance group solidarity.

4. *Group control.* Group solidarity makes group control much easier. If the group is acting as a unit, that is, if it is a controlled group, it can be aimed more precisely at its target. Its actions can be controlled by its own members to the satisfaction of all. The term "control" in this sense does not mean rigidity. On the contrary, attempts to maximize the group's success are fueled by flexibility and informality. In a well-controlled group, members will
   - work as a team, functioning as a unit
   - expend extra effort when deemed necessary for the group's success
   - work toward a common purpose
   - talk openly and frequently, offering and receiving information freely
   - volunteer their particular skills and knowledge where appropriate to help reach the group's goals

Donald Klopf, author of a book titled *Interacting in Groups,* suggests that a group's effectiveness in meetings can be improved by a *problem census*: a strategy for prioritizing the agenda so all the important topics are sure to be covered within the time constraints of the meeting. Attendees are informed in advance so that they can decide what topics they want discussed. Topics are written on a chalkboard so they can be easily seen by all, and then they are prioritized by group vote. Finally, the amount of time allotted for the meeting is divided by the number of topics to be discussed. Klopf also recommends that meetings be frequent enough so that group members are not continually bogged down by a long list of topics and potential problems can be nipped in the bud rather than held over for a later meeting.[5]

Advantages of Group Decision Making

Group decision making, also called *participative decision making,* benefits the organization by taking advantage of the combined knowledge and experience of its employees and encouraging a deeper commitment to implementation of any changes. Also, such participation often leads to the happy phenomenon of team spirit, which is one of the most powerful motivators of work performance and facilitators of smooth operation.

A group can generate more ideas for alternatives than an individual. In the words of Clark Wigley, problems are like beach balls: there is no one place you can stand on

Table 11.1 **Symptoms of Groupthink**

- An illusion of being invulnerable
- A tendency to defend the group's position against any objections
- A view that the group is totally moral—"the good guys"
- Stereotyped view of opponents
- A tendency to pressure group members who disagree to change their minds and conform
- An illusion that everyone agrees (because no one states an opposing view)
- The presence of self-appointed "mindguards"—people who urge other group members to go along with the group

Source: Irving L. Janis, *Groupthink: Psychological Studies of Policy Decisions and Fiascoes,* 2d ed. (Boston: Houghton-Mifflin, 1982).

the ball and see the whole ball. Likewise, "no matter where you stand in an organization, regardless of how much you get paid, how many degrees you have, or how many years of experience, there is no place where you can stand and see the whole problem."[6]

Disadvantages of Group Decision Making

Sometimes a group discussion becomes nonproductive, or even counterproductive. Disadvantages to group decision making are (1) the process is slower than for an individual, (2) there is a cost to the organization when employees spend their time in meetings rather than producing or selling, and (3) the group can reach an inferior decision by letting one person or a small subgroup dominate the process. Idea generation may stall for various reasons. *Groupthink,* mentioned earlier, is always a potential problem. In his book on the subject, Irving L. Janis describes groupthink as a failure to think independently and realistically because of a desire to enjoy consensus and closeness. Table 11.1 shows some symptoms of groupthink.

During the making of the movie, *The Bonfire of the Vanities,* many of the people involved had doubts about casting decisions and changes in the story line, but they did not tell the director, Brian DePalma. DePalma wondered about the wisdom of some of the decisions, but since no one objected, he convinced himself that his decisions were correct. The $50-million movie was a flop at the box office.[7]

When a group begins manifesting groupthink, it may be time for one member to play devil's advocate, challenging the position of the majority. The leader should seek to encourage quieter members to speak up and more dominant members to pipe down. Sometimes people are intimidated into groupthink by those with more forceful personalities.

Brainstorming

brainstorming
A technique for idea generation in which group members are encouraged to state their ideas, no matter how far fetched, without fear of criticism or comment until the process is complete.

A good antidote to groupthink is the practice of **brainstorming,** in which group members are encouraged to state their ideas, no matter how farfetched, without fear of criticism or comment until the process is complete. Figure 11.6 illustrates the process. Criticism can be death to a brainstorming session. To enforce the rule against it, David M. Armstrong at Armstrong International used the following idea: At the beginning of a meeting called to generate new-product ideas, he handed each member an M&M's candy and said, "You're allowed one negative comment during the meeting. Once you make that comment, you must eat your M&M's candy. If you don't have candy in front of you, you can't say anything negative."[8]

Figure 11.6 **The Brainstorming Process**

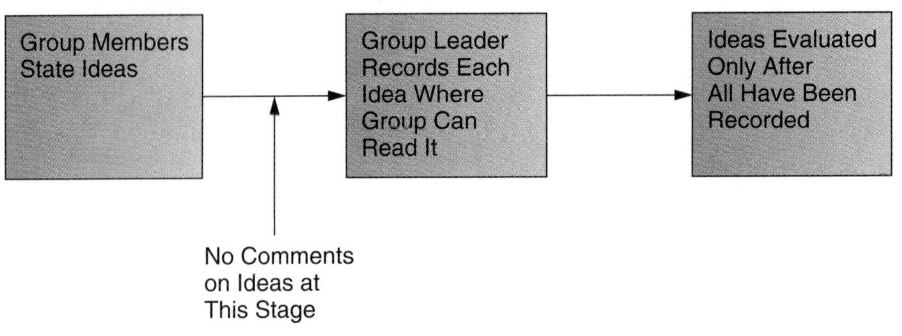

Hearing other people's ideas all the way through often stimulates group members' thinking in a positive way. Whatever a company can do to nurture creativity in its employees will probably be worth the effort somewhere down the line. "To encourage your employees to be more creative, you have to create an atmosphere that values their creativity," says Michael Michalko, a creativity consultant. "To do this, you've got to alleviate employees' fear of risk."[9] A good brainstorming session should be free of such risk.

Quick Quiz 11.2

1. Solidarity occurs naturally in a group where there are ____________ and ____________.
2. It is very important to encourage creativity in a ____________ session.

Informal Groups

As has been said in anger or in comfort many times, you can choose your friends but you can't choose your family. Similarly, although you cannot choose the people in your department or task force (unless you happen to be the one hiring), you *can* choose your informal group—and you surely will, since you will need it to meet your personal relationship needs as well as those work-related needs not met by the formal groups to which you are assigned.

Recall the explanation of formal versus informal communication in Chapter 6, on organizational communication. The network for informal communication is, in fact, an informal group. As time passes and friendships develop in the workplace, employees form informal groups that involve complex relationships that alter their job descriptions. Fast workers may help slow workers, or those especially skilled at one task may take on more than their share, trading off other tasks they dislike or are less skilled at. The way these changes occur depends on the informal structure of the group. Well-liked or high-status workers may receive a great deal of assistance; less appealing people may be ignored—even sabotaged, if they engender real hostility.

Multigroup Membership

Formal and informal groups frequently overlap. When Felicia accepted a post at the junior high school, she became a member of two formal groups—the teaching staff at the school and the teachers' union representing her district. She also decided to join a city-

Figure 11.7 **Informal Group Structures**

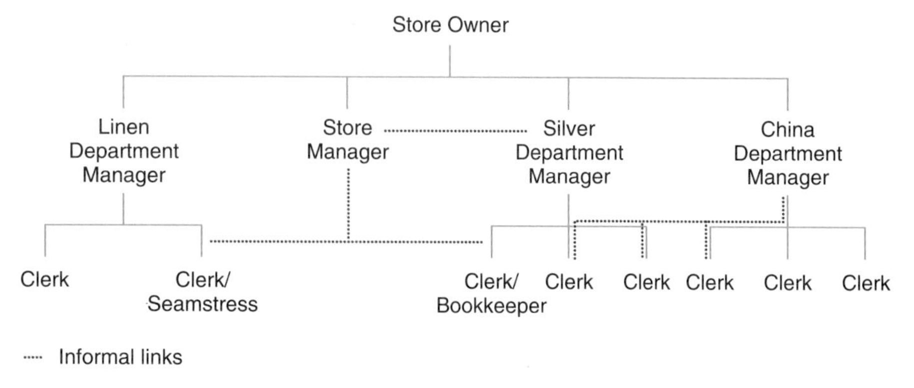

wide organization of black education professionals in order to receive moral support and to participate in service projects sponsored by the organization. In addition, the principal asked her to serve on a committee to plan an innovative math and science curriculum. And upon learning that Felicia likes to eat sushi, one of the other teachers invited her to join a group of four teachers who visit a local Japanese restaurant about once a month. One of the teachers in the informal sushi-eating group also belongs to the organization of black education professionals. All belong to the teachers' union. One is on the math and science committee. Thus, formal and informal groups overlap, and a person might belong to any number of both types, depending on inclination and job position.

The Importance of Informal Groups

Figure 11.7 shows how the relationships between informal groups at a small business coexist with those between the formal groups reflected on the organization chart. Note that the informal group, indicated by the dotted line, consists of the store manager, silver department manager, a clerk/seamstress, and a clerk/bookkeeper. Here the store manager is more dominant than the owner, unlike in the formal group. Another informal group is composed of the china department manager and three clerks. This manager appears to exert a dominant influence over people outside her sphere in the formal structure.

An organization is really a dichotomy of formal and informal groups. The formal groups are formed to achieve the organization's formal goals. However, figuratively speaking, they are only the tip of the iceberg (see Figure 11.8). The informal groups that make up the rest of the organization structure are formed to achieve the employees' personal goals, and they determine the course of the organization every bit as much as the formal ones do, and sometimes more. Some insight into human relations is extremely helpful in recognizing the existence and understanding the importance of such groups, since no organization chart reveals them.

Such informal groups can aid an organization by

1. helping people identify with the organization
2. getting things done by spreading information quickly
3. enhancing job satisfaction via rewarding social relationships
4. easing managers' work loads by helping to get things done
5. providing emotional outlets when employees are upset
6. helping managers gather employee feedback.

Figure 11.8 **The Organizational "Iceberg"**

In any organization there are really two organizations: (1) the formal organization, consisting of the formal reporting relationships, rules, and procedures, and (2) the informal organization, consisting of what really goes on in the organization, including beliefs and social relationships.

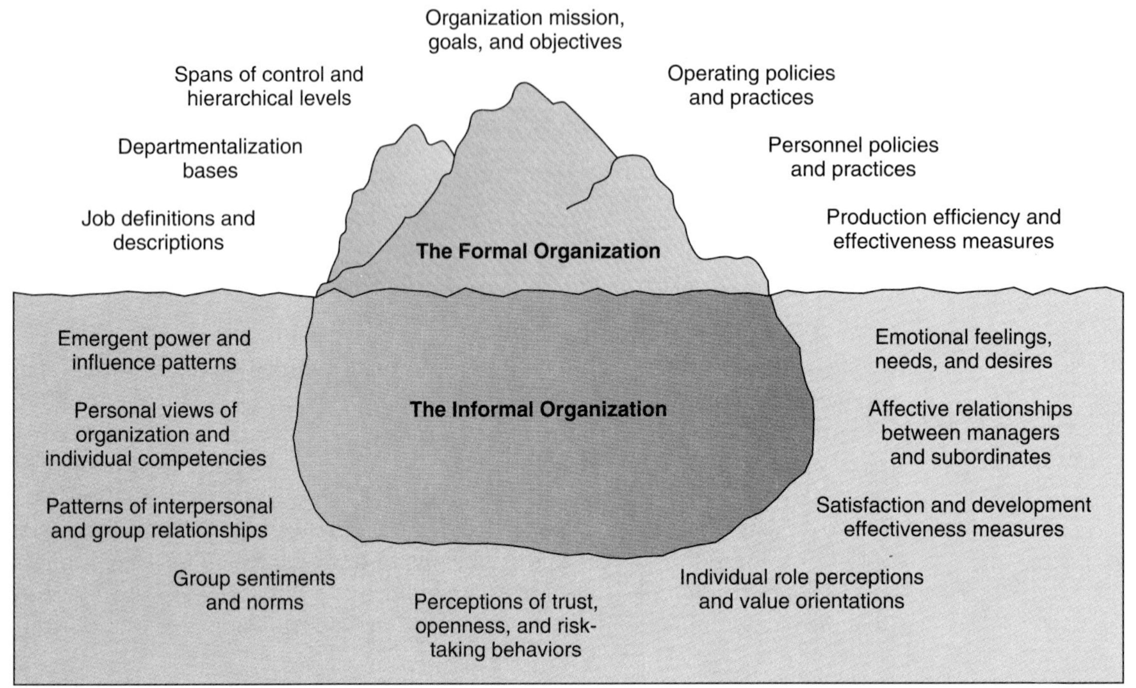

Source: Courtesy of R. J. Selfridge and S. L. Sokolik, "A Comprehensive View of Organizational Development," *MSU Business Topics* (1975): p. 47.

Getting Things Done. Informal groups can facilitate and supplement formal groups. Instead of waiting for information to come through formal channels, the marketing group can get started on its plan for the new product based on what it learns from its informal group, which is connected with top management. Instead of waiting two days until the formal contact person is back from vacation, a person can get a question answered through informal channels, or obtain assurance of the approval that will be forthcoming when the department head returns, saving valuable time. Figure 11.9 provides an illustration.

Enhancing Job Satisfaction. The social rewards provided by informal groups enhance overall job satisfaction. As a result, absenteeism and turnover are reduced, and productivity may be higher. A good belly laugh with coworkers over last night's popular TV show, an expression of concern about one's hay fever, an enjoyable exchange of theories on why the city's team lost that game in the last quarter—all these things make people feel better about their jobs. Even when the actual work becomes distasteful, social support from informal groups can see us through such temporary low periods. They are not enough to make up for having chosen the wrong vocation or position or receiving a woefully inadequate salary, but they are enough to cast the swing vote in borderline situations.

Figure 11.9 **How Informal Groups Save Time**

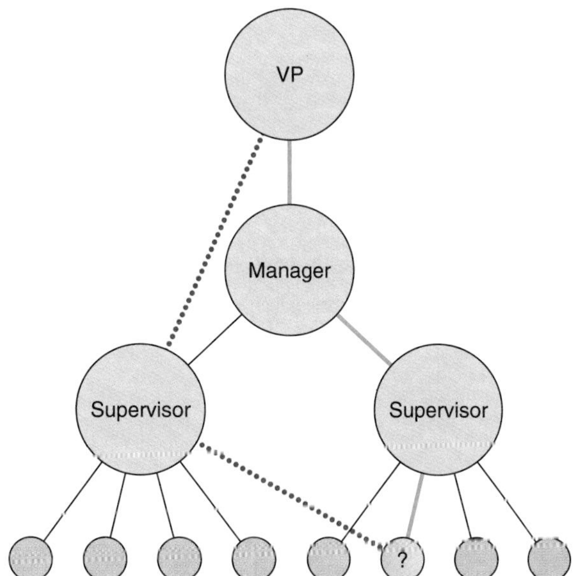

Providing Emotional Outlets. Sometimes all it takes to defuse a potentially explosive situation is being able to express the anger and frustration and have someone say, "I understand." And coworkers of an informal group *do* understand, because they are in the situation with you and they see the factors that distress you firsthand.

Easing Managers' Work Loads. Informal groups can quickly accomplish things quickly that a manager might have to struggle with over a much longer period of time—instructing this person, checking up on that one, correcting another. It may be wise for a manager to delegate responsibility to an informal group that he or she sees operating effectively. Recall how Sheri Poe of Ryka Inc. immersed herself in every aspect of her Massachusetts-based athletic-shoe company for two years, during which sales climbed from zero to $16 million. It took a crucial trade show, when Poe was torn between handling the myriad details of the show and doing interviews with retailers, for her to give responsibility to informal groups of her employees. Today she keeps tabs on operations through weekly meetings with the head of each department and lets the informal groups handle the details.[10]

Providing Employee Feedback. Informal groups process information both from and to higher management by means of the *grapevine*—the path along which informal communication travels. The grapevine contains a lot of information that would never be revealed by formal groups but can be beneficial to employees and the organization alike. But it also contains some misinformation, much of it gossip. When the vine veers too much toward gossip, it needs to be pruned.

As author Robert Genua says, "Gossip doesn't do anyone any good. It damages the efficiency and effectiveness of the organization, and it damages reputations, even if

Figure 11.10 **Authority in Formal Groups versus Power in Informal Groups**

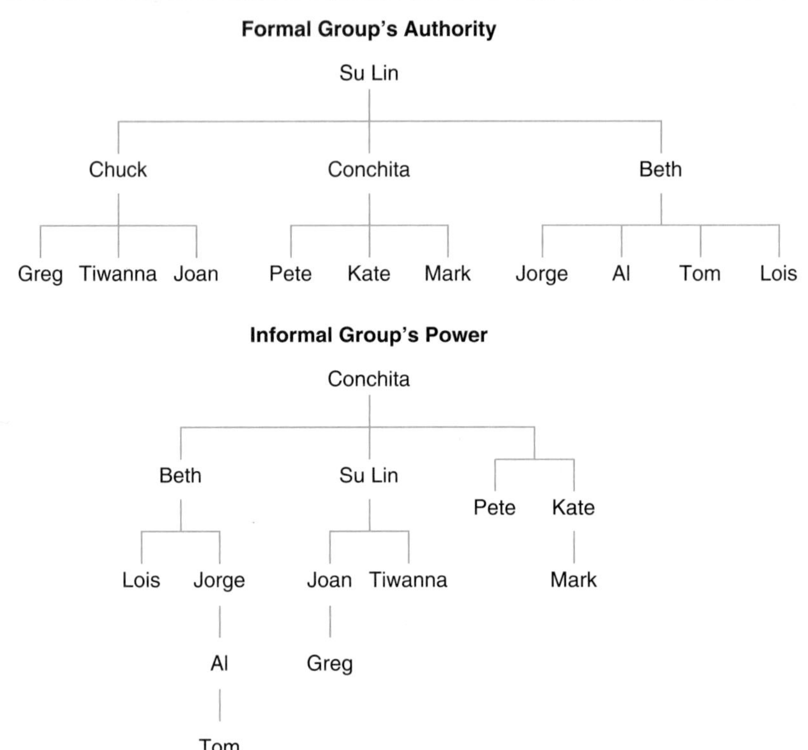

the rumors aren't true." Genua cites the example of a newly hired sales manager at a small company who was the subject of gossip to the effect that since he had not yet relocated his family, he was not committed to staying with the company. This news shook the other employees' trust in the manager and affected their work performance negatively. By the time it was learned that the new worker was indeed moving his family that very month, the company had already suffered from lowered productivity.[11] Genua points out that gossip costs employers in employee time and energy. He recommends the following actions to solve this problem:[12]

1. Establish a written credo, a model of acceptable office behavior that warns against gossip.
2. Make it clear that you disapprove of gossiping employees by walking through the office on a regular basis and halting near the culprits—disapprovingly.
3. For stubborn cases, speak to the gossipers individually.

Informal Leaders

authority
The official right to command, granted by the organization to the formal leader of a group.

Whereas the leader of a formal group is usually chosen by management, the leader of an informal group is decided upon by the members of the group. High marks for job performance may get the leader of a formal group promoted; the leader of an informal group may find his or her position in the group unaffected by work performance. A further difference between the leaders of formal and informal groups is more fundamental and applies to formal and informal leaders of a formal group, too (see Figure 11.10). While the formal group leader has **authority**, the official right to com-

power
The ability to influence, granted to an informal leader by the people being influenced.

mand granted by the organization, the informal leader has **power**, the ability to influence, granted by the people being influenced. This power can be used to achieve objectives of the informal group, such as convincing the department manager of the need for nonglare screens on computer terminals. It can also be used to advance personal goals, in which case personal ethics will determine how it is used.

The authority of the formal leader may or may not be accompanied by a certain degree of power issuing from the rights granted to the leader by the organization. For example, even a weak personality wields considerable power if he or she is granted the authority to hire and fire or recommend raises. Also, the power of the informal leaders is limited by the authority of others. An informal leader might plot insubordination, but a healthy raise or an authority-backed promise of a promotion can persuade cooperation. Similarly, the most charismatic of informal leaders cannot motivate employees who are severely underpaid or mistreated. If everyone knows the informal leader cannot change the circumstances causing the problems, his or her power is diminished.

In other words, the leaders of formal groups have more resources for controlling behavior, because they have authority to offer both physical and psychological rewards or punishments: money, a more desirable office or title, a less desirable assignment, a threat of termination. The informal leaders have only psychological rewards and punishments to offer, which have mostly to do with inclusion or exclusion from the group's social interactions. Sometimes the result is the formation of two or three fringe groups outside the formal group. Members of these groups may include not only those rejected from the group but also those wishing to enter it.

Thus, the power of informal groups must be reckoned with, but it will not necessarily win out over strong authority. If the formal groups are created by the organization and the informal ones by the employees, there will doubtless be differences between what appears on paper as the line of formal authority and what in reality are centers of informal power.

Office Politics

office politics
A calculated approach to obtaining a desired end by manipulating, or at least influencing, the emotions or actions of other people.

Using power often requires what is popularly termed **office politics**, a calculated approach to obtain a desired end by manipulating, or at least influencing, the emotions or actions of other people. Political behavior may be engaged in for constructive or destructive purposes. It may or may not be guided by ethical principles. A skilled office "politician" attempts to attain his or her ends while causing the fewest possible problems or bruised egos—at least for other powerful people. It is possible to engage in politically smart behavior that is nevertheless ethical. Of course, a truly ethical person is one who chooses the politically *harmful* course of action when ethics demand it.

Test your own taste for office politics by completing the "Self-Portrait" exercise now.

Even those who resolve to stay out of office politics usually find they cannot entirely. Almost all jobs involve human relations, and human relations involve politics. To deal well with informal groups, managers must understand their necessity, acknowledge their existence, and then try to reap the benefits they offer while curbing their harmful tendencies. The goal is to break down the walls between formal and informal groups and create a cooperative atmosphere. Here is where *diplomacy* and *compromise* come into play.

open groups
Groups that experience a great deal of change, due to frequent new entries and dropouts.

These admittedly political endeavors require that a manager stay on top of changes within the informal groups around him or her. The manager should note when the faces change as people drop out due to transfers, retirement, or strained personal relationships and new ones join. **Open groups** experience a great deal of change,

Self-Portrait

How Political Are You?

Select the response that best describes how you would behave on the job. Place the score for your response (1 to 5) on the line before each statement.

(5) Usually (4) Often (3) Sometimes (2) Seldom (1) Rarely

_____ I get along with everyone and try not to give my opinion on controversial issues.
_____ I strive to be recognized for my accomplishments.
_____ I trade favors with others.
_____ I say yes even if I'm not sure I can deliver; if I fail, I explain why it wasn't my fault.
_____ I form alliances and friendships that help me get what I want.
_____ I compromise when working with others.
_____ I'm familiar with the managers and activities of other departments.
_____ I develop interests and hobbies like those of my bosses.
_____ I try to network with my superiors so they will know me.
_____ I praise the work of others.

Add up your score to determine your political behavior; 10 is low, 50 high. The higher your score, the more political your behavior.

closed groups Groups that are more stable than open groups, usually due to a low organizational turnover rate.

with frequent new entries and dropouts. Others—usually due to a low turnover rate at the organization— are more **closed groups**, meaning that they are more stable.[13]

There are four basic ways for a manager outside the informal group to influence its operation:

1. Make it clear that any messages delivered to the group are important and worthy of the group's attention.
2. Use the authority given by the organization to good effect by speaking confidently and sticking to any rules that have been established and are generally considered reasonable. There is a time for flexibility and there is also a time for firmness.
3. When obedience is essential for the good of the formal group, do not allow the informal group to argue and disrupt the planned course of action without valid reason.
4. Know when there *is* valid reason to listen to objections, and then listen very carefully.

Perhaps there is no greater human relations lesson to master than knowing the right time to take the initiative and the right time to keep quiet and listen.

When Informal Groups Are Destructive

It is possible for an informal group to satisfy thoroughly the personal needs of its members while being quite destructive to the organization. Following are some of the ways that informal groups can hinder an organization's operation:

- distorting information or creating rumors
- developing the norm of fighting instead of helping management, thus creating conflicting goals within the organization
- disrupting the line of authority within formal groups

E. Claire Gaglione (center) is a first vice president in the consumer banking division of Republic New York Corporation. Skilled at human relations, she manages a group of employees who have won Republic's "Go for the Gold" award for profitability seven times, and she was named Manager of the Decade for her outstanding group leadership in the 1980s.
Photo source: Courtesy of Bloch Graulich Whelan.

- replacing job performance as the key to satisfaction
- heightening resistance to change
- increasing conformity to an undesirable, unprofitable, even prejudicial degree.

goal conflicts
Conflicts that occur when formal and informal groups have competing interests at stake.

When formal and informal groups have competing interests, that is, **goal conflicts**, organizational fighting can occur, usually between management and nonmanagerial employees or lower-management employees. Official authority will take precedence; even if the informal group succeeds in hurting the efficiency and effectiveness of the organization as a whole, it is not likely to achieve its goals at the expense of the organization's. Informal groups must coexist with the formal structure; they can strive to modify the formal structure, but when momentum builds toward tearing that structure down, the demise of the group is certain.

Quick Quiz 11.3

Mark each statement "true" or "false."

1. Informal groups can aid an organization by getting things done and spreading information quickly. ______
2. If a manager is overloaded with work, it may be wise for him or her to delegate some responsibility to an informal group that appears to be operating effectively. ______
3. Gossip can be extremely valuable to an organization. ______
4. The leader with the most authority is always the person with the most power. ______

organizational behavior
The way people behave in organizational settings, that is, in groups.

organizational culture
All aspects of the working environment but particularly the shared values and norms of employees.

Organizational Behavior and Culture

Organizational behavior is the way people behave in organizational settings—in groups. Consequently, the topic of **organizational culture**, which refers to all aspects of the working environment but particularly the values and norms accepted by employees, is integral to our discussion. One expert describes organizational culture as "who we are, what we believe is right, and how we do things around here."[14] Terrence E. Deal and Allan A. Kennedy have identified the following types of organizational cultures:[15]

Quality Highlights

Change from the Top Down at GE Med Systems

The old adage, "If it ain't broke, don't fix it," could have applied to the organizational culture at General Electric Medical Systems in Florence, South Carolina. The attitude that "managers think, workers do what they are told" was working fine.

The company had already bettered its bottom line by getting employees more involved, empowering them to make decisions. Overcoming entrenched beliefs in top-down management wasn't easy, however. The managers feared losing their power, and the employees weren't sure they wanted more responsibility.

Plant manager Maurice Dake realized that keeping employees involved meant proving the company's empowerment philosophy was more than skin deep. "It was difficult to keep the process going until we realized we needed to worry first about getting the process more ingrained in the corporate culture, and then take it to the bottom line." Thus began the company's plunge into changing the corporate culture. The firm provided more than 40 hours of values training, giving workers an introspective look at "why we work, who we are, and how other people see us."

Now the company is employee driven because people can see what's in it for them, says Dake. The bottom line is healthier even though the new culture is counter to most management philosophies that warn against getting personally involved with people. But Dake points out that the role of the manager is changing from directing the organization to developing people and nurturing constant renewal of the culture.

"We had changed people's way of participating, but we hadn't changed the real culture of the business. If you really change the culture, it's not something people hang up on a hook when they leave at night."

Source: *Total Quality,* October 1992, p. 6. Adapted from the Lakewood Publications video, *Empowering Your Workforce: What It Means and What It Takes.*

1. *Tough-Guy Macho* is a style well suited to some types of industry but disastrous for others. Decisions are made quickly, usually with a short-term orientation. Production is high, risks are high, and employees with an individualistic, self-confident personality fare best under this style.

   Sometimes, though, abusive behavior results from "macho"-style managers if they cannot achieve their goals legitimately. Dick Wilson of Alco Standard Corporation was transferred from a second-in-command position to a janitor's job (at full salary) when he declined to resign despite the hints of a new boss.[16]
2. *Work Hard–Play Hard* is a low-risk approach that attracts sociable, "people-oriented" employees and provides a comfortable working environment for most types of employees. In response, they generally give a good work performance. This culture may suffer a disadvantage in problem solving, however, since it does not value innovation as highly as harmony and stability.
3. *Bet-Your-Company* describes a high-risk culture that does value innovation and operates almost exclusively in a long-term orientation. Its weakness is its slowness, which can render it ineffective in adjusting to short-term changes. Visionary people who can tolerate slow feedback do well here. Others become very uncomfortable.
4. *Process* cultures assume low risks and produce slow feedback and unremarkable, though usually dependable, profits. Methodical people do well here if they are not highly creative, since the cautious atmosphere tends to discourage initiative.

These are only four possible cultures; many others exist. Often a company must change its culture in order to prosper—American automakers, challenged by Japanese imports, are prime examples. Other companies, such as the one profiled in the "Quality Highlights" box go even further, changing their culture to better their workers as well as their bottom line.

Monitoring and adjusting the organizational culture is essential to implementing organizational strategy. It has even been suggested that strategy makers might benefit from observing the culture of successful competitors, both for good ideas and to help anticipate their competitive strategy.[17]

In his book, *Corporate Tides,* Robert Fritz suggests that when organizational culture is not working well, organizational *structure,* which he defines as "the causal relationship that exists between two forces," may be the problem. Specifically, this is the conflict produced when two tension-resolution systems in the corporate culture fail to harmonize. He recommends setting clearer goals that are compared to a realistic description of current status to detect these problem structures.[18] Organizational structure will be explored later in this chapter.

The Organization as One Big Group

All the characteristics of groups can be applied to the organization when you consider it as one large group. Granted, it is composed of many smaller subgroups. Nevertheless, as a whole, an organization has its group roles, norms, and so forth, just as the smaller groups do. These tie together the organizational culture.

A force for group cohesiveness in the organization is symbolism, that is, ceremonies and rituals that honor good performance, such as a celebration of the "best employee of the month." Together with other organizational practices, such as the routine for introducing a new employee or bidding farewell to a retiring one, such experiences bind workers together the way a family bonds through holiday traditions. Not only will employees have a shared "history," they will view the organization as distinct from others by virtue of its particular "way of doing business."

Organizational Self-Esteem

The organization as a group has a certain level of *self-esteem,* just as individuals do. "When organizational self-esteem is low, employees spend work time reading help-wanted ads and daydreaming about other opportunities," says Jack Canfield, business consultant. "At social gatherings, when asked where they work, they mumble. Their commitment to the business goes no further than the next payday."[19]

David Thornburg, another consultant, notes that organizations with poor self-esteem tend to be ultracautious about risk, "a posture," says Robert McGarvey, "that rarely prospers in today's fast-changing economy. Pinpoint a high-self-esteem company, and, odds are, it's a leader." Still another consultant, and former psychology professor, Hanoch McCarty, offers Wal-Mart as an example of a company that has always emphasized corporate self-esteem. Wal-Mart employees are proud of where they work. They even have a company cheer. "Go into a Wal-Mart, and instantly you know the employees are glad to be there," says McCarty.[20]

Organizations can take concrete actions to improve their overall self-esteem. Good deeds are one way. You may recall that Ruppert Landscape Inc., in Ashton, Maryland, donated sod, foliage, and labor to change a nearby "Dust Bowl" into an attractive playground. Its gift to the community doubtless made the employees, especially those with children, feel proud to be associated with the company.[21]

Suppose a company begins recycling as an expression of environmental concern; employees who share that value will feel good about working for such an employer. Suppose it donates a percentage of profits to a children's hospital or some such charity. Suppose it does the right thing and recalls a product that might harm people even though it had the option to hide the evidence of such harm. Organizational self-esteem rises with ethical behavior.

Sam Walton (center) felt that motivated, satisfied employees would do their jobs better and better employees meant a better operation and more satisfied customers.
Photo source: © Eli Reichman.

Photo Exercise

What other leader in business or in your experience successfully generated high or low self-esteem among employees? How?

Organizational Structure

Since an organization is a very *big* group, its structure is of immense importance to the functioning of the group. Certain structures are better suited to certain types of organizations.

line employees
Those directly involved with production.

staff employees
Those who supplement—support and advise—the line employees with special expertise and are not directly involved with production.

Line and Staff. Two main types of employees are possible in an organization. **Line employees** are those directly involved with production. **Staff employees** serve to supplement—support and advise—the line employees with special expertise and are not directly involved with production. It is entirely possible for an organization to exist solely of line employees, in which case its structure is likely to be less complex than in one that uses both line and staff workers. Larger organizations tend to use more staff employees.

The group dynamics of a line-and-staff organization will probably be more complicated than those of a line organization. The potential for conflict is greater. Either line or staff workers may be perceived as having higher status. Group norms may be different for the two types of workers. Communication difficulties between the two may be more likely.

Job Specialization. The degree of *job specialization*—to what extent a complicated job is broken into simpler tasks—will determine some aspects of organizational structure. Again, a more complex structure will be necessary for a large organization with varying types of job specialization. If several strongly differentiated subgroups develop within the organization as a result of job specialization, an unhealthy competition could occur among them, putting the overall goals of the organization at peril. Also, communication is trickier when job specialization among different subgroups is very high. Such a situation cries out for effective *coordination* and *integration.* Human relations skills are vital to this type of organization.

chain of command
The arrangement of organizational authority, or levels of management.

span of control
The number of employees reporting to a manager or supervisor.

Chain of Command. There has been a lot of talk lately in the business world about a tendency toward "leaner" or "flatter" organization structures. The main idea is to speed up communication and decision making by reducing the number of steps involved. Compare the *tall* and *flat* structures in Figure 11.11. The **chain of command,** which is the arrangement of organizational authority, determines how tall or flat the structure is. A tall structure has more levels of authority than a flat one. The **span of control,**

Figure 11.11 **Tall versus Flat Organizational Structure**

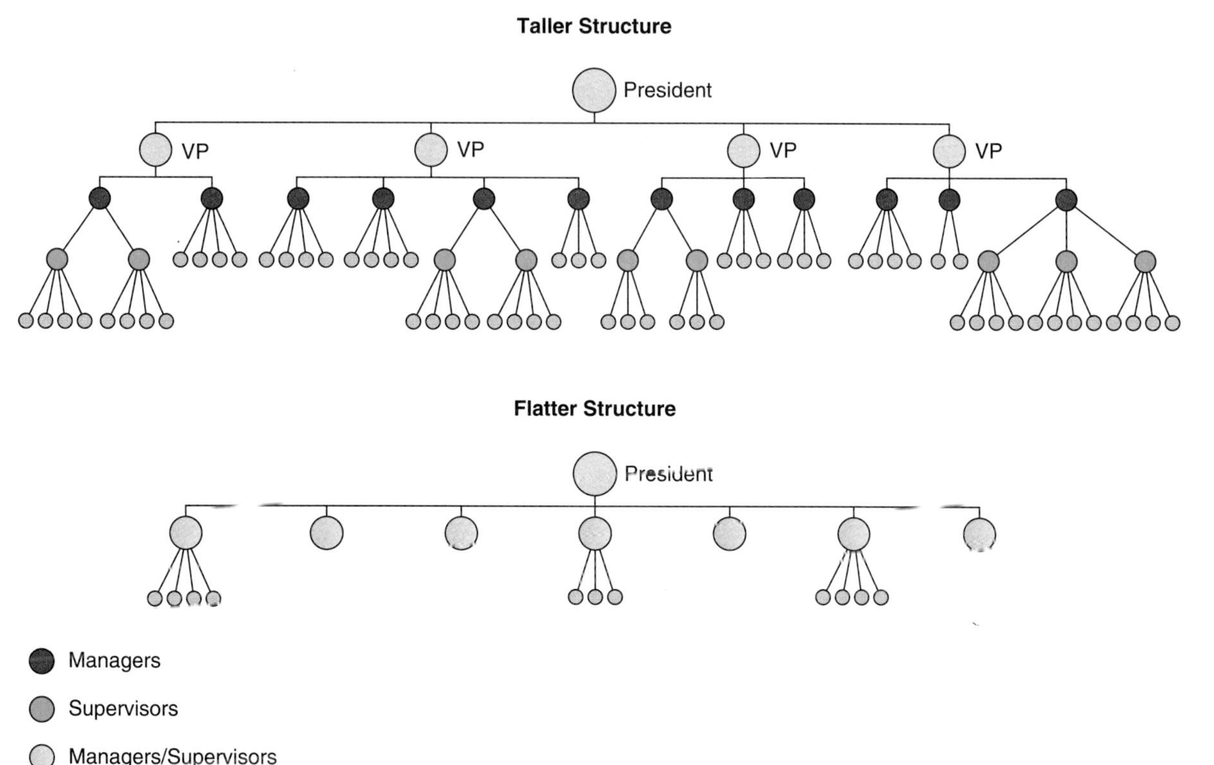

or number of employees reporting to a manager or supervisor, is small in a tall structure, where there are many levels of management, and broad in a flat one, where there are few levels.

Tall organizations have greater communication problems—and require more employees! That is one reason for today's trend toward "flattening" the structure. It is a natural consequence of *downsizing.* However, a too-flat structure can be harmful if it results in a manager being responsible for too many employees. Communication suffers here because employees do not receive enough individual attention. Questions may go unanswered, and motivation may decline from the lack of managerial feedback. Moreover, managerial burnout could occur. The ideal degree of "tallness" or "flatness" will vary with the organization.

centralized structures Those in which decision making is largely confined to top management.

decentralized structures Those in which much decision making is delegated to subgroups.

Centralization/Decentralization. In **centralized structures**, decision making can be largely confined to top management; in **decentralized structures** subgroups are given authority to make many decisions. Some organizations establish subgroups called *profit centers,* which make all their own decisions. Where employees have the necessary knowledge and judgment to make competent decisions, a decentralized structure is always going to be more efficient. Just think of the time saved if a decision can be immediately made and implemented rather than waiting for approval from headquarters! Of course, in many cases, employees do not possess the necessary knowledge and judgment, or they may not want the responsibility.

Rich Weber (right) is a line employee—in fact, a line mechanic at Nalley's, a division of Curtice Burns Foods. He is directly involved with the production of Adam's Old Fashioned Peanut Butter. Weber was able to save the company $25,000 by fabricating a new conveyor belt with just a "couple hundred dollars" in parts.

Photo source: Courtesy of Curtice Burns Foods, photography © 1993 Forest McMullin.

departmentalization
The subgrouping according to function, product, territory, customer, or some other criteria that occurs in organizations of any significant size.

Departmentalization. Organizations of any significant size demand **departmentalization**, or subgrouping into sections, branches, divisions, and so forth. These subgroups are usually made according to

- function
- product
- territory
- customer.

Combinations of these are possible as well, as are other criteria for departmentalization.

Modern Approaches to Structure. Many of today's organizations are altering standard structures. The current emphasis on *work teams* is one example (see Chapter 12).

Another trend is *intrapreneuring,* a term coined from "entrepreneuring" to suggest the same qualities of innovation and responsibility that are required to start one's own business, applied instead within an organization. Convincing entrepreneurial types to stay in a company obviously plays havoc with the structure; they must be offered immense freedom and substantial rewards. These people are risk takers, so there must be insulation against the adverse effects of their risks. They are essentially inventors, and inventing is a mysterious thing in itself. Consider Post-its, invented from a glue that failed to stick "properly" until the "inventor" realized it provided the perfect way to temporarily mark pages in his hymnbook without marring them. Writing in *Entrepreneur* magazine, Stephanie Barlow observes, "It's one of those charming facts of American business that most of the truly revolutionary products in our nation's history—we're talking about the biggies here; things like Coca-Cola, Post-its, and Apple computers—came from what could most charitably be described as pretty off-the-wall ideas."[22]

What kind of a group setting allows such creativity? More and more organizations are considering whether they can manage to provide such a setting, because the rewards are so great.

Matrix organizations have been around for a while, but they still represent a radical departure from the old structural choices because they violate the principle of *unity of command,* which states that an employee should report only to one person. The matrix system was devised by TRW Inc. cofounder Simon Ramo when other forms of departmentalization proved inadequate for managing complex technological developments in the aerospace industry and military-industrial ventures.[23] It is called a

To be successful, teams must be empowered to plan, control, coordinate, and continuously improve their work. In the photo at right is an empowered team at the Integrated Circuit Connector Products Division of AMP Incorporated, a division that won North Carolina's 1993 top quality award.

Photo source: Courtesy of AMP Incorporated.

Photo Exercise

How has working with a team helped you in your life?

"matrix" because functional and product lines of authority are overlaid, forming a matrix. Many employees belong to two subgroups in such a structure. Not only might they report to more than one supervisor, they may themselves become a temporary boss of those normally above them in the hierarchy of authority. Matrix structures break all the rules, but they appear to be the only structure that does work for some extremely complex projects.

Group dynamics can go haywire in a newly formed matrix structure. Group members have to reinvent the group roles and group norms of their new subgroups. Potential for conflict abounds. But the capacity to accommodate change exists, too.

In general, the push for *empowerment* is changing organizational structures. In the terms of the authors of the recently published book *Empowerment,* Cynthia D. Scott and Dennis T. Jaffe, the typical *pyramid* shapes of authority are changing to *circle* shapes, or *network* shapes. In the pyramid, decisions are made at the top, people are responsible for only one job and are tightly controlled, and communication is almost solely top-down. In the newer circle or network, the customer is the center and the people work cooperatively around the customer, with communication flowing in all directions and control coming through that communication. Responsibilities are broader, decision making is shared, and changes can be made quickly. As Scott and Jaffe point out, the key skill for any employee in these new structures is the ability to work with others—human relations skill.[24]

Quick Quiz 11.4

1. What type of people would fare well in a Bet-Your-Company type of organizational culture?
2. Ceremonies that honor good performance are a form of ____________ that benefits organizational culture.
3. Organizations, like individuals, can suffer from low self-____________.

Summary

- **Describe the two main types of formal groups in an organization.** Functional groups fulfill the ongoing needs in an organization by carrying out particular functions. Task groups (also called *project groups*) are set up to carry out a specific activity and are disbanded when the activity has been completed.

- **List the five stages of a group's life cycle and the four features of a mature, effective group.** A group's life cycle consists of orientation, dissatisfaction, resolution, production, and termination. A mature, effective group is marked by acceptance, good communication, group solidarity, and group control.
- **Name six characteristics of a group, and explain the significance of each.** *Group roles* are patterns of behavior related to a member's position in the group, such as leader or gatekeeper or compromiser; certain roles are needed by certain groups for them to be effective. *Group norms* are standards for acceptable or appropriate behavior; they can enhance or diminish a group's effectiveness. *Status* is a person's rank, or importance, in the group; people with higher status influence the formation of group norms. *Cohesiveness* is the degree of closeness among group members; it is important for an effective group. *Size* can range from two to any number, but informal subgroups tend to form in groups larger than twelve. Smaller groups are usually quicker at decision making and have better communication, but some tasks are so complex that a large group is necessary. *Homogeneity* refers to the sameness of the members of a group, that is, how much they have in common; homogeneous groups tend to be more harmonious than heterogeneous groups, but too much homogeneity can lead to the undesirable phenomenon of groupthink.
- **Discuss the advantages and disadvantages of group decision making.** A group can generate more ideas for alternatives than can an individual—for example, by the technique of brainstorming. However, disadvantages to group decision making are (1) the process is slower than for an individual, (2) there is a cost to the organization when employees spend their time in meetings rather than producing or selling, and (3) the group can reach an inferior decision by letting one person or a small subgroup dominate the process. If groupthink can be avoided, though, group decision making is beneficial to an organization in that it draws upon the varied skills, knowledge, and experience of its employees while also providing them with motivation for improved work performance and greater commitment to implementing any plans.
- **Explain how informal groups differ from formal groups.** Unlike formal groups, informal groups are not created by management and are not reflected on the organization chart. They are created by employees to meet personal needs as well as work-related needs that are not met by formal groups. The network for informal communication is, in fact, an informal group.
- **List some ways that informal groups can benefit an organization.** Informal groups can benefit an organization by helping people identify with the organization, getting things done, enhancing job satisfaction, easing managers' work loads, providing emotional outlets, and helping managers gather employee feedback.
- **List some ways that informal groups can hinder the operation of an organization.** Informal groups can hurt an organization when they distort information or create rumors and gossip, and when they create goal conflicts between managerial and nonmanagerial employees.
- **Compare various types of organizational cultures.** Some organizational cultures make quick decision making possible but at the cost of sometimes abusive behavior toward employees. Others are more people oriented but take few risks and thus suffer in the marketplace because of a lack of innovation. Still others are high risk, focusing on long-term results but therefore sometimes slow to make decisions and provide feedback to employees. Finally, some cultures produce dependable but unremarkable profits through a low-risk approach that provides job security but at the price of slow feedback to employees and an atmosphere that may discourage initiative. Symbolism and organizational self-esteem are important in organizational culture.
- **Compare various types of organizational structures.** Structure is determined by the line-and-staff configuration of an organization, degree of job specialization, chain of command (with its "taller" or "flatter" line of authority), degree of centralization in decision making, and type of departmentalization. Modern approaches to organizational structure involve work teams, intrapreneurship, and matrix structures.

Key Terms

groups (248)
formal groups (248)
informal groups (248)
functional groups (248)
task groups (248)
group roles (250)
group norms (251)
status (253)
cohesiveness (253)
homogeneous groups (254)
groupthink (254)
heterogeneous groups (254)
brainstorming (257)
authority (262)
power (263)
office politics (263)
open groups (263)
closed groups (264)

goal conflicts (264)
organizational behavior (265)
organizational culture (265)
line employees (268)
staff employees (268)
chain of command (268)
span of control (268)
centralized structures (269)
decentralized structures (269)
departmentalization (270)

Review and Discussion Questions

1. Think of your current job or the most recent job you have held. (If you have never been employed, consider your role as a student.)
   a. What formal groups are you a member of? For example, what organization employs you? What division or department do you work in?
   b. Why did you join each of these groups?

2. Identify whether the following are functional or task groups:
   a. a committee coordinating a company's move to a new location
   b. busboys at a Chinese restaurant
   c. a team responsible for identifying ways to reduce waste
   d. teachers in a high school science department

3. Mike Soliz, the assistant manager at a family restaurant, is responsible for leading employees in finding ways to respond to customer complaints of poor service. How can Mike make the group as effective as possible?

4. Why is it important to know about each of the following characteristics of a group?
   a. roles of group members
   b. status of group members

5. Tracey Washington heads a group of city recreational department employees who meet monthly to discuss ways to improve the department's programs. Tracey wants to encourage the group's cohesiveness so that its members will work hard. How can she do this?

6. Junko Nagano consistently comes to work early, but just as consistently refuses to follow unofficial policy and turn on the office lights, copier, and coffee maker. What group characteristic has she violated, and how can her coworkers pressure her to conform?

7. Can a group that is too cohesive be prone to groupthink? Why or why not? How can a group avoid groupthink?

8. Paul Zvonek, a factory foreman who captains the company softball team, has been approached by coworkers who are angry about new rules on punching the time clock. Does Paul have the power or authority to help them? What does Paul risk by getting involved?

9. What informal groups do you belong to? How do they influence your work or school life?

10. What effect does the organizational culture have on groups and on organizational structure?

A SECOND LOOK

As the only female Hispanic at a prominent Wall Street investment firm, Adela Cepeda found herself in an informal group of one despite her impressive credentials and experience. Use some of the terms you learned about in this chapter—group cohesiveness, homogeneous groups, group norms, and status—to discuss Cepeda's plight.

Independent Activity

Through a Child's Eyes

Children are naturally used to being put in groups, whether it be the classroom, Scouts, or sports teams. Yet despite their need to conform to group norms, children usually lack the discipline to be totally successful at working within a group.

Judge for yourself: Go to an organized sporting event—a Little League, PeeWee football, soccer, basketball, or hockey game—and watch the kids on the team. As you observe, ask yourself the following questions:

- How do the kids interact as group members? Are they working together toward a common goal—winning—or are their individual needs and personalities causing conflict?
- How cohesive is the group? How does the group's size or degree of homogeneity affect its cohesiveness?

- Have certain members adopted group roles?
- How do the groups behave within the organizational structure imposed by their coaches? How would you sum up the kind of culture or atmosphere the coach has established? Are the kids following the coaches' directions or a different set of group norms?

Skill Builder

Personal Values, Informal Groups

In this chapter's Group Activity, you will form informal groups with classmates with whom you may or may not have much of a bond. How important to you is the common link your group will form? Read the list below, and rate each item on a scale of most important (1) to least important (10). Are the items you rank as most important those which form the core of the informal groups to which you belong? Why or why not?

_____	Job	_____	Academic achievements
_____	Marriage or relationship	_____	Close friends
_____	Community activities	_____	Family
_____	Religion	_____	Intellectual pursuits
_____	Sports and exercise	_____	Material goods

Group Activity

Classroom Brainstorming Challenge (30 minutes)

Divide the class divides into groups of five or six people. Each group will brainstorm solutions to the following problem: The head librarian for an art museum's library has been directed to cut expenses by 15 percent. The library currently operates during the same hours as the museum (10 a.m. to 5 p.m. every day except Wednesday, when the museum is open until 9 p.m.). Half of the library's budget goes for salaries for the head librarian plus two reference librarians and a clerk. One-quarter of the budget goes to purchase books and periodicals, and another one-quarter goes to operating expenses such as the library's share of heating and lighting. Given this information, how can the library cut expenses with a minimal impact on the quality of its service?

1. Each group should pick a leader to record its ideas.
2. Group members should suggest ideas, and the leader should write them down where everyone can see them. No one is to comment on the ideas at this point.
3. When group members feel they are out of ideas, the group should discuss the ideas listed and pick the most promising one(s). The group leader should try to make sure that all group members contribute to this discussion.
4. As a class, discuss the following questions:
   a. Did hearing other people's ideas help you come up with more ideas?
   b. How did it feel to hear ideas without commenting on them? How did it feel to express ideas, knowing that no one was to criticize them?

c. How well did your group carry out this assignment? What could it have done better? Was it difficult to get everyone to participate?
d. Is brainstorming an appropriate technique for solving a problem such as this one? Why or why not?

Case Study

Too Big, Too Fast for Spartan Motors

"There are days when I wish we had 35 employees again," says Janine Nierenberger, director of personnel for Spartan Motors, remembering a simpler time more than ten years ago. Today, the Charlotte, Michigan, maker of chassis for fire trucks and motor homes bustles with nearly 400 workers, and Nierenberger has little time to reminisce.

Like most start-up companies, Spartan attracted individuals who enjoyed the feeling of being in a small family. They helped foster an informal organization without much reliance on a formal structure. They were used to communicating on a casual level, and being involved in creating the company.

Spartan's small size enabled it to move quickly and respond aggressively to the chassis market, and helped it grow to become a successful midsized company. But as their hard work helped make the company more financially successful and competitive, the employees lost their feelings of personal success and job satisfaction.

Spartan's growth fostered a need for greater structure, more procedures, and a division of responsibilities. As a formal structure superseded the informal structure on which the company was founded, these original employees became less involved, their freedom and responsibilities curtailed.

Now it looks as though the company may need to further departmentalize its structure, distancing the first employees even farther from what had been their primary task—running the organization.

"We used to be a family. The company was our life. Sixty-to seventy-hour workweeks weren't unusual," says Nierenberger. "Now it's a business; it isn't a little organization. We don't have the contact we once had, and that's a hard adjustment."

Case Questions

1. How have the benefits of the informal structure helped Spartan become so successful?
2. Which was more important to its success, its formal or informal structure?
3. Is goal conflict a potential problem for Spartan and its employees? What other ways can informal groups hinder the company?
4. How can the company keep its original work force happy while departmentalizing and maintaining a growth curve?
5. How can Spartan's management use the grapevine to its advantage?

Source: Rob Brookler, "HR in Growing Companies," *Personnel Journal* (November 1992): pp. 80B–80F.

Case Study

Consensus Rules at Drypers

There is no corner office at Drypers headquarters in Houston. No big cheese, no grand poohbah. In other words, no chief executive.

For that alone, the small disposable-diapers manufacturer might not be noteworthy. But the company's success without a single strong leader is: operating under the leadership of a group of five managing directors who share the office of chief executive, sales rose 24 percent in the last fiscal year.

The five managing directors—all with equal power and each with individual responsibility over an area, such as finance, marketing, or manufacturing—work as a team, sharing information and ideas. No major decisions are final until they arrive at a consensus. Reaching agreement among five individual minds and personalities means it takes longer to make a decision than it might with a single chief executive, but the Drypers co-CEOs think it works just fine. They say the decisions become inclusive, because all areas of the company, each represented by a decision maker, feel it is *their* decision. The result is an inclination to quickly put decisions into effect. Says managing director David Pitassi: "When you have a shared vision, it's a very powerful thing."

And, in this case, successful. Last year, the company developed and launched—all within a six-month span—technologically advanced, disposable training pants called Big Boy and Big Girl. The product's arrival was not only fast by industry standards, but response has been equally speedy; after only half a year on the market, the new line has a 20 percent market share in southeastern Texas.

Case Questions

1. Which group characteristics are most important for the Drypers management team? Do you think each of the five plays a defined role? How does that affect the group's claim of consensus?
2. What benefits stem from the company's group decision-making process? What dangers?
3. Do you think the Drypers co-CEO arrangement has had a positive or negative effect on the rest of the company's organizational structure? Why?
4. Will the Drypers co-CEO arrangement endure as the company grows? Why or why not? Would you enjoy working within this arrangement?

Source: Brian Dumar, "The New Non-Manager Managers," *Fortune,* February 22, 1993, p. 81.

Quick Quiz Answers

Quick Quiz 11.1

1. conflict
2. norms
3. groupthink

Quick Quiz 11.2

1. acceptance and communication
2. brainstorming

Quick Quiz 11.3

1. true
2. true
3. false
4. false

Quick Quiz 11.4

1. visionary people who can tolerate slow feedback
2. symbolism
3. esteem

PART OUTLINE

5

People Working Together

CHAPTER

12

Team Building

CHAPTER OUTLINE

Learning Objectives

- Explain how a real team differs from just a group of people working together.
- Identify three types of teams and discuss whether they are usually permanent or temporary in nature.
- Explain the role that participative management plays in team building, and give some reasons why managers often resist it.
- Discuss partnering as an alternative to team building.
- List some common causes of problems in team building.
- Describe what is involved in a team leader's, or coach's, job.
- Discuss some of the factors in successful team building.

Quiet Janitor Leads Connaught Labs

He dealt with waste every day as the Swiftwater, Pennsylvania, company's janitor, but no one guessed Harold Fraley would become an expert on waste control for Connaught Laboratories' Waste Reduction Always Pays (WRAP) team.

Least of all Harold.

"He was the least-educated man on our entire team, the opposite of what you would think of as a technical expert," recalls Bruce Kilby, WRAP team leader. "When the team first started meeting, he was really quiet." In fact, Fraley wanted off the seven-person team and had to be persuaded to stay. But once the team started brainstorming about the waste in the pharmaceutical company's plant, the quiet janitor realized he knew more about it than anyone else. Says Kilby, "He became the team expert and the implementation expert."

Fraley helped identify the worst of the plant's 60 waste streams, and he helped guide WRAP in reducing plant waste by 40 percent in just 11 months. Sadly, 6 months before the savings achieved by WRAP's efforts could be assessed, the 52-year-old janitor died. Recognizing the importance of Fraley's contribution to WRAP, team members shared their bonus with his family.

Source: Dirk Dusharme, "Quiet Janitor Becomes Team's 'Waste Guru,'" *Quality Digest,* May 1993, (800–527–8875). Photo source: Terry Vine/Tony Stone Images.

Authors Jon Katzenbach and Douglas Smith say that they set out to write their book, *The Wisdom of Teams,* with the idea that the word "team" is used too loosely, that "groups do not become teams simply because that is what someone calls them." They note that the "team" label is often applied to "amorphous groups in the hope of motivating and energizing them"—but it doesn't work.[1] There is more to team building

Figure 12.1 **Synergy from Teamwork**

When teamwork is operating, a team produces an effect that is more than the sum of its parts.

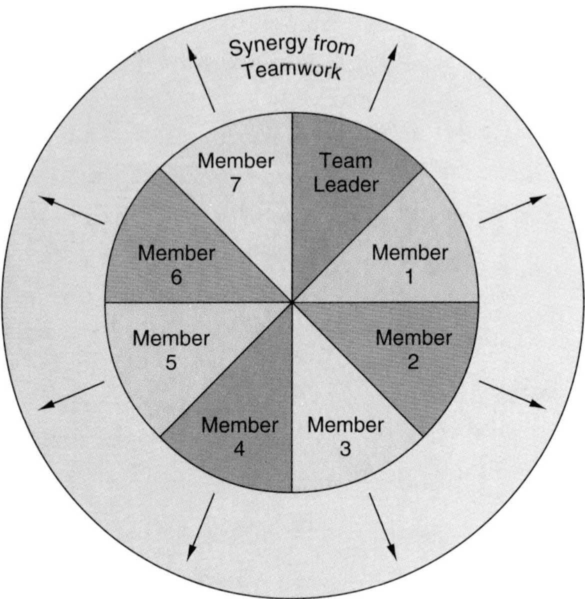

than labeling, as Bruce Kilby, Connaught Laboratories' WRAP team leader, discovered about team member Harold Fraley.

The Team: More than the Sum of Its Parts

teamwork
A way of accomplishing tasks in which a group of people pool their skills to achieve a common goal through commitment and cooperation.

synergy
The effect of achieving a greater result than team members could have achieved working individually.

team building
An active program in which groups of people are assembled and trained to work effectively together to achieve an agreed-upon goal.

Teamwork is a way of accomplishing tasks in which a group of people pool their skills to achieve a common goal through commitment and cooperation. Teamwork creates **synergy**, the effect of achieving a greater result than team members could have achieved working individually (see Figure 12.1).

Teamwork has three benefits for organizations. First, teamwork is a way of drawing on the skills of all workers. In today's complex marketplaces, a supervisor or manager cannot be expected to see all and know all. Second, teamwork can be highly motivating to employees. When they participate in problem solving and decision making, they become more committed to the solutions and take a greater interest in the fruit of their labors. Finally, teamwork improves the organization's performance overall. Of the Fortune 1000 companies surveyed that use teamwork, two-thirds reported improved productivity, customer service, and product quality.[2]

Teamwork does not just happen. An organization that wants to promote teamwork must usually undertake an active program of **team building**. Groups of people are assembled and trained to work effectively together to achieve an agreed-upon goal. Says expert Cathy E. Kramer, "It sounds relatively easy. Gather a group of employees together and let them apply their hands-on knowledge and experience to solve problems. Not only are they more likely to arrive at meaningful solutions, they will feel empowered by the process. There is only one catch. It is anything but easy."[3] Kramer goes on to say that getting teams to work in a "cohesive, creative, and meaningful manner requires careful planning, training, and evaluation," with the complete commitment of the employer.

The Work of Teams

collective work-product A result that reflects the joint, real contribution of team members.

The proof of teamwork is a **collective work-product**, a result that "reflects the joint, real contribution of team members."[4] Katzenbach and Smith present the following examples of "real" teams accomplishing real work:[5]

- In the 1980s a small group of railroaders, led by Bill Greenwood, took on most of the top management of Burlington Northern and created a multi-billion-dollar business in "piggybacking" rail services, despite vigorous resistance.
- A small group at Hewlett-Packard (Dean Morton, Lew Platt, Ben Homes, Dick Alberting, and a handful of others) revitalized the dying efforts of the Medical Products Group at that company by enhancing performance to a remarkable degree.
- A small group at Knight-Ridder fulfilled the "customer obsession" vision of its leader, Jim Batten, with the *Tallahassee Democrat* paper, by turning "a charter to eliminate errors into a mission of major change," bringing about a complete turnaround in the paper's fortunes.

Quad/Graphics credits teamwork for its phenomenal growth from a single press, 11 employees, and a 20,000-square-foot building in the early 1970s to its current imposing position as the largest privately held printing company in North America, with sales in excess of $500 million. Teamwork at this company is sacred. There is an ironclad commitment to breaking down differences between management and workers, who are entrusted with key decisions and are encouraged to be creative. Quad/Graphics has been able to respond "at a lightning pace" to opportunities, and both quality and productivity are high.[6]

Motorola has likewise made a firm commitment to foster teamwork. Thousands of work teams are set up each year. The company annually sponsors a problem-solving competition at all of its work sites, pitting one team against another. Motorola estimates that it saves $2.2 billion annually from quality programs that increasingly involve teamwork.[7]

Typology of Teams

Not all effective working groups are necessarily teams, nor are teams needed for every single group situation. Table 12.1 presents the differences between a working group that is not a team and one that has the distinguishing characteristics of a team.

Most teams can be classified in one of three major ways:[8]

1. *Teams that make recommendations.* Task forces, project groups, quality circles, safety groups, and audit groups are formed to make specific recommendations after studying a particular problem or situation. These teams are usually temporary.
2. *Teams that make or do things.* The people who are responsible for actual manufacturing, development, operations, marketing, sales, service, and so forth are usually part of a permanent, ongoing team. New-product development or process-design teams would be an exception.
3. *Teams that run things.* The people who are in charge of overseeing other people's work may compose a team, even though they may not recognize themselves as such. If they take a team approach to running the function or department or group of people under their authority and are accountable to one another, then they are indeed a team, albeit an informal one, and they may enjoy the benefits of

Table 12.1 **Not All Groups Are Teams: How to Tell the Difference**

Working Group	Team
• Has strong, clearly focused leader	• Has shared leadership roles
• Features individual accountability	• Features individual and mutual accountability
• Has a purpose the same as the broader organizational mission	• Has specific team purpose that the team itself delivers
• Has individual work-products	• Has collective work-products
• Runs efficient meetings	• Encourages open-ended discussion and active problem-solving meetings
• Measures its effectiveness indirectly by its influence on others (e.g., financial performance of the business)	• Measures performance directly by assessing collective work-products
• Discusses, decides, and delegates	• Discusses, decides, and does real work together

Source: Reprinted by permission of *Harvard Business Review.* Adapted from an exhibit from "The Discipline of Teams," by Jon R. Katzenbach and Douglas K. Smith, (March–April 1993), p. 113.

team dynamics such as synergy. These "teams at the top" will consist of only two to four people, and they are usually permanent in nature.

self-managed team One whose members direct their own work.

Regardless of the team's general purpose, it may have an assigned leader or be a **self-managed team**, whose members direct their own work. Members of self-managed teams rotate their own jobs, work schedules, and vacations and make all the decisions that affect their area of responsibility. For instance, at the GM Saturn plant, self-managed teams interview and approve their own members, decide how to run their work area, and take care of their own budgeting.[9] Self-managed teams are appropriate when the following conditions exist:[10]

- The work involves people with similar skills in a single location.
- Employees are willing and able to manage their own work as a team.
- Managers are able and willing to adopt a hands-off management style.
- The market is strong enough so the company can improve productivity without laying off workers as management is eliminated.
- The organization's policy and culture will support self-managed teams.
- The community will support self-managed teams.

Participative Management and Teams

Teamwork is a logical outgrowth of the participative management movement that emerged in response to increased emphasis on quality improvement. *Participative management* involves managers working with employees to set objectives and plan how to achieve them. Teamwork is, in fact, as expert Cathy E. Kramer puts it, the "driving force" of the quality and participation movements.[11]

Some managers do not like the idea of sharing their power in this manner. Those who, in terms of McClelland's motivation theory, have strong *affiliation* needs—a desire to maintain close and friendly personal relationships—may find participative management much to their liking. But those with strong needs for *power*—a desire to control, influence, or be responsible for other people or for results—resent losing

Quality Highlights

Freudenberg-NOK Shops for Kaizen

The old adage, "If you can't beat 'em, join 'em," has come into play in two industries hardest hit by overseas competition. The automobile and electronics industries are trying to beat their competitors by joining them in their use of lean manufacturing teams. Using what the Japanese call *kaizen,* or continuous improvement, their aim is to boost productivity on the shop floor by asking teams of employees to introduce dozens of small, inexpensive changes to make U.S. plants more competitive.

A two-year, $2 million investment in teams and their suggestions should help a foreign-owned, U.S.-based auto-parts maker achieve a direct payback of $12 million to $20 million.

Freudenberg-NOK's Ligonier, Indiana, plant is but one of the fourteen U.S. plants owned by the German-Japanese joint venture that is continually quality-checked by 12-member GROWTTH (Get Rid Of Waste Through Team Harmony) teams.

The teams work in short spurts, investigating problems and discussing improvements in one section of the plant. Over three days, for example, a team will work toward ambitious goals, such as boosting capacity by 20 percent, raising productivity by 15 percent, and reducing work-in-process by 50 percent. None of the quick-hit teams can actually produce plantwide gains that dramatic, but their suggestions are a launching pad for changes, often all implemented within a month. If their ideas work, they spread to other parts of the plant. Then comes the next shift of teams; in one year alone, 40 teams will move through the sprawling factory.

Team members can be honest without fear of losing their jobs or costing coworkers theirs. Chief executive Joseph Day smoothed the way for the teams by promising that no one would be laid off as a result of *kaizen* suggestions. Today, he thinks the teams will help double sales by the year 2000, to $1 billion, without adding people or factory space.

Source: James B. Treece, "Improving the Soul of an Old Machine," *Business Week,* October 25, 1993, pp. 134–136.

any control. A majority of managers seem to fall in this latter category. Management writer and consultant Thomas L. Brown says, "I've found few managers who are comfortable with the concept or practice of 'empowering' others."[12]

When managers view participative management as a threat, they will naturally resist it. The result can be disastrous. A token program is far worse than no program at all. When workers get enthusiastic about taking on more responsibility, having more say in their jobs, contributing more to the organization, and receiving more recognition and respect only to find themselves under the same old autocratic system, they cannot help but feel bitter.

What often happens is that company leaders announce a new emphasis on team building, offering employees the opportunity to develop new skills and enhance their performance, then fail to provide much opportunity to actually use those skills. "That's dangerous," says one company CEO, "because what you do is plant in people's minds the idea that this stuff doesn't really pay off." It is probably better to institute a program that covers only a few targeted areas than to offer a broad program that covers information the employees may never have the chance to apply.[13]

Token programs, moreover, are generally launched with much fanfare—slogans, T-shirts, coffee mugs bearing the logo of the program—which serves only to remind employees that "form is more important than substance" as they deal with their disappointment at finding their jobs essentially unchanged despite all the hoopla.[14] Such problems often develop from a hasty adoption of a team-building program without a careful outlining of how it will be implemented.

A company that embraces teams to boost quality and productivity and remain competitive can be hugely successful when it promises its employees that their suggestions to cut costs won't also cut their jobs. Read about it in the "Quality Highlights" box.

The Partnering Alternative. To overcome managerial resistance to participation, consultant and author Joanne Sujansky recommends *partnering,* in which the manager links up with each key worker in a project as a partner, in several one-on-one relationships rather than as a team. The partnering relationship with some employees may last for only the one or two days necessary for a particular task to be completed. This short-term relationship may be more enthusiastically received by power-conscious managers. Sujansky identifies the following roles for a manager taking on this partnering relationship:[15]

- *Coaching*—providing growth opportunities as well as corrective feedback and reinforcement for the partnered employee. The "coach is not playing, but is helping others to play."
- *Training*—either teaching the skills required for the job at hand or arranging for adequate instruction in them.
- *Modeling*—serving as a good example for the employee; making sure the employee sees his or her "partner" acting out the behaviors necessary for business success.
- *Facilitating*—working with the employee to make sure he or she learns how to solve problems, rather than just solving the problems *for* the employee.
- *Leading*—communicating a vision for the department or work areas (what would otherwise be the "team") and securing a commitment from each worker to strive for the realization of that vision.
- *Evaluating*—acting as a kind of "scorekeeper," observing and documenting work performed, assessing it, and giving performance reviews.

Much of the preceding applies equally well to leading a work team. In partnering, the team is replaced by a collection of twosomes consisting of the leader and each employee in turn. The aim is to duplicate the effect of teamwork without rousing the usual managerial objections to empowerment. One employee at a time, workers may not appear as threatening to a supervisor's power as they do en masse.

The Limits of Participation. As one expert notes, the hierarchy is still a reality of the modern business world—and "the fellow handling part-time maintenance duties on the production line is not 'equal' in all respects to the senior vice-president."[16] Not only do many managers make participative management impossible by their extreme reluctance to give up any authority or power, in some cases the nature of the business will not allow a fully equal participation by all of a team's members. Expert Richard Krieg, after endorsing the team-building, empowerment, participative management movement, adds this proviso: "The nature and degree of [worker] involvement [in decision making] should be carefully considered in light of corporate realities. High-performance practices don't imply the forfeiture of competition or the removal of managerial oversight."[17]

The current enthusiasm for team building has led to the establishment of some teams that should never have been born, that were simply not needed. "Let the work—the jobs that need doing—determine whether teams are the best answer," counsels management consultant Hank Karp. The higher the degree of interdependence among workers, the more teams are apt to accomplish. "You've got to look at it on a case-by-case basis," says Karp. "Teams may be a cure for some companies, but they're not a cure-all."[18]

team player
Someone who is willing to make a personal sacrifice for the good of the team.

The Individual in the Team. An effective team requires a skillful team leader and at least a few team members who could be described as **team players**—people willing to make a personal sacrifice for the good of the team. The sacrifice may be as small as

In corporate America, team building is even affecting sales forces, which are competitive by nature. Jack Pohanka, one of 180 Saturn dealers in the United States, is turning his salespeople into team players. He sent his employees off site for training that included the "trust fall," a backward leap off a 12-foot stepladder into the arms of fellow workers. A Saturn team is shown at right.
Photo source: © David Graham.

Photo Exercise

Do you think training tactics such as the "trust fall" are effective? Why or why not?

sharing the praise that could have been unshared ("I'm glad the board approved, but I want you to know that Nelly, Helmut, and Leon all contributed to the design") or as large as taking work home on weekends to achieve a team objective. How many groups designated as *work teams* number any team players among their members, and how many create the magic of teamwork?

The key element in involving people to the point where they actually create a functioning, productive team is *common commitment.* There must be a purpose that all can believe in and care about. This will serve as motivation. In one instance known to the author, an individual who quit his job in the fury of a perceived injustice gave notice to his supervisor this way: "*I quit!* You'll have a letter of resignation on your desk in the morning giving two weeks' notice—well, three weeks, I guess, or however long it takes for the McInerney project to be finished." He was quitting his company, but not his team. He was committed to the team goal and would stay with it until it was accomplished. In an effective team, each member feels responsible for the team's success as a whole. If the sentiment is, "Well, I did *my* part. It's not my fault if the thing doesn't work," then the team is in trouble.

Teams in Trouble

A study of 4,500 teams from more than 50 organizations revealed the following common causes of team trouble:[19]

- *Inadequate rewards and compensation for the team.* Most plans focus on rewarding individual performance, not team performance, and individual goals do not necessarily coincide with team goals.
- *Neglect of team issues in human resource development programs.* Most performance appraisals focus exclusively on individual performance with no consideration of team issues.
- *Information systems not geared to aid team efforts.* Access to pertinent information for a team is often difficult. Team members feel that they are constantly having to "reinvent the wheel."
- *Lack of top management commitment.* Most top management groups fear their staff cannot handle team leadership responsibilities, so they withhold the commitment that is vital to team success.
- *Organizational misalignment.* The organizational structure often unwittingly fosters internal competition, hampering team effectiveness.

Teamwork Highlights

Finger Pointing at Bausch & Lomb

Sometimes the workers make the effort. Without help from above, they empower themselves and create teams. Sometimes management tries. It empowers workers who destroy teams. But if some soothsayers are correct, by the year 2000, companies will be run by teams reporting directly to the CEO or board of directors. If that happens, both management and labor better get to work.

They've started at Data General Corp., where scientists formed a team without top management's attention or approval. Working late into the night, "borrowing" resources, and avoiding the scrutiny of senior management, the "skunkworks" team developed a new minicomputer way ahead of competitors.

Data General's team succeeded, purposefully, without help from above. But often teams fail in spite of help and encouragement from management.

In 1989, Bausch & Lomb put 1,400 workers into 38 self-directed work teams at its sunglasses plant. Management consultants taught 20 front-line supervisors the principles of being team leaders. But when team members arrived at different solutions than the supervisors, the latter group's need for hierarchy escalated a difference of opinion into bitter arguing. Three years later, about half the supervisors had not adjusted and had to be reassigned.

The company managed to force the two groups into a team mentality by paying each plant employee an end-of-year bonus based on the profitability of the plant.

But as for the team-management approach, plant manager Phil Lang says, "I thought it was a no-brainer. We spent a lot of time and money on professionals to teach motivation and leadership. But many people who were good soldiers under the old system just couldn't change."

Sources: Jon Katzenbach, "Manager's Journal: The Right Kind of Teamwork," *The Wall Street Journal,* November 9, 1992, p. A9; Aimee L. Stern, "Managing by Team Is Not Always as Easy as It Looks," *The New York Times,* July 18, 1993, p. F5.

- *Faulty distribution of work load.* Work loads frequently don't match the skills, knowledge, and abilities of the team members.

The conclusion of this study was that the answer to team success is "collaboration" of the sort that cannot take place unless departmental and functional barriers are broken down and internal competition minimized.

Two companies—one with teams created without management's knowledge, the other with teams created by management—can have very different results. See the "Teamwork Highlights" for details.

Work-team consultant Darrel Ray believes that another major pitfall in team building is the tendency toward *treating employees like children.* "Management has to approach team members like responsible adults," he says. When managers unthinkingly play the parent figure, immediately telling them what to do and what not to do and leaving them no decisions to make on their own, they disable their employees.[20] You may recall how Semco, a Brazilian manufacturer of pumps, mixers, and catering and other industrial equipment, goes to the opposite extreme in a country where companies traditionally treat their employees like children. Employees actually determine their own work hours and salaries and even evaluate the performance of their supervisors. Teams set their own productivity and sales goals and share earnings. The firm has survived the turmoil of the Brazilian economy and is operating debt free. "It's really very simple," notes company owner Ricardo Semler. "All we're doing is treating people like adults."[21]

Ignoring underperformers is another problem to watch out for. "When management saddles a team with a 'toad,' a worker who just doesn't cut it, the whole team grows resentful," says another team-building consultant, Judith Schuster. She claims that management is frequently guilty of purposely placing an unproductive worker on a team instead of firing him or her, in the hope that the team will correct the problem. Instead, such workers damage team performance.[22]

Quick Quiz 12.1

1. A task force formed to study ways to improve production time is an example of the type of team that ___________.
2. The phenomenon of team building grew out of what two movements?
3. The type of person who is willing to sacrifice personal glory for the good of the team is known as a ___________.
4. The key element in involving people to the point where they create an effective team is ___________.

Work Teams Compared to Sports Teams

The well-known management author, Peter Drucker, is one of many who has compared work teams to sports teams. Analogies between the sports world and the business world come easily. Drucker, however, has come up with an imaginative classification of work teams into three different types analogous to three different sports:[23]

- *Cricket:* Members of a cricket team play *on* the team but not *as* a team, being assigned fixed positions as the game goes on.
- *Soccer.* Soccer players have their own positions, but all move together in a style that is dictated by their coach.
- *Doubles tennis:* The doubles tennis pair is a small team having preferred rather than fixed positions. They cover for each other with total flexibility.

Ironically, Drucker describes himself as a "loner, not a team worker" and confesses himself to be a poor manager as a result, though no one would argue his acuity as a management observer.

Rules of the Game

Another management observer, Brian Baldock, presses the analogy to sports, advising, "Next time you consider the 'people' problems of your organization, consider comparing them with the world of your favorite sport. Whether it be tennis, golfing, or football, there are important lessons to learn." Baldock points out that despite all the fashionable talk of valuing people as an organization's most precious resource, there is far less action in this area than one might expect. He advises thinking in sports terms as an aid to developing successful work teams, since "the key to business success lies in achieving excellent performances from a team of ordinary people." He enumerates the vital ingredients as follows:[24]

- *Vision.* A clear, straightforward statement outlining the goal in tangible, measurable ways. Individual objectives of team members should demonstrate a total commitment to this vision, and "colleagues on the shop floor and in the boardroom alike must understand exactly what it means."
- *Leadership.* The leader must define the vision, the strategy, and the tactical or operational framework. He or she must then motivate workers to help with the plan and to implement it.
- *Communication.* House journals and corporate videos are not sufficient by themselves as communication, which has to be a two-way conversation. Feedback must be encouraged, including constructive criticism. Employees must be invited, and even exhorted, to provide such feedback, to make suggestions, to try innovative ideas—even to "take intelligent risks."

Thinking in sports terms can help develop successful work teams. At Tyson Foods, team spirit is developed at the annual softball tournament. In the photo, Ronnie Taylor, a supervisor on the day shift at Tyson Foods, participates as a Tyson softball team member.

Photo source: Courtesy of Kelly/Mooney.

Photo Exercise

Think of your own participation in sports. How does it prepare you for corporate team membership?

- *Coaching.* The subject of coaching, a hot topic in management and business circles today, is discussed in depth in the following section.

Coaches and Team Leaders

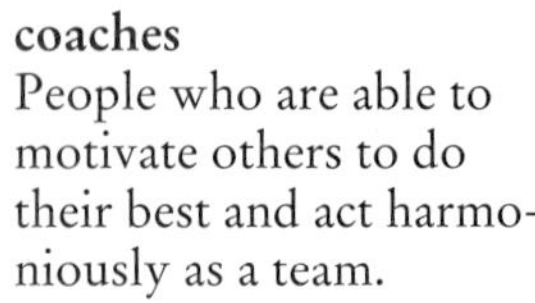

coaches
People who are able to motivate others to do their best and act harmoniously as a team.

The quality of the leaders is what makes or breaks team building. A good team leader is, to continue the sports analogy, a **coach**—someone who is able to motivate others to do their best, to exhort and encourage where necessary, and to bring the individuals in a group together to act harmoniously as a team. A coach is sometimes called a *facilitator,* because of the "helping" rather than "ruling" role that is played. Coaching is more than directing; it is a nurturing function, a way of helping employees develop their potential rather than simply delivering instructions to them and monitoring their work.

Let's return to sports for a minute and consider a football coach ordering his quarterback to throw a touchdown pass. The quarterback might understand the instructions and be quite willing to follow them, but unless he has received some coaching help, and unless the coach has prepared a game plan that provides for a receiver to catch the pass, the quarterback may instead throw an interception. So coaching is more than giving orders; it is helping people to fulfill the orders. It is, in short, a human relations job.

Coaches of teams in a work setting have a number of important duties:

- keeping the team on track and focused on good performance
- taking responsibility for the end result while team members take responsibility for how the result is accomplished
- making sure team members are adequately trained
- encouraging team members to express their ideas and feelings
- supporting team members' decisions
- calling in the resources that team members need to do their job
- smoothing relations between the team and other parts of the organization.[25]

Coaches rely heavily on two techniques. One is to answer team members' questions with other questions as a way to encourage people to solve their own problems. For instance, if a team member asks the coach what to do about overcoming a bad working relationship with someone in another department, the coach might ask, "Why do you think this problem arose?"

The other frequently used coaching technique is to let the team make its own mistakes. Whereas a supervisor might detect an error and issue an order to correct it, a coach will try to teach the employee how to avoid making such an error in the future, and how to check for it. Brian Azar, president of a training and consulting firm, explains the difference this way: "You're not merely working with your [people] to correct their deficiencies, you're coaching them to reach higher and higher levels of performance. By enlisting them in the pursuit of perfection, you'll enable them to capture excellence...."[26] Coaching is therefore an idea that fits in comfortably with empowerment.

People who are good managers or supervisors may not have what it takes to be a good team leader or coach. Management consultant Nancy Todd observes, "A team leader needs a balance of problem-solving and people skills."[27] These are some of the qualities of an effective team leader, according to Baldock:[28]

- trust in group members
- honesty in communication with group members
- long-term vision
- controlled temper
- competence at work
- optimistic personality
- open-minded attitude
- ability to summarize and clarify information for group members
- knowledge of group decision making and idea-generating techniques, such as brainstorming
- experience in leading meetings
- familiarity with team members' backgrounds and personalities
- experience as a team member.

Coaching a team is a delicate balancing act, requiring sensitivity and good judgment. Is a problem one that Jim should learn to solve, or do circumstances dictate that the leader quickly and efficiently solve it? Does William have good ideas that will need to be drawn out? Is Laticia likely to take over the meeting if you let her? Are the team members a highly educated, highly creative group that would fare poorly under tight control? Or are they unaccustomed to group discussions and in need of some clear-cut rules to get them going? Is the team's mission a sophisticated, complex one that requires a freer hand to generate the kind of thinking required, or is there a fairly straightforward goal best served by preventing a wide-ranging discussion? To some extent, formal training can help coaches develop these skills. However, team experience is invaluable, as Amy Katz, director of research for the Association for Quality and Participation (AQP), explains: "It's important to stay in touch with what it feels like to disagree with another team member, to go off on a tangent and have someone pull you back, or to feel so committed to something that you become a problem for the group."[29]

Quick Quiz 12.2

1. Peter Drucker compares work teams to which three different types of sports teams?
2. What are Drucker's four vital ingredients of a good team?
3. A coach should not only be a good leader but should also have experience as a ____________.

Team Building

Team building, as explained earlier, involves assembling a work team and training its members to work together effectively. Perhaps the word *building* in the term *team building* should be taken more literally than it usually is. There must be a foundation, a sturdy one, for the team; it must be created from the right materials (people with the skills and experience needed for the team's work); and it must proceed in an orderly fashion—clarifying its overall purpose before setting precise goals, setting goals before implementing plans, and so forth. Finally, it must have some rules that keep bored or unruly members in line, since not everyone will be continually thrilled with the work of the team. Team members need to be made accountable for their part in the team's work.

The synergy mentioned earlier is an invisible but vital element of a team. Group members must learn to rely on and contribute to group discussion and decision making rather than functioning solely as individuals. They must want success for the team's sake, not just their own. (Refer again to Table 12.1.) A good team, remember, is more than the sum of its parts. It is almost a mystical thing how a good group discussion can turn up ideas that the same people in separate cubicles, thinking hard, could never have come up with.

A major factor in a team's success is the type of people who are selected to be its members. Teams usually have a range of responsibilities, including technical and administrative tasks and problem solving.[30] Thus team members need not only certain job skills but also the ability to work well with others. When the new Saturn automobile-manufacturing plant in Tennessee was being staffed, for example, applicants filled out a 12-page assessment form that asked not only about skills but also about attitudes and behaviors.[31] Experience in other settings suggests that good team members are those who can get along, listen to one another, and be concerned about one another.[32]

Selecting members is only the beginning of team building. The group must then learn to work together effectively. This phase of team building starts with the managers or supervisors who have suddenly been thrown into the unaccustomed role of coach. They need to be trained in participative management skills, such as fostering a climate of openness and honesty and rewarding group rather than individual achievement. Managers and supervisors being transformed into coaches may also need counseling to help them cope with the anxieties of losing clear-cut authority. Often, organizations use the "cascade" approach to prepare team leadership—starting with the top executives, who then coach middle managers, who then coach supervisors, who then coach team members to assume leadership roles.

Another essential element of team building is training all members in a few essential group-related skills:

- how to set goals, make decisions, and solve problems as a group
- how to build and maintain good interpersonal relationships among team members
- how to communicate better both within the team and with other elements of the organization.[33]

People from within the organization may conduct this training, or an outside consultant might be brought in to conduct a specific program (or "intervention"). Table 12.2 presents some guidelines for such programs. Some techniques have worked well, and some have proved to be minimally effective in the long run, as you will see.

outdoor experiential training
Programs designed to build team spirit by involving coworkers in various outdoor activities.

Outdoor-based Training

Outward Bound is the best-known, but not the only, **outdoor experiential training** program. Such programs are designed to build team spirit and trust by involving

Table 12.2 **Guidelines for Team Building**

1. Establish urgency (time frame), performance standards, and direction.
2. Select members for skill and skill potential, not personality or position.
3. Pay particular attention to first meetings and actions.
4. Set some clear rules of behavior.
5. Set and seize upon a few immediate performance-oriented tasks and goals.
6. Challenge the team regularly with fresh facts and information.
7. Spend lots of time together.
8. Exploit the power of positive feedback, recognition, and reward.

Source: Adapted from Jon R. Katzenbach and Douglas K. Smith, "The Discipline of Teams," *Harvard Business Review,* March–April 1993, pp. 118–119.

coworkers in various outdoor activities, such as rafting, mountain climbing, or at least camping out for a night. The idea is that fresh air and physical activity facilitate learning and bonding.

A survey of 261 organizations found that 23 percent conducted some sort of outdoor-based training. The primary reason given for such training was "team building." Table 12.3 presents some additional information about the programs revealed by the survey. Some programs were voluntary and some were not; interestingly enough, the survey revealed no difference in results between volunteers and nonvolunteers. Nor were there any differences according to whether or not a group's supervisor attended. Some differences were noted, however. Mixed-gender groups scored better on problem solving and overall group effectiveness than groups consisting of mostly one gender. Mixed groups also reported enjoying the program more.

intact work groups Groups of workers who regularly interact and rely on one another.

The main determinant of success was whether participants were part of an **intact work group**, that is, a group of people who regularly interacted with and relied on one another. These groups reaped far more benefit from the program than nonintact groups. Overall, though, the programs appeared to be worthwhile in this particular survey.[34] Robert Weigand, manager of training and development at one of the organizations surveyed—a hospital—expressed this sentiment: "I think these programs are of value. I'm seeing some good group processes being transferred back to the workplace. And it couldn't have happened unless we took people somewhere else and got them to shed their suits and their titles."[35]

Others who have participated in such programs report only short-lived improvements in productivity—or none—and the programs are fairly expensive, ranging from an average of $200 to $500 per person per day, not including food and lodging or time lost from work. Moreover, the majority are offered on a voluntary basis. Robert J. Wagner, conductor of the survey just discussed, comments, "My hypothesis would be that nonvolunteers need team building a lot more than the volunteers." The outward-bound experience may be just a passing fancy, but time will tell.

Team Meetings

A more clearly fruitful technique for team building is training members in meeting-participation skills. "The team meeting," asserts Cathy E. Kramer, "is where team members do their most important work; [therefore] any effort to create an effective team needs to focus first and foremost on running an effective team meeting."[36] The team leader needs to be well versed in techniques for facilitating group decision

Table 12.3 **Survey Results on Outdoor-Based Training**

Where do outdoor programs take place?		*Who attends these programs?*	
Dedicated outdoor training center	37%	Top executives	53%
Camp	53	Middle managers	21
Resort	27	Salespeople	74
College campus	6	Nonmanagerial work force	5
Local park	6	First-line supervisors	5
State/national forest	6	Self-directed work teams	16
Other	6		
Does this facility have ...			
Low ropes course?	25%	*What type of evaluation does your organization use to assess the impact of outdoor-centered programs?*	
High ropes course?	5		
Both high and low ropes course?	55		
No ropes course?	15	Self-evaluations by trainees	74%
		Objective data	21
Who facilitates this program?		No formal evaluation is conducted	16
Internal trainers	20%	Managers' evaluations of trainees	16
External trainers	35	Focus group discussion	8
Both internal and external	45	Pre/post training evaluations	8

Source: Data from Richard J. Wagner, Ph.D. and Jennifer M. Lindner, University of Wisconsin–Whitewater.

making and be able to evaluate how well the team performs during a meeting. Other principles for a good team meeting include the following:

- a clear agenda
- a room conducive to teamwork
- a clear purpose
- a detailed orientation for new members.

In addition, do all members of the group understand the team's goals and their part in them? Do all feel committed to those goals? Do all have incentives for striving for those goals?

To keep the team functioning smoothly, the team leader needs to be open to and seek out feedback—even when it hurts. While working as an internal organizational development consultant at General Electric, Amy Katz was informed by a team member that she had become too vested in a particular project and was not recognizing and supporting other people's ideas during the meetings. "I was shocked that I had not been practicing what I had been preaching," recalls Katz. She warns, however, that the flip side of being too enthusiastic about a pet project is being "too participatory"—not taking charge when it is warranted, or failing to direct the discussion when necessary.[37]

Test your own abilities as a team leader and your skill at working with and delegating duties to other group members by completing the "Self-Portrait" exercise.

Katz also advises team leaders to pay attention to their own reactions during the meeting: "If you're confused, others are confused. If you're frustrated, others are frustrated. Confusion is an enormous source of low productivity both for individuals and groups. Reducing that confusion is a key part of the leadership task."[38] To minimize confusion, the group should begin a debate on the pros and cons of a proposed action only when everyone knows the goals, when all significant information has

Self-Portrait

How Well Can You Delegate?

Your ability to delegate work is a measure of your effectiveness as a team leader and an indicator of your ability to rely on and trust in others as part of your team. Answer the following statements true or false.

_____ 1. There are some tasks a team leader should never delegate.
_____ 2. If you want something done right, it is best to do it yourself.
_____ 3. Delegation is an important motivational tool.
_____ 4. Effective delegation involves transferring responsibility to another person.
_____ 5. The amount of work a team leader can delegate is determined by the competence of his or her team members.
_____ 6. The biggest problem with delegating is the increased possibility of mistakes.
_____ 7. Controls and feedback are necessary parts of every delegated task.
_____ 8. When delegating, team leaders can give varying degrees of responsibility and authority to team members.
_____ 9. Not every team leader has a need to delegate.
_____ 10. There are some tasks that should not be delegated because it takes more time to delegate them than to do them.

Answers: 1, 3, 5, 7, 8, and 10 are true; 2, 4, 6, and 9 are false.

Source: Adapted from David Engler, *Delegating Effectively* (Vital Learning Corp., 1986), pp. 5–7.

been transmitted to all team members, and when some more basic action has already been decided upon.

During each meeting, no one should be allowed to monopolize the discussion or persist in an argument over an issue that has already been decided. At the wrap-up of the meeting, decisions should be summarized (who should do what by when) and the team's productive efforts praised.

Sometimes special effort is necessary to prepare teams for effective meetings. Cindy S. Kane, quality manager for Electronic Systems Sector of Harris Corporation, says, "Having time together is important in developing a goal the team can rally around." A work team may spend an entire day off-site with a facilitator to reach agreements on such things as the following:[39]

1. how the team wants to work
2. how to manage team meetings
3. roles within the team
4. expectations of team members
5. how to handle conflicts when they occur.

Table 12.4 lists issues that might also be considered in advance of setting up the first team meeting. In addition, it is wise to establish how open team meetings should be—that is, should nonmembers be allowed to attend or speak?—and how long they should last. At the end of this initial meeting, as with others, the team's efforts to settle these difficult issues should be praised. "You don't have to do a lot of fanfare," says Kane, "but if you can get the manager or the team sponsor to reinforce their work, to just tell them that it's important, that's the best motivation you can give a team."

Table 12.4 **Issues in Team Meetings**

1. Will team members be representing other people or functions or only their own viewpoints?
2. What support are they getting for being on the team?
3. What reason do they have to make a meaningful contribution?
4. Is the team's work going to be extra?
5. Will it be over and above their normal jobs?
6. Will the manager give some tasks to another employee so that the team member will feel free to devote time to the team?
7. Will the team members be rewarded for being on the team?
8. Is it a controversial assignment?
9. Will this assignment enhance or hinder the careers of the team members?

Source: Cathy E. Kramer, "Improving Team Meetings," *Quality Digest,* May 1993, p. 78.

Goal Setting

goal setting
The establishment of attainable, precise, mutually understood goals that align well with the organization's overall strategic goals.

One of the universally accepted principles of team building is the necessity of **goal setting**: the establishment of attainable, precise, mutually understood goals that align well with the organization's overall strategic goals. Following are some guidelines for effective goal setting:[40]

- Goals must be specific and measurable. If stated in broad, general terms, they will probably be ignored since they cannot be tied to actual performance.
- Appropriately trained teams are better at goal setting. Management consultant Nancy Todd recommends "high-quality training of teams in the learning and practicing of problem-solving techniques." Facility in problem solving is useful in formulating goals.
- Expertise of people outside the team should be used where helpful. For example, a team might use a statistical consultant for data collection and analysis or might seek engineering help on design issues.
- Include in the goal setting a schedule for reporting to the rest of the organization on the progress of the team. Determine whether weekly or monthly reports are necessary, for example, and exactly what information they should contain. Establish whether the team needs approval from top management before advancing to another step in the project.

Regardless of the team's autonomy, management has a legitimate and necessary role in goal setting. With the exception of entrepreneurial situations, where a team creates a purpose entirely its own, most teams need management to clarify their charter, rationale, and performance standards. Of course, there must also be some flexibility for team members to modify those goals as their work progresses.[41]

Perhaps the most important rule in goal setting is specificity. Without specific goals, team members tend to get confused and work at cross-purposes. Examples of specific goals follow:[42]

- Respond to all customers within 24 hours.
- Reduce defect rate to zero while simultaneously cutting costs by 40 percent.
- Increase math scores of graduates by 40 to 95 percent.

When outdoor-based team building works, it is often because the team has a specific objective. For example, when a small group of people challenge themselves to get

Fortune magazine has named Rubbermaid America's most admired company. A manufacturer of approximately 5,000 products, the company attributes most of its product idea flow to a single source: teams. Twenty teams, each made up of five to seven people (one each from marketing, manufacturing, R&D, finance, and other departments), focus on a specific goal—product development for a specified product line such as kitchen accessories.
Photo source: © Chris Corsmeier.

over a wall, their differences fade as they focus on that specific goal.[43] The same principle is at work when they decide, for example, to reduce cycle time by 50 percent.

Characteristics of Effective Teams

Four characteristics seem to be the hallmark of effective teams:

1. *Size.* Teams should generally have fewer than 25 people. Larger numbers tend to break up into subgroups. The interpersonal dynamics involved in problem solving and decision making are more efficient in small groups. Larger groups also face logistical problems in finding enough space and enough time for meetings.
2. *Mix of skills.* Team members should have the complementary mix of skills necessary to do the team's work. Skills needed generally fall into three categories: technical or functional expertise, problem-solving or decision-making skill, and interpersonal skills. Unfortunately, team members are often assigned to a team primarily on the basis of personal compatibility or formal position in the organization without enough attention to the skill mix of the team.
3. *Agreement on how work will be done.* Team members must agree on who will do what particular jobs and how, and how all the jobs will fit together. This requires the common commitment discussed earlier as well as a candid assessment of which people are better suited to which jobs. Members also must decide on how decisions will be modified as deemed necessary and how progress will be evaluated. Most important, every member must be responsible for an equivalent amount of work, with all plainly and concretely contributing to the success of the team—including the team leader.
4. *Mutual accountability.* Companies such as Hewlett-Packard and Motorola have a performance ethic of mutual accountability that enables their teams to meet challenges with collective rather than individual effort. "We're all in this boat together" is the attitude. Without this attitude, a team is likely to fail. Yet mutual accountability can be enforced only so far. Schedules and reporting arrangements can be agreed on, but trust and commitment are at the heart of mutual accountability.

Mutual accountability involves trust and commitment, and thus honesty. Darrel Ray says bluntly, "Most of us believe we're honest, but in the workplace few are. Backstabbing and secrecy are more the norm. Lying, frequently by omission, is commonplace. But dishonesty means people miss learning what they need to know to do their jobs properly."[44] Assuming Ray's observations are valid at least some of the time for at least some team members, it is worth considering his recommendation of an "honesty hour" wherein members express what they do and don't like about what others are doing. The feedback should be beneficial, provided the rules of courtesy and a modicum of kindness are observed.

Conscience alone won't motivate everyone to join an "honesty" movement. Ray explains that compensation must be team based. If it is, those with a tendency to deny the blame and grab the glory will be enticed to put forth their best effort to accomplish the team's goals. Another advantage of team-based compensation is that it is often easier to measure a team's performance than an individual's.

Team building sometimes requires a lot of job sharing, too, so assembly-line thinking has to go. Suppose the drivers of a company find ways to speed up deliveries, but then they kill time at the loading bay because manufacturing is behind schedule and the drivers do not know how to help out. In a good team, all members feel responsible for the end goals of the team, so job sharing is a natural consequence whenever it is warranted.[45]

Finally, management consultant Nancy Todd warns that team leaders should recognize that even a good team will need to be nursed through periods of transition and anticlimax —for example, a period of elation after accomplishing one objective may be followed by a temporary depression or lack of enthusiasm for tackling a new problem. "Teams experience a roller-coaster effect. They have ups and downs, and leaders and members need to understand that so they don't get discouraged." Todd points out that a knowledge of the stages of group development can help leader and members alike weather the low periods.[46]

Clearly, the emphasis on team building in organizations of all types is here to stay. The Association for Quality and Participation (AQP), founded in 1977 as a nonprofit educational association dedicated to promoting increased quality and participation in the workplace, established the National Team Excellence Award in 1985 to recognize the achievements of teams throughout the United States. The momentum for team building that the AQP was responding to in the 1980s has not slackened in the 1990s. Despite failures, the principle of using work teams for many applications remains unchallenged: failures have simply pointed to the need for establishing teams in the right places and in the right way.

Quick Quiz 12.3

1. Which type of work group seems to benefit most from outdoor programs?
2. The most important rule in goal setting is ___________.
3. "We're all in the same boat together" applies to ____________.

Summary

- **Explain how a real team differs from just a group of people working together.** A real team produces a collective work-product, that is, it does real work that reflects the joint efforts of the group. It requires teamwork, which involves cooperation and consideration among a group of people, fostering optimal individual performances that then result in an optimal team performance. As a result of synergy, it produces an effect that is more than the sum of its parts.

- **Identify three types of teams and discuss whether they are usually permanent or temporary in nature.** There are teams that make recommendations, such as task forces, which are usually temporary in nature; teams that make or do things, such as a sales force or the marketing group, which are usually permanent in nature; and teams that run things, which are informal teams composed of just a few top managers who are in charge of others and may not even recognize themselves as a team. These are usually permanent in nature, too.

- **Explain the role that participative management plays in team building, and give some reasons why managers often resist it.** Participative management involves managers working with subordinates as a team in setting objectives and planning how to achieve them, so it is obviously integral to team building. Some managers do not like the idea of sharing their power in this manner. Indeed, most managers have stronger *power* needs (the desire to control, influence, or be responsible for other people or results) than *affiliation* needs (the desire to maintain close and friendly personal relationships).
- **Discuss partnering as an alternative to team building.** To avoid the resentment that so many managers exhibit toward participative management, partnering has been offered as an alternative to teaming. Here the manager links up with each key worker in a project as a partner, in several one-on-one relationships. The partnering relationship with some employees may last for only the one or two days that are necessary for a particular task to be done, and this shorter-term relationship is less threatening to many managers than a longer-term team relationship.
- **List some common causes of problems in team building.** Common causes of trouble are inadequate rewards and compensation for the team, neglect of team issues in human resource development programs, an information system not geared to aiding team efforts, lack of top management commitment, organizational misalignment, faulty distribution of work loads, treating employees like children, and ignoring underperformers.
- **Describe what is involved in a team leader's, or coach's, job.** A coach motivates others to do their best, exhorting and encouraging when necessary, and brings them together to act harmoniously as a team. Coaching is more than delivering instructions and monitoring work; it is a job that requires considerable human relations skills.
- **Discuss some of the factors in successful team building.** Vision, leadership, communication, and coaching are needed in work teams just as they are needed in sports teams. Outdoor-based team building has been effective in some cases. Team meetings are important to building a good team, and they should be well organized and prepared for. Specific goals are one of the most important factors in an effective team. Other important factors are team size (not too large), the skills mix of team members, agreement on how the work of the team will be done, and mutual accountability, which entails trust and commitment. Honesty is very important to build that trust and commitment and to ensure adequate communication throughout. A good deal of job sharing might be necessary among the members of a team, perhaps necessitating cross-training. Finally, it is important for the leader, in particular, to be knowledgeable about the stages of group development so as to prepare for the inevitable emotional ups and downs of the team.

Key Terms

teamwork (280)
synergy (280)
team building (280)
collective work-product (281)
self-managed team (282)
team player (284)
coaches (288)
outdoor experiential training (290)
intact work groups (291)
goal setting (294)

Review and Discussion Questions

1. Which type of team is each of the following, and is it permanent or temporary in nature?
   a. three accountants assigned to audit sales records
   b. four police officers overseeing cadet training
   c. a group of chefs and marketing managers developing new menu items
   d. six interdepartmental professors screening policy changes
2. What is synergy? Why is it important in team building?
3. Barbara Yien is close friends with her coworkers and subordinates. Reginald Ford prefers a more formal relationship with the people he supervises. Keeping in mind McClelland's motivation theory, who would more easily adapt to participative management? Why?
4. What is partnering and how does it work? List some partnering roles a manager can assume.
5. In which of the following companies would teams work best and why?
   a. a national office-products distributor with warehouses in six states

b. a temporary-services agency with three offices
c. a computer software firm dependent on quick market response
d. a telemarketing firm with a part-time work force

6. Heartfelt Greeting Card Co. is trying to make team management work in its factory. Although the company has set up an incentive program, so far the teams haven't become a unified work force. Why might the company's approach not be working, and how could team management be made successful?

7. What are some of the qualities of an effective team leader? Which do you think are the most important? Why?

8. A manufacturer of sporting goods has set up teams of employees to identify ways to cut costs. In what ways do you think such teams are similar to basketball teams? How can the leaders of these teams help them to be as productive as possible?

9. Sitting in the weekly team meeting, Nathan was confused about the new deadline for his department; jokes and gossip about weekend plans had interrupted a discussion about shipping orders. When he asked for clarification, another team member told him to loosen up. What team goals are in conflict at this meeting? What kind of team-building approach would help bring the team together? What role should the team leader play?

10. What characteristics of a group (listed in Chapter 11) are similar to those that build effective teams? How important is trust in team building? Why?

A SECOND LOOK

How would you characterize the team to which Harold Fraley belonged? What type of team does it appear to have been? What characteristics of effective teams does it seem to have had?

Independent Activity

Appraising Leadership

Reread the list of qualities on page 289 that Baldock identifies as key to being an effective leader. Think back on the supervisors, managers, or—if you have never worked—teachers you have had.

Make a list of their names; beside each name, check off those of Baldock's qualities they displayed. Scores will range from zero to four check marks.

Which of these leaders best displayed Baldock's qualities? How did their effectiveness in these areas affect your attitude and participation in teamwork? Do you find that the leader you liked best is also the one who best fulfills Baldock's list? Why or why not? Did an overabundance of one quality make up for the lack of another? Why? Which of these qualities do you think is most important? Least important? Why?

Skill Builder

HR Lab

Time for a third entry in your journal of observations on human relations in the classroom. Based on what you have learned in this chapter and your experiences in classroom exercises, do you think this class can easily be molded into teams? Why or why not? Has teamwork helped members of the class develop closer relationships with one another? Has it created tension between individuals or groups?

Based on your group experiences in this class, are there individuals in the class whom you think would be good team leaders? Poor team members? Explain why, based on the concepts you have learned in the previous four chapters. Did those people display those traits when you wrote your first "human relations laboratory" entry, or have they emerged in group activities? Explain.

Do you make a good team member? Specifically and honestly, which five members of the class would you prefer to be with on a work team? Why? Would the same five names appear on a list of five classmates with whom you would prefer to socialize? Why or why not? What are the underlying motivations for your relationships with those on the work team list and the friendship list, and how do they differ?

Group Activity

Team Building (45 minutes)

Divide the class into teams of three to five people. Each team should seek to accomplish the goal of its choice:

- Draw a map of campus.
- Design a common area for a dormitory.

After completing the task, team members should discuss the following questions:

1. Was a team leader chosen, or did one emerge? Why was either choice made? How effective was the leader? (Refer to Baldock's list of qualities of an effective leader on page 289.)
2. How did the team go about selecting a goal? Was the objective clear from the start?
3. Did the team resemble any of Drucker's sports teams—cricket, soccer, doubles tennis? If so, how?
4. Was the team meeting effective? Why or why not?

Case Study

Cincinnati Milacron Roars Back with Operation Wolfpack

Five years of losses were mounting and the wolves were at the door, or so it seemed to Daniel Meyer, the new CEO at Cincinnati Milacron Inc. Keeping the wolves at bay meant fighting back the same way: with Operation Wolfpack, a team-based effort to cut the fat from the organization and its processes and products.

Meyer also knew that getting the company back to its position as the premier maker of machine tools meant building in the agility to respond quickly to market demands. His approach, creating multidisciplinary teams to define and solve problems, is not original, but Milacron's use of the wolf-pack theme to give employees a keen sense of the urgency of change is.

"It's not a joke to us," says Meyer. "Wolves are survivors. They work in teams and they go out to kill." Improving cycle time, cost-effectiveness, and interdepartmental communication was not just a matter of staying ahead. It was all that stood between life and death for the entire organization.

The teams began tackling problems; though much of the program's success will be in the future, there already have been large-scale successes and payoffs. One "Wolfpack attack" reduced costs for one machine from $112,000 to $75,000. A reengineering project team reduced the number of fasteners in a machine from 2,542 to 709, for a savings of 70 percent.

To lower prices, the company began shaving its costs; it hopes to take 30 percent off the production cost of each machine by the mid-1990s. Milacron also cut its new-product cycle time in half, matching the quickness of its foreign competitors. Customers have noticed. Its new image as an organization able to compete and deliver on price, speed, and quality have resulted in black ink for the past three quarters.

Case Questions

1. What characteristics of the team are most important in Operation Wolfpack?
2. What kind of advantages are task groups providing Operation Wolfpack?
3. Do you think the company's use of teams will bring it long-term success or simply achieve short-term goals?

Source: "Milacron Survives in Dog-Eat-Dog Industry by Forming Wolfpack," *Total Quality,* September 1992, p. 6.

Case Study

Puritan-Bennett's Seven-Year Itch

Successful managers often make lousy team leaders because of rigid hierarchies that can pit supervisors, with their hard-earned authority, against newly empowered workers. But sometimes senior management is just as reluctant to fully empower those team managers, neglecting—sometimes deliberately, sometimes unconsciously—to provide the resources the leader and his or her team needs to do the job.

Wavering top-level support for team management has made for a long seven years at the Puritan-Bennett Corporation plant in Lenexa, Kansas. It was 1986 when the maker of respiratory equipment initiated team management in its product-development division. Team management was supposed to facilitate the development of a specific product, speeding it up from the industry average of three years. But today, one of the first Puritan-Bennett teams is still struggling to develop software that will improve its respirators. Roger J. Dolida, director of research and development at the plant, places the blame at management's door. He says management has never made the project a priority, an obvious fact to everyone the team has needed.

When the team of five engineers and a marketing manager needed someone from purchasing to help find suppliers for key components, management refused to free up another person. The executive in charge of the team was replaced three times, and each time, the new person focused mainly on projects he or she had initiated. The rare meetings the team had with its overseer might better be termed "hearings," held briefly at the end of other meetings. Team members spent months trying to get budgets approved.

Despite these setbacks and the growing amount of time they've consumed, as well as management's own intransigence, Puritan-Bennett refuses to kill the project. Customers were telling the company they needed the new software, so the project remained a "go." Two months ago, the company handed the team over to Dolida. He is not optimistic.

"If top management doesn't buy into the idea, if the specs don't get approved, teams can go nowhere," he says ruefully. "Once a team goes to hell, it's tough to pull them out."

Case Questions

1. What kind of approach would have worked better for Puritan-Bennett? Do you think the company just handed the project over, or was training involved?
2. What will be necessary on the part of management for this project to be completed?
3. Which of the common causes of team trouble described in the chapter apply to the problems experienced at Puritan-Bennett?
4. Do you think the team will be successful? Why or why not? What advice would you give team members?

Source: Aimee L. Stern, "Managing by Team Is Not Always as Easy as It Looks," *The New York Times,* July 18, 1993, p. F5.

Quick Quiz Answers

Quick Quiz 12.1

1. makes recommendations
2. quality and participative management
3. team player
4. common commitment

Quick Quiz 12.2

1. cricket, soccer, doubles tennis
2. vision, leadership, communication, coaching
3. team member

Quick Quiz 12.3

1. intact
2. specificity
3. mutual accountability

CHAPTER

13

Conflict and Change

CHAPTER OUTLINE

Learning Objectives

- Describe the different types of conflict that can occur in the workplace.
- Explain how conflict can sometimes have a positive rather than a negative effect.
- Discuss conflict and change as sources of stress.
- List methods of managing conflict.
- Identify sources of change in today's workplace.
- Discuss how resistance to change can be overcome.

Changing of the Guard at Hughes Aircraft

In the minds of many company veterans, the executive ranks of Hughes Aircraft Co. were filled with qualified CEO candidates. So when C. Michael Armstrong, a career IBM man, arrived to take the top spot at the Los Angeles firm, greetings from his new employees carried a trace of wariness and bitterness. If the appointment didn't work out, neither would the changes Hughes was undergoing as it explored new markets to replace shrinking military contracts. Fears were high that the company would drift without a strong helmsman—especially if he came from outside Hughes.

Armstrong confronted the doubts quickly and head on; he assured top executives he admired their talents and wanted them to be part of his team. In the same breath, he said they had a week to decide whether to join his efforts or clear out their desks. Armstrong's brashness gained their respect. He won their allegiance by demonstrating detailed knowledge about each of their careers.

His success in cultivating a sense of teamwork while confronting change has made Armstrong's restructuring plan a financial success. In the year since he took over, operating profits have leapt nearly 50 percent despite a $450 million acquisition of General Dynamics' missile business and a restructuring that closed 1.9 million square feet of Hughes plant and office space. Costs are down 30 percent.

"I don't think there's a prescription for American business that says hey, every 8 ½ years we ought to have somebody from the outside come in and take over," says Armstrong. "But I do think that the situation is sometimes obvious that an outside agent of change can be more effective than a natural successor."

Source: Jeff Cole, "Gentle Persuasion," *The Wall Street Journal,* March 30, 1993, pp. A1–A8. Photo source: © 1994 Comstock Inc.

Change! The familiar bottle is gone, and you are introduced to an awkward, cold, silver thing with which you are expected to maneuver food to your mouth. Conflict! The large parental figure looming above you is as dedicated to the proposition of you eating those strange green vegetables as you are to batting them away. Change again! Week later, a smile of happy anticipation curves your lips as you spy that same green vegetable, which you have now learned to savor.

Life without conflict and change would not be life as we know it on this planet. In the workplace, no less than in the rest of life, we must deal with conflict and change. Conflict may be personal or impersonal, positive or negative. Change may lead to good or bad results. Either way, a knowledge of human nature and group dynamics—in other words, human relations—can help you reap the benefits of a good situation or turn around a bad one. The story of Hughes Aircraft is a good example.

The Character of Conflict

conflict
The struggles that result from incompatible or opposing needs, feelings, thoughts, or demands within a person or between two or more people.

In the workplace, **conflict** refers to the struggles that result from incompatible or opposing needs, feelings, thoughts, or demands within a person or between two or more people. Conflict is inevitable, especially in a capitalistic system like ours. Organizations and individuals that are seeking wealth and power must compete for limited resources with others having the same goal, and so they experience conflict.

Conflict may be personal or impersonal. For example, if the schedule of one department is in conflict with that of another, it is entirely possible that no one's feelings will be hurt in resolving the conflict: the schedules simply have to be synchronized. This is an impersonal conflict. Or suppose office space is insufficient to accommodate a newly hired employee. This is an impersonal, logistical conflict of space. Perhaps the supply room can be converted to an office and the supplies moved to a broom closet. If, however, another employee must sacrifice office space to make room for the new hire, the conflict can become personal very quickly.

Suppose payroll is set up to compensate subcontractors on an hourly basis, but a new, important subcontractor insists on a flat fee based on a quotation for the entire job. An impersonal conflict exists between the two methods of accounting. But it might become personal if the subcontractor resents having to change his method of billing or someone in payroll faces additional work because of the subcontractor.

Another way to categorize conflict is according to whether it is intrapersonal, interpersonal, structural, or strategic (see Figure 13.1). An *intrapersonal* conflict involves only the individual and arises when a person has trouble selecting from among goals, such as

- two or more good choices
- two or more mixed choices
- two or more bad choices.

An *interpersonal* conflict involves two or more people with differing goals, beliefs, values, or even clashing personalities. Expert leadership can minimize such conflicts. Andrew S. Grove, CEO of Intel Corporation, says that constant interpersonal conflict such as bickering and complaining about one another is a symptom of inadequate leadership. Guidelines for acceptable behavior should be communicated and enforced to reduce this type of conflict.[1]

A *structural* conflict results from the way the organization is structured; for example, it may involve the conflicting goals of line and staff personnel or of different departments. Marketing wants to give customers whatever they ask for, while pro-

Figure 13.1 **Types of Conflict**

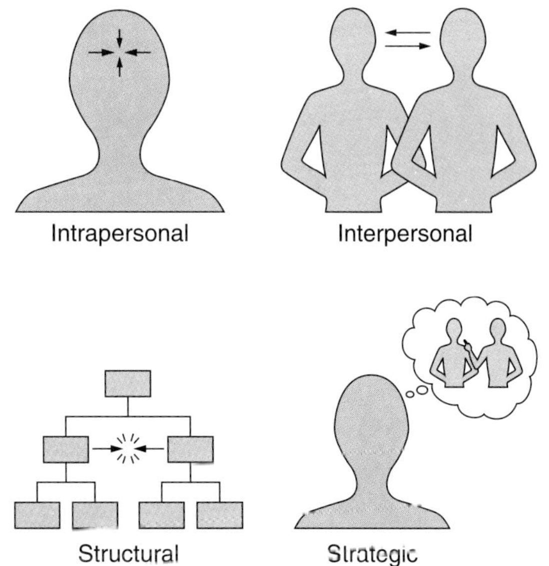

duction wants to make what it can easily and well. Advertising wants to spend more than the finance department is willing to give. Middle managers want more control than top managers are willing to give. First-line supervisors want more or less responsibility than higher-level managers deem appropriate. Richard Palermo, vice-president at Xerox Corporation, says that persistent long-term conflicts are generally structural ones.[2] Although some structural conflicts cannot be resolved, they can at least be minimized by proceeding in such areas cautiously and diplomatically.

Finally, a *strategic* conflict differs from other types in that it is intentionally brought about by management in order to achieve an objective. For example, a franchise oil-change organization might hold a contest to see which franchise can do the fastest and best oil change. Or a manager might tell two employees that they are both in the running for the supervisor's job when she retires next year. In both cases, the intention is to use competition to motivate employees to do exceptional work.

Conflict as a Force for Good

Sometimes, as in the case of strategic conflict, conflict is a positive force. In addition to its strategic benefits, it can signal a need for change and stimulate creative responses. A problem that is brought to light by conflict will more likely be dealt with, sometimes in ways that not only solve the problem, but actually enhance the organization's operation overall.

Although conflict is generally viewed as opposite to coordination and cooperation, it may actually promote coordination, particularly among departments of a high-technology company, provided those departments have interdependent goals. Recent studies suggest that "employees of different departments who believe their goals are cooperative, compared to competitive or independent, discuss their conflicts openly and constructively, which in turn helps them accomplish their tasks efficiently, serve customers, and strengthen their work relationships."[3]

Apparently, confrontation between opposing views—when goals are cooperative—leads people to explore the reasons for the opposing views. The result is a constructive discussion of conflicts that leads to better problem solving, decision making, and innovation.[4]

Conflict as a Source of Stress

Ongoing conflict produces *stress,* a physiological response to coping with the environment's demands—a faster heartbeat, higher blood pressure, and muscle tension. So does change, the subject of the latter half of this chapter. Let's consider the stress that results from conflict first.

Many of us are attracted to situations that contain certain types and degrees of conflict. For example, jobs described as "challenging" usually promise the need to resolve some conflict. That's part of what makes the job exciting. People tend to perform their best under just the right amount of stress. But if stress is excessive, the following problems can appear:

- decline in work performance
- increase in sick days
- increase in errors and accidents
- moodiness and irritability
- fatigue
- loss of enthusiasm
- overly aggressive behavior
- difficulty making decisions
- family problems
- apparent loss of concern for others' feelings
- feelings of inadequacy or inability to help others or oneself
- despair over the perceived impossibility of getting the work done in time.

A person experiencing these difficulties is more likely to promote conflict and also less able to manage it. So excessive conflict leads to excessive stress, which leads to more conflict—a vicious circle.

Stress that results from conflict dissipates when the conflict is resolved, but while you are waiting for that conflict resolution, communications consultant Carol Orsborn suggests you focus on what is within your control. You might even make a list of what you can and cannot change. "Take your attention off what you can't change, which is what most people focus on," she advises. Beverly Potter, an organizational psychologist and author of *Beating Job Burnout,* points out that feeling you lack control over your work situation is the main cause of stress (a point that we will return to shortly).[5] Some suggestions for relieving this kind of stress follow:

1. *Communication.* Have a talk with the boss or the coworkers who are creating the conflict for you. Beware of antagonizing them, though, by implying that everything is their fault. Simply lay the problem out and look together for solutions.[6]
2. *A break.* A slow walk, not for exercise, but to unwind, or simply a few minutes of clearing your mind and thinking of something restful can make you more productive and better able to either resolve the conflict or wait it out.[7]
3. *Humor.* Because laughter is relaxing—genuinely, physically relaxing to the muscles of your body—it can help ward off the assault of stress on your body. Interviews with former hostages, war veterans, airplane crash survivors, and cancer patients have revealed a common coping mechanism of humor.[8]

A heart attack is sometimes the ultimate expression of stress, and studies have found that people are more likely to have heart attacks if they hold high-demand, low-control jobs.[9] In other words, these people work under demanding conditions, but they have relatively little control over those conditions. Refer back to Table 9.1 on page 193 for a list of the most and least stressful jobs.

Lack of Power, Lots of Conflict

When we talk about a lack of control, we are talking about a lack of *power,* which is, in fact, control of circumstances and/or people. Power has long been linked with conflict, since power differences between people affect how they deal with conflict.[10] Interestingly, one study showed that power was negatively related to independent (that is, unrelated) goals: "People who feel their goals are unrelated do not see each other as powerful." Only when goals are interdependent does power emerge as a tool for conflict management.[11]

honor
Taking people at their word and then backing them up in their decisions.

Management expert Glenn Englund attributes a general trend toward a lack of power among employees to a lack of **honor**—taking people at their word and then backing them up in their decisions. He says he has been "struck by the abundance of powerless people, even among the most powerful people," meaning that decisions are frequently unimplemented or incompletely implemented, despite a plethora of detailed memos:

> A team member makes a decision. The other members of the team don't honor it. The decision gets directed to the supervisor, who makes another decision (perhaps even the same one). It also fails to be honored. As a result, other team members become timid, fearing that they too will lose the respect of their peers if they make a decision that similarly fails to be honored.[12]

Quick Quiz 13.1

1. A sales clerk who discovers a discrepancy between the items sold and the amount of money in her cash register at the end of the day faces a(n) ____________ conflict.
2. A paint manufacturer sets up _________ conflict by establishing a contest to see which sales reps can sell the most paint to retail stores.
3. _________ is a physiological response to coping with the environment's demands.
4. Stress is often caused by a lack of ____________.

Managing Conflict

After studying the subject in some depth, one researcher asserted, "Managing conflict is central to the basic mission of the organization."[13] Anyone who has witnessed the demoralization of a department or organization as a conflict raged out of control will acknowledge the truth of this sweeping statement. Without agreement—the opposite of conflict—people simply cannot work together. Thus, the development of good human relations skills involves the ability to manage conflict.

When a conflict first flares up, a good leader will immediately neutralize the situation by taking whatever steps are necessary to restore temporary peace while the problem is investigated. The wrong strategy for a particular type of conflict can worsen a situation, so it is important to select the right strategy. First, gather enough facts about the conflict in order to be able to analyze it accurately. Seek consultation when needed. Next, address the problem with respect for the feelings of all parties involved, and insist that they treat one another with the same respect. When the solution has been reached, communicate it clearly enough to avoid misinterpretations. Finally, be sure to deal with the root cause of a conflict, not just its symptoms, or it will recur.[14]

Some recognized strategies for conflict management are compromise, avoidance and smoothing, forcing a solution, and confrontation or problem solving. As pointed out, the wrong strategy can worsen a conflict. For example, compromise when one party to the conflict is clearly wrong and one clearly right may draw other employees into the conflict in response to the injustice they witness. Avoidance and smoothing may allow a conflict to fester until it erupts into a full-scale war. On the other hand, confrontation over a minor conflict that is better left ignored can produce more problems than it solves and distract attention from more important matters. If Federico complains that George is surly when asked to fix the camera, it might be better to advise him to ignore George's sour looks as long as he always fixes the machine without delay, especially since George is performing his work satisfactorily overall. Why call a meeting to investigate George's surliness? What can you possibly say to make him stop being surly? He doesn't like fixing the camera, but unless you're willing to assign someone with a sunnier disposition to the job, he will have to continue to do so.

Before reading further, turn to the "Self-Portrait" exercise and find out how you handle conflict.

Compromise

compromise
A conflict-management strategy in which each party to a conflict gets only part of what is wanted.

In **compromise**, each party gets part of what is wanted and gives up something, too. Compromise generally requires good communication in order to find out what each party is willing to give up or be flexible about. Some compromises are better—that is, more satisfying to all parties involved—than others. Compromise does not totally solve the problem giving rise to the conflict, but it makes the problem tolerable.

Avoidance and Smoothing

Minor frictions are often best ignored, as in the case of surly George. Let him grumble a little—it doesn't really inconvenience Federico to have to listen to a complaint or two. But when avoidance is the wrong conflict-management strategy, it can be disastrous. Serious problems demand attention. If George and Federico come to blows over the camera, somebody took the avoidance strategy too far. If a work team fails to meet its goals because of continual arguing and hurt feelings, someone's leadership skills are lacking.

A work team that failed to meet its project goal but more than met its company leader's expectations is profiled in the "Teamwork Highlights" box.

Forcing a Solution

Because ignoring or avoiding a conflict does not make it go away, the person in power may choose a more direct way of solving the conflict. In forcing a solution, that person single-handedly decides on an outcome and must be willing to take responsibility for the consequences. For instance, a team leader may cut short a heated discussion among team members about how long it will take to complete a project by simply imposing a deadline. That's forcing a solution, but the deadline must be realistic and the leader must be willing to do his or her part to help the team meet it. Forcing a solution may be the best approach in an emergency because it is simple and effective. A police chief or military leader is often called upon to force a solution. But, as illustrated above, the leader must be able to handle any fallout.

Self-Portrait

How Do You Handle Conflict?

Everyone has a basic style for handling conflicts. To identify the strategies you rely upon most, indicate how often each of the following statements applies to you. Next to each statement, write 5 if the statement applies often, 3 if the statement applies sometimes, and 1 if the statement never applies.

When I differ with someone ...

_____ 1. I explore our differences, not backing down, but not imposing my view either.
_____ 2. I disagree openly, then invite more discussion about our differences.
_____ 3. I look for a mutually satisfactory solution.
_____ 4. Rather than let the other person make a decision without my input, I make sure I am heard and also that I hear what the other person says.
_____ 5. I agree to a middle ground rather than look for a completely satisfying solution.
_____ 6. I admit I am half wrong rather than explore our differences.
7. I have a reputation for meeting a person halfway.
_____ 8. I expect to get out about half of what I really want to say.
_____ 9. I give in totally rather than try to change another person's opinion.
_____ 10. I put aside any controversial aspects of an issue.
_____ 11. I agree early on rather than argue about a point.
_____ 12. I give in as soon as the other party gets emotional about an issue.
_____ 13. I try to win the other person over.
_____ 14. I work to come out victorious, no matter what.
_____ 15. I never back away from a good argument.
_____ 16. I would rather win than end up compromising.

To score your responses, add up your total score for each of the following sets of statements:

Set A: statements 1–4	_____	*Set C:* statements 9–12	_____
Set B: statements 5–8	_____	*Set D:* statements 13–16	_____

A score of 17 or more on any set is considered high. Scores of 12 to 16 are moderately high. Scores of 8 to 11 are moderately low; scores of 7 or less are considered low.

Each set represents a different strategy for conflict management:

Set A = Collaboration (I win, you win)
Set B = Compromise (Both win some, both lose some)
Set C = Accommodation (I lose, you win)
Set D = Forcing/Domination (I win, you lose)

Source: Adapted from Stephen P. Robbins, *Training in Interpersonal Skills,* (Englewood Cliffs, N.J.: Prentice-Hall, 1989), pp. 214–216.

Confrontation/Problem Solving

The most direct and yet the most difficult way of resolving a conflict is to confront it in its entirety, listening to all sides and attempting to understand rather than place blame, and then to explore many possible solutions in order to find the one that will please everyone. Table 13.1 presents specific ways to resolve conflicts with this approach. This strategy makes a different assumption about conflict than do the others

Teamwork Highlights

The Grass Is Always Greener at Toro

Doing a job right is one thing, but what happens when you—and your coworkers—do it wrong? Reprimands, demotions, pink slips? Fear of suggesting change or creating conflict by your own mistakes is one way to ensure an organization will not be known for innovation.

At Toro Co., an engineering failure was made a success because of the lawn-mower manufacturer's risk-tolerant culture. Chairman Ken Melrose has made sure his workers know that "getting it right the first time" is a goal reserved for actual production—not for developing innovative new-product prototypes.

While developing a high-tech reel lawn mower, a team of engineers discovered a new technology for parts fabrication that was fast, low cost, and required no tooling. The team successfully tested a model in eight months. However, the model could not be successfully reproduced in full production, so Toro had to delay introducing the product for a year. It was a costly, as well as demoralizing, decision.

Melrose called the team members to his office for a meeting at which most believed they would be handed their pink slips. Instead, Melrose greeted them with balloons, lemonade, chocolate chip cookies, and a salute to their efforts.

Today, Toro's commercial engineering division leads all competitors because of its willingness to try new ideas and develop innovative products.

Source: "When Wrong Is Right," *Total Quality*, August 1993, p. 8.

discussed. They tend to assume that the parties have a *win-lose* conflict. In other words, the outcome will be that one person wins (gets the desired outcome) and the other loses—except in the case of compromise, in which both parties in a sense lose (creating a *lose-lose* conflict), since neither is satisfied and the decision is merely tolerable. In contrast, the confrontation problem-solving strategy assumes that many conflicts can result in a *win-win* situation, with everyone satisfied.

hidden agenda
A central concern that is left unstated.

Figure 13.2 shows the process of conflict resolution. Understanding the conflict is essential but not always easy, since those involved may have a **hidden agenda**, a central concern that is left unstated. If Heidi is angry about being passed over for the promotion that her coworker, Sean, got, she may initiate a conflict with Sean over some other, unrelated issue. Human relations skills may reveal hidden agendas to the person charged with resolving the conflict; if they don't, the conflict may drag on until its real cause either is forgotten or disappears (as if Sean takes a job at another company and Heidi moves up to his position).

Even when there is no hidden agenda, it may take a little work to understand the conflict completely. As Figure 13.2 indicates, it helps to state the problem specifically, in terms of actions and effects. Then listen to the response to make sure the problem has been correctly identified and described. If not, restate until it is. If the other party or parties to the conflict fail to acknowledge its existence, restate until they do. Finally, both or all parties can work on finding a solution together. Make sure they understand the solution they have agreed upon (restate it), and then implement it.

Quick Quiz 13.2

1. In ___________, each party gains something and loses something.
2. What strategy for managing conflict is sometimes the best for an emergency?
3. Confrontation/problem solving is a ___________-___________ approach to managing conflict.
4. Define "hidden agenda."

Table 13.1 **Guidelines for Confrontation/Problem Solving Approach to Conflict**

- Hold a meeting to discuss the problem. The atmosphere should be one of trust.
- Include everyone who is involved in the conflict. Let participants know this is a chance for them to give their side of the story.
- Allow everyone to present his or her position. Rather than allow the meeting to become an argument, simply note each viewpoint.
- Be suspicious about easy agreements. If the group seems to be arriving at a quick decision, it may mean people are uncomfortable with conflict and therefore are avoiding the problem.
- Do not allow the person with the most rank to control the process. One person's desires should not determine the outcome.
- Break the issue into parts. Determine what the major and minor concerns are. The solution should address the significant points you uncover.

Source: Adapted from "Maintenance Mainstream: Getting the Best Out of Conflict," *Maintenance Supervisor's Bulletin,* November 10, 1991, p. 3.

Change: The Only Constant

Human beings resist change, yet they also crave it. Here we encounter one of those paradoxes of human nature. We want "something different"—a new job, relationship, or house—but we recoil at all the adjustments we have to make to something new.

"Change is inevitable," said Benjamin Disraeli in a speech he made in 1867. Yet, "Change is not made without inconvenience, even from worse to better," as Richard Hooker observed in the sixteenth century. Therein lies the rational reason why people generally resist change.

The small company you've worked for boasts a bulletin board crowded with cartoons reflecting the varied senses of humor of your T-shirted, blue-jeaned coworkers and similarly casual-looking boss. A couple of you ride your bikes to work. You stay late when you have to, take work home when you have to, and take off when the work schedule lightens up. The company expands. You move to new, spacious offices with pristine, pale gray carpeting, and suddenly coffee cups—let alone packages of potato chips—are banned from the desks. Suits are the new mode of dress, so the bicycle riding is no longer practical. To add insult to injury, you are informed that you must obtain top management approval before taking work home, and the decision on whether to work late is no longer yours but management's. Your comfort-loving boss takes his blue-jeaned self to another company, leaving in his place a person who seems to come from an entirely different planet.

In the preceding scenario, you are likely to resent change for both practical and emotional reasons. Suppose, however, that you had become stale in your job at the small company with the creative bulletin-board notices and left it before it changed. You went to a new job at a company with spacious, luxuriously carpeted offices and rules against coffee drinking at your desk. But, in this case, you are excited about the new job and its new challenges. You find that you enjoy sprucing up in the morning for work. You lose weight, helped along by the company rules against potato chips, donuts, and coffee at your desk. You establish a good relationship with your boss there that is completely different in character from your relationship with your old boss, but just as satisfying in a different way. You are energized, motivated by the change. It was just what you needed.

For good or ill, changes keep coming in life and in business. "During earlier eras," says Daryl R. Conner, author of *Managing at the Speed of Change,* "you faced one

Figure 13.2 **Process of Conflict Resolution**

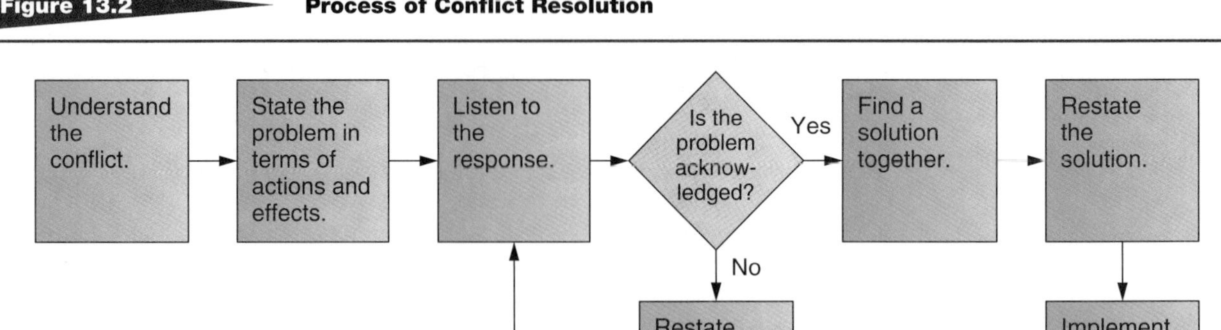

change at a time, and when it was over, you went back to the bench and rested. Today the problem is that most companies have 8 to 15 major change projects occurring simultaneously."[15] The changes are coming from all quarters: the economy, the social fabric of the nation (and the world), the global nature of competition, the educational deficiencies of today's work force, and even the current health-care crisis.

Social Changes Drive Business Change

The "traditional" family—father working full time, mother at home, children born after the parents' only marriage—is no longer the norm. The 1960 census found 43 percent of children living in such traditional families. By 1970, it was 37 percent; by 1980, only 27 percent; and by 1988, only 20 percent.[16] Divorce is commonplace, working mothers are commonplace, single working mothers are commonplace. With the diminished stability of the family, the employer has been called upon to help in ways once considered none of an employer's affair: by providing day-care and elder-care centers, job-hunting help for spouses of transferred employees, and time off for child care.

In addition, gender roles are changing. Women are placing more value on achievement at work than in the past. Men are placing more value on time spent with family than in the past. And in both cases, society as a whole approves of these choices more than it did in the past. The refusal of so many women to accept the role of sole child-care giver has put pressure on employers to consider family-related needs. The flurry of job-sharing, flextime, company day-care, and other such programs attests to that. So does the Family and Medical Leave Act, which requires employers of 50 or more people to grant 12 weeks of unpaid leave to care for a newborn baby or ill family member.

A number of companies that understand the permanence of these societal changes are giving executive status to managers who ensure that these changes are reflected within their work force. See "Diversity Highlights" box for an example.

Other trends in society that influence the workplace, or soon will, are the following:

- *The aging of the baby boomers.* Many companies are targeting aging baby boomers as customers.[17]

Diversity Highlights

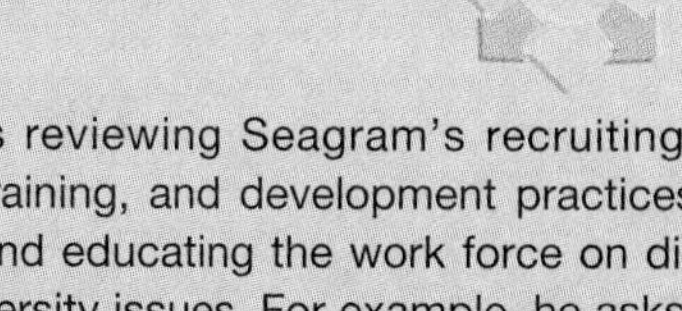

Engendering Diversity at Seagram

A recent study has upended the conventional wisdom that the advertising and communications fields are among the most open of all industries for women. Nearly two-thirds of women respondents identified an "old boys'" network and a sexist work climate as inhibiting their career progress. Male respondents denied this claim, and nearly all said women have equal opportunities in terms of salary, promotions, and responsibility. However, the study's salary survey backed the women's claim of inequity: not only are median incomes for men nearly twice those of women in publishing and advertising, but across the board, men are paid an average of $7,000 more per year than women at the start of their careers.

If the media aren't doing anything about this problem, at least one big advertiser is. Seagram, the New York–based beverage maker, recently created a new position, executive vice-president for diversity. It is not just a symbolic post; Robert Monroe, who holds the office, reports directly to company president Edgar Bronfman Jr. Says he: "Just as a brand requires leadership, so does this."

Formerly general manager for Seagram's southern region, Monroe is responsible for promoting ethnic and gender diversity within the beverage maker's work force. Aiming to eliminate racial and gender biases, he is reviewing Seagram's recruiting, training, and development practices and educating the work force on diversity issues. For example, he asks, if a woman is less assertive than a male coworker but just as effective, how should a manager evaluate her?

Despite the fears that such a review might engender, Seagram's push for diversity does not mean hiring or promotion quotas. Monroe says, "We have no hard numbers, but I guess it's like recognizing a duck. We will know when we've made progress."

Sources: Fred Danzig and Melanie Wells, "Old Boys'" Network Still Alive," *Ad Age,* May 24, 1993, p. 39; Jennifer Reese, "Mr. Diversity," *Fortune,* March 22, 1993.

- *The health-care crisis.* Whatever shape the reforms of the U.S. health-care system take, many industries are going to lose jobs, and many businesses are going to find it more expensive to provide health insurance for their employees.[18]
- *Smoking bans and health-promotion programs.* More than two-thirds of employers in a recent Bureau of National Affairs survey, conducted with the Society for Human Resource Management, report imposing total smoking bans or prohibiting smoking in common work areas. Just five years ago a similar survey showed that only one-third of employers had imposed any restrictions on smoking.[19]
- *The decline in job security and employee loyalty.* Along with downsizing has come an erosion of employee loyalty. As those employees who remain after downsizing see their coworkers lose their jobs, they realize their own are probably uncertain as well. Eastman Kodak cut 2,000 jobs; Siemens, 13,000; Daimler-Benz, 27,000; Philips, 40,000 since 1990; and IBM, 65,000 since 1992. The implicit contract that the big companies once had with their managerial and professional employees—long-term employment in exchange for loyalty—is "gone forever," says David Nadler, a management consultant who advises firms on how to restructure their businesses, "in almost every big American company, and now ... in Europe as well."[20]
- *The shrinking job market.* An M.B.A. is no longer the guarantee it once was of a high-level job, although the lack of one can hurt a job candidate's chances for some jobs.[21] For many graduates in many fields, the job market is minuscule compared to what it used to be. Sometimes being a member of a racial minority or being a woman is advantageous. One of President Clinton's administration staffers admits that, "in sifting through resumes you get to the point where you're not even looking at white men." Others disagree. Statistics show that unemploy-

ment has worsened for blacks relative to whites, and white males make up 82.5 percent of the Forbes 400 (those worth at least $265 million).[22]

The Skills Gap

Many of today's high school and college graduates lack the skills that businesses expect them to have as a result of their education.[23] There are so many of these job applicants that business has been forced into remedial training. Over half of organizations with 1,000 or more employees—Ford, Xerox, Polaroid, Eastman Kodak, and Motorola among them—are conducting basic skills or literacy programs.[24] Chrysler Corporation spent $5 million to advance some 4,000 workers to an eighth-grade level in reading, writing, and math.[25] Sometimes companies team up with colleges and universities—or, occasionally, with unions as a third partner. Others design an in-house basic skills program, with classroom tutoring or self-paced, interactive computer tutorials and videos. The most successful programs appear to be those that relate the teaching directly to organizational tasks.[26]

The federal government does its part, too. The Basic Skills Education Program (BSEP) was developed by the army in 1982 to combat illiteracy among soldiers, and in 1983 the Job Training and Partnership Act (JTPA) replaced the Comprehensive Employment and Training Act. As a result, approximately $4 billion is given to hundreds of individual **private industry councils (PICs)** to fund skills training. These PICs are composed of representatives from business, education, community agencies, and so forth, selected by local government officials to oversee the distribution of JTPA funds.[27]

private industry councils (PICs)
Organizations composed of representatives from business, education, and community agencies selected by local government officials to oversee the distribution of federal funds for skills training.

Deficiencies in basic skills such as reading and writing and math are not the only change contributing to the skills gap. So is the technology explosion. There is a continuing need for technical training to keep up with technological advances. Northeastern Illinois University and Motorola created a joint project called the Coalition of Universities and Businesses for Education (CUBE) in 1991 in which representatives from 24 schools named a business sponsor that was expected to help create and pay for changes in the way future teachers were educated. The idea is to help teachers teach in a more hands-on fashion, exposing students to the advanced technologies they will be confronting in the workplace.[28]

Downsizing, Reengineering, and Dislocation

Sacrificing the jobs of a few to save the jobs of many is a conflict that companies are increasingly facing. As mentioned earlier, many companies these days are streamlining in order to cut costs in a highly competitive, global marketplace. In addition, technological advances are reducing the need for traditional manufacturing workers with simple skills, who were nevertheless often relatively well paid. According to financial writer Ronald E. Yates, "The era of the lumbering battleship corporation that could fire broadsides of ill-aimed, sometimes poor-quality products into unsophisticated markets with relative impunity while using bloated crews of employees and seemingly bottomless fuel tanks of high-octane dollars, ended sometime in the early to mid-1980s."[29] The "International Highlights" box focuses on how one firm dealt with such changes to regain its competitive edge.

Unfortunately, downsizing—or simply shrinking the number of employees on the payroll—has become a distressingly common competitive technique. Another technique with a similarly unsettling effect is reengineering, or reorganizing the bureaucracy to make it flatter, with middle-aged middle managers often bearing the

International Highlights

Alcan Aluminum Pours It On

American companies have long complained that competing with low-wage foreign companies is a no-win situation: either they cut their own workers' pay or they move their plants overseas. But even those U.S. firms in old-line industries such as mining, steel, coal, and aluminum have made great strides in global competition. Although the wage disadvantage still exists, many companies' productivity gains have reduced labor costs to only a fraction of total expenses, making U.S. producers less labor intensive.

In the early 1980s, Alcan Aluminum Ltd. had fallen hopelessly behind its competitors. Its smelter in Sebree, Kentucky, couldn't compete with brand-new smelters with cheap power supplies in Canada and the Middle East. Alcan also couldn't match older, low-wage plants in Brazil and Mexico. Even though it had a freight advantage of about 7 percent, Alcan's costs were still higher than its foreign competitors'. Says plant manager Jim Martin, "This plant was assumed to be on its way out."

Yet while Alcan knew it couldn't beat foreigners' costs, it figured it could still serve the U.S. market. The key was improving productivity enough so that its cost disadvantage was lower than its freight advantage. It was a gamble that cost the company $70 million between 1987 and 1991, but it seems to have worked. The smelter doubled its production volume with 10 percent fewer workers.

Today, the Alcan plant in Sebree not only matches foreigners' costs at home, but Martin reports that it has even begun exporting to Mexico.

Source: Dana Milbank, "U.S. Productivity Gains Cut Costs, Close Gap with Low-Wage Overseas Firms," *The Wall Street Journal*, December 23, 1992, p. A2.

brunt of the layoffs. These employees are attractive targets because they are among the most expensive. "Many white-collar workers have become victims of their own success," comments James Medoff, a Harvard University economist. "By piling up 20 or 25 or 30 years of annual promotions and salary increases, they become targets when budget-cutting time rolls around."[30]

The surge in downsizing and reengineering is changing the structure of work in U.S. society as a whole. Many of the manufacturing and managerial jobs lost in the 1980s and 1990s will never come back. The jobs taking their place are mostly service jobs or jobs requiring specialized technical skills. Employees who are dislocated by either downsizing or reengineering therefore face some difficult new realities. They must usually try to find a similar job in a shrinking market or retrain for a new type of job. Although age discrimination is illegal, in reality the older workers may not be able to find a new job comparable to their old one and thus may be forced into either a less prestigious job or early retirement. Dislocated workers also lose their connection to an organization that may have provided a sense of stability and satisfying relationships with coworkers.

Some experts believe that employees and employers alike will have to adopt a new attitude toward work. "American companies that survive in the 1990s will have to find ways to position themselves so that their strategic resources are their people," notes Craig Moore, CEO of a company that operates renal dialysis centers in four states. Although companies that undertake downsizing or reengineering become leaner and more competitive, they are finding that, in the process, they have been cutting loose many of their most loyal, valued employees.[31] Workers, for their part, must learn to expect a series of job changes during their career. "College students coming out into the workplace today pretty much expect to have five or six career positions, some of them unrelated, over the course of their working lives," notes Robert Ripley, CEO of a manufacturing company in Illinois that he started when he was laid off by United Airlines during a round of downsizing.[32] In other words, for the foreseeable future, change will be a constant in most people's working lives.

The New "Temps"

Even highly skilled professionals are finding themselves reduced to temporary work in today's changing economy. At one time temporary workers were almost exclusively clerical or factory workers, but now, though they may be called "consultants," professionals are nevertheless temporary employees at many companies—saving those companies lots of money in benefits despite sometimes higher hourly pay. The new temps include doctors, lawyers, architects, scientists, and even top executives. Some of them like the freedom of the temporary-job life; others hate the insecurity.[33]

"The more I do this, the more I see how it fits into my life," says Jeffrey Roscoe, a computer analyst who for a year has worked for a top corporation at twice his previous salary and plans to spend more time as a musician with his more flexible schedule. Tax specialist Mary Ann Daniel likes the variety of temporary assignments. But David DiAntonio, a temporary architectural engineer at the Gillette Company, says, "My life is on hold because I could be out the door tomorrow. When permanent people say, 'You're just a temp,' it's like calling me a bad name."[34]

Temporary workers lose something that can be even more important than job security and vacations; they lose insurance benefits. This is a part of the current health-care crisis in the United States. Employers lose, too, because they can ill afford to have certain key professional temps leave them suddenly, which, of course, is the nature of the two-way street employer and employee occupy. And temps are understandably less loyal to an organization since they have no incentive for loyalty.

Relocation

The increase in dual-career families means less willingness to relocate at company demand. Indeed, at Mobil Corporation, female managers often resign for fear that their husbands won't go along with a move. Those husbands who do trail their relocated wives often have trouble finding suitable employment. The marriage may break up as a result. Mobil finds that a man generally will follow his wife only if she earns at least 25 to 40 percent a year more than he does. This trailing-husband problem is prompting companies to provide job-hunting help for "accompanying partners," as they call them:[35]

- Ciba-Geigy paid \$1,500 for job counseling for the husband of one of its transferred employees, a medical researcher.
- Monsanto paid \$1,000 for the job search of the husband of one of its transferred accountants.
- Sprint Corporation will spend up to \$4,000 to replace a relocated spouse's lost income for 60 days. It also tries to hire trailing spouses when it can.
- Marriott Corporation recently installed a computerized job-posting system that tracks its managerial vacancies nationwide and is available to both employees and their spouses.
- AT&T recently invited trailing spouses to use its four "resource centers," which were originally set up to provide outplacement help for employees who were victims of downsizing. Each person using a center gets a job counselor, access to a computerized job, secretarial help, access to a reference library, and an officelike setting to come to every day.

A recent study examined the relationship between the increasingly multicultural work force and willingness to relocate. Since Hispanics are underrepresented in many public and private organizations and are therefore a prime target for recruiting attempts, the researchers were particularly interested in seeing whether

Hispanics were less willing than non-Hispanics to relocate. They found that they were, in fact, less willing if the new employment area did not have a high percentage of Hispanics.[36]

Women Want Change

Insurance companies are now covering firms against sexual-harassment suits. One Boston-area company had a close brush with such a suit in 1992 and now pays a $25,000 annual premium for $1 million worth of coverage.[37] As discussed in an earlier chapter, the *glass ceiling*—the invisible barrier to career advancement faced by women and minorities—is getting increasing attention lately, too. "People are beginning to realize that nothing has changed at the top levels of management or on company boards. They're talking about the glass ceiling as if it's a hot, new issue because they're getting mad," says Wendy Reid Crisp, national director of the National Association for Female Executives.[38]

Yet numerous successful women report no bumping of heads against any glass ceiling. Antonia Shusta oversees 4,460 employees and $11 billion worth of business at Household International Inc. and before that occupied the fast track at Citibank. She credits both Citibank and Household with nurturing and investing in female talent, and she predicts that there will be a lot more female CEOs at major, publicly held corporations in the near future. "There are a lot of women breaking through into these senior management ranks, and I think that it is imminent, even if it doesn't always feel that way." Donna C. E. Williamson, corporate vice president in charge of Caremark International Inc., a health-cost management group, agrees: "It's just a matter of time before more women will become CEOs."[39]

So the marketplace has changed dramatically for some women, is changing now for others, and is expected to change for still others. Where it has not changed, it is being pressured to.

Quick Quiz 13.3

1. The most successful programs designed to increase basic skills of workers seem to be those that ____________.
2. In addition to job security and vacations, temporary workers also lose ____________.
3. The glass ceiling is defined as ____________.

Implementing Change

"We are by nature territorial creatures, bound by the force of habit. It is much more comfortable to stick to what we know," says one management expert.[40] Another expert observes, "If you don't feel awkward when you're trying something new, you're probably not really doing anything differently."[41] Change requires work. And it carries the risk of not being worth the work in the long run.

Because change is risky, decision makers should weigh the potential benefits of a proposed change against the costs of implementing it. Sometimes careful analysis shows that a lesser change will achieve adequate results without throwing the organization into turmoil. Honda, for example, is responding to an auto-industry slowdown by instituting subtle shop-floor changes at its three plants in Ohio, teaching all 10,000 workers how to maintain and repair their own machines rather than laying off workers.[42]

Sharon Hall (pictured), general manager of Avon Product's personal-care products group, deals with change in her company and career. Hall advises, "Always be doing some thing that contributes significant, positive change to the organization. That's the ultimate job security."
Photo source: © David Strick/Onyx.

Photo Exercise

Describe two significant, positive organizational changes that you have seen or read about. Why do you think these changes were important?

Change, you will remember, can be for good or ill. Thus sales management expert Jack Falvey cautions against too hasty an organizational change. Take time to evaluate and plan, he advises. "When you come right down to it, there's no real need to be fast on your feet—or to try and go with the latest guru's theories."[43]

Change as a Source of Stress

A major risk of change is the increased stress that it usually brings to the organization's labor force, leading to an increase in absenteeism, turnover, accidents, burnout, and grievances among unionized workers. The predictable result is a decrease in productivity.

Too much stress, of course, also has detrimental effects on individual workers, as you learned in Chapter 9. "Stress has become one of the most serious health issues of the twentieth century," proclaims the annual World Labour Report of the United Nations' International Labour Office. As we saw in Figure 9.1, it is a worldwide problem. But people react differently to the stress brought about by change. A ten-year study of Illinois Bell executives found that those who adapted best to stress tended to see changes as challenges to be risen to rather than as threats to be feared.[44]

Human relations experts should be alert to these signs of dysfunctional levels of stress among an organization's employees:

- constant fatigue
- low energy
- moodiness
- increased aggression
- excessive use of alcohol
- temper outbursts
- compulsive eating
- high levels of anxiety
- chronic worrying.[45]

When an individual displays one or more of these symptoms, you can focus on helping that person cope with stressful changes. Widespread symptoms like these, however, may indicate that organizational change is proceeding too quickly.

To compete against large chain stores such as WalMart, independent retailers such as Dave Skogen (right), president of Skogen's IGA Foodliners, must develop strategies to handle change: "It seems that every time a new competitor comes to town we work a little harder. They bring out something extra in us. We have to step it up a notch."
Photo source: © Scott McKiernan.

Photo Exercise

What changes might Dave Skogen have to make in his stores to deal with this increased competition? What steps can he take to minimize worker resistance to those changes?

Resistance to Change

Although some people like change, it is quite common for people confronted with change to resist it. They may resist either overtly (say, by objecting loudly and often) or covertly (by procrastinating in implementing change, for example). Such resistance can be aggravating to someone who has already embraced the need for change. Remember, however, that resistance can be beneficial. By forcing the organization's leaders to fully examine the implementation and implications of a proposed change, skeptics may actually help produce a better plan.

People resist change for a multitude of reasons, including the following:

- comfort with the status quo or force of habit
- fear of change or of the uncertainty that often accompanies change
- belief that problems don't exist, don't warrant change, or affect only the short term
- lack of trust in organizational leaders due to bad experiences with change in general or with a particular change
- incomplete or inaccurate information about the proposed change
- unwillingness to break with one's social group, which may oppose the change
- fear of a loss of personal power or prestige or of financial loss
- fear of being unable to perform respectably in changed circumstances
- anxiety about the effects of change on personal relationships at work or outside of work.

Overcoming any sort of resistance requires patience, understanding, and good communication skills—in other words, the stock in trade of human relations experts. An effective strategy for overcoming resistance incorporates four measures that help employees "buy into" change:[46]

- *Avoid surprises.* Surprises at work have a tendency to make people feel threatened and emotional, which is a barrier to accepting change. A calm, rational, measured approach is far more effective. Explain the need for change in terms that everyone will understand, and involve those who will be affected in planning for change.
- *Set the stage.* Management, top to bottom, must be seen to have a positive attitude toward the change. Managers must stress the benefits to both the organization and the employees. They are responsible for fostering the climate of trust and cooperation that will smooth the implementation of change.

- *Promote understanding.* Take every opportunity to answer the questions of those who will be affected. Give them information about what is going to happen to them at every stage. Reassure them that they will be trained and supported every step of the way. To do so, you must practice empathy—that is, you must seek to understand people's anxieties and needs and answer their unasked questions.
- *Make the change tentative.* Many organizations have benefited from a trial period, during which everyone has a chance to experience the change and tinker with the new program. If the general experience is negative, the program can be scrapped before the change is irrevocable. But if the general experience is positive, the organization will benefit from the refinements developed during the "shakedown cruise," and employees will more readily buy into the change.

Traits That Help Employees Change

In implementing organizational change, it helps to know who you can count on to tolerate or accept the program. Daryl R. Conner is CEO of ODR Inc., a consulting firm that helps corporations worldwide manage their way through change, and author of a book on adapting to change. He identifies the following qualities as common to employees who deal well with change:[47]

- *Positive attitude.* "They're not wearing rose-colored glasses, but when faced with a change, they see opportunities for success, not failure."
- *Flexibility.* "If doors are being slammed in their faces because of change, they find a new way to approach customers or colleagues." When restructuring or mergers leave an employee with a string of new bosses, this quality is especially important.
- *Goal-oriented attitude.* Setbacks resulting from a change in organizational policy are viewed as temporary setbacks. The employee does not let them derail him or her from pursuing previously established goals.
- *Organized approach.* Change can immobilize disorganized people. "You have to make sense out of the tremendous amount of data that is generated during the implementation of one or more changes. If not, the data is nothing more than noise, and it can prevent you from taking action."
- *Proactive attitude.* It is especially important to take the initiative in times of change. When a new idea is being adopted, you should immediately look for ways to apply it to your job.

The Learning Approach to Change

Successful change is also a function of the organization's style and structure. Ken Blanchard identifies an organization's "ability to learn" as its best asset for coping with and capitalizing on "the change and uncertainty present in almost every business market." In his company, he reports ongoing "experiments in progress," dividing learning into three operational parts:[48]

1. *Constantly striving to innovate.* Formal experiments are set up to test hunches on how to improve or innovate. Those that succeed change the way the company does business, but even those that fail "become part of our collective knowledge."
2. *Continually refining products and services.* The company has a system for updating its products that includes taking advantage of new technologies as they become available. Feedback from customers is continually sought.
3. *Applying knowledge in new ways to develop people and organizations.* An informal network for cross-training allows employees to develop interests in other

The move from a vertical departmental form of organization to a horizontal self-directed team form causes change for employees. When this change occurred at Kodak, this "zebra" team was formed in the black-and-white film division, and the members adapted so well that productivity, profitability, and morale soared.
Photo source: © John Abbott.

jobs or other areas of the company by being matched with employees who are willing to teach them. Top managers participate in "forum groups" in which they can learn from other executives.

Unfreeze—Change—Refreeze

Change can all too easily be undone. The secret to making lasting, effective change is to first overcome resistance to it, then ensure that the change is made and that it endures. Noted behavioral scientist Kurt Lewin has set forth a model for this process, which postulates the following stages in the change process:[49]

1. *unfreezing,* which occurs when people recognize a need for change
2. *changing,* which occurs when people begin trying to behave differently
3. *refreezing,* which involves making the new behavior part of oneself or part of the organization's regular processes.

The model reaffirms the idea that people must understand and acknowledge the need for the change if they are to accept it. In explaining the rationale for a change, the supervisor or manager should attempt to understand the employees' points of view and address their concerns.[50] Good communication skills can make the difference between success or failure at the "unfreezing" stage. An employee who does not get properly "unfrozen" cannot be properly changed and "refrozen."

Once the second stage begins, the key is to build on successes. As employees see the change achieving desirable results, they are more likely to go along with it and even embrace it.

Finally, there's follow-up. For the change process to be complete, employees must make the changed behavior part of their routine. However, because new procedures are less comfortable than old ones, employees may revert to their old practices when the initial pressure for change eases.[51] An important part of refreezing is for employees to be rewarded for behavior that shows they have made the desired change.

A Final Word on Implementing Change

The manager of a large work force at A. E. Staley has this advice: "In a time when the need for corporate change seems to be escalating—whether you're talking about downsizing, reorganizing, or whatever—it's very helpful to increase your sensitivity to what people are going through during the process of change."[52] Knowing what people are going through during the process of change is one of the fundamental areas of human relations knowledge. Knowing how to handle them—and yourself—during the process of change is one of the most valuable human relations skills because change, like conflict, is ever present in every life and in every workplace.

Quick Quiz 13.4

1. List the three parts of the learning approach to change.
2. Name the three stages of Kurt Lewin's model for change.
3. A study of Illinois Bell executives found that people who see changes as ___________ rather than ___________ adapt well to stress.

Summary

- **Describe the different types of conflict that can occur in the workplace.** Conflicts may be personal or impersonal; they can also be categorized as intrapersonal (occurring within an individual faced with difficult choices), interpersonal (occurring between two or more people with competing goals), structural (arising from the way the organization is structured), or strategic (arranged by the organization as a way of stimulating competition).
- **Explain how conflict can sometimes have a positive rather than a negative effect.** Conflict can have a positive effect when it is of the strategic type and so stimulates healthy competition, when it signals the presence of a problem that otherwise might not have been dealt with, and when it occurs among departments of a company that have interdependent goals, stimulating the kind of constructive discussion that leads to better problem solving, decision making, and innovation.
- **Discuss conflict and change as sources of stress.** Conflict leads to stress when it produces a feeling of lack of control or lack of power. Change can create stress when people fail to understand what will be required of them or why the change is necessary. A certain degree of conflict and change may be desirable, making a job more exciting and challenging, but if they become excessive, people suffer the physiological symptoms of stress—a faster heartbeat, higher blood pressure, and muscle tension. Those who adapt best to stress tend to see changes in life as challenges to be risen to rather than threats.
- **List methods of managing conflict.** Some recognized strategies for conflict management are compromise, avoidance and smoothing, forcing a solution, and confrontation or problem solving. The wrong strategy can worsen a conflict, so it is important to select the right one. A good leader will do what is necessary to bring temporary peace into a conflict situation as soon as it flares up and then gather information, seek consultation if necessary, and decide on the best course of action.
- **Identify sources of change in today's workplace.** Sources of change in the workplace are changes in society such as the decrease in traditional families and changes in gender roles, with an accompanying need for more family-related help from employers; the health-care crisis; the shaky economy and shrinking job market and the decline in job security and in employee loyalty, along with the increase in temporary employees; an increased protest by some women against the glass ceiling; an increasing reluctance to relocate; and a skills gap resulting from a deficiency in basic skills and literacy among today's work force plus a problem in keeping up with technology.
- **Discuss how resistance to change can be overcome.** A successful strategy for overcoming resistance to change avoids surprises, sets the stage by enlisting the

enthusiastic participation of management, promotes employee understanding of the effects of change, and makes the change tentative until it has been tested. Traits that seem to help people adapt to change are a positive attitude, flexibility, a goal-oriented attitude, an organized approach, and a proactive attitude. Regardless of an employee's personal traits, an organizational culture characterized as a learning environment eases resistance by making change an accepted part of competing in the marketplace. A noted theory of change postulates three phases for overcoming resistance: unfreezing, in which employees are made to understand the desirability of a change; changing, which is implemented by building upon successes; and refreezing, in which follow-up is conducted to make sure the changed behavior endures and that employees do not lapse into old behaviors.

Key Terms

conflict (304)
honor (307)
compromise (308)
hidden agenda (310)
private industry councils (PICs) (314)

Review and Discussion Questions

1. What is conflict? Can a conflict be beneficial? Explain.

2. Matt Zycharski is the darkroom supervisor at a large photography lab. One day his boss says that although he realizes Matt is going on vacation to Hawaii next month, he'd like him to consider staying to ensure that things go smoothly when three new employees join his group and a number of large orders are expected.
   a. What is the nature of the conflict in this situation? In other words, what two goals are impossible for Matt to achieve at the same time?
   b. What are some possible ways to resolve this conflict? List as many solutions as you can think of.
   c. Which solution do you think Matt should embrace? How could he present it to his boss?

3. Identify each of the following conflicts as interpersonal, intrapersonal, structural, or strategic:
   a. A salesperson does not want to take telephone messages for her coworkers because she thinks she has a better chance of being the department's top performer if her coworkers do not return their calls.
   b. One of the clerks in a shoe store is much older than the others and he does not spend much time talking to them. The other clerks criticize him for not being a team player.
   c. The production department at an electric-train company has set a goal to make parts faster, while the quality-control department wants to slow production to reduce the rate of defects.
   d. A college student interning for the summer at a trade association is offered a full-time position and has to choose between returning to school or accepting the job.

4. What are the drawbacks of managing conflict by compromising? Is it ever a good idea to compromise? Explain.

5. Maureen Duong supervises the cashiers and baggers at a supermarket. Although she knows several of them have been upset about the hours she has scheduled for them, she believes that people should not argue and avoids discussing the subject. Maureen posts the following week's schedule just before leaving for the day. What is wrong with her approach to conflict management? What would be a better way to manage this conflict?

6. Donnell Brown, the manager of a furniture warehouse, has noticed that one of his employees regularly comes to work in a surly mood. Although the employee is getting his work done, his attitude seems to be affecting the other employees.
   a. How can Donnell initiate conflict resolution with this employee? How should he describe the problem?
   b. If the employee responds to Donnell's statement of the problem by saying, "I'm fine, don't worry about me," what should the manager do and say?

7. The managers of a soft-drink bottling company decide that production workers will each learn several jobs and rotate among those jobs. They have read that this technique improves productivity and they believe that the workers will be happier because their jobs will be more interesting. However, many of the employees and their supervisors are reluctant to make the change. What could explain their resistance?

8. How can management overcome resistance to change among its work force? How can management build on successes to ensure that a change is implemented successfully?

9. In a business world filled with change, are human relations skills more or less important? Why?

10. What skills help employees adapt to change? Can you think of any others?

A SECOND LOOK

In taking over as CEO of Hughes Aircraft, what techniques for managing conflict and implementing change did C. Michael Armstrong use?

Independent Activity

Unfreeze—Change—Refreeze

Think of a time during your life when you were forced to make a major change—transfer schools, drop an athletic activity you loved, change majors, or some such. Now that you know a few techniques for handling change, think about how you might have approached this change differently. Next, consider a change that you anticipate taking place in your life during the next few months or years—graduation, a move across the country, a new job, marriage, and so forth. Using the unfreeze—change—refreeze model, map out how you would like to handle this change successfully.

Skill Builder

The Many Faces of Conflict

Refer back to your score on the "Self-Portrait." According to the test, which strategy do you rely upon most? Are you comfortable with your customary approach, or would you like to change? How can you do that?

Think of some conflict situations you have been in recently, whether with your supervisor or instructor, family, friends, or coworkers.

- What was the cause of the conflict?
- How was it discussed? (For example, who was at fault? Who was angry? Who raised his or her voice?)
- How was it resolved? What strategy did you use?
- Did you feel like a winner, a loser, or neither?
- Could the conflict have been resolved more successfully? How?

Second, think about the different ways you handle conflict.

- How does your strategy for dealing with conflict today differ from the way you dealt with conflict as a child? Explain.
- How does your handling of conflict at work (or in class) differ from your handling of conflict at home? Explain.

Group Activity

Conflict Challenge (30 minutes)

This exercise is based on role playing. Four or five class members should take the role of a "Conflict Resolution Board," and the rest of the class should divide into two groups. The Conflict Resolution Board should leave the room for ten minutes while the two opposing groups debate the following issue, each taking one side of the argument.

Group A wants to hold a demonstration in a central area on campus grounds to protest the school's investments in businesses that do not engage in socially or environmentally responsible practices. Group B believes that the demonstration is inappropriate, will disrupt classes, and should not be held on campus property.

After the two groups debate for ten minutes or so, the Conflict Resolution Board should return. The board should decide how it wants to hear the arguments (for example, from one spokesperson from each group) and then what type of conflict resolution it will choose to settle the matter (compromise, forcing a solution, confrontation/problem solving).

Case Study

GM Workers Battle Change

When it was built at the beginning of World War II to make B-24 Liberator bombers, the Willow Run, Michigan, industrial plant was the largest in the world. Fifty years later, the factory—now used to assemble General Motors cars—has been slated for closing as part of GM's organizational restructuring. Despite a court fight led by the plant's union and local officials, a state appellate court ruled that, despite taking $13.5 billion in tax abatements in 1984 and 1988, GM is not bound to keep the plant open indefinitely.

The nation's largest car company has already begun shifting production to its Arlington, Texas, plant. Four hundred of Willow Run's workers have transferred there; those who remain will lose their jobs.

The 2,000 Willow Run workers facing unemployment are not alone among GM workers. Since a new management team with a mandate for change was appointed by the board of directors in 1991, no job—from assembly-line worker to executive chef—has been safe. Change has been both symbolic, such as closing the executive dining room, and substantive. In less than two years, the cadre of GM middle managers who once checked every move at the operating divisions has been cut from 13,000 people to 2,000. Although GM said in 1991 that it would shed 74,000 employees by 1995, that figure now looks conservative.

Sacred cows also are at risk: Ideas that not too long ago would have been considered as heresy are now openly discussed. For example, GM is considering converting a factory to building trucks for Toyota and building a small pickup truck in the United States for sale by Isuzu Motors Ltd., GM's struggling Japanese affiliate.

In one of the biggest changes, marketing executives are learning how to sell cars one at a time, instead of selling thousand-vehicle lots to rental car fleets. A Chevrolet executive compares the process of giving up fleet sales to quitting cigarette smoking.

The stress of change for those who remain employed at GM is great but perhaps not as great as for those who are losing their jobs. Workers at the Willow Run factory plan one more appeal, this one to the state supreme court.

"We hope for the best, but we know in our hearts that we are not going to get the best," says 33-year-old Cheryl Caincross, who has worked at the Willow Run plant for 15 years. "We just want it settled. We want to get on with our lives."

Case Questions

1. What is the nature of the conflict between GM and its workers? Is it intrapersonal, interpersonal, structural, strategic, or a combination? Why?
2. Could a compromise between GM and its work force be reached? Explain.
3. How well do you think GM is handling change and resistance to change within its work force? Why?

4. What kinds of stress are GM workers facing? What contributes to these stresses? How could GM help? What are some ways for employees to reduce stress?
5. Can you suggest some conflict-management techniques for GM to use in future plant closings and layoffs?

Sources: *Chicago Tribune,* August 5, 1993, sec. 3, p. 1; Joseph B. White, "GM's Overhaul of Corporate Culture Brings Results But Still Faces Hurdles," *The Wall Street Journal,* January 13, 1993, p. A3.

Case Study

UPS Delivers Attitude Adjustment

The brown UPS truck is still a familiar sight, but the world it travels in has changed. United Parcel Service is no longer the undisputed king of the hill. New kids in town, such as Federal Express, and new technologies, such as fax machines, are aggressively stealing business from the Atlanta-based company.

It wasn't that "Big Brown" *couldn't* change with the times. It just didn't want to. Says an executive at Eastman Kodak, "Every time we'd ask them about special services or discounts, I'd hear back the same thing: 'It's not in our best interest.' Well, that's not what I was hearing from their competitors."

But under CEO Kent C. "Oz" Nelson, that "we-know-best" attitude has changed. Customer service and flexibility are paramount. And in order to better compete, UPS has invested roughly $2 billion in new technology to keep up-to-the-minute tabs on shipments.

One strategic change was particularly wrenching; switching its emphasis from home deliveries to corporate customers has affected the perception of UPS both inside and outside the company. Home deliveries had been UPS's bread and butter since its founding in 1907. But in the 1990s, delivering a pallet-load of VCRs to a single store is far more profitable than delivering one VCR to a rural home.

To emphasize the change, UPS has raised residential rates an average of more than 11 percent a year since 1991; by comparison, commercial rates have grown less than 4 percent a year. The move has alienated many catalog retailers; UPS's daily shipments from such retailers are off by 100,00 packages a day. Pricing flexibility has worked both ways, however, and attracted some catalog merchants. As part of an agreement to keep ground and air rates down, Lands' End Inc. has switched its overnight-air contract from industry leader Federal Express to UPS.

So far, the drive for change has met little resistance from managers and supervisors in the field. Retraining helped. More than 500 managers attended week-long seminars in which they were coached to think in terms of customer service. UPS's compensation plan played an even bigger role in executive compliance. "We have 25,000 owner-managers who have virtually every cent they own invested in stock of this company," says Nelson. "They knew that if we didn't change, somebody would, and there'd go your life savings."

Change has not sat as well with the union drivers. The head of the Teamsters, which represents 165,000 drivers and package sorters, has long complained of the way UPS treats his members. For instance, some drivers are told to make 15 deliveries or pickups an hour, no matter the weather or traffic conditions. Strikes still loom as a future possibility.

Case Questions

1. What do you think of the changes at UPS? How would you feel as an employee? As a catalog customer? How well do you think UPS is handling change and resistance to change within its work force?
2. How important has money been as a motivator for employees to accept change? Why? What could motivate union workers? Explain.

3. What human relations techniques could UPS use to better labor relations and avoid a strike by its union?
4. What kinds of stress do you think UPS workers are under during these changes? Does a lack of power contribute to these stresses?

Source: "After A U-Turn, UPS Really Delivers," *Business Week,* May 31, 1993, pp. 92–93.

Quick Quiz Answers

Quick Quiz 13.1

1. intrapersonal
2. strategic
3. Stress
4. power or control

Quick Quiz 13.2

1. compromise
2. forcing a solution
3. win-win
4. A hidden agenda is a central concern that is left unstated.

Quick Quiz 13.3

1. relate teaching directly to organizational tasks
2. health-care benefits
3. barrier denying women and minorities the opportunity to advance their careers

Quick Quiz 13.4

1. constantly striving to innovate, continually refining products and services; applying knowledge in new ways to develop people and organizations
2. unfreezing, changing, refreezing
3. challenges; threats

CHAPTER

14

Job Design and Enrichment

CHAPTER OUTLINE

Learning Objectives

- Discuss the philosophy behind job redesign.
- Identify various methods of job enrichment.
- Explain how responsibility is used in job enrichment and why authority and accountability are usually involved as well.
- List and define the five core job dimensions.
- Discuss the relationship of training to job enrichment.

Stuck in a Rut—and Loving It

Drew Melton doesn't aspire to a corner office and a company car from his employer, Prospect Associates Ltd. It's a good thing he doesn't. Melton started out three years ago as a copy-machine chief operator and that's still his job title today.

Some would consider it a dead-end job. But not Melton, who has built a veritable Xerox fiefdom at the Rockville, Maryland, health communications and policy consultancy. Within two weeks of being hired, Melton was telling the company's president how he could run document production better and faster. He was given both the freedom and the authority to do things his way.

Today, Melton is busy giving advice to Prospect's harried consultants, who rely on him to give their proposals a professional look. And though Melton hasn't climbed the corporate ladder, he has become more valuable to the company by honing his skills and expanding the scope of his job description. His reward: respect from the company's professional staff and a salary increase of more than 40 percent. And because there is no pressure on him to move up, Melton is free to follow a horizontal career path and continue to do the job he loves.

"They're listening to my ideas, and that's where I'm making changes and contributing to the company," says Melton.

Source: Donna Fenn, "Bottoms Up," *Inc.*, July 1993, p. 58. Photo source: © Chris Hartlove.

The oldest human relations challenge—existing long before the term "human relations" was used in an employment setting—is how to get the worker to work: to work faster, better, more carefully, more conscientiously, more fervently. Very few people are independently wealthy, so most work because they have to, not because they want to. Free to pursue their heart's desire, many would choose some other activity than the one they are currently being paid for by an organization. So the more that the "have to" of a job can be changed to "want to," the harder and better an employee is likely to work and the more satisfied he or she is likely to be, meaning less absenteeism and turnover for the organization. This is the main reason for designing enriched jobs. The result of success is employees like Drew Melton of Prospect Associates Ltd., who love their job and contribute their best effort to it.

Mending Past Mistakes

The mistake made by the *scientific management* crowd early in the twentieth century was in concentrating on the fact that most employees had to work, ignoring the possibility that improving the quality of their work lives could also improve their performance. Thus, the only task for the employer in getting the most and best work out of employees was to match their abilities to the jobs. Is he strong enough to lift that lever? Is she nimble-fingered enough for the sewing machine, or the typewriter? Pleasant-voiced enough for telephone answering? Does he have the appropriate education? Does she have enough experience? The idea was to match the employee to the job, screening out those who did not match—never to change the *job.* People were viewed as a kind of work equipment. Like any other machine, they had to be kept in good working order (cold rooms were heated for their comfort and hot ones cooled; breaks were even provided). But if someone's attitude toward the job led to a poor performance, then he or she was obviously the wrong person for that job, and another person must be found. The concept of job redesign was yet unborn.

As behavioral scientists moved into the management field in greater force, more emphasis was placed on training employees to match their jobs. Still, the job was treated as something fixed and immutable, something to be worked around and adapted to. The person could be altered (by training) to fit the job better, but the idea of altering the job to better suit the person was a revolutionary one when it came.

Picture one of those robots used to paint automobiles in some plants. If it lays the paint on too thickly or thinly, it is adjusted. This was the old way of approaching human workers. Adjust them to do the job better. The new approach, which is actually the underlying philosophy of the entire field of human relations, is that employees should not be viewed as robots to be adjusted. For one thing, a simple mechanical adjustment will not suffice. For another, they are worthy of having their needs considered, not just the needs of the workplace.

Job Redesign

When the old scientific management ideas were reassessed with the human factor in mind—the universal need for meaning and variety and responsibility in work—the dramatically different idea of **job redesign** was born: changing a job's characteristics to make it more enjoyable, satisfying, and challenging. This meant a partial retreat from *job specialization,* wherein a complicated job was broken up into smaller, simpler tasks. Job specialization was a brilliant idea, a good thing; it speeded up production tremendously. But sometimes too much of a good thing is bad. The numbing boredom of the assembly line is what prompted the beginnings of the job-redesign movement.

job redesign
Changing a job's characteristics to make it more enjoyable, satisfying, and challenging.

Creativity—or the ability of an individual to overcome that boredom through his or her own initiative or skills—is important in creating job satisfaction. Check your own creativity quotient by completing the "Self-Portrait" exercise now.

Observers began to ask, was the efficiency of the assembly line worth the deadening effect on the worker? In fact, was it even as efficient as it could be? Bored employees worked more slowly and less carefully than motivated ones. Machines work faster when they have less to do, but people do not necessarily follow the same

Self-Portrait

How Creative Is Your Thinking?

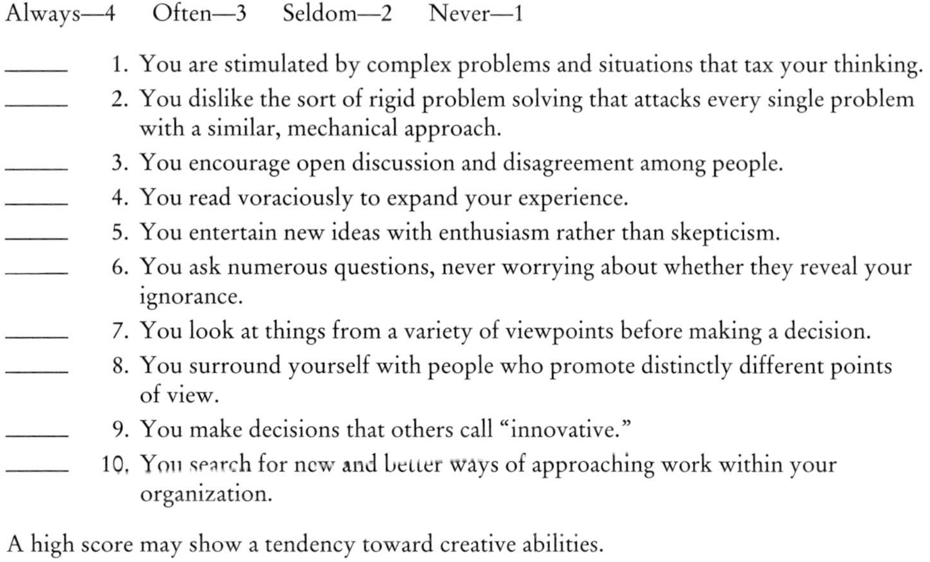

Put a number next to each statement to indicate whether that statement is always, often, seldom, or never true of you.

Always—4 Often—3 Seldom—2 Never—1

_____ 1. You are stimulated by complex problems and situations that tax your thinking.

_____ 2. You dislike the sort of rigid problem solving that attacks every single problem with a similar, mechanical approach.

_____ 3. You encourage open discussion and disagreement among people.

_____ 4. You read voraciously to expand your experience.

_____ 5. You entertain new ideas with enthusiasm rather than skepticism.

_____ 6. You ask numerous questions, never worrying about whether they reveal your ignorance.

_____ 7. You look at things from a variety of viewpoints before making a decision.

_____ 8. You surround yourself with people who promote distinctly different points of view.

_____ 9. You make decisions that others call "innovative."

_____ 10. You search for new and better ways of approaching work within your organization.

A high score may show a tendency toward creative abilities.

Source: Craig R. Hickman and Michael A. Silva, "What's Your Creativity Quotient?" *Working Woman,* September 1985, p. 30.

pattern. The quality of a machine's work does not vary according to emotions, feelings of self-esteem, or perceptions of meaningfulness. But people who care about what they are doing do it better. People who take pride in their work do better work. How could Joe take pride in attaching one little piece to another, the same little piece to the same other piece, over and over and over, hour after hour? Yet he could take pride in being responsible for an entire machine. He could say, "I made that," and therefore care about how well it was made.

So the revolutionary concept of actually making the job more difficult—adding back some of the complexity that specialization had removed, for the sole purpose of benefiting human emotions and thus influencing human performance—was developed. Another way of accomplishing the same purpose was to let employees change jobs for a while, introducing variety to their work lives. We are talking about *job enlargement* and *job rotation* here, which we will discuss in detail in this chapter. Once management looked at the human emotions involved in the workplace, many other ideas came flowing—ways of making life at work more pleasant, more fulfilling. The "quality of work life" became a familiar phrase. Motivation became a subject of renewed study.

It all came together under the term *job enrichment,* a clear indication of the change in priorities: jobs are "enriched" in order to please and satisfy people. The job, not the person, was to be changed. Job redesign is based on the belief that employee attitudes and work performance will automatically improve if the job is appropriately changed. W. Edwards Deming said, "We are all born with intrinsic motivation, self-esteem, dignity, an eagerness to learn. Our present system of management crushes all that

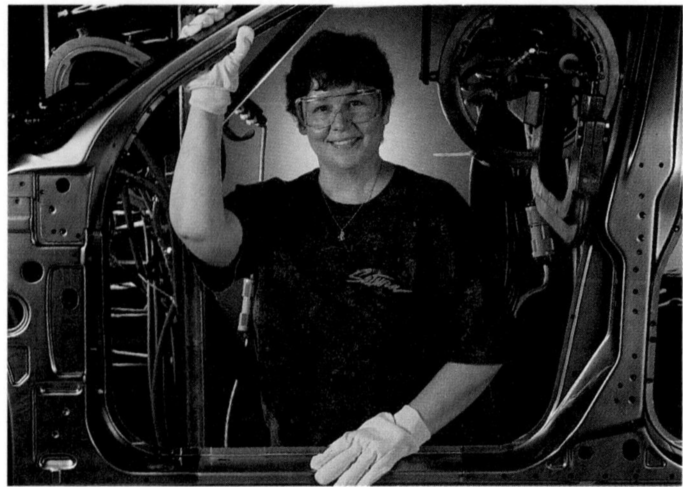

Deborah Wikaryasz, a line worker for Saturn, does more than just assemble fixtures on the left side of each Saturn. She belongs to a team that hires workers, approves parts from suppliers, chooses its equipment, and handles administrative matters such as its budget.
Photo source: © Dan Dry.

Photo Exercise

Does Deborah's job appeal to you? Why?

out."[1] In the quality-improvement movement launched by Deming and developed by the Japanese, then translated back into American businesses, jobs were changed to bring out the best in workers—to stir up their motivation, their eagerness to learn, their pride in doing a good job. This was the genesis of job redesign.

The Quest for Quality in Work Life

quality of work life (QWL)
A concept that refers to how well employment opportunities meet a range of employee needs.

Deming's work inspired the Japanese-led approach to improving quality by involving employees in more decision making. What was involved was a consideration of the **quality of work life (QWL),** a concept referring to how well employment opportunities met a range of employee needs. QWL principles have received much attention in both American and Japanese companies since their introduction in the 1960s. The concept is that of a fair exchange: give the employee a higher quality of life while at work, and he or she will give you back a higher quality performance. A key QWL idea was to allow employees to assemble an entire product rather than just a tiny piece of it on the assembly line. *Task identity* will be discussed later in this chapter. Following is a list of QWL principles. Note how they blend Japanese and American ideas.

- opportunities for personal growth (American)
- employee involvement in decision making (Japanese)
- job security (Japanese)
- mutual trust between management and employees (Japanese)
- enhanced communication (American)
- emphasis on cooperation rather than competition among employees (Japanese)
- job redesign to make work more interesting and thus more satisfying (American).

Note that although only the last item specifically mentions job design, several others would or could involve job design of some type. For example, an enriched job often offers opportunities for personal growth, invites employee involvement in decision making, and requires or leads to mutual trust between management and workers.

Quick Quiz 14.1

Mark "true" or "false" next to each statement.

1. Scientific management practices laid the groundwork for today's QWL principles.

   ______

In this AT&T factory in Batam Island, Indonesia, a trainer from Singapore gives on-the-job training to a new employee. Such training has enabled Indonesian workers to perform new and more challenging jobs.
Photo source: © Munshi Ahmed.

2. Actually making a job more difficult—adding some challenge and complexity to it—may be part of job redesign. ______

Job Enrichment

job enrichment
The incorporation of motivating factors into a job.

Job enrichment is the incorporation of motivating factors into a job. It can be provided by job rotation, job enlargement (with or without added responsibility), or various forms of individualistic treatment such as flexible working schedules, "family-friendly" policies, and so forth. In every case, the human being who performs the job comes first, the job second. It is worth repeating that this difference in priority is what constitutes job redesign, or job enrichment.

Job Rotation

job rotation
Moving employees from job to job to give them more variety.

cross-training
Training in the skills required to perform more than one job; necessary for job rotation.

Job rotation involves moving employees from job to job to give them more variety. For example, the employees in a production department may take turns operating all the machines in the factory. **Cross-training**, or training in the skills required to perform more than one job, is necessary for job rotation, and the opportunity to learn new skills through cross-training can in itself motivate employees. The management of Highland Park Hospital in Highland Park, Illinois, developed a plan for cross-training with the goal of cutting costs for nursing personnel. As a side benefit, however, management saw a motivational effect when the nurses viewed cross-training as a way to make their work more interesting.[2] Although job rotation may have some bottom-line benefits for some organizations, as it did for Highland Park Hospital, it is often instituted solely for the purpose of enriching jobs. It may even increase company costs to train people for more than one job, but the costs are counted worthwhile if the result is more motivated employees.

Pride in a company's product or service is another great motivator for employees (see the "Teamwork Highlights" box for an example).

Job Enlargement

job enlargement
An effort to make a job more interesting by adding more duties to it.

Job enlargement is an effort to make a job more interesting by adding more duties to it. Like job rotation, this approach assumes that variety in a job makes it more satis-

Teamwork Highlights

Zymol Employee Waxes Poetic

Probably the most effective way to enhance the workplace is to hire someone who is already an avid fan of the product or service an organization is selling.

Laurence Zankowski is a prime example of the kind of enthusiasm that cannot be bought. Zankowski was an auto detailer who thought Zymol Enterprises' organic car wax was the greatest thing since sliced bread. Price was no object—even at $40 for an eight-ounce jar and four-digit prices for customized blends in larger quantities. "I'd buy two jars," says Zankowski. "One to use, and one to keep in my cupboard to look at."

When Zankowski found out that the wax was produced nearby, in North Branford, Connecticut, he visited corporate headquarters. Then he began to call the company—constantly, he says—"at least three times a week."

Less than a year later, Zankowski has a wide-ranging job description at Zymol. It includes manning the phones for technical and customer-service support; sales and marketing (he traveled to BMW headquarters to discuss the intricacies of a Zymol finish); new-product development (he is pitching a CD-ROM laser-disc cleaner to companies such as Microsoft); and graphics support (helping with the logo for a special Harley-Davidson wax).

When he first started at Zymol, Zankowski says he found records of his calls in the logbooks, saying, "It's Laurence again." His fervor hasn't changed, and it's helped him design his own jobs. "My passion for the product is what keeps me going," he says. "Because of this, I'm willing to bend over backward for the company."

Source: Alessandra Bianchi, "True Believers," *Inc.*, July 1993, p. 72.

fying, thus increasing motivation. The difference is that variety is provided by adding permanent duties to a given job rather than having an employee change jobs.

The enlargement of the job may involve either horizontal or vertical loading. **Vertical loading** refers to increasing the depth of the job by adding responsibility, authority, autonomy, and/or accountability (all discussed shortly). **Horizontal loading**, in contrast, refers to simply adding job activities without any additional responsibility or autonomy. Some experts tend to reserve the term *enlargement* for horizontal loading, making a distinction between job enlargement and enrichment, and regarding vertical loading as applying specifically to enrichment. However, we will discuss enlargement here as a type of job enrichment, thus encompassing both horizontal and vertical loading.

vertical loading Increasing the depth of a job by adding responsibility, authority, autonomy, and/or accountability.

horizontal loading Adding job activities to a job without any additional responsibility or autonomy.

Responsibility. Let's look first at the vertical loading of **responsibility**, which can be defined as an obligation to perform certain duties and make certain decisions. Adding responsibility is one of the most popular ways of enriching jobs. The more responsible job is a more challenging job, and the more challenging job is presumed to be more rewarding. For example, instead of requiring salespeople in a department store to call a supervisor whenever a customer comes to them with a complaint, the store might authorize them to handle complaints as they see fit. They would have to call the supervisor only if solving the problem would cost the store more than some set amount, say $500.

responsibility The obligation to perform certain duties and make certain decisions.

The summary of a job's responsibilities is its **job description**. A properly designed job description communicates job content to employees, establishes performance levels that employees must maintain, and serves as a guide that employees can follow to help the organization reach its objectives.[3]

job description A summary of a job's responsibilities.

Authority. As the preceding example of the department-store salespeople indicates, added *authority*, the right to command or perform, usually goes along with added responsibility. Generally speaking, it has to. When an employee is charged with a responsibility for which he or she is given insufficient authority, big problems arise. In

Table 14.1 **Seven Responsibility Relationships among Managers**

General Responsibility—The individual guides and directs the execution of the function through the person accepting operating responsibility.

Operating Responsibility—The individual is directly responsible for execution of the function.

Specific Responsibility—The individual is directly responsible for executing a specific or limited portion of the function.

Must Be Consulted—The individual, if the decision affects his or her area, must be called on before any decision is made or approval is granted to render advice or relate information, but not to make the decision or grant approval.

May Be Consulted—The individual may be called on to relate information, render advice, or make recommendations.

Must Be Notified—The individual must be notified of action that has been taken.

Must Approve—The individual (other than persons holding general and operating responsibility) must approve or disapprove.

most cases, though, the need for authority is clearly a practical necessity, and so it is automatically provided. Suppose a service station manager is responsible for pumping gas and repairing automobiles. The manager has complete authority to perform these jobs for which he is responsible. In addition, he has the authority to delegate either activity to his assistant. He should, in turn, give his assistant authority to order parts, to command certain other attendants to help, and to do anything else necessary to complete the repair jobs.

accountability
The management philosophy that employees are held accountable for how well they use their authority and live up to their responsibilities.

Accountability. Also accompanying responsibility is **accountability**, the management philosophy that employees are held accountable for how well they use their authority and live up to their responsibilities. The concept of accountability implies that some type of penalty or punishment will be forthcoming if the employee does not fulfill his or her responsibilities. Also implied in the concept, however, is the notion that some kind of reward follows a good performance of responsibilities. Most people are motivated by accountability. Those who fear it or dislike it may be subpar performers or may, rightly or wrongly, perceive their work situation as unfair. Certainly, if responsibility is assigned without commensurate authority, a person would be justified in arguing against being made accountable. But in that case, the employee should protest the assigning of responsibility from the beginning.

Managerial versus Nonmanagerial Responsibility. Managerial jobs can differ greatly in terms of responsibility, and since responsibility is such a key part of a manager's job, it is important that areas of managerial responsibility be clarified. Table 14.1 shows seven possible areas. To be avoided are **responsibility gaps**, where no manager is responsible for an important activity, and **overlapping responsibilities**, where more than one manager is responsible for something that could be handled by only one.

responsibility gaps
When no employee is responsible for an important activity.

overlapping responsibilities
When more than one employee is responsible for something that could be handled by only one.

For nonmanagerial employees, such participative management and empowerment expressions as self-directed teams serve to enrich jobs by adding responsibility, authority, and accountability. Of course, this means managers are sharing their responsibility, authority, and accountability. Sad to say, some view the sharing as a loss—the opposite of job enrichment for them. It doesn't have to be that way. Managers with good human relations skills generally find that when their employees' jobs are enriched, their own jobs are, too. Table 14.2 presents some guidelines for sharing responsibility with employees.

Table 14.2 **Guidelines for Sharing Responsibility**

- Give employees freedom to pursue tasks in their own way.
- Establish mutually agreed-upon results and performance standards related to delegated tasks.
- Encourage an active role on the part of employees in defining, implementing, and communicating progress on tasks.
- Entrust employees with completion of whole projects or tasks whenever possible.
- Explain relevance of delegated tasks to larger projects or to departmental or organizational goals.
- Give employees the authority necessary to accomplish tasks.
- Allow employees not ordinarily available access to information, people, and departments necessary to perform the delegated task.
- Provide training and guidance necessary for employees to complete delegated tasks satisfactorily.
- When possible, delegate tasks on the basis of employee interests.

Does Enlargement Always Work? A possible problem with job enlargement is that employees may become overloaded with duties, or they may be assigned too much responsibility to handle comfortably. A study on the effects of job enlargement on clerical positions found increased job satisfaction and improved customer service overall, but employees tended to make more errors.[4] Obviously, it is important to make sound decisions on when to stop the horizontal and vertical loading.

Of course, sometimes job enlargement doesn't work because the employees resent any added duties or do not like being given any added responsibility. They might just want to get home on time and forget the job until tomorrow morning, when they are required to think about it. The evidence indicates, however, that most people respond positively to job enlargement. People generally seem to like work if you give them half a chance. Maybe they are there only because they have to be, but that doesn't mean they can't derive some satisfaction out of performing well and taking on new challenges.

Rotation or Enlargement?

The line between job rotation and job enlargement may become blurred when there is no formal program. For example, cross-training in an informal atmosphere may evolve into both rotation and enlargement as employees pitch in and help according to the work that needs doing—here adding a duty to their regular job, there leaving their regular job to temporarily perform another. The workers have to have authority to make decisions for such a happy arrangement to work. In addition, they have to be committed, motivated, and competent employees. They may also have to be nonunionized employees, since many labor contracts restrict informal switching of duties.

Customer Contact

Job enrichment aims to make jobs more interesting, more challenging, and also more meaningful. A good way to make a job more meaningful is to give employees some contact with the people who receive and use their products or services. For example, a group of production workers might be able to visit a customer who is having trouble operating a machine the company manufactures. The workers would not only be able to help the customer, they might also get some ideas on how to make the machine better. Accounting personnel might meet with the people in the company who use their reports to make sure they understand and are satisfied with the reports. Note that the "customer" in this latter case is an internal one. Other employees can be customers if they depend on and benefit from the work of their fellow employees.

Treat Employees as Individuals

flextime
A program offering employees flexible working hours.

compressed workweek
The performing of a full week's work in four 10-hour days instead of the usual five 8-hour days.

job sharing
The division of one full-time job into two part-time jobs.

Individualistic treatment, such as offering **flextime**—a choice of flexible working hours—is still another way to enrich a job. Workers might be given the choice of arriving earlier than usual when they want to leave early or working on weekends so that they can take off during the week. The **compressed workweek** is another possibility, in which employees "compress" a full week's work into four days instead of the usual five, working four 10-hour days instead of five 8-hour days. In one study of over 500 corporations, 93 percent offered employees some choice in working schedules, usually flextime or the compressed workweek.[5]

Job sharing, in which two workers split one full-time job into two part-time jobs, is another way to meet the needs of individuals. Understanding the importance of meeting individual needs has led to the development of "family-friendly" policies at many organizations. For example, GE Medical Systems in Milwaukee allowed Pam Burns to shift from working full time to working three days a week when she became pregnant with her second child—while retaining full health benefits. Consequently, instead of quitting, as she had planned, Pam stayed on, with the idea of switching back to full-time status when her youngest child starts kindergarten.[6]

Northeast Utilities encourages job sharing to help its employees who are finding it difficult to juggle family needs with full-time work. The company will even do the necessary recruiting for a job-sharing partner. Most companies that offer job sharing report enthusiastic responses from employees. At one San Francisco law firm, two legal secretaries planned their pregnancies so that each could cover for the other during her maternity leave.[7]

Quaker Oats has a slew of such "family-friendly" policies: flexible work schedules and unpaid family leave to care for a new baby, sick child, or elderly parent; an offer to match 25 cents to every dollar an employee sets aside to pay for child care; a "Mothers' Room" for breast-feeding mothers; and a telephone counseling service operated by former teachers to answer the questions of parents of school-age children. Says Robert Montgomery, vice-president of human resources, "There was a time when companies expected employees to not let their families interfere with work. Today that can't be done."[8]

Telecommuting is the way some organizations adapt to individual employee needs. Instead of physically going to the office, the telecommuting employee works at home and communicates with the employer electronically by computer. Continental Traffic Services set up one of its data processors at home with a computer and modem in order to avoid losing her when she decided to quit as a result of her long commute. The arrangement worked so well that three more employees were similarly set up. On-line monitoring showed a 35 percent increase in their productivity.[9] FourGen tried the same thing when it could not afford to add space for three needed programmers. When productivity for the telecommuters rose by 25 percent, the company sent seven more workers home.[10]

Of course, telecommuting can have its downside. A telecommuting employee does not have continuous personal interaction—and feedback—from a supervisor and coworkers. It is also difficult to set up an impromptu emergency meeting, and any problems with computer or communications hardware can be more difficult or time consuming to solve. But these problems seem to be outweighed by the benefits for many professionals.

Quality Highlights

Language Instruction Helps Workers Improve Jobs

When work-force diversity and the move toward quality programs seemed to be at loggerheads, a Springfield, Virginia, ink manufacturer decided it needed help promoting English among it workers.

SICPA, a 100-employee company, wanted to prepare its production workers for changes brought about by new manufacturing technologies. The firm also anticipated problems with its planned move to Total Quality Management, which would require workers to track down and write down more information.

SICPA hired a firm to teach English to a class of 13 Hispanic, Cambodian, and African workers. SICPA paid for the materials and instruction, half of which was on company time.

"I was concerned about attendance, but we didn't have a problem," says Katherine Hartman, SICPA's human resources manager. "They really enjoyed it, and everyone in the class improved. Some have gone on to a local community college to take English on their own."

Benefits of the English instruction have gone beyond an improved ability to speak and understand English; SICPA's workers have become better workers. They developed confidence, and began to participate and show more initiative; they now ask questions when they don't understand something. In sum, these workers now see their own potential and their own contributions to the company.

Source: Roberta Maynard, "Improving English Skills," *Nation's Business,* May 1993, pp. 68–69.

Companies That Dare to Be Different

Some employers today do more than acknowledge and accommodate employees' individuality and the legitimacy of their life outside the job—they share it. As seen in the "Quality Highlights" box, one employer helps employees learn English. Other employers help employees care for their aging parents, put children through school, and improve the community.

Another such company is Wilton Connor Packaging Inc., which has hired a large number of recent immigrants through a Catholic refugee service and now brings teachers from a nearby community college to the company to teach English and high-school-equivalency classes. The human relations director helps employees deal with landlords, doctors, and government officials. The company even bought a washer and dryer and hired a launderer because so many of its immigrant employees were living in apartments without washing machines. Furthermore, this commendable company sends three vans to pick up workers every morning and take them to work, stopping to drop children off at day care. How can Wilton Connor Packaging afford to be so good? It takes advantage of the local government's funding support for classes and transportation, and, through wise management, has kept costs to a minimum.[11]

Hemmings Motor News pays 100 percent of its employees' health and dental premiums and provides a family leave policy far more generous than that mandated by the government. It does more than the federal Family and Medical Leave Act stipulates and was doing so long before the law was enacted. Instead of 12 weeks' unpaid leave for the birth or adoption of a child and for other family events, Hemmings provides the first 6 weeks at two-thirds pay and, after 12 weeks off, employees can return to work part time if they prefer, rather than full time. Both Hemmings and Wilton Connor provide full benefits for part-time work and flexible hours for all employees.[12]

When Ridgeview Hosiery Inc. discovered that the day care available in the area was substandard, it opened its own AA-rated center. Lancaster Laboratories did the same and is now planning an on-site day-care facility for employees' aging parents as well. The company subsidizes the programs for employees. Ridgeview also brings in school guidance counselors to talk with employees about their children on company time. G. T. Water Products Inc. responded to the poor quality of public schools in the area by opening its own schoolhouse, free to employees' children![13]

Quick Quiz 14.2

1. Define *cross-training.*
2. A manager who decides to increase the depth of her administrative assistant's job by asking her to prepare a report on a competing product is practicing ___________ loading.
3. The most obvious potential problem with job enlargement is that ___________.
4. A working couple with small children might ask each of their employers if they could practice ___________, ___________, or ___________ in order to meet the demands of both work and family.

Dimensions and Design

core job dimensions
Areas in which jobs might conceivably be enriched: skill variety, task identity, task significance, autonomy, and feedback.

The five **core job dimensions** addressed in designing enriched jobs were identified by J. R. Hackman and G. R. Oldham in their *job characteristics model* more than a decade ago:[14]

1. skill variety
2. task identity
3. task significance
4. autonomy
5. feedback.

job diagnostic survey
A survey that allows employees to measure each core job dimension according to their own perception of their job.

motivation potential score (MPS)
The result of a job diagnostic survey; it shows whether a job can be enriched by altering one or more of its core dimensions.

Figure 14.1 shows how two particular jobs might compare on these points. Figure 14.2 shows how these dimensions tie in with attempts at job enrichment. Hackman and Oldham also devised a **job diagnostic survey** that allows employees to measure each core job dimension according to their own perception of their job. The result is a **motivation potential score (MPS)**, which shows whether the job can be enriched by altering one or more of its core dimensions:

$$\left(\frac{\textit{Skill variety} + \textit{Task identity} + \textit{Task significance}}{3}\right) \times \textit{Autonomy} \times \textit{Feedback}$$

For some jobs, one or another of these dimensions cannot be redesigned. For example, only so much skill variety can be offered by a VCR-repair job. The company that repairs VCRs cannot have the same people who repair the machines design advertising or type business correspondence, and it would make no sense to have them handle the billing or the telephones. But some jobs have been dramatically enriched by expanding one or more of these dimensions. By allowing a marketing assistant to set up her own schedule for coordinating the different functions of a specific project, rather than handing her a chart prepared by someone else, a company might free her to do a better job while simultaneously making her a happier, more *autonomous* worker (thus strengthening one of the core job dimensions—autonomy). Let's look at some other ways of tinkering with the five core dimensions.

Skill Variety

skill variety
The degree to which a job requires differing skills and abilities.

Both job enlargement and job rotation are ways of increasing a job's **skill variety**, which refers to the degree to which it requires differing skills and abilities. If variety is the spice of life, it cannot but help the quality of work life as well.

Broadly speaking, most skills are either *motor skills,* physical in nature, or *cognitive skills,* intellectual in nature. Many people find it a pleasant balance to have a job that requires both. However, a lot of variety can be provided in just the cognitive area. A job that draws on many different types of thinking skills, some creative, some organizational

Figure 14.1 **Comparison of Core Dimensions of Two Selected Jobs**

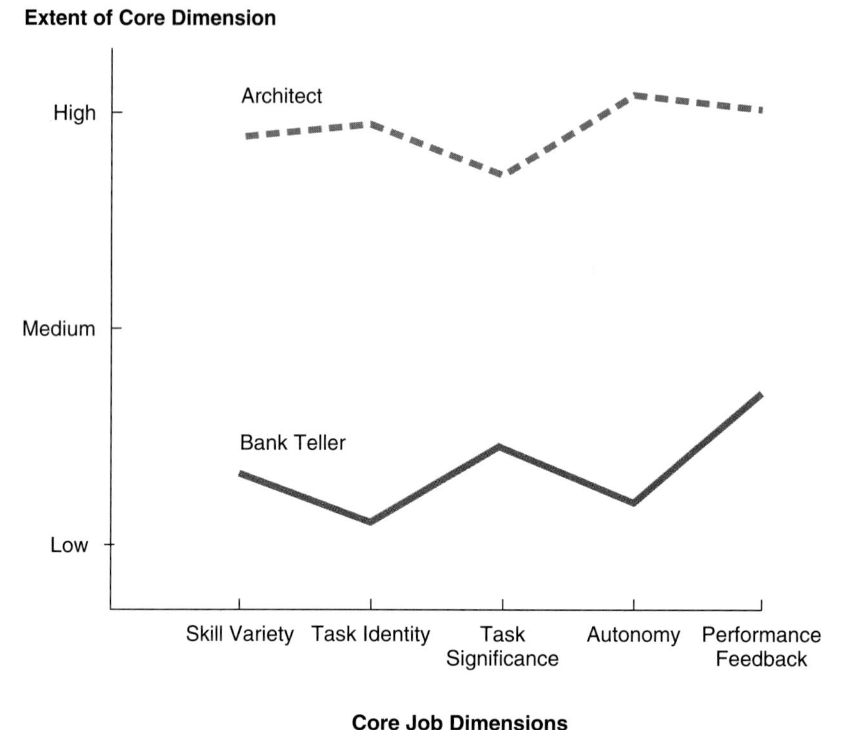

in nature, for example, can usually satisfy a person's desire for skill variety. Jobs that primarily depend on motor skills—even a considerable variety of motor skills—may require the addition of a cognitive component to satisfy the need for skill variety.

Task Identity

task identity
The degree to which a job requires completion of a whole or identifiable piece of work.

Task identity is the degree to which a job requires completion of a whole or identifiable piece of work. The assembly line kills task identity. It provides speed, but at the cost of that powerful motivator—pride in one's work. It is hard to be proud of a tiny piece of something that has no meaning by itself and may not even be visible once a product is fully assembled. You have to be able to *identify* it in order to take pride in it. Partial job specialization is the answer at some factories, so that workers can at least point to an identifiable portion of a product as their own work if it is not practical for them to produce the entire product.

This concept is not limited to manufacturing. Consider a proofreader. If she is assigned to a complete book, she can derive more satisfaction from having caught some errors in it than if she proofreads only a few galleys while others proofread other portions of the book. For one thing, she will have had the pleasure—and it is a pleasure for a proofreader—of finding more errors to be corrected.

Task Significance

In Greek mythology, Sisyphus was a king who earned the wrath of Pluto, god of the underworld, and was condemned to eternally push a heavy stone up a long hill, only

Figure 14.2 **Various Means for Implementing Job Enrichment**

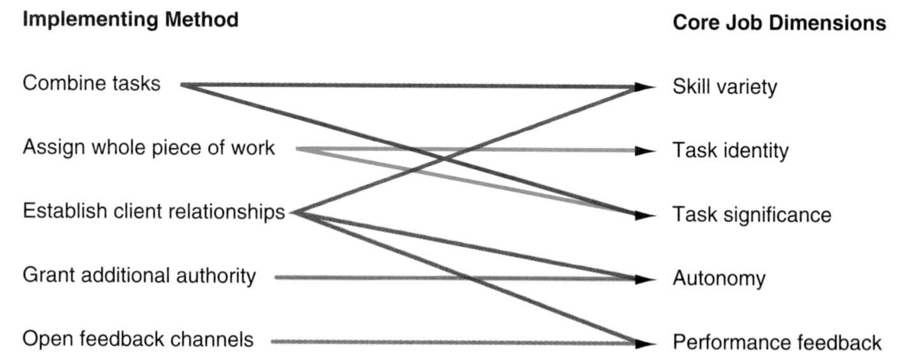

Source: Based on J. Richard Hackman and Greg R. Oldham, *Work Redesign* (pg. 135), © 1980 by Addison-Wesley Publishing Company, Inc. Reprinted by permission of the publisher.

to have it roll down again as soon as he reached the top. So the task was unending, and all his work was futile. When a job seems meaningless, when it seems to accomplish nothing of lasting value, it needs to be redesigned to increase its **task significance**, meaning the degree to which it has a perceptible impact on something or someone. All workers resent "busywork." Suppose the waitresses and waiters at a small coffee shop are told to wipe down the already wiped-down ketchup bottles and sugar containers when no customers are present just to "look busy." Suppose a secretary is asked to reorganize files that were organized a week ago. Suppose a police officer is instructed to fill out arrest forms in triplicate just so no one has to photocopy them. All of these situations are bound to create resentment in the employees because none of these tasks is viewed as significant.

task significance
The degree to which the results of a job have a perceptible impact on something or someone.

Task significance is more important to some people than others. These are the people who look for a job that "helps someone" or "influences someone," and they may even take a cut in pay to get it. But all of us need some degree of task significance to keep motivated. The paycheck may be reason enough to report for work, but it is not reason enough by itself to make us care about how well we do our work. Suppose you were paid to inspect the quality of a product, but every time you found a flaw, your discovery was ignored and the product was sent off without correction. Your job would have no task significance, no impact. Despite a good paycheck, it would probably frustrate you.

Autonomy

autonomy
The degree of freedom and independence a job affords in making work-related decisions.

Autonomy is freedom, independence—the right to make your own decisions in performing a job. It is what gives workers a sense of power, of control, over their work. Since the feeling of a lack of control can contribute to stress, increasing autonomy may be a way to relieve stress in some situations. The idea cannot be taken too far, though. An overzealous employee without a deadline might nitpick a project to death before being willing to turn it over to top management for inspection. A perfectionist might drag a project out to three times its desirable time frame. And a happy-go-lucky soul who has somehow escaped the development of a work ethic and finds all his or her satisfaction in nonwork activities might abuse too much freedom. Usually, however, a healthy dollop of autonomy improves the recipe for job satisfaction and has a motivating effect.

Diversity Highlights

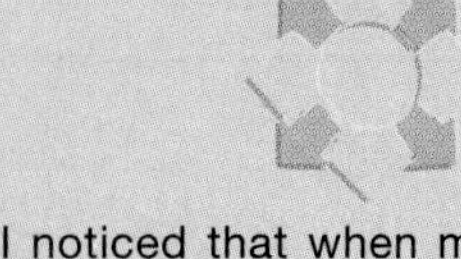

Skill—and Disdain for Tradition—Spark M-R Electronics

Despite her status as owner of a $3-million electronics company, you won't find Melva Roesler in a suit and pearls, sitting behind a big desk. In what she calls her "power suit" of jeans and tennis shoes, Roesler is more likely to be sitting at a workbench beside her production staff, assembling and checking control panels. It's a nontraditional way to get work done—just the way she likes to work.

Roesler, president of M-R Electronics, wasn't on the fast track to success when she dropped out of school at 16 to get married. She had two children before she was 20 and quit her job as a "wireman" at an electronics company when her more traditional husband said he wanted her to stay home. Less than a year later, at her employer's insistence and her husband's urging (he missed the second income), she was back at work. But this time, it was as an independent contractor.

She set up shop in her living room, got a business license, and went to work putting together systems. Her client list grew, as did her reputation as a manufacturing engineer. "When I told my husband I was going to start a business, he just smirked and said something patronizing," Roesler recalls.

That was just the first reality check for Roesler, who has since divorced. Electronics is traditionally a male-dominated field, and sexism was a constant problem during her first years as an entrepreneur. "My former husband worked with me for a while, and I noticed that when my male clients and vendors automatically walked up to him instead of me, he didn't always steer them in the right direction. I had to remind him who was boss."

Roesler is fair but tough with her employees. "I have a problem with people who don't want to work; I worked so hard to get to where I am." But whatever problems she encounters, Roesler never blames them on being a woman. In the late 1970s, she was dumbfounded by growing complaints that men wouldn't let women do anything. "I thought, 'What do you mean? I can't even get a day off!'"

Source: Erika Kotite, "Wired In," *Entrepreneur*, February 1993, p. 168.

As seen in the "Diversity Highlights" box, autonomy can also mean the ability to do things in a nontraditional manner—especially if you are the boss.

Vertical loading increases autonomy by eliminating the steps between approving an action and taking an action. Thus, a worker makes his own decisions about matters that might have been reserved for a supervisor, or she inspects her own work and corrects it as necessary instead of responding to someone else's inspection. Vertical loading obviously requires giving a worker more knowledge as well as more authority. It may entail a special training program.

Feedback

As discussed earlier in this text, *feedback,* or information on our job performance, is vital to motivation. In addition, it is a practical necessity for performing well. You need to know where you are failing in order to correct your performance. You also need to know what you are doing well in order to continue it.

Unfortunately, managers often lose sight of the fact that the feedback they value themselves is just as important to their employees. In one study that asked workers to rank ten motivational factors and then asked their supervisors to guess how they had ranked the factors, workers gave highest priority to "full appreciation for work done," which supervisors ranked eighth.[15]

Consultant Will Kaydos observes that "the only way to make training stick is to make feedback about performance an integral part of day-to-day operations." He says that it takes months for most people to learn the essential skills of their job and a year or two to learn "all the intricacies that make the difference between acceptable

In the photo, employees of The Print & Copy Factory watch a tape of a previous company-training session. Educating employees can give a company an edge over the competition.
Photo source: © Robert Holmgren.

Photo Exercise

If your employer offered training, what skills would you most like to improve?

and excellent performance." Kaydos strongly urges performance measurement and feedback to reinforce training and bolster its results.[16]

Quick Quiz 14.3

1. The equation involving Hackman and Oldham's core job dimensions yields a ____________.
2. Task ____________ is hard to preserve on an assembly-line job.
3. ____________ is one way to increase a job's autonomy.

Training and Job Enrichment

Training is a way of meeting the job designer halfway. If duties are added to make the job more satisfying, for example, the employee may need training in order to handle those duties. If job rotation is being used to add skill variety, training will be necessary to equip the rotating workers for the new jobs. Training, or education, then, is often what allows a company to engage in job redesign.

"Education gives us our competitive edge. Anybody can hire smart people. It's what you do with them that makes the difference," says Lawrence Weinbach, managing partner and CEO of Arthur Andersen, the world's third largest accounting and consulting organization. Unlike many U.S. companies, Arthur Andersen provides its most intensive training for new employees at the start of the career ladder. Most courses are taught by people from line operations. "In our culture, it's an honor to teach," says Herbert W. Desch, the organization's chief training officer.[17]

Training at Detroit Diesel is a cooperative venture between management and the union. It is the result and the cause of extensive job redesign, in which roles have changed so that "supervisors are expected to be coaches and part of the team," according to Jim Brown, the union shop chairman. Jim Bachman, one of the trainers, describes it this way: "It used to be that people came in and did the same task, day in and day out. Now, people have multiple jobs and responsibilities. In my area ... people like to change jobs. They feel more important and better about themselves."

Companies are discovering that just like permanent employees, temporary workers need to be trained to avoid excessive turnover and low productivity. In the photo, Norell Services in Memphis teaches high-speed packing techniques to temp workers bound for Nike.
Photo source: © 1993 Ed Kashi.

Both Brown and Bachman agree there is more "pitching in and helping." In fact, the union and management have bargained a new labor contract that reduced 44 job classifications to 14, and then to 11. The result of these enriched jobs? Decreased absenteeism and increased productivity, quality, and sales.[18]

Fiat Auto regards its training program as a part of an "integrated factory" approach that leads to:[19]

- resourceful and multifunctional workers
- teamwork as a daily method of operation
- increased responsibility for individual workers
- continuous improvement
- maximum utilization of human resources.

It appears, then, that effective training means effective job-enrichment programs. Some suggestions for effective training programs follow:[20]

1. *Evaluate the training program's success in improving work performance.* Careful evaluation of the results of training will reveal ways that the program can be improved, methodologies adjusted, and individual trainers advised where necessary to change their training style. Pretraining evaluation questionnaires are a good idea, too, to help trainees focus on what they should be learning from the program.
2. *Make sure that training goals harmonize with overall organizational goals.* This means trainers must thoroughly understand organizational goals and be committed to them. Furthermore, the training should address these goals in order of priority. For example, cutting costs should not be addressed last if it is in fact a top-priority goal.
3. *Involve line managers in developing the training program.* Manager involvement is important not only in developing the training objectives and deciding on the best way to achieve them, but also in helping trainees implement what they have learned when they return to their redesigned jobs. Without follow-up attention, the time and money spent for training could be wasted.
4. *Choose the appropriate method for the particular trainees and the particular situation.* Some trainees, and some situations, call for individual coaching rather than a group setting; some need hands-on practice rather than classroom lectures and demonstrations.
5. *Administer tests before training as well as after.* It is helpful to determine levels of expertise *before* training through pretests which can measure the results of the

training and help direct its emphasis. Role playing, practice sessions, and job simulations can be used for such testing in addition to questionnaires and interviews.

6. *Measure the impact of training on the organization by some quantifiable means.* Increased sales, cost savings, improved work output, reduced errors, reduced customer complaints, and even a decline in absenteeism can indicate the impact of the training, which can then be compared with its cost to see if it is a worthy investment. Though much of the impact—such as higher morale or job satisfaction—may not be directly measurable, it should translate into such concrete results as lower turnover and absenteeism, more productivity, and higher quality.

Will Kaydos cautions that although people learn, they also "unlearn" without follow-up and continual feedback, not only because they may lapse into old ways of doing their jobs but also because of turnover. As a result, "the fully trained organization that exists today can look quite a bit different a year from now."[21] So training is an ongoing operation, one that needs continual evaluation and updating. Moreover, as Steven M. Hronec at Arthur Andersen comments, training needs to be "very responsive to [the] changing marketplace." Hronec says that Arthur Andersen's clients' needs are changing, "and I expect training to be able to be done very quickly, very focused, and in a way that responds to these changes."[22] Some industries need to change their training programs frequently because of their marketplace. But even those that do not should still reassess their programs in light of accumulated information on how well or poorly their trainees perform—and on continuing insights gleaned from the business world on effective training methods in general.

The prevailing sentiment seems to be an increasing approval of investing in training. Companies have not cut back on their training budgets in recent years, despite economic downturns.[23] Also, training is being seen more as a continuing need, not limited to teaching basic skills, but appropriate for advanced education of almost everyone at an organization. A lifelong learning goal is being established at many organizations, with the idea that all jobs can be enhanced and further enriched and that no one ever knows everything there is to know. Employees who welcome that approach are seeing some good opportunities for making their job more and more what they "want to" do as well as what they "have to" do.

Quick Quiz 14.4

Mark "true" or "false" next to each statement.

1. Unions generally resist management efforts to train employees. ______
2. Training goals should harmonize with overall organizational goals. ______

Summary

- **Discuss the philosophy behind job redesign.** The philosophy behind job redesign is that people should not be treated as machines and that, instead of altering them to fit the job, the job should be changed to provide meaning and variety and responsibility, making it more enjoyable, satisfying, and challenging. The idea is that employee attitudes and work performance will automatically change if the job is changed.
- **Identify various methods of job enrichment.** Methods of job enrichment include job rotation, which involves moving employees from one job to another to provide more variety; job enlargement, which involves adding job activities, also to provide variety, and sometimes adding responsibility as well to make a job more meaningful and challenging; increased customer contact to make a job more meaningful; and individualistic treatment such as offering flexible working schedules, "family-friendly" policies, and telecommuting.
- **Explain how responsibility is used in job enrichment and why authority and accountability are usually involved as well.** One of the most popular ways of enriching jobs is adding responsibility, since the more

responsible job is a more challenging job, and the more challenging job is presumed to be more rewarding. In most cases, along with responsibility goes authority, which is the right to command or perform certain job activities, and accountability, which means being held liable for results.

• **List and define the five core job dimensions.** The five core job dimensions are (1) skill variety, which is the degree to which a job requires differing skills and abilities, both motor and cognitive; (2) task identity, which is the degree to which a job requires completion of a whole or identifiable piece of work; (3) task significance, which is the degree to which the results of a job have a perceptible impact on something or someone (its meaningfulness); (4) autonomy, which is the degree of freedom and independence a job affords; and (5) feedback, which is information on how well or poorly the job is being performed.

• **Discuss the relationship of training to job enrichment.** Training is related to job redesign in that it may be necessary to help an employee reap the benefits of an enriched job. Employees trained to handle enriched jobs can provide a company with an important competitive edge. Some suggestions for effective training programs are to (1) evaluate the training program's success in improving work performance so that it can be modified where necessary, (2) make sure that training goals harmonize with overall organizational goals, (3) involve line managers in developing the training program, (4) choose the appropriate method—perhaps individual coaching rather than classroom instruction—for the particular trainees and the particular situation, (5) administer tests before and after training, and (6) measure the impact of training on the organization by some quantifiable means. Follow-up is advised to keep trainees from "unlearning," or lapsing into old habits.

Key Terms

job redesign (330)
quality of work life (QWL) (332)
job enrichment (333)
job rotation (333)
cross-training (333)
job enlargement (333)
vertical loading (334)
horizontal loading (334)
responsibility (334)
job description (334)
accountability (335)
responsibility gaps (335)
overlapping responsibilities (335)
flextime (337)
compressed workweek (337)
job sharing (337)
core job dimensions (339)
job diagnostic survey (339)
motivation potential score (MPS) (339)
skill variety (339)
task identity (340)
task significance (341)
autonomy (341)

Review and Discussion Questions

1. What is job redesign? How does it differ from job specialization? Which is more human relations oriented and why?

2. What are the motivational benefits of job rotation and job enlargement? Which would work best for you?

3. Do the following examples involve vertical or horizontal loading:
   a. A weekend handyman is asked to take on a homeowner's entire kitchen remodeling project.
   b. A full-time teacher is asked to teach two additional classes.
   c. A public relations manager is given responsibility for the firm's biggest client.
   d. A marketing manager fills in while the CEO takes a two-week vacation.

4. Phyllis Greene, a dental hygienist for a growing practice, has been asked to assume a dual role as office manager. She will handle the appointment book and most billing procedures. How can Phyllis ensure that enlarging her job will involve vertical, rather than horizontal, loading? How can she make sure she has authority and doesn't get overloaded? Describe what would make this a successful job-enlargement situation.

5. What are the roles of responsibility, authority, and autonomy in job enrichment? Which is most important to you?

6. As the newcomer to the marketing department, Sami Hassan was happy to take on the responsibility for writing the company's annual report. Two senior coworkers were in charge of gathering material from other departments and working with the printer and artist. When Sami missed his first deadline because he received material late, the company's president warned him that a late annual report would cost Sami his job. With material still arriving late, Sami worked until midnight every night for two weeks to write the report.

How could this situation have been better resolved? What action should Sami have taken? The president?

7. What are the five core job dimensions? Give an example of each. How do they tie in with attempts at job enrichment? Which is most important to you?

8. Everbright Light Bulb Co. is proud of its tradition. It still uses the same employee-training program it established 37 years ago, focusing exclusively on how to make light bulbs. Recently the company began experiencing quality-control problems. What changes would you suggest to make the company's training program more effective?

9. How have organizational attitudes toward training changed in recent years? How can companies and their employees best benefit from this change in attitudes?

10. Luis Santos squeaked by in high school and landed a job at the carpet mill where his uncle worked. After eight years there, he was unhappy when the company initiated a cross-training program. How can the company get Luis to respond positively to the program? What motivational factors might work? Why? What training approach might work best for Luis? Why?

A SECOND LOOK

Explain how Prospect Associates Ltd. allowed copy-machine chief operator Drew Melton to enrich his own job. What motivational factors existed for Melton? What lesson can other companies glean from this example?

Independent Activity

"But Someone's Got to Do It"

List ten jobs or careers you think are most in need of job enrichment. Explain your choices. Would enriching these jobs make them more appealing to you? Why or why not?

Now take a few minutes to interview workers who hold those jobs (try for at least five). Ask them how they feel about what they do for a living:

- Do they like their job? Why or why not?
- If they could change one aspect of the job, what would it be?
- What would make their jobs better?
- In what specific ways have their jobs been enriched already (for example, through more responsibility)?
- In what ways do their jobs fulfill the five core job dimensions?
- Have they tried to communicate their needs to their supervisors? What was the result?

After interviewing these workers, have your views of these jobs changed? For better or worse? Why?

Skill Builder

Designing Jobs

Think of a job you or a friend have had. What part of the job was particularly satisfying? What was not? List those characteristics.

Using the five core job dimensions (skill variety, task identity, task significance, autonomy, and feedback), redesign the job to improve it. Think of ways that you could convince a team member or supervisor that your changes would be better for both you and the company.

Group Activity

Classroom Training Challenge (30 minutes)

One or more students should volunteer to teach the class a skill. If possible, volunteers should have some time to prepare their training session before the class in which this exercise takes place. Perhaps a few trainers will want to work as a team. Here are suggestions for skills to teach (or trainers can choose their own):

- how to change a software program in a computer
- how to arrange the classroom for an office conference
- how to set up audiovisual equipment.

After the training session, the class should discuss the following questions:

1. How can you evaluate whether this training was successful? If possible, conduct an evaluation of what the class learned. What do the results of this evaluation indicate?
2. What training techniques were used? Would additional or alternative techniques, such as one-on-one coaching, have made the skill easier to learn?
3. Appraise the trainers: how effective were their teaching methods? Did they provide feedback to those whom they were teaching?

Case Study

Employee Autonomy Promotes Initiative at Carrier

It sits on a pothole-filled road across from a big chicken processor in a remote town, but the Carrier Corp. plant in Arkadelphia, Arkansas, could be a model for the future of U.S. manufacturing. The plant, which manufactures compressors for air conditioners, looks more like an insurance office than a factory: it has a sleek, one-story design and is heavily automated.

The lean, 150-member work force, however, is what really distinguishes the plant. Its workers are not the typical lunch-pail crowd but carefully picked, nonunion workers granted unheard-of autonomy. Their authority, says one worker, means taking care of the "100 problems that managers never knew existed."

Job applicants must complete a grueling six-week course and be interviewed by managers and factory coworkers; only 1 of every 16 hopefuls is hired. Once on the job, however, all workers have a say in how the plant operates. They can shut down production if they spot a problem and, within limits, order their own supplies.

For example, when an employee told supervisor Tracy Bartels he needed new gloves, she handed him a catalog. "Isn't it somebody's job to do that?" he asked her. Says Bartels, "They're the ones who are going to use it; they might as well decide what they're going to use." Carrier does have safeguards against misuse, however; each department places flexible ceilings on how much workers can buy without management approval.

Flexibility is crucial throughout the plant. Carrier teaches workers several jobs so that, if one is sick, another can fill in quickly. And no job is off limits to women. Women work beside men in every area and can handle every job. The plant was designed so that no one has to lift anything heavier than 12 pounds. "Why should there be any barriers in our plant?" asks Thomas L. Kassouf, president of Carrier's compressor division.

Because the workers themselves took the initiative to learn how to install the plant's machinery, they have a sense of ownership and the pride that goes with it. Their familiarity with their machines means they don't have to wait for maintenance workers to fix a machine that breaks down; they do it themselves. And they check the quality of the finished product constantly, rather than at prescribed intervals.

Keeping quality high in its work force and its products may help Carrier achieve Kassouf's goal—selling Arkansas compressors to Japan.

Case Questions

1. What Japanese or American aspects of Theory Z were put to use in creating Carrier's quality of work life (QWL)?
2. Cross-training is already at work at Carrier. Do you think job rotation would be a good idea in this factory? Flextime or job sharing? Why or why not?
3. What are some examples of how vertical loading has increased worker autonomy at Carrier?
4. How well does Carrier fulfill the five core job dimensions necessary in designing enriched jobs? Explain.

Source: Erle Norton, "Future Factories," *The Wall Street Journal,* January 13, 1993, pp. A1–A2.

Case Study

Deloitte & Touche Helps Workers Balance Life's Demands

On June 1, 1993, Elizabeth Rader became the first partner to work part time at Deloitte & Touche, the country's third-largest accounting firm. By cutting her 50-hour workweek by 40 percent, Rader was able to spend more time with her two sons. As her hours decreased, she retained her benefits but her pay was reduced to reflect her shorter workweek.

The flexible work schedule for partners is one of several "family-friendly" benefits the New York–based firm has offered recently to increase productivity and reduce its annual departure rate for women of 20 to 25 percent. Among the current benefits of the "Work/Life Balance Program" are hot lines for child-care, adoption-assistance, and education information and tax-season day care.

These programs, and Rader's ability to switch to part-time work, reflect the renewed desire of the nation's accounting firms to increase the number of women in the profession. Today, despite industry efforts to improve the status of women, only 5 percent of the partners at the nation's 6 largest accounting firms are women. Of Deloitte's 1,500 partners, only 77 are female. Various societal and cultural obstacles are blamed for the low percentage. Deloitte's chairman, J. Michael Cook, attributes the problem to the expectations that working women must "balance personal commitments" to their families.

Despite these obstacles, Cook says Deloitte will lower its turnover rate among female partners—now higher than among men—and promote more women to partnership ranks. Cook estimates that 20 percent of Deloitte's 80 new partners this year will be female, up from between 10 percent and 13 percent over the past three years. Though he hopes by the year 2000 to have a "much more" significant number of women partners at the firm, Cook concedes it may take a decade or more for many women to become partners because the firm picks partners from professionals hired about a dozen years before.

The fact that women make up more than half of the entry-level employees—and 20 percent of managers—at the 6 biggest accounting firms makes Ellen P. Gabriel hopeful. A partner at Deloitte, Gabriel was recently named national director of the firm's new committee on the advancement of women. "With current demographics, this program will enable us to become competitive in the future," she says. "And, as the mother of a six-year-old girl, I feel such programs will give her more opportunities in the future."

However well the family-care programs work, Deloitte would do well to heed the results of the task force it set up in 1992 to find out why women were leaving the company. The in-house panel of 13 partners interviewed 80 top-performing, exiting employees—75 percent of them women. It was not family concerns but the company's failure to take them seriously as professionals that was most often cited as their reason for quitting.

Case Questions

1. What other types of individualistic treatment might be necessary to increase the number of women in large accounting firms? Should programs for other minorities also be initiated? Why or why not?
2. Which of the five core job dimensions are lacking for female accountants? Why?
3. How could better human relations management help Deloitte retain more of its female work force?
4. What kind of training approaches would be helpful?

Sources: Michelle Litvin, "Extended Family," *Chicago Tribune,* May 23, 1993, sec. 6, p. 1; Lee Berton, "Deloitte Wants More Women for Top Posts in Accounting," *The Wall Street Journal,* April 28, 1993, pp. B1–B7.

Quick Quiz Answers

Quick Quiz 14.1

1. false
2. true

Quick Quiz 14.2

1. Cross-training is training in the skills required to perform more than one job.
2. vertical
3. employees may become overloaded with duties
4. flextime; a compressed workweek; job sharing

Quick Quiz 14.3

1. motivation potential score (MPS)
2. identity
3. Vertical loading

Quick Quiz 14.4

1. false
2. true

PART OUTLINE

6

Special Topics

CHAPTER

15

International Opportunities

CHAPTER OUTLINE

Learning Objectives

- Explain how the globalization of business came about.
- List some reasons for a U.S. organization to globalize its business.
- Contrast a transnational organization with a traditional international or multinational one.
- Discuss some effects of the globalization of business on U.S. organizations.
- Explain why cultural awareness is vital in an age of globalization.
- Identify some of the adjustments that an employee in a foreign country may have to make.
- Identify some of the management issues that complicate global operations.

Front Porch Swings It with CompuServe

Jeff Freeman grew up in Chatsworth, Georgia, population 5,000. But he knew there was a wider world out there, especially after he got his first computer in high school. By age 16, he was dialing up local bulletin boards to retrieve copies of software programs and talk with other callers. At college, he met his wife, Mary, at a party given by a local computer-bulletin-board operator. Jeff left school to come home and help run the family business, but his interest in computers never flagged. In 1991, he and Mary launched Front Porch Computers, a personal-computer mail-order business. Spending less than $200 a month to run classified ads on CompuServe, the nation's leading on-line service, the Freemans have built their small-town firm into a $4-million-a-year international powerhouse. The company sells IBM personal-computer clones, modems, and other computer devices to customers as far away as Europe, South America, and Asia; its client list includes Calvin Klein Germany, based in Dusseldorf, and Bahrain Petroleum Corp., based in Bahrain.

The Freemans still work from home, though they've set up shop in a nearby storefront and hired three part-time employees to answer phones. Though profit margins are slim—only 5 to 10 percent—Jeff is confident of their ability to survive. They earned customers by offering low prices and standing behind their products. Today, he says, "The better name recognition you have, the less you have to compete on price."

Jeff admits they owe their company's success—and its very existence—to CompuServe; without that link, he says, business would be "nowhere." Chatsworth is a limited market; the

Freemans' store is the first and only computer store the town is likely to have. And in today's global market, selling computers by ones and twos is no way to make a profit.

Source: Rosalind Resnick, "Front Porch on the World," *Nation's Business,* September 1993, p. 17. Photo source: Photo by John Dickerson.

Like Front Porch Computers, more organizations than ever before are engaging in international business—not so much because they want to, but because they must. Foreign competition is too stiff and foreign opportunities are too inviting to be ignored.

As we've seen throughout this text, business is about more than dollars and cents: it is about people. Thus, global competition among companies involves global competition among workers. As one author has written, "Foundry workers in Louisiana compete with foundry workers in Howrah, India. Garment workers in Manhattan compete with their counterparts in Hong Kong and Seoul."[1]

In this globalized business world, the study of human relations assumes increased importance. Universal human emotions and needs notwithstanding, people of different cultures sometimes act differently, react differently, and interpret events differently. Germans and English people tend to understate their positive feelings, for example, while Italian, Spanish, and Latin American people tend to exaggerate them.[2] A Muslim regards any gestures made with the left hand as offensive, whereas an American does not. Understanding these differences helps us communicate better with each other.

cultural stereotypes
Assumptions that individuals from certain cultures embody certain characteristics believed to be associated with that culture.

At the same time, we should be wary of being led astray by **cultural stereotypes**—value judgments that pass for cultural knowledge. The idea, for example, that the people of one culture are more hardworking or more trustworthy than those of another is harmful, not helpful, to human relations. A healthy respect for individual differences among people should keep us from this pitfall. The more informed a person is about the *facts* pertaining to people of other cultures, the more effective he or she is likely to be in human relations as the globalization of business continues.

The Global Economy

globalism
The increasing interrelationship of the various parts of the world due to trade and technology developments.

Trade among nations has always existed, but never to the degree we see today. ***Globalism*** is the term used to describe the increasing interrelationship of the various parts of the world as a result of developments in both trade and technology. Today the world economy is so interrelated that significant fluctuations in one nation are usually felt by the other major players.

U.S. workers are directly affected by globalism. More than 5 million U.S. workers owe their employment to exports. Each billion dollars' worth of products sold overseas generates 25,000 new jobs. On the other hand, more than a million jobs are lost yearly as a result of our importing products rather than manufacturing them.[3] Figure 15.1 shows the trade deficits for 1992 and part of 1993. Even those workers who do not work directly for organizations with international operations may therefore be affected by globalism.

The Rise of Globalism

Immediately following World War II, the United States was the world's undisputed economic leader. Western Europe and Japan were wrecked economically, and the Third World was not yet industrialized. As these economies developed (quite often with American help), many U.S. companies found opportunities overseas.

Figure 15.1 **Trade Deficit Statistics**

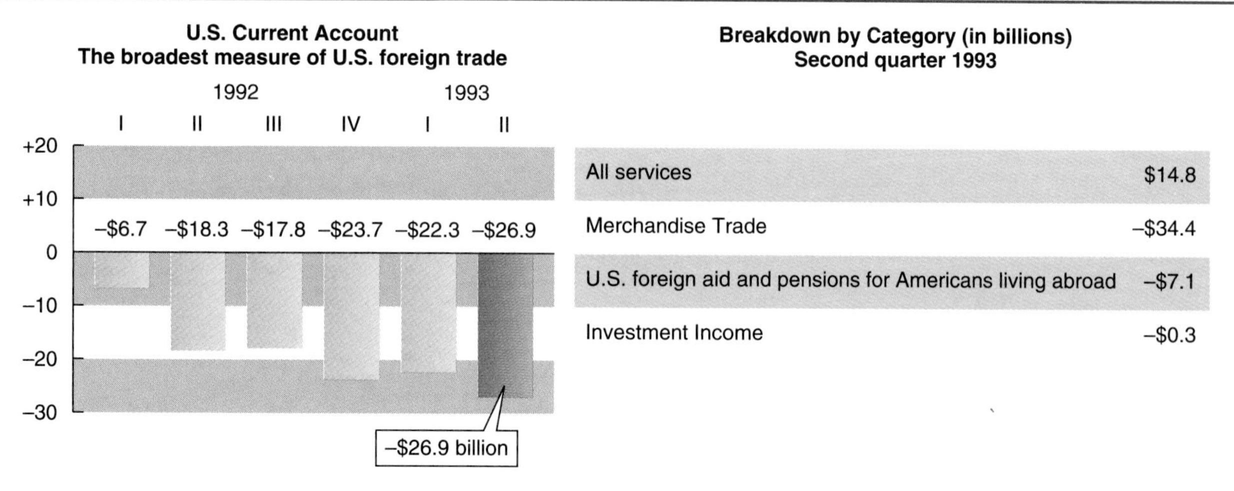

Breakdown by Category (in billions)
Second quarter 1993

All services	$14.8
Merchandise Trade	−$34.4
U.S. foreign aid and pensions for Americans living abroad	−$7.1
Investment Income	−$0.3

Source: *Daily Southtown,* September 15, 1993, p. B1. Reprinted by permission of AP/WIDE WORLD PHOTOS.

American business as a whole dominated the global marketplace until the end of the 1960s. At that time the world economy began to change dramatically. Four factors figured prominently in the change:

1. Industrialization picked up speed in many previously unindustrialized nations, such as Taiwan, Brazil, and Malaysia, to name just a few. Then these nations started exporting.
2. Because of increasing industrialization, the standard of living rose in many nations, leading to expanded markets and increased consumer demand.
3. Technological advances brought global communication and transportation, homogenizing consumer tastes, accelerating the rate of new-product development, and requiring more technical skills of many workers.
4. The recession of the early 1980s combined with a strong U.S. dollar to make U.S. exports too expensive on the world market, forcing U.S. companies to compete with the less expensive products of other countries.

In the 1980s, as businesses in other countries gained strength, American businesses often seemed to lose ground. Wealthy investors from other parts of the world bought up U.S. companies and real estate, and foreign competitors learned to beat the Americans at their own game. Figures 15.2 and 15.3 give some idea of the scope of international activity in this country during the past couple of decades. In addition, we now must compete internationally in industries representing about 70 percent of the goods we produce.[4] Today Japan, Germany, Canada, and Korea are among those nations challenging the United States in the marketplace. It is a rare U.S. organization today that can avoid the impact of globalism.

The trend is toward even freer global trade. For instance, the United States, Canada, and Mexico recently negotiated the *North American Free Trade Agreement (NAFTA).* This pact reduces or eliminates trade barriers among the three countries on a wide range of goods and services. NAFTA was controversial because many believed it would encourage U.S. companies to set up shop in Mexico, where workers can be paid far less than they are in this country. Others were convinced that NAFTA would ultimately create jobs by opening up new markets, especially in Mexico. The

Figure 15.2 **Goods Made in the United States by Foreign Companies**

Anglo-Dutch

Royal Dutch Shell: Shell Oil.
Unilever: Wisk, All, Breeze, Rinso, Lux, Dove, Caress, Lifebuoy, Signal, Aim, Close-up, Pepsodent, Imperial, Mrs. Butterworth's Syrup, Lawry's seasonings, Lipton teas and soups, Wish-Bone salad dressings, Knox gelatin, Lucky Whip.

France

Club Mediterranée: resorts and youth camps.
Société Bic: pens and lighters.
Pernod Richard: Wild Turkey Bourbon, Michelin tires.

Norway

Olsen, Lehmkul Families: Timex watches.

Switzerland

Nestlé: Nescafé, Taster's Choice, Libby's canned foods, Stouffers restaurants and frozen foods, Nestea, Nestlé chocolate bars.
Sandoz: Ovaltine.

Germany

BASF: auto paint, chemicals.
Tengelmann Group: A&P.
Bayer: Alka-Seltzer, One-A-Day Vitamins, SOS pads, plastics, herbicides, typesetting equipment.
Bertelsmann: Bantam books.
Hugo Mann: Fed-mart department stores.
Continental: General Tires.

Brazil

Copersucar: Hills Brothers Coffee.

Japan

Bridgestone Tire: Firestone tires.
Brother Industries: Business machines.
Honda: Accord and Acura cars, lawnmowers, motorcycles, and electronic parts.
Matsushita: Quasar TV sets.
Nissan: trucks.
Sharp: TV sets and microwave ovens.
Sony: Records, videotapes, and audio disks.

Sweden

Electrolux: Eureka vacuum cleaners, Frigidaire, Westinghouse, Kelvinator, and Gibson microwave ovens and air conditioners.

United Kingdom

B.A.T.: Kool, Viceroy, Belair, Raleigh cigarettes, Saks Fifth Avenue and Gimbels department stores.
Beechum Group: McLeans, Aquafresh, Sucrets, Cling Free, Brylcream, Calgon.
British Petroleum: BP, Sohio, Boron gasoline, Purina animal feeds.
W. Lyons: Baskin-Robbins.
Reckirt and Culman: French's mustard.
Grand Metropolitan: L&M cigarettes, Pearle Vision Centers, Pillsbury (Burger King, Green Giant, Jeno's, Vandekamp, Haagen-Dazs).

Canada

Campeau Corp: Federated Department Stores.

Source: Samuel C. Certo, Stewart T. Husted, and Max E. Douglas, *Business,* 3e, © 1990, pp. 694, 695. Reprinted by permission of Prentice Hall, Englewood Cliffs, New Jersey.

Commerce Department, for example, estimates that 19,100 American jobs are created for every $1-billion increase in U.S. manufacturing exports. The 600,000 American jobs that existed in 1993 because of trade with Mexico were predicted to jump to 1 million by 1995.[5] At this point it seems that NAFTA is indeed increasing cross-border trade and thus the job-producing capacity of all three nations.[6]

Figure 15.3 **Companies That Were U.S. Owned in the 1970s and Foreign Owned by the 1990s**

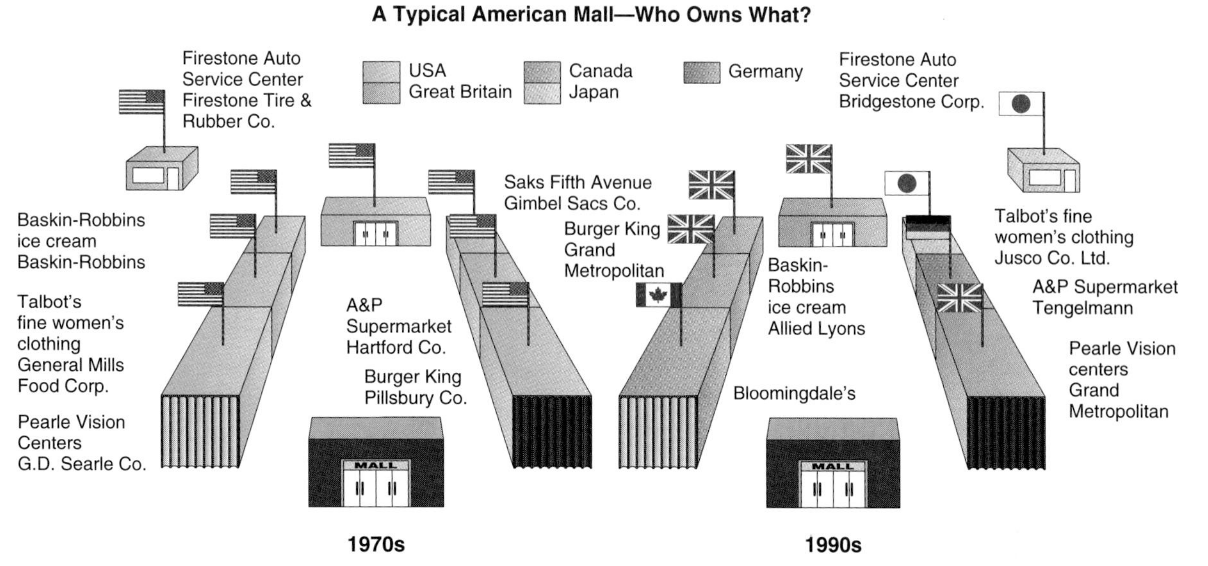

Source: Samuel C. Certo, Stewart T. Husted, and Max E. Douglas, *Business,* 3e,© 1990, pp. 694, 695. Reprinted by permission of Prentice Hall, Englewood Cliffs, New Jersey.

The evolving European Union (EU) is an even more comprehensive pact. It seeks to reduce trade barriers and to foster political and economic cooperation among an expanding roster of European nations. However, this arrangement is unlikely to benefit the United States the way NAFTA does. Some fear that the EU will become a "Fortress Europe" closed to imports of U.S. and other foreign products. To maintain a place at the table, some large American corporations are starting or buying European companies. General Motors bought half of Saab-Scandia for this purpose.

The need to compete globally—to produce more products and services of better quality and for less cost—has given rise to all the hot topics in modern human relations: quality improvement, downsizing, team building, participative management, cultural diversity. In turn, modern human relations practices are crossing borders, as the "Diversity Highlights" box demonstrates.

One other element of globalism that affects the practice of human relations is the development of international quality standards. For example, to sell certain products in Europe, companies must document that their quality assurance systems comply with *ISO 9000,* a series of standards developed by the International Organization for Standardization (ISO). The goal is to ensure consistent quality in such critical products as medical devices. Even products that are not required to meet the standards register with ISO 9000, however, to gain a competitive edge.[7] ISO 9000 (which has been described as a kind of "Good Housekeeping Seal of Approval" for the international marketplace) has now been adopted by 91 countries.[8] A director of quality assurance and training in the United States, Michael J. Apfelberg, says that, by requiring documentation of the systems a company uses to assure quality products, ISO 9000 helps "you identify training needs. ISO 9000 really gives you all the material you need as far as determining what needs to be done to perform the job properly."[9] In this and many other ways, increasing globalism is affecting the work of human relations professionals.

Diversity Highlights

Britain's Kwik-Fit Fine-Tunes for Diversity

It's a small world when it comes to trends in the workplace. Just as political correctness and an emphasis on work-force diversity are worldwide trends not confined to the United States, team building is a concept growing in global popularity.

Sometimes, however, a company's attempts to combine these theories and shake things up runs into trouble. Take the case of the British firm Kwik-Fit, the largest car-repair company in Europe. Since the company's founding 21 years ago, the 2,000 mechanics at Kwik-Fit's 610 outlets have all been men. It was a statistic that company chief Tom Farmer was determined to change. At the company's national convention in Scotland last year, he announced that within four years, one in four Kwik-Fit mechanics would be female.

An aggressive recruiting campaign attracted a lot of publicity with its unusual wording: "Female fitters wanted." Across the country, Kwik-Fit garages began building women's restrooms and other amenities to welcome the first females to their teams.

But the laws governing the workplace are also gaining international acceptance; in Britain, as in the United States, employers are prohibited from reserving jobs for specific categories of people. Farmer's zealous effort toward equal opportunity violated the country's anti-discrimination laws. Despite applauding Kwik-Fit's goal, Britain's Equal Opportunities Commission objected to the hiring campaign's form. So while Kwik-Fit can continue its search for female mechanics, it cannot advertise positions to be filled exclusively by women.

Source: Veronique Mistiaen, "The Right Idea, The Wrong Approach," *Chicago Tribune,* September 5, 1993, sec. 6, p. 1.

The Risks and Rewards of Globalism

Global competition has forced U.S. businesses to reach for greater quality and productivity. But the result of intensifying globalism has been a profound shift in the American labor market—for some Americans, lost jobs or reduced wages. As businesses have streamlined, they have laid off huge numbers of middle managers. Other U.S. companies have abandoned industries in which they can no longer compete effectively or have shifted production to other countries where the costs are lower. For example, after 12 years of assembling Magnavox televison sets at a North American Phillips Corporation plant, Allen McAmis was laid off and his $13-an-hour job moved to Juarez, Mexico, where it pays $2 an hour. This case represents one reason why some people view global competition in a negative light.[10]

comparative advantage The theory that a country should specialize in the products it can supply more efficiently and economically than other products.

Despite the pain of such shifts on the human scale, in economic terms these shifts are rational. In 1817, David Ricardo advanced the theory of **comparative advantage**—that a country should specialize in the products it can supply more efficiently and economically than other products. This way it makes better use of its natural resources, technology, and labor force. The theory of comparative advantage argues in favor of dropping trade barriers so that each country can concentrate on doing what it does best and depend on others for what they do best.

In part, the upheaval in U.S. industry is due to shifts in comparative advantage. Today American high-tech and service industries enjoy a competitive edge internationally. However, various American manufacturing industries have been losing their comparative advantage as trade barriers have fallen. Some experts attribute the decline to manufacturers' insufficient investment in research and new-product development, others to the relatively high wages of American workers. In any case, the result is the loss of some jobs as companies downsize, move operations to countries that offer cheaper labor, or even are driven out of business by the competition.

Globalism does have its rewards, however. Many American companies today take advantage of the comparative advantages of various countries by designing their product in one country, manufacturing certain components in certain other countries, assembling the product in still another country, and then marketing it everywhere. The profits enrich the U.S. economy. It also appears that, on the whole, the economies of the United States, Japan, and the nations of western Europe have improved as they have competed in areas of strength; evidence suggests that Mexico, China, and India will follow suit.[11] The unfortunate outcomes of increasing globalism may thus be outweighed by the new jobs that are created and the competitive spur to many nations' productivity.

Trade protection—import barriers or export assistance—is not the solution to the dilemma of disappearing jobs because it is designed "precisely to avoid the need for higher productivity."[12] The effect of Japanese competition on the once-complacent U.S. auto industry proves this point. Instead, the answer for those who view increased international trade with pessimism appears to be more training to upgrade the skills of U.S. workers. Such companies as Deere, Ford, and Motorola are keeping more jobs at home this way. Other tactics include more investment in technology and more innovative management programs to upgrade the productivity of U.S. workers. All of the relatively new ideas of job enrichment, empowerment, and team building are being explored by employers in an effort to achieve a comparative advantage in smart, flexible, committed workers.

Organizations That "Go Global"

Most U.S. companies see opportunities in the international marketplace. For one thing, while the U.S. population maintains steady growth, the populations in other countries are exploding. The World Bank estimates that China, India, and Indonesia combined had more than 2 billion people, that is, 40 percent of the world's population, in 1990.[13] There are huge markets out there, beyond U.S. borders. Protection from domestic risk is another compelling reason for companies to go global. The principle is the same as that behind an investor having a diversified portfolio. Every country has its ups and downs in the economic cycle, many of which are unpredictable. By having operations in more than one country, an organization spreads its risk.

Organizations that "go global" face a variety of challenges, however: cultural differences among the workers in different countries, a lack of economic and technological development in some countries, a difficult political structure, a demographic makeup that may require a change in marketing strategies, and difficulties in obtaining or transporting natural resources needed for production.[14] Nevertheless, many U.S. companies have decided to do business in other countries.

Classification of Global Companies. Organizations that "go global" don't all do it to the same degree. Any organization that engages in some degree of business in other countries is an **international organization**, but only an organization that conducts a large amount of business in other countries is a **multinational corporation (MNC)**. Many of the biggest American companies derive more than half of their revenue from foreign markets: Dow Chemical, Coca-Cola, NCR, Colgate-Palmolive, and Gillette, to name a few.[15]

international organization
An organization that engages in some degree of international business.

multinational corporation (MNC)
A corporation that conducts a large amount of business in nations other than that where it is headquartered.

McDonald's may be the quintessential MNC, with more than 13,000 restaurants in 66 countries. Its restaurant in Moscow is the busiest, serving more than 40,000 customers every day.[16] "We won't stop opening McDonald's franchises until there is one in everyone's backyard," says William Hallett, staff director for international restaurant development. "Our challenge is expanding high-growth markets. We are targeting having a presence in unique sites." Kiosks are being used to do this in busy locations, such as in a Taiwan hospital right next to the counter where patients check in.[17] Plans are also being made to open a franchise in Israel, and Israeli farmers have already begun growing a special strain of McDonald's-approved potatoes for its french

Colgate-Palmolive Company's Suavitel fabric softener dominates the Latin American market, where Colgate's market share is 60 percent or higher and sales are growing.
Photo source: Courtesy of COLGATE-PALMOLIVE COMPANY.

fries, since there is a ban on importing frozen french fries into the country.[18] Still, McDonald's receives more of its income from the United States than from its worldwide markets.

The great opportunities in the global marketplace have prompted some MNCs to change from being home-based companies with worldwide interests to being worldwide companies with a global point of view. This new attitude is expressed by the term ***transnational organization***, suggesting an organization that names "the world" as its address, irrespective of where its plants are physically based, and claims no loyalty to any one particular nation. These organizations conduct their operations wherever they deem most suitable. That is not to say that they take no interest in the communities in which they do business. Many support their host countries with vigor. For example, it is estimated that in 1994 the total charitable contribution of Japanese corporations operating in the United States will be $1 billion.[19]

transnational organization
An organization that conducts operations wherever deemed most suitable in the world, without considering any particular country its home base.

Adjustments in Management Philosophy. Although the United States has been shifting from a manufacturing-based economy to a knowledge-based and service-based economy for a long time, it was not until recently that management approaches began to reflect that fact. Today, service industries such as health care, travel, recreation, food service, entertainment, and insurance provide far more jobs than does manufacturing. Yet, as Karl Albrecht observes, "Our management philosophies have been slow to adapt to the changing reality. Although fewer people do work that needs to be standardized, controlled, and held to minimum variability, the Western view has remained mostly one of determinism and control."[20]

We have been pushed into changing that view. The Japanese applied the quality-improvement concepts of W. Edwards Deming and others to all aspects of management with astounding success. To meet Japanese competition, U.S. companies finally decided to copy what worked. Philip Crosby led the quality-improvement movement in the United States with his book *Quality Is Free.* A PBS program called "If Japan Can, Why Can't We?" turned the spotlight on Deming's teachings. Total quality management (TQM) and variations thereof revolutionized Xerox Corporation, Motorola, and other big companies, and the Malcolm Baldrige National Quality Award became a popular subject of study.[21]

Gradually, a customer orientation grew. Tom Peters and Bob Waterman's *In Search of Excellence* reported that virtually all successful companies operated with a customer orientation instead of the traditional command-and-control style, whether in manufacturing or service industries. Then the Scandinavian Airlines System (SAS) made an impressive turnaround with its heavily customer-oriented *service management* approach when all major European airlines were taking an economic nosedive. The validity of the authoritarian style of management was further challenged. *Service America! Doing Business in the New Economy* by Karl Albrecht and Ron Zemke drew from the SAS success story and several others to win the argument for service management as far as many U.S. organizations were concerned. The result is a "market-driven, customer-focused, value-creating, culture-based approach" that Albrecht refers to as the "total customer-value package."[22]

Globalism can take much of the credit for this adjustment in management philosophy. Consider Donnelley, until recently a completely American giant that produced catalogs, phone books, and magazines. It has constructed plants in Singapore and Mexico; begun joint ventures in Thailand, Hong Kong, France, and Spain; opened a sales office in South Korea; and purchased printing, computer documentation, and translation companies in Britain, Ireland, and the Netherlands. The company prints comic books in Bangkok, telephone books for Prague and Gibraltar, documents for China, and children's books in Mexico. While only 8 percent of last year's revenues came from abroad, Donnelley expects that figure to grow by at least 40 to 50 percent a year in the next decade. Listen to the explanation, from John R. Walter, chairman and chief executive:

> We don't have some wild desire to be outside the borders of the United States. We go with our customers. Certain client groups, including computer hardware and software concerns, telecommunications companies, and financial houses, are going overseas and want Donnelley to go with them.[23]

Thus globalism is not just an opening of borders to companies from other countries. It is the impetus for a profound change in the way companies do business.

Quick Quiz 15.1

1. A human relations professional who recommends a job candidate for a position based on beliefs about the candidate's ethnic background is succumbing to ___________.
2. Four major factors in the genesis of globalism from the late 1960s to the early 1980s were increased industrialization, an increased standard of living, the recession of the 1980s, and ___________.
3. The main reason why some people objected to NAFTA was concern about ___________.

Cultural Awareness

culture
The knowledge, beliefs, values, and behaviors that characterize a society.

A nation's **culture** consists of the knowledge, beliefs, values, and behaviors that characterize its society. Mistakes issuing from ignorance about another country's culture can be devastating. Consider Procter & Gamble's gaffe in Poland when it marketed a shampoo with TV commercials that showed a woman emerging from a swimming pool and then going into a shower. "We don't have swimming pools, and most of us don't have showers. We have baths," explained the president of a Warsaw market-

Gillette has learned the knack of selling to the global emerging middle class, as in this store in Shanghai. The company has also had great success in selling in Latin America, where it made $178 million in operating profits vs. $256 million in the U.S. last year.

Photo source: © Adrian Bradshaw/ SABA.

Photo Exercise

What are some ways that selling might be similar or different in China, Latin America, or the United States?

research institute. P&G also distributed free samples to Polish homes, a maneuver that was interpreted as trying to sell "the garbage they can't sell in the West." Eventually the shampoo, called Wash & Go, became the ignominious subject of a pun, "Wash your hair, and it goes away," and, inexplicably, the name of a vodka drink in Warsaw bars.[24]

Business Culture, Customs, and Language

It is all too easy to make a mistake when doing business with people of other cultures because languages and customs vary so much around the world. For example, offering a gift to a business colleague is strictly forbidden in China though perfectly acceptable in Japan and eagerly anticipated and expected in Arab cultures.[25] If you set an appointment too far in the future in the Middle East, you run the risk of having it ignored. In Asia, it might be rescheduled by a Buddhist for a more religiously favorable date.[26] You can inquire after someone's family and heartily offend the Arab or fail to do so and heartily offend the Mexican.[27] So let's say you try to keep quiet and practice "active listening." You can still offend English or Danish people by standing too close to them. Or you can project an attitude of coldness and lack of interest to the Latin by standing too far away.

The best human relations skills in the world are defeated by a wrong choice of words, and when one language is being translated into another, the wrong choice of words is often possible:

- The slogan, "Let Hertz put you in the driver's seat," translated into Spanish as, "Let Hertz make you a chauffeur."[28]
- The slogan, "Come alive with Pepsi," was scrapped in Asia when its true translation was discovered: "Bring your ancestors back from the dead."[29]
- Gillette had to change the name of its Trac II razor when it found out that it meant "fragile" in some Romance languages.[30]
- Chevrolet learned in time not to market its Nova car in Spanish under that name, since it would translate as "it doesn't go."
- The General Motors slogan, "Body by Fisher," translates into Japanese as "Corpse by Fisher."[31]

To avoid such embarrassing and costly gaffes, companies that intend to do business overseas are well advised to employ the services of someone who is completely familiar with the idiom of the host country.

As globalism takes hold, U.S. companies are finding themselves doing business with some interesting new partners as well as some familiar old ones. The following sections describe the general business culture in a few countries that are currently drawing the attention of American businesses.

Japan. The Japanese have traditionally been taught self-denial and acceptance of privation, but Japanese culture is changing, primarily as a result of increasing affluence. Still, "when the goal is individual well-being, their inexperience often leads to confusion." The result, according to recent surveys, is a lower level of personal satisfaction than Americans on practically every quality-of-life issue; 81 percent of Americans were satisfied with their overall quality of life, compared with only 67 percent of Japanese.[32]

Differences between Japanese and American culture have been abundantly reported, but perhaps one of the most telling differences is that the Japanese, unlike the Americans, have a word, *karoshi,* meaning "being worked to death." Working for Hitachi Ltd. of Japan, one Canadian, Ming Ho, described how workers regularly stayed long past official quitting time and often came in on weekends to work voluntarily. "You'd be seen as slacking off if you didn't stay overtime." Since the company knows that its employees are putting in 12-hour days, every other Wednesday it holds a "Healthy Day," when workers are encouraged to leave the office at the official quitting time. "And people would treat it like a holiday," says Ho. "Everyone would be so happy."[33] Attitudes are changing, however: spouses of those who actually have been "worked to death" are beginning to sue.[34]

Some other Japanese differences noted by Ho were the following:[35]

- The companies involve themselves in the personal lives of their employees to the extent that some, like Hitachi, even provide company-subsidized dormitories to single people, who qualify for a subsidized apartment when they marry. Hitachi also offers loans to employees saving for homes and provides subsidized cafeterias at work and in the dorm.
- Tennis, badminton, soccer, and baseball clubs are sponsored by many employers.
- A Tea Ceremony Club at Hitachi allows male workers to meet female workers. Japanese workers rarely socialize outside their company or marry outside it.
- Employees are hired because of a combination of their grades in school and their personalities, not their expertise. A chemical engineer, for example, might be hired to design computer chips, something completely unrelated to his field.
- As a result of assigning employees to jobs not directly related to their expertise, training needs are sometimes great, with some employees being unproductive for two or three years before they have received sufficient training.
- Employees are expected to sweep their own offices and empty their own trash—part of developing a "family" feeling.
- Women are treated poorly, groped by men on the tightly packed trains that take employees to work and expected to quit as soon as they become engaged to marry. No maternity leave or day-care help is provided.
- Employees must leave phone numbers where they can be reached at all hours, even when they go on vacation. Visitors must write down their name, company, person they are visiting, and time of arrival and departure.
- The "family" feeling engendered by many company rules does produce intense loyalty in most employees, especially those who have been there for a long time. Salary raises are primarily linked to length of service.

Canadian leviathan Diversey Corporation has succeeded beautifully in Japan with Nippon Diversey, so its advice is probably worth heeding: outstanding service, says a company representative, is key in Japan. Its service standards are very high. Also important is a respect for "the Japanese way" of doing business. In other words, a knowledge of and sensitivity to Japanese culture is essential to success in that nation.[36]

England. British culture, so like our own American culture in many ways, is also very unlike it in many others. Take the class system. Despite John Majors's vow to turn Britain into a "classless society," the British still work hard to place a person in that very class system, noting nuances of accent, dress, and taste—and asking subtle questions—to do so. The ways of classifying people have, however, undergone some changes as a result of the changing nature of many jobs and the changing role of women in the workplace. New money is mingled with old, and celebrities vie with nobility for higher status. Still, attempts to eradicate class consciousness are clearly futile: As recently as 1991, when asked to place themselves in a class by a survey, all but 6 percent did so. Sixty-five percent said they were "working-class," which is what most self-identified "middle-class" Americans would be called in Britain.[37]

Russia. Russia's business culture is in transition as its political and economic system shifts from authoritarian communism toward democracy and capitalism. Thus, although Russia for the most part is European in outlook, the business traveler is likely to encounter contradiction and confusion.

Some Russians, uncomfortable with recent changes, cling to the old ways of doing business. In the old managed economy, people were used to pursuing goals set at a higher level; bribes and favors helped to overcome the sclerosis of an overdeveloped bureaucracy. People who didn't show up for work could be prosecuted for "parasitism."

A new class of entrepreneurs has arisen in Russia, however. Certainly the streets of Moscow reveal a "raucous, frantic, gold-rush style of petty capitalism."[38] Conspicuous consumption and the icons of success are far more acceptable than they once were.

China. Like Russia, China is a command economy in the throes of change, and its workers are beginning to throw off apathy and adopt entrepreneurial attitudes. However, unlike in Russia, the government of China still has an iron grip on the economy, going so far as to employ prisoners in the manufacture of goods for export.

Market research in China is practically nonexistent, but some estimate that this country has 100 million consumers affluent enough to buy Western goods. Still, cultural differences can complicate marketing in China. Procter & Gamble, for example, ran into an interesting reason for some Chinese resistance to one of its hair-care products: "Chinese eat rice; Westerners eat wheat. The [shampoo's] ingredients just do not fit the Chinese [hair texture]," said one consumer, Zhang Yong De. Other P&G products, however, are selling extremely well, and more plants and joint ventures are planned. The Chinese urban dweller tends to have a comparatively large disposable income since rents are proportionately very low.[39]

The Dutch-owned Unilever and Japanese giant Kao are making inroads into China, too. Colgate-Palmolive is constructing a new toothpaste factory there. Johnson & Johnson is making Band-Aids in Shanghai and plans another factory to produce baby shampoo.[40] AT&T's vice-president for business development in Asia predicts, "Over the next couple of years, China will be the hottest market in the world."[41]

Poland. Polish culture is theoretically more like American culture than is Chinese culture, but many differences still exist. Although Poles were very happy to see the fall of Soviet communism and the rise of a more market-oriented economy, advertisements that would work in the United States may fall flat in Poland. It is a land of "sen-

Long-term relationships that developed during more than a decade of work in Russia gave Edward Wierzbowski's small TV production company an edge over his global giant competitors. His company, Global American, was the first to persuade Russian TV executives to sell commercial air time to western companies. Wierzbowski is pictured at right.
Photo source: © Chuck Kidd.

sitive and emotional" people, according to Mariola Czechowska, managing director of Young & Rubicam in Warsaw. Colgate has produced a television commercial for Ajax cleanser that features a blond woman dancing from room to room as she cleans to the tune of Bizet's *Carmen,* singing passionately about Ajax. Colgate's Warsaw manager, Richard Mener, led a team of copywriters who decided to substitute phrases such as "touching softly" for "cleaning" to appeal to Polish romanticism. The ad was a hit.[42]

Tips for Global Marketers

Although English is now considered the universal business language, American business customs have not supplanted those in other countries. Even when U.S. companies traded mostly with Western Europe, business travelers were advised to learn about the nuances of local custom. Today, when trade has expanded to regions that have far less in common with American culture, that advice is even more valuable. Always keep in mind, too, that cultures are changing as globalism introduces new outside influences.

Experts agree on the importance of researching a culture before trying to enter its market. Research firms such as Research International, Burke International, Starch INRA Hooper Inc., SRG International, and A. C. Nielsen sell a lot of information gathered by surveys, interviews, and analyses to companies that are not equipped to conduct their own research overseas. General Data-Comm, a $200-million supplier of computer networking equipment based in Connecticut, buys some such knowledge and gathers its own information firsthand on twice-yearly world tours. Thomas Buchert, director of Japanese operations for the company, says this research has allowed access to markets the company would otherwise have found difficult or impossible to enter.[43]

Quick Quiz 15.2

1. Mistakes are easy when doing business with people of other cultures because ____________ and ____________ vary so much.
2. In Russia, China, and Poland, what is the most significant feature of the business culture?
3. What country is predicted by many to become the "hottest market in the world"?

The International Work Force

MNCs and transnationals may have three types of employees:

expatriates
Workers who live in a country of which they are not a citizen.

host-country nationals
Citizens of a country in which the plant or branch of a foreign-based organization is located.

third-country nationals
Citizens of one country who work in another country for an organization headquartered in still another country.

culture shock
A state of confusion, anxiety, and stress related to the need to make cultural adjustments.

1. **Expatriates** live and work in a country of which they are not citizens.
2. **Host-country nationals** are citizens of a country in which the plant or branch of a foreign-based organization is located.
3. **Third-country nationals** are citizens of one country who work in another country for an organization headquartered in still another country.

Organizations that operate in the global workplace often employ all three types. However, the use of host-country nationals is increasing because it is less expensive—the employee does not have to be physically moved to another country, nor does he or she require training in a new culture's customs, language, tax laws, and so forth. Expatriates and third-country nationals, in contrast, need to adjust to the culture in which they have been posted.

Adjusting to a New Culture

Upon arrival in a foreign land, many people experience **culture shock**, a state of confusion, anxiety, and stress related to the need to make cultural adjustments. The food, weather, and language may be different. They may have to drive on the "wrong" side of the street. Their new coworkers may have different productivity norms and employment attitudes. The Japanese, for example, are notorious for their hard-driving work ethic, whereas some other cultures encourage a relaxed attitude that Americans can find quite frustrating. In Germany you might be criticized if you don't leave at the official quitting time. In some nations it is important to begin a meeting promptly. In others it is rude—a little small talk is the norm.

Following are some of the areas in which expatriates may have to make adjustments:

- language and nonverbal communication
- legal environment
- social behavior
- workplace behavior
- work-related ethical standards
- political climate
- physical environment.

The more knowledge you have about these elements of a culture, the better off you will be.

A sensitivity to others' reactions can help smooth over any offenses caused by gaps in your knowledge. Do practice active listening. Be observant. Notice your companion's expressions. Above all, maintain a respectful and considerate attitude inside, where it doesn't show, and your outside mannerisms are less likely to offend.

The Expatriate Personality. Not everyone can easily adapt to a new culture. Those suffering from *ethnocentrism*, the belief that one's own culture is superior to all others, make poor workers in a foreign land no matter how fluent they are in the language or how well versed in the customs.

Even if a person is free of attitude problems stemming from ethnocentrism, he or she might find adaptation to a new culture more difficult than someone else because of personality differences. There are those who relish the excitement of foreign relocation and those who dread the discomfort. Check out your own attitudes on working abroad by taking the "Self-Portrait" exercise.

Self-Portrait

Would You Be a Good Transnational Employee?

Mark "true" or "false" next to each statement.

_____ 1. I would rather work at corporate headquarters in New York than at regional headquarters in Singapore.

_____ 2. If I were transferred to another country, I would prefer to live in an area where citizens of the local culture live rather than in an American compound.

_____ 3. I don't trust the judgment of host-country managers because they are not close to corporate headquarters.

_____ 4. I think I could learn a lot from employees in our different worldwide offices.

_____ 5. I'll wait and learn the German language once I've moved there.

_____ 6. I already know all I need to know about the Japanese people.

_____ 7. I'd rather focus my attention on one country than on several at once.

_____ 8. I've never traveled outside the United States.

_____ 9. I read the international business sections of the newspapers every day.

_____ 10. Consumers in Japan may have very different needs and wants than those in China.

Score: Responses of "true" to statements 2, 4, 9, and 10 as well as responses of "false" to statements 1, 3, 5, 6, 7, and 8 indicate receptiveness to the requirements of transnational employment.

Source: Adapted from N. J. Adler and S. Bartholomew, "Managing Globally Competent People," *The Executive* 6, no. 3 (1992): p. 54.

Lifestyle and Social Custom. Lifestyle differences can be significant. U.S. managers generally have more leisure time and less pressure than their Japanese counterparts. On the other hand, an American who transferred to Paris reports, "I am enjoying a quality of life that is different [here].... Europeans live better and appreciate life and its complexities more than the typical North American." However, another European transplant says in frustration, "It's almost impossible to do business during August [in Europe].... In the United States, a business person tends to sneak off for a day or two. The European thinks nothing of taking a month." Japanese posted to the United States often say they find life less stressful here and the standard of living higher. "I live much better here than I do in Tokyo," says one, and many agree. Others, though, express anxiety about the higher crime levels in the United States and can't wait to go home.[44]

American expatriates are similarly anxious about the political instability in some countries. Unanticipated upheaval may necessitate a sudden return home or—worse yet—an act of terrorism might put expatriates in extreme danger. Many MNCs purchase ransom and extortion insurance and train expatriate managers in techniques to avoid being kidnapped.[45]

Expatriates' families also struggle with lifestyle adjustments, such as a new school for the children. In some countries, wives of expatriate employees may face unfamiliar restrictions on the freedom of women.

American women who are posted overseas are not exempt from such discouraging customs. Regardless of their rank at home, they have to be prepared to overcome the discrimination against women that is culturally acceptable in many other countries. One woman's experience is recounted in the "International Highlights" box.

repatriation
The process of bringing an employee back to his or her home country.

The Return Home. **Repatriation**, the process of bringing an employee back to his or her home country, has its own set of challenges, particularly for those who have

International Highlights

The Global Glass Ceiling

Her years of hard work in Chicago hadn't prepared Vesna Tomic for the humiliation she endured in Tokyo. Tomic, an international telecommunications consultant, and a woman colleague were snubbed there by executives who refused to take their business cards, yet accepted cards from the men who were with them. Exchanging cards is a very important part of doing business in Japan; the gesture indicated that the men did not consider the women part of the business proceedings. The women ignored the snub, and later in the negotiations, Tomic's colleague began to speak Japanese. Jaws dropped and business cards were extended.

Tomic's conclusion? Women have to work twice as hard for international success. From the Middle East and Asia to Latin America, female entrepreneurs confront not only language and cultural differences but gender barriers as well.

It's a set of problems professional women thought they had overcome, at least in the United States, says Stephanie Derderian of The Cultural Transitions Group. Rarely do businessmen in other countries encounter female business owners, so they're often at a loss as to proper behavior. Their responses vary from ignoring women to treating them condescendingly.

For women, says Derderian, the first step is allowing your foreign counterparts to get used to you. She advises finding someone to introduce you to the right people. Karen Post, owner of a Houston ad agency, agrees. "Foreign men treat you better if you go through someone they know."

But whether you are a woman or a man, the key to overcoming the discomfort of others within their own culture is empowering yourself with knowledge. Studying the culture before you visit will arm you with knowledge and allow you to better understand the difference between outright discrimination and cultural discrepancies.

Your cultural differences, be they gender or race based, should not be hidden. Instead, present yourself confidently and be polite yet businesslike. Being well prepared by knowing your business objectives and the subjects of discussion thoroughly is the best way to communicate your effectiveness in international circles.

In sum, exercising the human relations skills you have learned will help open the door to global business success.

Source: "Culture Shock," *Entrepreneur,* July 1993, p. 198.

lived long in one or more foreign lands. Sometimes people become accustomed to certain advantages in their overseas style of living and miss it when they return home. Sometimes they idealize their homeland so much while they are gone that it can only fail to live up to expectations when they return. And sometimes they simply acquire certain habits that are hard to shake. One repatriate tried to bargain with the checkout cashier at a Kmart store during her first week back in the United States before belatedly remembering it was not the custom here.[46]

To ease expatriates' return, many organizations provide counseling for the repatriation experience. A written agreement specifying what the returned employee's new duties will be at home and what path his or her career is likely to take may also be negotiated before the employee takes a foreign assignment.

Managing an International Work Force

Human relations cannot be just American human relations, or even Western human relations, in most organizations today. If your organization does not go abroad for business, people of other cultures may well come to you and work beside you. One way or another, everybody is going to need to learn how to get along with each other in an increasingly multicultural world. Table 15.1 lists some of the requirements for successful management of employees in or from different countries.

One of the most sensitive issues in the management of employees in other countries is the relationship between workers and management. In Mexico, for example,

Table 15.1 **Requirements for Transnational Managers**

1. *Global perspective.* Understanding of the worldwide business environment rather than just focusing on relationships between one or two foreign countries and headquarters.
2. *Local responsiveness.* Readiness to respond to the needs and wants of many different cultures.
3. *Synergistic learning.* Working with and learning from people from many different cultures simultaneously.
4. *Transition and adaptation.* Knowledge of how to learn what is needed about a culture—any culture—in order to adapt to living in it.
5. *Cross-cultural interaction.* Ability to interact cross-culturally on a daily basis rather than just on particular foreign assignments.
6. *Collaboration.* Attitude of equality and mutual respect in interacting with foreign colleagues.
7. *Foreign experience.* Background of "transpatriation" rather than expatriation and career goals that include its continuation.

Source: Adapted from N. J. Adler and S. Bartholomew, "Managing Globally Competent People," *The Executive* 6, no. 3 (1992): p. 54.

workers are more tolerant of an autocratic management style than are workers in the United States or even in Spain.[47] European workers, on the other hand, have strong unions that expect to play a role in management decision making:[48]

- General Motors and Ford in Germany have unionists sit on the board of directors.
- The Gaullist party in France is calling for employee share-ownership programs, and the first action of the new prime minister was to call in the trade unions to discuss the country's economic problems.
- IBM in Sweden has fully unionized operations, including managerial staff.

There are an overwhelming number of differences in working arrangements—hours in the workweek, annual days of vacation, and so on—in various countries. Some are fixed by law, others by unwritten agreement, others by long custom, also unwritten.

Compensation is another area that requires flexibility. *The Wall Street Journal* reports that in most countries the difference between the average pay of managers and the average pay of employees is relatively minor but that "Americans are a breed apart."[49] American CEOs can earn 50 or even 100 times what nonmanagerial workers earn; the figure for Japan, for example, is closer to 10 times.[50]

Another difference in managerial compensation is that U.S. employees must pay many of their own expenses whereas foreign companies, or governments, often foot the bill. For example, U.S. managers have to pay more for their medical care (even when they have good insurance coverage) than the employees of most other countries. In Japan, many companies help pay for vacations and certain living expenses in addition to salaries. In many parts of Europe, the company pays all gasoline bills, including from vacations.[51]

Pay plans for expatriates are especially complicated. Following is a list of just a few of the possible elements of an international paycheck:

- foreign-service premium
- host-country housing cost
- home-country housing deduction
- relocation (mobility) allowance
- language training

The importance of the global marketplace is clearly seen in London's fashionable West End: advertising surrounding the Piccadilly Circus intersection represents many different countries.

Photo source: © The Stock Market/ Robert Matheson, 1992.

Photo Exercise

How many different countries can you identify from the ads/signs found in this photo?

(Answer: Panasonic and TDK—Japan; Coca-Cola and McDonald's—U.S., Burger King—Britain; Fosters—Australia; Sanyo—Japan; Carlsberg—Denmark; Boots and H. Samuels—Britain)

- repatriation allowance
- hardship premiums or hazard pay
- wire-transfer allowance
- home leave
- shipment or storage of household goods
- hypothetical home-country tax deduction.

A sophisticated computer program may be necessary to compute such paychecks.[52]

In the global workplace, expatriates, host-country nationals, and third-country nationals all require training—not only in job-related skills but in human relations skills. Managers who devise training programs thus need to take into consideration the cultures in which they will operate. For instance, many American managers believe that experiential training works best; Asians and Arabs prefer to have skills demonstrated to them by others instead. Interactive videos aren't of much use in Japan, where employees learn best in teams. Faced with such diverse learning styles, the human relations professional in a transnational organization must learn to be flexible. Consider the experience of Johnson Wax, which has a fully developed team-building course. The company does not offer it to employees at its Brazilian plants, however, because Brazilians place such a high value on teamwork (and are so practiced in it) that they would be offended if asked to take a formal course.[53] In this area, you could say, Brazilian workers have a comparative advantage over Johnson Wax's other workers. This is just one more example of the rewards to be reaped from operating in a global workplace.

Quick Quiz 15.3

1. A German citizen who works in Berlin for an American-based company is called a ____________.
2. An American family transferred to Moscow may experience the confusion and anxiety known as ____________.
3. Active listening, observation of expressions, and ____________ are all good methods of showing sensitivity to other people's reactions.
4. Readjusting to life in one's homeland is part of the process of ____________.

Summary

- **Explain how the globalization of business came about.** Some reasons for the globalization of business are that, after World War II, (1) many previously unindustrialized nations became industrialized and began exporting; (2) the standard of living rose in many nations, leading to expanded markets and increased consumer demand; (3) technology brought global communication and transportation and required more technical skills of many workers; and (4) the recession of the 1980s combined with a strong U.S. dollar to make U.S. exports too expensive, forcing U.S. companies to compete with the less expensive products of other nations.
- **List some reasons for a U.S. organization to globalize its business.** The main reason for a U.S. organization to globalize its business is to meet foreign competition. If, in doing so, it sets up operations in foreign countries, it can reduce transportation costs and gauge customer response more accurately. Another compelling reason is to take advantage of the opportunities available in the world marketplace. The expanding population of other countries compared to that of the United States means more consumers and bigger markets. Still another reason is protection against domestic risk by diversifying investments across countries.
- **Contrast a "transnational" organization with a traditional international or multinational one.** A transnational organization views the world, rather than one specific country, as its address, no matter where it has originated. Its employees are encouraged to become knowledgeable about the cultures of many different nations, not just one or two.
- **Discuss some effects of the globalization of business on U.S. organizations.** The globalization of business has had good and bad effects. Many new jobs have been created because of today's globalized business world, but many have also been lost as companies have downsized, moved plants to cheaper-labor countries, or been driven out of business by foreign competition. In some cases wages have been reduced. In others, jobs have been enriched and/or training provided. Quality improvement, downsizing, team building, participative management, and cultural diversity programs are all results of U.S. organizations' attempt to compete with increasing foreign competition and to harvest international opportunities.
- **Explain why cultural awareness is vital in an age of globalization.** The trend toward globalization of business has made multicultural awareness a high priority for people who want to advance their careers and organizations that want to succeed. Experts agree that international research of cultures is important before attempting to enter markets. Cultures in countries such as Russia, Japan, England, China, and Poland are changing; keeping abreast of these changes and practicing good human relations skills such as active listening and a respectful attitude means that companies and organizations can communicate needs to each other more successfully.
- **Identify some of the adjustments that an employee in a foreign country may have to make.** Expatriates may have to adjust to differences in language and nonverbal communication, legal environment, social and workplace behavior, work-related ethical standards, political climate, and physical environment.
- **Identify some of the management issues that complicate global operations.** Workers in other countries often have different expectations of the relationship between management and workers; in Europe, in particular, unions are often involved in management decision making. Compensation varies considerably from country to country, although most do not experience the wide gap between executive pay and worker pay that characterizes U.S. compensation systems. Other countries also tend to provide more nonwage benefits than does the United States, such as housing and vacation expenses. Compensation for expatriates, too, may include a wide array of allowances for special expenses. Finally, training practices have to be adjusted to account for cultural differences.

Key Terms

cultural stereotypes (354)
globalism (354)
comparative advantage (358)
international organization (359)
multinational corporation (MNC) (359)
transnational organization (360)
culture (361)
expatriates (366)
host-country nationals (366)
third-country nationals (366)
culture shock (366)
repatriation (367)

Review and Discussion Questions

1. What are the four factors detailed in the text as leading to today's globalization? Which do you think was the most important? Why? Can you think of other factors?

2. How does globalization hurt U.S. workers? How does it benefit the U.S. economy? Overall, do you think globalization is good or bad?

3. What is comparative advantage? Would it work today in a globalized world? Why or why not?

4. Moreno Textiles is facing increased competition for its richly detailed fabrics; in the last two years, it has lost 10 percent of its market share to firms in eastern Europe. What are some ways Moreno can combat this threat? Does it have a comparative advantage?

5. What is the difference between international and multinational organizations? What is a transnational organization? How would the human relations skills required of employees differ?

6. Applying the five basic aspects of human relations, how are the interrelationships between countries similar to those between members of an organization?

7. Chip's Video Shack, located in a Seattle neighborhood with a growing Indian and Malaysian population, has been the area's major video-rental store for a decade. The neighborhood's new residents, however, are bypassing his shop, full of the latest Hollywood hits, and renting movies of their native countries from a corner fruit market. Friends tell him to close up and relocate, but Chip wants to stay. How can he win these new customers?

8. Are the following expatriates, host-country nationals, or third-country nationals?
   a. Isabel, a Frenchwoman working in Egypt for a Swiss firm
   b. Gordon, a Canadian painter living in New Mexico
   c. John, an American plant manager working in Italy for a transnational corporation
   d. Cito, a Venezuelan working for the UN in Iceland.

9. What are some ways to ease the adjustment for an employee in a foreign country? What would most help you adjust?

10. After three years in Europe, Tetsu Hikada was happy to return home to Japan. However, the adjustment back to 12-hour work days and six-day work weeks was more difficult than he had expected, and his work and home life suffered. How could his company help him make a smoother transition? How compatible are work attitudes in Europe and Japan?

A SECOND LOOK

What comparative advantages does Front Porch Computers enjoy in the global marketplace? What problems of cultural awareness do you suppose affect a business of this type?

Independent Activity

Prepare for an Overseas Assignment

Imagine that you work for a company that has offered you a position in Japan, Europe, Russia, China, or another area that interests you. What steps would you take to prepare for your assignment, independently and with your employer's help?

Skill Builder

Take Note of Gestures

In order to understand nonverbal communication in other cultures, it's a good idea to start with an awareness of meaningful gestures in your own culture. Make a list of gestures—the handshake, raised eyebrows, thumbs up, and the like—that you commonly use, along with their meaning. The next time you use them, be aware of their meaning and the response they generate in others.

Group Activity

Practice Cultural Awareness (20 minutes)

Divide into groups of four or five students. One student in each group will be designated as an employee transferred from Russia or Japan to the United States to work as part of a team including the other students in the group. With the transferee's input, the other students should discuss how they will make the Russian or Japanese employee comfortable both in daily life and as a team member. Be aware of the pitfalls of stereotypes! Discuss how to avoid them if they come up.

Case Study

Campbell Soups Up Foreign Sales

"Carpe Futurum," or "Seize the Future," is the cry of Campbell Soup's CEO, David W. Johnson. The Camden, New Jersey, company's red-and-white cans and its cherubic Campbell's Kids are an American institution. But Johnson does not want the company to be rooted in tradition; a veteran of job stints in South Africa and Hong Kong, he is determined to turn the insular American corporation, now weathering stagnant domestic growth, into a global force in food.

By the year 2000, he wants no less than half of Campbell revenues—which approached $6.3 billion in fiscal 1992—to come from outside the United States. It's an uphill climb; foreign sales have held steady at less than 26 percent for the past four years. Diet is a function of local culture, and because it is not as universal or as easily marketable as soap, cigarettes or soda, prepared food is one of the toughest sales overseas.

Facing cultural obstacles and a lack of brand recognition are the first steps as Campbell enters a global scene already populated by its biggest domestic competitors, H.J. Heinz Co. and CPC International Inc. There has been some success: in western Europe, its Pepperidge Farm cookies, renamed Biscuits Maison, are quickly gaining a following.

Campbell is finding that its canned brands, though much beloved by American consumers, aren't as easily transplanted. Although cream of mushroom soup is a surprise hit among westernized Chinese, Italians shudder at canned pasta; it's "Oh no, Spaghettios." And while the average Pole consumes five bowls of soup a week—three times the American average—98 percent of Polish soups are homemade. A canned soup, let alone a foreign brand, just cannot compete with Mom. The company's advertising, aimed at working mothers, emphasizes convenience. Lee Andrews, Campbell's new product manager in Warsaw, acknowledges that learning what sells will take time. "We can't shove a can in their faces and replace Mom."

By creating new products that appeal to distinctly regional tastes, however, Campbell is making its own successes. A fiery cream of chile poblano soup is a hit in Mexico. In Hong Kong, watercress and duck-gizzard soup is popular.

The latter success is a product of cultural and culinary research in the Hong Kong test kitchen Campbell opened in 1991. The investment is a showcase of Campbell's determination to reach two billion Asian consumers. Though fewer than 1 in 20 varieties tested may hit the marketplace, the Chinese average of one bowl of soup a day per person can mean a big payoff for Campbell. Competing means using local, often exotic, ingredients, but Campbell draws the line on some Asian favorites. You won't find dog soup or shark's fin soups (most species are endangered). But minds—and palates—remain open. Snake soup was recently tested.

Case Questions

1. What global factors led to Campbell's entry into the global market? Do you think it was a smart move? Why or why not?

2. How likely is Campbell to become a multinational company? A transnational? Explain. In what countries might the company have the most success? The least?
3. What kind of comparative advantage does Campbell have over its competitors? Why? Any disadvantages?
4. How effective has Campbell been in learning about other cultures? Have its employees been well trained? What advice would you give them?
5. How likely is the company to achieve Johnson's goal of making half of its revenues from foreign sales? Why?

Source: Joseph Weber and Pete Engardio, "Campbell: Now It's M-M-Global," *Business Week,* March 15, 1993, pp. 52–54.

Case Study

Detroit Vets Tackle Czechs' Tatra

The situation was desperate and the solution unorthodox. But to the government of the Czech Republic and those who live and carve out a living in the East Moravian company town of Koprivnice, working a miracle takes miracle workers.

So they called the Americans to rescue the Czech Republic's Tatra truck plant, which has long provided paychecks for the entire region, at one time employing 16,000 people. Tatra's brawny trucks have a towering reputation in the former East bloc and Third World, but like many other businesses in eastern Europe, Tatra is now awash in debt. Its best customers are broke, and its work force has been cut by a third. Unable to pay lenders and suppliers nearly $136 million in debts, the huge plant halted production in April 1993; by July, the plant had put out only 800 trucks—4,000 fewer than during its heyday. By August, pink slips had gone out to 1,650 more workers, more than 16 percent of the remaining 10,000 workers.

The miracle workers from the West are led by Gerald Greenwald, once heir apparent to Lee Iacocca at Chrysler; he is backed up by David Shelby and Jack Rutherford, both formerly of Navistar International and Ford Motor Co. They call themselves GSR Inc.

The Americans took on the job on the condition that they handle it mostly from their offices in Chicago and Aspen, Colorado. The idea is to return the truck plant to profitability by 1995; if they succeed, they stand to gain a 15 percent stake in Tatra—without expending any of their own financial capital. Any required investments have to come out of Tatra's pockets once a deal has been worked out with creditors.

Residents of Koprivnice gush about what the Americans will do for Tatra. "Look what they did for Detroit," says a fruit vendor. But others with a clearer understanding of the task undertaken by GSR raise their eyebrows, especially at the terms that make the Americans' job at Tatra a salaried, part-time, no-risk, long-distance one.

"You've got to get your hands dirty," says a Czech-based Western manager of a Fortune 500 company's efforts here. "You've got to be there, day in and day out. To say, 'Do this,' and then hope it will be done—that just doesn't work."

The Americans disagree. Rutherford, a truck and tractor specialist for 30 years, counters that he controlled and operated 60 plants around the world without ever visiting a lot of them. "Did that make a difference? I don't think so," he says. "Besides, we have fax machines now. We have satellite phones. It's not like we're going to be out of touch."

Greenwald says Tatra is not an overly complicated situation. More than a decade ago, he was one of the heroes of the Chrysler rescue, acting as chief negotiator with the banks. The company's rebound from the brink of bankruptcy made his boss a folk hero and enhanced Greenwald's reputation as a miracle worker. He contends there is only one basic difference between Chrysler's situation and Tatra's. "When I walked into Chrysler, it had severe cash problems, its management had lost confidence, and worst of all, it had a lousy product. Tatra," he notes, "at least has a sound product."

Case Questions

1. What effect will the Americans' absence have on Tatra's success? How could working there full time increase their chances for success?
2. What information will they be lacking by not being on-site as true expatriates? What kind of human relations skill training might help them better understand the situation and how they are perceived?
3. Do their statements show that the Americans suffer from an ethnocentric attitude? Why or why not?
4. What effect would their failure have on Czechs' perception of Americans? Do you think the Americans should play down their reputations as miracle workers? Explain.

Source: Neil King Jr., "Three Americans Try To Work Miracle At Czech Republic's Tatra Truck Plant," *The Wall Street Journal,* July 7, 1993, p. A7.

Quick Quiz Answers

Quick Quiz 15.1

1. **cultural stereotyping**
2. **technological advances leading to global communication**
3. **loss of American jobs**

Quick Quiz 15.2

1. **language; culture**
2. **the switch to market economies**
3. **China**

Quick Quiz 15.3

1. **host-country national**
2. **culture shock**
3. **a respectful and considerate attitude**
4. **repatriation**

CHAPTER

16

Ethics and Social Responsibility

CHAPTER OUTLINE

Business Ethics

Ethics Codes

Ethics Training

The Perimeters of Privacy

Our Right to Health and Safety

The Environment: Everyone's Concern

Whistleblowers

Ethics Abroad and at Home

It's Legal, but Is It Right?

It's Right, but Is It Necessary?

Social Responsibility and the Company Soul

Going the Extra Mile

Charity Begins with Employees

Caring about Consumers and the Community

Global Responsibility

Social Responsibility Is Here to Stay

Summary

Self-Portrait: How Ethical Are You?

Teamwork Highlights: Birkenstock Task Force Makes an Imprint

Diversity Highlights: No Free Lunch for Denny's

Learning Objectives

- Explain the difference between business ethics and social responsibility.
- Discuss ethics codes and ethics training.
- List some ethical issues of privacy.
- Discuss ethical concerns in regard to health and safety.
- Identify some of today's ethical problems and dilemmas.
- Name some ways that an organization can be socially responsible.
- Discuss why social responsibility is likely to prevail in the future.

Stride Rite's Exit Leaves Big Shoes to Fill

Stride Rite has done plenty of good deeds. Public-service plaques line the walls of its Cambridge, Massachusetts, headquarters. The shoe company has contributed 5 percent of its pretax profit to a foundation, sent 100,000 pairs of sneakers to strife-torn Mozambique, paid Harvard graduate students to work in a Cambodian refugee camp, given scholarships to inner-city youths, permitted employees to tutor disadvantaged children on company time, and pioneered on-site facilities for day care and elder care.

But just a few blocks away from its new headquarters, in Boston's tough, inner-city Roxbury neighborhood, stands Stride Rite's old corporate headquarters, where 2,500 people once made Keds sneakers and Sperry Top-sider shoes. With local unemployment near 30 percent, Stride Rite's citations for good works ring hollow. The jobless workers see a bleak future. "Where are you supposed to go?" asks Miguel Brandao, a Cape Verde immigrant who worked at the plant for 11 years. "There is no place to go."

The company says it had little choice over the past two decades but to pull out of Roxbury—and the rest of New England—and shift most of its production overseas. As much as they wish to link corporate and social responsibilities, the company's directors concede that their primary obligation is to their stockholders. If Stride Rite cannot compete, say executives, it cannot afford its social programs and, just possibly, cannot survive. "It was a difficult decision," admits chairman Ervin Shames. "Our hearts said, 'stay,' but our heads said, 'move.'"

Source: Joseph Pereira, "Split Personality," *Utne Reader,* September/October 1993, pp. 61–66. Photo source: © 1993 Marilyn Humphries/Impact Visuals.

Table 16.1 Ethical Scandals in Business

- Exxon Corporation's oil spill at Valdez, Alaska after Exxon's management had asserted the impossibility of such a disaster.
- Wall Street crime such as racketeering, mail fraud, and insider trading by Ivan Boesky, Dennis Levine, and Michael Milken.
- Housing and Urban Development (HUD) transactions with private escrow agents, allowing the embezzlement of millions of dollars.
- British Airways' breach of the Data Protection Act in tapping into Virgin Atlantic's computer to obtain customer information and breach of the libel laws in its charges against British Airways' chairman, Richard Branson.

Sources: "HUD Embezzlement Probe Ordered," *USA Today/International Edition,* June 13, 1988, p. 3; and "Tactics and Dirty Tricks," *The Economist,* January 16, 1993, p. 23.

business ethics
Moral values that determine business conduct.

social responsibility
The responsibility of organizations to contribute to the well-being of their customers, their employees, their community, and society as a whole.

Ethics are moral values that determine conduct. Just as individuals have moral values, so do organizations, expressed as **business ethics**—ethics applied to a business situation. Closely related is the subject of **social responsibility**, the responsibility of organizations to contribute to the well-being of their employees, their customers, their community, and society as a whole, as illustrated by the Stride Rite vignette.

The idea of business ethics has no doubt existed as long as business itself has existed. However, social responsibility is a fairly recent concept, and the idea that an organization has any responsibility beyond making a profit is still foreign to some people. In general, though, the public has come to expect organizations to assume some degree of social responsibility, and the trend has been to expect more and more.

Although business ethics and social responsibility are certainly related, they are not identical. Just because an organization engages in ethical business practices (for instance, setting prices fairly) doesn't mean it assumes social responsibility (for instance, donating products to individuals who cannot afford to buy them). Further complicating matters, large companies in particular may engage in both ethical and unethical practices and may practice social responsibility in one area (say, the community) while ignoring it in another (say, the environment).

Business Ethics

The first formal course in business ethics was offered by Harvard Business School in 1915. A string of scandals much later in the century (see Table 16.1) prompted a proliferation of such courses at business schools throughout the country. In the 1970s, the study of ethics as part of management education increased, and it became a standard part of the curriculum during the 1980s.[1] Ninety percent of all business schools offer ethics classes today and, globally, more than 20 research units study the topic. In addition, a plethora of business-ethics journals is being published.[2] Finally, prominent individuals associated with various aspects of industry have backed their business philosophies with cold cash. John Shad, former chairman of the Securities and Exchange Commission, recently created a $20-million trust fund for the Harvard Business School specifically to develop a curriculum in business ethics for M.B.A. candidates. Television producer Norman Lear donated $1 million to underwrite the Business Enterprise Trust, which will honor companies and "whistleblowers ... who demonstrate courage, creativity, and social vision in the business world."[3]

Figure 16.1 **The Johnson & Johnson Code of Ethics**

We believe our first responsibility is to the doctors, nurses, and patients, to mothers and all others who use our products and services.
In meeting their needs everything we do must be of high quality.
We must constantly strive to reduce our costs in order to maintain reasonable prices.
Customers' orders must be serviced promptly and accurately.
Our suppliers and distributors must have an opportunity to make a fair profit.

We are responsible to our employees, the men and women who work with us throughout the world.
Everyone must be considered as an individual.
We must respect their dignity and recognize their merit.
They must have a sense of security in their jobs.
Compensation must be fair and adequate, and working conditions clean, orderly and safe.
Employees must feel free to make suggestions and complaints.
There must be equal opportunity for employment, development, and advancement for those qualified.
We must provide competent management, and their actions must be just and ethical.

We are responsible to the communities in which we live and work and to the world community as well.
We must be good citizens—support good works and charities and bear our fair share of taxes.
We must encourage civic improvements and better health and education.
We must maintain in good order the property we are privileged to use, protecting the environment and natural resources.

Our final responsibility is to our stockholders.
Business must make a sound profit.
We must experiment with new ideas.
Research must be carried on, innovative programs developed and mistakes paid for.
New equipment must be purchased, new facilities provided, and new products launched.
Reserves must be created to provide for adverse times.
When we operate according to these principles, the stockholders should realize a fair return.

Ethics Codes

Figure 16.1 shows the ethics code for Johnson & Johnson (J&J), which is fairly typical of large U.S. corporations' codes. Why do most big firms have a written code of ethics? A code that is highly publicized within the organization can have a profound effect on employee behavior. Employees who believe that the organization for which they work is ethical are probably more apt to act ethically themselves. An established, written code of ethics supports employees who may encounter difficult situations. "Many people stumble into unethical behavior without thinking about what they're doing," notes Thomas Dunfee, a social responsibility professor at the Wharton School of Business in Philadelphia. "There is thoughtlessness rather than willful violation. That's why a code is a valuable tool. It provides a checklist before we commit to an action."[4]

In addition, the J&J code states that the company is responsible not only to its customers and stockholders but also to its own employees, citing that everyone must be considered as an individual, be treated with dignity and respect, be compensated fairly, and so forth. Finally, a code of ethics establishes boundaries of behavior that cannot be crossed without consequence—whether reprimand or termination.

Even when a company has a written code of ethics, it can run into ethical problems. For instance, in 1992 the FDA warned J&J that the company was selling two of its specialized surgical products without proper clearance. Company spokespeople

Self-Portrait

How Ethical Are You?

The importance of ethical behavior to the career prospects of different people varies. The following test will help you determine if ethics are likely to play an important role in your career.

_____ 1. If my boss asked me to lie to cover one of his or her mistakes, I would
   a. quit.
   b. lie.
   c. say it made me uncomfortable.
   d. do it this time but refuse if it became a pattern.

_____ 2. If I discovered that I had unintentionally violated an important regulation, I would
   a. file a report acknowledging my mistake.
   b. wait and see if it was as important a violation as it seemed.
   c. discuss the situation with my boss.
   d. try to straighten out the error and talk to my boss if I could not.

_____ 3. If I observed a fellow employee stealing from the company, I would
   a. report the employee.
   b. keep an eye on the employee.
   c. discuss the situation with my boss.
   d. try to make the employee return what he or she stole.

_____ 4. If I knew my boss and another coworker were having an affair, I would
   a. transfer to another department.
   b. ignore it.
   c. wait to see if I was affected.
   d. talk to my boss to clear the air.

_____ 5. If a headhunter approached me with an attractive job offer, I would
   a. talk it over with my boss before proceeding.
   b. ask my current employer to beat the outside offer.
   c. meet the representative of the outside firm and talk to my boss if I was serious about leaving.
   d. ask my employer to make his best offer and then take the highest offer.

claimed that J&J had had "extensive discussions with an FDA official" before launching the product and were told that approval was not necessary.[5] What was the company's ethical responsibility in this case? Who was most likely to be harmed by the misunderstanding—customers (doctors and patients) or stockholders? Should J&J have removed the product from the market?

Ethics Training

Companies often use their ethics code as the focus of *ethics training.* Such training may be restricted to reviewing the code and ensuring that all participants understand its tenets, or it may involve in-depth discussions of ethical dilemmas. Citibank even uses a board game, The Work Ethic, which poses 100 dilemmas for group discussion at staff meetings. Martin Marietta uses "Gray Matters: The Ethics Game," a series of 55 ethical scenarios, including how to explain an absence due to a hangover ("tell the truth").[6]

Just as college and university courses in ethics are proliferating, there has been an increase in the numbers and types of businesses deciding that ethics training is needed for their decision makers. Even attorneys are being targeted. A professor of a course

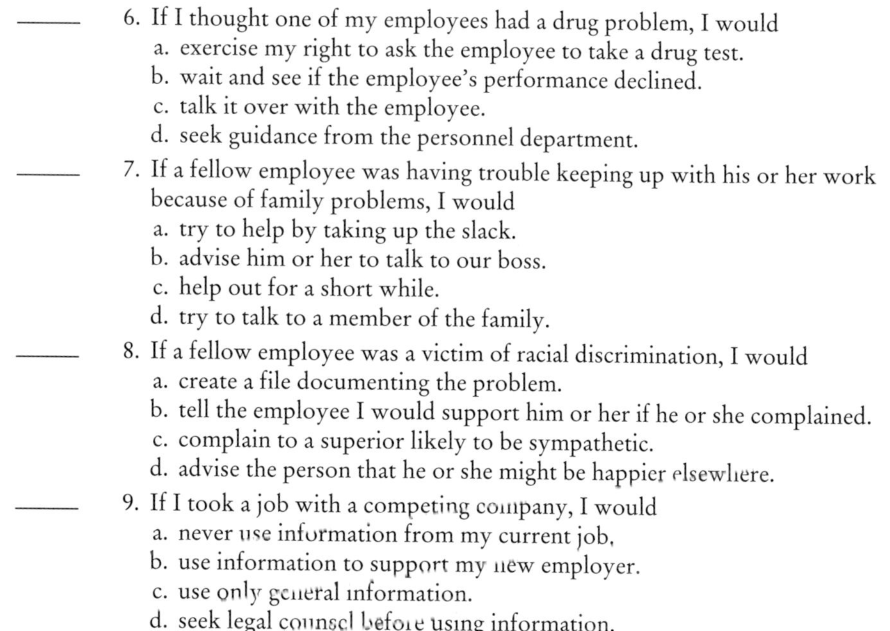

_____ 6. If I thought one of my employees had a drug problem, I would
  a. exercise my right to ask the employee to take a drug test.
  b. wait and see if the employee's performance declined.
  c. talk it over with the employee.
  d. seek guidance from the personnel department.

_____ 7. If a fellow employee was having trouble keeping up with his or her work because of family problems, I would
  a. try to help by taking up the slack.
  b. advise him or her to talk to our boss.
  c. help out for a short while.
  d. try to talk to a member of the family.

_____ 8. If a fellow employee was a victim of racial discrimination, I would
  a. create a file documenting the problem.
  b. tell the employee I would support him or her if he or she complained.
  c. complain to a superior likely to be sympathetic.
  d. advise the person that he or she might be happier elsewhere.

_____ 9. If I took a job with a competing company, I would
  a. never use information from my current job.
  b. use information to support my new employer.
  c. use only general information.
  d. seek legal counsel before using information.

If you answered (a) most often, you have a strong sense of ethics but tend to be rigid. You will run into ethical conflicts in your career unless you find a very like-minded company. If you answered (b) most often, you are too willing to compromise on ethics. You will run into trouble if your job requires you to exercise judgment without clear guidelines. If you answered (c) most often, you have a strong sense of ethics balanced with flexibility. You can act ethically and succeed in most organizations but will leave those that are wholly unethical. If you answered (d) most often, you are unwilling to deal with ethical conflicts. You will run into trouble when others sense that you avoid hard issues.

for attorneys believes teaching these professionals how to be more ethical is a growth industry. "I think lawyers are desperately in need of the training," he comments.[7] Actually, the complexities brought about by information technology, increasing diversity, and the increasing globalization of business have made ethics training more of a necessity today for almost every field of endeavor. Test your own degree of ethical behavior by completing the "Self-Portrait" exercise now.

The Valley of Decision. Andrew Stark, professor of management at the University of Toronto, sees a problem in the way business schools generally choose to teach their business ethics courses: "If in some instance it turns out that what is ethical leads to a company's demise, [the teaching is] so be it." No businessperson, Stark contends, is going to sacrifice his or her company that way,[8] especially since what is ethical might be open to debate. For example, the spotted owl controversy of several years ago pitted this particular endangered species against the jobs of lumberjacks. Reasonable arguments were made on both sides. When people's jobs can be kept only at the price of people's health or life, as in the case of an unsafe nuclear power facility, there is no argument. But so many decisions revolve around suppositions and predic-

Foreign investors are swarming to China, hoping to benefit from double-digit growth. But risks are great and rising. U.S. pension fund managers are increasingly investing funds with Chinese money managers who talk of 40 or 50 percent prospective return. U.S. pension funds helped build this new entertainment center in Guangzhou.

Photo source: Forrest Anderson/Gamma Liaison.

Photo Exercise

Is it ethical to invest pension funds in high-risk foreign markets?

tions, relative advantages and disadvantages, and arguments between people of good faith on opposing sides. Making an ethical decision is just not always simple.

What people need to know, says Stark, is how to juggle the "confusing mix of self-interest, altruism, and other influences"—in other words, the "mixed motives" that are so often involved in business decisions. He observes that a further problem is the tendency of college courses to wrestle with broad questions such as, "Is capitalism ethically justifiable?" instead of more practical, relevant matters.[9]

Robert Solomon of the University of Texas bases his teaching on Artistotle's concept of virtue, which translates to a surprisingly practical approach to business ethics—promoting the qualities of sensitivity, courage, persistence, and honesty, and "a willingness to do what is necessary with an insistence on doing it humanely." The result is compromise. Compromise is likewise the result of the similarly practical approach of Laura Nash of the Boston University Graduate School of Management, who says that in resolving ethical dilemmas, people should think of their business in terms of "covenants"—with employees (subordinates, coworkers, and superiors), customers, and suppliers. Keeping the covenants requires some compromises, and business actions cannot be totally altruistic, but they can be guided to minimize harm to any parties to the covenants.[10]

It Isn't Always Easy Being Ethical. Suppose you are a manager who receives the news that your unsatisfactory employee, Herman, is quitting because he did not get a raise. You are relieved, but you know that if a prospective employer asks for a reference, an honest answer will surely ruin Herman's chances for the new job. You don't want to sentence Herman to the unemployment line and, truthfully, you don't want him to remain in your employ. But what is your responsibility to the employer considering hiring Herman? A personal ethic of honesty would dictate that you tell the truth. But a person with good human relations skills can tell the truth graciously, citing positive qualities in Herman that might predict his success in another type of job, in another company.

On a larger scale, consider the ethical dilemma faced by Genzyme, a Massachusetts-based manufacturer of pharmaceuticals including "orphan drugs" for rare diseases (which cost a great deal to research and produce for a small number of people). Genzyme's product Ceredase, which treats the rare Gaucher's Disease, can cost up to $200,000 per year. The company claims that its profits on the drug are low by industry standards and offers the drug free to patients without insurance.[11] The cost of the drug is outrageous. But the company invested in its research and development and is further practicing social responsibility by giving the drug to those in need. In this case, what *is* the clear ethical path?

The Perimeters of Privacy

In the 1800s, many companies insisted that their laborers go to church on Sunday. During the early 1900s, female schoolteachers in many states were not allowed to marry. And only 80 years ago, Ford Motor Company was still sending social workers to employees' homes "to determine whether their habits and finances were worthy of bonuses."[12]

The United States has become much more sensitive to privacy rights as we head into the twenty-first century. Your employer is not supposed to question your religious beliefs, let alone order you to prayer meeting, and you cannot be questioned as to your marital status. However, soaring health-care costs have prompted a new nosiness about your physical health and therefore personal lifestyle.

Furthermore, the Computer Age makes it possible for many people and agencies, including your employer, to review other aspects of your personal life, such as your credit history. A currently debated issue is whether the employer is obligated to tell a job applicant what was discovered on a credit check or an FBI check of any criminal history. Legislation has been proposed to force credit bureaus to divulge to the consumer, free of charge, what information they have collected.[13]

Legally, employers are required in some instances to respect employees' privacy; in others, they are not. Says one observer, "Today the companies that employ us seem to know everything from our charities to our cholesterol counts, including how much we save, what our credit rating may be, whether our children are toilet trained (the day-care center needs to know), who our heirs are, and what model of car we prefer to rent."[14]

AIDS and Other Health Problems. Another privacy issue concerns the grim specter of AIDS. No decision making is necessary in this case: the law prohibits anyone from passing on information about an employee's HIV status to other employees. Indeed, all employee health records are legally private. The **Americans with Disabilities Act (ADA)** forbids discrimination against people with any kind of health problem, including AIDS, and prevents employers from screening out high-risk (unhealthy) job candidates. Although an employer can make a job conditional on the candidate's passing a physical examination, only a defect that prevents current job performance is a legitimate condition. Future prognoses are not legally relevant.[15]

Americans with Disabilities Act (ADA) An act that forbids discrimination against people with any kind of health problem, including AIDS and substance abuse.

Before passage of the ADA, H&H Music, a Houston retail chain, was able to switch the insurance plan for an employee discovered to have AIDS. H&H switched the employee with AIDS to a policy that had a $5,000 lifetime cap on benefits, while it kept its other employees on their $1-million plans. The courts upheld its right to do this.[16]

Only 10 percent of employees (and their families) accounted for about 70 percent of total medical costs to employers in 1993. If not for the ADA, employers would surely attempt to screen out that 10 percent in the hiring process or terminate them when their poor health status became evident.

Smoking, Bungee Jumping, and Living Dangerously. An organization's ethical—and financial—concern for employees' health can infringe on privacy rights. For example, does your employer have the right to tell you not to smoke when you are at home? Some say yes. Turner Broadcasting has refused to hire smokers since 1986.

North Miami requires applicants to sign an affidavit that they have not used tobacco products for the previous year.[17]

In a survey by the National Consumer's League, 80 to 96 percent of respondents complained that companies have no business asking questions related to employees' health.[18] Some states have passed laws shielding smokers from discrimination. A few have gone further and passed laws to protect employees from employer infringement on other off-duty behaviors such as bungee jumping and other activities deemed dangerous by insurance companies. Best Lock Corporation fired a machine operator for having a couple of drinks every night after his shift ended, which indicates how far the invasion into privacy can go unless state laws intervene.[19]

The Debate on Drug Testing. The reason for drug testing to detect cocaine, amphetamines, heroin, and other controlled substances in the urine is understandable enough: it is the best way for an organization to protect itself from the poor performances and possibly disastrous mistakes of drug-dependent employees. The federal government requires that all contractors who do more than $20,000 worth of business with Washington conduct random tests on their workers. Many companies test all new hires. Motorola tests all employees every three years.[20]

Although the reason for such testing is clear, some argue that it still may not be justified. The occasional report of a falsely positive test stirs fresh alarm at this invasion of privacy. The problems that drug abusers cause for their coworkers, however, fuel the counterarguments defending the tests.

Although drug testing is legal, publishing the results of the testing is not. Employees who are battling alcoholism or drug addiction are legally entitled to confidentiality.

Even Your Mind May Not Be Private! In the 1960s, many types of psychological tests were ruled illegal invasions of privacy unrelated to work performance due to their delving into such subjects as whether job candidates felt they "deserved severe punishment for their sins."[21] Today the pen-and-pencil "honesty" or "integrity" tests are a target of protest. They also ask some deeply personal questions in an effort to reveal the candidate's overall trustworthiness. Lie-detector tests, once a staple of many businesses, have been outlawed.

Electronic Monitoring. A bill was introduced in 1993 to restrict employers' eavesdropping on customer service operators to those with fewer than 60 days on the job.[22] Of course, a valid argument can be made for electronic monitoring—how else can supervisors evaluate certain kinds of performance? But electronic surveillance smacks too much of Big Brotherism to avoid criticism.

Managerial workers sometimes have less privacy than lower-level workers. Generally, the CEO can tap into the computer database of a managerial employee to check his or her progress on a job at any time. Employers have the right to read workers' e-mail (electronic mail), as proved in the following case: Two Nissan employees who traveled the United States training car dealers, sales staff, and mechanics in how to use the company's e-mail system used that system themselves for some racy conversations with students and disparaging remarks about a supervisor. The conversations were read by that very supervisor, who overrode the employees' passwords to do so. Their grievance was rejected by the courts.[23]

Our Right to Health and Safety

The Occupational Health and Safety Act (OSHA) forced employers to consider employees' health and safety to a degree. Some have gone further than the law requires. Smoking bans and "wellness" programs that actively seek to promote good health enter the area of social responsibility, which we will discuss later. Good *ergonomics*—the science of fitting the physical workplace to the worker—has recently become an ethical issue. Although carpal-tunnel syndrome (contracted by workers who spend much time at computer keyboards) is not as serious as black lung disease (contracted by coal miners), it is nevertheless a work-related injury that can be prevented by an ergonomically correct environment. Computers cause a host of physical problems, from the aforementioned syndrome to eyestrain, and some 60 million workers use computers daily. By the year 2000, an estimated 75 percent of all jobs will involve the use of a video display terminal.[24] Thus, the Computer Age has brought new health issues to the ethical forefront.

An ethical dispute arises in the special case of jobs that cause sterility or may result in birth defects in the fetus of a female employee. Does an organization have the right to bar women from such jobs? Do women have the right to sue an organization for sterility or birth defects resulting from workplace hazards?

Businesses are held accountable for the health of both their employees and their customers. After an outbreak of E. coli bacterial infections from its hamburgers, Jack in the Box instituted a program of seven separate quality-control checks for its hamburger meat. Scores of restaurant companies reviewed their cooking procedures for all types of food since, as the representative of one dinner-house chain said, "It could happen to anyone."[25]

The Environment: Everyone's Concern

No one wants to be thought of as a tree hater; no one is in favor of dirty air and water; no one wants to kill the grasses and flowers of the earth; no one enjoys the sight of a grease-laden duck drowning in an oil slick. But when environmental protection is pitted against that other green thing—money—scruples often fail.

At a recent meeting of the Royal Society of Arts, the following hypothetical problem was posed to a panel: Suppose you, as chairman of a huge for-profit organization, learn that it will take a staggering amount of money to rectify environmental harm caused by a product. Would you conceal the matter to save the money? All averred that, without a doubt, they absolutely, positively would not hesitate to make the necessary reparations. Simon Duffy, group finance director of Thorn EMI, formerly of Guinness, had posed the question. "I am delighted to think you would all make that decision," he said, "but, in my opinion, you are not that representative." In his personal experience, of three companies in such a situation, not one had chosen the virtuous path. It is worth noting, however, that one of the panelists, Robert Horton of Railtrack, formerly of BP, had faced just such a problem in his time in the United States and had spent $40 million to make environmental amends.[26]

Since the Clinton administration has vowed to cut pesticide use in the United States, products based on the ethics of avoiding harm to the environment may enjoy increased success in the 1990s. An agricultural spray called ENVIReppel, for example, produced by Guardian Spray Corporation, fights insects with a garlic and pepper solution instead of harmful chemicals. Ecogen Inc., a large biotechnical company, produces NoMate, a substance that disrupts the mating process of tomato pinworms. These safer products, however, are usually somewhat less effective than the poisonous chemicals that companies such as Dow Chemical produces—perhaps 80 percent effective compared with 99 percent, says Phil Hutton of the Environmental Protection Agency (EPA). And "a little cosmetic injury on food is important. If it doesn't look good, people won't eat it."[27] Consumers, then, can hinder the goal of environmental safety as much as producers do.

Usually, though, the problem is money. Money wouldn't be much good on a planet with unbreathable air, undrinkable water, and poisonous food, but the temptation to push the limits as far as possible is always there in the business world. Perhaps those who break the laws comfort themselves with the thought that "it isn't really that bad," and perhaps it isn't. But it could be, later. That is why ethical people—and whistleblowers, discussed next—are so valuable to have around when decisions that affect our physical environment are being made.

Whistleblowers

whistleblowers
People who are willing to risk their jobs in order to report unethical practices of the companies they work for.

Whistleblowers are people who are willing to risk their jobs in order to report unethical practices of the companies they work for. In years past, virtue practically always had to be its own reward for the whistleblower, since he or she often lost the job and had to substitute a lesser one, but today many whistleblowers are rewarded for their actions. Consequently, the whistleblower may actually be someone scheming to advance his or her wealth. That is what Chester Walsh, a former General Electric (GE) employee who exposed a defense-contract fraud, was accused of. He was awarded $11.5 million for his action, but the Justice Department turned against him as the investigation proceeded, charging that Walsh gathered evidence of the fraud for four years before filing the suit and never reported his suspicions to anyone at GE. As a result, GE asked for reform of the False Claims Act, a federal statute that allows employees to sue their employers on behalf of the government and collect as much as a quarter of the assessments and fines, thus offering a type of "bounty."[28]

Society owes much to the whistleblowers who halted their companies from dumping pollutants into our drinking water under cover of night or exposed information about defective products that their companies had deemed too expensive to recall, to name just two examples. Some of these people were genuine ethical heroes—rare in any culture and any business.

Ethics Abroad and at Home

Ethics vary from culture to culture, based on each culture's norms and values. The Foreign Corrupt Practices Act prohibits U.S. businesses from bribery but, in many parts of the world, bribery is viewed as part of the cost of doing business. Jeannette R. Scollard, author and lecturer, tells of an American entrepreneur who discovered, after purchasing a Caribbean island, that "nothing could be accomplished until a massive dispensation of bribes was first negotiated." He had to sell to a European entrepreneur who was not constrained by the U.S. Foreign Corrupt Practices Act.[29]

Uruguayan essayist and author Mario Benedetti notes that big corporations have ways other than bribery with money (or even blonde "secretaries") to accomplish their purposes. Political influence, the promise of a favorable vote in an international organization, the cover-up of "carefully orchestrated scandals," offers of privatization, and so forth can accomplish the same ends.[30]

International business espionage is also a problem. The information that the French government had targeted a "hit list" of U.S. aerospace companies for industrial espionage has been cited by some as evidence for making the Central Intelligence Agency (CIA) help U.S. businesses keep competitive internationally. Amy Borrus, a writer for *Business Week,* grants the appropriateness of the CIA protecting U.S. trade secrets from foreign governments but cautions against its use to spy out foreign business secrets. She quotes Michael Sekora, president of Technology Strategy Planning Inc. and a former Defense Intelligence Agency official, as saying, "If you really want to hurt the [foreign offenders, like the French in this example], you limit their access to technology in general and counterattack. You sever some U.S. research agreements with them and deny access to U.S. labs."[31] International business obviously raises a host of ethical decisions for U.S. companies.

Human rights issues influence business ethics (and social responsibility) as well. For instance, the Chinese government engages in what many Westerners view as horrendous human rights violations. Thus, some people argue that American companies should not do business in or with China. Levi Strauss has announced plans to leave China because of its "pervasive violation of human rights." (It should be noted that the company has sold little there.) Firms such as AT&T and Boeing, which stand to gain a lot from the Chinese market and plan to increase their presence there, admit that the country's human-rights record is indeed dismal. Child labor, convict labor, forced sterilization of women, and imprisonment for political and religious beliefs all flourish in China. State-owned Capital Steel in Beijing works its employees 365 days a year.[32] A growing number of companies, including Reebok International and Sears, Roebuck and Company, are pressuring their Chinese contractors to observe certain human-rights policies.

It's Legal, but Is It Right?

Some actions that are technically legal—and profitable for a company's shareholders—might be deemed unethical because they generate a profit at the expense of someone else's well-being. Consider the subject of the **hostile takeover**—an acquisition of one company by another despite the acquired company's unwillingness. Many jobs are lost when the new owners take charge.

hostile takeover
An acquisition of one company by another despite the acquired company's unwillingness.

golden parachute
The provision of a few years' annual pay plus benefits to executives who lose their jobs because of acquisitions.

leveraged buyouts (LBOs)
The borrowing of huge amounts against a firm's equity to purchase equity in other firms, which can then be sold at a profit.

Consider, too, the **golden parachute**, which provides a few years of annual pay plus benefits to executives who lose their jobs because of acquisitions and does nothing for the nonmanagerial workers or lower-level managers—who are presumably hurt far worse. Similarly generous arrangements are often made for top managers who leave a company for other reasons, such as early retirement. Ralston Purina Company paid William H. Lacey, former head of its pet food and grocery businesses, $1.4 million in severance after his retirement (at age 52) following several unprofitable quarters for the company.[33] It's legal, but is it ethical?

Leveraged buyouts (LBOs) have been questioned on ethical grounds as well. Here managers borrow huge amounts on their firm's equity to purchase equity in other firms, which they can then sell at a profit. The idea is to break a company into parts that can be sold for higher profits than the company could as a whole. Again, many jobs are lost as a result of the breakup.

Downsizing—laying off employees to achieve a leaner corporate structure—can help a floundering firm survive and a prospering one prosper even more. Moving operations to cheaper-labor countries is another way to improve a company's financial status. But is it ethical to shove all those Americans out of their jobs? Of course, if no one is laid off, eventually *everyone* might be, since the company might go under. In steering a middle course, firms sometimes offer employees the option of pay cuts. Early retirement packages are another inducement used to avoid layoffs. The best choice appears to be training to upgrade employees to higher-level jobs.

It's Right, but Is It Necessary?

Two opposing courses of action may have equally compelling advantages, and both may be ethically pure. When one moral good is pitted against another, decision making gets really difficult. In the mid-1980s, Control Data Corporation did good

John Trent worked for 23 years for Digital Equipment. In May 1992, he opted for an early retirement package instead of being forced out of the company. With four children, Trent now works as a car-service driver for 10 hours a day for minimum wage plus tips, and his wife Joan is a waitress.
Photo source: © Steve Lewis.

Photo Exercise

Is it ethically correct for workers like John Trent to be removed from their jobs for the economic benefit of the company?

things for its employees and society by starting employee assistance programs (discussed later) and building plants in the inner city, but it did so at the expense of profits. The result was replacement of the chairman and restructuring.[34] The company's efforts at social responsibility may have gone beyond the realm of practicality, since they led to a restructuring.

Quick Quiz 16.1

Mark "true" or "false" next to each statement.

1. An employer must inform employees that one of their coworkers is HIV positive. ______
2. These days, whistleblowers almost always lose their jobs. ______
3. Bribery is considered unethical worldwide. ______
4. A company can practice good human relations and take care of its employees during downsizing by training them for higher-level jobs. ______

Social Responsibility and the Company Soul

enlightened self-interest A self-interest that is not in conflict with the social welfare but is tempered by it.

Adam Smith's *The Wealth of Nations,* published in 1776, claimed that business should pursue its own self-interest. No capitalistic society challenges that tenet, but it has been modified in recent years by the prevailing view of **enlightened self-interest**, meaning a self-interest that is not in conflict with the social welfare but is tempered by it. The modern idea is that profit making should not be a company's sole goal; it might well be the primary goal, but not the only one.

Actually, for-profit organizations usually see their main goal as maximizing *shareholder wealth,* which is not exactly the same as maximizing profit. Sometimes annual reports even state this to be the primary goal. It is achieved by maximizing the value of a firm's common stock rather than raising its profit. Shareholder wealth can in fact decline despite rising profits because of the mechanics of the risk-return trade-off. The price of common stock reflects both profit and the risk assumed by the firm and thus reflects the actual wealth of the shareholders.[35]

Today, businesses have so much more to consider than profit—the past and present effects of discrimination, the spoiling of our air and water, the decline in educational fitness of graduates, and the day-care and elder-care needs of dual-career

Teamwork Highlights

Birkenstock Task Force Makes an Imprint

Encouraging and empowering employees, both in their jobs and in their outside interests, can create a synergy that benefits both the employees and their organization. In at least one case, the environment has benefited, too.

Birkenstock Footprint Sandals had always embraced a wide variety of environmentally conscious practices, but back in 1989, a marketing department employee thought that the Novato, California, company could go further.

She approached her boss, who encouraged her to form what would become a 12-member "eco-task force." The group, whose members represented all company departments, began to study and draft suggestions on how the cork-heeled sandal maker and its distributors, as well as other businesses, could improve recycling efforts and decrease the amount of energy used in daily operations.

The task force grew so popular that Birkenstock granted its members one hour a week of company time to spend on related ideas. Among the group's accomplishments: an in-house environmental library, a guide to nontoxic resources, a newsletter on relevant internal activities, and monthly meetings with neighboring businesses to share ideas on conservation.

Birkenstock's interest in and support of its employees' concerns has strengthened its ties with its work force. While the team helped the company cut energy costs, together they were building a more motivated and loyal group of workers who can boast of high productivity and low turnover. The company's vice-president, Mary Jones, says Birkenstock tries to create an environment where employees can contribute and feel enthusiastic about what they are doing. She adds, "I'm really here to help out."

Source: Howard Rothman, "The Power of Empowerment," *Nation's Business*, June 1993, p. 49.

families. If an organization wants to be socially responsible, it has lots of ways to be so. And as you can read about in the "Teamwork Highlights" box, being socially responsible can benefit an organization and its employees.

Going the Extra Mile

Community, state, and federal governments set minimum rules for zoning, waste disposal, safety, and so forth, to guard the social welfare, and these rules have become more numerous and specific as time goes on (see Table 16.2). Following these laws, not only to the letter but also in spirit—that is, not looking for ways to legally skirt around them—is part of being socially responsible. An organization might give attention, for example, to ergonomics that will make its employees more comfortable, not just safe.

In a sense, manufacturing a needed product at a fair price and resisting the temptation to increase profits at the expense of quality is an expression of social responsibility, too. The organization that does this is not only providing for customers' needs but also providing employment. Creating a pleasant, comfortable working environment (ergonomics again) and giving fair compensation and benefits to employees is another part of social responsibility.[36] Training can be, too. It is estimated that more than 50 million workers need additional training to enable peak efficiency in current jobs, at a cost of about $30 billion a year. Expert Richard M. Krieg says, "The systems necessary to accomplish this task are not currently in place."[37] Socially responsible organizations are addressing that need.

Finally, voluntary social activities, donations to charitable organizations, corporate sponsorship of local or national nonprofit organizations or community projects (like tutoring inner-city schoolchildren), and even support for the arts may be undertaken to contribute to society's welfare. For instance, as one of its many socially responsible programs, the huge pharmaceutical company Merck donated cotton linens and clothing to the Good Samaritan House, an emergency shelter for women and children in Selma, California. This was not a random gesture. The shelter is located in the San Joaquin

Table 16.2 **Primary Functions of Several Federal Agencies Involved with Social Responsibility Legislation**

Federal Agency	Primary Agency Activities
Equal Employment Opportunity Commission	Investigates and conciliates employment discrimination complaints that are based on race, sex, or creed
Office of Federal Contract Compliance Programs	Ensures that employers holding federal contracts grant equal employment opportunity to people regardless of race or sex
Environmental Protection Agency	Formulates and enforces environmental standards in such areas as water, air, and noise pollution
Consumer Product Safety Commission	Strives to reduce consumer inquiries related to product design, labeling, etc., by promoting clarity of these messages
Occupational Safety and Health Administration	Regulates safety and health conditions in nongovernment workplaces
National Highway Traffic Safety Administration	Attempts to reduce traffic accidents through the regulation of transportation-related manufacturers and products
Mining Enforcement and Safety Administration	Attempts to improve safety conditions for mine workers by enforcing all mine safety and equipment standards

Source: Samuel C. Certo, Stewart W. Husted, Max E. Douglas, *Business,* 3e, © 1990, p. 76. Reprinted by permission of Prentice Hall, Englewood Cliffs, New Jersey.

Valley, where Merck Agvet markets a product designed to control mites in cotton fields. "The Good Samaritan House serves the community in which our farmers live and produce fiber," explains Michael J. Kelly, executive director for sales for Merck Agvet U.S. Operations.[38] Such actions enhance the corporate image, which helps a firm compete, so in the end, even those who advocate profit or shareholder wealth as the only legitimate goal of business might approve of some socially responsible actions.

Charity Begins with Employees

Let's look first at the ways organizations can exercise their social conscience in regard to those closest to them—their own employees. Work life, personal life, and family welfare may all be targeted for help.

Minorities and Women. Some organizations are more aggressive than others in attempting to make amends for past discrimination against women and minorities in employment. For example, the auto industry is called "one of the most racist businesses" by Robert A. Hill, president of the National Association of Minority Automobile Dealers.[39] Under pressure from civil rights groups, the auto companies have made special efforts to recruit minorities and women, but sometimes it appears their heart is not in it. Ford Motor Company, for example, is being sued by graduates of its minority dealer training program on the grounds that the company lured them into poor locations where they were bound to fail. Women rarely seem to obtain dealerships.[40]

In contrast, the accounting profession is using workshops, flexible work arrangements, and specialized career planning to bring women up to the higher ranks of management, and now 20 percent of managers for the six biggest firms are women.[41]

Firms seeking to become more socially responsible in redressing the wrongs of racial and gender discrimination often institute programs (called "Valuing Diversity"

Diversity Highlights

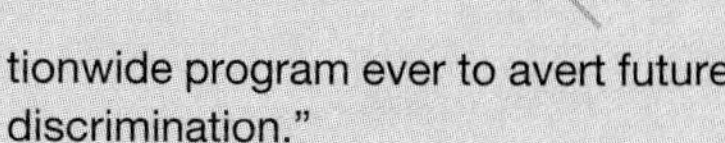

No Free Lunch for Denny's

Robin Thompson wore a suit identical to those worn by the rest of the Secret Service detail that stopped for breakfast at the Denny's in Annapolis, Maryland. Not that it should have mattered. Denny's was not a restaurant where coats and ties were necessary for service; only shoes and shirts were required.

But Thompson, along with the 5 other African-American agents in the 21-member contingent, didn't get breakfast. Although the entire detail was seated in the same section, identically dressed down to the gun strapped over their shoulder, Thompson says only the white members of the party were served. "I was somewhat invisible that day."

He did not remain invisible. The black agents filed a discrimination suit against Denny's Inc., a division of Flagstar Companies Inc.

Since the lawsuit, Denny's has terminated the manager of the restaurant for failure to report a complaint of alleged discrimination involving customer service. But the chain denied any wrongdoing, blaming the incident on "slow service."

Denny's was already on the defensive; the Annapolis incident occurred on the same day a federal court in California was ordering the company to stop discriminating against blacks. The U.S. Justice Department said it had substantiated allegations that Denny's discriminated against blacks in more than 300 California restaurants. Overall, the chain was hit with 4,300 complaints of racial bias from coast to coast.

In just over a year, the suit was settled and the company was ordered to begin what the Justice Department called "the largest nationwide program ever to avert future discrimination."

Denny's was ordered to pay a record $46 million to black patrons as well as nearly $9 million in lawyers' fees for the black customers. It also was ordered to retrain employees, feature minorities in its ads, and hire an outside lawyer to monitor its civil rights compliance. In addition, Denny's will conduct 625 unannounced tests next year to ensure that its 1,500 restaurants stop refusing to serve blacks, imposing cover charges on them, demanding that they pay in advance, or presenting other conditions not required of whites.

Sources: Jerry Thomas, "Invisible Patrons Demand to Be Seen," *Chicago Tribune,* June 10, 1993, section 3, pp. 1–5; *Chicago Tribune,* May 25, 1994, section 1, p. 3.

or a similar term) for deepening employees' sensitivity to multicultural issues. A board game, The Diversity Game, even exists for this purpose.[42]

Some companies, however, are unable to learn the lessons of and abide by the laws banning racial or gender discrimination and have to be forced to change their ways. One such company is profiled in the "Diversity Highlights" box.

Physically Challenged Employees. The ADA has set legal guidelines for being fair to physically challenged employees and job candidates, but some socially responsible companies go further and actively recruit the physically and mentally challenged. Those that do usually report good results. Jack Kaeufer, a business owner who began hiring those with disabilities ten years after experiencing a temporary disability himself, speaks for several when he says that physically challenged people "are committed to their jobs, and I'd recommend them to any employer."[43]

Goodwill Industries, The National Easter Seal Society, and other such organizations give organizations a lot of support in hiring and training the physically challenged. The federal government also issues special tax credits, and state and federal job training programs reimburse the employer for a portion of training costs. "We make a determined effort to perfectly match our [physically challenged] workers with the employers' job requirements," says Judith J. Smith of an Easter Seal program in Alabama. "We rarely see a disability impact the job performance if the worker and job position are properly matched."[44]

Take Good Care of Yourself. It is not only socially responsible for an organization to help employees stay healthy, it is also cost effective. The average cost of providing

Table 16.3 **Costs to DuPont in Medical Claims and Sick Days**

A study of 46,000 DuPont employees showed the following costs in medical claims and sick days for the average

• smoker	$960
• overweight person	401
• alcohol abuser	369
• person with elevated cholesterol	370
• person with high blood pressure	343

Source: "Can Smoking or Bungee Jumping Get You Canned?" *Fortune,* August 9, 1993, p. 92.

health insurance had risen to about $4,000 per employee in 1993, up from just over $1,600 in 1983. Since the ADA prohibits an organization from screening out the employees that account for most of these costs, the only course left is to try to keep everyone as healthy as possible. Consider the following:[45]

- A four-year study by Control Data Corporation found that medical claims for overweight employees were 11 percent higher than for those of normal weight, and those for smokers were almost 20 percent higher than for nonsmokers.
- U-Haul discovered that a few hundred of its 18,500 employees were responsible for 44 percent of the company's medical costs and that their illnesses were the type that a healthier lifestyle could have prevented.
- Hershey Food Corporation discovered that 30 percent of its premium costs were related to preventable health risks.

Table 16.3 provides related information found in a study of DuPont's employees in the late 1980s.

Various companies are trying to lower health costs by either rewarding healthy habits or penalizing unhealthy ones monetarily. Here are some examples:[46]

- Southern California Edison in Rosemead, California, gives a $10 monthly rebate on health insurance to employees who pass a voluntary health-risk screening.
- Johnson & Johnson gives warm-up clothes, cookbooks, and other health-related gifts to those participating in health promotion activities.
- U-Haul International requires a $5 contribution for health insurance from smokers and those who do not fall within weight guidelines.
- Baker Hughes Inc. charges a $10 additional health insurance premium per month for smokers.
- Hershey penalizes (or rewards) workers according to their cholesterol count, blood pressure readings, weight, and smoking and exercising habits.

Some companies believe in the stick as well as the carrot and actually punish employees who do not hew to the healthy lifestyle: Butterworth Hospital of Grand Rapids, Michigan, docks employees who do poorly on physical health tests or refuse to cooperate with its health program up to $25 per biweekly paycheck (the "good" employees get up to $25 extra).[47]

And just what is involved in the "healthy lifestyle"? Some employers ask their workers to drink only moderately; others ask for teetotalers. Some keep track of their weight and blood pressure and even their cholesterol count. Some want to know if they are using their seat belts when they drive, having a healthful breakfast before work, indulging in too much red meat and not enough vegetables, or enjoying risky hobbies like scuba diving, motorcycling, or bungee jumping.[48] Add to that list skydiving and mountain climbing for Multi-Developers Inc.[49] And unless a state specifically protects jobs from this new kind of "dangerous hobby" discrimination, a person can indeed be fired because of it. Some companies simply go too far, many charge, in assuming this particular social responsibility.

Do financial health incentives work? Money might not be an effective motivator for making lifestyle changes. When Security Pacific National Bank offered $120 to employees who passed a health-risk screening, only 10,000 of 200,000 showed up. The vice-president of corporate health promotion, Gina Brandenburg, believes that those who participated did so because of a genuine interest in their own health, not for the financial incentive.[50] However, more and more companies seem to be going this route in an attempt to keep health costs down.

Helping Employees Help the Community. Sometimes the welfare of employees and of the community can be benefited in one stroke. An increasing number of companies have programs that encourage employees to "reenergize" themselves by engaging in philanthropic efforts such as creating affordable housing for the working poor or tutoring inner-city schoolchildren. Xerox Corporation's Social Service Leave Program grants sabbaticals for such purposes. A daily newspaper in Virginia, *The Virginian-Pilot,* promotes a variety of "personal-growth" ventures for its staff, including academic study, hiking the Appalachian Trail or undertaking another such adventure, and volunteer work.[51]

Helping Employees with Their Families. Company-sponsored day-care and elder-care programs, flexible working arrangements that allow employees to juggle work and family responsibilities, family and medical leave policies, and employment assistance for spouses of employees are some of the ways organizations today help their employees' families. The increasing numbers of single-parent families and dual-career couples make this kind of help more and more necessary, and the public today is expecting employers to provide it. A Boston consulting firm even offers a board game, Smart Moves, which aims to open managers' eyes to employees' concerns about balancing work and family.[52]

Employee Assistance Programs (EAPs). To deal with today's escalating problem of substance abuse, as well as mental illness and various personal problems of employees, socially responsible organizations often establish *employee assistance programs (EAPs).* These programs attempt to identify troubled employees and either directly provide or refer them to the help they need. They are based on the idea that personal problems often underlie problems in work performance. It is assumed that substance abusers will not admit their problem unless confronted with proof of a poor performance. EAPs sprang from the job-related alcoholism programs that began in the 1940s. Currently there are more than 13,000 such programs in the United States.[53]

Passage of the Drug Free Workplace Act in 1988 encouraged organizations to establish EAPs, since it requires those that receive federal grants or contract amounts of more than $25,000 to have a written drug-use policy that entails advising employees where to obtain counseling. Furthermore, EAPs help an organization comply with the ADA, which requires that they make "reasonable accommodations" to help disabled employees improve work performance, and those suffering from alcoholism or drug addiction are specifically included.

Stress Management Programs. Because of the current interest in the effect of stress on work performance, many organizations are attempting to help their employees

Managerial burnout can result from stress. Providing stress management programs by helping bosses come to terms with their anxieties when they must fire employees is Donald Rosen (seated, center) of the Menninger Clinic.

Photo source: © Max Aguilera-Hellweg.

learn how to manage stress. Excessive stress has been revealed as the cause for many psychological problems, psychosomatic symptoms, and even lack of job satisfaction and commitment.[54]

Seminars on stress management and time management, exercise programs, relaxation exercises, assertiveness training, and even biofeedback and meditation training are being provided by various organizations as a means of combating the deleterious effects of stress. In addition, some firms are looking for ways to redesign jobs to eliminate the sources of excessive stress.

Caring about Consumers and the Community

When critics charged fast-food chains with being socially irresponsible in selling high-fat, high-cholesterol products that contribute to heart disease and other ailments, McDonald's set out to prove it wasn't so. It created the McLean burger, a "healthy," reduced-fat burger—which flopped. In fact, some wits renamed it the "McFlopper." It was less filling, but it didn't taste good. Still, McDonald's had tried.[55]

Other companies have seen some of their socially responsible actions in this area fail as well. Many companies that were promoting "healthy" fares have turned to "hearty" ones (read that as "more fat and thus more taste") as sales declined. KFC abandoned its skinless chicken promotion, Burger King pushes fried pork sandwiches, Wendy's features burgers with bacon and cheese, and Pizza Hut recommends cookies to go with its double pizzas.[56]

The Company as Community Citizen. Organizations today are expected to function as citizens of their community by contributing to the public welfare. Most donate money to one or more good causes, and some even donate staff time to improving the local community. For instance, State Farm Insurance developed the Good Neighbor Award in cooperation with the National Science Teachers Association. The award is given to science teachers who use their own creativity to encourage students to increase their knowledge of the natural world. One teacher received the award for creating a program in which students collected live specimens in and around Delaware Bay then classified and studied them in order to understand the ecology of the area. State Farm contributes $5,000 to the award recipient's school.[57]

Recycling Shows Caring. A company is legally and ethically prohibited from causing pollution, but some socially responsible firms go further in protecting the environment by instituting voluntary recycling projects. Kinko's Copy Centers in Ventura, California, recycles entire trees, planting a new one for every tree mulched into copy-paper stock. It also coordinates a program that urges consumers to buy live pines from participating nurseries for Christmas trees and return them in January for permanent planting.[58] AT&T recycled enough paper in 1989 to save 374,000 trees and 55,000 barrels of oil plus more than $1 million in waste-disposal costs.[59]

Global Responsibility

An American company might have a clean record at home but be using suppliers in other countries who commit horrendous human-rights or environmental abuses. Consumers today often hold such companies responsible. It is not easy to police foreign operations, but a lot of companies are doing their best:[60]

- Atlanta-based Home Depot has demanded assurances from its foreign suppliers that they do not use child labor or convict labor.
- H.J. Heinz will buy tuna only from the foreign fishing boats that use techniques that avoid hurting dolphins.
- Sears refuses to import forced-labor products from China.
- Phillips-Van Heusen threatens to terminate orders to apparel suppliers that violate its broad ethics, environmental, and human-rights code.
- Dow Chemical insists on suppliers conforming, not just to local pollution and safety laws, but to the more stringent U.S. laws.
- A persistent false rumor that McDonald's suppliers were grazing their cattle on cleared rain-forest land led to a written policy statement that the company banned the practice.
- Levi Strauss arranged to help educate children in Bangladesh who are working for its suppliers but could not be fired without impoverishing entire families.

Social Responsibility Is Here to Stay

Milton Friedman, the best-known advocate for businesses ignoring social responsibility, insists that the profit motive leads to a better society—that as companies seek their own best interest, capitalism flourishes and benefits all. He believes that pursuing altruistic aims of social responsibility constitutes a conflict of interest since, in doing so, managers are spending other people's (shareholders') money.[61] But public pressure on organizations to be socially responsible has overwhelmed this argument in most quarters. Large firms today are expected to make substantial donations of those shareholders' money to various charities. Boycotts are even sometimes threatened if a company's contributions are perceived as inadequate. In essence, a company's profit-making ability may depend in large part on how socially responsible the public perceives it to be.

Some companies have made a name for themselves because of their socially responsible profile. Ben & Jerry's is one. This ice cream producer has named one flavor Rainforest Crunch and devotes a portion of its profits to the preservation of the real rain forest. Its Cookies 'n' Cream ice cream is produced with the help of people recruited from among the homeless. The Body Shop, profiled at the end of this chapter, is another company known as much for its social conscience as for its products—cosmetics and soaps. The owner, Anita Roddick, led campaigns against the Gulf War and for the promotion of condom use. These two companies have joined with three dozen more to form Businesses for Social Responsibility, a group dedicated to "revolutionizing how business in America operates" by emphasizing a variety of causes, from environmental protection to family leave policies.[62]

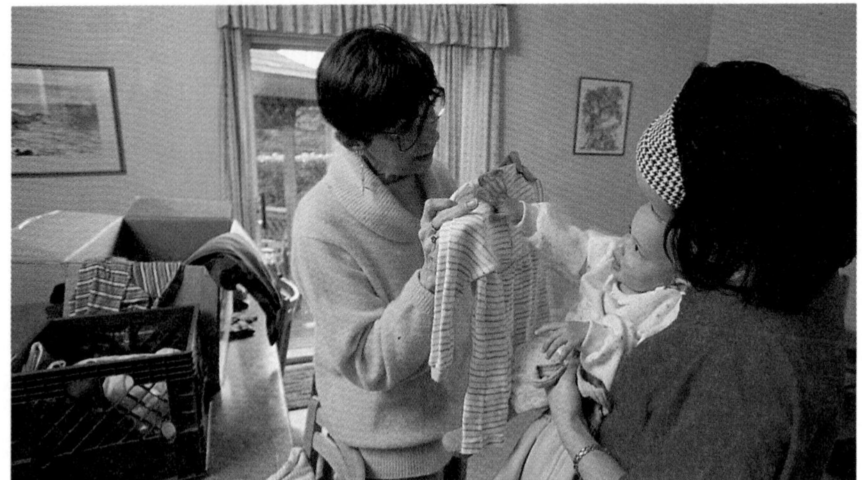

Mail-order company Hanna Andersson donates children's clothing to women's shelters. Through its Hannadowns program, customers receive a 20 percent credit for mailing back clothes their infants have outgrown. The clothes are laundered and given to needy families or to women's shelters.
Photo source: © Robbie McClaran.

Some issues of social responsibility generate almost universal agreement, but others, like Anita Roddick's opposition to the Gulf War, do not. A company runs the risk of losing customers over controversial issues, and most steer clear of them. Children's charities are a popular choice for donations. Clean air and water are basic to everyone's happiness and so "safe" causes. There are enough social needs to go around, and there are enough public voices demanding business's help to keep every organization interested in doing something for the world besides providing a product or service.

Quick Quiz 16.2

1. The view that business's pursuit of its own self-interest need not conflict with the social welfare is called ___________.
2. An employee who is found to be an alcoholic might benefit from the company's ___________.
3. H.J. Heinz company practices international social responsibility by ___________.

Summary

- **Explain the difference between business ethics and social responsibility.** Business ethics are moral values that determine business conduct. Some actions that are legal are nevertheless unethical. Social responsibility encompasses business ethics but goes beyond them in assuming a responsibility to contribute to the well-being of employees, customers, the local community, and society as a whole.
- **Discuss ethics codes and ethics training.** By putting its ethical guidelines in writing and publicizing them, an organization can help motivate and remind employees to adhere to them. Ethics training may be centered around the ethics code, or it may involve the discussion of complex ethical dilemmas. Ethics courses at business schools have proliferated in recent years. The complexities brought about by information technology, increasing multicultural diversity, and the increasing globalization of business have made ethics training more of a necessity today for almost every field of endeavor.
- **List some ethical issues of privacy.** Privacy rights are involved in today's information technology, which makes an individual's credit history available to employers; electronic monitoring systems, which allow an employer to listen in on employees' telephone calls and read their electronic mail; health records, which are legally deemed confidential; mandatory drug testing, which is carried out whether or not there is reason to

suspect drug use; "honesty" tests, which ask very personal questions; and health and safety policies that attempt to regulate employees' personal smoking, eating, and recreational habits.

- **Discuss ethical concerns in regard to health and safety.** Employers are legally and ethically bound to provide a safe workplace for their employees, to produce a safe product for their customers, and to refrain from polluting the environment. The Computer Age has brought some new health and safety problems to the ethical forefront, making the science of ergonomics more important. Society owes a debt of gratitude to whistleblowers who halt the illegal and unethical actions of their companies.

- **Identify some of today's ethical problems and dilemmas.** U.S. organizations that do business in countries where bribery is rampant are put at a competitive disadvantage. Those that have plants in countries where human rights violations occur have difficulty controlling foreign operations yet are held responsible for them by the American public. Issues involving questionable ethics are hostile takeovers, golden parachutes, leveraged buyouts, downsizing, and moving plants to cheaper-labor countries.

- **Name some ways that an organization can be socially responsible.** Areas of social responsibility include (1) improving the quality of a product or service even if doing so reduces profits somewhat; (2) contributing to the quality of employees' work lives through good ergonomics, training opportunities, fair compensation and benefits, and efforts to redress the effects of discrimination; (3) contributing to the quality of employees' personal lives through health-promotion policies, employee assistance programs (EAPs), stress management programs, programs to help balance work and family needs, and opportunities for "personal growth," including volunteer social work; (4) contributing to the welfare of the community through charitable donations and sponsorship of nonprofit organizations and programs; and (5) aiding environmental protection through such activities as recycling.

- **Explain why social responsibility is likely to prevail in the future.** Some argue against social responsibility because they believe that the profit motive leads to a better society—that as companies seek their own best interest, capitalism flourishes and benefits all. They believe that pursuing altruistic aims of social responsibility constitutes a conflict of interest since, in doing so, managers are spending other people's (shareholders') money. This argument is not likely to prevail, however, since public pressure on organizations to be socially responsible has been increasing. As a result, a company's profit-making ability may well depend in large part on how socially responsible the public perceives it to be.

Key Terms

business ethics (378)
social responsibility (378)
Americans with Disabilities Act (ADA) (383)
whistleblowers (386)
hostile takeover (387)
golden parachute (387)
leveraged buyouts (LBOs) (387)
enlightened self-interest (388)

Review and Discussion Questions

1. Do you think ethics should be a major concern of human relations? Why or why not?

2. In each of the following situations, what would have been the ethical thing for the employees to do?* What criteria did you use to decide? What would you have done in that situation? Why?
   a. One fall, managers of Toys "R" Us sent employees to Child World stores to buy large quantities of items that had been heavily discounted. The items were then resold by Toys "R" Us.
   b. Three students at Stanford University reported that their summer employers had asked them to call up competitors, asking for information. They were to pretend that they were doing research for school.

3. How valuable is an ethics code? How should a company penalize employees who break it?

4. Sanjay Dharti is warehouse manager at an import-export company. One day, a truck driver there took him aside and said, "Do you know that Michael (a warehouse worker) has been taking home supplies like tape, nails, and staples to work on personal projects?" What should Sanjay do?

5. Assume that Michael, the warehouse worker in question 4, was found to be pilfering and was disciplined. Upset, he decides to act on some safety prob-

*Examples are taken from Kenneth Labich, "The New Crisis in Business Ethics," *Fortune*, April 20, 1992, pp. 168, 172.

lems he has observed and complained about, and he reports them to the local office of the Occupational Safety and Health Administration. When Sanjay, Michael's boss, finds out that the warehouse will be investigated by OSHA, he is furious. It seems to him that Michael is nothing but trouble. What should Sanjay do?

6. What are some expressions of social responsibility on the part of the organization? On the part of the individual?

7. What socially responsible actions are you a part of as an individual? As a member of a group or organization? How important is human relations in your actions?

8. Like many companies, Gracey Inc. will hold a party in December for its employees and their guests. What guidelines can you offer for how to behave at such an event? Should the behavior of the employees and the company president differ? Why or why not?

9. Mavis Foley, an overweight smoker, has been asked by her employers in a small office to diet and quit smoking because the company's medical-insurance premiums are skewed by her unhealthy lifestyle. Mavis is upset and insulted, particularly because she is aware of the equally bad—but secret—habits of her coworkers. What should she do? Does the company have a right to ask Mavis to change her lifestyle? What other approach might the company have taken?

10. What is the difference between business ethics and social responsibility? Do you think one has more relative value to human relations? Explain.

A SECOND LOOK

Stride Rite broke no laws when it moved production overseas, but was the company's move ethical? Socially responsible? What factors lay behind the company's move? Do you think it was justified? Name some measures the company might have undertaken to keep its jobs in the United States.

Independent Activity

Technology's Human Touch

Think about the organizations profiled in the opening vignettes and case studies of these final two chapters. Two of the companies in Chapter 15—Front Porch Computer and Tatra—are highly dependent on technology for their very existence. In this chapter, although human relationships seem to be more responsible for the success of the companies, Stew Leonard's stores are doing well despite his abuse of technology.

With these organizations in mind, how do you think human relationships and personal communications will be affected by rapid advances in technology? Answer the question in memo form and illustrate your ideas with examples of what your workplace—be it a restaurant, store, factory, or office—will be like in 25 years.

Skill Builder

Human Relations Laboratory

This course in human relations is now drawing to a close. Take some time to reflect on what you have learned and apply it to this classroom, your "human relations laboratory."

Consider some of the same questions you did in your first lab entry:

- How have relationships changed within the classroom? Are those changes reflected in the seating arrangements?
- How does this room appear to you today? Give a physical description.
- What are your impressions of the classroom atmosphere?
- Your impressions of the instructor?

Compare your responses to those you wrote in your first lab memo. Apply the similarities and/or differences in your answers to the following questions:

- How can the human resources practices and concepts you have learned be applied to the members of this class? For example, how effectively do the people within the class communicate? How much more or less effectively do they communicate today than they did at the start of this course?
- Is the passage of time the major factor in fostering better communication, or is it a result of classroom small-group activities?
- How have the class's informal groups changed, and have the roles people play in these groups been affected?
- How have the concepts of human relations and human relations management been applied in the classroom?
- How have your feelings changed about your role in this classroom group?
- Do you think you have a better understanding of others and will function better in a diverse workplace due to what you've learned about human relations?

Group Activity

Classroom Ethics Challenge (30 minutes)*

Each student should complete the following survey anonymously, circling all the answers that apply. The instructor should tabulate the results and distribute them for discussion at the next class session.

For each item in the survey, the class should discuss the following questions:

- Which answer(s) were selected by most students?
- What is the justification for the answers selected?
- How would you respond if you were the coworker of an employee who acted in this way? If you were his or her boss?
- How would your career be affected if your boss knew you had acted in the way indicated by the survey response?

Survey for Class Exercise

Which of the following actions would you take? Circle the letters of as many choices as apply to you.

I would

______ 1. Put false information in my resume
  a. if necessary in order to get a job.
  b. only about minor details.
  c. if most people were doing it.
  d. never.

______ 2. Tell a competing company secrets about my employer's products or procedures
  a. in order to land a job with the competitor.
  b. in exchange for $100.
  c. in exchange for $1 million.
  d. never.

*This exercise is based on a suggestion submitted by James Mulvehill of Mankato, Minnesota.

_____ 3. Cheat on a test used as the basis for promotions
   a. if I had a family to support.
   b. if I thought the test was unfair.
   c. if my coworkers were doing it.
   d. never.

_____ 4. Use the office copier
   a. to make a copy of my dentist's bill.
   b. to make six copies of a report related to my charitable work.
   c. to make 50 copies of my resume.
   d. never.

_____ 5. Pad my expense account for a business trip
   a. if I believed I was underpaid.
   b. only for small amounts that my employer wouldn't miss.
   c. only when I was experiencing financial problems.
   d. never.

_____ 6. Call in sick when I'm not sick
   a. if I'm worn out from working on a big project.
   b. if my child was sick.
   c. if I need to recover from the weekend.
   d. never.

_____ 7. Lie about my boss's whereabouts when he or she takes a long, liquid lunch
   a. only if specifically instructed to do so.
   b. if the boss gives me a generous raise in return.
   c. only when the person asking is my boss's superior.
   d. never.

Case Study

Stew Leonard's Dairy Turns Sour

Stew Leonard thought it important to pass along his values to his staff, and with his folksiness and integrity, he became known as the Mister Rogers of food retailing.

His Norwalk, Connecticut, supermarket, Stew Leonard's, is listed by Ripley's *Believe It or Not* as the world's biggest dairy store, but the listing doesn't take into account the circuslike experience of shopping there. Leonard's animated megamarket includes dancing milk cartons, a petting zoo with live geese and goats, and employees in duck costumes waddling down the aisles. Leonard himself was often at the door, sometimes in a cow suit, greeting some of the 200,000 customers who flocked to his two stores every week.

But Stew Leonard is no longer greeting customers. The one-time milkman, called a marketing genius by Wall Street and a folk hero by his customers, is today called a criminal by the Internal Revenue Service. Leonard and the executives of his $200 million business have pleaded guilty to what has been called the largest criminal tax case in Connecticut history, as well as the biggest computer-driven tax-evasion scheme in the nation.

Customers, many who come by tour bus to wander the 20-foot-wide aisle that meanders through the 10-acre complex, have a hard time believing it. So do most of Leonard's 1,300 employees. Over the years, Leonard had been hailed for his adherence to the values of an old-fashioned family enterprise. But, according to the IRS, Leonard also had one foot in the future, pulling off "a crime of the twenty-first century."

Using a customized computer-software program, Leonard was able to reduce sales data on an item-by-item basis and skim $17 million in cash, mostly during the 1980s. Computer tapes containing the real financial figures were destroyed, and the company's auditors were given the understated books. Leonard was able to divert even more money by requiring customers to pay cash when buying gift certificates.

Each day, say prosecutors, cash was emptied from the registers into a "money room," where it was counted, then placed in bags and dropped down a chute into the "vault room." Most of this cash was carried to the Caribbean, where Leonard owns a second home. Leonard's brother-in-law, an executive at the store, kept nearly $500,000 hidden in a false panel in his basement.

Leonard has agreed to pay $15 million in restitution and faces up to five years in prison. In the meantime, he faces new charges that his store short-weighted hundreds of food packages.

Yet neither the charges nor his confession of guilt has hampered business. Leonard's son says business is steady. "We were packed today. Our customers are extremely supportive and sympathetic," claims Stew Leonard, Jr.

And the customer is always right. It says so on a three-ton slab of granite at the store's entrance.

Case Questions

1. Why do you think Stew Leonard committed these acts? What might have deterred him? Can he be trusted to run a company again?
2. Why do you think customers and employees continue to support Leonard? Would you?
3. Would an ethics code or ethics training be of value at the store? Why or why not?
4. Compared with acts of violence, how serious do you consider Leonard's crimes? How would you sentence him?

Source: Richard Behar, "Skimming the Cream," *Time*, August 2, 1993, p. 49.

Case Study

The Body Shop's Social Whirl

Anita Roddick, founder of the Body Shop and Britain's best-known female entrepreneur, has transformed herself from a penniless hippie to one of the country's five richest women. But she hasn't lost her youthful idealism; while building a 900-store international retailing empire, she continues to tirelessly promote worthy social causes.

Slogans and messages exhorting customers to save whales and fight for human rights are scattered among the all-natural, fruit-scented soaps and peppermint foot lotions sold at a Body Shop. The stores' recycled shopping bags and trucks also serve as billboards; a recent AIDS awareness saying is one of Roddick's favorites: "If you think you're too small to have an impact, try going to bed with a mosquito."

The Body Shop puts its money where Roddick's mouth is—for example, sponsoring projects to save the whales and to end the testing of cosmetics on animals (Body Shop products are tested on human volunteers). The company's new "Trade Not Aid" project searches the world for indigenous peoples willing to squeeze oil from Brazil nuts or make paper from water hyacinths—anything that could provide the natives with income and the Body Shop with sales.

Having agitated Britons with high-profile campaigns touting condom use, she has teamed in the United States—where she has 200 stores—with three dozen American firms to "revolutionize how business in America operates" by promoting such progressive policies as environmentally sound manufacturing. The Body Shop's new headquarters makes good on that idea. There is no air conditioning; ventilation is natural. The walls are filled with ozone-friendly insulation, and timber is supplied from managed plantations that are replanted as trees are cut down. Visitors are ferried between buildings by battery-operated taxis; the batteries are recharged by wind turbines.

During the 1992 presidential election, Roddick used her U.S. stores to sign up 50,000 new voters. That November, she opened a store in Harlem, all profits from which will be plowed back into the community. Soon after, she launched an assault on U.S. government policy, urging customers to tell members of Congress to spend less money defending Europe and more on children, the elderly, the infirm, the homeless, and the unemployed.

Some people react indignantly to such sermons. Says one London paper, "Roddick represents causes attractive to the liberal conscience, yet this goodness is used, remorselessly, to sell vanity products. You wash your hair in global concern. And it is debatable whether the wizened peasants on the walls are dignified or patronized."

In the United States, one mall owner banned a Body Shop poster of a baby's bottom because it showed too much flesh. Another charged that a deodorant slogan urging people to turn their "armpits into charm pits" encouraged homosexuality. The Body Shop's activism doesn't always sit easily in the shopping malls and airport lobbies where the stores are based, but Roddick and company have no plans to stop preaching.

Case Questions

1. Do you agree with those who think Anita Roddick goes too far? Why or why not?
2. What are the limits for a company's social responsibility? For an individual's? Why is there a difference?
3. Does its sense of social responsibility mean the Body Shop is an ethical company? Explain.
4. Will the philosophy of the Body Shop continue to be the key to its success, or will Roddick's activism backfire?
5. Is the chain one you would feel good about buying from or working for? Why or why not?

Source: Philip Elmer-Dewitt, "Anita the Agitator," *Time,* January 25, 1993, pp. 52–54.

Quick Quiz Answers

Quick Quiz 16.1

1. false
2. false
3. false
4. true

Quick Quiz 16.2

1. **enlightened self-interest**
2. **employee assistance program**
3. **buying tuna only from foreign fishing boats that use techniques to avoid hurting dolphins**

Notes

Chapter 1

1. Frederick W. Taylor, *The Principles of Scientific Management* (New York: Harper, 1911).

2. Lillian M. Gilbreth, *The Quest of the One Best Way* (New York: Society of Industrial Engineers, 1924).

3. Frank B. Gilbreth, Jr., and Ernestine Gilbreth Carey, *Cheaper by the Dozen* (New York: Thomas Y. Crowell, 1948).

4. Arthur G. Bedeian, *Management,* 2d ed. (Hinsdale, Ill.: The Dryden Press, 1989).

5. John Dos Passos, *The Big Money* (New York: Harcourt Brace, 1936), p. 20.

6. William J. Dickson, "Hawthorne Experiments," in Carl Heyel, ed. *The Encyclopedia of Management,* 2d ed. (New York: Van Nostrand Reinhold, 1973), pp. 298–302.

7. J. M. Juan, ed., *Quality Control Handbook,* 3d ed. (New York: McGraw-Hill, 1974).

8. Michelle Iaffaldano and Paul Muchinsky, "Job Satisfaction and Job Performance: A Meta-Analysis," *Psychological Bulletin* 97, 1985, pp. 251–273.

9. "Reengineering: Milacron Survives in Dog-Eat-Dog Industry by Forming Wolfpack," *Total Quality Newsletter,* September 1992, p. 6.

10. Sharon Nelton, "Winning with Diversity," *Nation's Business,* September 1992, p. 18.

11. "A Beijing Battle for McDonald's," *Chicago Tribune,* January 14, 1994, sec. 3, p. 3.

Chapter 2

1. J. M. Juran, ed., *Quality Control Handbook,* 3d ed. (New York: McGraw-Hill, 1974).

2. "Quality-Speak: A Manager's Glossary," *Working Woman,* March 1993, p. 26.

3. John Hillkirk, "New Award Cites Teams with Dreams," *USA Today,* April 10–12, 1992, pp. 1A-2A.

4. Nancy K. Austin, "The Lowdown on Quality," *Working Woman,* March 1993.

5. Jaclyn H. Park, "Quality on Tap," *GSB Chicago* (Chicago: University of Chicago Graduate School of Business, Spring 1992), pp. 20–25.

6. Ronald E. Yates, "For Motorola, Quality an Olympian Effort," *Chicago Tribune,* January 27, 1992, sec. 4, p. 1.

7. Ronald E. Yates, "Managing Quality: Certainty Not Part of the Equation," *Chicago Tribune,* January 27, 1992, sec. 4, pp. 1, 2.

8. Philip B. Crosby, *Quality Is Free* (New York: McGraw-Hill, 1979).

9. W. Edwards Deming, *Out of the Crisis* (Cambridge, Mass.: Massachusetts Institute of Technology Press, 1986).

10. "Deming's Demons," *The Wall Street Journal,* June 4, 1990, R39, p. 41.

11. Ibid.

12. John A. Byrne, "The Prophet of Quality," *Business Week,* January 28, 1991, p. 14.

13. William G. Ouchi, *Theory Z—How American Business Can Meet the Japanese Challenge* (Reading, Mass.: Addison-Wesley, 1981).

14. Herbert Stein and Murray Foss, "How Bad Is It: The Bottom Line," *Audacity,* Spring 1993, pp. 20–21.

15. Daniel Benjamin, "Losing Its Edge: Germany Is Troubled by How Little Work Its Workers Are Doing," *The Wall Street Journal,* May 6, 1993, p. A1.

16. Ibid.

17. Cynthia Hanson, "Working Smart," *Chicago Tribune,* May 23, 1993, sec. 6, p. 9.

18. Ibid.

19. Ibid.

20. Brian Azar, "Striking a Balance," *Sales & Marketing Management,* February 1993, p. 35.

21. Austin, "The Lowdown on Quality."

22. David Woodruff, "Where Employees Are Management," *Business Week,* 1992, p. 66.

23. David L. Goetsch, *Industrial Supervision in the Age of High Technology* (New York: Merrill, 1992), p. 461.

24. Crosby, *Quality Is Free.*

25. Woodruff, "Where Employees Are Management."

26. "Quality-Speak: A Manager's Glossary."

27. Eugene Sprow, "Insights into ISO 9000," *Manufacturing Engineering,* 1992, pp. 73–77.

28. Jerry G. Bowles, "Quality '92: Leading the World-Class Company," *Fortune,* September 21, 1992, special advertising section, p. 63.

29. "Quality Movement News," *Total Quality Newsletter,* April 1993, p. 8.

30. Sprow, "Insights into ISO 9000."

31. "Quality-Speak: A Manager's Glossary."

32. Sprow, "Insights into ISO 9000."

33. "Quality-Speak: A Manager's Glossary."

34. Austin, "The Lowdown on Quality," p. 22.

35. Jeremy Main, "Is the Baldrige Overblown?" *Fortune,* July 1, 1991, pp. 62–65.

36. Ibid.

37. Marian Harmon, "Internal Award Programs: Benchmarking the Baldrige to Improve Corporate Quality," *Quality Digest,* May 1992, pp. 20–24.

38. E. C. Huge, *Total Quality: An Executive's Guide for the 1990s* (Homewood, Ill.: Richard D. Irwin, 1990). See Chapter 5, "Measuring and Rewarding Performance," pp. 70–88. Also see W. E. Deming, *Out of Crisis* (Cambridge, Mass.: MIT Center for Advanced Engineering Study, 1986).

39. Leonard Berry, "Improving Service," *Marketing Management* 1, no. 3 (1992).

40. Ibid.

Chapter 3

1. Adam Smith, *The Wealth of Nations* (New York: McGraw-Hill, 1985).

2. "Who Gets Hurt," *Business Week,* August 10, 1992, p. 52.

3. Robert S. Goldman, *Work Values: Six Americans in a Swedish Plant,* report by New York State School of Industrial and Labor Relations, Cornell University, March 1975.

4. Walter Kiechel III, "How We Will Work in the Year 2000," *Fortune,* May 17, 1993, p. 39.

5. Glen E. Salmon, principal software engineer, Asia Products Development, Lotus Development Corporation.

6. "Who Gets Hurt."

7. Janean Huber, "Home Inc.," *Entrepreneur,* March 1993, p. 78.

8. Janean Huber, "Homing Instinct," *Entrepreneur,* March 1993, p. 83.

9. Louise Washer, "Home Alone: Small Business Strategies," *Working Woman,* March 1993, p. 46.

10. Huber, "Home Inc."

11. Barbara Brabec, *National Home Business Report* (newsletter), Naperville, Ill., 1993.

12. Kiechel, "How We Will Work," p. 40.

13. Ibid.

14. James Brian Quinn, *Intelligent Enterprise* (New York: Free Press, 1993).

15. "Typing without Keys," *Newsweek,* December 7, 1992, p. 22b.

16. "How to Rid Your Company of VDT Health Hazards," *Working Woman,* March 1990.

17. Glen E. Salmon, principal software engineer, Asia Products Development, Lotus Development Corporation.

18. "How to Rid Your Company"; and "Seven Ways to a Healthier Work Environment," *Supervisory Management,* April 1992, p. 4.

19. Ibid.

20. "Typing without Keys."

21. "VDT Radiation Threat Remains a Mystery," *Chicago Tribune,* November 8, 1992, pp. 3–4.

22. "No Ceilings, No Doors," *Working Woman,* April 1993, p. 44.

23. "Quality '93: Empowering People with Technology," *Fortune,* September 20, 1993, p. 122.

24. Fernando Bartolome, "Nobody Trusts the Boss Completely—Now What?" *Harvard Business Review,* March-April 1989, p. 142.

25. Ibid.

26. Thayer C. Taylor, "Getting in Step with the Computer Age," *Sales & Marketing Management,* March 1993, pp. 52–59.

27. Ibid., p. 57.

28. Ibid.

29. Ibid., p. 59.

30. Stephen Gondert, "The 10 Biggest Mistakes of SFA (And How to Avoid Them), *Sales & Marketing Management,* February 1993, pp. 52–57.

31. "Take a Clean Sheet of Paper," *The Economist,* May 1, 1993, p. 67.

32. Ibid.

33. Ibid., p. 68.

34. Ibid.

35. "Levi Strauss Uses Information Systems to Empower Employees," *TotalQuality,* August 1993, p. 6.

36. Ibid.

37. "Quality '93," p. 153.

38. Ibid., p. 67.

39. Ibid., pp. 134–136.

40. Craig Brod, *Technostress: The Human Cost of the Computer Revolution* (Reading, Mass.: Addison-Wesley, 1984).

41. H. L. Capron, *Instructor's Guide* for *Computers and Data Processing,* 2d ed. (Menlo Park, Calif.: Benjamin Cummings Publishing, 1983), p. 4.

42. Victoria B. Elder, Ella P. Gardner, Stephen P. Ruth, "Gender and Age in Technostress: Effects on White Collar Productivity," *Government Finance Review* 3 (December 1987), pp. 17–21.

43. Ibid.

44. "Levi Strauss Uses Information Systems to Empower Employees," *TotalQuality,* August 1993, p. 6.

45. "PC I Love You," *Entrepreneur,* December 1992, p. 53.

46. Brod, *Technostress.*

47. Taylor, "Getting in Step," p. 57.

48. Craig Brod, "Technostress," *Review,* September 1984, p. 28.

49. William A. Faunce, *Problems of an Industrial Society* (New York: McGraw-Hill, 1968).

50. Fred Luthans, *Organizational Behavior,* 2d ed. (New York: McGraw-Hill, 1977), pp. 91–92.

51. P. B. Doeringer, *Turbulence in the American Workplace* (New York: Oxford University Press, 1991).

52. Eric Flanholtz, Yvonne Randle, and Sonya Sackmann, "Personnel Management: The Tenor of Today," *Personnel Journal* 66 (June 1987): p. 64.

53. Elizabeth Erlich, "America's Schools Still Aren't Making the Grade," *Business Week/International Edition,* September 19, 1988.

54. Kiechel, "How We Will Work," p. 39.

55. Ibid., p. 41.

Chapter 4

1. Allen L. Otten, "People Patterns," *The Wall Street Journal,* December 7, 1992, p. B1.

2. "Workforce 2000: Attracting and Retaining Hispanic Employees," *Management Review,* November 1992, p. 9.

3. Lena Williams, "The Scramble to Manage a Diverse Workforce," *The New York Times,* December 15, 1992, p. C2.

4. Sharon Nelton, "Winning with Diversity," *Nation's Business,* September 1992, p. 19.

5. Leon E. Wynter, "Business & Race," *The Wall Street Journal,* February 21, 1993, p. B1.

6. Williams, "The Scramble."

7. Maggie Mahar, "The Truth about Women's Pay," *Working Woman,* April 1993, p. 53.

8. Christine L. Williams, "The Glass Escalator: Hidden Advantages for Men in the 'Female' Professions," *Social Problems* 39 (1992): 253–267.

9. "How to Keep Women Managers on the Corporate Ladder," *Business Week,* September 2, 1991, p. 64.

10. *Colby,* August 1992, p. 79.

11. Mahar, "The Truth about Women's Pay," p. 100.

12. Juliet B. Schor, *The Overworked American: The Unexpected Decline of Leisure* (New York: Basic Books, 1991), cited in Barbara Reskin and Irene Padavic, *Women and Men at Work* (Thousand Oaks, Calif.: Pine Forge Press, 1994), p. 150.

13. "Policies and Training Can Help Firms Discourage Harassment," *Tarrant Business,* March 4–10, 1991.

14. "Male College Grads: The Racial Pay Gap Is Widening," *Business Week,* March 18, 1991, p. 20.

15. O. C. Ferrell and Geoffrey Hirt, *Business: A Changing World* (Homewood, Ill.: Richard D. Irwin, 1993), p. 265.

16. Ibid.

17. American Indian College Fund, 21 West 68th Street, Suite 1F, New York, NY 10023.

18. Nelton, "Winning with Diversity," p. 22.

19. David Jamieson and July O'Mara, *Managing Workforce 2000* (San Francisco: Jossey-Bass, 1991).

20. Nelton, "Winning with Diversity."

21. Ferrell and Hirt, *Business: A Changing World,* p. 270.

22. This section draws on Ferrell and Hirt, *Business: A Changing World,* pp. 275–278.

23. Marilyn Loden and Judy B. Rosener, *Workforce America! Managing Employee Diversity as a Vital Resource* (Homewood, Ill.: Business One Irwin, 1991).

24. Personal communication from Donald N. Kelly, North Hennepin Community College, Fall 1993.

25. W. A. Brown, "How to Write an Affirmative Action Plan," *American Demographics,* March 1993, pp. 56-58.

26. Ferrell and Hirt, *Business: A Changing World,* p. 278.

27. Loden and Rosener, *Workforce America!*

28. Alice Cuneo, "Diverse by Design," *Business Week/Reinventing America,* 1992, p. 72; Williams, "The Scramble," p. C2; R. Roosevelt Thomas, Jr., "From Affirmative Action to Affirming Diversity," *Harvard Business Review,* March-April 1990, pp. 107–117; and Wynter, "Business & Race," p. B1.

29. "Managing Diversity," *Inc.,* January 1993, p. 33.

30. R. Roosevelt Thomas, Jr., "From Affirmative Action to Affirming Diversity," *Harvard Business Review,* March–April 1990, p. 113.

31. "Labor Letter," *The Wall Street Journal,* February 2, 1992, p. A1.

Chapter 5

1. Based on a discussion in Michael A. Hitt, R. Dennis Middlemist, and Robert L. Mathis, *Management: Concepts and Effective Practice,* 2d ed. (St. Paul, Minn.: West Publishing Company, 1986), pp. 404–405.

2. Marshall McLuhan, *The Medium Is the Message* (New York: Random House, 1967).

3. David Jackson, "Memos an Art Form at City Hall," *Chicago Tribune,* April 26, 1992, sec. 1, pp. 1, 16.

4. "The Politics of Meeting Seating," *Working Woman,* May 1992, p. 21.

5. Michael L. Hecht, Peter A. Anderson, and Sidney A. Ribeau, "The Cultural Dimensions of Nonverbal Communication," *Processes and Effects,* pp. 168–177; David Matsumoto, Harald G. Wallbott, and Klaus R. Scherer, "Emotions in Intercultural Communication," *Processes and Effects,* pp. 226–227, 229, 242; Sondra Thiederman, *Bridging Cultural Barriers for Corporate Success: How to Manage the Multicultural Work Force* (New York: Lexington Books, 1991).

6. Hecht et al., "The Cultural Dimensions," p. 172; and Matsumoto et al., "Emotions in Intercultural Communication," p. 242.

7. Hecht et al., "The Cultural Dimensions," p. 172.

8. Diane Bone, *The Business of Listening* (Menlo Park, Cal.: Crisp Publications, 1988).

9. Letitia Baldrige, *The Complete Guide to Executive Manners* (New York, N.Y.: (Rawson Associates) Macmillan, 1985).

10. LeaAnn Anderson, "Say What?" *Entrepreneur,* May 1993, p. 111.

11. Ibid.

12. Much of the following discussion is based on information from Anderson, "Say What?" pp. 113–115.

13. Ibid, p. 113.

14. William V. Haney, *Communication and Interpersonal Relations: Text and Cases,* 6th ed. (Homewood, Ill.: Richard D. Irwin, 1992), p. 290.

15. Anderson, "Say What?" p. 113.

16. Ibid., p. 115.

17. Ibid.

18. Brian Azar, "Phone Reps Need Motivating Too," *Sales & Marketing Management,* October 1992, p. 58.

19. Dennis Fox, "Ringing Up Prospects," *Sales & Marketing Management,* March 1993, p. 77.

20. Based on information in Azar, "Phone Reps."

21. David W. Johnson, *Reaching Out—Interpersonal Effectiveness and Self-Actualization* (Englewood Cliffs, N.J.: Prentice-Hall, 1981), pp. 43–44.

22. Gerald L. Manning and Barry L. Reece, *Selling Today: An Extension of the Marketing Concept,* 5th ed. (Boston:Allyn & Bacon, 1992).

23. Fernando Bartolome, "Nobody Trusts the Boss Completely—Now What?" *Harvard Business Review,* March–April 1989, p. 137.

24. Cynthia Hanson, "Working Smart," *Chicago Tribune,* July 11, 1993, sec. 6, p. 9.

25. Ibid.

26. William Wordsworth, *The Prelude,* Book IV (Ithaca, N.Y.: Cornell University Press, 1977).

27. Tony Mauro, "Justice's Gentle Reminder: She's Not a He," *USA Today,* November 14, 1991, p. 3A.

28. "The Spare Sex," *The Economist,* March 28, 1992, pp. 17–18, 20.

Chapter 6

1. Fernando Bartolome, "Nobody Trusts the Boss Completely—Now What?" *Harvard Business Review,* March–April 1989, p. 142.

2. "Quality '93: Empowering People with Technology," *Fortune,* September 20, 1993, p. 147.

3. Ibid., pp. 122, 126.

4. Richard T. Hurley, "The Truth about American Workers," *Industry Week,* May 3, 1993, p. 37.

5. "BAD Program Nets Good Ideas," *Quality Digest,* May 1993, p. 10.

6. Ibid.

7. *Profiles in Quality: Blueprints for Action from 50 Leading Companies* (Boston: Allyn & Bacon, 1991), p. 46.

8. Teri Lammers, "The Effective Employee-Feedback System," *INC.*, February 1993, p. 109.

9. Bartolome, "Nobody Trusts the Boss Completely," p. 135.

10. Ibid., p. 142.

11. CPC International Inc., 1991 Annual Report, p. 17.

12. Patti Doten, "Flying Rumors May Mean a Crash Landing," *Chicago Tribune*, January 14, 1992, sec. 5, pp. 1, 7.

13. Lindsey Novak and Lauren Spier, "Workplace Solutions: When Gossip Gets Back to the Boss," *Chicago Tribune*, February 16, 1992, sec. 8, p. 1.

14. Doten, "Flying Rumors."

15. Arthur Bedeian, *Management*, 2d ed. (Hinsdale, Ill.: The Dryden Press, 1989), pp. 498–499.

16. Vicki Vaughan, "The Electronic Grapevine," *The Orlando Sentinel*, October 28, 1993, p. E1.

17. Keith Davis, *Human Behavior at Work: Organizational Behavior*, 5th ed. (New York: McGraw-Hill, 1972), pp. 278, 280.

18. Based on Mortimer R. Feinberg, "How to Get the Grapevine on Your Side," *Working Woman*, May 1990, p. 23.

19. Vaughan, "The Electronic Grapevine," p. E4.

20. Ibid.

21. Ibid.

22. Bartolome, "Nobody Trusts the Boss," p. 142.

23. "New AT&T Phone Carries Still Video Images, Sound," *The Wall Street Journal*, May 12, 1993, p. B6.

24. Stephanie Barlow, "Voice of Reason," *Entrepreneur*, March 1993, p. 49.

25. Karl Albrecht, "Customer-Friendly Communication," *Quality Digest*, March 1993, p. 23.

26. Stan Kossen, *Creative Selling Today*, 3d ed. (New York: Harper & Row, 1989), pp. 233–234.

27. Dennis Fox, "Ringing Up Prospects," *Sales & Marketing Management*, March 1993, p. 76.

28. Albrecht, "Customer-Friendly Communication," p. 22.

29. Fox, "Ringing Up Prospects," p. 76.

Chapter 7

1. *Industry Week*, November 2, 1992, p. 32.

2. Abraham Maslow, *Eupsychian Management* (Homewood, Ill.: Richard D. Irwin, 1965).

3. Michael P. Cronin, "Piquing Employee Interest," *Inc.*, August 1992, p. 83.

4. Ibid.

5. Kenneth Blanchard, "How to Turn Around Department Performance," *Supervisory Management*, March 1992, p. 3.

6. D. C. McClelland, "Toward a Theory of Motive Acquisition," *American Psychologist*, May 1965, pp. 321–333.

7. James A. Belasco, "How Do I Empower People?" *Supervisory Management*, January 1992, p. 12.

8. Blanchard, "How to Turn Around Department Performance."

9. Belasco, "How Do I Empower People?"

10. Stephen Franklin, "The Wisest Capital Investment," *Chicago Tribune*, December 20, 1992.

11. "Teaching Business to Train," *Business Week/Reinventing America*, 1992, pp. 82–90.

12. Otis Port, "Lev Landa's Worker Miracles," *Business Week*, September 21, 1992, p. 72.

13. Clay Carr, "Planning Priorities for Empowered Teams," *Journal of Business Strategy* (September-October 1992): p. 43.

14. Glenn R. Englund, "Viewpoint," *Personnel Journal*, (August 1992): p. 32.

15. Franklin, "The Wisest Capital Investment."

16. Ibid.

17. Ibid.

18. "Experts in Overalls," *Business Week/Reinventing America*, 1992, p. 90.

19. "Teaching Business to Train," p. 82.

20. Franklin, "The Wisest Capital Investment."

21. Ibid.

22. "Teaching Business to Train," p. 86.

23. "National Safety Council Launches Training Program," *Quality Digest*, October 1992, p. 7.

24. "Teaching Business to Train," p. 86.

25. Ibid., p. 90.

26. John Schermerhorn, Jr., William N. Gardner, and Thomas N. Martin, "The Trouble with Bob: A Drama in Managerial Life," *Executive Female*, September-October 1991, pp. 42–47.

27. Jay Schuster and Patricia Zingheim, "How to Closely Link Pay and Performance," *Boardroom Reports*, September 1, 1992, pp. 3–4.

28. "Study: More Companies Link Compensation to Quality," *Total Quality*, April 1992, p. 6.

29. Andrea Gabor, "After the Pay Revolution, Job Titles Won't Matter," *The New York Times*, May 17, 1992, p. F5.

30. "Stock Options Foster Commitment," *Personnel Journal*, (November 1992).

31. John A. Parnell, "Five Reasons Why Pay Must Be Based on Performance," *Supervision*, February 1991, pp. 6–8.

32. William Keenan, Jr., "From Bad to Worse," *Sales & Marketing Management*, Nov. 1992, p. 37.

33. Ibid., p. 42.

34. "Linking Directors' Pay to Companies' Fortunes," *The Wall Street Journal*, October 13, 1992, p. B1.

35. George Gendron, "FYI: Schwarzkopf on Leadership," *Inc.*, January 1992, p. 11.

36. Gabor, "After the Pay Revolution."

37. Will Kaydos, "Motivating by Measuring Performance," *Quality Digest*, May 1992, pp. 53–54, 75.

Chapter 8

1. *Boardroom Reports*, August 15, 1992, p. 2, citing Paul B. Malone III, *Abuse 'Em and Lose 'Em* (Annandale, Virginia: Synergy Press, 1992).

2. Jeff Cole, "Gentle Persuasion: New CEO at Hughes Studied Its Managers, Got Them on His Side," *The Wall Street Journal*, March 30, 1993, p. A1.

3. Ibid.

4. Roger Ailes, "Lighten Up! Stuffed Shirts Have Short Careers," *Newsweek*, Management Digest special advertising section, May 18, 1992, p. 10.

5. Kenneth Blanchard, "How to Turn Around Department Performance," *Supervisory Management*, March 1992, p. 3.

6. Bill Powell and Hideko Takayama, "Who's Better Off?" *Newsweek*, March 22, 1993, p. 54.

7. Peter L. Thigpen, "Creating the Covenant," *Quality Digest*, August 1992, pp. 63-64.

8. Joseph T. Straub, "Keep Your Distance without Losing Rapport," *Supervisory Management*, April 1992, p. 3.

9. Ibid.

10. Sondra Thiederman, *Bridging Cultural Barriers for Corporate Success: How to Manage the Multicultural Work Force* (Lexington, Mass.: Lexington Books, 1991), p. 80.

11. Bradford McKee, "A Business in Crisis Has No Time for Democracy," *Nation's Business*, July 1992, pp. 8, 17.

12. Based on a character and scene created by Adele Scheele, "Are You a Bad Boss?" *Working Woman*, April 1992, p. 32.

Chapter 9

1. *Psychology Today*, May-June 1993, p. 15.

2. "Job Stress Claims Increase Dramatically in California," *Los Angeles Times*, March 31, 1990, pp. A23–A25.

3. H. S. Friedman and S. Booth-Kewley, "The 'Disease-Prone' Personality," *American Psychology* 42 (1987): pp. 539–555.

4. M. Osborn, "Workers Stretched to the Limits," *USA Today,* September 8, 1992, p. 1.

5. Sandra Lotz Fisher, "Stress, Part I: Warning Signs and Identifying Characteristics," *Sales & Marketing Management,* November 1992, p. 94.

6. Ibid.

7. Frank B. McMahon, Judith W. McMahon, and Tony Romano, *Psychology and You* (St. Paul, Minn.: West Publishing, 1993), p. 480.

8. Marilyn Elias, "Women's Job, Home Conflicts Raise Heart Risk," *USA Today,* March 3, 1992, p. 1D; Steve Johnson, "You Think You've Got Stress—Join the Club," *Chicago Tribune,* March 25, 1993, p. 26.

9. C. Lee, S. J. Ashford, and P. Bobko, "Interactive Effects of Type A Behavior and Perceived Control of Worker Performance, Job Satisfaction, and Somatic Complaints," *Academy of Management Journal* 33 (December 1990): pp. 870–882.

10. Ibid.

11. J. B. Stewart, "Scenes from a Scandal: The Secret World of Michael Milkin and Ivan Boesky," *The Wall Street Journal,* October 2, 1991, pp. B1, B8.

12. D. A. Girdano, G. S. Everly, Jr., and D. E. Dusek, *Controlling Stress and Tension: A Holistic Approach,* 3d ed. (Englewood Cliffs, N.J.: Prentice-Hall, 1990), p. 37.

13. Steve Johnson, "You Think You've Got Stress—Join the Club," *Chicago Tribune,* March 25, 1993, p. 1.

14. Elias, "Women's Job, Home Conflicts Raise Heart Risk."

15. R. Zemke, "Workplace Stress Revisited," *Training,* November 1991, p. 35.

16. J. C. Latack, "Career Transitions with Organizations: An Exploratory Study of Work, Non-Work, and Coping Strategies," *Organizational Behavior and Human Performance* 34 (1984): pp. 296–322; E. H. Shein, *Career Dynamics: Matching Individual and Organizational Needs* (Reading, Mass.: Addison-Wesley, 1978).

17. Ibid.

18. D. C. Feldman and B. A. Weitz, "Career Plateaus Reconsidered," *Journal of Management* 14 (1988): p. 71.

19. Zemke, "Workplace Stress Revisited," p. 36.

20. Girdano et al., *Controlling Stress and Tension,* pp. 140–141.

21. R. Hogan and J. Morrison, "Work and Well-Being: An Agenda for the '90s." Paper presented at the American Psychological Association and National Institute for Occupational Safety and Health Conference, Washington, D.C., November 1990.

22. J. E. Driskell and E. Salas, "Group Decision Making under Stress," *Journal of Applied Psychology* 76 (June 1991): pp. 473–479.

23. J. Bales, "Work Stress Grows, but Services Decline," *The APA Monitor* 22 (November 1991): p. 32.

24. Ann Japenga, "Sabotage at Work," *Los Angeles Times,* May 3, 1990, pp. E1, E16.

25. Zemke, "Workplace Stress Revisited," pp. 35–39.

26. M. Malik, "All Stressed Up and No Place to Go," *Modern Office Technology,* February 1993, p. 27.

27. D. I. Nelson and C. Sutton, "Chronic Work Stress and Coping: A Longitudinal Study and Suggested New Directions," *Academy of Management Journal* 33, no. 4 (1990): pp. 859–869.

28. K. E. Kram and D. T. Hall, "Mentoring as an Antidote to Stress during Corporate Trauma," *Human Resource Management* (Winter 1989): pp. 493–511.

29. G. Parliman and E. Edwards, "Employee Assistance Programs: An Employer's Guide to Emerging Liability Issues," *Employee Relations Law Journal* 7 (1991): pp. 593–601.

30. M. T. Matteson and J. M. Ivancevich, *Controlling Work Stress* (San Francisco: Jossey-Bass, 1987).

31. J. M. Ivancevich, *American Psychologist* 45 (1990): p. 254.

32. D. C. Ganster and J. Schaubroeck, "Work Stress and Employee Health," *Journal of Management* 17 (1991): pp. 235–271.

33. "Meditation, the New Balm for Corporate Stress," *Business Week,* May 10, 1993, p. 86.

34. "Fear and Stress in the Office Take Toll," *The Wall Street Journal,* November 6, 1990, sec. B, p. 1.

35. J. S. Shepherd, "Manage the Five C's of Stress," *Personnel Journal* 69 (July 1990): pp. 64–68.

36. "How Jim Howard Gets So Much Done," *Boardroom Reports,* September 1, 1992, pp. 13–14.

37. Clark Brooks, "Minimizing Stress," *Southtown Economist,* August 8, 1993.

38. Ibid.

39. Brooks, "Minimizing Stress."

40. Ibid.

41. C. W. Metcalf, *Lighten Up: Survival Skills for People under Pressure* (Reading, Mass.: Addison-Wesley, 1993).

42. Kristen Hillary Neri, "Now or Never," *Entrepreneur,* September 1993, p. 115.

Chapter 10

1. All information on Typewatching comes from Otto Kroeger and Janet M. Thuesen, "It Takes All Types," *Newsweek,* September 7, 1992, pp. 8–10.

2. J. S. Wiggins, *Personality and Prediction: Principles of Personality Assessment* (Reading, Mass.: Addison-Wesley, 1973); B. Kleinmutz, "Why We Still Use Our Heads Instead of Formulas: Toward an Integrative Approach," *Psychological Bulletin* (1990): pp. 296–310.

3. Sandra Lotz Fisher, "Stress, Part I: Warning Signs and Identifying Characteristics," *Sales & Marketing Management,* November 1992, p. 94.

4. Lini S. Kadaba, "A Wakeup Call," *Chicago Tribune,* December 20, 1993, section 5, p. 5.

5. J. Greenberg, "The Protestant Work Ethic and Reactions to Negative Performance Evaluation on a Laboratory Task," *Journal of Applied Psychology* 62 (1977): pp. 682–690.

6. R. P. Vecchio, "The Function and Meaning of Work and the Job: Morse and Weiss (1955) Revisited," *Academy of Management Journal* 23 (1980): pp. 361–367.

7. Robert McGarvey, "Attitude Adjustment," *Entrepreneur,* March 1993, p. 170.

8. Ibid., pp. 172–173.

9. Ronald E. Yates, "Downsizing's Bitter Pill," *Chicago Tribune Magazine,* November 21, 1993, p. 16.

10. Ibid., p. 15.

11. L. Kohlberg, "Stage and Sequence: The Cognitive-Developmental Approach to Socialization," in *Handbook of Socialization Theory and Research,* ed. D. A. Goslin (Chicago: Rand-McNally, 1969), pp. 347–400.

12. Janean Huber, "Homing Instinct," *Entrepreneur,* March 1993, pp. 84, 86.

13. LeaAnn Anderson, "Say What?" *Entrepreneur,* May 1993, p. 115.

14. Kenneth Blanchard, "Creating a Learning Environment," *Quality Digest,* March 1993, pp. 20–21.

15. Lena Williams, "Scrambling to Manage a Diverse Work Force," *The New York Times,* December 15, 1993, p. C2.

16. E. G. C. Collins and E. B. Blodgett, "Sexual Harassment: Some See It … Some Won't," *Harvard Business Review,* March-April 1981, pp. 76–95.

17. "Emotions in Intercultural Communication," *Processes and Effects,* p. C2.

18. Ibid.

19. Ibid., p. 239.

20. Stephanie Barlow, "Great Shakes," *Entrepreneur,* December 1992, p. 48.

21. Robert McGarvey, "Good Vibrations," *Entrepreneur,* April 1993, p. 162.

22. Kenneth Blanchard, "Remembering Business Etiquette," *Quality Digest,* November 1992, p. 14.

Chapter 11

1. Bradford McKee, "Turn Your Workers into a Team," *Nation's Business,* July 1992, pp. 36–38.

2. R. B. Lacoursiere, *The Life Cycle of Groups: Group Developmental Stage Theory* (New York: Human Service Press, 1980).

3. "What They Don't Know *Will* Hurt Us," *Industry Week,* May 3, 1993, p. 7.

4. David T. Bottoms, "Status: Cleaning up the Mess," *Industry Week,* May 3, 1993, pp. 15–16.

5. "Got a Problem?" *Entrepreneur,* March 1993, p. 56.

6. Clark Wigley, "Working Smart on Tough Business Problems," *Supervisory Management,* February 1992, p. 1.

7. Aimee L. Stern, "Why Good Managers Approve Bad Ideas," *Working Woman,* May 1992, pp. 75, 104.

8. David M. Armstrong, "Management by Storytelling," *Executive Female,* May-June 1992, pp. 38–41.

9. Ibid.

10. *Working Woman,* March 1990, p. 77.

11. Stephanie Barlow, "Pssssst!" *Entrepreneur,* April 1993, p. 48.

12. Ibid.

13. R. C. Ziller, "Toward a Theory of Open and Closed Groups," *Psychological Bulletin* 64 (1965): p. 164.

14. Clay Carr, "Planning Priorities for Empowered Teams," *Journal of Business Strategy* (September–October 1992): p. 44.

15. Terrence E. Deal and Allan A. Kennedy, *Corporate Cultures* (Reading, Mass.: Addison-Wesley, 1988), pp. 107–127.

16. Elizabeth Lesly, "Good-Bye Mr. Dithers," *Business Week,* September 21, 1992.

17. Bernard C. Reimann and Yoash Weiner, "Corporate Culture: Avoiding the Elitist Trap," *Business Horizons,* March–April 1988, p. 44.

18. Tracy E. Benson, "Your Structure May Be Killing You," *Industry Week,* November 2, 1992, p. 13.

19. Robert McGarvey, "Good Vibrations," *Entrepreneur,* April 1993, p. 162.

20. Ibid. p. 163.

21. "A Company's Gift to Its Diverse Work Force," *Nation's Business,* November 1992, p. 18.

22. Stephanie Barlow, "Turn It On!" *Entrepreneur,* May 1993, p. 52.

23. Arthur Bedeian, *Management,* 2d ed. (Hinsdale, Ill.: The Dryden Press, 1989), pp. 207–208.

24. Cynthia D. Scott and Dennis T. Jaffe, *Empowerment* (Los Altos, Calif.: Crisp Publications, 1991), p. 12.

Chapter 12

1. Jon R. Katzenbach and Douglas K. Smith, "The Discipline of Teams," *Harvard Business Review,* March-April 1993, pp. 111, 112.

2. Edward E. Lawler III, Susan Albers Mohrman, and Gerald E. Ledford, Jr., "Study Shows Strong Evidence That Participatory Management Pays Off," *Total Quality,* September 1992, pp. 1–4.

3. Cathy E. Kramer, "Improving Team Meetings," *Quality Digest,* May 1993, p. 75.

4. Katzenbach and Smith, "The Discipline of Teams," p. 112.

5. Ibid., p. 111.

6. Richard M. Krieg, "The New Era: Workers as Assets," *Chicago Tribune,* July 23, 1993, sec. 1, p. 15.

7. Ibid.

8. Katzenbach and Smith, "The Discipline of Teams," pp. 116–119.

9. S. C. Gwynne, "The Right Stuff," *Time,* October 29, 1990, pp. 74–84.

10. Jack D. Orsburn, Linda Moran, Ed Musselwhite, and John H. Zenger, *Self-Directed Work Teams: The New American Challenge* (Homewood, Ill.: Business One Irwin, 1990), p. 40.

11. Kramer, "Improving Team Meetings."

12. Thomas L. Brown, "Is There Power in Partnering?" *Industry Week,* May 3, 1993, p. 13.

13. "Token Programs Are a Bitter Pill," *Industry Week,* May 3, 1993, p. 44.

14. Ibid.

15. Joanne Sujansky, *The Power of Partnering* (San Diego: Pfeiffer & Company, 1991).

16. Brown, "Is There Power in Partnering?"

17. Krieg, "The New Era."

18. Robert McGarvey, "Dream Team," *Entrepreneur,* May 1993, p. 144.

19. "Why Teams Don't Work," *Sales & Marketing Management,* April 1993, p. 12.

20. McGarvey, "Dream Team."

21. "Treating People Like Adults Isn't Just Fantasy," *The Globe and Mail,* July 6, 1993, p. B18.

22. Ibid.

23. "Do as I Say," *Management Today,* July 1993, p. 79.

24. Brian Baldock, "Harnessing the Team's Talents," *Management Today,* July 1993, p. 5.

25. Beverly Geber, "From Manager into Coach," *Training,* February 1992, pp. 25–31.

26. Brian Azar, "Striking a Balance," *Sales & Marketing Management,* February 1993, p. 35.

27. Cathy E. Kramer, "Improving Team Meetings," p. 80.

28. Baldock, "Harnessing the Team's Talents"; Kramer, "Improving Team Meetings," p. 76.

29. Kramer, "Improving Team Meetings," p. 75.

30. Orsburn et al., *Self-Directed Work Teams: The New American Challenge,* p. 65.

31. Beverly Geber, "Saturn's Grand Experiment," *Training,* June 1992, p. 31.

32. Alfredo S. Lanier, "Alex Warren: Bridging the Gap between Cultures and Technologies," *GSB Chicago* (University of Chicago Graduate School of Business), Winter 1991, pp. 9–13.

33. Richard M. Hodgetts, *Modern Human Relations at Work,* 5th ed. (Fort Worth, Tex.: The Dryden Press, 1993), p. 420.

34. Betsy Wiesendanger, "Games Managers Play," *Sales & Marketing Management,* February 1993, p. 41.

35. Ibid.

36. Kramer, "Improving Team Meetings," p. 75.

37. Ibid., p. 76.

38. Ibid.

39. Ibid.

40. Ibid., p. 78.

41. Katzenbach and Smith, "The Discipline of Teams," p. 112.

42. Ibid., p. 113.

43. Ibid., p. 114.

44. McGarvey, "Dream Team," p. 146.

45. Ibid.

46. Kramer, "Improving Team Meetings," p. 80.

Chapter 13

1. Andrew S. Grove, "How to Manage Office Friction," *Working Woman,* August 1990, pp. 24, 26.

2. Thomas A. Stewart, "The Search for the Organization of Tomorrow," *Fortune,* May 18, 1992, pp. 92–98.

3. Dean Tjosvold, Valerie Dann, and Choy Wong, "Managing Conflict between

Departments to Serve Customers," *Human Relations* 45, no. 10 (1992): p. 1038.

4. Ibid., pp. 1035–1050.

5. Clark Brooks, "Minimizing Stress," *Southtown Economist,* August 8, 1993.

6. Ibid.

7. Ibid.

8. C. W. Metcalf, *Lighten Up: Survival Skills for People under Pressure* (Boston: Addison-Wesley, 1993).

9. Marilyn Elias, "Women's Job, Home Conflicts Raise Heart Risk," *USA Today,* March 3, 1992, p. 1D; Steve Johnson, "You Think You've Got Stress—Join the Club," *Chicago Tribune,* March 25, 1993, p. 26.

10. J. Pfeffer, *Power in Organizations* (Boston: Pittman, 1981).

11. Tjosvold et al., "Managing Conflict," pp. 1038, 1049.

12. Glenn R. Englund, "Honor Thy Co-workers," *Personnel Journal,* August 1992, p. 30.

13. Tjosvold et al., "Managing Conflict," p. 1047.

14. Joe Carbone, "Keeping Peace on the Job," *Supervisory Management,* December 1992, p. 2.

15. Cynthia Hanson, "Working Smart: Don't Let Waves of Change Swamp Your Career," *Chicago Tribune,* August 15, 1993, sec. 6, p. 9.

16. "Traditional Families Have Thin Tradition," *The Wall Street Journal,* May 12, 1993, p. B1.

17. "Aging Boomers Are New Target for Maybelline," *The Wall Street Journal,* April 13, 1993, p. B1.

18. Lee Smith, "The Coming Health Care Shakeout," *Fortune,* May 17, 1993, pp. 70–75.

19. "Bans Douse Workplace Smoking," *Industry Week,* May 3, 1993, p. 8.

20. "The Death of Corporate Loyalty," *The Economist,* April 3, 1993, p. 63.

21. Betsy Wiesendanger, "The M.B.A.: Is It Relevant in Sales?" *Sales & Marketing Management,* May 1993, pp. 58–61.

22. David Gates, "White Male Paranoia," *Newsweek,* March 29, 1993, pp. 49, 51–52.

23. E. Dole, "'Ready, Set, Work,' Says Labor Secretary," *Training and Development Journal* 44, no. 5 (1991): pp. 17–22.

24. B. Filipczak, "What Employers Teach," *Training* 29, no. 10 (1992): pp. 43–55.

25. Ibid.

26. B. L. Bell, "Illiteracy: It's Cheaper to Train Them," *Supervisory Management* 36, no. 9 (1991): pp. 4–5.

27. J. J. Laabs, "How Federally Funded Training Helps Business," *Personnel Journal* 71, no. 3 (1992): pp. 35–39.

28. Meg McSherry, "Schools, Businesses Make Uneasy Partners," *Daily Southtown,* August 20, 1993, pp. 1, 4.

29. Ronald E. Yates, "Downsizing's Bitter Pill," *Chicago Tribune Magazine,* November 21, 1993, p. 16.

30. Ibid., p. 18.

31. Ibid., p. 40.

32. Ibid., p. 18.

33. Susan Diesenhouse, "In a Shaky Economy, Even Professionals Are 'Temps,'" *The New York Times,* May 16, 1993.

34. Ibid.

35. Joann S. Lublin, "Husbands in Limbo: As More Men Become 'Trailing Spouses,' Firms Help Them Cope," *The Wall Street Journal,* April 13, 1993, p. A1.

36. Jack E. Edwards, Paul Rosenfeld, Patricia J. Thomas, and Marie D. Thomas, "Willingness to Relocate for Employment: A Survey of Hispanics, Non-Hispanic Whites, and Blacks," *Hispanic Journal of Behavior Sciences* 15, no. 1 (February 1993): p. 121.

37. Gates, "White Male Paranoia," p. 49.

38. Nancy Ryan, "For 3, No Encounter with the Glass Ceiling," *Chicago Tribune,* May 31, 1993, p. 1.

39. Ibid., p. 2.

40. Brian Baldock, "Harnessing the Team's Talents," *Management Today,* July 1993, p. 5.

41. Ken Blanchard, "The Seven Dynamics of Change," *Quality Digest,* May 1992, p. 18.

42. "Honda Sticks to Its Way," *The Economist,* June 1993.

43. Jack Falvey, "Getting Organized," *Sales & Marketing Management,* April 1993, p. 16.

44. Steve Johnson, "You Think You've Got Stress—Join the Club," *Chicago Tribune,* March 25, 1993, p. 1.

45. J. Clifton Williams, *Human Behavior in Organizations* (Cincinnati: South-Western, 1982), pp. 212–213. Cited in Samuel C. Certo, *Modern Management: Quality, Ethics, and the Global Environment,* 5th ed. (Boston: Allyn and Bacon, 1992), p. 367.

46. Certo, *Modern Management: Quality, Ethics, and the Global Environment,* p. 362. Based on "How Companies Overcome Resistance to Change," *Management Review,* November 1972, pp. 17–25. See also Hank Williams, "Learning to Manage Change," *Industrial and Commercial Training* 21 (May/June 1989): pp. 17–20.

47. Hanson, "Working Smart," p. 9.

48. Ken Blanchard, "Creating a Learning Environment," *Quality Digest,* March 1993, p. 21.

49. Kurt Lewin, "Frontiers in Group Dynamics: Concept, Method, and Reality of Social Sciences—Social Equilibrium and Social Change," *Human Relations,* June 1947, pp. 5–14.

50. Ken Blanchard, "Six Concerns in the Change Process," *Quality Digest,* June 1992, pp. 14, 62.

51. Blanchard, "The Seven Dynamics of Change," p. 78.

52. Jill Andresky Fraser, "Managing Emotions in the Workplace," *Working Woman,* April 1993.

Chapter 14

1. "Deming's Demons," *The Wall Street Journal,* June 4, 1990, pp. R39, R41.

2. Rosemary F. Lyons, "Cross Training: A Richer Staff for Leaner Budgets," *Nursing Management,* January 1992, pp. 43–44.

3. Bruce Shawkey, "Job Descriptions," *Credit Union Executive* 29 (Winter 1989/1990): pp. 20–23.

4. M. A. Campion and C. L. McClelland, "Interdisciplinary Examination of the Costs and Benefits of Enlarged Jobs: A Job Design Quasi-Experiment," *Journal of Applied Psychology* 76 (1991): pp. 186–198.

5. K. Christensen, "Here We Go into the 'High Flex' Era," *Across the Board* 27, no. 7 (1990): pp. 22–23.

6. "Employees Take Pains to Make Flextime Work," *The Wall Street Journal,* August 18, 1992, p. B1.

7. Cindy Lampner, "Part-Time Goes Professional," *Resources,* 2nd Quarter 1992, p. 2.

8. Eileen Ogintz, "Quaker Takes Hand in Helping Families," *Chicago Tribune,* September 23, 1992, sec. 3, pp. 1, 4.

9. "Telecommuter Tips," *Inc.,* June 1993, p. 35.

10. Ibid.

11. Michael P. Cronin, "One Life to Live," *Inc.,* July 1993, p. 56.

12. Ibid.

13. Ibid.

14. J. Richard Hackman and Greg R. Oldham, *Work Redesign* (Reading, Mass.: Addison-Wesley, 1980).

15. Ellyn E. Spragins, "Keeping Good People," *Inc.,* June 1993, p. 36.

16. Will Kaydos, "Managing by Measuring Performance," *Quality Digest,* March 1993, p. 44.

17. Patricia A. Galagan, "Training Keeps the Cutting Edge Sharp for the Andersen

Companies," *Training and Development Journal* (January 1993): pp. 30–35.

18. Raymond A. Note, John R. Hullenbeck, Barry Gerhart, and Patrick M. Wright, "Detroit Diesel Corporation: An Evolution of Tasks and Attitudes," *Human Resource Management: Gaining a Competitive Advantage* (Burr Ridge, Ill.: Austen Press, 1993).

19. "Fiat Auto Starts 'Cultural Revolution,'" *Quality Digest,* May 1993, p. 9.

20. Anita Van de Vliet, "Assess for Success," *Management Today,* May 1993, pp. 60–65.

21. Kaydos, "Managing by Measuring Performance."

22. Galagan, "Training Keeps the Cutting Edge Sharp."

23. Van de Vliet, "Assess for Success," p. 60.

Chapter 15

1. Arthur Bedeian, *Management,* 2d ed. (Hinsdale, Ill.: The Dryden Press, 1989), p. 620.

2. "How Culture Can Affect Your Study," *International Business,* March 1993, p. 103.

3. "U.S. Trade Deficit Widens 20.7 Percent," *Daily Southtown,* September 15, 1993, p. B1.

4. Louis Rukeyser, *Business Almanac* (New York: Simon & Schuster, 1988), p. 265.

5. Jack Kemp, "NAFTA Means Trade, Jobs and Money," *Chicago Tribune,* September 13, 1993, sec. 1, p. 14.

6. "The Fruits of NAFTA: Early Trade Figures Show Impressive Gains," *The San Diego Union-Tribune,* June 8, 1994, p. B8.

7. Suzan L. Jackson, "What You Should Know About ISO 9000," *Training,* May 1992, pp. 48–52.

8. Leslie Brokaw, "ISO 9000: Making the Grade," *Inc.,* June 1993, p. 98.

9. Bridget Kinsella, "TQM Tries to Measure Up," *Graphic Arts Monthly,* April 1993, pp. 45, 46.

10. "The Global Economy: Who Gets Hurt," *Business Week,* August 10, 1992, p. 48.

11. "He Wants Your Job," *The Economist,* June 12, 1993, p. 15.

12. Ibid., p. 16.

13. "Dossier: Telecommunications in Asia, Malaysia, Thailand," *International Business Newsletter,* June 1993, p. 12.

14. Charles W. Lamb, Jr., Joseph F. Hair, Jr., and Carl McDaniel, *Principles of Marketing,* 2d ed. (Cincinatti: South-Western, 1994), pp. 68–80.

15. *Forbes,* July 23, 1990, pp. 207–210.

16. Howard Witt, "The Big Mac Revolution," *Chicago Tribune Magazine,* July 25, 1993, p. 12.

17. William H. Duvall III, "Golden Arches Reaching Every Corner of Globe," *The Doings,* April 12, 1993, p. 19.

18. "McDonald's Will Operate in Israel with Local Fries," *The Wall Street Journal,* June 25, 1993, p. A5A.

19. Richard M. Krieg, "The New Era: Workers as Assets," *Chicago Tribune,* July 23, 1993, sec. 1, p. 15.

20. Karl Albrecht, "A Review of Quality History," *Quality Digest,* May 1993, pp. 20, 99.

21. Ibid., pp. 99–101.

22. Ibid., p. 102.

23. Susan Carey, "Donnelley Follows Its Customers Around the World," *The Wall Street Journal,* July 1, 1993, p. B9.

24. Gail E. Schares, "Colgate-Palmolive Is Really Cleaning Up in Poland," *Business Week,* March 15, 1993, p. 56.

25. Lennie Copeland, "Training Americans to Do Business Overseas," *Training,* July 1983, p. 12.

26. Michael A. Hitt, R. Dennis Middlemist, and Robert L. Mathis, *Management: Concepts and Practice,* 2d ed. (St. Paul: West Publishing Co., 1986), pp. 607, 608.

27. Copeland, "Training Americans to Do Business Overseas."

28. C. W. Park and Gerald Zaltman, *Marketing Management* (Hinsdale, Ill.: The Dryden Press, 1987), p. 578.

29. Ibid.

30. *Fortune,* April 14, 1986, p. 44.

31. Ibid.

32. Robert Levine, "Why Isn't Japan Happy?" *American Demographics,* June 1992, pp. 58–59.

33. Danielle Bochove, "Culture Shock Proves a Major Component of Work-Study Tour," *The Globe and Mail,* July 6, 1993, p. B16.

34. Steve Johnson, "You Think You've Got Stress—Join the Club," *Chicago Tribune,* March 25, 1993, sec. 1, p. 26.

35. Bochove, "Culture Shock Proves a Major Component of Work-Study Tour."

36. Mark Nusca, "Service Key to Success in Japan," *The Globe and Mail,* July 6, 1993, p. B15.

37. "The Class of 1992," *The Economist,* September 5, 1992, pp. 62–64.

38. Natalie Perkins, "The Big Mac Revolution," *Chicago Tribune Magazine,* July 25, 1993, p. 10.

39. "Enticed by Visions of Enormous Numbers, More Western Marketers Move into China," *The Wall Street Journal,* July 12, 1993, pp. B1, B6.

40. Ibid., p. B1.

41. David P. Hamilton, "After Initial Fuzziness, AT&T Clears Up Signal to Asia," *The Wall Street Journal,* June 30, 1993, p. B6.

42. Schares, "Colgate-Palmolive Is Really Cleaning Up in Poland."

43. Aimee Stern, "Do You Know What They Want?" *International Business,* March 1993, p. 102.

44. Amanda Bennett, "But for Many Executives, Pay Is One Thing and Play Is Another," *The Wall Street Journal,* October 12, 1992, p. B5.

45. "The Miniboom in Kidnapping Coverage," *Business Week,* March 19, 1990, p. 100.

46. Robert L. Mathis and John H. Jackson, *Personnel/Human Resource Management,* 6th ed. (St. Paul: West Publishing, 1991), p. 536.

47. Norman R. Page and Richard L. Wiseman, "Supervisory Behavior and Worker Satisfaction in the United States, Mexico, and Spain," *The Journal of Business Communication,* vol. 30, no. 2 (1993): pp. 161–177.

48. Denis MacShane, "Playing Fair with Labor," *The Arizona Daily Star,* July 25, 1993, pp. 1F, 35.

49. "Executive Pay: An International Survey," *The Wall Street Journal,* October 12, 1992.

50. MacShane, "Playing Fair with Labor," p. 36.

51. "Executive Pay."

52. L. P. Crandall, "Getting through the Global Payroll Maze," *Personnel Journal* (August 1992): p. 76.

53. M. J. Marquardt and D. W. Engel, *Global Human Resources* (Englewood Cliffs, N.J.: Prentice-Hall, 1993); and B. Gerber, "A Global Approach to Training," *Training,* September 1989, pp. 42–47.

Chapter 16

1. Samuel C. Certo, *Modern Management: Quality, Ethics, and the Global Environment,* 5th ed. (Boston: Allyn and Bacon, 1992), p. 86.

2. "How to Be Ethical, and Still Come Top," *Business,* June 5, 1993, p. 7.

3. Leonard J. Brooks, Jr., "Corporate Codes of Ethics," *Journal of Business Ethics* (February/March 1989), 117–29; James Srodes, "Mr. Diogenes, Call Your Office," *Financial World* Vol. 158, no. 13 (June 27, 1989).

4. Robert McGarvey, "Do The Right Thing," *Entrepreneur,* vol. 20, October 1992, p. 140.

5. "Johnson & Johnson Gets FDA Warning," *The Wall Street Journal,* December 10, 1992, p. B8.

6. "Games Employers Play," *Working Woman,* March 1993, p. 41.

7. Richard B. Schmitt, "Ethics Courses for Lawyers Draw Comers," *The Wall Street Journal,* July 8, 1993, p. B2.

8. Andrew Stark, "What's the Matter with Business Ethics?" *Harvard Business Review,* May–June 1993.

9. Ibid.

10. Ibid.

11. John Schwartz and Carolyn Friday, "Beating the Odds in Biotech," *Newsweek,* October 12, 1992, p. 63.

12. Lee Smith, "What the Boss Knows about You," *Fortune,* August 9, 1993, p. 89.

13. Ibid.

14. Ibid.

15. Ibid., p. 91.

16. "Does the Boss Know You're Sick?" *Fortune,* August 9, 1993, p. 91.

17. "Can Smoking or Bungee Jumping Get You Canned?" *Fortune,* August 9, 1993, p. 92.

18. Shari Caudron, "Are Health Incentives Disincentives?" *Personnel Journal* (August 1992): p. 37.

19. "Can Smoking or Bungee Jumping Get You Canned?"

20. "Does the Boss Know You're Sick?" pp. 90–91.

21. Ibid., p. 89.

22. Ibid.

23. "Whose Office Is This Anyhow?" *Fortune,* August 9, 1993, p. 93.

24. Michele Mohr, "The Human Factor," *Daily Southtown,* September 9, 1993, p. D1.

25. Richard Martin, "Push for Safety: A Quiet Crusade," *Nation's Restaurant News,* June 21, 1993, p. 75.

26. "Conspicuous Virtue," *Management Today,* July 1993, p. 80.

27. Wendy Bounds, "Fighting Bugs with Garlic and Peppers," *The Wall Street Journal,* July 12, 1993, p. B1.

28. Amal Kumar Naj, "Whistle-Blower at GE to Get $11.5 Million," *The Wall Street Journal,* April 26, 1993, p. A3.

29. Jeannette R. Scollard, "Here Comes the Bribe," *Entrepreneur,* July 1993, p. 284.

30. "A World of Scandal: And the Call for a Cleanup," *World Press Review,* May 1993, p. 8.

31. Amy Borrus, "Why Pinstripes Don't Suit the Cloak-and-Dagger Crowd," *Business Week,* May 17, 1993, p. 39.

32. Frank Gibney, Jr., "The Trouble with China," *Newsweek,* May 17, 1993, p. 46.

33. "Ex-Ralston Official Got $1.4 Million in Severance," *The Wall Street Journal,* January 15, 1993, p. A3.

34. "Helping Workers Helps Bottom Line," *Employee Benefit Plan Review,* July 1990; Eric J. Savitz, "The Vision Thing: Control Data Abandons It for the Bottom Line," *Barron's,* May 7, 1990, pp. 10–11.

35. Jeff Madura and E. Theodore Veit, *Introduction to Financial Management* (St. Paul: West Publishing, 1988), pp. 6–7.

36. Ibid., p. 8.

37. Richard M. Krieg, "The New Era: Workers as Assets," *Chicago Tribune,* July 23, 1993, sec. 1, p. 15.

38. "Merck Agvet Donates Clothing and Linens to Emergency Shelter," *The Daily* (company newsletter), Merck & Co., Inc., January 11, 1993, p. 1.

39. "Hardly a Showroom for Equal Opportunity," *Business Week,* February 15, 1993, p. A37.

40. Ibid.

41. Lee Berton, "Deloitte Wants More Women for Top Posts in Accounting," *The Wall Street Journal,* April 28, 1993, pp. B1, B7.

42. "Games Employers Play."

43. Richard J. Maturi, "Able and Willing," *Entrepreneur,* February 1993, p. 154.

44. Ibid., p. 156.

45. Caudron, "Are Health Incentives Disincentives?" p. 35.

46. Ibid., pp. 35–37.

47. "Can Smoking or Bungee Jumping Get You Canned?"

48. Ibid.

49. Caudron, "Are Health Incentives Disincentives?" p. 37.

50. Ibid.

51. Cynthia Hanson, "Working Smart: Energize Your Career by Taking Time Out to Renew," *Chicago Tribune,* September 19, 1993, sec. 6, p. 9.

52. "Games Employers Play."

53. D. A. Masi, *The AMA Handbook for Developing Employee Assistance and Counseling Programs* (New York: AMACOM, 1992), pp. 1–35.

54. S. E. Sullivan and R. S. Bhagat, "Organizational Stress, Job Satisfaction, and Job Performance: Where Do We Go from Here?" *Journal of Management* 18 (1992): pp. 353–374.

55. Richard Gibson, "Back to Fat: Too Skinny a Burger Is a Might Hard Sell, McDonald's Learns," *The Wall Street Journal,* April 15, 1993, p. A1.

56. Ibid.

57. Magazine advertisement published by State Farm Insurance.

58. "They Recycle Whole Trees," *Inc.,* June 1993, p. 49.

59. Stephanie E. Ferm, "The Environmentally Conscious Home Office."

60. "The Supply Police," *Newsweek,* February 15, 1993, p. 48.

61. Milton Friedman, "Does Business Have Social Responsibility?" *Bank Administration,* April 1971, pp. 13–14.

62. "Quality Digests," *Quality Digest,* March 1993, p. 14.

Glossary

accountability The management philosophy that employees are held accountable for how well they use their authority and live up to their responsibilities.

achievement-power-affiliation theory A content theory based on the assumption that through their life experiences, people develop needs for achievement, power, and affiliation.

active listening Hearing what the speaker is saying, seeking to understand the facts and feelings the speaker is trying to convey, and stating what you understand that message to be.

affirmative action A method of providing equal employment opportunities to certain groups of people hurt in the past by unfair, discriminatory employment practices.

alienation Feelings of powerlessness and isolation and a view of one's work as meaningless and devoid of satisfaction.

Americans with Disabilities Act (ADA) An act that forbids discrimination against people with any kind of health problem, including AIDS and substance abuse.

anchoring-and-adjustment effect When the perception represents an adjustment from an "anchoring" reference point.

aptitude tests Preemployment intelligence tests that aim to predict performance by measuring cognitive ability in verbal, numerical, perceptual, spatial, or reasoning areas.

artificial intelligence A computer's version of human reasoning and thinking.

assertiveness training Training that teaches how to say no to the demands of others when saying no is appropriate.

assimilation The belief that minorities should become as much like the majority as possible.

attitude A specific emotion toward a person, object, or situation.

attribution Assigning causes to outcomes in the process of interpretation.

authority The official right to command, granted by the organization to the formal leader of a group.

autocratic leaders Leaders who depend primarily on their formal authority to lead others and tend to subscribe to Theory X assumptions.

automated technology Technology that allows some types of human labor to be performed mechanically or electronically, generally involving the use of a computer, with little or no human input.

autonomy The degree of freedom and independence a job affords in making work-related decisions.

behavior modification The use of reinforcement and punishment to motivate people to act in desired ways.

benchmarking The practice of using examples of successful competitors to spur continuous improvement.

biased perception Seeing only a stereotype and basing conclusions on that.

biofeedback A technique of developing an awareness of such automatically controlled bodily functions as pulse rate, blood pressure, body temperature, and muscle tension and thus being able to control them to some extent.

brainstorming A technique for idea generation in which group members are encouraged to state their ideas, no matter how far fetched, without fear of criticism or comment until the process is complete.

burnout A state of emotional exhaustion in which motivation is lost and continued high performance is rendered impossible; it results from ongoing, excessive stress.

business ethics Moral values that determine business conduct.

business-process reengineering A complete redesigning of business processes rather than refinement or adjustment of existing processes. It focuses on the continuing nature of such processes rather than viewing them as many discrete tasks.

centralized structures Those in which decision making is largely confined to top management.

chain of command The arrangement of organizational authority, or levels of management.

climate The emotional tone of the group where the communication occurs.

closed groups Groups that are more stable than open groups, usually due to a low organizational turnover rate.

coaches People who are able to motivate others to do their best and act harmoniously as a team.

coaching A leadership style that involves encouraging employees with lots of feedback and guidance.

cohesiveness The degree of closeness among group members.

collective work-product A result that reflects the joint, real contribution of team members.

communication barriers Things that disrupt the communication process—that create problems in encoding, transmitting, and decoding a message.

communication process The process in which a sender encodes a message and transmits it to a receiver, who decodes the message and responds with feedback.

comparable worth The concept that equal pay should exist not just for the same jobs but for jobs of equal importance to society and demanding equal levels of knowledge and skill.

comparative advantage The theory that a country should specialize in the products it can supply more efficiently and economically than other products.

compressed workweek The performing of a full week's work in four 10-hour days instead of the usual five 8-hour days.

compromise A conflict-management strategy in which each party to a conflict gets only part of what is wanted.

computational infrastructure A computer-based system supporting the routine operations of a business.

conflict The struggles that result from incompatible or opposing needs, feelings, thoughts, or demands within a person or between two or more people.

content theories Theories that focus on the incentives of motivation.

continuous quality improvement (CQI) Closely allied with TQM, with emphasis on the notion that quality can—and should—always be improved.

contrast effect When contrast to a reference point makes something seem smaller or greater than it really is.

controlling function Making sure that work goes according to plan.

core job dimensions Areas in which jobs might conceivably be enriched: skill variety, task identity, task significance, autonomy, and feedback.

cross-training Training in the skills required to perform more than one job; necessary for job rotation.

cultural stereotypes Assumptions that individuals from certain cultures embody certain characteristics believed to be associated with that culture.

culture The knowledge, beliefs, values, and behaviors that characterize a society.

culture shock A state of confusion, anxiety, and stress related to the need to make cultural adjustments.

cybernetic technology Technology that allows machines to be self-regulating; labor performed by a machine is thus controlled by another machine, further reducing human input.

decentralized structures Those in which much decision making is delegated to subgroups.

decoding Interpreting a message.

democratic leaders Leaders who invite participation in planning from subordinates, delegate responsibility, and allow employees flexibility in carrying out their duties. They tend to subscribe to Theory Y assumptions.

departmentalization The subgrouping according to function, product, territory, customer, or some other criteria that occurs in organizations of any significant size.

discrimination The practice of limiting people to certain categories of jobs (usually the lowest paid and least desirable)—if they are hired at all—solely on the basis of stereotypes.

distress The scientific term for excessive or undesirable (unhealthy) stress.

diversity The coexistence of many types of people in a particular setting.

downsizing Cutting the size of an organization by eliminating jobs in order to give it a flatter structure and make it more responsive to change; laying off employees to achieve a leaner corporate structure.

downward communication When someone at a higher level in the organization sends a message to someone at a lower level.

employee assistance programs (EAPs) Employer-provided programs that offer counseling for stress-producing problems.

employee involvement teams Teams that plan ways to improve quality in their area of an organization.

empowerment Giving employees the authority to make decisions that affect their jobs; the responsibility for self-management.

encoding Translating the ideas behind a message into such symbols as words, pictures, gestures, or facial expressions.

enlightened self-interest A self-interest that is not in conflict with the social welfare but is tempered by it.

equity theory Theory that people tend to compare the ratio of their rewards to their work effort against what they perceive to be the ratio for others.

ergonomics The science concerned with the human characteristics that must be considered in designing and arranging tasks and equipment used in the workplace so that they are used most effectively and safely; also called *human engineering.*

ethnocentrism The belief that one's own culture is superior to all others.

eustress The challenge that motivates us to reach for a goal.

expatriates Workers who live in a country of which they are not a citizen.

expectancy The perceived probability that a certain behavior will lead to a certain outcome.

expectancy-valence theory Theory that the strength of motivation equals the perceived value of the outcome times the perceived probability of the behavior resulting in the outcome.

externalizing Description of people who believe external forces largely control them; they have an external *locus of control.*

feedback A message sent by the receiver in response to the sender's message; information on our job performance.

financial incentives Payments for meeting or exceeding objectives.

flextime A program offering employees flexible working hours.

formal communication Communication specifically geared toward achieving the goals of the organization and that follows the lines of the organizational chart.

formal groups Groups set up by management in order to meet organizational objectives.

frustration An unsettled, dissatisfied feeling that produces a number of negative reactions.

functional groups Groups that fulfill the ongoing needs in an organization by carrying out a particular function.

gatekeepers Those who determine what information will be conveyed to the decision makers in the organization.

general adaptation syndrome Generalized reactions to any stressor; also known as the stress response.

glass ceiling An unspoken agreement among senior managers to prevent women or minorities from rising to their ranks.

globalism The increasing interrelationship of the various parts of the world due to trade and technology developments.

goal conflicts Conflicts that occur when formal and informal groups have competing interests at stake .

goal setting The establishment of attainable, precise, mutually understood goals that align well with the organization's overall strategic goals.

golden parachute The provision of a few years' annual pay plus benefits to executives who lose their jobs because of acquisitions.

grapevine The path along which informal communication travels in an organization.

graphic scale An attempt to measure attitudes by offering the respondent a choice of positions ranging from strong agreement with a statement to strong disagreement; also called the *Likert Scale.*

group norms Standards for appropriate or acceptable behavior.

group roles Patterns of behavior related to the member's position in the group.

groups Two or more people who in some way interact with one another and think of themselves as being a group.

groupthink A phenomenon in which the people in a group all think so much alike that new ideas are unlikely.

halo effect A form of anchoring and adjustment in which a perception in one area influences perceptions in other, unrelated areas.

Hawthorne effect An improvement in job performance resulting from feelings of self-worth.

health promotion programs Programs that encourage employees to practice healthy living habits; also called "wellness" programs.

heterogeneous groups Groups made up of people of different ages, education levels, races, personalities, work experiences, and so forth.

hidden agenda A central concern that is left unstated.

hierarchy of needs theory Theory that people first try to satisfy physiological needs, then security, social, esteem, and finally self-actualization needs.

homogeneous groups Those in which members have a lot in common.

honor Taking people at their word and then backing them up in their decisions.

horizontal loading Adding job activities to a job without any additional responsibility or autonomy.

host-country nationals Citizens of a country in which the plant or branch of a foreign-based organization is located.

hostile takeover An acquisition of one company by another despite the acquired company's unwillingness.

human relations Interactions with other people.

human relations skills The ability to work effectively with other people.

hygiene factors According to Herzberg's two-factor theory, aspects of employment that produce dissatisfaction by virtue of their absence.

image The way others perceive us.

impersonal communication Communication in which the recipients have no opportunity to respond with questions or express reactions.

inferences Conclusions drawn from available evidence, instead of statements based solely on that evidence.

informal communication Communication directed toward meeting individuals' needs.

informal groups Groups that result when individuals in the organization develop relationships to meet personal needs.

information overload An excess of information.

intact work groups Groups of workers who regularly interact and rely on one another.

intelligence A person's ability to learn and reason.

internalizing Description of people who believe they have much control over their own circumstances; they have an internal *locus of control.*

international organization An organization that engages in some degree of international business.

interpersonal communication The process by which persons send and receive and interpret messages.

ISO 9000 A series of quality standards developed by the International Organization for standardization (ISO) for products in the world market.

job description A summary of a job's responsibilities.

job diagnostic surveys A survey that allows employees to measure each core job dimension according to their own perception of their job.

job enlargement An effort to make a job more interesting by adding more duties to it.

job enrichment The incorporation of motivating factors into a job.

job redesign Changing a job's characteristics to make it more enjoyable, satisfying, and challenging.

job rotation Moving employees from job to job to give them more variety.

job satisfaction A favorable emotion toward work.

job sharing The division of one full-time job into two part-time jobs.

laissez-faire leaders Leaders who expect employees to discharge their duties without prompting, to ask for guidance when they need it, and to perform well for the sake of their own self-esteem.

lateral communication Communication between two people at the same level in an organization.

leaders Those who can influence the behavior of others in desired directions.

leveraged buyouts (LBOs) The borrowing of huge amounts against a firm's equity to purchase equity in other firms, which can then be sold at a profit.

liaisons People who are the first to learn and pass on information in the informal communication system of an organization.

line employees Those directly involved with production.

locus of control Extent to which people feel in control of circumstances. Those with an external locus of control believe they are largely controlled by external forces. Those with an internal locus of control believe they have much control over their circumstances.

Malcolm Baldrige National Quality Award An annual award administered by the U.S. Department of Commerce.

management by objectives (MBO) A system that provides rewards when employees meet or exceed the objectives they have helped set.

management by walking around A style of management that involves walking around the employment area and thereby making oneself accessible to employees' questions and observations.

management information system (MIS) A formal method of gathering, processing, and disseminating all the information an organization needs.

Managerial Grid A device that identifies five types of leadership according to the degree of concern for people and for production.

mechanistic technology Technology that allows some types of human labor to be performed by a machine, usually with human input.

meditation A relaxation technique in which you focus your thoughts on something—a phrase, a word, a symbol, or even just the act of breathing—other than day-to-day concerns.

medium The method chosen for transmitting a message.

mirroring A technique for creating rapport by feeding back the same kinds of phrases and style of talking, including the same speed and volume of speech, to the other speaker.

motivating factors Job characteristics that create job satisfaction.

motivation Giving people incentives to act in desired ways.

motivation potential score (MPS) The result of a job diagnostic survey; it shows whether a job can be enriched by altering one or more of its core dimensions.

multiculturalism The belief that the diversity of employees is an asset and policies promoting diversity and equality create a competitive advantage.

multinational corporation (MNC) A corporation that conducts a large amount of business in nations other than that where it is located.

networking The process of developing a wide range of contacts inside and outside the organization.

networks The channels used by people to send and receive messages.

nonverbal cues Facial expressions, tone or pitch of voice, body positions, gestures, and degree of eye contact.

objective self-awareness An awareness of one's own role in causing outcomes.

office politics A calculated approach to obtaining a desired end by manipulating, or at least influencing, the emotions or actions of other people.

open-door policy The practice of telling employees that they are welcome to discuss problems with a manager at any time.

open groups Groups that experience a great deal of change, due to frequent new entries and dropouts.

organization A group of individuals brought together for a common purpose and structured in a way that should best serve that purpose.

organizational behavior The way people behave in organizational settings, that is, in groups.

organizational culture All aspects of the working environment but particularly the shared values and norms of employees.

outdoor experiential training Programs designed to build team spirit by involving coworkers in various outdoor activities.

overlapping responsibilities When more than one employee is responsible for something that could be handled by only one.

participative management A management style that involves managers working with employees as a team in setting objectives and planning how to achieve them.

perception A way of seeing and interpreting reality, based on subjective factors, such as experiences and values; people's interpretation of reality or what they think about what they observe.

perceptual adaptation Learning to condition your mind to handle stressors you cannot control.

perceptual congruence The extent to which people share the same perceptions.

perceptual grouping Organizing data received into familiar patterns in order to facilitate interpretation.

perceptual set The expectations of the perceiver.

perfectionism The attempt to do things perfectly.

performance standards Measures of what is expected in terms of quantity and quality.

personality The behavioral and emotional characteristics that distinguish an individual.

power The ability to influence, granted to an informal leader by the people being influenced; control of circumstances and/or people.

prejudices Negative perceptions based on stereotypes.

private industry councils (PICs) Organizations composed of representatives from business, education, and community agencies selected by local government officials to oversee the distribution of federal funds for skills training.

process control Improving the process of production.

process theories Theories that focus on the way motivation operates.

procrastination Putting off what needs to be done.

product quality control Improving the product itself.

Pygmalion effect The direct relationship between expectations and performance.

quality approach A business orientation in which all members of the organization are involved in improving quality in order to satisfy customers.

quality control An organization's efforts to prevent or correct defects in its goods and services.

quality of work life (QWL) A concept that refers to how well employment opportunities meet a range of employee needs.

reinforcement theory Theory that people behave as they do because of the consequences they experience as a result of their behavior.

repatriation The process of bringing an employee back to his or her home country.

responsibility The obligation to perform certain duties and make certain decisions.

responsibility gaps When no employee is responsible for an important activity.

robotics The specific field of automated technology that utilizes robots: machines that duplicate, or better, human physical movements.

role ambiguity When the job requirements are unclear to the worker.

role conflict When a worker has conflicting job requirements; when a person has two different roles that call for conflicting types of behavior.

role overload When the requirements of a job are greater than the ability of the worker.

role underutilization When the requirements of a job fail to fill the worker's time or utilize the worker's ability.

scientific management The merging of people and the work environment to produce optimum results.

selective perception Seeing only what you want or expect to see.

self-concept The opinion you have of yourself and the way you picture yourself.

self-managed team One whose members direct their own work.

self-serving attribution Assigning causes in a way that reflects favorably on ourselves.

semantic differential scale An attempt to measure attitudes that offers a choice of positions ranging from one adjective (such as "good") to the opposite adjective (such as "bad").

sexual harassment Unwelcome sexual advances or physical or verbal conduct of a sexual nature that in any way influences a person's employment situation.

situational leadership An approach in which the particular leader, followers, and situation determine the leadership style chosen. The term refers to *contingency theories of leadership.*

skill variety The degree to which a job requires differing skills and abilities.

social comparisons Influences on our perception by other people's expressed perceptions.

social responsibility The responsibility of organizations to contribute to the well-being of their customers, their employees, their community, and society as a whole.

span of control The number of employees reporting to a manager or supervisor.

staff employees Those who supplement—support and advise—the line employees with special expertise and are not directly involved with production.

statistical process control (SPC) Method in which operators use statistics to monitor quality on an ongoing basis during manufacturing.

statistical quality control Looking for defects in parts of finished goods selected through sampling.

status A person's rank, or importance, in the group.

stereotyping Making a judgment about an individual based on generalizations or preconceived ideas about a group to which that individual belongs.

stress The body's response to environmental demands.

stress management programs Programs that educate employees about stress and/or train them in stress management techniques.

subjective perception Seeing everything from your own point of view and discounting others' perceptions.

subliminal influences Influences on our perception that we are not consciously aware of.

synergy The effect of achieving a greater result than team members could have achieved working individually.

task groups Groups set up to carry out a specific activity and disbanded when the activity is completed; also called *project groups*.

task identity The degree to which a job requires completion of a whole or identifiable piece of work.

task significance The degree to which the results of a job have a perceptible impact on something or someone.

team building An active program in which groups of people are assembled and trained to work effectively together to achieve an agreed-upon goal.

team player Someone who is willing to make a personal sacrifice for the good of the team.

teamwork A way of accomplishing tasks in which a group of people pool their skills to achieve a common goal through commitment and cooperation.

telecommuting Working at home by means of a computer and telephone linkup.

Theory X assumptions Belief that people tend to dislike work and thus avoid it when possible, making tight control by a leader necessary.

Theory Y assumptions Belief that people tend to want meaningful work and can therefore be encouraged to use self-direction and self-control in accomplishing employment objectives.

Theory Z A method of management that emphasizes formal planning, employee participation, frequent cross-training, and a focus on long-term results.

third-country nationals Citizens of one country who work in another country for an organization headquartered in still another country.

time management Controlling the use of time.

total quality management (TQM) An organizationwide focus on continuously improving every business process involved in producing and delivering goods or services.

transactional analysis The theory that there are three *ego states* in social transactions: the child, parent, and adult.

transnational organization An organization that conducts operations wherever deemed most suitable in the world, without considering any particular country its home base.

two-factor theory Theory that dissatisfaction results from the absence of hygiene factors and satisfaction results from the presence of motivating factors.

Type A Classification describing people who are aggressive, competitive, and hard driving.

Type B Classification describing people who are more easygoing and relaxed than Type A people, enjoy more non-work-related activities, and are more flexible in their attitude toward work.

upward communication Communication that flows from a lower level in the organization to a higher level.

valence The value a person places on the outcome of a particular behavior.

values A person's beliefs about what is morally right and wrong or what has worth and what does not.

vertical loading Increasing the depth of a job by adding responsibility, authority, autonomy, and/or accountability.

whistleblowers People who are willing to risk their jobs in order to report unethical practices of the companies they work for.

work ethic An attitude of valuing work for its own sake and seeing virtue and dignity in any type of hard work.

zero defects A quality-control technique based on the view that all members of the organization should work toward creating products and services that are free of problems.

Index

Key terms and the page on which they are defined appear in boldface type. A lowercase n after a page number indicates that a specific individual is listed only once in the notes on that page. A double n (nn) designation after a page number indicates that an individual is cited more than once in the notes on that page.